MONASTIC COMMUNITIES AND CANONICAL CLERGY
IN THE CAROLINGIAN WORLD (780–840)

MEDIEVAL MONASTIC STUDIES

VOLUME 8

General Editors
Janet Burton, University of Wales Trinity Saint David
Karen Stöber, Universitat de Lleida

Editorial Board
Frances Andrews, University of St Andrews
Edel Bhreathnach, School of History, University College Cork
Guido Cariboni, Universita Cattolicà del Sacro Cuore di Milano
Megan Cassidy-Welch, Australian Catholic University
James Clark, University of Exeter
Albrecht Diem, Syracuse University
Marilyn Dunn, University of Glasgow
Sarah Foot, Oxford University, Christ Church
Paul Freedman, Yale University
Alexis Grélois, Université de Rouen
Johnny Grandjean Gøgsig Jakobsen, University of Copenhagen
Martin Heale, University of Liverpool
Emilia Jamroziak, University of Leeds
William Chester Jordan, Princeton University
Jozsef Laszlovszky, Central European University Budapest
Julian Luxford, University of St Andrews
Colman O Clabaigh, Glenstal Abbey
Tadhg O'Keeffe, University College Dublin
Antonio Sennis, University College London
Kurt Villads Jensen, Stockholms Universitet

Monastic Communities and Canonical Clergy in the Carolingian World (780–840)

Categorizing the Church

Edited by
RUTGER KRAMER, EMILIE KURDZIEL, *and* GRAEME WARD

BREPOLS

British Library Cataloguing in Publication Data
A catalogue record for this book is available from the
British Library.

© 2022, Brepols Publishers n.v., Turnhout, Belgium.

All rights reserved. No part of this publication
may be reproduced, stored in a retrieval system, or
transmitted, in any form or by any means, electronic,
mechanical, photocopying, recording, or otherwise
without the prior permission of the publisher.

ISBN 978-2-503-57935-1
E-ISBN 978-2-503-57936-8
DOI 10.1484/M.MMS-EB.5.114927

ISSN 2565-8697
E-ISSN 2565-9758

Printed in the EU on acid-free paper.
D/2022/0095/37

Dedicated to Miriam Czock and Janneke Raaijmakers,
who asked all the right questions

Table of Contents

Acknowledgements   11

Institutions, Identities, and the Realization of Reform:
An Introduction
Rutger KRAMER, Emilie KURDZIEL, Graeme WARD   13

The Monastic Reforms of 816–19: Ideals and Reality
Charles MÉRIAUX   33

Origins

The Organization of the Clergy and the *canonici* in the Sixth Century
Sebastian SCHOLZ   49

Choreography and Confession: The *Memoriale qualiter* and
Carolingian Monasticism
Albrecht DIEM   59

Confusion and the Need to Choose? A Fresh Look at the
Objectives Behind the Carolingian Reform Efforts in
Capitularies and Conciliar Legislation (*c.* 750–813)
Brigitte MEIJNS   99

Old Norms, New Boundaries

What is a *canonicus*? The Carolingians and the Rethinking of
Ecclesiastical *ordines*
Emilie KURDZIEL   131

Reduce, Reuse, Recycle: Episcopal Self-Reflection and the
Use of Church Fathers in the *Institutio canonicorum*
Rutger KRAMER and Veronika WIESER   179

Loose Canonesses? (Non-)Gendered Aspects of the Aachen *Institutiones*
Michael EBER   217

Reception and Reflection

'Superior to Canons, and Remaining Inferior to Monks': Monks, Canons, and Alcuin's Third Order
Stephen LING   241

This is a Cleric: Hrabanus Maurus's *De institutione clericorum*, Clerical Monks, and the Carolingian Church
Cinzia GRIFONI   267

The 'Apostates' of Saint-Denis: Reforms, Dissent, and Carolingian Monasticism
Ingrid REMBOLD   301

Debating the *una regula*: Reflections on Monastic Life in Ninth-Century Manuscripts from St Gall
Johanna JEBE   323

Reform in Practice

Monks Pray, Priests Teach, Canons Sing, and the Laity Listens: The *Regula Benedicti* and Conceptual Diversity of Sacred Space in Carolingian Discourse
Miriam CZOCK †   355

Cathedral and Monastic: Applying Baumstark's Categories to the Carolingian Divine Office
Renie CHOY   381

Implementing Liturgical Change in Ninth-Century Lyon: Authority, Antiphoners, and Aachen 816
Graeme WARD   403

Ordering the Church in the *Ordines Romani*
Arthur WESTWELL   425

Index   447

List of Illustrations

Johanna Jebe

Figure 12.1. *Regula Benedicti*, prologus with text-critical apparatus (ll. 6, 11, 13); St Gall, Stiftsbibliothek, Cod. Sang. 914, p. 6. Around 820. Reproduced with the permission of the Sankt Gallen Stiftsbibliothek. 330

Figure 12.2. *Regula Benedicti*, first page of the prestigious new copy for the community; St Gall, Stiftsbibliothek, Cod. Sang. 915, p. 27. Middle of the ninth century. Reproduced with the permission of the Sankt Gallen Stiftsbibliothek. 338

Arthur Westwell

Figure 16.1 The script of Cod. 349; St Gall, Stiftsbibliothek, Cod. Sang. 349, p. 55. Late eighth century. Reproduced with permission of the Sankt Gallen Stiftsbibliothek. 437

Figure 16.2. Script and use of rubrication in Pal.lat.574; Città del Vaticano, Biblioteca Apostolica Vaticana, Pal. lat. 574, fol. 155^r. End of the eighth century. © 2021 Biblioteca Apostolica Vaticana. Reproduced by permission of Biblioteca Apostolica Vaticana, with all rights reserved. 440

Acknowledgements

This volume was sponsored by the SFB 'Visions of Community' (VISCOM; Austrian Science Fund, F42-G18), a comparative project coordinated from the *Institute for Medieval Research* (ÖAW) and the University of Vienna from 2011 to 2019. This project aimed to look at the way religious ideas and ideals influenced the formation and consolidation of individual communities. In many ways, the chapters presented here fit perfectly with VISCOM's research agenda, as the question of what a community should be, and how it should act within larger political and religious frameworks is at the core of these deliberations as well.

In addition to VISCOM, this book and this project have also benefited greatly and continue to benefit from the involvement of the *Centre d'études supérieures de civilisation médiévale* (CESCM-UMR 7302) and the Université de Poitiers. It has also been sponsored by the Région Nouvelle Aquitaine through the programme *Aquitania Monastica* (chaire régionale d'histoire monastique) and the Radboud Institute for Culture and History (RICH).

Last, but definitely not least, the editors want to thank Nicola Edelmann for her tireless efforts in helping to prepare this book for production, and Marieke Ceelaert for her help preparing the index.

RUTGER KRAMER, EMILIE KURDZIEL,
GRAEME WARD

Institutions, Identities, and the Realization of Reform

An Introduction

In the short story *Ein Bericht für eine Akademie* (*A Report to an Academy*), written by Franz Kafka and published in the German magazine *Der Jude* in November 1917, a chimpanzee, called 'Red Peter' by his capturers, addresses an otherwise unspecified academy, telling them the story of how he had become human.[1] It is not a happy story, its poignancy amplified by the ape's wry humour.[2] His original assignment, he starts, was to tell the assembled crowd about his 'previous life as an ape', but he could not comply with that request because his 'achievement would have been impossible if [he] had stubbornly wished to hold […] onto the memories of [his] youth'. In fact, he continues, 'Giving up that obstinacy was the highest command that I gave myself'.

What follows is a recollection of Red Peter's capture, his confinement, and his realization that, in order to be let out of his cage, he needed to convince his capturers that he is one of them. The wording is deliberate. Red Peter was looking for a 'way out' (*Ausweg*), even if this did not mean gaining his 'freedom' (*Freiheit*). Freedom, after all, was the ability to do what you want and be who you are. Our speaker, on the other hand, wanted to continue existing outside of his cage. This meant adapting to the whims of the humans around him, indulging in their vices, wearing their clothes, speaking their language. He had to forgo the freedom he had known in the jungle, and settle for 'human freedom' instead: the 'self-controlled movement' of a trapeze artist, executed in accordance with the expectations of onlookers and the means they had

---

1 Franz Kafka, 'Ein Bericht für eine Akademie'; online at <http://ds.ub.uni-bielefeld.de/viewer/image/1667317/1/LOG_0000/> [accessed 8 September 2021]. The English translation is made by Ian Johnston and is available online at <http://johnstoi.web.viu.ca//kafka/reportforacademy.htm> [accessed 8 September 2021].
2 Our reading of this short story was inspired by the remarks about its reception, adaptation, and interpretation by Winkler, 'Achter de coulissen van het theaterstuk *Bewustzijn*', esp. pp. 15–16 and 27–28. See also Sokel, 'Identity and the Individual'.

given themselves. 'A mockery of sacred nature!', Red Peter calls this, but nonetheless a means to an end. In what is implied to be his last moment of freedom, '[He], a free ape, submitted [himself] to this yoke', and began to shed his old identity of a nameless chimpanzee, and learn to live with his new name (which he detests) and the obligations that came with it.

Metamorphosis; adaptation; change; and self-awareness — these are recurring themes in this story, and indeed throughout Kafka's entire oeuvre. They are also the subject of this book.

Identities

The protagonists of this volume — monks, canonical clerics (*canonici*),[3] and religious women in the Carolingian world, roughly from the eighth to the tenth century — have all been faced with an experience similar to that of the ape narrating the *Report*. No matter how they were designated ('monks', 'canonical clerics' (or 'canons'), 'nuns', 'canonesses', or otherwise), these would be men and women who had chosen to live a life of apparent unfreedom under a monastic rule or the exigencies of clerical life, with a view towards the ultimate freedom that awaited them in Heaven.[4] They walked a narrow path toward salvation, feeling enabled rather than hindered by the 'sweet yoke' of Christ as described in the Gospel of Matthew.[5] The comparison runs deeper still. Although Kafka's story betrays a deeply satirical view of the intersection between appearance, (learned) behaviour and identity, it touches upon several issues that might have been as familiar to early medieval monks as they were to modern monkeys (or rather, apes). Their identity, too, became caught up in the development of the world around them, a world that was shaped by imperial initiatives, ecclesiastical priorities, debates about order, and attempts to order these debates.[6] Such was the challenge to the men and women religious of the Frankish realm in the later eighth and ninth centuries;

---

3 The meaning of the word *canonicus* between the sixth and the ninth centuries and the categorization of the particular kind of ecclesiastics associated with that term is discussed in the chapters by Scholz, Kurdziel, and Ling in this volume.
4 See also Dey, 'Bringing Chaos Out of Order'.
5 Matthew 11. 29–30 (Douay-Rheims Version): 'Take up my yoke upon you, and learn of me, because I am meek, and humble of heart: and you shall find rest to your souls. For my yoke is sweet and my burden light'.
6 The historiography on this subject is vast, and will mostly be covered by the bibliographies of the individual chapters in this book. Several key monographs, presenting a bird's-eye view of these complex developments, are worth mentioning here, however: Claussen, *The Reform of the Frankish Church*; Gaillard, *D'une réforme à l'autre*; Klueting, *Monasteria semper reformanda*; McKitterick, *The Frankish Church*; Vanderputten, *Monastic Reform as Process*; Schieffer, *Die Entstehung von Domkapiteln*; Meijns, *Aken of Jeruzalem*; Howe, *Before the Gregorian Reform*, and of course the venerable study by Ladner, *The Idea of Reform*.

their ability to live the way they wanted would be dependent on their ability to adapt to the (new) rules set by society.

The early ninth century in particular was marked by a period of intense reflection and renegotiation of clerical and monastic identities. This process culminated, during the reign of Louis the Pious (r. 814–40), in a series of councils held in Aachen between 816 and 819, key moments in Carolingian ecclesiastical legislation. According to the established grand narrative, the Carolingian court used this momentum to enforce a (re)definition of the canonical and monastic orders and to impose upon all religious communities the duty to make it clear where they stood — that is to choose between implementing the *Regula Benedicti* or one of the two normative texts drafted in 816: the *Institutio canonicorum* for men or the *Institutio sanctimonialium* for women. It had apparently become paramount to figure out which members of the clergy belonged to which group, and to ensure that everybody would be properly categorized and made aware of the expectations that came with any given category. This may not have been completely new ideas, nor an exclusive purview of the Carolingian 'reformers'. Besides, it will be one of the objectives of this book to re-evaluate this interpretative scheme, but the fact is that attempts to properly 'categorize' the Church definitely increased in density at the turn of the ninth century.

The stated goal of this reorganization was *correctio*.[7] And *correctio* was not limited to merely changing one's habits and external behaviour. As Charlemagne put it in the *Admonitio generalis* of 789, the ecclesiastics of the Frankish realm were faced with the challenge of becoming 'either *real* monks, or *real* canonical clerics (*canonici*)'.[8] The internalization of the proposed reforms implied here meant that they had to undergo an internal metamorphosis that went deeper than merely changing their habit. These calls to transformation and above all the debates surrounding them constitute the subject of this book. More broadly, its authors aim to re-ignite the discussion on the (re)ordering of the Western Church between the middle of the eighth and the end of the tenth century by rethinking the usual grand narrative.

Recent interdisciplinary work has shown the possibilities of reading the sources usually associated with 'reform' or seen as 'reformative' against the grain, and to re-think the attempts at re-categorizing the ecclesiastical order(s) within the Frankish realm. Many active thinkers have been brought

---

7 For a classic statement, see Schramm, 'Karl der Große', esp. p. 341; Smith, '"Emending evil ways and praising God's omnipotence"' (at pp. 189–90) offers a clear summary of what the word *correctio* could comprise. Cf. also a forthcoming volume devoted specifically to the subject: Westwell, Rembold, and Van Rhijn ed., *Rethinking the Carolingian Reforms*.
8 *Admonitio generalis* (789), ed. by Mordek, Zechiel-Eckes, and Glatthaar, 75, p. 228: 'Clericis. Ut illi clerici, qui se fingunt habitu vel nomine monachos esse et non sunt, omnimodis videtur corrigendos atque emendandos esse, ut vel veri monachi sint vel veri canonici'. On the reasons to translate *Canonicus* by 'canonical cleric' rather than 'canon', see Kurdziel's contribution in this volume.

out from under the shadow of the ubiquitous Benedict of Aniane.[9] The idea that the Carolingians sought to uniformize the institutions in their empire at all costs is being questioned once more.[10] New light has also been shed on the names and descriptions given by contemporary onlookers to what we nowadays refer to as 'reforms'.[11] Our understanding of the way Carolingian government functioned in the service of the Church — and *vice versa* — has deepened, as has our understanding of the normative value of monastic rules and regulations as well as, very importantly, canon law.[12] This book should be seen in the context of these studies and the ongoing debates that cross them — not as an end point, but a new impulse for further discussion.

Changing the Focal Length: Old Issues, New Perspectives

This volume is the result of a workshop held in Vienna in May 2017 under the title 'Categorizing the Church: Debates about Religious Communities in the Carolingian World'. This meeting followed a series of sessions organized at the International Medieval Congress in Leeds in 2016, itself the consequence of a debate at the same conference in the preceding year, when the point was raised, during a session on 'canonical' reforms, that it is still unclear *why* exactly 'canons' became so prevalent in the Western Europe reform discourse of the eighth and ninth centuries. Why did the Carolingians care so much about who was a monk and who was a 'canon' (or a canonical cleric)?

A well-established model holds that, during the course of the seventh and eighth centuries, the boundaries between monastic and clerical communities had become blurred; as a result, successive Carolingian rulers, from Charles Martel (r. 718–41) onwards, supported various attempts to restore or re-establish them, by urging that monks observed a *regula*, or clergy adhered to the requirements of the *canones*.[13] At the same time, there is an assumption that as part of this process of differentiation, the fusion between monastic and non-monastic ways of life deepened. Communities of clerics became

---

9 Benedict's influence is most forcefully stated in Semmler, 'Benedictus II'. See, however, Rousseau and Diem, 'Monastic Rules'. Oexle, *Forschungen*, also remains useful.
10 Most recently, Patzold, 'Prozesse der Vereinheitlichung?'. See also, for instance, McKitterick, 'Unity and Diversity'. Contra: Close, *Uniformiser la foi pour unifier l'Empire*.
11 Barrow, 'Developing Definitions of Reform'; Barrow, 'Ideas and Applications of Reform'; Vanderputten, *Monastic Reform as Process*; but see also Walsham, 'Migrations of the Holy'; and Barrow, 'Le terme "réforme"'.
12 Kramer, *Rethinking Authority*; Patzold, *Presbyter*. On the production and value of normative texts: Mordek, 'Fränkische Kapitularien'; Hartmann, *Die Synoden der Karolingerzeit*; Hartmann, *Kirche und Kirchenrecht*; Hartmann and Grabowsky ed., *Recht und Gericht*; Rousseau and Diem, 'Monastic Rules'. See also the introduction to the recent edition of *Admonitio generalis*, ed. by Mordek, Zechiel-Eckes, and Glatthaar.
13 See also the methodological remarks by Reuter, '"Kirchenreform" und "Kirchenpolitik"'.

increasingly monasticized through the normative rules they were expected to follow: bishop Chrodegang of Metz (r. 742–66), for instance, repackaged the *Regula Benedicti* for the cathedral clergy at Metz.[14] In a parallel process, monastic communities became increasingly clericalized: monks were increasingly expected to be ordained so as to allow them to celebrate Mass and fulfil pastoral roles within the vicinities of their monasteries.[15]

These, and other, aspects of the institutional and cultural changes which occurred in the Church during the Carolingian period, have all been studied more or less extensively in the past century. However, in most cases, the studies in question tended either to isolate a single instance of the phenomenon, or to see them all as the result of a single, empire-wide initiative pushed by the court. Moreover, considerably more attention has been devoted to the study of male monasteries than groups of cathedral clergy, collegiate churches, or female religious houses, with the result of a biased (or at least incomplete) 'monastic' and 'male' oriented vision.[16]

In order to avoid reproducing these biases, several important choices were made while preparing this volume. The first of these was to broaden our chronological horizon, so as to be able to place the 'moment' represented by 816–19 in a wider context. Put differently: we intended to observe the changes and reforms made visible during the early years of Louis the Pious's reign with telescopic vision — although with microscopic precision. If the book puts the spotlight on the Aachen councils of 816–19 and their textual results, this temporal sequence should be considered as much as a starting point as an end point, a stage in a longer process, whose prolegomena and continuations are just as much at the heart of the reflection undertaken here. The period of 816–19 is to us a pivotal vantage point rather than a goal *per se*.

Our second choice was to investigate monastic and clerical (or 'canonical') normative texts and initiatives as a singular *corpus*, while also illuminating the diverse range of communities affected by them. It is, indeed, only by changing our focus from a strictly monastic point of view to the wider angle of this phenomenon in its entirety, that we can hope to discern the desired direction of these reforms, the nuances seen from the top and the many variants that only become visible when zooming in at a local level. For the same reason, we have tried to consider male and female institutions and voices in equal measure. However — and this is an important point — as is so often the case, the perspective of the discourse offered to us is almost exclusively masculine: as much as we have attempted to give female religious and their communities pride of place, discerning a gendered vision of the proposed

---

14 As most fully explained by Claussen, *The Reform of the Frankish Church*. But see now also the PhD thesis by Ling, 'The Cloister and Beyond'.
15 Gaillard, *D'une réforme à l'autre*, p. 127. See further the contribution of Cinzia Grifoni in this volume.
16 On this, see Diem, 'The Gender of the Religious'.

reforms that takes into account the patriarchal and kyriarchal biases inherent in the sources, remains an avenue for future research.[17]

Top-Down vs. Bottom-Up — Central vs. Local

Another underlying idea to this volume is that the attempts at reorganizing the Church should not be seen as having been imposed unilaterally from the top down. The palace and the court did, of course, play an important role in shaping Carolingian ecclesiastical politics, but not necessarily, as has long been thought, a decisive one; they most definitely did not operate in a vacuum. On the one hand, the 'Carolingian reforms' of the 'Frankish Church' may be regarded as a series of measures to be implemented and obeyed at a community's peril. On the other hand, they could also be seen as an ongoing debate, arbitrated by those with a stake in the improvement of the *ecclesia*, with a view towards establishing a mutually agreed-upon bandwidth within which salvation could be pursued.

Over the preceding decades, much has been made of the 'reforms' propagated by the Carolingian court and imposed on the Church by means of a combination of political and intellectual coercion, economic stimuli, and genuine piety. Following in the footsteps of, especially, Josef Semmler's influential studies on this subject, most of these analyses have one thing in common, in that they tend to fall for the seductive rhetoric of the sources, that this was a mere top-down and programmatic reform effort sponsored by the Carolingian rulers, and nothing else.[18] Recently, these 'reforms' have been recognized as being built on more local foundations rather than simply the will of an emergent dynasty.[19]

Admittedly, normative texts such as the *Institutiones canonicorum et sanctimonialium* (816) were issued in the name of the emperor, imperial capitularies such as the *Capitulare monasticum* (817) enacted change, and successive Carolingian rulers supported the creation of many new communities and reorganization of existing ones. To improve the *ecclesia* was, after all, a responsibility of any ruler following in the wake of Constantine, who, despite

---

17 The contribution by Michael Eber in this volume may provide a starting point for this kind of study.
18 As explained by Charles Mériaux in this volume. References to Semmler's extensive work can be found throughout the volume's other contributions, but see esp. those of Brigitte Meijns and Emilie Kurdziel. See also, Kottje, 'Einheit und Vielfalt'; Kottje, 'Einleitung'; Geuenich, 'Kritische Anmerkungen'.
19 For instance, see Vanderputten, *Monastic Reform as a Process*; van Rhijn, 'Royal Politics in Small Worlds'; Kramer, '"…ut normam salutiferam cunctis ostenderet"'. Of note are also the recent dissertations by Gibson, 'Rewriting History', Hosoe, '*Regulae* and Reform', and Hohman, 'Carolingian Sermons', who all attempt to bridge the gap between imperial ideals and local practice by looking at reforms through the lens of hagiography and sermons.

his problematic legacy, set a standard for the politicization of the Western Church when he presided over the ecumenical Council of Nicaea in 325.[20] And yet, 'improvement' was not a royal or imperial prerogative. It was as much a crucial concern to regional and local ecclesiastical leaders (whether archbishops, bishops, or abbots), but also to local communities and actors (priests, for instance).

It is true that within the fledgling Church of early medieval Western Europe, the idea existed that salvation depended on the resolve and responsibilities of people who found themselves higher up on the hierarchical ladder. For the Frankish Church under the Carolingian dynasty in the eighth and ninth centuries, this translated into a political theory perhaps best exemplified by the 'exhortation to share responsibilities' described by Olivier Guillot already in 1983 on the basis of a cross-section of sources from the first half of the reign of Louis the Pious.[21] This was a time when the Carolingian experiment was in full swing and the so-called crisis years of 829–33 had not yet caused a comprehensive re-appreciation of the system upon which the empire rested.[22] It seemed straightforward enough, based as it was in Isidore's famous maxim that 'the word king comes from doing what is right'.[23] Part of what was 'right', in this view, was to ensure that the ruler would surround himself with people willing to share in this duty and divide the burdens of responsibility that came with operating at the top of the hierarchy.[24] The fact that these people shared in the responsibilities of rulership — that they held a *ministerium* — had implications for the loyalty they exercised towards their ruler and which they expected from their subjects.[25] Thus, Carolingian government was dependent on the willingness of elites to do their part without bureaucratic or authoritarian prompting, and to improve what needed improving even if this meant criticizing their superiors.[26]

---

20 Pohl, 'Creating Cultural Resources for Carolingian Rule'; For other examples, see also Raaijmakers and van Renswoude, 'The Ruler as Referee'.
21 Guillot, 'L'exhortation'; but see also Davis, 'A Pattern of Power'.
22 Gaillard, 'De l'interaction entre crise et réforme'. Cf. also Kramer, *Rethinking Authority*, pp. 19–58.
23 Isidore of Seville, *Etymologiarum sive Originum libri XX*, ed. by Lindsay, IX. 3. 4; trans. by Stephen A. Barney, p. 200: 'Kings are so called from governing, and as priests (sacerdos) are named from "sacrificing" (sacrificare), so kings (rex) from governing (regere, also meaning "keep straight, lead correctly"). But he does not govern who does not correct (corrigere); therefore the name of king is held by one behaving rightly (recte), and lost by one doing wrong. Hence among the ancients such was the proverb: "You will be king (rex) if you behave rightly (recte); if you do not, you will not"'.
24 De Jong, 'Charlemagne's Church', pp. 125–29.
25 Helbig, '*Fideles Dei et regis*'; Costambeys, Innes, and MacLean, *The Carolingian World*, pp. 131–53.
26 Bührer-Thierry, 'Pensée hiérarchique et différentiation sociale'; see also, in the same volume, Oexle, 'Mönchtum und Hierarchie'.

At the top of this house of cards we find the phenomenon that, in simplified terms, tends to be referred to as 'Carolingian'.[27] As a concept, it is suffused with ideas about court-centred, top-down legislation, which adds another layer to the observation that talking about 'Carolingian reforms' only allows us to glimpse a part of the picture. Reform was always an elite discourse. Nonetheless, even in a Carolingian context, it should be seen as a two-way street. It was not due to the sole initiative of the rulers, nor to the sole input from the bottom up. The Frankish realm was not a simple hierarchy where the elites determined what needed to happen. Rather, it provided a structure propped up by interdependent relations, and within which everybody was encouraged to admonish everyone else.[28] In this system, improving the Church and the Empire was the result of a continuous feedback loop in which mutual criticism and shared responsibilities fed into each other and, ideally, motivated the people in a position to effectuate changes as they were deemed necessary. Thus, even if the changes described in this volume were the purview of those people with a stake in the religious aspects of life in the Carolingian Empire (bishops, abbots, kings), they relied on the support and acceptance of the communities under their wing. Despite the essential role played by individual movers and shakers, the changes we see were the result of experimentation on a smaller scale before they could be recognized and harnessed for the greater good of the empire — the *ecclesia*.[29]

Thus, local priests, smaller communities, and individual brokers — what John Howe has called 'Hinge People' — were in fact instrumental in ensuring whatever changes were wrought actually took root in society.[30] Even when they ended up resisting these tendencies, their concerns would fuel ongoing developments and foment new insights.

It is important to stress the dynamic interplay between the various stakeholders here, as that is ultimately how this volume positions itself vis-à-vis

---

27 Thinking of a 'Carolingian system' means that it is, to a certain extent, unavoidable to buy into the Carolingian propaganda upon which the system rested. Cf. Costambeys, Innes, and MacLean, *The Carolingian World*, pp. 9–16, esp. p. 14: '[Carolingian] longevity rested in part on their success in creating and imposing ways of thinking that self-consciously re-defined the Frankish world *as* Carolingian'. See also already Fichtenau, *The Carolingian Empire*, who, on p. vii, describes the Carolingian Empire as a 'compromise between such a claim to universal lordship and the [...] spiritual, political and social conditions [...] in western Europe', and cautions historians to treat 'the history of ideas as if it were something apart and devoid of practical consequences [...] especially when the gulf between the two is as great as it was in the reign of Charles the Great'. For a general framework that holds up well, see also Contreni, 'The Carolingian Renaissance'.
28 Matthew Innes talks of 'an articulated hierarchy which the centre claimed to control', which he contrasts with the pyramidal structure of Merovingian and Ottonian rulership. Innes, *State and Society in the Early Middle Ages*, p. 180.
29 Keeping in mind the methodological remarks in Walsham, 'Migrations of the Holy'.
30 Howe, *Before the Gregorian Reform*, pp. 254–61; see also van Rhijn, 'Priests and the Carolingian Reforms'.

previous scholarship. The chapters in this book go beyond simply studying the actions taken by the powers that be. Rather, they pay particular attention to local contexts and initiatives around the years 816–19 — especially in the two last sections. This allows the authors to shed new light on the dynamic relationships between imperial pronouncements and local undertakings, making clear that sometimes there was a direct connection, but often local developments just ran their own course. Observable changes were probably more often than not the result of a complex symbiosis of central requirements or encouragements and local logics.

Needless to say, we do not claim to fully get to the bottom of this symbiosis. The chapters in this volume are intended to open up new reflections on the role played by local communities in this process.[31] We have continued with this endeavour in the course of a second conference, organized in Poitiers in 2018, which explicitly focused on individual communities, tracing their evolution between the eighth and eleventh century.[32] One of the stated aims of that conference was to explore the impact (or lack thereof) of the proposals formulated at a central level in 816–19. Taking a longer time-frame and scrutinizing the continuations and transformations of communities allowed us to re-examine this vital period and analyse, firstly, to what extent certain local practices and experiments have influenced the rules formulated at a central level, in what was a dynamic process of communication involving individual communities rather than purely the impetus from the court; and secondly, whether or not 816–19 indeed constituted a pivotal moment in the history of the organization of the Church and of ecclesiastical communities, and if it was ever experienced as such. Moreover, focusing on individual communities made it possible to explore further what differentiated, in practical terms and not from a normative viewpoint, canonical clerics from monks, *sanctimoniales* from nuns, and the extent to which any real difference existed between such categories for contemporary observers. One should indeed refrain from looking at those communities or analysing them through the very framework of the reformers, who aimed precisely at imposing one interpretation of what a canonical cleric or a monk (and their respective lives) should be.

Debating In and Through Texts

This second meeting has resulted in a special issue of the *Cahiers de Civilisation Médiévale* (2022), which focuses on what characterizes religious communities on a concrete and institutional level — and how they defined themselves. The current volume lays the groundwork for that sequel by highlighting the

---

31 See co-authored book by Bernard Zeller and others, *Neighbours and Strangers*.
32 *Categorizing the Church II: Clerical and Monastic Communities in the Carolingian World (8th–10th)*, International workshop held in Poitiers the 10–12 October 2018.

role played by texts and their production in the wake of the recategorization of ecclesiastical orders. It is our hope to be able to study this process, as well as the surrounding debates, on its own terms. One way of doing this is by zooming in on normative texts. These are indeed the primary locus of formulation of reform or calls to reform. In this category, we comprise capitularies, acts of general or regional councils, but also religious rules of life (sometimes defined as infra-normative).[33] The detailed re-reading of texts like the *Institutiones canonicorum* and *sanctimonialium*, the Merovingian *Memoriale qualiter* or capitularies from the 780s, their modes of production and the rhetorical devices used to justify their existence form the bulk of several chapters of this volume. All these studies shed light on the mechanisms driving the reform experiment and the way members of the 'inner circle' would present themselves as propagators of change. Precise examination of specific manuscripts, of the *Regula Benedicti* for instance, also show how the codices we have served as a conduit between local perspective and universal ideas — and *vice versa*.

Other texts and narrative sources are, however, equally useful in discerning the points of view of the many participants in this debate. Letters, polemical treatises, and liturgical commentaries all open up a window to situated views and attitudes towards the proposed changes, before and after 816. For instance, hagiographical narratives have often been used to provide an implicit or explicit commentary on the initiatives deployed by the imperial court or, more locally, the episcopal household.[34] Such responses are also perceptible in slight alterations of the content, omitted passages, or marginal glosses in the manuscripts themselves (something which recent work on early medieval practices of annotation has amply highlighted),[35] such as in subsequent narratives, that may not have been intended by the original copyist or author. Each of these texts are expressions of support or resistance — showing engagement or awareness of the larger developments at hand.

This volume examines such texts as responses to ongoing initiatives and/or to the norms formulated at the central level, and more broadly as individual manifestations of an empire-sized discourse community, rather than isolated productions or new phenomena.[36] Two types of codices have been privileged here: those reproducing one or the other of the rules of life promoted in 816–19 (i.e the *Regula Benedicti*, the *Institutio canonicorum* or the *Institutio sanctimonialium*) and liturgical manuscripts, paying particular

---

33 Coccia, 'Regula et vita'.
34 Isaïa, 'L'hagiographie contre la réforme' and Krönert, 'Réformer la vie monastique'.
35 Teeuwen and van Renswoude ed., *The Annotated Book in the Early Middle Ages*; for focused examples of such an approach, see Pezé, *Le virus de l'erreur* and Chambert-Protat, Delmulle, Pezé, and Thomson ed., *La controverse carolingienne sur la prédestination*.
36 On the concept of a 'discourse community', see Porter, *Audience and Rhetoric*, pp. 82–102 and p. 106; Evans, 'Audience and Discourse Community Theory', pp. 1–5; Swales, *Other Floors*, pp. 194–207; Wuthnow, *Communities of Discourse*, pp. 9–19.

attention to revisions, variants, or marginal annotations that might inform us about how the ongoing debate and proposals for change were received and lived, followed closely or adapted. Textual reception, manuscript production, and annotation were after all part of this same ongoing process in which male and female religious would, in the end, reflect on their own position in life and in the *ecclesia*. It is a worthwhile exercise to think about texts in this dynamic way and we hope the impulses given in this volume will open up new avenues of systematic research into the way manuscripts, for instance those containing the *Regula Benedicti*, the *Institutio canonicorum*, or another kind of *florilegium* of normative texts, should be seen as carriers of and responses to reform during the ninth, tenth, and eleventh centuries (and beyond).[37] Exploring the 'reform movement' along these lines will allow us to arrive at a more complex and nuanced, and *ipso facto* a more realistic, answer to the following question: how did reform actually work in the Carolingian era?

Reform — *correctio, emendatio* — was obviously not a Carolingian thing. 'Reforms' were part of the very being of the medieval Church, just as categorizing religious order was a perennial issue. To be part of the clergy or of a religious community was to be part of an ongoing process of improvement that was set into motion when the apostle Paul wrote the first of his letters to the emergent Christian communities in the Eastern Mediterranean.[38] The authors in this book acknowledge that these reformers were latching on to a long tradition of taking responsibility (and credit) for developments that they could not always quite control. Still, unsurprisingly, the way the Carolingians went about their attempt at categorizing the Church was typical for the context within which it all took place. The scale at which those responsible tended to operate; the way abbots, bishops, and kings interacted; and maybe even the specific amalgamation of Roman imperial, Frankish elite, and Christian intellectual ideologies underpinning their attempts all indicate a particular flavour to these improvements that make them 'Carolingian'. Underpinning this volume is the idea that the Carolingian project was aimed at making sense of and channelling the diversity *within* the ecclesiastical structures under their responsibility, while also dealing with the impulses coming from below, rather

---

37 See, on this point specifically, the contribution by Steven Vanderputten in the upcoming issue of *Cahiers de Civilisation Médiévale*. A new edition of the *Institutio sanctimonialium* is presently being prepared by Dominik Trump (Köln), which will undoubtedly enhance our understanding of this issue.

38 Although coming at it from a distinctly 'Protestant' angle, Bradbury, *Perpetually Reforming*, at pp. 1–6 (in a chapter appropriately titled 'The Problem with Church') correctly points out that even the attempt to define what the Church is already changes it. See also the review of this book by Avis, review of Bradbury, *Perpetually Reforming*, pp. 230–31: 'Historically, reform has meant rectifying bad pastoral practice (abuses), reconstructing the organization, restoring unity and refocusing on the gospel'. Both agree that the modern conception of 'reform' is closely tied up with the sixteenth-century Reformation (also argued, for instance, by Walsham, 'Migrations of the Holy').

than erasing that diversity.[39] In order to deal with the diversity within the *ecclesia*, the purported leaders seemed to have been aware that they needed to embrace rather than extinguish the many voices in this debate, and could not exclude the people who had most to gain (or lose) by their participation: the monks, clerics (or 'canons'), nuns and 'canonesses' who were tasked with living up to the expectations of the people credited with being 'reformers' in the modern discourse. Their identity as members of religious communities thus became an invitation to participate in the aforesaid ongoing conversation about and among themselves.

The contributions in this volume offer snapshots of these conversations. In the course of fifteen chapters, divided among four sections, they shed new light on the self-reflection engaged in by the participants, and in turn allow us to reflect on the way we regard 'reforms' and their impact on the lives of those affected.

The Book

Origins

Following a summary and reassessment of the influential scholarship of Josef Semmler by Charles Mériaux, the first section traces themes vital to understanding the pre-history of the reform councils of the early reign of Louis the Pious. First, Sebastian Scholz examines the meaning of *canonici* in sixth-century Francia and beyond, providing some much-needed insight into the use of the term prior to the canonical initiatives taken under the Carolingians: while the term generally seems to refer to those clerics of the episcopal churches and municipal parishes who were listed in registers and were given sustenance by the bishop, these *canonici*, however, did not emerge as an autonomous group, as previous scholarship has often assumed. Next, Albrecht Diem takes a fresh look at the *Memoriale qualiter*, a significant but overlooked eighth-century source for studying Carolingian monasticism, arguing that 'reform texts' are not just indicative of changing practices, but also of the theological and spiritual background informing these practices. Finishing this section, Brigitte Meijns studies the motivations of those sponsoring the reform councils by asking to what extent their initiatives were fuelled by 'confusion or the necessity to choose' between one type of communal life or the other. She argues that the ambitions and concrete measures of the Carolingian reformers were not so much framed in terms of ending confusion but that they were inspired by a desire to tackle very specific problems, indiscipline in particular, and ultimately by the ambition to restore proper order in society.

---

39 Swanson, 'Unity and Diversity'; McKitterick, 'Unity and Diversity'.

Old Norms, New Boundaries

The next section focuses on the media and messages surrounding the 816–19 councils. Emilie Kurdziel begins by investigating the categories of *canonicus*, monks, nuns, and *canonicae* at the turning point of the ninth century. She argues that in normative sources, the word *canonicus* was not used to refer to 'canons', which is a later concept, but to any cleric who was not a monk. This implies that the normative texts issued at a central level between 780 and 820 and dealing with '*monaci*' and '*canonici*', including the *Institutio canonicorum*, were not addressing monks and 'canons' as we usually think, but the whole clergy at once. In this respect, the *Institutio canonicorum* was a deeper and bolder attempt at change than is usually thought, in so far as it offered an ethical model to every cleric who had not taken monastic vows and an institutional model of organization for every church (except the ones served by monks). The attempted reform was therefore much more far-reaching than generally imagined. The chapters by Rutger Kramer and Veronika Wieser and by Michael Eber then zoom in on the *Institutio canonicorum* and the *Institutio sanctimonialium*, that is, the two central texts through which the imperial centre communicated its admonitions regarding non-monastic communities. Treating, in turn, the way the patristic foundation of these texts informs the central argument made by the bishops, and the way their arguments reinforce gender patterns present in Carolingian ecclesiastical culture by mapping masculine power structures onto female communities, these chapters should be seen as a starting point for further research into not just the reception, but also the inception of these texts.

Reception and Reflection

We then move on to an exploration of the way key reform concepts were variously scrutinized, reformulated, implemented, and even resisted. Steve Ling focuses on Alcuin of Tours' elusive 'third order' — a distinctive response to questions about the enclosed life posed in the early ninth century. He suggests that while it ultimately lost out to the more prevalent and simpler dichotomy between monks and canons, it was reflective of a wider school of thought within the Frankish Church. Cinzia Grifoni's contribution then considers the contents, purposes, and intended audience of Hrabanus Maurus's *De institutione clericorum*, as well as the historical context in which it originated. Specifically, it compares the vision of the clergy elaborated by Hrabanus at Fulda in 819 with that developed at the Carolingian court and transmitted by the *Institutio canonicorum* of 816, showing that the abbot was willing to be flexible about the circumstances, but remained clear as to what a cleric should strive to be. Moving to another major monastery, Ingrid Rembold next re-interprets the 'apostates' of Saint-Denis and the conflict over the reform of this eminent community. The debate centred on Saint-Denis draws attention to the competing and evolving visions of reform which were operative in the

Carolingian world, and, in so doing, revisits the role of the Aachen reform councils themselves. Lastly, Johanna Jebe focuses on a local debate about good monastic practice through a detailed analysis of two codices (MSS Sang. 914 and 915), which allows for a comparative evaluation of how monastic ideals were perceived around 817 and 850 respectively.

Reform in Practice

The final chapters in the book advance a number of perspectives on the one practical aspect of ecclesiastical life that underpins all attempts to regulate the performance of collective, organized worship: the liturgy. It starts with Miriam Czock's contribution, which examines the way the attempts at categorizing communities intersected with local perspectives on sacred space. Looking closely at sources produced in relation to the endeavours of 816/17, it emerges that, no matter how nuanced, sacred space was conceptualized distinctively for monks, the clergy, or the laity. Concepts of sacred space were thus tailor-made to emphasize the separation of monks and their tasks from all other Christians. Then follows Renie Choy, who assesses the influence of Anton Baumstark's division between monastic and cathedral offices on the reception of the Carolingian reform councils, and juxtaposes local variance with attempts to establish some kind of gold standard. Closing off this section, and the book, are two contributions which further reveal the tension between universal ideals and local realities. Graeme Ward's contribution focuses on the controversial attempts of Amalarius of Metz to implement liturgical change in Lyon in the 830s and asks how they link back to 816. Arthur Westwell, finally, looks at manuscripts containing the so-called *ordines romani* in order to gauge the extent to which monastic and canonical communities would treat this common source differently according to their needs.

Reforming Identities, Categorizing Communities

Under the broad heading of 'Categorizing the Church', this volume thus seeks to examine and explore a range of distinct but interrelated aspects of the reform attempt of the early years of the reign of Louis the Pious, and to re-think old debates and perspectives on the nature and concerns of Carolingian 'reformers', by offering, among other things, new analyses of fundamental texts. In addition to placing the 816–19 councils in their historiographical context, the various chapters also illuminate vital themes of their pre-history and reception. Throughout what follows, local perspectives clash with universalizing aspirations; shared sources are altered through the specific needs of communities; and imperial interests make way for regional concerns (and vice versa). In fact, not all the authors are in agreement with one another — Steve Ling, for instance, offers a view that diverges from the interpretation offered by Emilie Kurdziel — but we see this as a strength rather than a weakness: a reflection of the reform processes we study. The contributions, taken together, show the problems inherent in adhering to a Grand Narrative of reform, not only by letting the sources speak for themselves, but also by taking on board the messiness that came with trying to distinguish between monks, clerics, female religious, and everybody else. Didn't these difficulties remain part of the ecclesiastical discourse for centuries to come?

Ultimately, the attempts to categorize or to re-categorize the Church and its members, and the resultant proliferation of texts are the result (and at the same time also the driver) of a broad public debate, whose central questions were: What does it mean fundamentally to be a cleric or a monk or a female religious? How to best adhere to this ideal? And how could each ecclesiastic, at his own rank and level, take part in it? The fundamental issue at stake was, in other words, a reassessment of clerical and monastic identities. These were obviously not new questions, but they became the subject of a lively public debate culminating in the first decades of the ninth century: a debate fuelled and encouraged by the court and its closest advisers but involving virtually the whole Church, including the *simplices*, from one end of the empire to the other.[40] And a debate whose local textual expressions and ramifications had not all been anticipated, such as its lasting consequences for ecclesiastical institutions and the history of the Church in the West.

Unlike the chimpanzee in Kafka's story, we cannot be sure that the Carolingians ever 'achieved what [they] wished to achieve'. Neither do we think that the present book answers all the questions it raises in this regard. But as Red Peter warns his audience in closing, 'You should not say it was not worth the effort'.

Works Cited

Primary Sources

Die Admonitio generalis Karls des Großen, ed. by Hubert Mordek (†), Klaus Zechiel-Eckes (†), and Michael Glatthaar, *Monumenta Germaniae Historica: Fontes iuris Germanici antiqui in usum scholarum separatim editi (Fontes iuris)*, XVI (Hannover: Hahn, 2012)

Isidore of Seville, *Etymologiarum sive Originum libri XX*, ed. by Wallace Martin Lindsay, 2 vols (Oxford: Clarendon, 1911); trans. by Stephen A. Barney and others, *The Etymologies of Isidore of Seville* (Cambridge: Cambridge University Press, 2006)

---

40 On the Carolingian debate culture, and the participation of simple clerics or monks to theological debates, see Pezé, *Le virus de l'erreur*, 369–428.

Kafka, Franz, 'Ein Bericht für eine Akademie', in Franz Kafka, *Ein Landarzt: Kleine Erzählungen* (Munich/Leipzig: Kurt Wolff, 1920), pp. 145–89; online at <http://ds.ub.uni-bielefeld.de/viewer/image/1667317/1/LOG_0000/> [accessed 8 September 2021]. The English translation is made by Ian Johnston and is available online at <http://johnstoi.web.viu.ca//kafka/reportforacademy.htm> [accessed 8 September 2021]

Secondary Works

Avis, Paul, review of John P. Bradbury, *Perpetually Reforming: A Theology of Church Reform and Renewal* (London: Bloomsbury, 2013), *Theology*, 117.3 (2014), 230–31

Barrow, Julia, 'Ideas and Applications of Reform', in *The Cambridge History of Christianity*, vol. 3: *Early Medieval Christianities, c. 600–c. 1100*, ed. by Thomas F. X. Noble and Julia M. H. Smith, The Cambridge History of Christianity, 3 (Cambridge: Cambridge University Press, 2008), pp. 345–62

———, 'Developing Definitions of Reform in the Church in the Ninth and Tenth Centuries', in *Italy and Early Medieval Europe: Papers for Chris Wickham*, ed. by Ross Balzaretti, Julia S. Barrow, and Patricia Skinner (Oxford: Oxford University Press, 2018), pp. 501–11

———, 'Le terme "réforme" est-il adapté pour décrire les changements qui s'opèrent dans les communautés cléricales entre le IXe et le Xe siècle?', *Ordonner l'Église II: Communautés cléricales et communautés monastiques dans le monde carolingien (8e–10e s.)*, ed. by Emilie Kurdziel, forthcoming

Bradbury, John P., *Perpetually Reforming: A Theology of Church Reform and Renewal* (London: Bloomsbury, 2013)

Bührer-Thierry, Geneviève, 'Pensée hiérarchique et différentiation sociale: quelques réflexions sur l'ordonnancement des sociétés du haut Moyen Âge', in *Hiérarchie et Stratification Sociale dans l'Occident Médiéval 400–1100*, ed. by Dominique Iogna-Prat, François Bougard, and Régine Le Jan, Collection Haut Moyen Âge, 6 (Turnhout: Brepols, 2008), pp. 363–90

Chambert-Protat, Pierre, Jérémy Delmulle, Warren Pezé, and Jeremy C. Thomson, eds, *La controverse carolingienne sur la prédestination: Histoire, textes, manuscrits* (Turnhout: Brepols, 2018)

Claussen, M. A., *The Reform of the Frankish Church: Chrodegang of Metz and the* Regula canonicorum *in the Eighth Century* (Cambridge: Cambridge University Press, 2004)

Close, Florence, *Uniformiser la foi pour unifier l'Empire: contribution à l'histoire de la pensée politico-théologique de Charlemagne* (Bruxelles: Académie royale de Belgique, 2011)

Coccia, Emanuele, '*Regula et vita*: Il diritto monastico e la regola francescana', *De Medio Aevo*, 1 (2013), 169–212

Contreni, John, 'The Carolingian Renaissance: Education and Literary Culture', in *The New Cambridge Medieval History*, vol. 2: *c. 700–c. 900*, ed. by Rosamond McKitterick (Cambridge: Cambridge University Press, 1995), pp. 709–57

Costambeys, Marios, Matthew Innes, and Simon MacLean, *The Carolingian World* (Cambridge: Cambridge University Press, 2011)

Davis, Jennifer, 'A Pattern of Power: Charlemagne's Delegation of Judicial Responsibilities', in *The Long Morning of Medieval Europe: New Directions in Early Medieval Studies*, ed. by Jennifer Davis and Michael McCormick (Aldershot: Ashgate, 2008), pp. 235–46

Dey, Hendrik, 'Bringing Chaos Out of Order: New Approaches to the Study of Early Western Monasticism', in *Western Monasticism ante litteram: The Spaces of Monastic Observance in Late Antiquity and the Early Middle Ages*, ed. by Hendrik Dey and Elizabeth Fentress, Disciplina Monastica, 7 (Turnhout: Brepols, 2011), pp. 19–41

Diem, Albrecht, 'The Gender of the Religious: Wo/men and the Invention of Monasticism', in *The Oxford Handbook of Women and Gender in Medieval Europe*, ed. by Judith M. Bennett and Ruth Mazo Karras (Oxford: Oxford University Press, 2013), pp. 432–46

Fichtenau, Heinrich, *The Carolingian Empire: The Age of Charlemagne*, trans. by Peter Munz (Oxford: Blackwell, 1957)

Evans, Karin, 'Audience and Discourse Community Theory', in *Theorizing Composition: A Critical Sourcebook of Theory and Scholarship in Contemporary Composition Studies*, ed. by Mary Lynch Kennedy (Westport, CT: Greenwood, 1998), pp. 1–5

Gaillard, Michèle, *D'une réforme à l'autre (816–934): Les communautés religieuses en Lorraine à l'époque Carolingienne*, Publications de la Sorbonne: Série Histoire Ancienne et Médiévale, 82 (Paris: Éditions de la Sorbonne, 2006)

——, 'De l'interaction entre crise et réforme: la politique monastique de Louis le Pieux et de Benoît d'Aniane', in *La Productivité d'une Crise: Le Règne de Louis le Pieux et la Transformation de L'Empire Carolingien*, ed. by Philippe Depreux and Stefan Esders, Relectio: Karolingische Perspectiven, 1 (Ostfildern: Thorbecke, 2018), pp. 313–27

Geuenich, Dieter, 'Kritische Anmerkungen zur sogenannten "anianischen Reform"', in *Mönchtum — Kirche — Herrschaft 750–1000: Josef Semmler zum 65. Geburtstag*, ed. by Dieter R. Bauer, Rudolf Hiestand, Brigitte Kasten, and Sönke Lorenz (Sigmaringen: Thorbecke, 1998), pp. 99–112

Gibson, Kelly, 'Rewriting History: Carolingian Reform and Controversy in Biographies of Saints' (unpublished PhD dissertation, Harvard University, 2011)

Guillot, Olivier, 'L'exhortation au partage des responsabilités entre l'empereur, l'épiscopat et les autres sujets, vers le milieu du règne de Louis de Pieux', in *Prédication et Propagande au Moyen Âge: Islam, Byzance, Occident — Penn-Paris-Dumbarton Oaks Colloquia III, Session des 20–25 Octobre 1980*, ed. by George Makdisi, Dominique Sourdel, and Janine Sourdel-Thomine (Paris: Presses Universitaires de France, 1983), pp. 87–110

Hartmann, Wilfried, *Die Synoden der Karolingerzeit im Frankenreich und in Italien*, Konziliengeschichte. Reihe A: Darstellungen (Paderborn: Schöningh, 1989)

——, *Kirche und Kirchenrecht um 900: die Bedeutung der spätkarolingischen Zeit für Tradition und Innovation im kirchlichen Recht* (Hannover: Hahn, 2008)

Hartmann, Wilfried, and Annette Grabowsky, eds, *Recht und Gericht in Kirche und Welt um 900* (Munich: R. Oldenbourg, 2007)

Helbig, Herbert, '*Fideles Dei et regis*: zur Bedeutungsentwicklung von Glaube und Treue im hohen Mittelalter', *Archiv für Kulturgeschichte*, 33 (1951), 275–306

Hohman, Laura A., 'Carolingian Sermons: Religious Reform, Pastoral Care, and Lay Piety' (unpublished PhD dissertation, Catholic University of America, 2016)

Hosoe, Kristina Marie, '*Regulae* and Reform in Carolingian Monastic Hagiography' (unpublished PhD dissertation, Yale University, 2014)

Howe, John, *Before the Gregorian Reform: The Latin Church at the Turn of the First Millennium* (Ithaca: Cornell University Press, 2016)

Innes, Matthew, *State and Society in the Early Middle Ages: The Middle Rhine Valley, 400–1100* (Cambridge: Cambridge University Press, 2000)

Isaïa, Marie-Céline, 'L'hagiographie contre la réforme dans l'église de Lyon au IXe siècle', *Médiévales*, 62: *Hagiographie et réforme dans l'Occident latin (VIe-XIIIe s.)*, ed. by Charles Mériaux and Stéphane Gioanni (2012/1), 83–104

Jong, Mayke de, 'Charlemagne's Church', in *Charlemagne: Empire and Society*, ed. by Joanna Story (Manchester: Manchester University Press, 2005), pp. 103–36

Klueting, Edeltraud, *Monasteria semper reformanda: Kloster- und Ordensreformen im Mittelalter* (Münste: LIT, 2005)

Kottje, Raymund, 'Einheit und Vielfalt des kirchlichen Lebens in der Karolingerzeit', *Zeitschrift für Kirchengeschichte*, vierte Folge XIV, 76 (1965), 323–42

———, 'Einleitung: monastische Reform oder Reformen?', in *Monastische Reformen im 9. und 10. Jahrhundert*, ed. by Raymund Kottje and Helmut Maurer (Sigmaringen: Thorbecke, 1989), pp. 9–13

Kramer, Rutger, '"… ut normam salutiferam cunctis ostenderet": représentations de l'autorité impériale dans la Vita Benedicti Anianensis et la Vita Adalhardi', in *Normes et Hagiographie dans l'Occident Chrétien (ve-xvie siècles): Actes du Colloque International de Lyon, 4–6 Octobre 2010*, ed. by Marie-Céline Isaïa and Thomas Granier (Turnhout: Brepols, 2014), pp. 101–18

———, *Rethinking Authority in the Carolingian Empire: Ideals and Expectations during the Reign of Louis the Pious (813–828)*, The Early Medieval North Atlantic (Amsterdam: Amsterdam University Press, 2019)

Krönert, Klaus, 'Réformer la vie monastique ou réformer l'empire? La vie d'Eigil de Fulda par Brun Candidus (vers 840)', *Médiévales*, 62: *Hagiographie et réforme dans l'Occident latin (VIe-XIIIe s.)*, ed. by Charles Mériaux and Stéphane Gioanni (2012/1), 49–65

Ladner, Gerhard, *The Idea of Reform: Its Impact on Christian Thought and Action in the Age of the Fathers* (Cambridge: Harvard University Press, 1959)

Ling, Stephen, 'The Cloister and Beyond: Regulating the Life of the Canonical Clergy in Francia, from Pippin III to Louis the Pious' (PhD thesis, University of Leicester, 2016)

McKitterick, Rosamond, *The Frankish Church and the Carolingian Reforms 789–895* (London: Royal Historical Society, 1977)

———, 'Unity and Diversity in the Carolingian Church', in *Unity and Diversity in the Christian Church*, ed. by Robert N. Swanson (Oxford: Blackwell, 1996), pp. 59–82

Meijns, Brigitte, *Aken of Jeruzalem? Het ontstaan en de hervorming van de kanonikale instellingen in Vlaanderen tot circa 1155* (Leuven: Leuven University Press, 2000)

Mordek, Hubert, 'Fränkische Kapitularien und Kapitulariensammlungen: Eine Einführung', in Hubert Mordek, *Studien zur fränkischen Herrschergesetzgebung: Aufsätze über Kapitularien und Kapitulariensammlungen ausgewählt zum 60. Geburtstag* (Frankfurt am Main: Peter Lang, 2000), pp. 1–53

Oexle, Otto Gerhard, *Forschungen zu monastischen und geistlichen Gemeinschaften in westfränkischen Bereich: Bestandteil des Quellenwerkes* Societas et Fraternitas, Münstersche Mittelalter-Schriften, 31 (Munich: Wilhelm Fink, 1978)

———, 'Mönchtum und Hierarchie im Okzident', in *Hiérarchie et Stratification Sociale dans l'Occident Médiéval 400–1100*, ed. by Dominique Iogna-Prat, François Bougard, and Régine Le Jan, Collection Haut Moyen Âge, 6 (Turnhout: Brepols, 2008), pp. 185–204

Patzold, Steffen, *Presbyter: Moral, Mobilität und die Kirchenorganisation im Karolingerreich* (Stuttgart: Anton Hiersemann, 2020)

———, 'Prozesse der Vereinheitlichung? Unitas, concordia und pax in der karolingischen Welt', in *Entscheiden und Regieren: Konsens als Element vormoderner Entscheidungsfindung in transkultureller Perspektive*, ed. by Linda Dohmen and Tilmann Trausch (Bonn: Vandenhoeck & Ruprecht, 2020), pp. 197–219

Pezé, Warren, *Le virus de l'erreur: La controverse carolingienne sur la double prédestination: Essai d'histoire sociale* (Turnhout: Brepols, 2017)

Pohl, Walter, 'Creating Cultural Resources for Carolingian Rule: Historians of the Christian Empire', in *The Resources of the Past in Early Medieval Europe*, ed. by Clemens Gantner, Rosamond McKittenck, and Sven Meeder (Cambridge: Cambridge University Press, 2015), pp. 15–33

Porter, James, *Audience and Rhetoric: An Archaeological Composition of the Discourse Community* (Englewood Cliffs: Prentice Hall, 1992)

Raaijmakers, Janneke, and Irene van Renswoude, 'The Ruler as Referee in the Theological Debates: Reccared and Charlemagne', in *Religious Franks: Religion and Power in the Frankish Kingdoms: Studies in Honour of Mayke de Jong*, ed. by Rob Meens, Dorine van Espelo, Bram van den Hoven van Genderen, Janneke Raaijmakers, Irene van Renswoude, and Carine van Rhijn (Manchester: Manchester University Press, 2016), pp. 51–71

Reuter, Timothy, '"Kirchenreform" und "Kirchenpolitik" im Zeitalter Karl Martells: Begriffe und Wirklichkeit', in *Karl Martell in seiner Zeit*, ed. by Jörg Jarnut, Beihefte der Francia, 37 (Sigmaringen: Thorbecke, 1994), pp. 34–59

Rhijn, Carine van, 'Priests and the Carolingian Reforms: The Bottlenecks of Local *correctio*', in *Texts and Identities in the Early Middle Ages*, ed. by Richard Corradini, Rob Meens, Christina Pössel, and Philip Shaw (Vienna: Österreichische Akademie der Wissenschaften, 2006), pp. 219–38

———, 'Royal Politics in Small Worlds: Local Priests and the Implementation of Carolingian correctio', in *Kleine Welten: ländliche Gesellschaften im Karolingerreich*, ed. by Thomas Kohl, Steffen Patzold, and Bernhard Zeller (Ostfildern: Jan Thorbecke, 2019), pp. 237–52

Rousseau, Philip, and Albrecht Diem, 'Monastic Rules (4th–9th c.)', in *The Cambridge History of Medieval Monasticism in the Latin West*, vol. 1: *Origins to the Eleventh Century*, ed. by Isabelle Cochelin and Alison Beach (Cambridge: Cambridge University Press, 2020), pp. 162–94

Schieffer, Rudolf, *Die Entstehung von Domkapiteln in Deutschland*, Bonner historische Forschungen, 43 (Bonn: Röhrscheid, 1976)

Schramm, Percy Ernst, 'Karl der Große: Denkart und Grundauffassungen — Die von ihm bewirkte Correctio ("Renaissance")', *Historische Zeitschrift*, 198 (1964), 306–45

Semmler, Josef, 'Benedictus II: una regula — una consuetudo', in *Benedictine Culture, 750–1050*, ed. by Willy Lourdaux and Daniel Verhelst, Mediaevalia Lovaniensia, Series I, Studia, 11 (Leuven: Leuven University Press, 1983), pp. 1–49

Smith, Julia M. H., '"Emending evil ways and praising God's omnipotence": Einhard and the Uses of the Roman Martyrs', in *Conversion in Late Antiquity and the Early Middle Ages: Seeing and Believing*, ed. by Kenneth Mills and Anthony Grafton (Rochester: University of Rochester Press, 2003), pp. 189–223

Sokel, Walter H., 'Identity and the Individual, or Past and Present: Franz Kafka's *A Report to an Academy* in a Psychoanalytic and a Sociohistorical Context', in *The Myth of Power and the Self: Essays on Franz Kafka*, ed. by Walter H. Sokel (Detroit: Wayne State University Press, 2002), pp. 268–91

Swales, John M., *Other Floors, Other Voices: A Textography of a Small University Building* (Mahwah: Lawrence Erlbaum, 1998)

Swanson, Robert N., 'Unity and Diversity, Rhetoric and Reality: Modelling "the Church"', *Journal of Religious History*, 20.2 (1996), 156–75

Teeuwen, Mariken, and Irene van Renswoude, eds, *The Annotated Book in the Early Middle Ages: Practices of Reading and Writing* (Turnhout: Brepols, 2018)

Vanderputten, Steven, *Monastic Reform as Process: Realities and Representations in Medieval Flanders, 900–1100* (Ithaca: Cornell University Press, 2013)

Walsham, Alexandra, 'Migrations of the Holy: Explaining Religious Change in Medieval and Early Modern Europe', *Journal of Medieval and Early Modern Studies*, 44.2 (2014), 241–80

Westwell, Arthur, Ingrid Rembold, and Carine van Rhijn, eds, *Rethinking the Carolingian Reforms* (Manchester: Manchester University Press, forthcoming)

Winkler, Marieke, 'Achter de coulissen van het theaterstuk *Bewustzijn*: Over *Monkey Business* (2003) van Jan Lauwereyns', in *Tegen de Schenen: Opstellen over Recente Nederlandse en Vlaamse Literatuur*, ed. by Jos Muijres and Marieke Winkler (Nijmegen: Vantilt, 2018), pp. 13–29

Wuthnow, Robert, *Communities of Discourse: Ideology and Social Structure in the Reformation, the Enlightenment, and European Socialism* (Cambridge, MA: Harvard University Press, 1989)

Zeller, Bernhard, Charles West, Francesca Tinti, Nicolas Schroeder, Marco Stoffella, Miriam Czock, Carine van Rhijn, Steffen Patzold, Thomas Kohl, and Wendy Davies, *Neighbours and Strangers: Local Societies in Early Medieval Europe* (Manchester: Manchester University Press, 2020)

CHARLES MÉRIAUX*

The Monastic Reforms of 816–19

Ideals and Reality

The grand monastic reform movement associated with the start of the reign of Louis the Pious (814–40) is generally thought to have been inspired by a single person: Benedict of Aniane (d. 821). Similarly, there is one name usually associated with the wave of historical research into this phenomenon in the second half of the twentieth century: that of the influential historian Josef Semmler (1928–2011).[1] In this chapter, rather than try to assess his entire oeuvre — an endeavour that would no doubt be left incomplete, even if we limit ourselves to his work on the Carolingian monastic world — I will highlight several approaches Semmler has taken to the monastic reforms in the early ninth century in the course of his research, and to put these into perspective. As such, I will first treat the texts that are seen to be the carriers of these reforms, before delving into their reception, the social and political implications of the proposed reforms, and finally, the implications of the reforms for the use of monastic space — an approach that is currently *en vogue* in French medieval studies.

Writing Reforms

In order to treat the work done on the reforms set in motion by Louis the Pious and Benedict of Aniane during the councils held in the summers of 816 and 817 and the winter of 818–19, no matter how briefly, it is necessary to start with an overview of the available documentation — especially since the circumstances of their composition and redaction remains unclear still. This remains true

---

* My thanks to Émilie Kurdziel and Rutger Kramer for the invitation in Vienna and to Rutger Kramer for translating this paper. Any remaining errors are my own.
1 Finger, 'Josef Semmler'; for a first overview on the monastic reform, see Semmler, 'Le monachisme occidental'; Rosé, 'Fondations et réformes'.

> **Charles Mériaux** is Professeur des Universités at the Université de Lille, Institut de recherches historiques du Septentrion UMR 8529.

Monastic Communities and Canonical Clergy in the Carolingian World (780–840): Categorizing the Church, ed. by Rutger Kramer, Emilie Kurdziel, and Graeme Ward, MMS 8 (Turnhout: Brepols, 2022), pp. 33–45
BREPOLS ❦ PUBLISHERS   DOI 10.1484/M.MMS-EB.5.128527

even if we acknowledge that it falls beyond the scope of this chapter to also dwell on the rules for canons, the *Institutio canonicorum* that may have been inspired by the measures taken by Chrodegang for his clerical community in Metz in the mid-eighth century,[2] or on the *Institutio sanctimonialium*, that 'règle a minima destinée aux communautés féminines ne souhaitant pas suivre la règle monastique'.[3] Concerning monastic communities, on the other hand, the point of reference has long remained the 'monastic capitulary', a text counting eighty-three chapters according to the edition by Victor Boretius in the first volume of the *MGH* collection *Capitularia Regum Francorum* from 1883.[4] In the edition made for the *Corpus Consuetudinum Monasticarum* series headed by Dom Kassius Hallinger, however, Josef Semmler demonstrated that this capitulary actually had been compiled from a capitulary counting thirty-six chapters promulgated in 816, and another capitulary, this one counting forty-two different chapters, dating to the summer of 817 in order to fill the gaps left by its predecessor.[5] In this second capitulary, additions to the *Regula Benedicti* are given so as to make its observance more attractive to the monastic communities within the Carolingian Empire. This, in part, explains the disparate character of these chapters.[6]

The remainder of the contemporary normative texts leaves much to be desired, given that it is limited to the letters by Emperor Louis the Pious to the archbishops who were not present at the reform councils,[7] the *Notitia de servitio monasteriorum* of 819,[8] and several decisions laid down in the so-called *Capitulare ecclesiasticum* issued in the winter of 818–19.[9] To this may be added several passages from Ermoldus Nigellus's *Carmen in honorem Hludovici* and from Ardo's *Vita Benedicti Anianensis*, as well as the *Concordia regularum* composed by that same Benedict of Aniane between 816 and 821 — a text which has been newly edited by Pierre Bonnerue in 1999.[10]

In addition to these strictly normative texts, composed by members of the entourage of Louis the Pious, the *réécritures* of a number of saints' lives, and the attempts to bring their contents in line with the standards set by the court by proposing that their protagonists were the first ones to follow these

---

2 Claussen, *The Reform of the Frankish Church*; Semmler, 'Die Kanoniker und ihre Regel im 9. Jahrhundert'.
3 Gaillard, *D'une réforme à l'autre*; Schilp, *Norm und Wirklichkeit*; Schilp, 'Die Wirkung der Aachener Institutio sanctimonialium'.
4 *Capitulare monasticum*, ed. by Boretius, pp. 344–49.
5 *Capitulare monasticum*, ed. by Semmler, pp. 452–81.
6 Gaillard, *D'une réforme à l'autre*, p. 135.
7 *Hludowici ad archiepiscopos epistolae*, ed. by Boretius, pp. 338–42.
8 *Notitia de servitio monasteriorum*, ed. by Boretius, pp. 349–52; Wagner, 'Zur Notitia de servitio monasteriorum'.
9 *Capitulare ecclesiasticum*, ed. by Boretius, pp. 275–80.
10 *Ermoldi Nigelli Carmen in honorem Hludovici*, ed. by Dümmler, pp. 4–79; Ardo, *Vita Benedicti abbatis Anianensis*, ed. by Waitz, pp. 200–20; Benedictus Anianensis, *Concordia regularum*, ed. by Bonnerue.

new norms, should also be seen as carriers of the proposed reforms.[11] These *réécritures* were the result of local initiatives, such as happened in Ghent in Flanders, where the *Vita Bavonis* provides us with an excellent example of a hagiographical composition meant to accompany and support the reform movement. Saint Bavo was the eponymous patron of one of the two monasteries founded in the city in the mid-seventh century (the other one being dedicated to Saint Peter). Both communities opted for the canonical life, at least until the middle of the tenth century. Both were also led by the lay abbot Einhard from 819 until his death in 840 — Einhard being one of the most well-known courtiers of the Carolingian court at the time of course, as well as abbot of Saint-Wandrille and Saint-Servatius in Maastricht. From a literary point of view, the *Vita Bavonis* is undoubtedly a product of the first phase of the so-called Carolingian Renaissance, with its literary stylings and borrowings from classical authors.[12] Evidently, oral traditions about the saint persisted in Ghent at the start of the ninth century, which the author had had to take into account even if they were reduced to mere echoes. Bavo was a seventh-century aristocrat who, after the death of his wife, abandoned the secular life in pursuit of an eremitic lifestyle. Nonetheless, the author wants to make readers think that the cell of the saint was situated inside the monastery — something which is manifestly not the case.

The first lesson of the text concerns the discipline of the monastic life imposed on hermits by the Carolingian court, as they are asked to join a community just like Bavo had done. In doing so, the author insists on the kind of stability that was characteristic of the *Regula Benedicti*. Other such traits are also developed, such as obedience to the abbot or the requirement to assist during the liturgical office. The only challenge was to reconcile all this with the fact that Bavo did not exactly conform to the ideal of a 'Benedictine' monk in the early ninth century. Paradoxically, however, a recluse like Bavo, living in a cell but supported by monks of a nearby community, represented an ideal of sanctity — very demanding, for sure, but also very compatible with the canonical life which allowed for a greater degree of autonomy in their daily lives. Moreover, this text also highlights the many links that Bavo retained with the local community, notably with the secular clergy in the area — something which definitely would have spoken to the canons in Ghent. Through such efforts, the *Vita Bavonis* thus shows how narrative traditions about a patron saint's life could be adapted to accommodate reforms, such as those that would have been brought to Ghent by the court of which Einhard, leader of the community, remained an integral part.

---

11 Isaïa and Granier ed., *Normes et hagiographie dans l'Occident médiéval*; Goullet, *Écriture et réécriture hagiographiques*; Gioanni and Mériaux ed., *Réforme(s) et hagiographie dans l'Occident latin*; Mériaux, 'Bishops, Monks and Priests', pp. 150–53; Helvétius, 'Les modèles de sainteté'.

12 *Vita Bavonis*, ed. by Krusch, pp. 534–46; Declercq, 'La *Vita prima Bavonis*', pp. 595–626.

The Reception of Reforms: Differences between and among Communities

Josef Semmler's work has largely focused on assessing the impact the reforms of 816–19 had on the communities within the empire — to what extent they were simply accepted or indeed met with resistance.[13] To take but one well-documented example, the difficulties that emerged in the monastery of Fulda crystallized less around the reforms themselves, and more on the place the monks aspired to give their foundation within the imperial monastic system that emerged under Louis the Pious.[14] From 812 on, the monks of Fulda were in conflict with their abbot Ratgar, whose megalomania and excessive spending on the construction of a new abbatial church caused problems within the community. The larger point, however, was that they spoke out against the fact that Fulda was increasingly turning into a hub of political and cultural power. This situation necessitated considerable efforts on their part, which they resented. In response, the emperor allowed the deposition of Ratgar and the election of a new abbot, named Eigil. A possible solution to the crisis was offered by Eigil himself in his redaction of the *Vita Sturmi*, which aimed at showing that both the introduction of the *Regula Benedicti* and the close collaboration with the sovereign were in line with ancient traditions established by Boniface, which had in turn inspired Sturm, the first abbot of Fulda.[15] However, it fell to another hagiographical text, the *Vita Eigilis*, composed about twenty-five years after the events, to revisit the crisis caused by Ratgar's deposition. This *Vita Eigilis* consists of two parts, one in prose, the other in verse. An ambitious work, its narrative shows how it was influenced by the context of the 830s, when Fulda was affected by the crises that shook the entire empire. When Brun Candidus edited the *Vita Eigilis* in the 840s, the narrative this time would serve the double function of becoming a 'mirror' for the monks in order to quell the present conflict, but also a 'mirror' for the rulers who were encouraged to restore peace and concord to the empire.[16]

In certain monastic foundations of the empire, the reception of the proposed reforms went beyond the simple choice between *ordo monasticus* or *ordo Canonicus*. As shown by several examples from the North of Gaul, other possibilities existed that showed that, even if the adoption of the *ordo monasticus* does not seem to have been a problem for large communities such as Saint-Amand or Saint-Vaast in Arras, altogether more curious situations did emerge.[17] In Sithiu (Saint-Bertin), the community was cut into two distinct

---

13 Semmler, 'Benedictus II.'; for the example of Saint-Denis, see Semmler, 'Saint-Denis'.
14 Raaijmakers, *The Making of the Monastic Community of Fulda*.
15 Eigil, *Vita Sturmi*, ed. by Pertz.
16 *Vita Aegil*, ed. by Becht-Jördens; Krönert, 'Réformer la vie monastique'.
17 Mériaux, *Gallia irradiata*, pp. 247–49 and 316–18.

groups in 820 under the abbacy of Fridugisus, who had been archchancellor of Louis the Pious since 819. Out of this split grew a monastic community around the church of Saint-Bertin, and a canonical community around the church of Saint Audomar (Saint-Omer). As shown by Brigitte Meijns, however, the interpretation that this amounted to a veritable conflict actually only goes back to the chronicler Folcuin, writing over a hundred years later. In his work, the events of the 820s are placed in the context of the monastic reforms imposed by the count of Flanders around the year 944.[18] Contrary to the Carolingian reforms, these tenth-century measures were not accepted by a part of the religious living there. Up until that time, they seemed to have continued living on more or less equal footing during the ninth and tenth centuries, under the authority of a single abbot.

Similarly interesting forms of symbiosis between monastic and canonical foundations existed throughout the ninth century, as shown by Daniel Misonne and, again, Brigitte Meijns, who talks of 'secular chapters that depend on Benedictine abbeys'.[19] While adopting the *ordo monasticus*, a number of larger communities profited from the decisions made in Aachen in 816–19 by supporting small canonical communities that were charged with defending their interests and possessions situated further from the centre. The best-documented case is that of the canons of the abbey of Centula (Saint-Riquier) in the ninth century. At other places, like the monastery of Lobbes in the tenth century, the community of canons would even take care of the liturgy in the principal basilica around the tomb of Saint Ursmer, patron of the monastery. Such cases become more prevalent in the tenth and eleventh centuries, but some of them undoubtedly go back to the reforms of 816–19. Still, we should be on guard against an all-too vertical or hierarchical interpretation of such measures. Recent research has shown that the reception of monastic reform measures should not be seen in terms of outright adoption or rejection of the Rule of Saint Benedict as imposed by the imperial court and its circle of reformers. Similarly, the superior status of the *ordo monasticus* is not a given. Instead, paradigmatic cases like Saint-Denis or Fulda are more the exception than the rule, which held that solutions were developed locally by the communities themselves as they sought to deal with the impetus from above.

Monasticism and Society

Our understanding of the broad societal implications of the reform efforts initiated in 816–19 has progressed considerably from the 1970s onward, largely due to new critical research into a new type of hitherto neglected source material. These were the necrologies and commemorative documents,

---

18 Meijns, 'Chanoines et moines à Saint-Omer'.
19 See Misonne, 'Chapitres séculiers', and Meijns, 'Communautés de chanoines'.

produced by prayer confraternities established not only between religious foundations (monastic or canonical), but also between those foundations and the lay aristocracy, from the rulers and their entourage downward. Studied by Gerd Tellenbach and his students in Freiburg, or by Karl Schmid, Joachim Wollasch, and their colleagues in Münster (from amongst whom the name of Otto Gerhard Oexle should definitely be mentioned), these texts stand witness to the observation that the reform movement was not limited to intra-monastic musings, aimed at reinforcing discipline and spreading the *Regula Benedicti*. The lists of names, when properly studied, allow us to reconstruct entire networks of people who were active parties in the reform efforts, showing that they were not only the brainchild of Benedict of Aniane. Moreover, they indicate the means by which these reforms were financed (a considerable amount was raised by benefices from prayers for the dead), and help us understand their ultimate goals (the integration of the monasteries in larger frameworks, which were simultaneously spiritual, political, ecclesiastical, and cultural). They sketch a picture of places of intense social exchange and practice — an image that the normative texts of 816–19 do not allow us to see.[20]

While studying the confraternities centred on the monastery of Reichenau, put to writing in 824, Dieter Geuenich concluded that Benedict of Aniane did not occupy a central place in this network — even if he had died only three years previously.[21] He only appears at the start of the list of names of the monks of Marmoutier, the community he led before founding the monastery of Inda. In the course of the same research, the importance of fraternities around a bishop was also highlighted. This in turn demonstrated how the reforms were not uniquely royal and monastic. For the longest time, they had been spiritually and practically supported by episcopal initiatives as well. Their contribution is made visible already in a canon from the Council of Ver (755), in which monks are required to submit to the *episcoporum potestas*, as Semmler showed quite some time ago.[22]

In the course of his research on the *nomina amicorum viventium* from 824, Dieter Geuenich, for his part, reminds us that the monastic reforms were always part of a much grander initiative. The presence of a wide array of different dignitaries such as Hilduin (who brought the monastic reform movement to Saint-Denis), Einhard (abbot of the monastery of Saint-Wandrille, but also of canonical foundations in Ghent), or even Fridugisus (who had just created a community that was simultaneously monastic and canonical in Sithiu), shows that the entourage of Louis the Pious was always more concerned

---

20 For an excellent overview, see Oexle, 'Les moines d'Occident'; Treffort, *L'Église carolingienne et la mort*; Le Jan, 'Nomina viventium, nomina defunctorum'.
21 Geuenich, 'Gebetsgedenken und anianische Reform'.
22 *Concilium Vernense*, ed. by Boretius, 3, p. 33: 'Ut unusquisque episcoporum potestatem habeat in sua parrochia, tam de clero quam de regularibus vel secularibus, ad corregendum et emendandum secundum ordinem canonicam spiritale, ut sic vivant qualiter Deo placere possint'; Semmler, '*Episcopi potestas* und karolingische Klosterpolitik'.

with the integration of individual monasteries into the wider political milieu, than with enforcing a choice between the *ordo monasticus* and the *ordo canonicus*. The *Notitia de servitio monasteriorum*, for instance, is particularly explicit when it comes to the three kinds of service — economical, military, and spiritual — that were expected of religious foundations. In the text, a distinction is made between those who owed *dona et militia*, those who owed 'sola dona sine militia', and finally those who were only expected to contribute 'nec dona nec militia' but 'solae orationes pro salute imperatoris vel filiorum eius et stabilitate imperii'.[23] We find a clear illustration of how that worked in practice when, from 828 onwards, the monks of Fulda were asked to perform a thousand masses in support of a Frankish military expedition, led by Louis the German, against the Bulgars.[24]

Despite the importance of the documents promulgated in 816–19, the monastic reforms and the acceptance of the *Regula Benedicti* remained a lengthy process. Carloman had already called for these measures in 742; Charlemagne encouraged them from 802 onwards; and Benedict of Aniane intensified the movement rather than beginning it. As shown by Otto Gerhard Oexle, the *Regula Benedicti*, with its insistence on *stabilitas*, was not only attractive to those propagating reforms from the top down, but also catered to the needs of those operating from the bottom up. It offered a 'forme spécifique de la vie sociale' to which laypeople were also invited as they benefited from the communal prayers as well.[25] In the end, the research done on these confraternity networks has done much toward opening the study of the reform movement to include not only the point of view of high institutions — the Church and the royal/imperial court — but also the perspective from the local and regional social groups that had to deal with the implications of the reforming initiatives throughout the early Middle Ages.

Open Spaces, (En)closed Spaces

While the monastic reform movement certainly turned monasteries into places where social praxis was imposed upon the inhabitants, it also allowed for innovative and differentiated uses of space in its wake.[26] For the purpose of this chapter, I will limit myself to a few remarks on the consequences of the reforms for a very specific phenomenon: the way the movement allowed monasteries to take charge of the cult of saints.[27] From the seventh century

---

23 Oexle, 'Les moines d'Occident', p. 264; see above, Note 8.
24 Oexle, 'Les moines d'Occident', pp. 253–64; *Epistolarum Fuldensium fragmenta*, ed. by Dümmler, p. 518.
25 Oexle, 'Les moines d'Occident', pp. 257–58.
26 Lauwers ed., *Monastères et espace social*.
27 Bath-Sheva, *Le pèlerinage à l'époque carolingienne*; Mériaux, 'Les sanctuaires du haut Moyen Âge'; Smith, 'L'accès des femmes aux saintes reliques'.

onwards, we witness the development of tensions between the desire to open the grand basilicas to the faithful and increasing flocks of pilgrims on the one hand, and the imposition, by Queen Balthild, of a monastic rule of life on the communities that served these altars.[28] In many cases, the Carolingian monastic reform movement, with its insistence on enclosure of the monks and nuns, seemingly ran counter to the idea that important sanctuaries should remain open to the public. This is, incidentally, one of the main reasons why in many cases a community opted to forgo the *Regula Benedicti* in favour of a rule for canons, such as happened in Saint-Martin of Tours.

Commenting on Chapter 52 of the *Regula Benedicti*, on the oratory of the monastery, an undated capitulary of Charlemagne specifies that 'there where the bodies of the saints rest, there should be a second oratory where the brethren can pray separately'.[29] In 794, the capitulary issued in the wake of the Council of Frankfurt called for the construction of oratories dedicated to monastic offices inside the cloister — implying that the church where the saintly relics were situated could be visited by the faithful.[30] Similarly, when the abbot Angilbert had the churches of Centula/Saint-Riquier rebuilt, the chosen arrangement of the buildings, together with the new liturgical scheme he developed, indicated that the main church, with its extraordinary collection of relics gathered by his predecessors, would be open to the lay public during certain feast days. The two other oratories, on the other hand, dedicated to Saint Mary and Saint Benedict, were and remained reserved for the exclusive use of the monks.[31]

In Gaul, the echoes of larger-scale architectural transformations may be found in many narrative texts. In the mid-ninth century, in Elnone/Saint-Amand, it was told how the relics of Saint Amandus were supposedly moved in the seventh century to a church outside the monastery, because it was larger and accessible to women as well. This narrative, however, makes it seem as if a problem that would have only emerged during the reforms of Benedict of Aniane had already been solved a long time ago.[32] In the course of the ninth century, a new equilibrium was gradually established. For example, while it remained strictly forbidden for laypeople — and especially women — to enter the confines of Sithiu/Saint-Bertin, whose monks even refused entry to countess Elftrude of Flanders in 918, this inflexibility towards the lay population was made possible in part by the fact that their neighbours, the canons of Saint-Omer, did open their church

---

28 Dierkens, 'Prolégomènes à une histoire des relations culturelles'.
29 *Duplex legationis edictum*, ed. by Boretius, 7, p. 63: 'Ut ubi corpora sanctorum requiescunt aliud oratorium habeatur, ubi fratres secrete possint orare'.
30 *Capitulare Francofurtense*, ed. by Werminghoff, 15, p. 168: 'De monasterio ubi corpora sanctorum sunt: ut habeat oratorium intra claustra ubi peculiare officium et diuturnum fiat'.
31 Hariulf, *Chronicon Centulense*, ed. by Lot, II. 7–11, pp. 53–76 and 296–306.
32 *Vita Amandi secunda*, ed. by Krusch, p. 472; Mériaux, 'Les sanctuaires du haut Moyen Âge', p. 82.

to the flock.[33] More generally, the monastic reform movement thus forced every community to redefine its own boundaries in whatever way they felt corresponded to their (perceived) relation with the wider world. That way, they could address both their needs and duties as monks (or nuns), and the obligations that came with being a sanctuary for prestigious saints' cults.[34] In a 1997 article on the tombs of saints in the Frankish world, Werner Jacobsen mentions the many possibilities open to monastic authorities in this regard.[35] In places where the enclosure would be strictly guarded, it was evidently not necessary to adapt a crypt in the abbatial church with the express purpose of hosting pilgrims, since the faithful would merely be relegated to an outside oratory. Similarly, if the faithful were allowed to enter the main sanctuary at certain points in the year, such as was the case in Saint-Riquier, it would not be necessary to engage in an extensive rebuilding process. Conversely, the construction of a crypt would become all but unavoidable for churches where the body of a saint was an intrinsic part of the local community, and/or where lay people were welcomed on a more regular basis.

***

In conclusion, we can safely say that not only were the monasteries themselves opened up during the Carolingian reform movement, but also that the study of this phenomenon has benefited from an increasingly broad approach and fresh perspectives gained from looking at new source material — an approach first hinted at by Josef Semmler and his contemporaries. From a purely institutional history, to a history of texts, to a history that mostly takes into account the impulses given by those people most affected by the measures — be they lay or ecclesiastical — the way the reforms have been studied over the past twenty years show how researchers are increasingly exploring the full social and political implications of this new wave of monastic reforms. In all this, it is recognized that the conditions on the ground and the reception of 'new' ideas was as important as the circumstances under which reform measures were formulated at court. In so doing, modern research now also allows us to reassess the centrality of the reforms in the contemporary discourse.

---

33 *Gesta abbatum Sithiensium*, éd. by Holder-Egger, 103 and 106, pp. 627–28; Mériaux, 'Les sanctuaires du haut Moyen Âge', p. 83.
34 Mériaux and Noizet, 'Moines, chanoines et espace urbain en Flandre'.
35 Jacobsen, 'Saints' Tombs in Frankish Church Architecture'; Crook, *The Architectural Setting of the Cult of Saints*.

Works Cited

Primary Sources

Ardo, *Vita Benedicti abbatis Anianensis*, ed. by Georg Waitz, in *Monumenta Germaniae Historica: Scriptores*, xv. 1 (Hannover: Hahn, 1887), pp. 200–20

Benedictus Anianensis, *Concordia regularum*, ed. by Pierre Bonnerue, Corpus Christianorum Continuatio Medievalis, 168 (Turnhout: Brepols, 1999)

Capitulare ecclesiasticum, ed. by Alfred Boretius, in *Monumenta Germaniae Historica: Capitularia regum Francorum*, I (Hannover: Hahn, 1883), no. 138, pp. 275–80

Capitulare Francofurtense, ed. by Alfred Werminghoff, in *Monumenta Germaniae Historica: Concilia*, II. 1 (Hannover: Hahn, 1896), no. 19, pp. 165–71

Capitulare monasticum, ed. by Alfred Boretius, in *Monumenta Germaniae Historica: Capitularia regum Francorum*, I (Hannover: Hahn, 1883), no. 170, pp. 344–49

Capitulare monasticum, ed. by Josef Semmler, in *Corpus Consuetudinum Monasticarum*, vol. 1: *Initia Consuetudinis Benedictinae: Consuetudines saeculi octavi et noni* (Siegburg: Franz Schmitt, 1963), pp. 452–81

Concilium Vernense a. 755. Jul. 11, ed. by Alfred Boretius, in *Monumenta Germaniae Historica: Capitularia regum Francorum*, I (Hannover: Hahn, 1883), no. 14, pp. 33–37

Duplex legationis edictum, ed. by Alfred Boretius, in *Monumenta Germaniae Historica: Capitularia regum Francorum*, I (Hannover: Hahn, 1883), no. 23, pp. 62–64

Eigil, *Vita Sturmi*, ed. by Georg Heinrich Pertz, in *Monumenta Germaniae Historica: Scriptores*, II (Hannover: Hahn, 1829), pp. 366–77

Epistolarum Fuldensium fragmenta, ed. by Ernst Dümmler, in *Monumenta Germaniae Historica: Epistolae*, v (Hannover: Hahn, 1899), pp. 517–33

Ermoldus Nigellus, *Carmen in honorem Hludovici*, ed. by Ernst Dümmler, in *Monumenta Germaniae Historica: Poetae*, II (Berlin: Weidmann, 1884), pp. 4–79

Gesta abbatum Sithiensium, ed. by Oswald Holder-Egger, in *Monumenta Germaniae Historica: Scriptores*, XIII (Hannover: Hahn, 1881), pp. 606–35

Hariulf, *Chronicon Centulense*, ed. by Ferdinand Lot, *Chronique de l'abbaye de Saint-Riquier (Ve siècle–1104)* (Paris: Picard, 1904)

Hludowici ad archiepiscopos epistolae, ed. by Alfred Boretius, in *Monumenta Germaniae Historica: Capitularia regum Francorum*, I (Hannover: Hahn, 1883), no. 169, pp. 338–42

Notitia de servitio monasteriorum, ed. by Alfred Boretius, in *Monumenta Germaniae Historica: Capitularia regum Francorum*, I (Hannover: Hahn, 1883), no. 171, pp. 349–52

Vita Aegil, ed. by Gereon Becht-Jördens, *Vita Aegil Abbatis Fuldensis a Candido ad Modestum edita prosa et versibus: Ein Opus geminum des IX. Jahrhunderts* (Marburg: Selbstverlag, 1994)

Vita Amandi secunda, ed. by Bruno Krusch, in *Monumenta Germaniae Historica: Scriptores Rerum Merovingicarum*, v (Hannover: Hahn, 1910), pp. 450–85

Vita Bavonis, ed. by Bruno Krusch, in *Monumenta Germaniae Historica: Scriptores Rerum Merovingicarum*, IV (Hannover: Hahn, 1902), pp. 534–46

Secondary Works

Albert, Bath-Sheva, *Le pèlerinage à l'époque carolingienne*, Bibliothèque de la Revue d'histoire ecclésiastique, 82 (Louvain-la-Neuve: Revue d'histoire ecclésiastique, 1999)

Claussen, Martin A., *The Reform of the Frankish Church: Chrodegang of Metz and the Regula canonicorum in the Eighth Century*, Cambridge Studies in Medieval Life and Thought, 4th series, 61 (Cambridge: Cambridge University Press, 2004)

Crook, John, *The Architectural Setting of the Cult of Saints in the Early Christian West (c. 300–c. 1200)*, Oxford Historical Monographs (Oxford: Oxford University Press, 2000)

Declercq, Georges, 'La *Vita prima Bavonis* et le culte de saint Bavon à l'époque carolingienne', in *Scribere sanctorum gesta: Recueil d'études d'hagiographie médiévale offert à Guy Philippart*, ed. by Étienne Renard, Michel Trigalet, Xavier Hermand, and Paul Bertrand, Hagiologia, 3 (Turnhout: Brepols, 2005), pp. 595–626

Dierkens, Alain, 'Prolégomènes à une histoire des relations culturelles entre les îles britanniques et le continent pendant le haut moyen âge: La diffusion du monachisme dit colombanien ou iro-franc dans quelques monastères de la région parisienne au VIIe siècle et la politique religieuse de la reine Bathilde', in *La Neustrie: Les pays au nord de la Loire de 650 à 850*, ed. by Hartmut Atsma, Beihefte der Francia, 16.2 (Sigmaringen: Thorbecke, 1989), pp. 371–93

Finger, Heinz, 'Josef Semmler (1928–2011)', *Francia*, 40 (2013), 469–71

Gaillard, Michèle, *D'une réforme à l'autre (816–934): les communautés religieuses en Lorraine à l'époque carolingienne*, Histoire ancienne et médiévale, 82 (Paris: Publications de la Sorbonne, 2006)

Geuenich, Dieter, 'Gebetsgedenken und anianische Reform — Beobachtungen zu den Verbrüderungsbeziehungen der Äbte im Reich Ludwigs des Frommen', in *Monastische Reformen im 9. und 10. Jahrhundert*, ed. by Raymund Kottje and Helmut Maurer, Vorträge und Forschungen, 38 (Sigmaringen: Thorbecke, 1989), pp. 79–106

Gioanni, Stéphane, and Charles Mériaux, ed., *Réforme(s) et hagiographie dans l'Occident latin (VIe–XIIIe siècle)*, Médiévales, 62 (Saint-Denis: Presses universitaires de Vincennes, 2012)

Goullet, Monique, *Écriture et réécriture hagiographiques: Essai sur les réécritures de Vies de saints dans l'Occident médiéval (VIIIe–XIIIe s.)*, Hagiologia, 4 (Turnhout: Brepols, 2005)

Helvétius, Anne-Marie, 'Les modèles de sainteté dans les monastères de l'espace belge du VIIIe au Xe siècle', *Revue bénédictine*, 103 (1993), 51–67

Isaïa, Marie-Céline, and Thomas Granier, ed., *Normes et hagiographie dans l'Occident médiéval (VIe–XVIe siècle)*, Hagiologia, 9 (Turnhout: Brepols, 2014)

Jacobsen, Werner, 'Saints' Tombs in Frankish Church Architecture', *Speculum*, 72 (1997), 1107–43

Krönert, Klaus, 'Réformer la vie monastique ou réformer l'Empire? La Vie d'Eigil de Fulda par Brun Candidus (vers 840)', *Médiévales*, 62 (2012), 49–66

Lauwers, Michel, ed., *Monastères et espace social: Genèse et transformation d'un système de lieux dans l'Occident médiéval*, Collection d'études médiévales de Nice, 15 (Turnhout: Brepols, 2015)

Le Jan, Régine, '*Nomina viventium, nomina defunctorum*: les interactions entre vivants et morts dans les *libri memoriales* carolingiens', in *Les vivants et les morts dans les sociétés médiévales*, Histoire ancienne et médiévale, 158 (Paris: Éditions de la Sorbonne, 2018), pp. 121–34

Meijns, Brigitte, 'Chanoines et moines à Saint-Omer: Le dédoublement de l'abbaye de Sithiu par Fridogise (820–834) et l'interprétation de Folcuin (vers 962)', *Revue du Nord*, 83 (2001), 691–705

——, 'Communautés de chanoines dépendant d'abbayes bénédictines pendant le haut Moyen Âge: L'exemple du comté de Flandre', *Revue bénédictine*, 113 (2003), 90–123

Mériaux, Charles, *Gallia irradiate: Saints et sanctuaires dans le nord de la Gaule du haut Moyen Âge*, Beiträge zur Hagiographie, 4 (Stuttgart: Franz Steiner, 2006)

——, 'Les sanctuaires du haut Moyen Âge en Gaule (VIe–XIe siècle)', in *Ordini religiosi e santuari in età medievale e moderna*, ed. by Lucia M. M. Olivieri (Bari: Edipuglia, 2013), pp. 73–84

——, 'Bishops, Monks and Priests: Defining Religious Institutions in Writing and Rewriting Saint's Lives (Francia, 6th–11th Centuries)', in *Hagiography and the History of Latin Christendom (500–1500)*, ed. by Samantha Kahn Herrick, Reading Medieval Sources, 4 (Leiden: Brill, 2020), pp. 143–60

Mériaux, Charles, and Hélène Noizet, 'Moines, chanoines et espace urbain en Flandre (X^e-XIe siècles)', in *Cluny: Les moines et la société au premier âge féodal*, ed. by Dominique Iogna-Prat, Michel Lauwers, Florian Mazel, and Isabelle Rosé, Art & Société (Rennes: Presses universitaires de Rennes, 2013), pp. 65–78

Misonne, Daniel, 'Chapitres séculiers dépendant d'abbayes bénédictines au Moyen Âge dans l'ancien diocèse de Liège', in *La vita comune del clero nei secoli XI e XII*, vol. 1 (Milano: Vita e pensiero, 1962), pp. 412–32

Oexle, Otto Gerhard, 'Les moines d'Occident et la vie politique et sociale dans le haut Moyen Âge', *Revue bénédictine*, 103 (1993), 255–72

Raaijmakers, Janneke, *The Making of the Monastic Community of Fulda (c. 744–c. 900)*, Cambridge Studies in Medieval Life and Thought, 4th series, 83 (Cambridge: Cambridge University Press, 2012)

Rosé, Isabelle, 'Fondations et réformes à l'époque carolingienne', in *Monachesimo d'Oriente e d'Occidente nell'alto Medioevo*, Settimane di studio della fondazione Centro italiano di studi sull'alto Medioevo, 64 (Spoleto: Centro italiano di studi sull'alto Medioevo, 2017), pp. 397–459

Schilp, Thomas, *Norm und Wirklichkeit religiöser Frauengemeinschaften im Frühmittelalter*, Veröffentlichungen des Max-Planck-Instituts für Geschichte, 137 (Göttingen: Vandenhoeck & Ruprecht, 1998)

——, 'Die Wirkung der Aachener "Institutio sanctimonialium" des Jahres 816', in *Frühformen von Stiftskirchen in Europa: Funktion und Wandel religiöser Gemeinschaften vom 6. bis zum Ende des 11. Jahrhunderts; Festgabe für Dieter Mertens zum 65. Geburtstag*, ed. by Sönke Lorenz and Thomas Zotz, Schriften zur südwestdeutschen Landeskunde, 54 (Leinfelden-Echterdingen: DRW, 2005), pp. 163–84

Semmler, Josef, 'Episcopi potestas und karolingische Klosterpolitik', in *Mönchtum, Episkopat und Adel zur Gründungszeit des Klosters Reichenau*, ed. by Arno Borst, Vorträge und Forschungen, 20 (Sigmaringen: Thorbecke, 1974), pp. 305–95

——, 'Benedictus II. Una Regula — Una Consuetudo', in *Benedictine Culture (750–1050)*, ed. by Willem Lourdaux et Daniel Verhelst, Mediaevalia Lovanensia, Series I, Studia XI (Leuven: Leuven University Press, 1983), pp. 1–49

——, 'Saint-Denis: von der Bischöflichen Coemeterialbasilika zur Königlichen Benediktinerabtei', in *La Neustrie: Les pays au nord de la Loire de 650 à 850*, ed. by Hartmut Atsma, Beihefte der Francia, 16.2 (Sigmaringen: Thorbecke, 1989), pp. 75–123

——, 'Le monachisme occidental du VIIIe au Xe siècle: Formation et réformation', *Revue bénédictine*, 103 (1993), 68–89

——, 'Die Kanoniker und ihre Regel im 9. Jahrhundert', in *Studien zum weltlichen Kollegiatstift in Deutschland*, ed. by Irene Crusius, Veröffentlichungen des Max-Planck-Instituts für Geschichte, 114, Studien zur Germania Sacra, 18 (Göttingen: Vandenhoeck & Ruprecht, 1995), pp. 62–109

Smith, Julia, 'L'accès des femmes aux saintes reliques au haut Moyen Âge', *Médiévales*, 40 (2001), 83–100

Treffort, Cécile, *L'Église carolingienne et la mort: Christianisme, rites funéraires et pratiques commémoratives*, Collection d'histoire et d'archéologie médiévale, 3 (Lyon: Presses universitaires de Lyon, 1996)

Wagner, Heinrich, 'Zur Notitia de servitio monasteriorum von 819', *Deutsches Archiv für Erforschung des Mittelalters*, 55 (1999), 417–38

Origins

SEBASTIAN SCHOLZ

The Organization of the Clergy and the *canonici* in the Sixth Century

There have been mixed results from the many research studies on the organization of the clergy and the importance of the *canonici* in the sixth century. Probably, this is also because there are only three citations of the term *canonicus* in the canons from the sixth century, and only two further references to the term in the remaining texts. There is no record of the word for the duration of the seventh century. The textual interpretation of the word *canonicus* already poses problems. Heinrich Schäfer held the view that the *canonici* concern the clerics who were found 'to be tried and tested in the canonical legislation'.[1] Arnold Pöschl traced the original foundation of the term to the κανονικοὶ ψάλται, 'the regular singers of the psalms' as they were referred to in Canon 15 of the Council of Laodicea (364?).[2] He therefore associated the dissemination of the *canonici* in the West with the widespread emergence of daily periodic worship according to the *Ordo psallendi*.[3] But the derivation of the term *canonici* from the κανονικοὶ ψάλται was quite controversial. Josef Siegwart assumed that the definition was probably originally derived from the word *canon* in the sense of 'list'.[4] During the sixth century one would have perceived the *canonicus* as the individual who appears in a list of the clerics. However, by the eighth century *canonicus* was already understood in the sense of 'in accordance with the rule'.[5]

In Pöschl's opinion, the duties in singing the psalms also led to a kind of *vita communis* among the *canonici*.[6] This idea has also gained broad acceptance

---

1 Schäfer, *Pfarrkirche*, pp. 85–97; cf. further Schieffer, *Entstehung*, p. 124 with n. 132.
2 *Concilium Laodicenum*, ed. by Bruns, 15, p. 75.
3 Pöschl, *Bischofsgut*, pp. 51–56.
4 Siegwart, *Die Chorherren- und Chorfrauengemeinschaften*, pp. 3–6.
5 Schieffer, *Entstehung*, pp. 124–25 with n. 133.
6 Pöschl, *Bischofsgut*, pp. 57–58.

Sebastian Scholz is Professor of Early Medieval History at the University of Zurich.

in the research literature. However, Rudolf Schieffer correctly warned against treating the evidence for the *cleric community* in the bishop's entourage in the sense of a community which abided by written fixed legislation. It was mainly the practical foundations of daily periodic worship that provided the verifiable evidence for the communities.[7]

It is clear from these opening remarks that it is challenging to give the precise definition of the *canonicus*. Moreover, its integration within the context of the other clerics is unclear. For this reason, I would like to focus here on examining which statements are reasonably implied by the sources. However, before I continue to examine the meaning of the *canonicus* in the sixth century, it is perhaps useful to highlight the relationship between clerics and monks at that time. A brief reference should suffice to the decisions of the Council of Agde in 506 that ruled in Canon 27 that:

> No one should dare to establish or found a new monastery without the consent or approval of the bishop. Unless their abbot has given them the authority, the monks moving around may not be ordained for an office of the clergy either in the cities or in the parishes. […] If it is necessary for one of the monks to be ordained as a cleric, the bishop may do so with the approval and in accordance with the will of the abbot.[8]

Monks and clerics are portrayed in this text as clearly separate from each other.[9] A monk may be ordained as a cleric only in exceptional cases. The possible assumption that the *canonici* could be clerics who live according to a monastic rule therefore becomes implausible.

The concept of the *canonicus* was first used in Gaul at the Council of Clermont in 535. This Burgundian council, which was convoked by the Frankish King Theudebert I, issued the following decree in Canon 15:

> If any presbyter or deacon is known neither in the city nor in the parishes to serve as *canonicus*, but rather lives on the small country estates and in devotion to the holy office celebrates divine liturgy in the oratories, he should on no account attend the main festivals — the Lord's nativity, Easter and Pentecost, nor other celebrations if these are special festivals, in any other place than with his bishop in the city. Moreover, all citizens of noble birth should in the same manner come into the cities to their bishops on the pre-designated festival days. If they disregard this in blind

---

7 Schieffer, *Entstehung*, pp. 109–11; cf. also Meijns, *Aken of Jeruzalem?*, pp. 23–27; Godding, *Prêtres*, p. 225.
8 *Concilium Agathense a. 506*, ed. by Munier, 27, p. 205: 'Monasterium novum nisi episcopo aut permittente aut probante nullus incipere aut fundare praesumat. Monachi etiam vagantes ad officium clericatus, nisi eis testimonium abbas suus dederit, nec in civitatibus nec in parrociis ordinentur. […] Si enim necesse fuerit clericum de monachis ordinari, cum consensu et voluntate abbatis praesumat episcopus'. This translation and all further translations in this text by Sebastian Scholz; cf. *Concilia Galliae et aevi Merovingici selecta*, ed. by Scholz passim.
9 Cf. Predel, *Vom Presbyter*, pp. 237–39.

audacity on those very festival days when they scorn being present in the city, they should be excluded from the community.¹⁰

In his book on the emergence of the chapters in Germany, Rudolf Schieffer correctly observed that the word *canonicus* was certainly not newly introduced in Clermont, but rather was already assumed to be a familiar term. Based on the preceding research Schieffer concluded that the *canonici* named in Clermont were different from the other clerics because they completed the ceremonial liturgical worship, for they were the only ones in the position to do so in the city and the larger parishes. The clerics from the small oratories would have had to come to the city for this purpose.¹¹ While this explanation seems plausible, a more detailed examination hardly makes it compelling. The crucial aspect of the decree issued at the Council of Clermont is the reference to the bishop. Only together with the bishop can clerics from the oratories on the small rural estates celebrate the main festivals. And this regulation applies not only for the clerics, but also for residents of the estates as well. This aspect reveals the endeavour of the bishops to improve the discipline of the faithful and their bond with the religious community, and thus at the same time to strengthen the influence of the church. If rich landlords and their clerics basically stayed away from the episcopal church service and celebrated the major church festivals like Easter and Christmas in their private oratories on the rural estates, this contradicted the Christian central idea of *communio*, the community of all Christians whether they were landowners or slaves. Furthermore, everyone should listen to what the bishop preached about conducting a Christian way of life and abide by this accordingly.¹²

Nevertheless, Canon 15 of the Council of Clermont includes an important reference to the meaning of the word *canonicus*: the presbyters and deacons living on the small rural estates are compared with the canons in the city and in the parishes. The canons thus seem to represent the clear majority of clerics.

Canon 12 of the Council of Orléans in 538 reveals a similar comparison:

If the clerics decline to carry out the assigned services on any occasion, like the others and as an apology for not fulfilling their duty they plead the protective power of several people, and believe that under this kind of

---

10 *Concilium Arvernense a. 535*, ed. by Maassen, 15, p. 69: 'Si quis presbyter adque diaconus, qui neque in civitate neque in parrochiis canonecus esse dinuscitur, sed in villolis habitans, in oraturiis officio sancto deserviens celebrat divina mysteria, festivitatis praecipuas: Domini natale, pascha, pentecosten et si quae principalis festivitatis sunt reliquae, nullatenus alibi nisi cum episcopo suo in civitate teneat. Quicumque etiam sunt cives natu maiores, pari modo in orbibus ad pontifices suos in praedictis festivitatibus veniant. Quod si qui inproba temeritate contimpserint, hisdem festivitatibus, in quibus in civitate adesse dispiciunt, communione pellantur'.
11 Schieffer, *Entstehung*, pp. 100–02.
12 Cf. Scholz, *Die Merowinger*, pp. 81–82 with reference to the corresponding legislation in Orléans (511); Predel, *Vom Presbyter*, pp. 61–64.

pretext they may disrespectfully treat their bishops through disobedience, they should by no means be counted among the other clerics living as *canonici*, so that the others are not spoiled by this impertinence. Moreover, they should not receive any kind of assistance or gifts from church property together with the *canonici*.[13]

Those clerics who in their appeal to the protection of powerful men refuse to carry out their assigned duties are compared with the 'other clerics living as *canonici*'.[14] Because of their behaviour, unlike the other canons they should receive no assistance or gifts from church property. Here, too, the clear majority of clerics is evidently on the same level as the *canonici*. They are described as those who according to the Council of Orléans in 511 should have at their disposal a quarter of church property for their care,[15] and to whom the bishop could assign land, the same as he did for for the monks, as a mark of favour.[16]

Two texts by Gregory of Tours have been associated with this canon. Gregory reports that Bishop Baudin of Tours (546–52) had established a *mensa canonicorum*,[17] and Gregory writes of St Patroclus (b. about 500, d. 576):

> Soon after he had accepted the office of the deaconry, he had time for fasting; he was glad of the night vigils, practised reading and dedicated himself so intently to constant prayer that he did not come to the meal at the *mensa canonicorum* with the other clerics. When the arch-deacon heard this, he complained angrily about him and said, 'Either take your meal with the other brothers or leave us. For it does not seem right that you neglect to eat with those whom, as one assumes, you practise the liturgy'.[18]

Arnold Pöschl assumed that this was a reference to Patroclus being removed from the circle of the *canonici* with whom he was associated

---

13 *Concilium Aurelianense a. 538*, ed. by Maassen, 12, p. 77: 'Si qui clerici ministeria suscepta quacumque occasione agere, sicut et reliqui, detractant et excusationem de patrociniis quorumcumque, ne officium inpleant, praetendunt hac sacerdotes suos sub huiusmodi causa aestimant per inoboedientia contemnendos, inter reliquos canonicos clericos, ne hac licentia alii vitientur, nullatinus habeantur neque ex rebus ecclesiasticis cum canonicis stipendia aut munera ulla percipiant'.

14 Meijns, *Aken of Jeruzalem*, p. 25, distinguishes based on this text between clerics with 'ministeria suscepta' and the canons. But this is not the meaning of Canon 12.

15 *Concilium Aurelianense a. 511*, ed. by Maassen, 5, p. 4.

16 *Concilium Aurelianense a. 511*, ed. by Maassen, 23, pp. 7–8; *Concilium Aurelianense* (541), ed. by Maassen, 18, p. 91.

17 Gregory of Tours, *Libri historiarum decem*, ed. by Krusch and Levison, X.16, p. 533: 'Hic instituit mensam canonicorum'.

18 Gregory of Tours, *Liber vitae patrum*, IX. 1, p. 253: 'Nec multo post diaconatus officium sumens, vacabat ieiuniis, delectabatur vigiliis, exercebatur lectione atque in oratione assidua prumptus effundebatur, ut nec ad convivium mensae canonicae cum reliquis accederet clericis. Quod audiens archidiaconus, frendens contra eum, ait: "Aut cum reliquis fratribus cibum sume, aut certe discede a nobis. Non enim rectum videtur, ut dissimules cum his habere victum, cum qui bus eclesiasticum implere putaris officium"'; cf. Schieffer, *Entstehung*, p. 108.

through his service.[19] Robert Godding even identifies in both statements by Gregory of Tours a reference to a *vita communis* of the *canonici* who had supposedly belonged to the bishop's 'entourage'.[20] However, here the *canonici* do not even emerge as an autonomous group. The first text refers only to the institution of the *mensa canonicorum*, while the second describes the *clerici* who dine at the *mensa canonicorum*. In other words, the institution of the *mensa canonicorum* is the general table where the clerics of the episcopal church could take their meals. The *Vita* of Caesarius of Arles, which was written shortly after his death in 542,[21] describes the meals arranged by him:

> In the house of his church, whether he was present or absent, a meal was always prepared for the clerics and for everyone who came here. For as long as he (Caesarius) was alive nobody came to Arles as though it were a foreign city, but rather as though he arrived in his own house.[22]

Here, the hospitality in the *domus ecclesiae* was not even reserved for the clerics. Rather, it was open for all those who came from outside. The statements cited above by Gregory of Tours give no indication of the exclusivity of the *mensa canonicorum*. In this case, the needy also probably had access to the table. The Council of Mâcon in 585 demanded that the house of the bishop should offer its hospitality to everyone without regard for the person.[23]

Until now in the quoted texts the *canonici* generally seems to have been used to refer to the clerics at the episcopal churches. Obviously, however, there were different communities of clerics within the church. Canon 13 of the Council of Orléans in 541 ruled:

> If any of the office holders should dare to consult concerning official activities with clerics from any arbitrary community who serve at the altar and[24] whose names are listed in the church registers, he should know that, if he does not improve himself under the reprimand of his bishop, he does not have the peace of the church.[25]

---

19 Pöschl, *Bischofsgut*, pp. 55–56.
20 Godding, *Prêtres*, p. 225.
21 Klingshirn, *Caesarius of Arles*, p. 8.
22 *Vita Caesarii*, ed. by Krusch, I. 62, p. 483: 'In domo vero ecclesiae suae, sicut illo praesente, ita absente, convivium semper praeparatum est clericis sive quibuscumque advenientibus. Nullus illo superstite tamquam ad extraneam civitatem, sed tamquam ad propriam domum Arelato venit'.
23 *Concilium Matisconense a. 585*, ed. by Maassen, 13, p. 170.
24 *Vel* must here be translated as 'and', cf. Schäfer, *Pfarrkirche*, p. 93.
25 *Concilium Aurelianense a. 541*, ed. by Maassen, 13, p. 90: 'Si quis iudicum clericus de quolibit corpore venientes adque altario mancipatus vel quorum nomina in matricula ecclesiastica tenentur scripta, publicis actionibus adplicare praesumpserit, si a sacerdote commonitus emendare noluerit, cognoscat se pacem ecclesiae non habere'; cf. Sternberg, *Orientalium more secutus*, pp. 113–14.

According to an edict of the *Codex Theodosianus*, clerics were exempt from paying the *munera*[26] to which this canon refers. It mentions various clerical communities whose common attribute consists in serving at the altar and being recorded in the church register. If Josef Siegwart's suggested interpretation of the term *canonicus* as 'somebody who appears in a list' is appropriate, then those clerics whose names appear in the register would correspond to the *canonici* mentioned at the Councils of Clermont in 535 and Orléans in 538. This is also supported by the second canon of the Council of Agde in 506:

> The defiant clerics, so far as the status of their dignity allows, should be improved by the bishops; and if they perhaps arrogantly despise the community with (the clerics) from their previous grade and neglect to come to church or to fulfil their duty, they should be removed from the community; indeed, so that when duly improved by the penance, they are again entered into the list of their grade and regain their dignity.[27]

According to this canon all the clerics of a specific ordination grade were entered in a separate list; this is plausible from an administrative viewpoint. Their names were deleted from the register for as long as they were excommunicated. They were only re-entered in the register after they had completed the penance.

The final canon, in which the *canonici* are mentioned, is Canon 20 of the Council of Tours in 567:

> But many, if not all arch-presbyters who live in the country, as well as the deacons and sub-deacons are regarded with mistrust by the people because they stay with their wives. Therefore, it was decided to observe this and that if an arch-presbyter remains in his village or travels to his country estate, one of his *lectores canonici* or on any account one of the clerics accompanies him and should have his bed in the room where the former rests, so that he can bear witness. However, seven of the sub-deacons, lectors, or laypersons should be permitted to ensure that they spend their weeks alternately and entirely with him. Those who deviate from this should be beaten with the cane.[28]

---

26 *Codex Theodosianus*, ed. by Mommsen and Meyer, XVI. 2. 2, p. 835; cf. Dockter, *Klerikerkritik*, p. 109 and pp. 128–29; however, this privilege was revoked by Valentinian III in 441, Valentinian III, *Novella X*, ed. by Meyer, pp. 91–92; this does not seem to have been taken into account in the canon.

27 *Concilium Agathense a. 506*, ed. by Munier, 2, p. 193: 'Contumaces vero clerici, prout dignitatis ordo permiserit, ab episcopis corrigantur, et si qui prioris gradus, ut elati superbia, communionem fortasse contempserint aut ecclesiam frequentare vel officium suum implere neglexerint, peregrina eis communio tribuatur; ita, ut cum eos paenitentia correxerit, rescripti in matricula gradum suum dignitatemque recipiant'.

28 *Concilium Turonense a. 567*, ed. by Maassen, 20, p. 127: 'Archipresbiteri vero vicani et diaconi et subdiaconi non quidem omnes, sed plures in hac suspicione tenentur a populo, quod cum coniugibus suis maneant. Pro qua re hoc placuit observare, ut quocienscumque archepresbiter seu in vico manserit seu ad villam suam ambulaverit, unus lectorum

The *lectores canonici* in this description are compared with the other clerics. The arch-presbyter[29] should take one of his *lectores canonici* or on all accounts one of his clerics with him so that they can bear witness that he has no sexual intercourse with his wife. The *lector canonicus* would therefore be a *lector* who appears in the register of lectors in that rural parish which is led by the arch-presbyter. He gains special mention here because in general it was probably his duty to remain with his arch-presbyter. This could explain the unusual choice of wording which only appears in this text. However, the involvement overall of seven individuals from the group of sub-deacons, lectors, or also laypersons was required for the supervision of the arch-presbyter.

Finally, I would like to take a moment to concentrate on the aspect of the *vita communis*, since this always plays a role in the discussion concerning the *canonici*. However, it is notable that those sources which give indications of a *vita communis* never refer to *canonici*. One of the most significant records of the existence of at least some vestiges of a *vita communis* among the episcopal clerics in the sixth century is Canon 13 of the Council of Tours in 567 which states:

> The bishop should treat his wife like a sister, and he should manage both the church as well as his own house through holy life conduct, so that no mistrust whatsoever is directed against him.[30] And although he lives a chaste life by God's grace in accordance with the testimony of his clerics, as they live both with him in one room as well as accompany and follow him wherever he always is, and the presbyters, deacons, and also the crowd of younger clerics stay with him with God's help: nevertheless, the rooms should be so far apart because of the jealousy of our Lord and be separate from the proximity (to the wife's room), so that those who are educated to attain the hope (of the resurrection) through the service of the clerics are not blemished by close contact with the female servants.[31]

---

canonicorum suorum aut certe aliquis de numero clericorum cum illo ambulet et in cella, ubi ille iacet, lectum habeat pro testimonio. Septem tamen inter subdiaconus et lectores vel laicus habeat concessus, qui vicissim septemanas suas cum illo facere omnino procurent; qui distulerit, fustigetur'.

29 For more about the term cf. Godding, *Prêtres*, pp. 243–53.
30 Cf. *Concilium Arvernense a. 535*, ed. by Maassen, 13, p. 68, which refers, however, to presbyters and deacons.
31 *Concilium Turonense a. 567*, ed. by Maassen, 13 (12), p. 127: 'Episcopus coniugem ut sororem habeat et ita conversatione sancta gubernet domum omnem tam ecclesiasticam quam propriam, ut nulla de eo suspitio quaqua ratione consurgat. Et licet Deo propitio clericorum suorum testimonio castus vivat, quia cum illo tam in cella quam, ubicumque fuerit, sui habitant eumque prosecuntur et presbiteri et diaconi vel deinceps clericorum turba iuniorum Deo adiutore conversantur: sic tamen propter zelotem Deum nostrum tam longe absint mansionis propinquitate divisi, ut nec hi, qui ad spem recuperandam clericorum servitute nutriuntur, famularum propinqua contagione polluantur'.

A certain form of the *vita communis* is manifested here. Some of the clerics live together with the bishop and sleep in his quarters, while the other presbyters, deacons, and younger clerics should stay close to their bishop, as long as this is possible. Gregory of Tours writes of Bishop Aetherius of Lisieux that his bed was surrounded by many beds of his clerics.[32] The ruling of the council therefore seems to have been put into practice.

If one considers overall the few citations of the word *canonici* in the sixth century, it is clear that the term is certainly not new in this period. The older textual interpretations of the word *canonicus* understand the term in different ways, but only Josef Siegwart assumed that the definition was probably originally derived from the word *canon* in the sense of 'list'. The analysis of the available texts shows that the term generally seems to refer to those clerics of the episcopal churches and municipal parishes who were listed in the registers and were given sustenance by the bishop. But there is no reference to a kind of *vita communis* among the *canonici* as Pöschl means. The *mensa canonicorum* is not a table reserved for the canons, but rather an institution to provide sustenance for those clerics who appeared in the register and were therefore entitled to receive care.

Works Cited

Primary Sources

Codex Theodosianus, ed. by Theodor Mommsen and Paul Martin Meyer, *Theodosiani libri XVI cum Constivtionibvs Sirmondianis et Leges novellae ad Theodosianvm pertinentes*, vol. I. 2 (Berlin: Weidmann, 1905)

Concilia Galliae et aevi Merovingici selecta. Edita, translata notisque instructa a Sebastian Scholz – Ausgewählte Synoden Galliens und des merowingischen Frankenreichs, ed., trans., and with a commentary by S. Scholz (forthcoming)

Concilium Agathense a. 506, ed. by Charles Munier, in *Concilia Galliae*, Corpus Christianorum Series Latina, 148 (Turnhout: Brepols, 1963)

Concilium Arvernense a. 535, ed. by Friedrich Maassen, in *Monumenta Germaniae Historica: Concilia*, I (Hannover: Hahn, 1893), pp. 65–71

Concilium Aurelianense a. 511, ed. by Friedrich Maassen, in *Monumenta Germaniae Historica: Concilia*, I (Hannover: Hahn, 1893), pp. 2–14

Concilium Aurelianense a. 538, ed. by Friedrich Maassen, in *Monumenta Germaniae Historica: Concilia*, I (Hannover: Hahn, 1893), pp. 72–86

Concilium Aurelianense a. 541, ed. by Friedrich Maassen, in *Monumenta Germaniae Historica: Concilia*, I (Hannover: Hahn, 1893), pp. 86–99

---

32 Gregory of Tours, *Libri historiarum decem*, ed. by Krusch and Levison, VI. 36, p. 307; cf. Godding, *Prêtres*, p. 224.

Concilium Laodicenum, ed. by Henry T. Bruns, Canones Apostolorum et conciliorum saeculorum IV, V, VI, VII (Berlin: Reimer, 1839)

Concilium Matisconense a. 585, ed. by Friedrich Maassen, in *Monumenta Germaniae Historica: Concilia*, I (Hannover: Hahn, 1893), pp. 163–73

Concilium Turonense a. 567, ed. by Friedrich Maassen, in *Monumenta Germaniae Historica: Concilia*, I (Hannover: Hahn, 1893), pp. 121–38

Gregory of Tours, *Decem libri historiarum*, ed. by Bruno Krusch and Wilhelm Levison, Gregorii Turonensis opera, vol. 1: *Libri historiarum X*, in *Monumenta Germaniae Historica: Scriptores rerum Merovingicarum*, I. 1, 2nd edn (Hannover: Hahn, 1951), pp. 1–537

Gregory of Tours, *Liber vitae partum*, ed. by Bruno Krusch, in *Monumenta Germaniae Historica: Scriptores rerum Merovingicarum*, I. 2 (Hannover: Hahn, 1885)

Valentinian III, *Novella X*, ed. Paul M. Meyer, in *Leges Novellae ad Theodosianum pertinentes* (Berlin: Weidmann, 1905), pp. 91–92

Vita Caesarii, ed. by Bruno Krusch, in *Monumenta Germaniae Historica: Scriptores rerum Merovingicarum*, III (Hannover: Hahn, 1896), pp. 433–501

Secondary Works

Dockter, Hanno, *Klerikerkritik im antiken Christentum* (Göttingen: V&R unipress, 2013)

Godding, Robert, *Prêtres en Gaule mérovingienne*, Subsidia hagiographica, 82 (Brussels: Société des Bollandistes, 2001)

Klingshirn, William E., *Caesarius of Arles: The Making of a Christian Community in Late Antique Gaul* (Cambridge: Cambridge University Press, 1994)

Meijns, Brigitte, *Aken of Jeruzalem? Het ontstaan en de hervorming van de kanonikale instellingen in Vlaanderen tot circa 1155* (Leuven: Universitaire Pers, 2000)

Pöschl, Arnold, *Bischofsgut und mensa episcopalis: Ein Beitrag zur Geschichte des kirchlichen Vermögensrechtes* (Bonn: Hahnstein, 1908)

Predel, Gregor, *Vom Presbyter zum Sacerdos*, Dogma und Geschichte, 4 (Münster: LIT, 2005)

Schäfer, Heinrich, *Pfarrkirche und Stift im Deutschen Mittelalter* (Stuttgart: Ferdinand Enke, 1903)

Schieffer, Rudolf, *Die Entstehung von Domkapiteln in Deutschland*, Bonner Historische Forschungen, 43 (Bonn: Röhrscheid, 1976)

Scholz, Sebastian, *Die Merowinger* (Stuttgart: Kohlhammer, 2015)

Siegwart, Josef, *Die Chorherren- und Chorfrauengemeinschaften in der deutschsprachigen Schweiz vom 6. Jahrhundert bis 1160*, Studia Friburgensia, N.F., 30 (Freiburg: Universitätsverlag, 1962)

Sternberg, Thomas, *Orientalium more secutus: Räume und Institutionen der Caritas des 5. bis 7. Jahrhunderts in Gallien*, Jahrbuch für Antike und Christentum, Ergänzungsbd. 16 (Münster: Aschendorff, 1991)

ALBRECHT DIEM*

Choreography and Confession

The Memoriale qualiter *and Carolingian Monasticism*

The first volume of the *Corpus Consuetudinum Monasticarum* contains a short treatise titled *Memoriale qualiter in monasterio religiose ac studiose conuersare uel Domino militare oportet idipsum cotidie repetendo* (A reminder of how to faithfully and eagerly live the monastic life, or to fight in the Lord's service. It is necessary to repeat this daily).[1] The work is tentatively dated to the last decades of the eighth century, thus roughly a generation before the reform councils of 816/7.[2] With thirty-nine known manuscripts, the *Memoriale qualiter* counts among the most widely disseminated textual witnesses of the Carolingian monastic reforms.[3] Only Benedict of Aniane's *Collectio capitularis*,

---

* This chapter is a contribution to the Spezialforschungsbereich F 4202 'Visions of Community', funded by the *Fonds zur Förderung der wissenschaftlichen Forschung* (FWF), the *Faculty of History and Cultural Sciences of the University of Vienna*, and the *Austrian Academy of Science*. I am also grateful to the *Humanities Center at Syracuse University* for receiving a Faculty Fellowship during the spring semester 2019, which allowed me to complete this chapter. I would also like to thank Julian Hendrix, Rutger Kramer, and Matthew Mattingly for reading and commenting on different versions of this text and allowing me to benefit from their expertise and Isabelle Cochelin for sharing her notes on the *Memoriale qualiter* with me.

1 *Memoriale qualiter*, ed. by Morgand. For an English translation of the *Memoriale qualiter* in its version for monks, see Mattingly, 'The Memoriale Qualiter'. The title given in Morgand's edition appears only in one manuscript that, in his view, represents the most authentic text: Merseburg, Domstiftsbibl., MS I 136 [olim 58], fols 25ᵛ–35ʳ. Other titles include *Ordo monasticus secundum doctrinam sancti Benedicti* (manuscript group 1); *Memoriale qualiter in monasterio conuersare debemus* (group 2); *Ordo qualiter agendum sit monachis in monasteriis constitutis et sub regula beati patris Benedicti degentibus* (group 3); *Ordo in monasterio qualiter a fratribus religiose ac studiose conuersari uel domino militare oportet idipsum cotidie repetendo* (group 4); *Traditio de ordine monachorum* (group 7). On the different manuscript groups, see Note 33 below.

2 *Memoriale qualiter*, ed. by Morgand, pp. 224–25.

3 Aside from the manuscripts used in Morgand's edition, the text appears in the following manuscripts: Admont, Bibl. des Benediktinerstifts, MS 497; Brno, Státní Vědecká Knihovna, MS NR 34; Brussels, KBR, MSS 15111–15128 (479); Budapest, MNM, MS lat. 329; Melk,

---

Albrecht Diem is Associate Professor at Syracuse University.

Monastic Communities and Canonical Clergy in the Carolingian World (780–840): Categorizing the Church, ed. by Rutger Kramer, Emilie Kurdziel, and Graeme Ward, MMS 8 (Turnhout: Brepols, 2022), pp. 59–97

Smaragdus's *Expositio Regulae*, and the *Institutio canonicorum* are preserved in more manuscripts.

I will provide an exploration of the *Memoriale qualiter* which consists of two parts. First, I focus on the textual transmission, reception, and structure of this largely understudied text and, in particular, on the relationship between its two versions addressing monks and nuns. I argue that the *Memoriale qualiter* not only engages with the *Regula Benedicti* but also expands upon a seventh-century Rule for nuns, the *Regula cuiusdam ad uirgines*.[4] Parts of the text may originally have been written for a female community. The second part focuses on the content of the *Memoriale qualiter* and discusses three of its central aspects within the broader context of Carolingian monastic reform: the notion of the unceasing *opus Dei* beyond the liturgical Hours, its effects on monastic discipline, and the imperative of continuous confession. As such, this study will serve as a stepping stone for a broader exploration of the practice of confession within the early medieval monastic world.

The *Memoriale qualiter* is generally viewed as the first monastic customary that appropriates and expands upon the *Regula Benedicti*.[5] Because of its transmission along with the *Collectio Capitularis*, which was drawn up by Benedict of Aniane, the text has sometimes been ascribed to the great monastic reformer himself. His authorship cannot be excluded conclusively, but given the observations presented in this study, it is rather unlikely.[6] In some later manuscripts it is presented as a part of the *Regula Benedicti*. We can certainly dismiss this possibility, although the ascription to Benedict certainly enhanced the authority of the work, particularly in the high and late Middle Ages.[7]

The content of the *Memoriale qualiter* has thus far received remarkably little scholarly attention, aside from a study of Claudio Morgand, which focuses on confession, liturgy, and the gatherings in the chapter house, and which surveys how these issues are addressed in texts that possibly influenced the *Memoriale qualiter*.[8] Marilyn Dunn points to parallels between the *Memoriale qualiter* and the *Regula Magistri* that could support her thesis that the *Regula Benedicti* predates the *Regula Magistri*.[9] A recent article by Katie Ann-Marie Bugyis reflects on the impact of the provisions on confession in

---

Stiftsbibl., MS 1093 (olim 423); Munich, BSB, MS Clm 14678; Munich, BSB, MS Clm 14952; Munich, BSB, MS Clm 17459. All manuscripts are, along with links to manuscript catalogues and, if available, digitized images, documented on <http://www.earlymedievalmonasticism.org/texts/Memoriale-Qualiter.html> [accessed 25 May 2021].

4 *Regula cuiusdam ad uirgines*, ed. by Diem, *The Pursuit of Salvation*, pp. 37–151.
5 On monastic customaries, see Cochelin, 'Downplayed or Silenced'; Cochelin, 'Customaries'.
6 There are no connections in regard to language or ideas between *Memoriale qualiter* and Benedict of Aniane's other works, especially the *Excerptus diuersarum modus penitentiarum*, ed. by Semmler.
7 This applies to manuscripts of group 1 and 2 (see below, note 33).
8 Morgand, 'La discipline pénitentielle'. Much of Morgand's observations are reproduced in the apparatus of his edition.
9 Dunn, 'The Master and St Benedict', pp. 108–09.

the *Memoriale qualiter* on female monastic life in medieval England.[10] Only Matthew Mattingly's short introduction to his translation of the *Memoriale qualiter* addresses the content of the text and the work as a whole.[11] Isabelle Cochelin gracefully shared with me her notes on the *Memoriale qualiter* for her forthcoming work on monastic customaries.

We do not know exactly when the text was produced, but given its textual transmission we can assume that monastic reformers involved with the Aachen Council of 817 regarded the *Memoriale qualiter* as an important document to promote their agenda. It may not have been written for this purpose, but it became part of a portfolio of texts that was disseminated after the Aachen reform councils, serving the purpose of explaining and expanding the *Regula Benedicti* and resolving the problems resulting from turning a text that was 250 years old and hopelessly anachronistic into a unifying norm for monastic life in the Carolingian kingdoms.[12] Turning the *Regula Benedicti* into the '*sancta regula*'[13] meant discussing and interpreting the text, submitting it to exegesis, expanding it, and reconciling it with long-established practices.[14] The *Memoriale qualiter* was seen as an important contribution to this endeavour.

Aside from appearing in a large number of manuscripts, the *Memoriale qualiter* also has a remarkable reception history. Four sections of the text appear in the interpolated version of Chrodegang of Metz's *Regula canonicorum* from the second half of the ninth century.[15] Moreover, large parts of it have been

---

10 Bugyis, 'The Practice of Penance'.
11 Mattingly, 'The Memoriale Qualiter', pp. 62–66.
12 On the role of the *Regula Benedicti* in the Carolingian world, see Diem, 'The Carolingians'; Diem, 'Inventing the Holy Rule'.
13 On the use of *sancta regula*, see, for example, *Breuiarium ecclesiastici ordinis*, ed. by Hallinger, p. 38, l. 15; Theodomar, *Epistola ad Theodoricum*, ed. by Winandy and Hallinger, 1, p. 129, l. 17; 12, p. 132, l. 6; 17, p. 133, l. 21; 18, p. 133, l. 28; 34, p. 136, ll. 31–32; Theodomar, *Epistola ad Karolum regem*, ed. by Hallinger and Wegener, 2, p. 160, l. 1; *Capitula in Auuam directa*, ed. by Frank, 7, p. 335, l. 9; *Capitula qualiter*, ed. by Frank, 1, p. 353; *Statuta Murbacensia*, ed. by Semmler, 1, p. 441, l. 17.
14 On reading and interpreting the *Regula Benedicti*, see, for example, *Synodus et conuentus exeuntes anno 802*, ed. by Boretius, p. 105; *Concilium Moguntiense a. 813*, ed. by Werminghoff, p. 259; *De cursu diurno uel nocturno*, ed. by Semmler, p. 46, ll. 11–13; *Synodi primae Auisgranensis decreta authentica*, ed. by Semmler, 1, p. 457; Benedict of Aniane, *Collectio Capitularis*, ed. by Semmler, 1, p. 516; Ardo, *Vita Benedicti Anianensis*, ed. by Waitz, 18, p. 206; 20, p. 208; 29, p. 211; 36–38, pp. 215–17.
15 *Regula canonicorum interpolata*, ed. by Bertram, 14, pp. 194–95 quotes *Memoriale qualiter*, ed. by Morgand, 1.1, pp. 230–31. *Regula canonicorum interpolata*, ed. by Bertram, 18, pp. 196–97 quotes, but also revises, *Memoriale qualiter*, ed. by Morgand, 2. 5–7, pp. 234–38, leaving out some passages but also describing some of the liturgical provisions in greater detail. *Regula canonicorum interpolata*, ed. by Bertram, 19, p. 197 quotes from *Memoriale qualiter*, ed. by Morgand, 8–9, pp. 238–40. *Regula canonicorum interpolata*, ed. by Bertram, 23, p. 198 quotes *Memoriale qualiter*, ed. by Morgand, 6.18, p. 260.

rephrased and inserted into the *Regularis Concordia*, the main document of the monastic reforms in Anglo-Saxon England, which was produced around 966.[16]

Claudio Morgand, the editor of the text, provides in his apparatus a large number of source references (especially to monastic Rules) without, however, clearly indicating where he finds similarities and parallels in content and where we can say with high certainty that a specific text has been used for the composition of the *Memoriale qualiter*.[17] If we eliminate instances of parallels, shared ideas, and cross refences linking the *Memoriale qualiter* to other Carolingian reform texts, the list of sources the author undoubtedly used shrinks to two or three: the *Regula Benedicti*, the *Regula cuiusdam ad uirgines*, and, possibly, the *Regula Magistri*.[18]

Among these sources, the *Regula cuiusdam ad uirgines* deserves the most attention because the author of the *Memoriale qualiter* not only used words and phrases from this Rule but also incorporated some of its central ideas — to the extent that the text could be read not only as a *consuetudo* exemplifying and expanding the *Regula Benedicti* but also as an expansion of the *Regula cuiusdam ad uirgines*.

The *Regula cuiusdam ad uirgines* was written around the middle of the seventh century, most likely for the monastery of Faremoutiers and possibly other convents founded in the orbit of Luxeuil and in the perceived tradition of the Irish monastic founder Columbanus. The text shows an overwhelming number of parallels with Jonas of Bobbio's *Vita Columbani* in phrasing,

---

16 *Regularis Concordia*, ed. and trans. by Symons. Chapter 1, pp. 10–24 (titled *Ordo qualiter*) largely paraphrases the *Memoriale qualiter*. The text expresses in a similar way to the *Memoriale qualiter* the importance of an unceasing *opus Dei* and a liturgization of all daily activities. We find a number of allusions to the *Memoriale qualiter*, but also a couple of passages that are quoted almost verbatim, especially prayers. Both texts describe in the same words how to rise for the *opus Diuinum* by making the sign of the cross and saying Psalm 50. 17 ('Domine labia mea aperies') and the complete Psalm 69 ('Deus in adiutorium'). Moreover, the *Regularis Concordia* inserts from the *Memoriale qualiter* a prayer at the beginning of the day. The *Regularis Concordia* largely quotes and partly paraphrases the provisions of the *Memoriale qualiter* for the daily gathering in the Chapter house, for beginning work, and for the beginning of Compline. On the date of this text, see Barrow, 'The Chronology'.

17 Morgand lists, among others, the *Regula Pauli et Stephani*, the *Regula Columbani*, Fructuosus's *Regula monachorum*, and Cassian's *Collationes*. I checked his references, which indeed point to similarities but never to an extent that would prove a direct use of these texts and adaptation of these texts.

18 There are several parallels between the *Regula Magistri* and the *Memoriale qualiter* that support that the author of the *Memoriale qualiter* used the *Regula Magistri*. None of them, however, provides definitive proof. *Memoriale qualiter*, ed. by Morgand, 1. 1, p. 230 prescribes like *Regula Magistri*, ed. by de Vogüé, 30. 14, II, p. 164 to say Psalm 50. 17 at the moment of awakening. *Memoriale qualiter*, ed. by Morgand, 1.1, p. 232 on spitting, sneezing, and covering spittle with one's foot in order to avoid other brothers soiling their habits reminds the reader of *Regula Magistri*, ed. by de Vogüé, 47. 21–24, p. 216. *Memoriale qualiter*, ed. by Morgand, 4, p. 248 and *Regula Magistri*, ed. by de Vogüé, 12. 2, II, p. 34 both use the phrase 'semel et secundo uel tertio' (instead of 'semel et iterum atque tertio', as the *Regula Benedicti* does).

vocabulary, style, and content, which has led me to the conclusion that Jonas himself was the author of the *Regula cuiusdam ad uirgines*.[19] The Rule expresses, probably in the purest way, what Jonas of Bobbio considered Columbanus's monastic programme.[20] This means that the *Memoriale qualiter* formed a port of entry of 'Columbanian' monastic ideals into the Carolingian debates on monastic reform — by taking a loop through a female monastic tradition.

The *Regula cuiusdam ad uirgines* itself can be read as a commentary and a reaction to the *Regula Benedicti* which took a foothold in Columbanian monasteries at the time when Jonas wrote the text. Jonas used and rephrased numerous chapters of the *Regula Benedicti* but developed a monastic programme that was profoundly different both on a practical level and with regard to its theological framework.[21] We have, thus, as I will show in my analysis of the text, the situation of using a critical response to the *Regula Benedicti* written in the Columbanian orbit for producing a highly influential Carolingian exemplification and expansion of this very Rule.

As such — but also in various other regards — the *Memoriale qualiter* complicates the story of Carolingian monasticism and monastic reform. It forms part of the very fragmented narrative that links the *Regula Benedicti* in the context of its origin and earliest reception to the triumph of this Rule in the Carolingian period and it may shed light on the question of *how* monasteries that used other monastic Rules shifted towards the observance of the *Regula Benedicti*.

Structure, Transmission, and Impact of the *Memoriale qualiter*

Claudio Morgand's edition is, as any edition, far from perfect. Aside from giving the text a title that appears, in fact, only in one single manuscript,[22] he inserted chapter divisions that do not appear in any of the textual witnesses. Dividing the *Memoriale qualiter* into chapters may be helpful for quoting the text but it obfuscates that the work is transmitted (and was read) as one continuous and unstructured treatise. Based on its content, however, we can divide the work into two clearly distinguishable parts. The main part is an outline of a daily

---

19 Diem, *The Pursuit of Salvation*, pp. 155–90. See also Diem, 'Das Ende des monastischen Experiments', pp. 81–136; Diem and van der Meer, *Columbanische Klosterregeln*. Jonas of Bobbio, *Vita Columbani*, ed. by Krusch, pp. 144–294. For an English translation and extensive commentary on the text, see Jonas of Bobbio, *Life of Columbanus*, trans. by O'Hara and Ian Wood.
20 See Diem, *The Pursuit of Salvation*, pp. 11–34.
21 See Diem, *The Pursuit of Salvation*, pp. 331–562; Diem and van der Meer, *Columbanische Klosterregeln*, pp. 48–108.
22 See Note 1 above.

monastic routine from the moment of awakening to the moment of falling asleep, which Morgand divides into five sections (I. *De nocturnis horis*; II. *De prima et officio capitula*; III. *De opere manuum*; V. *De refectione*; VI. *De collatione et completorio*). This part will henceforth be indicated as the *Cursus*. Between the sections on manual work and on meals, this *Cursus* is interrupted by a long insertion that Morgand titles *Exhortationes de bona obseruantia*, which is unrelated to the rest of the text and consists of twenty-five short precepts on various aspects of monastic life that are presented in no clear order. This section, which is henceforth indicated as the *Exhortationes*, is largely based on the *Regula Benedicti* though some of the precepts show similarities to other monastic Rules. Differently from the *Cursus*, the *Exhortationes* show no clear ties to the *Regula cuiusdam ad uirgines*. My contribution will mostly focus on the *Cursus* of the *Memoriale qualiter* and save an analysis of the *Exhortationes*, which are equally interesting, for another occasion.

We can find for both the *Cursus* and the *Exhortationes* similar (though unrelated) examples in the Carolingian monastic corpus. The *Cursus* is reminiscent of the treatise *De cursu diurno uel nocturno*,[23] the *Ordo Casinensis* I,[24] the *Ordo diurnus Anianensis*,[25] and the *Capitula in Auuam directa*.[26] All of these provide an outline of monastic (mostly liturgical) activities at specific moments of the day. The *Exhortationes*, for its part, shows formal similarities to the *Capitula Notitiarum*,[27] the *Capitula qualiter*,[28] the *Synodi primae Aquisgranensis acta praeliminaria*,[29] but also to Benedict of Aniane's *Collectio Capitularis*.[30]

The disparity between the *Cursus* and the *Exhortationes* and the rather arbitrary place of the *Exhortationes* within the *Cursus* makes it likely that we are dealing with two works of different origins that were at some point forged together to become the *Memoriale qualiter* as it is preserved. It is possible that this hybrid was created only for the purpose of being disseminated along with the acts of the Aachen reform councils. There are no manuscripts that contain only one part or the other, but in one manuscript, which contains a female version of the *Memoriale qualiter*, the *Exhortationes* appear at a different place, just before the last section on Compline.[31] An analysis of the *Memoriale qualiter* needs to address the *Cursus* and the *Exhortationes* separately and assume that observations on one part do not necessarily apply to the other,

---

23 *De cursu diurno uel nocturno*, ed. by Semmler, pp. 47–50.
24 *Ordo Casinensis* I, ed. by Leccisotti, Hallinger, and Wegener, pp. 101–04.
25 *Ordo diurnus Anianensis*, ed. by Molas and Wegener, pp. 311–17.
26 *Capitula in Auuam directa*, ed. by Frank, pp. 333–36.
27 *Capitula Notitiarum*, ed. by Frank, pp. 341–45.
28 *Capitula qualiter*, ed. by Frank, pp. 353–54.
29 *Synodi primae Aquisgranensis acta praeliminaria*, ed. by Semmler, pp. 435–36.
30 Benedict of Aniane, *Collectio Capitularis*, ed. by Semmler, pp. 515–36.
31 *Memoriale qualiter* II, ed. by Morgand, 7, pp. 277–81. On this version see below, pp. 66–71.

but as far as its reception and the impact is concerned, it is necessary to look at the work as *one* text.

Morgand was, to his great frustration, unable to create a stemma for the *Memoriale qualiter*.[32] Based on shared variants, he tentatively divided the thirty manuscripts he used for his edition into seven groups.[33] Each of these groups shares significant variants with each of the other groups, which makes it impossible to establish a clear relationship between them. Morgand decided therefore to identify the group that represents the largest common denominator, which is group 5, as providing the most authentic version of the text. He assessed the other groups on the basis of the number of variants as closer or more remote from the presumed original text. His reconstruction of the *Memoriale qualiter* almost entirely represents the text of the two manuscripts of group 5 (one of which is incomplete).[34] All variants, many of them bearing the same authority as the presumed original text, are documented in Morgand's massive apparatus criticus.

The fact that we have seven groups of manuscripts that share variants in almost any conceivable combination could be explained by assuming that there was a 'norm exemplar' of the *Memoriale qualiter* that has been copied several, maybe even numerous, times in one production process with the copies being superficially compared to each other. Most of the early manuscripts combine the *Memoriale qualiter* with Benedict of Aniane's *Collectio Capitularis*, which indicates that such a 'mass production' of copies of the *Memoriale qualiter*

---

32 *Memoriale qualiter*, ed. by Morgand, pp. 202–20.
33 I have documented the groups with hyperlinks to manuscript catalogues and digitized manuscripts on <http://earlymedievalmonasticism.org/texts/Memoriale-Qualiter.html>. **Group 1**: Rome, BC, MS 54 (olim B IV 21), s. XI; BnF, MS lat. 2860, s. XIII; Cambridge, University Libr., MS Dd. 4.58, s. XIII[in]; fols 103[v]–105[v]; BAV, MS Reg. lat. 127, 1361–1367; Trier, Stadtbibl., MS 1238/601, s. XV; Trier, Stadtbibl., MS 1259/586, s. XV; Paris, Bibl. de l'Arsenal, MS 968, s. XVI; Avignon, BM, MS 712, s. XVI; BnF, MS lat. 12885, AD 1455; Vienna, ÖNB, MS lat. 2655, s. XV. **Group 2** largely (but not exclusively) consists of manuscripts from England: Turin, BN, MS G.V. 4, s. X; BL, MS Harley 5431, s. X[ex]; Cambridge, CCC, MS 57, s. XI; BAV, MS Barb lat. 646, s. XI; BL, MS Cotton Tiberius A III, s. XI; BL, MS Cotton Titus A IV, s. XI[med]; BnF, MS lat. 15025, s. XIII; Cambridge, University Libr., MS Ll. 1.14, s. XI. **Group 3** consists of manuscripts related to Montecasino: Montecassino, Bibl. dell'Abazia, MS 175, s. X; Montecassino, Bibl. dell'Abazia, MS 179, s. XI; Montecassino, Bibl. dell'Abazia, MS 442, s. XI; BAV, MS Vat. lat. 13501, s. XI[ex]. **Group 4** consists of four late medieval manuscripts: Montecassino, Bibl. dell'Abazia, MS 418, s. XVI; Avignon, BM, MS 732, AD 1645; Valenciennes, BM, MS 246. AD 1647; Zürich, ZB, MS Rh. 134, s. XV. **Group 5** provides, in Morgand's view, the most authentic text: Merseburg, Domstiftsbibl., MS I 136 (58) and Rouen, BM, MS 1385 [U 107]. **Group 6** consists of only one manuscript, Tours, BM, MS 284 s. XI, which stands close to group 5. **Group 7** contains the *Memoriale qualiter* in a version for nuns, which is only preserved in one manuscript, Montpellier, Bibl. de l'École de la Médicine, MS H 85, s. XI.
34 Rouen, BM, MS 1385 [U 107] contains only parts of the text. Morgand almost exclusively follows Merseburg, Domstiftsbibl., MS I 136 (58) as *codex optimus*.

would have taken place soon after the Aachen council of 817 as part of the process of disseminating Benedict of Aniane's work.

Morgand's decision to reconstruct the text entirely on the basis of manuscripts of group 5 makes sense, but since all groups have, by lack of a stemma, equal authority, his edition should be used with caution and along with its apparatus criticus. If, for example, we compare the parts of the *Memoriale qualiter* in the interpolated Chrodegang Rule with Morgand's edition, we see that the interpolator used a version that shows close proximity to group 5 but also shares variants with most of the other groups in various combinations.[35] This means that Morgand, at least for the sections that overlap, should have used the interpolated Chodegang Rule as a corrective for his editorial decisions.

The *Memoriale qualiter* II

To make things more complicated, the *Memoriale qualiter* is preserved in a version addressing a community of monks (in thirty-eight manuscripts) and another one written for nuns, which we find in only one manuscript where the text is integrated into the *Institutio sanctimonialium*.[36] Morgand provides a separate edition of the version for nuns as *Memoriale qualiter* II — a problematic title since this version has, in its manuscript, no title at all.[37] The text of the *Memoriale qualiter* II is about a quarter longer than the *Memoriale qualiter* for monks. Almost all of its expansions contain instructions for ritual and liturgy, many of which pertain to the liturgical Hours while the version for monks exclusively focuses on liturgical instructions outside the Hours.[38] In order to show where the *Memoriale qualiter* II deviates from the version addressing monks, Morgand published it in two columns. The left column contains the text that overlaps with the *Memoriale qualiter* for monks, the right column the parts that have been added or changed. With the exception of a short section on manual labour,[39] the entire *Memoriale qualiter* for monks is reproduced in the *Memoriale qualiter* II.

Among all treatises in the *Corpus Consuetudinum Monasticarum* and, in fact, all texts produced in the context of the Carolingian monastic reforms, the *Memoriale qualiter* is the only one that is preserved in a male and a female version. As Katrinette Bodarwé has shown, there is little evidence showing

---

35 The *Regula canonicorum* goes twice with group 1; four times with group 2; twice with group 3; once with group 4; once with groups 1, 2, 3, and 4; and once with groups 2 and 4.
36 Montpellier, Bibl. de l'École de la Médicine, MS H 85, fols 98–102.
37 *Memoriale qualiter* II, ed. by Morgand, pp. 267–82. The text begins with the words 'Nocturnis horis […]' and ends with '[…] roget poni ori suo custodiam', thus without the final sentence of the *Memoriale qualiter* I.
38 See especially *Memoriale qualiter* II, ed. by Morgand, 3. 8–9, pp. 271–73.
39 *Memoriale qualiter*, ed. by Morgand, 8–10, pp. 238–40.

how the attempt of unification under the *Regula Benedicti* affected Carolingian female communities. None of the few female adaptations of the *Regula Benedicti* is older than the tenth century.[40] If the single manuscript of the *Memoriale qualiter* II had been lost, we would have had no idea that one of the most important reform documents was considered applicable to both sexes.

There are, aside from the *Institutio sanctimonialium*, no Carolingian reform texts preserved that specifically address female communities or explicitly address all religious communities regardless of the sex of their inhabitants, which indicates that convents were hardly on the agenda of monastic reform. Acts of Carolingian councils and *Capitularia* impose enclosure on female foundations and, in a side line, require that they either have to live *regulariter* or, as canonical houses, follow the *Institutio sanctimonialium*, which is entirely different from its counterpart, the *Institutio canonicorum*.[41]

Not much has been done with the version of the *Memoriale qualiter* for monks, but the *Memoriale qualiter* II has been ignored almost completely, even by Katie Ann-Marie Bugyis, who studied the impact on confessional and penitential practices of the *Memoriale qualiter* on English female Benedictine life. Morgand identified some of the expansions we find in the *Memoriale qualiter* II as liturgical provisions linked to the Cluniac reforms and therefore assumed that the female *Memoriale qualiter* has been produced at some point between the early tenth century and the twelfth century when the only extant manuscript has been written.[42]

There are a number of reasons for challenging the dating and the relation between both versions of the *Memoriale qualiter* as proposed by Morgand. Based on his assumption that the *Memoriale qualiter* II is a tenth-century

---

40 Bodarwé, 'Eine Männerregel für Frauen', pp. 260–72: Bodarwé lists as the earliest examples of female versions of the *Regula Benedicti* the Old English female adaptation of the *Regula Benedicti* that was probably produced in the late tenth century (preserved in later manuscripts, e.g. BL, MS Cotton Claudius D III), a version preserved in a tenth-century Spanish manuscript (Madrid, RAH, MS Aemilianensis 62), fragments of a ninth-century manuscript of the *Regula Benedicti* that has been adapted for a female community in the tenth or eleventh century (Regensburg, Bischöfliche Zentralbibl., MS Cim. 8), and a complete female revision of the *Regula Benedicti* produced around 990, now preserved in Bamberg, SB, MS Msc. Lit 142.

41 E.g. *Pippini regis capitulare*, ed. by Boretius, 5, p. 34; *Caroli magni capitulare primum*, ed. by Boretius, 3, p. 45; *Capitulare missorum generale a. 802*, ed. by Boretius, 18, p. 95; *Capitulare missorum specialia*, ed. by Boretius, 5, p. 100; *Capitula ecclesiastica ad Salz data a. 803/04*, ed. by Boretius, 5, p. 119; *Capitula originis incerta a. 813*, ed. by Boretius, 4, p. 175; *Concilium Germanicum a. 742*, ed. by Werminghoff, 7, p. 4; *Pippini regis capitulare a. 782–86*, ed. by Boretius, 3, p. 192; *Pippini capitulare Papiense*, ed. by Boretius, 11, p. 199; *Statuta Rhispacensia*, ed. by Boretius, 21, p. 228; *Concilium Foroiulense a. 796/97*, ed. by Werminghoff, 12, pp. 193–94; *Concilium Arelatense a. 813*, ed. by Werminghoff, 7–8, p. 251; *Concilium Moguntiense a. 813*, ed. by Werminghoff, 13, p. 264; *Concilium Moguntiense a. 813*, ed. by Werminghoff, 19–20, p. 266. On the *Institutio sanctimonialium*, see Schilp, *Norm und Wirklichkeit religiöser Frauengemeinschaften*.

42 *Memoriale qualiter*, ed. by Morgand, pp. 263–65.

Table 3.1 Variants of the *Memoriale qualiter* and the *Exhortationes*

These are the variants in Chapter 1:

	group 5 / Morgand's edition	**Memoriale qualiter II**	**other groups**
p. 230, l. 1	*in primis*	om.	with groups 2, 3
l. 2	*primum signum sibi sanctae crucis imprimat*	*primum sibi sancte crucis signum imprimat*	with group 4
p. 231, ll. 2–3	*sibi; tunc referat gratias deo ita dicendo Gratias*	*sibi; ita dicendo Gratias*	with group 2
l. 6	*seruitus nostra*	*seruitus mea*	with groups 1, 3, 4, 6

These are the variants in Chapter 6:

	group 5 / Morgand's edition	**Memoriale qualiter II**	**other groups**
l. 4	*sicut praecipit regula*	om.	with group 3
l. 8	*incipiant Completam*	*et incipiant Completorium*	with groups 3, 4, and parts of group 1
l. 4	*gratias deo Gratias*	*gratias deo, ita dicendo Gratias*	group 1: *ita referendo*; 2 and 6: *dicendo*
l. 6	*qualiter mane*	*quatinus mane*	with group 4
l. 4	*mane surgens postulauit*	*mane postulauit*	with group 1
l. 5	*a domino aperire*	*aperiri a domino*	with group 1
l. 5	*ponere*	*poni*	with parts of group 2
l. 6	*Hi affectus […] reducuntur*	om.	with groups 1 and 3

Variants from the *Exhortationes* (beginning)

	group 5 / Morgand's edition	**Memoriale qualiter II**	**other groups**
l. 2	*ex fratribus alterum*	*ex sororibus aliam*	with groups 1 and 4
l. 6	*abbas uero domnus et pater uocetur*	*abbatissam autem dominam et matrem uocent*	with groups 2 and 3
l. 8	*aliud nullus*	*aliud nullum*	with group 2
l. 9–p. 242, l. 242	*aut Plane, quod saepe sanctum Augustinum legimus testificasse, aut Certe*	*aut Certe*	with group 3 and parts of group 4
l. 4	*aliqua*	om.	with group 3
l. 5	*in faciem*	om.	with group 2
l. 5	*eadem*	om.	with groups 1 and 4
l. 7	*ante omnia*	om.	with most of group 2
l. 3	*iunior dicat*	*dicat soror*	group 4: *dicat iunior*
ll. 5–6	*iuxta regulam nostram*	om.	only in *Memoriale qualiter II* and MS *V*
ll. 6–7	*Et expleto […] Benedictite*	om.	with groups 1, 4, and 6
p. 245, ll. 1–2	*et iterum […] Benedicite*	om.	with groups 1 and 4, different text in group 3
l. 5	*in quolibet*	*in quolibet loco*	with group 1, most of group 2, and 4

revision that largely deviated from the version of *Memoriale qualiter* for monks, Morgand decided not to integrate the textual variants of the *Memoriale qualiter* II into his apparatus criticus. Had he done so, this would have shown that, just like the fragments in Chrodegang's Rule, the *Memoriale qualiter* II shares variants indiscriminately with almost every other manuscript group that Morgand identified. This shows, on the one hand, that the *Memoriale qualiter* II should have been taken into account in Morgand's edition of the *Memoriale qualiter* for monks and, on the other hand, that the *Memoriale qualiter* II may have been based on a female version that had been produced very early in the textual transmission, possibly at the same time as the other copies but not in the tenth century.

Table 3.1 shows variants from Chapters 1 and 6 of the *Memoriale qualiter* for monks and of the beginning of the *Exhortationes*.

Given the fact that the *Cursus* of the *Memoriale qualiter* is based on the *Regula cuiusdam ad uirgines*, I would even go one step further: it is possible that at least the *Cursus* was originally written for a female community and was later adapted for monks and distributed as a monastic reform document.[43] A possible place of origin would be the monastery of Chelles which was founded by Queen Balthild. The *Vita* of Bertila, the first abbess of Chelles, was strongly influenced by the *Regula cuiusdam ad uirgines* and the monastery seems to have adopted the *Regula Benedicti* in the course of the eighth century.[44] A text like the *Memoriale qualiter* would have helped to facilitate a transition from the *Regula cuiusdam ad uirgines* to the *Regula Benedicti* by creating a 'customary' that retained various traditions that had been practised in the monastery and reconciled them with the new Rule. Chelles, however, only stands in for possible other, not as well-documented, seventh-century female foundations that may have used the *Regula cuiusdam ad uirgines* and later adopted the *Regula Benedicti*.[45]

The *Memoriale qualiter* refers seven times to a *regula*, three times in the *Cursus* and four times in the *Exhortationes*. In the case of the *Exhortationes*, the wording of the *Memoriale qualiter* clearly points to the *Regula Benedicti*.[46] Two of the references to the *regula* in the *Cursus* also clearly refer to the *Regula*

---

[43] Davril and Palazzo, *La vie des moines*, p. 86 describe the text as 'coutumier rédigé à l'usage d'une communauté des moniales de la fin du VIIIe siècle' without providing evidence for this assumption. It is unclear whether this ascription is the product of a slip of the pen or of an analysis that has not been documented.

[44] On the dependence of the *Vita Bertilae* on the *Regula cuiusdam ad uirgines*, see Diem, *The Pursuit of Salvation*, pp. 179–81 and pp. 611–12.

[45] On monasteries that may have used the *Regula cuiusdam ad uirgines*, see Muschiol, *Famula Dei*, p. 73.

[46] *Memoriale qualiter*, ed. by Morgand, 4. 2, p. 241 refers to *Regula Benedicti*, ed. by de Vogüé, 63. 11–12, II, p. 646. *Memoriale qualiter*, ed. by Morgand, 4. 5, p. 243 refers to *Regula Benedicti*, ed. by de Vogüé, 63. 15–17, II, p. 646. *Memoriale qualiter*, ed. by Morgand, 4. 12, p. 247 refers to *Regula Benedicti*, ed. by de Vogüé, 33. 1, II, p. 562, etc.

Benedicti,[47] but the third stands closer to the *Regula cuiusdam ad uirgines*,[48] which indicates that the monastery for which the *Cursus* was written, could indeed have used both monastic Rules. The *Memoriale qualiter* ends with the requirement to bring the provisions provided in the text 'back to memory' (*ad memoriam reducuntur*). This would support the idea that it was meant to preserve monastic practices that might be abandoned and forgotten in the process of adopting the *Regula Benedicti*.[49]

Another observation supports the precedence of a female *Memoriale qualiter*. The *Memoriale qualiter* II refers in one of the sections that cannot be found in the *Memoriale qualiter* for monks, to a *Hora Secunda* as liturgical Hour.[50] The *Hora Secunda* only exists in texts related to Columbanian monastic traditions, particularly in the *Regula cuiusdam ad uirgines* and in the *Regula Donati*.[51] This might indicate that the *Memoriale qualiter* II contains a trace of an original version of the text that had been omitted in the *Memoriale qualiter* for monks because the *Hora Secunda* had become obsolete.

The possibility that a text that was produced for a specific female community was later adapted to become a guideline for monks is by no means outlandish. A number of female communities, particularly Caesarius's foundation in Arles, Radegund's monastery in Poitiers, and the monastery of Faremoutiers, which was founded shortly after Columbanus's death, were highly innovative,

---

47 *Memoriale qualiter*, ed. by Morgand, 5. 12, p. 255 '[...] Et sicut docet regula, nullius uox ibi audiatur, nisi solius legentis, nisi certe pro aedificatione aliquid exinde preuiter dicatur', clearly refers to *Regula Benedicti*, ed. by de Vogüé and Neufville, 38. 8–9, II, p. 574, but also shows parallels in content with *Regula cuiusdam ad uirgines*, ed. by Diem, 9. 13–18, p. 102. *Memoriale qualiter*, ed. by Morgand, 6. 17, p. 259: 'Post Uesperas hora competenti facto signo omnes in unum conueniunt in capitulo uerpertino et legatur scriptura quae aedificet audientes, quamtum hora permittit, sicut praecipit regula' clearly refers to *Regula Benedicti*, ed. by de Vogüé/Neufville, 42. 5–6, II, p. 584.

48 Compare *Memoriale qualiter*, ed. by Morgand, 3. 9, pp. 239–40: 'Cum **ad opus diuinum horis** canonicis **auditum fuerit signum**, sicut continetur in regula, relinquentes statim quicquid **in manibus** est, sic tamen ut non pereat, tunc conueniant simul ad introitum oratorii' to *Regula cuiusdam ad uirgines*, ed. by Diem, 8. 1, p. 96: 'Quandocumque uel diurnis uel nocturnis horis **ad opus diuinum signum** insonuerit, mox cum summa festinatione surgendum est, ac si praeco regis insonet, omni opere, quod **in manibus** habebatur, postposito' and to *Regula Benedicti*, ed. by de Vogüé/Neufville, 43. 1–2, II, p. 586: 'Ad horam **diuini** officii, mox **auditus fuerit signus**, relictis omnibus quaelibet fuerint **in manibus**, summa cum festinatione curratur, cum grauitate tamen, ut non scurrilitas inueniat fomitem'.

49 *Memoriale qualiter*, ed. by Morgand, 6. 19, p. 261: 'Hi affectus in unum collecti citius ad memoriam reducuntur/reducantur'. This final sentence appears only in Group 2 and 5. All other groups omit the requirement to entrust the text to memory.

50 *Memoriale qualiter* II, ed. by Morgand, 4, p. 269: 'Hora secunda signo pulsato eant calciatum. Deinde lotae ingrediantur oragorium et decantent tacito sicut in nocte septem psalmos'.

51 *Regula cuiusdam ad uirgines*, ed. by Diem, 3. 17–20, p. 78; 6. 20–23, p. 92; 8. 7, p. 96; 12. 3, p. 110; *Regula Donati*, ed. by Zimmerl-Panagl, 19. 2, p. 157; 20. 1, p. 158. See also Muschiol, *Famula Dei*, p. 118.

controversial, and experimental foundations that established new practices that were adopted by communities of monks and nuns alike.[52]

The most striking example of an instructive text initially addressing a female community that later become a general guideline is a letter written by Caesarius of Arles to his sister Caesaria and her community of virgins, which is usually indicated after its opening term as the letter *Vereor*. The text is a staunch admonition of the nuns to protect their virginity and to understand the monastery as a battleground against vices. *Vereor* is preserved in only three manuscripts addressing a female community but in at least twelve manuscripts as *Epistola ad monachos* (the three oldest manuscripts are Carolingian). Parts of the letter have been inserted into Caesarius's *Regula ad monachos* but also into the *Institutio sanctimonialium*.[53]

Benedict of Aniane collected for his *Codex regularum* (the most extensive collection of early medieval monastic normative texts) both Rules for monks and Rules for nuns.[54] In his *Concordia Regularum* he used various chapters from Rules for nuns (especially from the *Regula cuiusdam ad uirgines*) as material to be compared to the *Regula Benedicti*. He changed the grammatical gender of all female monastic Rules and made them look like Rules for monks.[55] Smaragdus of St Mihiel used in his *Expositio Regulae S. Benedicti* much of the material arranged by Benedict of Aniane, probably without realizing that it was originally written for female monasteries.[56] Extant communities of nuns may not have mattered much to Carolingian monastic reformers, but that does not mean that the textual witnesses of female monastic experiments were disregarded. The *Memoriale qualiter*, at least its *Cursus*, very likely transmitted a female monastic experience — either directly by having been composed for a female community and then adapted as a text for monks, or indirectly by incorporating ideas that were originally expressed in a Columbanian Rule for Nuns.

So much for the history of the text. It is now time to focus on its content.

---

52 Diem, 'The Gender of the Religious'. On Caesarius's foundation, see Klingshirn, 'Caesarius's Monastery for Women'; on Radegund's foundation: Dailey, *Queens, Consorts, Concubines*; on Faremoutiers: Diem, *The Pursuit of Salvation*, pp. 191–241.

53 Caesarius of Arles, *Epistola a uirgines*, ed. by de Vogüé and Courreau, trans. by Klingshirn, pp. 129–39. For a list of manuscripts and its reception history see <http://www.earlymedievalmonasticism.org/texts/Caesarius-Ep-Vereor.html> [accessed 19 April 2022]. For an analysis of the letter: Rudge, 'Texts and Contexts', esp. pp. 55–59 and 160–67; Diem, *The Pursuit of Salvation*, pp. 276–81.

54 The *Codex Regularum* is preserved in one Carolingian manuscript, Munich, BSB, MS Clm 28118. See Engelbert ed., *Der Codex Regularum* (facsimile edition). For a description see also <http://www.earlymedievalmonasticism.org/manuscripts/Munich-Clm-28118.html> [accessed 19 April 2022] with hyperlinks to the digitized manuscript.

55 Benedict of Aniane, *Concordia Regularum*, ed. by Bonnerue, II. See also the index of vol. I, pp. 244, 246, 254–55.

56 Smaragdus, *Expositio*, ed. by Spannagel and Engelbert.

A Choreography of Monastic Life

The *Cursus* of the *Memoriale qualiter* begins with the following provision (in Matthew Mattingly's translation):

> To begin with, at the night Hours, when a brother has arisen from his bed for the Work of God, he first invokes the holy Trinity by making the sign of the cross. He then says the verse 'Lord open my lips', (Psalm 50. 17) followed by the psalm 'God come to my assistance' (Psalm 69) in its entirety with the 'Gloria'. He may then attend to nature's needs before hastening to the oratory as he prays the psalm 'To you, Lord, I have lifted up my soul' (Psalm 24). He enters the oratory with all reverence and care so as not to disturb the others praying. Then, as he lies prostrate in the appropriate place, he pours forth prayers in the Lord's presence, more from the heart than from the mouth and in such a way that his voice might be closer to God than to himself. Then he gives thanks to God, saying, 'To you I give thanks, almighty Father, who have deigned to watch over me this night. I earnestly pray for your mercy, compassionate Lord, that you might grant that I may live this coming day in your holy service with humility and discretion so that it may be pleasing to you'.[57]

This first provision shows parallels with Chapter 14 of the *Regula cuiusdam ad uirgines* which addresses the nuns' sleep. At the moment the nuns awaken they have to make the sign of the cross and say Psalm 69 (*Deus in adiutorium*).[58] Elsewhere in the Rule, Jonas of Bobbio emphasizes that the nuns' behaviour at the moment of awakening needs to be submitted to thorough control by the prioresses who are supposed to strictly punish any form of negligence.[59] The requirement of making the sign of the cross as an apotropaic act and

---

57 *Memoriale qualiter*, trans. by Mattingly, pp. 66–67; ed. by Morgand, 1. 1, pp. 230–31: 'In primis, nocturnis horis, cum ad opus diuinum de lectulo surrexerit frater, primum signum sibi sanctae cruds imprimat per inuocationem sanctae trinitatis; deinde dicat uersum Domine labia mea aperies; inde psalmum Deus in adiutorium meum intende totum cum Gloria. Tunc prouideat sibi corpoream necessitatem naturae, et sic ad oratorium festinet psallendo psalmum Ad te, domine, letuaui anintam meam, cum summa reuerentia et cautela intrans, ut aliis orantibus non impediat; et tunc prostratus in loco congruo effundat preces in conspectu domini, magis corde quam ore, ita ut illius uox uicinior sit deo quam sibi; tunc referat gratias deo ita dicendo Gratias tibi ago, omnipotens pater, qui me dignatus es in hac nocte custodire; deprecor clementiam tuam, misericors do mine, ut concedas mihi diem uenturum sic peragere in tuo sancto seruitio cum humilitate et discretione, qualiter tibi complaceat seruitus nostra'.

58 *Regula cuiusdam ad uirgines*, ed. by Diem, 14. 15, p. 118: 'Ad cursum uero cum festinatione surgentes signum crucis fronti inferatur, simulque sub silentio dicatur: deus in adiutorium meum intende'.

59 *Regula cuiusdam ad uirgines*, ed. by Diem, 2. 18–19, p. 74: 'Similiter ad omnes cursus nocturnos hoc est faciendum, ut sciant quae cum feruore uel quae cum tepiditate ad cursum adsurgunt. Et eas, quas tarditate uel segnitia culpabiles reppererint, prout culpa uel aetas fuerit, aut increpatione aut flagello corripiant'.

immediately asking God for help makes sense for Jonas, who explicitly states that the mind and flesh of his nuns have attracted sins while their nuns had been paralysed by sleep and that the devil could take control over a nun while sleeping.[60] There are various examples of using the sign of the cross as a tool for warding off evil,[61] but no other monastic Rule requires making the sign of the cross at the moment of awakening.

The *Memoriale qualiter* thus expands what we find in the *Regula cuiusdam ad uirgines* by adding two other prayers (and a bathroom visit), but it also picks up on an idea that is central to the *Regula cuiusdam ad uirgines*: that the *opus Dei* not only pertains to the liturgical Hours but that everything a member of the community does between the moment of awakening and the moment of falling asleep is to be considered *opus Dei*. As such, every act has to be submitted to the greatest scrutiny, ritualized and 'liturgized'. The *Regula cuiusdam ad uirgines* is built entirely around the idea that everything a nun does throughout the day (and even in her sleep) is a matter of salvation or eternal damnation and that there are, within monasteries, neither spaces nor times that are more or less holy than others.[62] Consequently, the *Regula cuiusdam ad uirgines* contains numerous references to liturgical activities outside the Hours, and the *Memoriale qualiter* vastly expands on them.[63]

The imperative of the unceasing *opus Dei* manifests itself in the *Regula cuiusdam* not only by adding liturgical provisions related to various daily activities (arising out of bed, the beginning of work, meal times, confession, going to sleep), but also by controlling the nuns' bodily movement and submitting them to an elaborate 'choreography' that makes the body itself a liturgical object, and by imposing a strict control over every spoken word and over anything that causes noise.[64] All monks (or, in the *Memoriale qualiter* II, nuns) are in constant, restrained, and carefully choreographed movement,

---

60 *Regula cuiusdam ad uirgines*, ed. by Diem, 6. 20, p. 92: 'Quicquid post conpletorium per opace noctis spacia mens uel caro per fragilitatemm deliquerit, post secundam per confessionem curandum est expiari'; 8. 7, p. 96: 'Nam foris omnino non segregentur, ne a somno detentae dormiant aut in aliquo maligno hosti adeundi detur occasio'; 14. 7–8, p. 118: 'Neque se ad inuicem, id est facie ad faciem, respiciant, sed una post aliam quiescens dormiat, ne antiquus hostis, qui ore libenti animas uulnerare cupit, aliquid fraudis iaculando inmittat, ut colloquendo mortalia excitet desideria'.

61 *Regula Magistri*, ed. by de Vogüé, 8. 30, I, p. 404; 15.34, II, p. 68; 47. 24, II, p. 216; Columbanus, *Regula coenobialis*, ed. by Walker, 2, p. 146, ll. 6–10; 3, pp. 146–48; 9, p. 150, ll. 13–14; 15, p. 164, ll. 26–27.

62 Diem and van der Meer, *Columbanische Klosterregeln*, pp. 79–108; Diem, *The Pursuit of Salvation*.

63 *Regula cuiusdam ad uirgines*, ed. by Diem, 2. 17, p. 74; 3. 12, pp. 76–78; 5. 24, p. 88; 6. 14–16, p. 90; 6. 28–30, p. 94; 9. 8, p. 100; 10. 15, p. 106; 12. 11, p. 112; 12. 16–17, p. 112; 12. 24–28, p. 114; 20. 7–8, p. 132. Matthew Mattingly observed that the *Regula Benedicti* rarely addresses such liturgical activities. See Mattingly, 'The Memoriale Qualiter', p. 63.

64 *Regula cuiusdam ad uirgines*, ed. by Diem, 2. 18, p. 74; 3. 9, p. 76; 7. 3, p. 94; 8. 1–4, p. 96; 9. 15, p. 102; 10. 12, p. 106; 22. 4, p. 142; 22. 10, p. 144; 22. 15, p. 138; 22. 20–23, pp. 140–42; 24. 4, p. 144; 24. 8–9, p. 144.

which includes walking in a dignified manner, prostrating themselves, bowing, kneeling, rising, and standing. Here are all choreographic instructions of the *Cursus* placed in a row. This is monastic aerobics:

> When a brother has **arisen** from his bed for the Work of God, he first invokes the holy Trinity by making the sign of the cross [...] He **enters the oratory with all reverence** and care so as not to disturb the others praying. Then [...] **he lies prostrate** in the appropriate place [...] After the completion of the Night Office there is complete silence at the interval, **as much in voice as in movement**, whether through coming in or the sound of any other affair [...] Now, at the break of day, when the signal has sounded, all **hasten quickly with cheerful hearts**, as if the kind and merciful God is pleased with them, to render Morning Lauds, with a ready mind, measured voices which are neither too drawn out nor abbreviated, and with great sincerity and respect [...] When this is completed, they assemble for the chapter. **With faces turned to the east they reverence the cross**, and the rest of **brothers bow** wherever they may be [...] In a like manner **they bow whenever they are assembled** [...] They are to **pray while kneeling** [...] **Arising again**, together they say the verse 'Look on your servants', (Psalm 89. 16) all the way to the end of the psalm adding the 'Glory to the Father' **with a bow**. [...] **Arising together** from the chapter, **all stand and say three times the verse**, begun by the superior, 'God come to my assistance' (Psalm 69. 1), adding the 'Glory to the Father' **while kneeling** [...] When he has heard the signal at the canonical Hours for the divine office, just as it is contained in the Rule, **he immediately puts down whatever is in hand**, but in such a manner that the work is not lost [...] Then they come together at the entrance of the oratory [...] and they say the verse [...] 'You are blessed, Lord God who have helped me and consoled me' (Psalm 85. 17), three times, adding the 'Glory to the Father' which is prayed **while kneeling**. After the prayer is complete, **they arise** and say, 'May the almighty Lord have mercy on us. Amen' (Psalm 66. 2) [...] Now when they have heard the bell (*cymbalum*), **they move quickly and in order, without any noise**, entering the refectory after washing their hands. They **reverence the cross with their faces turned toward the east**. When the second bell has sounded they proceed to the table, where together the whole congregation says the verse and the Lord's prayer **while kneeling** [...] At the time that the superior blesses the food and drink and whatever else, **he does not sit but says the blessing while standing** [...] Let the young immediately **arise for this task, standing in line by seniority** [...] The junior who puts a cup into the hand of one who is sitting **bows his head in humility**; and the one who receives it, also **with his head bowed in humility**, gives thanks to God who provides it and says '*Benedicite*'. [...] When he returns it **each one bows humbly**. When they have completed the work of mixing the wine, **they bow as they look to the cross, and**

then turn bowing towards the lord abbot, and then in a circle to all the brothers. And thus **they walk quickly back to their tables** [...] **Arising from the table** after the verse is said, the left choir **exits first in order, then afterwards the right, with the lord abbot last**, all chanting the fiftieth psalm deliberately and not too fast. When they have entered the oratory, chanting, **they bow up to the 'Gloria', and then at the 'Gloria' they kneel**. After the Lord's Prayer and the short readings, as much as there is time for, they **then rise and depart in silence** [...] When the reading is complete, **all arise together** and the lord abbot says, 'Our help is in the name of the Lord'; and all respond, 'Who made heaven and earth' (Psalm 123. 8). Then, leaving in silence, they **enter reverently** for Compline [...] **They are to walk with great care** in the church and in the dormitory.[65]

The *Memoriale qualiter* also expands on the *Regula cuiusdam ad uirgines* in its strong emphasis of silence, restrained voice, and avoiding noise. Most monastic Rules address silence extensively, but none integrates it as much into a programme of unceasing *opus Dei* as the *Regula cuiusdam ad uirgines*.[66] We find the same concerns in *Memoriale qualiter* expressed in these passages:

Then, as he lies prostrate in the appropriate place, he pours forth prayers in the Lord's presence, **more from the heart than from the mouth and in such a way that his voice might be closer to God than to himself** [...] After the completion of the Night Office **there is complete silence at the interval** [...] All hasten quickly with cheerful hearts [...] to render Morning Lauds, **with a ready mind, measured voices which are neither too drawn out nor abbreviated** [...] Then, when Morning Lauds are finished, **there is attentive silence for praying and reading** [...] Then they go either together or separately to their assigned work, **observing the silence** [...] **They should say nothing else, unless engaged in some activity for which it will be necessary to speak with due care** [...] At the time for the meal, after they have completed the office, they wait in the church in the choir **saying the psalms silently**. Now when they have heard the bell (*cymbalum*), they move quickly and in order, **without any noise**, entering the refectory after washing their hands [...] After the superior has given the blessing they sit at table in seniority **and in complete silence** [...] And, just as the Rule teaches, **the voice of no one is to be heard there**, except for the one reading, unless, perhaps, something is briefly said afterwards for edification [...] Then they ring the bell softly and the brothers say '*Benedicite*' **in a slow, even voice** [...] Now if the

---

65 *Memoriale qualiter*, trans. by Mattingly, pp. 66–74.
66 See *Regula cuiusdam ad uirgines*, ed. by Diem, 1. 4–6, p. 63; 3. 7–10, p. 76; 4. 11, p. 82; 4. 19–22, p. 84; 7. 3, p. 94; 12. 9–12, p. 112; 12. 18–19, p. 112; 12. 22, p. 114; 14. 5–8, p. 118; 14. 15, p. 118; 19. 9–11, p. 130; 22. 4–5, p. 136; 22. 22–23, pp. 140–42; 23. 7, p. 142.

> wine is the sort that will have to be mixed in the cups, the cellarer **gives a signal discreetly** to the server […] Again the cellarer **sounds the bell softly**, and the brothers say '*Benedicite*' **slowly and in unison** […] After the Lord's Prayer and the short readings, as much as there is time for, they then rise **and depart in silence** […] Then, **leaving in silence**, they enter reverently for Compline […] The same office having been completed, **the greatest silence is to be kept. There should be silent prayer with mouth and heart** […] When a brother comes to his own bed, where he settles in, he says the psalm 'God come to my assistance' (Psalms 69), and after the 'Gloria' he says the verse '**Lord put a guard over my mouth**' (Psalms 140. 3), etc., and just as in the morning when he arose and **asked the Lord to open his lips, now resting may he ask him to put a guard over his mouth**.[67]

Documenting all liturgical activities outside the Hours would mean reproducing almost the entire *Cursus* of the *Memoriale qualiter*. A list of all Psalms and Psalm verses to be sung outside the liturgical Hours might suffice: Psalm 50. 17; Psalm 69; Psalm 24; Psalm 137. 2; Psalm 115. 15; Psalm 69. 1; Psalm 89. 16; Psalm 123. 8; Psalm 69. 1; Psalm 123. 8; Psalm 85. 17; Psalm 66. 2; Psalm 123. 8; Psalm 69; Psalm 140. 3. Additionally, the *Memoriale qualiter* inserts a morning and a night prayer, that both emphasize the idea that a member of the community is 'on duty' day and night:

> To you I give thanks, almighty Father, who have deigned to watch over me this night. I earnestly pray for your mercy, compassionate Lord, that you might grant that I may live this coming day in your holy service with humility and discretion so that it may be pleasing to you.[68]

> I give thanks to you, holy Lord, all-powerful Father, who deigned to watch over me this day through your holy mercy; grant that I may pass this night with a pure heart and body in such a way that in the morning when I arise, I may offer you pleasing service.[69]

---

67 *Memoriale qualiter*, trans. by Mattingly, pp. 66–74.
68 *Memoriale qualiter*, trans. by Mattingly, p. 67, ed. by Morgand, 1. 1, p. 231: 'Gratias tibi ago, omnipotens pater, qui me dignatus es in hac nocte custodire; deprecor clementiam tuam, misericors domine, ut concedas mihi diem uentumm sic peragere in tuo sancto seruitio cum humilitate et discretione, qualiter tibi complaceat seruitus nostra'. Morgand identifies similarities with an *Oratio ad matutinas* in the *Gelasian Sacramentary*, ed. by Wilson, III, no. 84, p. 291: 'Gratias tibi agimus, Domine sancte, Pater omnipotens, aetene Deus, qui nos transacto noctis spatio ad matutinas horas perducere dignatus es; quaesumus, ut dones nobis diem hunc sine peccato transire, quatenus ad uesperum gratias referamus'.
69 *Memoriale qualiter*, trans. by Mattingly, p. 74; ed. by Morgand, 6. 18, p. 260: 'Gratias tibi ago, domine sancte pater omnipotens, qui me dignatus es in hac die custodire per tuam sanctam misericordiam; concede mihi hanc noctem mundo corde et corpore sic pertransire, qualiter mane surgens gratum tibi seruitium exsoluere possim'. Morgand identifies similarities with an *Oratio ad vesperum* in the *Gelasian Sacramentary*, ed. by Wilson, III, no. 85, p. 293: 'Gratias

All three elements — the monastic choreography, the restraint of one's voice, and liturgical activities that structure the day outside the Hours — may not be entirely absent in the *Regula Benedicti* but they play there, all in all, a rather marginal role.[70] The same applies for the other Carolingian *Ordines*: the *Ordo Casinensis* I says little about movement but refers to silence a number of times;[71] the *Ordo diurnus Anianensis* contains a few references to movement and hardly anything on silence;[72] the *Capitula in Auuam directis* contains five references to movement and mention silence once.[73] The fact that almost the entire *Memoriale qualiter* revolves around these three themes sets it apart from all the other textual contributions to the Carolingian monastic reform process. They may also have been the reasons why Carolingian reformers considered the text so important.

Very few sections of the *Cursus* (such as the bathroom breaks and the requirement to cover one's spittle with a foot to prevent other member of the community soiling their habits when prostrating themselves on the ground)[74] cannot be tied to the topics of unceasing *opus Dei*, silence and noise prevention, and monastic choreography — with one exception: the *Memoriale qualiter* contains various references to the practice of confession, which, again, sets the text apart from all other textual witnesses of the Carolingian reform initiatives.

Confession

The *Regula Benedicti* requires, as the fifth stage of humility (Chapter 7), that a monk confesses all evil thoughts to the abbot and that he confesses his guilt and his misdeeds to God.[75] In his chapter on the *Instruments of good work* (Chapter 4), Benedict prescribes that evil thoughts need to be smashed against Christ (*ad Christum allidere*) and revealed to a spiritual

---

tibi agimus, Domine, custoditi per diem: gratias tibi exsoluimus custodiendi per noctem: repraesenta nos, quaesumus, Domine, matutinis horis incolumes, ut nos omni tempore habeas laudatores'.
70 See *Regula Benedicti*, ed. by de Vogüé/Neufville, 35. 16–18, II, p. 568: prayer at the end of the weekly kitchen service; 53. 14, p. 614: prayer after washing the feet of the guests. See Mattingly, 'The Memoriale qualiter', p. 64.
71 *Ordo Casinensis* I, ed. by Leccisotti, Hallinger, and Wegener, 1–4 and 10, pp. 101–03.
72 *Ordo diurnus Anianensis*, ed. by Molas and Wegener, p. 316.
73 *Capitula in Auuam directa*, ed. by Frank, pp. 333–36.
74 *Memoriale qualiter*, ed. by Morgand, 1. 1, p. 232. The *Regula Magistri*, ed. by de Vogüé addresses the problem of coughing and sneezing in 47. 21–23, II, p. 216. The fact that both texts address a similar theme does, in my opinion, not necessarily point towards a direct connection. I would cautiously assume that monks and nuns had to deal with running noses ever since monasticism emerged.
75 *Regula Benedicti*, ed. by de Vogüé/Neufville, 7. 44–48, I, p. 484. See also Chapter 4. 50, which defines to smash evil thoughts.

elder and that a monk needs to confess past sins to God in daily prayer with tears and sighing.[76] Moreover, Benedict states that sins lying hidden in the soul should be revealed only to the abbot or to a spiritual elder but not to the community.[77] Yet the *Regula Benedicti* neither demands a daily confession (aside from a daily confession to God) nor does the text stipulate a ritual or liturgy of confession or tie confession to penance, intercessory prayer, or the forgiveness of sins.

The *Cursus* in the *Memoriale qualiter* requires a confession at five moments of the day, more often than any other guideline of monastic life. As such, the *Memoriale qualiter* implements the rather vague imperative of confession, as we find it in the *Regula Benedicti*, in the most radical way by turning it into one of the central monastic activities and fully integrating it into the 'liturgy at large' that encompasses the entire monastic day.

Morgand and Mattingly observe that the practice of regular confession in the *Memoriale qualiter* can be traced to Columbanian monasticism. They list Columbanus's *Regula coenobialis*, which requires two daily confessions of all acts 'because confession and penance frees from death',[78] the *Regula Donati*, which expands on Columbanus by requiring three confessions,[79] and the *Regula cuiusdam ad uirgines*, which also requires three confessions.[80] Moreover, the *Regula cuiusdam ad uirgines* states that humble and immediate confession along with intercessory prayer by the community leads to a mild judgment. The text describes how the nuns have to reveal their guilt at daily gatherings of all nuns.[81] It is especially the *Regula cuiusdam ad uirgines* that impacts most of the confessional practices of the *Memoriale qualiter*.

According to the *Memoriale qualiter*, the day begins and ends with a tearful confession to God of all sins:

> After the completion of the Night Office there is complete silence at the interval, as much in voice as in movement, whether through coming in or the sound of any other affair, so that each one may be allowed, without disturbing another, to confess his sins to the Lord with groaning, sighing, and tears, and with weeping to request mercy and forgiveness for themselves from the all-powerful Lord.[82]

---

76 *Regula Benedicti*, ed. by de Vogüé/Neufville, 4. 50 and 4. 57, I, p. 460.
77 *Regula Benedicti*, ed. by de Vogüé/Neufville, 46. 5, II, pp. 596.
78 Columbanus, *Regula coenobialis*, ed. by Walker, 1, pp. 144–46.
79 *Regula Donati*, ed. by Zimmerl-Panagl, 19. 3–4, p. 157; 23, pp. 159–60.
80 *Regula cuiusdam ad uirgines*, ed. by Diem, 6. 19–23, pp. 91–93.
81 *Regula cuiusdam ad uirgines*, ed. by Diem, 3. 15, p. 78; 6–7, pp. 88–94; 16. 5–10, p. 124; 22. 17–18, p. 140.
82 *Memoriale qualiter*, trans. by Mattingly, p. 67; ed. by Morgand, 2. 2, p. 233: 'Post expletionem uero Nocturnae in ipso interuallo summum silentium fiat tam in uoce quam et in actu uel incessu seu sono alicuius rei, ut liceat unicuique absque alterius inquietudine peccata sua cum gemitu et suspirio et lacrimis domino confiteri et ueniam uel remissionem pro ipsis ab omnipotente domino flendo postulare'.

> The same office [Compline] having been completed, the greatest silence is to be kept. There should be silent prayer with mouth and heart, as they recollect their sins with tears and weeping, lamentation or sighs, in such a way that one does not disturb another.[83]

This could be read as an expansion of the provisions we find in the *Regula Benedicti*, turning its general imperative of confessing misdeeds and evil thoughts to God with sighing and tears into a ritual that is integrated in the daily liturgical programme.

Morgand provides in his study on the confessional practices of the *Memoriale qualiter* various biblical and patristic references to the 'confession to God' that also include Chapter 6 of the *Regula cuiusdam ad uirgines*, which integrates the confession to God into a larger argument that explains how confession may lead to the forgiveness of sins.[84]

After the first introspective confession and before the last one, the *Memoriale qualiter* requires a verbal confession that is also integrated into a broader liturgical process:

> When this office is completed, before the fiftieth psalm, in turn they make their confessions, simply and with humble hearts, eagerly praying for one another.[85]
>
> Then, leaving in silence, they enter reverently for Compline. Let them pray with an attentive mind, give their confessions by turns, and then begin Compline.[86]

Morgand assumed that in this ritual one individual monk confesses to another one (*uicissim/alternatim* — in turn) and that they pray for each other's forgiveness.[87] In accordance with the *Regula cuiusdam ad uirgines*, I suggest that *uicissim/alternatim* rather means that all monks have to confess their sins *in turn* to a spiritual superior and that the entire community prays for their sins. This would be the ritual the *Regula cuiusdam ad uirgines* requires at three moments of the day:

> But we must introduce the Hours at which it is appropriate to wash away daily offences. Whatever the mind or flesh commits through frailty during

---

83 *Memoriale qualiter*, ed. by Morgand, 6.17, p. 260: 'Expleto eodem officio summum silentium custodiatur, et ore et corde fiant orationes secrete, recordatio peccatorum cum fletu et lacrimis et gemitu seu suspirio, ita ut unus alium non noceat'.

84 *Regula cuiusdam ad uirgines*, ed. by Diem, 6. 1–18, pp. 88–91.

85 *Memoriale qualiter*, trans. by Mattingly, p. 68; ed. by Morgand, 2. 5, p. 234: 'Iterum conuenientes ad primam, dum percompletur ipsud officium, ante psalmum quinquagesimum donent confessiones suas uicissim pariter supplici corde certatim pro se orantes'.

86 *Memoriale qualiter*, trans. by Mattingly, p. 74; ed. by Morgand, 6. 17, p. 259: 'Recepto silentio, cum reuerentia intrent ad Completam, orent cum intentione mentis, dent confessiones suas alternatim, incipiant Completam'.

87 Morgand, 'La discipline pénitentielle', pp. 29–32.

the dark time of the night after Compline, must be seen to be atoned through confession after the Second Hour. But whatever it has committed out of tepidity by deed, look, hearing or thought at daytime, has to be judged at the Ninth Hour after the service is carried out so that it be cleansed. But whatever stain the mind contracts later, after the Ninth Hour, ought to be confessed before Compline. The abbess, however, has to be eager that, entering the common room after having ended prayer, she does not allow anyone to go outside before confession is given. Likewise, this ought to be done after the Ninth [Hour] and before Compline.[88]

An idea central to the *Regula cuiusdam ad uirgines* (but not to Columbanus's Rule) is that *confessio* is aligned with prayer of the community for the forgiveness of sins. The *Memoriale qualiter* follows this notion and in this regard clearly deviates from the *Regula Benedicti*. Here is how Jonas expresses this idea:

> In such a way does Scripture encourage us by saying: *Confess your offences to one another, and pray for each other* (James 5 16). It is known how much love of the mild judge has been poured upon us, so that the misdeed contracted through wretched acts is dissolved by mutual prayer. The comfort of praying for each other should therefore be granted so that, in praying for each other, protection is obtained.[89]

Lastly, the *Memoriale qualiter* requires that a monk who has committed a transgression should reveal this at the daily meeting at the chapter house and profess his sin:

> After this, he who is at fault asks for pardon; and, according to the kind of fault, he receives a judgment. Whether in the chapter or in any other assembly or place, when the brother asks for pardon from the lord abbot, the prior or dean, or any other of the seniors, the senior asks, 'What is the case, brother?' The one who seeks pardon should then answer before all

---

88 *Regula cuiusdam ad uirgines*, ed. by Diem, 6. 19–23, p. 92: 'Sed quibus horis congruentibus cotidiana delicta sunt abluenda, a nobis inserendum est. Quicquid post conpletorium per opace noctis spacia mens uel caro per fragilitatem deliquerit, post secundam per confessionem curandum est expiari. Quicquid uero diurno actu uel uisu, auditu, cogitatu tepescendo deliquit, nonae horae expleto cursu, ut purgetur, censendum est. Post uero quicquid ab hora nona mens maculae adtraxerit, ante conpletam confitendum est. Illud tamen abbatissa studere debet, ut post secundam scolam ingrediens peracta oratione nullam foras egredi permittat, nisi prius detur confessio. Similter et post nonam uel ante conpletorium faciendum est'.
89 *Regula cuiusdam ad uirgines*, ed. by Diem, 6. 14–16, p. 90: 'Sic nos scriptura dicendo ortatur: Confitemini alterutrum peccata uestra, et orate pro inuicem. Quanta clementis iudicis pietas erga nos diffusa dinoscitur, ut quod actibus erumnosis facinus contractum fuit, mutua praece soluatur! Detur ergo mutuae orationis solacium, ut inuicem orando capiatur presidium'.

else, 'The fault is mine, lord'. If indeed he says anything else before this, he should be judged at fault because of it.[90]

The *Memoriale qualiter* explains that the humility a monk expresses in this act determines the judgment of his sin and that this judgment in present life will free him from being judged guilty in the afterlife.

> Indeed whichever brother seeks pardon for his fault, in proportion as he humbles himself and acknowledges himself culpable, he is to be judged mercifully and lightly by the superior. For it is necessary that all our sins — whether of thought, word, or deed — should always be judged in the present life through true confession and humility so that we might not be guilty of them after death.[91]

Here the *Memoriale qualiter* expands on the provisions we find in Chapter 22 of the *Regula cuiusdam ad uirgines* which describes confession at the daily gatherings of nuns. A nun who confesses, needs first to prostrate herself on the ground and admit to being guilty. Then she rises, confesses her sins, and receives her assignments.[92] At another place, the *Regula cuiusdam ad uirgines* prescribes, entirely in line with the *Memoriale qualiter*, that the grade of humility and satisfaction determines how a transgression is to be judged. There is no notion of tariffed penance involved.[93]

This is what we find on confession in the *Cursus*. The *Exhortationes* addresses confession briefly, building upon the *Regula Benedicti* as well, but take the text into an entirely different direction that does not really relate to the confessional discourse in the *Cursus*. The *Exhortationes* addresses the spontaneous disclosure of acts and thoughts in an entirely non-ritualized manner — entirely in line with the *Regula Benedicti*. This indicates, again, that we should look at the *Cursus* and the *Exhortationes* as originally two different texts:

---

90 *Memoriale qualiter*, trans. by Mattingly, p. 68; ed. by Morgand, 2. 7, p. 237: 'Post haec, qui culpabilis est, postulet ueniam, et secundum modum culpae iudicium recipiat. Et tam in capitulo quam et in quolibet conuentu uel loco, quando ueniam postulat frater ad domnum abbatem aut praepositum uel decanum aut qualemcumque de senioribus, cum ille senior dixerit Ouae est causa, frater? ille qui ueniam postulat, primum omnium respondat Mea culpa, domne; si uero aliud quodcumque ante dixerit, iudicetur exinde culpabilis'.

91 *Memoriale qualiter*, trans. by Mattingly, p. 68; ed. by Morgand, 2. 7, p. 238: 'Quisquis uero frater ueniam postulat pro culpa, quantum plus se hurniliat et se culpabilem asserit, tanto rnisericorcliter ac leuius a priore iuclicetur; necesse est enim ut omnes nostras neglegentias, id est cogitationum, linguae uel operis, in praesenti uita per ueram confessionem et humilitatem semper iuclicentur, ut non post mortem nos reos faciant'.

92 *Regula cuiusdam ad uirgines*, ed. by Diem, 22. 18–19, p. 140: 'Ad confessionem ueniens prius prostrata supra humum suam culpam esse dicat. Sic postquam surgere iubetur, suam confessionem manifestet. Quando ad aliquod opus fieri commeatus rogatur, uenia prius petatur, et sic de opere, quod fiendum est, commeatus rogetur'.

93 *Regula cuiusdam ad uirgines*, ed. by Diem, 3. 15, p. 78: 'Si humili satisfactione patefiant, prout humilitas confitentis cernitur, ita delinquentis culpa iudicetur'.

If a brother has treated carelessly, ruined, split, broken, or damaged anything in the storeroom, in the refectory, in the kitchen, or anywhere else, immediately he is to hurry back in order to ask for pardon. If it is possible, he holds the thing that he has damaged in his hand while lying prostrate on the ground, seeking pardon, making known what he has done.[94]

For impure acts, harmful thoughts, or improper speech let them always hasten back to confession: for it is better that we accuse the devil than ourselves, since if we always make known his evil suggestions, he will be less able to harm us.[95]

Both the *Regula cuiusdam ad uirgines* and the *Cursus* of the *Memoriale qualiter* provide for their respective periods of production the most extensive descriptions and rationales of a daily monastic *confessio*. The Merovingian *Regula cuiusdam ad uirgines* expands upon — but also alters — the requirement of daily confession as laid out in Columbanus's Rule, which linked confession of deeds to acts of tariffed penance.[96] The Carolingian *Memoriale qualiter* uses the *Regula cuiusdam ad uirgines* and expands, in a similar manner, on the *Regula Benedicti*. Both give confession a ritual form and integrate it into a wider liturgical framework.

The Carolingian Context

The uniqueness and the radicality of the confessional programme of the *Memoriale qualiter* can be assessed if we compare the text with other provisions on confession that can be found in the corpus of Carolingian reform texts and beyond.[97] There is no uniform concept, theology, or practice of confession in the Middle Ages — far from it. Confession is sometimes, but certainly not always, tied to *paenitentia*, occasionally to intercessory prayer, and sometimes to the seven deadly sins. It has no sacramental character before the twelfth century. Bishops, priests, monastic superiors of both genders, or even lay

---

94 *Memoriale qualiter*, trans. by Mattingly, p. 70; ed. by Morgand, 4. 7, p. 245: 'Si aliquid in cellario, in refectorio, in coquina, uel in quolibet frater neglexerit, perdiderit, fuderit, fregerit, aut aliquid damnum intulerit, statim recurrat ad ueniam postulandam, et si talis res est quam neglexent, in manu teneat in terra prostratus ueniam postulando, ostendens quid contigerit'. Cf. *Regula Benedicti*, ed. by de Vogüé/Neufville, 46, II, pp. 594–96.
95 *Memoriale qualiter*, trans. by Mattingly, p. 71; ed. by Morgand, 4. 13, p. 249: 'Pro immundis uero et nociuis cogitationibus uel ineptis locutionibus semper ad confessionem recurrant: Melius enim est ut diabolum accusemus quam nos, quia si semper manifestamus iniquiam eius suggestionem, minus nos nocere poterit'. Compare to *Regula Benedicti*, ed. by de Vogüé/Neufville, prologue. 5, I, p. 414; 7. 44–48, II, p. 484.
96 Columbanus, *Regula coenobialis*, ed. by Walker, 1, pp. 144–46.
97 For a similar assessment of the confessional programme of the *Regula cuiusdam ad uirgines*, see Diem, *The Pursuit of Salvation*.

people appear in our sources as confessors. Confession can be required as part of a public penance. Some texts require confession once a year, others twice a year, before the main Christian holidays, as preparation for the Eucharist, whenever felt to be needed, or, as in our case, on a daily basis. Confession can focus on thoughts, dreams, and intentions and leave their assessment to the confessor; it can focus on deeds and leave thoughts and intended but uncommitted sins aside, or it can be just a profession of sinfulness according to a standardized text that does not reveal specific sins. It can be used as a tool of gaining insight into oneself, as a disciplinary tool to create shame, or be understood as causing remission of sins and forgiveness, or to escape eternal damnation. It can be informal and incidental but also part of an elaborate ritual. Some, but certainly not all, texts addressing confession assign the confessor the authority to absolve confessants from their sins. Theological texts addressing confession disagree whether confession leads to absolution and at which point this happens: when showing contrition and the intention to confess, when confessing, through a priestly act, or after completion of an imposed penance.[98]

If we study medieval confession, we have to deal with a wonderful conundrum. On the one hand, we have Michel Foucault's thought-provoking propositions that medieval Christian tradition shaped the Western individual as a 'confessing animal' and turned confession into the predominant technique of producing truth, and that the ascetic practice of confession formed the beginning of a new genealogy of subjectivity.[99] On the other hand, we need to accept that there *is* no medieval confession and that *confessio* falls apart into a myriad of different practices, rituals, theological rationales, contents, and objectives.

Limiting oneself to the Carolingian period only slightly reduces the variety and complexity of confession.[100] So we should by no means assume that confession as it is laid out in the *Memoriale qualiter* was generally practised among Carolingian monks and nuns. Oddly, it seems that confession was not on the agenda of monastic reform and unification. There are scattered references to confession in Carolingian monastic texts, but they show no coherence at all. Here is an overview:

---

[98] The most important studies on the history of confession include: Lea, *A History of Auricular Confession*; Watkins, *A History of Penance*. More recent studies include Biller and Minnis ed., *Handling Sin*; Murray, *Confession and Authority*; Tentler, *Sin and Confession*. One common trait of most studies of the history of confession is to approach confession largely in the context of penitential practices or the sacraments, which ignores that many references to confession, including those discussed here, are tied neither to *paenitentia* nor have a sacramental character.
[99] On the 'confessional animal', Foucault, *The History of Sexuality*, I, pp. 17–35. On confession and subjectivity, Foucault, *Confessions of the Flesh*.
[100] On Confession in the Carolingian context, see Watkins, *A History of Penance*, II, pp. 632–722; Bachrach, 'Confession in the Regnum Francorum'.

The monastic *ordo* that Benedict of Aniane's hagiographer Ardo inserted into his *Vita Benedicti Anianensis* requires that monks visit all the altars of the monastery once a day, pray the Lord's prayer at the first altar and confess their transgressions (*delicta*) at the following ones. This rather points to a confession to God than to a confession to the community.[101]

We would expect to find references to confession in Benedict of Aniane's *Excerptus diuersarum modus penitentiarum* but this is not the case. This indicates that a regular and ritualized confession was not part of Benedict's monastic vision or, at least, no matter of concern. Yet in his *Concordia Regularum* Benedict of Aniane not only quotes the chapters on confession from the *Regula cuiusdam ad uirgines* but supplements them with a lengthy quotation from Jonas of Bobbio's *Vita Columbani* that describes how two nuns incurred eternal damnation for their refusal to confess why they had tried to escape from the monastery.[102] This is the one and only instance of Benedict of Aniane quoting a narrative text in his *Concordia Regularum*, which means that he considered it important that those reading the *Concordia Regularum* at least took notice of this rather unusual practice.[103]

The *Supplex Libellus* of 812 mentions *confessio* as a sideline. As part of the grievances against the squandering of resources and the abuse of power in Fulda, the supplicants request that the sick should be kept in the monastery to prevent their dying without *confessio* and the *uiaticum*,[104] which points to the practice of deathbed confession as part of the last rites. None of the other texts collected in the *Corpus Consuetudinum* mentions deathbed confession.

The two most prolific sources on monastic life in the Carolingian period are the commentaries to the *Regula Benedicti* by Smaragdus of St Mihiel and Hildemar of Corbie. Both of them address confession in different ways. Smaragdus emphasizes the importance of confession to God,[105] defines confessing one's sinfulness as an essential act of humility,[106] but never does he refer to a regular, ritualized confession that would be related to *paenitentia*, intercessory prayer, or the forgiveness of sins.[107] In his commentary on Benedict's *Fifth Step of Humility* Smaragdus stresses that confession to the abbot, on the one hand, increases self-awareness and, on the other hand, entails a confession

---

101 *Ordo diurnus Anianensis*, ed. by Molas and Wegener, p. 316, ll. 9–10 = Ardo, *Vita Benedicti Anianensis*, ed. by Waitz, 38 (52), p. 217: 'His tribus per diem uicibus circumire cuncta precepit altaria, et ad primum ex eis orationem dominicam dicant et simbolum, ceteris orationem dominicam uel sua confiteantur delicta'.
102 Benedict of Aniane, *Concordia Regularum*, ed. by Bonnerue, 15. 12, II, pp. 156–57 quotes from *Vita Columbani* II, ed. by Krusch, 19, pp. 272–75.
103 Benedict of Aniane, *Concordia Regularum*, ed. by Bonnerue, 15. 12, II, pp. 156–58.
104 *Supplex Libellus*, ed. by Semmler, 5, p. 323.
105 Smaragdus, *Expositio*, ed. by Spannagel and Engelbert, Prologue. 1, p. 8.
106 Smaragdus, *Expositio*, ed. by Spannagel and Engelbert, Prologue. 29, p. 41.
107 Smaragdus, *Expositio*, ed. by Spannagel and Engelbert 4. 50, pp. 130–31; 4. 57, pp. 136–37; 4. 74, pp. 146, 7. 18–19, pp. 172, 7. 53, p. 186; 7. 66, p. 191.

to God who is represented by the abbot. Here, as well, there is no indication of a regular or a ritualized confession.[108]

There is only one indirect hint that Smaragdus assumes that the monks begin the day with some sort of an introspective confession. In his commentary he warns against returning to bed after Nocturns to avoid being polluted by a wet dream.[109] He quotes in this context Cassian on having oneself cleansed through confession before dawn, which might refer to something similar to the morning confession mentioned in the *Memoriale qualiter*.[110]

Hildemar's *Expositio Regulae Sancti Benedicti* comments on confession in several chapters which provide an equally confusing impression. First of all, Hildemar gives a rare — but indirect — hint of the existence of auricular confession to a priest and the confessional secret in a rather curious context. In order to prevent a monk who had committed sodomy from being ordained as a priest, the abbot needs, in case of doubt, to talk to the priest who acts as confessor of the candidate. If a monk has committed sodomy, the priest should talk to him and discourage him from accepting the offer of ordination. If the monk still wants to be ordained, the priest should give a discreet hint to the abbot that he may not be a good candidate.[111]

Hildemar does not, however, imply that his monks have to submit themselves to a ritual of confession that is aligned either with intercessory prayer or with receiving absolution or with the imposition of penance. There is an instance of daily *confessio* at Compline which could either mean that individual monks confess their transgressions or that the community as a whole confesses their sinfulness.[112] Yet monks have to confess to their abbot or to their spiritual superior, all instances of vainglory, murmuring,[113] negligences in kitchen service, or transgressions while on a journey,[114] but Hildemar is primarily concerned with the abbot or spiritual elder keeping secret what is revealed to him.[115] Moreover, the abbot has to have regular pastoral conversations with each monk in which he encourages them to reveal whether they live their monastic life with the correct motivation — i.e. not out of vainglory.[116]

In the context in which we would expect the most detailed references to a confessional programme, his commentary on the *Fifth Step of Humility*, Hildemar

---

108 Smaragdus, *Expositio*, ed. by Spannagel and Engelbert, 7. 44–48, pp. 183–84.
109 Smaragdus, *Expositio*, ed. by Spannagel and Engelbert, 8. 3–5, p. 196.
110 Cassian, *Institutiones*, ed. by Guy, III. 5, p. 106; Cassian, *Collationes*, ed. by Pichery, XXIII. 3, III, pp. 141–42.
111 Hildemar, *Expositio Regulae*, ed. by Mittermüller, 62. 1–3, p. 570.
112 Hildemar, *Expositio Regulae*, ed. by Mittermüller, 20. 5, p. 322: 'In completorio uero, cum iacet in oratione, et cum primum signum dimissum fuerit, facit abbas signum, ut confiteantur; confessione autem facta omnes pariter surgant. Sed ut mihi uidetur, melior est ille primus sensus quam secundus'.
113 Hildemar, *Expositio Regulae*, ed. by Mittermüller, 5. 17–19, pp. 197–98.
114 Hildemar, *Expositio Regulae*, ed. by Mittermüller, 62. 3–4, pp. 609–10.
115 Hildemar, *Expositio Regulae*, ed. by Mittermüller, 4. 55, pp. 170–71.
116 Hildemar, *Expositio Regulae*, ed. by Mittermüller, 5. 3–4, pp. 189–90.

only remarks that overtly committed sins also need to be confessed,[117] and reflects on the nature of evil thoughts.[118] He remains, however, entirely vague on the practice of confession and mostly focuses on the biblical references to confessing towards God and confessing towards oneself.[119] If we want to pin down what confession actually is, Hildemar leaves us in a state of utter confusion.

The text that probably comes closest to the *Memoriale qualiter* in regard to confession is a letter of Theodomar, the abbot of Montecasino, in which he explains the monastic practices of his monastery to an unknown *uir gloriosus* named Theodoric. According to this letter, the monks of Montecassino confess their thoughts, deeds, emotions, and dreams twice a day:

> Twice a day, that is in the morning and in the evening, we give confession to each other. In the morning we confess if we transgressed at night in thoughts or dreams; in the evening if we lapsed in anything in word, in the heart or in deeds.[120]

Theodomar's letter, unlike the *Memoriale qualiter*, does not mention intercessory prayer or place confession into a specific liturgical context. Aside from the daily confession, Theodomar's letter mentions a *confessio diligens* at Compline on Saturday in the context of the question of at which time it is appropriate to make genuflections, which are to be made at the occasion of this *confessio*.[121]

Another text from Montecassino, the *Ordo Casinensis* I, refers to an *interrogatio* that should take place every day before the Third Hour, which could also point to a confessional practice similar to what the *Memoriale qualiter* prescribes for the chapter gathering.[122] One branch of the early manuscript transmission of the *Memoriale qualiter* consists of manuscripts from Montecasino, which indicates that the monks there indeed practised regular daily confession, which may have distinguished them from other monasteries in the north.

Another important witness, the first version of the *Regula canonicorum* by Chrodegang of Metz, addresses confession from yet another perspective.

---

117 Hildemar, *Expositio Regulae*, ed. by Mittermüller, 7. 42–43, p. 234.
118 Hildemar, *Expositio Regulae*, ed. by Mittermüller, 7. 44, pp. 242–46.
119 Hildemar, *Expositio Regulae*, ed. by Mittermüller, 7. 45–47, pp. 246–48; see also Hildemar, *Expositio Regulae*, 4. 57–58, pp. 173–75.
120 Theodomar, *Epistula ad Theodoricum Gloriosum*, ed. by Winandy and Hallinger, c. 23, p. 134: 'Bis in die, mane scilicet et uesperi, confessionem ad inuicem facimus: mane confitentis, si quid noctu cogitatione uel illusione deliquimus, uesperi autem, si quid uerbo, corde uel opere excedimus'.
121 Theodomar, *Epistula ad Theodoricum Gloriosum*, ed. by Winandy and Hallinger, c. 21, p. 134: '[…] Siue cum die sabbatorum ante Completorium apud beati patris confessionem diligentiam facimus'.
122 *Ordo Casinensis* I, ed. by Leccisotti, Hallinger, and Wegener, 2, p. 101: '[…] Ut iuxta regularem auctoritatem usque ad interrogationem non loquatur. Ista interrogatio a sapientibus consideranda est, ut paucis comprehendant'.

The text requires that clergy have to confess twice a year to their bishop but may confess to another cleric whenever needed. *Matricularii* need to confess twice a year to a priest.[123]

What such a confession might look like, is shown in the *Ordo confessionis* ascribed to Othmar of St Gall, which is preserved along with the *Regula Benedicti* in a manuscript of St Gall from the early ninth century and in a manuscript from Lorsch. It describes how someone is supposed to confess to a priest and provides a very extensive list of major and minor transgressions, ranging from swearing and cursing to murder, bestiality, and masturbation.[124] The text is followed by an Old-High German confession for a lay person.[125] It is remarkable that this *Ordo confessionis* resurfaces in an abbreviated version (omitting, for example, bestiality and masturbation) in the interpolated version of the *Regula canonicorum* from the late ninth century, which also requires clerics to confess thrice a year.[126] The same interpolated *Regula canonicorum* incorporates, but also alternates, most provisions on confession from the *Memoriale qualiter*.[127] All of this shows that different confessional practices could easily be blended together. It is a mesh that creates a mess.

A last — post-Carolingian — source to be taken into account in the context of confession is the *Regularis Concordia*, which, like the interpolated *Regula canonicorum*, applies at least parts of the confessional practice laid out in the *Memoriale qualiter*. The text does not, as the *Memoriale qualiter*, require that the monks use the time between Nocturns and Prime for a remorseful *confession* to God,[128] but says something similar in other words: 'Through great compunction of the soul and recollecting his sins, he may efficaciously reach the ears of the merciful Lord and obtain pardon for all his misdeeds by the grace granted by Christ'.[129]

The *Regularis Concordia* also omits the first confession after Prime but describes the confession during the chapter gathering. As in the *Memoriale*

---

123 Chrodegang of Metz, *Regula canonicorum*, ed. by Bertram, 14, p. 36; 34, p. 50.
124 Othmar of St Gall, *Ordo confessionis*, ed. by Wasscherschleben, p. 437.
125 St Gall, Stibi, Cod. Sang. 916, pp. 166–69; BAV, MS Pal. lat. 485, fols 2–3ᵛ (from Lorsch). The Old-High German text is edited in Steinmeyer ed., *Die kleineren althochdeutschen Sprachdenkmäler*, no. XLVI, pp. 323–24.
126 *Regula canonicorum interpolata*, ed. by Bertram, 32, pp. 201–02.
127 *Regula canonicorum interpolata*, ed. by Bertram, 18, p. 196: 'Conuenientes cleri ad primam canendam in ecclesia, completo officio ipso, ante psalmum quinquagesimum, donent confessiones suas uicissim, dicentes: "Confiteor Domino et tibi, frater, quod peccaui in cogitatione, et in locutione, et in opere; propterea precor te, ora pro me". "Misereatur tui omnipotens Deus, et indulgeat tibi omnia peccata tua, liberet te ab omni malo, conseruet te in omni bono, et perducat te ad uitam aeternam. Supplici corde certatim pro se orantes, hoc sibi faciunt"'. The text turns, thus, the confession after Prime from a personal confession into a collectively spoken statement of sinfulness.
128 *Memoriale qualiter*, ed. by Morgand, 2, p. 233.
129 *Regularis Concordia*, ed. and trans. by Symons, 1. 15, p. 12: 'per magnam animi compunctionem [et peccaminum suorum recordationem], aures minisericordis Domini efficaciter penetret ac scelerum omnium Christi annuente gratia, ueniam obtineat'.

qualiter, the gathering in the chapter gives monks the opportunity to confess, to receive a rebuke from their superiors, and to ask for forgiveness. The *Regularis Concordia* paraphrases the *Memoriale qualiter* with these words:

> For it is meet that in all our negligences, whether of thought, word or deed, we should be judged in this present life by sincere confession and humble penance lest, when this life is over, our sins declare us guilty before the judgment-seat of Christ.[130]

The *Regularis Concordia* depicts this act as *negocium spiritualis purgaminis* (duty of spiritual purgation). Subsequently, the *Regularis Concordia* describes an entirely different confessional ritual that cannot be found in the *Memoriale qualiter* but reminds us of the evidence we find in Hildemar's *Expositio*: a weekly confession on Sunday of the state of one's conscience to one's assigned spiritual father or his replacement:

> […] and this in such wise that each monk shall by humble confession reveal the state of his conscience to his spiritual father or, if he be absent, to whomsoever acts in his place. And if the number of the brethren be such that all cannot make their confession on that day, let them do so on the next, that is on Monday. Nor shall the *schola* even, on the score of their tender age, ever omit this duty but, although they are as yet untroubled by temptations, let them make their confession in the customary way as the elder brethren do. If, moreover, a brother, urged by some temptation of soul or body, needs to confess at any other time, let him by no means delay to have recourse to the healing remedy of confession.[131]

Subsequently, the monks take communion unless they are 'conscious of the guilt of sin or of weakness of the flesh'. Out of its context, it seems that the *Regularis Concordia* is to a large extent concerned about confessing sexual transgressions. Following the model of the *Memoriale qualiter*, the *Regularis Concordia* imposes a third round of confession at Compline: 'When the bell is rung for Compline there shall be a space for prayer after which, at a sign from the prior, the brethren shall offer to one another the healing remedy of confession'.[132]

It seems that, along with extensively using the *Memoriale qualiter* for modelling the 'liturgy at large', the *Regularis Concordia* took over confessional practices from two traditions: the regular confession at three points a day, which includes a confession in the chapter, but also the weekly confession as a

---

130 *Regularis Concordia*, ed. and trans. by Symons, 1. 21, p. 18: 'Quanto enim quis se humiliauerit seseque culpabilem reddiderit, tanto misericordius ac leuius a priore debet iudicare; necesse est enim ut in omnibus neglegentiis nostris, it est cogitationum, lingue uel operum in praesenti uita per ueram confessionem et humiliem paenitudinem iudicemur, ne post istius uitae decursum reos nos ante tribunal Christi statuant'.
131 *Regularis Concordia*, ed. and trans. by Symons, 1. 22, p. 18.
132 *Regularis Concordia*, ed. and trans. by Symons, 1. 27, p. 23.

preparation for taking the Eucharist. The *Regularis Concordia* calls confession both a *remedium* and a *purgatio* and explicitly relates it to the forgiveness of sins. In this regard, the text moves beyond what we find in the *Memoriale qualiter* itself.

In sum, references to confession in Carolingian texts and in the *Regularis Concordia* provide no coherent picture of monastic confession in the Carolingian period at all and indicate that confession, if it was part of the monastic routine, was performed in various manners and not an object of reform and unification at all. Among all these sources, however, the *Memoriale qualiter*, which expands in this regard on the *Regula cuiusdam ad uirgines*, assigns to the practice of confession by far the most important role within the daily monastic routine.

Conclusion

In her studies of medieval customaries, Isabelle Cochelin makes a distinction between normative and 'inspirational' uses and urges us not to read customaries simply as norms to be implemented.[133] Regardless of whether we should consider the *Memoriale qualiter* indeed as 'Benedictine' customary or as something else, the tension between a normative and inspirational understanding applies here as well. Its *Cursus* may have been written as an attempt to preserve practices in a process of reform; its *Exhortatio* reads like an exemplification of an existing norm, the *Regula Benedicti*. The hybrid of both texts was probably meant to be a contribution to reform discussions and as a suggestion of how to understand and implement the *Regula Benedicti* — an 'inspirational' text rather than a norm to be implemented. As such it did, however, contribute to producing new works that were themselves probably intended to be normative rather than inspirational, such as the interpolated *Regula canonicorum* and the *Regularis Concordia*.

My observations on the *Memoriale qualiter* remain preliminary and might form a point of departure for various further investigations (which should focus more on the *Exhortationes* than I do here). More than most textual witnesses of the Carolingian monastic reforms, the *Memoriale qualiter* bridges the 'pre-Benedictine' past with the period of monastic reform and opens the door to a field deserving a much more systematic exploration.

Another door that the *Memoriale qualiter* opens leads to the diversity of, possibly competing, monastic theologies. Scholars now agree that there was no Carolingian reform movement leading to one clear result — 'una regula, una consuetudo', but rather an endless chain of discussion of 'best practice' created a monastic life that, under the disguise of following the *Regula Benedicti*, remained just as diverse as it had been before the first endeavours of reform. The *Memoriale qualiter* is much more than just a hybrid collection of norms

---

133   Cochelin, 'Customaries'.

and guidelines; it is a text with underlying theological assumptions waiting to be unpacked, and, as such, a reminder that the Carolingian monastic diversity was not just a diversity of practices and institutional forms but also a diversity of monastic theologies.

The programme of the *Cursus* consists, on the one hand, of the assumption of an unceasing *opus Dei* — the idea that liturgy and liturgical discipline are by no means restricted to the Hours of prayer but that in fact everything a member of a religious community does, and even says, has to be submitted to the same standards and ritualized in the same way as the liturgical Hours themselves. This idea is also central to the *Regula cuiusdam ad uirgines* and it manifests itself not only in numerous prayers to be said outside of the Hours but in a strict 'choreography' of movements and voice, which begins at the moment of awakening and extends to the moment of falling asleep. If we were to strip the *Memoriale qualiter* of everything related to movement, prayers, and silence, hardly anything would be left. One of the most remarkable elements of the liturgized daily routine is the requirement to confess in a ritualized form five times per day. Neither the *Regula Benedicti* itself nor any of the reform texts or commentaries to the Rule submit monks or nuns to a similarly strict regime of introspection and daily confession.

The *Cursus* (and maybe the *Exhortationes* as well) may originally have been written as an attempt to reconcile traditions upheld by a specific community with their adopting the *Regula Benedicti*. In the case of the *Cursus* this may have been a community following Jonas's Rule, thus probably a community of nuns. At a later moment the *Memoriale qualiter* became a widely disseminated document for monastic reform aligned with Benedict of Aniane's *Collectio Capitularis*. This means that two individual voices in the process of adaptation to the *Regula Benedicti* were, among the many we find in the first volume of the *Corpus Consuetudinum*, singled out to be disseminated widely — probably as contributions to a discussion rather than as norms to be followed. This shows itself in the way that words and ideas in the *Memoriale qualiter* were processed and revised in the interpolated *Regula canonicorum* and in the *Regularis Concordia*.

Morgand's edition, if not studied along with the 'small print' of its apparatus, obfuscates a third layer of meaning. The *Memoriale qualiter* was a *Memoriale qualiter* only at the very beginning of its dissemination. The change of its title (*Ordo qualiter agendum sit monachis in monasteriis constitutis et sub regula beati patris Benedicti degentibus; Ordo in monasterio qualiter a fratribus religiose ac studiose conuersari uel domino militare oportet idipsum cotidie repetendo; Traditio de ordine monachorum*, etc.), and the ever-changing combinations with other texts show that, as much as its words remained meaningful, its use and function may have drastically changed throughout the Middle Ages.

With all its open ends and open questions, the *Memoriale qualiter* can, in any case, be read as an invitation to take the entire corpus of Carolingian monastic reform texts seriously, not only as quarries for specific practices but as theological and spiritual programmes and documents of various concepts of community and rationales for monastic life that are worth studying on their own terms. The first volume of the *Corpus Consuetudinum Monasticarum* may bear many more surprises for future research.

Works Cited

Manuscripts

Admont, Bibliothek des Benediktinerstifts, MS 497
Avignon, Bibliothèque municipal, MS 712
———, MS 732
Bamberg, Staatsbibliothek, MS Msc. Lit 142
Brno, Státní Vědecká Knihovna, MS NR 34
Brussels, Bibliothèque Royale, MSS 15111–15128 (479)
Budapest, Magyar Nemzeti Muzeum, MS lat. 329
Cambridge, Corpus Christi College, MS 57
Cambridge, Cambridge University Library, MS Dd. 4.58
———, MS Ll. 1.14
Città del Vaticano, Biblioteca Apostolica Vaticana, MS Barb lat. 646
———, MS Pal. Lat. 485
———, MS Reg. lat. 127
———, MS Vat. lat. 13501
London, British Library, MS Cotton Claudius D III
———, MS Cotton Tiberius A III
———, MS Cotton Titus A IV
———, MS Harley 5431
Madrid, Real Academia de la Historia, MS Aemilianensis 62
Melk, Stiftsbibliothek, MS 1093 (olim 423)
Merseburg, Domstiftsbibliothek, MS I 136 [olim 58]
Montecassino, Biblioteca dell'Abazia, MS 175
———, MS 179
———, MS 418
———, MS 442
Montpellier, Bibliothèque de l'École de la Médecine, MS H 85
Munich, Bayerische Staatsbibliothek, MS Clm 14678
———, MS Clm 14952
———, MS Clm 17459
———, MS Clm 28118
Paris, Bibliothèque national de France, MS fonds latin 2860
———, MS fonds latin 12885
———, MS fonds latin 15025
Regensburg, Bischöfliche Zentralbibliothek, MS Cim. 8
Rome, Biblioteca Casanatense, MS 54 (olim B IV 21)
Paris, Bibliothèque de l'Arsenal, MS 968

Rouen, Bibliothèque Municipale, MS 1385 [U 107]
St Gall, Stiftsbibliothek, Cod. 916
Turin, Biblioteca Nazionale, MS G.V. 4,
Tours, Bibliothèque municipal, MS 284
Trier, Stadtbibliothek, MS 1238/601
———, MS 1259/586
Valenciennes, Bibliothèque municipal, MS 246
Vienna, Österreichische Nationalbibliothek, MS lat. 2655
Zurich, Zentralbibliothek, MS Rh. 134

Primary Sources

Ardo, *Vita Benedicti Anianensis*, ed. by Georg Waitz, in *Monumenta Germaniae Historica: Scriptores*, xv.1 (Hannover: Hahn, 1887), pp. 198–220
Benedict of Aniane, *Collectio Capitularis*, ed. by Josef Semmler, in *Corpus Consuetudinum Monasticarum*, vol. 1: *Initia Consuetudinis Benedictinae: Consuetudines saeculi octavi et noni* (Siegburg: Schmitt, 1963), pp. 515–36
———, *Concordia Regularum*, ed. by Pierre Bonnerue, Corpus Christianorum Continuatio Medievalis, 168, 168A, 2 vols (Turnhout: Brepols, 1999)
———, *Excerptus diuersarum modus penitentiarum*, ed. by Josef Semmler, in *Corpus Consuetudinum Monasticarum*, vol. 1: *Initia Consuetudinis Benedictinae: Consuetudines saeculi octavi et noni* (Siegburg: Schmitt, 1963), pp. 563–82
Breuiarium ecclesiastici ordinis, ed. by Kassius Hallinger, in *Corpus Consuetudinum Monasticarum*, vol. 1: *Initia Consuetudinis Benedictinae: Consuetudines saeculi octavi et noni* (Siegburg: Schmitt, 1963), pp. 25–44
Caesarius of Arles, *Epistola a uirgines*, ed. by Adalbert de Vogüé and Joël Courreau, *Sources Chrétiennes*, 345 (Paris: Editions du Cerf, 1988), pp. 294–336; trans. by William Klingshirn, *Caesarius of Arles: Life, Testament, Letters*, Translated Texts for Historians, 19 (Liverpool: Liverpool University Press, 2004), pp. 129–39
Capitula in Auuam directa, ed. by Hieronymus Frank, in *Corpus Consuetudinum Monasticarum*, vol. 1: *Initia Consuetudinis Benedictinae: Consuetudines saeculi octavi et noni* (Siegburg: Schmitt, 1963), pp. 333–36
Capitula ecclesiastica ad Salz data a. 803/04, ed. by Alfred Boretius, in *Monumenta Germaniae Historica: Capitularia Regum Francorum*, i (Hannover: Hahn, 1883), no. 42, pp. 119–20
Capitula Notitiarum, ed. by Hieronymus Frank, in *Corpus Consuetudinum Monasticarum*, vol. 1: *Initia Consuetudinis Benedictinae: Consuetudines saeculi octavi et noni* (Siegburg: Schmitt, 1963), pp. 341–45
Capitula originis incertae, 813 vel post, ed. by Alfred Boretius, in *Monumenta Germaniae Historica: Capitularia Regum Francorum*, i (Hannover: Hahn, 1883), no. 79, p. 175
Capitula qualiter, ed. by Hieronymus Frank, in *Corpus Consuetudinum Monasticarum*, vol. 1: *Initia Consuetudinis Benedictinae: Consuetudines saeculi octavi et noni* (Siegburg: Schmitt, 1963), pp. 353–54

Capitulare missorum generale, 802 initio, ed. by Alfred Boretius, in *Monumenta Germaniae Historica: Capitularia Regum Francorum*, I (Hannover: Hahn, 1883), no. 33, pp. 91–99

Capitulare missorum specialia, ed. by Alfred Boretius, in *Monumenta Germaniae Historica: Capitularia Regum Francorum*, I (Hannover: Hahn, 1883), no. 34, pp. 99–102

Caroli magni capitulare primum, ed. by Alfred Boretius, in *Monumenta Germaniae Historica: Capitularia Regum Francorum*, I (Hannover: Hahn, 1883), no. 19, pp. 44–46

Cassian, *Collationes*, trad. by Eugène Pichery, vol. 3: Jean Cassien, *Conférences (XVIII–XXIV)*, Sources chretiennes, 64 (Paris: Editions du Cerf, 1959)

——, *Institutiones*, ed. by Jean-Claude Guy, Sources Chrétiennes, 109 (Paris: Editions du Cerf, 1965)

Chrodegang of Metz, *Regula canonicorum*, ed. by Jerome Bertram, *The Chrodegang Rules* (Aldershot: Ashgate, 2005)

Columbanus, *Regula coenobialis*, ed. by G. S. M. Walker, *Columbani opera* (Dublin: Dublin Institute for Advanced Studies, 1957), pp. 142–69

Concilium Arelatense a. 813, ed. by Albert Werminghoff, in *Monumenta Germaniae Historica: Concilia*, II. 1, *Concilia aevi Karolini*, I (Hannover: Hahn, 1906), no. 34, pp. 248–53

Concilium Foroiulense a. 796/97, ed. by Albert Werminghoff, in *Monumenta Germaniae Historica: Concilia*, II. 1, *Concilia aevi Karolini*, I (Hannover: Hahn, 1906), no. 21, pp. 177–95

Concilium Germanicum a. 742, ed. by Albert Werminghoff, in *Monumenta Germaniae Historica: Concilia*, II. 1, *Concilia aevi Karolini*, I (Hannover: Hahn, 1906), no. 1, pp. 1–4

Concilium Moguntiense a. 813, ed. by Albert Werminghoff, in *Monumenta Germaniae Historica: Concilia*, II. 1, *Concilia aevi Karolini*, I (Hannover: Hahn, 1906), no. 36, pp. 258–73

De cursu diurno uel nocturno, ed. by Josef Semmler, in *Corpus Consuetudinum Monasticarum*, vol. 1: *Initia Consuetudinis Benedictinae: Consuetudines saeculi octavi et noni* (Siegburg: Schmitt, 1963), pp. 45–50

Engelbert, Pius, ed., *Der Codex Regularum des Benedikt von Aniane: Faksimile der Handschrift Clm 28118 der Bayerischen Staatsbibliothek München* (St Ottilien: Eos Editions, 2016)

Hildemar, *Expositio Regulae*, ed. by Rupert Mittermüller (Regensburg: Pustet, 1880)

Jonas of Bobbio, *Vita Columbani*, ed. by Bruno Krusch, in *Monumenta Germaniae Historica: Scriptores rerum Germanicarum in usum scholarum separatim editi*, XXXVII (Hannover: Hahn, 1905), pp. 144–294

——, *Life of Columbanus, Life of John of Réome, and Life of Vedast*, trans. by Alexander O'Hara and Ian Wood, Translated Texts for Historians, 64 (Liverpool: Liverpool University Press, 2017)

Memoriale qualiter in monasterio religiose ac studiose conuersare uel Domino militare oportet idipsum cotidie repetendo, ed. by Claudio Morgand, in *Corpus*

Consuetudinum Monasticarum, vol. 1: *Initia Consuetudinis Benedictinae: Consuetudines saeculi octavi et noni* (Siegburg: Schmitt, 1963), pp. 177–282; trans. by Matthew Mattingly, 'The Memoriale Qualiter: An Eighth Century Monastic Customary', *American Benedictine Review*, 60.1 (2009), 62–75

Oratio ad matutinas, ed. by Henry A. Wilson, in *Gelasian Sacramentary: Liber sacramentorum romanae ecclesiae* (Oxford: Oxford University Press, 1894), III, no. 84, p. 291

Oratio ad vesperum, ed. by Henry A. Wilson, in *Gelasian Sacramentary: Liber sacramentorum romanae ecclesiae* (Oxford: Oxford University Press, 1894), III, no. 85, p. 293

Ordo Casinensis I, ed. by Tommaso Leccisotti, Kassius Hallinger, and Maria Wegener, in *Corpus Consuetudinum Monasticarum*, vol. 1: *Initia Consuetudinis Benedictinae: Consuetudines saeculi octavi et noni* (Siegburg: Schmitt, 1963), pp. 101–04

Ordo diurnus Anianensis, ed. by Clemente Molas and Maria Wegener, in *Corpus Consuetudinum Monasticarum*, vol. 1: *Initia Consuetudinis Benedictinae: Consuetudines saeculi octavi et noni* (Siegburg: Schmitt, 1963), pp. 311–17

Othmar of St Gall, *Ordo confessionis*, ed. by F. W. H. Wasscherschleben, *Die Bussordnungen der abendländischen Kirche nebst einer rechtsgeschichtlichen Einleitung* (Halle: Graeger, 1851), p. 437

Pippini regis capitulare, ed. by Alfred Boretius, in *Monumenta Germaniae Historica: Capitularia Regum Francorum*, I (Hannover: Hahn, 1883), no. 14, pp. 33–37

Pippini regis capitulare a. 782–86, ed. by Alfred Boretius, in *Monumenta Germaniae Historica: Capitularia Regum Francorum*, I (Hannover: Hahn, 1883), no. 91, pp. 191–93

Pippini capitulare Papiense, ed. by Alfred Boretius, in *Monumenta Germaniae Historica: Capitularia Regum Francorum*, I (Hannover: Hahn, 1883), no. 94, pp. 198–200

Regula Benedicti, ed. by Adalbert de Vogüé and Jean Neufville, vol. 1: *Introduction: Prologue–Chapitres I–VII*, vol. 2: *Chapitres VIII–LXXIII: Index et Tables*, Sources Chrétiennes, 181–82 (Paris: Editions du Cerf, 1975)

Regula cuiusdam ad uirgines, ed. and trans. by Albrecht Diem, *The Pursuit of Salvation: Community, Space, and Discipline in Early Medieval Monasticism* (Turnhout: Brepols, 2021), pp. 37–151

Regula Donati, ed. by Victoria Zimmerl-Panagl (nach Vorarbeiten von Michaela Zelzer), Corpus Scriptorum Ecclesiasticorum Latinorum, 98, Monastica, 1 (Berlin: De Gruyter, 2015)

Regula longior canonicorum Seu Regula S. Chrodegangi interpolata, ed. by Jerome Bertram, in *The Chrodegang Rules: The Rules for the Common Life of the Secular Clergy from the Eighth and Ninth Centuries; Critical Texts with Translations and Commentary* (Aldershot: Ashgate, 2005), pp. 184–228

Regula Magistri, ed. by Adalbert de Vogüé, *La Règle du Maître*, vol. 1: *Prologue–Chapitre 10* and 2: *Chapitres 11–95*, Sources Chrétiennes, 105–06 (Paris: Editions du Cerf, 1964–1965)

Regularis Concordia, ed. and trans. by Thomas Symons (London: Thomas Nelson and Sons, 1953)

Smaragdus of St Mihiel, *Expositio in regulam S. Benedicti*, ed. by Alfred Spannagel and Pius Engelbert, *Corpus Consuetudinum Monasticarum*, vol. 8 (Siegburg: Schmitt, 1974), pp. 3–337

Statuta Murbacensia, ed. by Josef Semmler, in *Corpus Consuetudinum Monasticarum*, vol. 1: *Initia Consuetudinis Benedictinae: Consuetudines saeculi octavi et noni* (Siegburg: Schmitt, 1963), pp. 436–50

Statuta Rhispacensia Frissingensia Salisburgensia, ed. by Alfred Boretius, in *Monumenta Germaniae Historica: Capitularia Regum Francorum*, I (Hannover: Hahn, 1883), no. 112, pp. 226–30

Steinmeyer, Elias von, ed., *Die kleineren althochdeutschen Sprachdenkmäler* (Berlin: Weidmann, 1916)

Supplex Libellus, ed. by Josef Semmler, in *Corpus Consuetudinum Monasticarum*, vol. 1: *Initia Consuetudinis Benedictinae: Consuetudines saeculi octavi et noni* (Siegburg: Schmitt, 1963), pp. 319–27

Synodus et conuentus exeuntes anno 802, ed. by Alfred Boretius, in *Monumenta Germaniae Historica: Capitularia Regum Francorum*, I (Hannover: Hahn, 1883), p. 105

Synodi primae Aquisgranensis acta praeliminaria, ed. by Josef Semmler, in *Corpus Consuetudinum Monasticarum*, vol. 1: *Initia Consuetudinis Benedictinae: Consuetudines saeculi octavi et noni* (Siegburg: Schmitt, 1963), pp. 435–36

Synodi primae Auisgranensis decreta authentica, ed. by Josef Semmler, in *Corpus Consuetudinum Monasticarum*, vol. 1: *Initia Consuetudinis Benedictinae: Consuetudines saeculi octavi et noni* (Siegburg: Schmitt, 1963), pp. 457–68

Theodomar Abbatis Casinensis, *Epistula ad Theodoricum Gloriosum*, ed. by Jacques Winandy and Kassius Hallinger, in *Corpus Consuetudinum Monasticarum*, vol. 1: *Initia Consuetudinis Benedictinae: Consuetudines saeculi octavi et noni* (Siegburg: Schmitt, 1963), pp. 127–36

——, *Epistola ad Karolum regem*, ed. by Kassius Hallinger and Maria Wegener, in *Corpus Consuetudinum Monasticarum*, vol. 1: *Initia Consuetudinis Benedictinae: Consuetudines saeculi octavi et noni* (Siegburg: Schmitt, 1963), pp. 137–75

Vita Columbani II, ed. by Bruno Krusch, in *Monumenta Germaniae Historica: Scriptores rerum Germanicarum in usum scholarum separatim editi*, XXXVII (Hannover: Hahn, 1905), pp. 295–320

Secondary Works

Bachrach, David S., 'Confession in the Regnum Francorum (742–900): The Sources Revisited', *Journal of Ecclesiastical History*, 54.1 (2003), 3–22

Barrow, Julia, 'The Chronology of the Benedictine "Reform"', in *Edgar, King of the English, 959–75*, ed. by Donald Scragg (Woodbridge: Boydell, 2008), pp. 211–23

Biller, Peter, and Alastair J. Minnis, ed., *Handling Sin: Confession in the Middle Ages* (Woodbridge: Boydell & Brewer, 1998)

Bodarwé, Katrinette, 'Eine Männerregel für Frauen: Die Adaption der Benediktsregel im 9. und 10. Jahrhundert', in *Female vita religiosa between*

Late Antiquity and the High Middle Ages: Structures, Developments and Spatial Contexts, ed. by Gert Melville and Anne Müller (Münster: LIT, 2011), pp. 235–72

Bugyis, Katie Ann-Marie, 'The Practice of Penance in Communities of Benedictine Women Religious in Central Medieval England', *Speculum*, 92.1 (2017), 36–84

Cochelin, Isabelle, 'Customaries as Inspirational Sources', in *Consuetudines et Regulae: Sources for Monastic Life in the Middle Ages and the Early Modern Period*, ed. by Carolyn Marino Malone and Clark Maines (Turnhout: Brepols, 2014), pp. 27–72

——, 'Downplayed or Silenced: Authorial Voices behind Customaries and Customs (Eighth to Eleventh Centuries)', in *Shaping Stability: The Normation and Formation of Religious Life in the Middle Ages*, ed. by Krijn Pansters and Abraham Plunkett-Latimer, Disciplina Monastica, 11 (Turnhout: Brepols, 2016), pp. 153–73

Dailey, Erin Thomas A., *Queens, Consorts, Concubines: Gregory of Tours and Women of the Merovingian Elite* (Leiden: Brill, 2015)

Davril, Anselme, and Eric Palazzo, *La vie des moines au temps des grandes abbayes X^e–XIIIe siècles* (Paris: Hachette, 2000)

Diem, Albrecht, 'Das Ende des monastischen Experiments: Liebe, Beichte und Schweigen in der *Regula cuiusdam ad virgines* (mit einer Übersetzung im Anhang)', in *Female vita religiosa between Late Antiquity and the High Middle Ages: Structures, Developments and Spatial Contexts*, ed. by Gert Melville and Anne Müller (Münster: LIT, 2011), pp. 81–136

——, 'Inventing the Holy Rule: Some Observations on the History of Monastic Normative Observance in the Early Medieval West', in *Western Monasticism ante litteram: The Spaces of Monastic Observance in Late Antiquity and the Early Middle Ages*, ed. by Hendrik Dey and Elizabeth Fentress, Disciplina Monastica, 7 (Turnhout: Brepols, 2011), pp. 53–84

——, 'The Gender of the Religious: Wo/Men and the Invention of Monasticism', in *The Oxford Companion on Women and Gender in the Middle Ages*, ed. by Judith Bennett and Ruth Mazo-Karras (Oxford: Oxford University Press, 2013), pp. 432–46

——, 'The Carolingians and the *Regula Benedicti*', in *Religious Franks: Religion and Power in the Frankish Kingdoms; Studies in Honour of Mayke de Jong*, ed. by Rob Meens, Dorine van Espelo, Bram van den Hoven van Genderen, Janneke Raaijmakers, Irene van Renswoude, and Carine van Rhijn (Manchester: Manchester University Press, 2016), pp. 243–61

——, *The Pursuit of Salvation: Community, Space, and Discipline in Early Medieval Monasticism* (Turnhout: Brepols, 2021)

Diem, Albrecht, and Matthieu van der Meer, *Columbanische Klosterregeln: Regula cuiusdam patris, Regula cuiusdam ad virgines, Regelfragment De accedendo* (St Ottilien: EOS, 2016)

Dunn, Marilyn, 'The Master and St Benedict: A Rejoinder', *The English Historical Review*, 107.422 (1992), 104–11

Foucault, Michel, *The History of Sexuality*, vol. 1 (New York: Pantheon Books, 1978)

———, *Confessions of the Flesh: The History of Sexuality*, vol. 4, trans. Robert Hurley (New York: Pantheon Books, 2021)

Klingshirn, William E., 'Caesarius's Monastery for Women in Arles and the Composition of the "Vita Caesarii"', *Revue Bénédictine*, 100 (1990), 441–81

Lea, Henry Charles, *A History of Auricular Confession and Indulgences in the Latin Church*, 3 vols (Philadelphia: Lea Brothers, 1896)

Mattingly, Matthew, 'The Memoriale Qualiter: An Eighth Century Monastic Customary', *American Benedictine Review*, 60.1 (2009), 62–75

Morgand, Claudio, 'La discipline pénitentielle et l'Officium capituli d'après le Memoriale qualiter', *Revue Bénédictine*, 72 (1962), 22–60

Murray, Alexander, *Confession and Authority in the Medieval Church* (Oxford: Oxford University Press, 2015)

Muschiol, Gisela, *Famula Dei: Zur Liturgie in merowingischen Frauenklöstern* (Münster: Aschendorff, 1994)

Rudge, Lindsay, 'Texts and Contexts: Women's Dedicated Life from Caesarius to Benedict' (Ph.D., St Andrews, 2006)

Schilp, Thomas, *Norm und Wirklichkeit religiöser Frauengemeinschaften im Frühmittelalter: Die Institutio sanctimonialium Aquisgranensis des Jahres 816 und die Problematik der Verfassung von Frauenkommunitäten*, Studien zur Germania Sacra, 21 (Göttingen: Vandenhoeck & Ruprecht, 1998)

Tentler, Thomas N., *Sin and Confession on the Eve of the Reformation* (Princeton: Princeton University Press, 2016)

Watkins, Oscar Daniel, *A History of Penance: Being a Study of the Authorities (A) For the Whole Church to A.D. 450 (B) For the Western Church from A.D. 450 to A.D. 1215* (New York: Franklin, 1961)

BRIGITTE MEIJNS

Confusion and the Need to Choose?

A Fresh Look at the Objectives Behind the Carolingian Reform Efforts in Capitularies and Conciliar Legislation (c. 750–813)*

Introduction

Traditionally, the local situation in the religious community of Saint-Martin in Tours in the years 801–02 takes a prominent place in scholarship concerning the Carolingian efforts to make a clear distinction between canons and monks. In the wake of a dramatic incident — the violation of the right of asylum in a religious building by a fugitive cleric — three contemporary letters inform us about the nature of the *servi Dei* who served this important saint's shrine and place of pilgrimage.[1] The first is a letter by Charlemagne in which he lashes out at his trusted friend and advisor Alcuin who was, at that time, the head of Saint-Martin.[2] According to the emperor, the community of Saint-Martin and its religious had often been criticized for their way of life: 'Sometimes you say you are monks, at other times you say you are canons, and occasionally you say you are neither (*neutrum*)'.[3] To do away with what he considered their bad reputation ('ad malam famam abolendam'), the emperor sent Alcuin to instruct the brethren of Saint-Martin in the right way of life (*rectam viam instruere*)

---

* I am very grateful to the organizers of the conference, Emilie Kurdziel, Rutger Kramer, and Graeme Ward, for their stimulating comments on earlier drafts of this chapter.
1 On this particular episode see Felten, *Äbte und Laienäbte im Frankenreich*, pp. 233–40; Noizet, 'Alcuin contre Théodulphe', pp. 113–29; Meens, 'Sanctuary, Penance and Dispute Settlement', pp. 277–300; Kramer, 'The Exemption that Proves the Rule', pp. 231–61; Kramer, *Rethinking Authority*, pp. 88–89; Ling, 'The Cloister and Beyond', pp. 25 and 151–52, and Ling's chapter in this volume.
2 Alcuin, *Epistolae*, ed. by Dümmler, no. 247, pp. 399–401. On the transmission of these letters see Meens, 'Sanctuary, Penance and Dispute Settlement', p. 277 n. 1.
3 Alcuin, *Epistolae*, ed. by Dümmler, no. 247, p. 400: 'Aliquando enim monachos, aliquando canonicos, aliquando neutrum vos esse dicebatis'.

Brigitte Meijns is Professor of Medieval History at KU Leuven.

Monastic Communities and Canonical Clergy in the Carolingian World (780–840): Categorizing the Church, ed. by Rutger Kramer, Emilie Kurdziel, and Graeme Ward, MMS 8 (Turnhout: Brepols, 2022), pp. 99–127

but, apparently, to no avail.[4] In his reply, Alcuin stood up for the members of his community. Calling God as his witness, he declared that their reputation was wholly undeserved: 'In as far as everyone can see and hear, they celebrate the office in honour of God in Christ's churches in such a way that — I most truthfully declare — I have not seen others in whatever place do in a more perfect manner, nor intercede more diligently on behalf of your preservation and of the stability of the Christian realm on a daily basis'.[5] In a letter addressed to Archbishop Arn of Salzburg from around the same time, Alcuin speaks of a *tertius gradus*, a way of life situated in between canons and monks, which is superior to the way of life of the canons and inferior to that of the monks: 'These [religious living according to this *tertius gradus*] are not to be scorned, because they are found in the highest degree (*maxime*) in the house of God'.[6]

The emperor's reproach and Alcuin's mention of a third position have been discussed many times in the abundant literature on the Carolingian reform project.[7] Moreover, the emperor's and Alcuin's words have been understood as strong proof of the indistinct nature of contemporary religious life and of the lack of clear dividing lines between the monastic and canonical regimens at the time.[8] The Saint-Martin case has been considered as compelling evidence of the state of confusion which characterized many religious communities in the second half of the eighth century and around the turn of the ninth century. It is generally assumed that the confusion displeased the Carolingian kings and their learned entourage and fuelled their desire to unambiguously

---

4 Alcuin, *Epistolae*, ed. by Dümmler, no. 247, p. 400: 'Et nos, consulendo vobis, et ad malam famam abolendam, magistrum et rectorem idoneum vobis elegimus et de longinquis provintiis invitavimus, qui et verbis et admonitionibus vos rectam vitam instruere et, quia religiosus erat, bonae conversationis exemplo potuisset informare. Sed pro dolor […]'.

5 Alcuin, *Epistolae*, ed. by Dümmler, no. 249, pp. 401–02: 'In quantum vero videri poterit et cognosci, digne Deo faciunt officia in ecclesiis Christi, sicut — verissime testor — perfectius non vidi alios in quolibet loco celebrantes nec diligentius consuetudine cotidiana pro vestra incolomitate et christiani inperii stabilitate intercedere'.

6 Alcuin, *Epistolae*, ed. by Dümmler, no. 258, p. 416: 'Pridem plura scripsi, quapropter modo pauca scribere ratum duxi, hoc solum suadens vestram sanctam auctoritatem in Deo et pro Deo loqui et in Deo confidere, ut diligenter examinetur, quid cui conveniat personae, quid canonicis, quid monachis, quid tertio gradui, qui inter hos duos variatur; superiori gradu canonicis et inferiori monachis stantes. Nec tales spernendi sunt, quia tales maxime in domo Dei inveniuntur'; Semmler, 'Monachus — clericus — canonicus', pp. 14–15 (on the notion of *tertius ordo*).

7 Including in Ling's chapter in this volume.

8 A small selection from the vast scholarly production: Dickinson, *The Origins of the Austin Canons*, pp. 15–16 (concerning Saint-Martin: 'a curious undetermined state'); Dereine, 'Chanoines', cols 363–65 ('rapprochement', 'confusion'); Schieffer, *Die Entstehung von Domkapiteln in Deutschland*, pp. 126–29 ('eine monastisch-klerikale Symbiose'); Semmler, 'Reichsidee', p. 46 ('eine solche Zwitterstellung', when describing the situation in Saint-Martin); Semmler, 'Pippin III.', pp. 131–32 ('Scheidung der *ordines*'); Semmler, 'Mönche und Kanoniker', p. 81 ('eine tiefgreifende Verwischung der Unterschiede'), and p. 81 ('Unter diesen Auspizien blieben die Grenzen zwischen den beiden Ordines fließend'); Semmler, 'Benedictus II.', p. 5; Marchal, 'Was war das weltliche Kanonikerinstitut', p. 784 ('die Vermischung des *ordines*'); De Jong, 'Carolingian Monasticism', pp. 628–29.

distinguish clerics and monks. The existence of this confusion, and the wish of certain abbots and bishops to eradicate it, set the Carolingian rulers on a path which inevitably led to the clear definitions and razor-sharp division proposed at the Aachen reform councils in the years 816 and 817.

In traditional scholarship, confusion is often presented as one, or even the principal, reason for the encompassing reform programme. According to the grand narrative, the Carolingian process of categorization was inspired by a genuine wish to end a disturbing confusion in contemporary religious houses. But was the Carolingian reform endeavour really as straightforward as this? The question may seem somewhat guileless but answering it proves to be far from easy since the historian has to pierce not just one, but two layers of rhetoric. First, there is the layer of modern historical scholarship, which — as we will see shortly — has framed the Carolingian reform efforts in a very particular way. Second, there are the Carolingian sources themselves which have to be interpreted with care. In what follows, it will become clear that conclusive evidence of confusion in eighth- and ninth-century religious communities is remarkably hard to find in Carolingian capitularies and conciliar *acta*. Nor are there many traces in contemporary sources of religious men or women struggling with their own spiritual identity. The conspicuous absence of confusion in legislative texts from the Carolingian period on the one hand, and the omnipresence of confusion in the modern master narrative on the other is therefore not only problematic; this state of affairs inevitably raises questions concerning the very nature of Carolingian religious life.

In what follows, I will therefore critically reassess this notion of confusion, which is of tantamount importance to our understanding of the motives behind the Carolingian reform. I will begin with a succinct discussion of the way the reform activities and their objectives have been represented and interpreted in scholarship. Then I will turn to the royal and conciliar legislative sources themselves to check whether modern scholarly discourse accurately derives from these texts or rather imposes modern preconceptions upon them. After analysing the objectives and aims as expressed in some of the most important capitularies and councils from the early days of the Carolingians until the five reform councils of 813, I will briefly discuss the situation on the ground in some of the religious communities in the same period.

Restoring Order and Separating the Orders in the Church

For many decades, our understanding of the Carolingian reform activity with regard to the orders in the church has been dominated, amongst others, by the many learned articles of Josef Semmler.[9] His ideas and his way of representing

---

9   See previous footnote for a selection of some of his most influential articles, and the contribution by Charles Mériaux in this volume.

and explaining what happened during the latter half of the eighth century and the first decades of the ninth century have influenced generations of scholars.[10] In Semmler's view, two ideas were closely intertwined. First, there is the idea that the church and religious life as a whole was in a deplorable state at the moment Pippin III came to power in 751, and was in urgent need of improvement. Hence, all initiatives were aimed at restoring order in the one Christian empire. Secondly and consequently, restoring order implied clearly distinguishing between monks and clerics. This is couched in terms of separating the *ordines* in the Church because each group (the canons and the monks) had a specific task, for which a suited material basis was called for. The need for separation was a direct result of the fact that the distinction between canons and monks had somehow become blurred. Over the course of time, canons and monks had become increasingly similar. The Belgian scholar and specialist of the *ordo canonicus*, Charles Dereine, spoke of a 'rapprochement' between the two religious ways of life, resulting in a state of confusion.[11] In his article 'Reichsidee und kirchliche Gesetzgebung' from 1960, Semmler uses the term *Zwitterstellung*, referring to a hybrid or ambiguous kind of religious life, the result of evolution over time, which had produced 'Kanonikermönche oder Mönchskanoniker'.[12] Consequently, from the middle of the eighth century onwards, all efforts were directed at avoiding any further confusion by delimiting the spheres of monks and canons and by setting clear boundaries between the *ordines*. Therefore, religious men and women were compelled to choose between a contemplative monastic life, based on the Rule of St Benedict, or a canonical way of life, as described in ancient canon law, in the Rule of Bishop Chrodegang of Metz for his cathedral canons, and finally, from 816 onwards, in the *Institutio canonicorum Aquisgranensis*.

In a nutshell, a church in crisis constituted the starting point of, and the reason for, the Carolingian reform endeavour. The master narrative also strongly articulates the need to distinguish monastic from canonical life as one of the remedies to counter confusion. But to which degree does this scholarly interpretation actually agree with the language of the Carolingian sources? Perhaps a fresh look at the normative sources, and especially at the way specific objectives have been formulated in these contemporary texts, might give us additional or alternative insights into the Carolingian plans. For this analysis, I focused on some of the important legislative documents of

---

10 An early criticism can be found in Oexle, *Forschungen*, pp. 127–33, where the supposed crisis in religious communities is refuted by a detailed study of the situation in Saint-Martin of Tours. In the same vein: Noizet, *La fabrique de la ville*, pp. 34–35.
11 Dereine, 'Chanoines', cols 363–65.
12 Semmler, 'Reichsidee', p. 46: 'Mit der klaren Scheidung der Ordines durch die Reformgesetzgebung Ludwigs d. Frommen vertrug sich eine solche Zwitterstellung, die historisch in manchen Gemeinschaften gewachsen war, künftig nicht mehr. In der Tat sind in der Folgezeit diese Kanonikermönche oder Mönchskanoniker verschwunden, die Existenzberechtigung war ihnen abgebrochen'.

the sons of Charles Martel and of Charlemagne himself, mostly capitularies and acts of synods and councils from the second half of the eighth century until the five reform councils in the summer of 813.[13] In doing so, I paid close attention to the two central themes which have dominated historical scholarship so far, i.e. that of a church in crisis, and, subsequently, the desire to make a separation between the religious orders with the intention of ending the reigning confusion.

A Church in Crisis?

As Timothy Reuter already observed in 1994, the image of a church in dire neglect and in desperate need of restoration is almost exclusively found in documents written by or under the influence of Boniface and other Anglo-Saxon missionaries.[14] Representative examples are Boniface's letter to Pope Zachary (742) and the prologues of the *Concilium Germanicum* (742) and of the council of Ver (755), both presided by Boniface.[15] Consequently, we need to be very careful with this reform discourse, expressed in terms of *correctio*, *emendatio*, or *restauratio* and we have to ask ourselves to what degree the state of affairs depicted in these sources truthfully reflects the situation on the ground. Products of reform logic, these texts powerfully voice the necessity of the changes they want to initiate. Recent research into monastic reform in the tenth century and into the general church reform of the eleventh and twelfth century has convincingly emphasized the trappings of reform rhetoric.[16] Situations which the reformers wanted to change are deliberately painted

---

13 For this chapter's purpose I have conveniently considered these capitularies and conciliar acts as a whole, but, evidently, as recent research has abundantly shown, each set of conciliar acts or capitularies originated in a very specific historical context which influenced its contents as well as the phrasing of these texts and was the product of a complex and ongoing process of negotiations. However, notwithstanding chronological and geographical nuances, several general ideas are voiced again and again in this corpus of texts, as this chapter hopes to demonstrate. Cf. McKitterick, *Charlemagne*, pp. 233–63 (on the capitularies); Mordek, *Studien zur fränkischen Herrschergesetzgebung*; Hartmann, *Die Synoden der Karolingerzeit*; Patzold, *Wissen über Bischöfe im Frankenreich*, pp. 61–80; Kramer, *Rethinking Authority*, pp. 61–69.
14 Reuter, '"Kirchenreform" und "Kirchenpolitik"', pp. 35–37.
15 Boniface, *Epistolae*, ed. by Dümmler, no. 50, pp. 298–302; trans. by Emerton, no. 50, pp. 78–83; *Concilium in Austrasia habitum Q.D. Germanicum a. 742*, ed. by Werminghoff, p. 1; *Concilium Vernense a. 755*, ed. by Boretius, Prologue, p. 33. Cf. Riché, 'Le christianisme en occident', pp. 660–62; Claussen, *Reform of the Frankish Church*, pp. 47–50 and Ling, 'The Cloister and Beyond', pp. 66–67 (on the prologue of Ver).
16 Constable, *Reformation of the Twelfth Century*, pp. 125–67; Van Engen, 'The Future of Medieval Church History', pp. 492–522, especially 514–15; Innes, *Introduction to Early Medieval Western Europe*, pp. 469–70; Barrow, 'Ideas and Applications of Reform', pp. 345–62; Cushing, *Reform and the Papacy*; Miller, 'New Religious Movements', pp. 211–29; Vanderputten, *Monastic Reform as Process*; Walsham, 'Migrations of the Holy', pp. 241–80;

in the darkest colours in order to justify their reform enterprise, which was not always welcomed by those who were considered to be in need of reform. When the reformers' rhetoric is compared with descriptions of the local situation in near-contemporary local sources, often a completely different and more nuanced picture emerges. Regrettably, this gripping sequence of decadence, followed by inevitable reform which then brings about a period of flourishing still looms large in traditional narratives concerning reform, no matter the historical period under discussion.[17]

Hence, detailed studies of the individual religious communities are of fundamental importance in order to check the reliability of the depiction in the Carolingian normative sources. Do the local circumstances as described in these sources confirm the general picture of the capitularies and councils? If so, the researcher must tread carefully. Sources produced in the religious communities as well may boast reform rhetoric. These accounts are very often written after the events with the express intent of justifying institutional changes within that community. The *Vita secunda* of St Hubert by Jonas of Orléans, written shortly after the transformation of the canonical community of Andage in the Belgian Ardennes into a Benedictine abbey in 817, blames the decadent canons for the poor state their house was in.[18] Negligent canons who do not care much for liturgy, discipline, and the material well-being of their community is a recurrent theme, not just in Carolingian times but also in numerous episodes of reform throughout monastic history. But are we to take this explanation, which entails a clear value judgment, at face value? The fact that this explanation template pops up so frequently in texts written by the monks who replaced the canons raises serious questions with regard to its credibility.

Rapprochement and Confusion between the Orders?

Whereas the paradigm of decadence and ensuing reform put forward in modern scholarship directly derives from the rhetoric of certain Carolingian sources, the idea of rapprochement and concomitant confusion is much less so. After analysing the language in the capitularies and in the canons of the councils of the second half of the eighth century until 813, one comes to the rather unexpected conclusion that the notion of confusion seems to belong,

---

Melve, 'Ecclesiastical Reform in Historiographical Context', pp. 213–21; Rosé, 'Fondations et réformes à l'époque carolingienne', pp. 397–460; Barrow, *The Clergy*, pp. 91–96; Leyser, 'Review Article: Church Reform', pp. 478–99; Howe, *Before the Gregorian Reform*, pp. 6–12.

17 Constable, 'Renewal and Reform in Religious Life', pp. 37–67.
18 Ionas ep. Aurelianensis, *Vita et translatio sancti Hucberti*, ed. by De Smedt, p. 30: '[cella] per excessum temporis vetustate nimia collapsa et deficientibus habitatoribus paene fuerat annullata'; Dierkens, 'La Christianisation', pp. 319–26; Dubreucq, 'La *vita secunda sancti Hucberti*', pp. 365–86.

to a great extent, to modern scholarly discourse. Latin words expressing confusion or some kind of mix-up of the different forms of religious life are conspicuously absent in the Carolingian texts. In fact, nouns such as *perturbatio, confusio*, or synonyms thereof, or the verbs *turbare, (per)miscēre, perrumpere*, or *confundere* are nowhere to be found in the capitularies and canons addressing the 'reform' of the clergy.

If we focus not so much on the particular choice of words but look more at the intended meaning of certain legislative measures, the lack of clarity with regard to the different religious lifestyles shimmers through only in a few instances. Canon 77 of the *Admonitio generalis*, directed to the clerics, tackles the problem of clerics who feign ('qui se fingunt') to be a monk because of their dress or name.[19] These clerics need to be corrected in order that they either become true monks ('vel veri monachi sint') or true canons ('vel veri canonici').[20] The measure implies that at least some members of the clergy looked like monks or considered themselves to be monks although, according to the reformers, they did not live the appropriate life. Hence, they had to change their ways so as to live either a fully monastic life or a canonical one. Secondly, according to Canon 3 of the *Capitula originis incertae* (813?), inquiries have to be made into the way canons and monks are living, 'in order that each of them lives either canonically or *regulariter*, not in like manner (*non similiter*)'.[21] Here we could have a strong indication that both ways of life could be very similar, although caution is called for as the words *non similiter* seem to be corrupted, according to the editor. The same canon pops up in the Council of Arles from 813 (Canon 6). However, here, the *non similiter* is left out and replaced by a quote from Paul's Epistle to the Corinthians (1 Corinthians 7. 20) urging everyone to stay true to the chosen vocation.[22] Finally, Canon 25 of the Council of Tours of 813 discusses those *monasteria monachorum* where the Rule of St Benedict, which had been respected there in the past, made way for a more relaxed way of life due to negligence. In these cases, a

---

19 Cf. Garver, '"Go humbly dressed as befits servants of God"', pp. 203–30.
20 *Die Admonitio generalis*, ed. by Mordek, Zechiel-Eckes, and Glatthaar, 75, p. 228: 'Clericis. Ut illi clerici, qui se fingunt habitu vel nomine monachos esse, et non sunt, omnimodis videtur corrigendos atque emendandos esse, ut vel veri monachi sint, vel veri canonici'.
21 *Capitula originis incertae*, ed. by Boretius, 3, p. 175: 'Providendum omnimodis ac diligenter exquirendum, qualiter canonici vivant necnon et monachi, ut unusquisque eorum secundum ordinem canonice ac regulariter vivant, et non similiter; id est, ut refectoria et dormitoria una simul observentur, quemadmodum iamdudum in capitulis nostris iniunctum habemus'. The canon imposes the use of a refectory and dormitory by canons and monks alike and presents this obligation as an elucidation (*id est*) of the preceding sentence. To a certain extent, this provision emphasizes the similarities rather than the desired distinction between the two orders.
22 *Concilium Arelatense a. 813*, ed. by Werminghoff, 6, p. 251: 'Providendum necesse est unicuique episcopo, qualiter canonici vivere debeant necnon et monachi, ut secundum ordinem canonicum vel regularem vivere studeant, ut ait apostolus: Unusquisque in que vocatione vocatus est, in ea permaneat'.

return to the original state is recommended and the abbots have to study the way of life as set out in the Rule of St Benedict. The emphasis on abbatial responsibility is inspired by the fact that there were other monasteries with a small number of monks who had promised their abbots to live according to the Rule, but where the abbot himself lived 'more like a canon than a monk' ('magis canonice quam monastice') among his brethren.[23] So, from this injunction, we learn that certain leaders of monastic communities seemed to be living differently than their inmates and apparently upheld a lifestyle which the reformers associated more with a canonical regime.

These four Carolingian canons, two of them from the 813 councils, presuppose some kind of blurring of religious standards of living. The canon from the *Admonitio generalis* is aimed at those clerics who wrongfully dress like monks or declare themselves to be monks, and in the 813 Council of Tours, specific abbots who live more like canons while directing a monastic community are admonished to closely study the Rule of St Benedict.[24] Both instructions more or less explicitly address the problem of indistinctness. Clearly, the indistinctness is considered problematic by the legislator, not by the persons — clerics or abbots — concerned. A strong *similiter* is present in the *Capitula originis incertae*, yet the words are hard to read in the manuscript. Nonetheless, if there had been grand-scale confusion or rapprochement between the *ordines*, it is surprising that the problem is not more extensively discussed in these sources. Moreover, we have to consider the aim of the 813 councils. As Rutger Kramer recently argued, these assemblies probably functioned more as advisory committees to the Carolingian court to spur on the reform movement in the empire rather than being uniformizing reform councils in their own right. Likewise, the canons these councils produced could be understood more as suggestions addressing particular issues within an ongoing process of debate, than directives from above for all to follow.[25] But no matter the exact interpretation, advice to make clear-cut distinctions hardly takes centre stage.

In any case, the mixing of canonical and monastic ways of life is not as directly broached as, for instance, in the *Missae expositionis geminus codex* (c. 814), attributed to Amalarius of Metz.[26] When mentioning in his *De officio candelabrorum* the different regimens in the Church, the author speaks of

---

23 Kramer, *Rethinking Authority*, pp. 87–88.
24 On the practical ways monks and nuns may have engaged with the Rule of St Benedict as a response to the councils' recommendation to follow this rule: Diem, 'The Carolingians and the *Regula Benedicti*', pp. 243–61.
25 Kramer, *Rethinking Authority*, pp. 70–91; Cf. also Nelson, 'Charlemagne and the Bishops', pp. 367–69 and Scholz, 'Normierung durch Konzile', who argues that the major objective of the 813 councils was a discussion of the precise relationship between the religious and the secular spheres as he observes that a desire to keep both spheres separated permeates many canons of these councils.
26 Cf. the contributions by Stephen Ling and Graeme Ward in this volume.

'those who live separately (*separatim*) in a contemplative way — the monks —, of those who live separately in an active manner — the canons —, and of a mix (*mixtim*) of those who live a contemplative life and those devoted to an active life'.[27] The adverb *mixtim* is striking, but still, we should not necessarily consider this straightaway as evidence of a fusion between the different religious lifestyles. Here, *mixtim* seems to stand in sharp contrast with the *separatim*, twice mentioned in the previous part of the sentence. Taking into account that the author might have wanted to depict an opposition between the words, the sentence then points to the fact that in certain places, monks and canons lived side by side and not in separate communities (*separatim*). This implies a certain *cohabitation* of monks and canons in particular institutional circumstances, which was a feature of some of the important Frankish basilical communities, as we shall see in the second part of this chapter, rather than a fusion of their regimens.

Tackling Immoral Behaviour

How then do these normative sources phrase the need to make a distinction between the monastic and canonical way of life? How do they articulate the obligation to choose between one of two religious regimens? And in which particular contexts do the relevant regulations appear? When investigating the language of the earlier Carolingian capitularies and conciliar acts, one is struck by the implicitness of the message they convey. Although modern scholarship couches the reform in terms of making a division and the need to choose, the legislative measures almost nowhere explicitly state that a choice is called for. Actually, statements like 'all religious have to choose between the life of the monks or that of the canons' are not present as such, nor are Latin terms referring to 'distinguishing' (*distinguere, discernere, discretio, distinctio, differentia*) or 'choosing' (*deligere*) in the context of the categorization of the clergy. Only the use of the conjunctions *sive* or *seu* in a disjunctive sense (meaning 'whether … or') or in combination with other disjunctive particles like *aut* or *-ne* are indications that nevertheless some kind of choice was expected.[28]

---

27 Amalarius of Metz, *Missae expositionis geminus codex*, ed. by Hanssens, p. 273: 'Quia nostra ecclesia habet separatim degentes in contemplativa vita, ut sunt monachi, et habet separatim morantes in activa vita, ut sunt canonici, et habet mixtim hos qui in contemplativa vita degunt et qui in activa […] Quos utrosque nostra ecclesia mixtim tenet, quia tales simul in una civitate habitant, simul in uno vico, simul in uno castello'; cf. Ling in this volume, who translates *mixtim* as a mix of contemplative and active.

28 Examples can be found in the *Admonitio generalis*, ed. by Mordek, Zechiel-Eckes, and Glatthaar, 70, p. 222 ('seu alii canonici observantiae ordines vel monachici propositi congregationes'), and 75, p. 228 ('veri monachi sint, vel veri canonici'); in the *Capitula de causis cum episcopis et abbatibus tractandis*, ed. by Boretius, 10, p. 163 ('aut clericus aut monachus […] in ecclesia vel canonicorum vel monachorum'), and 11, p. 164 ('ut suus clericus vel monachus'); in the Council of Mainz: *Concilium Moguntinense a. 813*, ed. by

Evidently, the very fact that in many instances canons and monks are treated separately in the chapters of capitularies and councils implies that both groups were systematically thought of as different observances that merited separate attention. Still, an unambiguous obligation to make a clear-cut distinction (*discretio*) between canons and monks, as is the case in the report of the 786 Legatine Synod held in Northumbria, is noticeably absent.[29] Whereas the Carolingian legislation abounds with measures frequently describing in some detail how the life of the monks, that of the nuns, and that of the clerics and canons should be, only in a minority of capitularies and conciliar acta are both regimes of religious life discussed together and in some kind of opposition. It is interesting to have a closer look at those particular instances when the religious lifestyles are set against each other in order to learn more about the context in which these sentences appear and about the motives that lay behind these decisions.

The Council of Ver in 755 is considered to be the very first expression of the reformers' desire to separate canons and monks.[30] However, eleven years earlier, in the Austrasian capitulary of Lestinnes, the first canon addresses the problem of the religious regimens and juxtaposes the different options. Reform rhetoric resonates in this canon, which stipulates that every member of the clergy ('omnis aecclesiastici ordinis clerus'), the bishops, the priests, and the deacons with their clerics (meaning the clerics in lower orders) have to abide by the legislation of the ancient fathers and must promise that they will regain (*recuperare*) the ecclesiastical law with regard to conduct,

---

Werminghoff, 23, p. 267 ('sive in canonico sive in monachico ordine'), in the Council of Chalon-sur-Saône: *Concilium Cabillonense a. 813*, ed. by Werminghoff, 40, pp. 281–82 ('in monasterio aut canonico aut regulari').

29 *Councils and Ecclesiastical Documents*, ed. by Haddan and Stubbs, 4, III, p. 450: 'Ut episcopi diligenti cura provideant, quo omnes canonici sui canonice vivant, et monachi seu monachæ regulariter conversentur, tam in cibis quam in vestibus, ut discretio sit inter canonicum et monachum et secularem […]'. Cubitt, *Anglo-Saxon Church Councils*, pp. 153–90, lays bare strong ideological, stylistic, and textual links between a considerable number of the twenty decrees of the Legatine Synod and Alcuin's views, as reflected in his oeuvre. She convincingly argues that the scholar, who was a member of the legation, had a hand in the composition of the document. However, Canon 4, which mentions the word *discretio*, is not discussed by Cubitt. Cf. also Ling, 'The Cloister and Beyond', pp. 117–18. The term *discretio* is used in Canon 10 regarding the life of the clerics of the Council of Mainz (813) when a distinction is called for between those who say that they have left the world and those who still serve it. *Concilium Moguntinense a. 813*, ed. by Werminghoff, 10, p. 263: 'Discretionem igitur esse volumus atque decrevimus inter eos, qui dicunt se saeculum relinquisse, et adhuc saeculum sectantur'.

30 *Concilium Vernense a. 755*, ed. by Boretius, 11, p. 35; De Clercq, *Législation religieuse franque*, p. 135: 'Nous voyons ici pour la première fois une terminologie qui deviendra classique dans la législation religieuse carolingienne: les clercs doivent observer les canons et les moines la règle'; Semmler, 'Mönche und Kanoniker', pp. 77–79; Semmler, 'Monachus — clericus — canonicus', pp. 9–10; Semmler, 'Pippin III.', pp. 131–32: 'Im Jahre 755 klingt zum erstenmal eines der großen Themen karolingischer Klostergesetzgebung an: die Scheidung der *ordines* der *monachi* und der *canonici*'.

doctrine, and office.[31] Abbots and monks, on the other hand, have received the Rule of St Benedict in order to restore regular monastic life. This sentence is immediately followed by the directive that clerics who live together with women, and who thus pollute the holy places and the monasteries they live in, are to be removed and brought to penance. If thereafter they resume their old way of life, they are subject to the legislation of an earlier council. The same goes for monks and nuns. In this matter, the referenced council is the *Concilium Germanicum* of 742. The sixth canon of this council takes measures against 'fornicating' — to use the reform rhetoric — amongst nuns, clerics, and monks.[32] It also juxtaposes clerics and monks, but, still, both categories have to undergo the same kind of punishment (one year of penance in prison). In both instances, the mention of the two distinctive ways of life takes place in the context of disciplinary measures with regard to the moral behaviour of the religious. The insistence on these measures reveals a genuine concern for the reputation of the religious men and women in question.

In several other instances when the existence of two specific ways of religious life is brought up, it occurs when discussing the quality of religious life in general. Canon 70 of the *Admonitio generalis* aspires to settle the life of the priests. Here, as well, the two lifestyles are mentioned: 'seu alii canonici observantiae ordines vel monachici propositi congregationes', again in the context of guaranteeing the *bona conversatio*, the good conduct, and the *bonae mores*, the good moral behaviour of the priests.[33] Canon 23 of the same capitulary underlines that neither monks nor clerics were to be involved in

---

31 *Concilium Liftinense a. 743*, ed. by Werminghoff, 1, p. 7: 'Et omnis aecclesiastici ordinis clerus, episcopi et presbiteri et diaconi cum clericis, suscipientes antiquorum patrum canones, promiserunt se velle aecclesiastica iura moribus et doctrinis et ministerio recuperare. Abbates et monachi receperunt sancti patris Benedicti regulam ad restaurandam normam regularis vitae. Fornicatores et adulteros clericos, qui sancta loca vel monasteria ante tenentes coinquinaverunt, praecipimus inde tollere et ad poenitentiam redigere; et si post hanc definicionem in crimen fornicationis vel adulterii ceciderint, prioris synodus iudicium sustineant, similiter et monachi et nonne'. Cf. van Rhijn, *Shepherds of the Lords*, p. 40.

32 *Concilium in Austrasia habitum Q.D. Germanicum a. 742*, ed. by Werminghoff, 6, p. 4: 'Statuimus similiter, ut post hanc synodum, que fuit XI. Kalendas Maias, ut, quisquis servorum Dei vel ancillarum Christi in crimen fornicationis lapsus fuerit, quod in carcere poenitentiam faciat in pane et aqua et, si ordinatus presbiter fuisset, duos annos in carcere permaneat en antea flagellatus et scorticatus videatur, et post episcopus adaugeat. Si autem clericus vel monachus in hoc peccatum ceciderit, post tertiam verberationem in carcerem missus vertentem annum ibi paenitentiam agat. Similiter et nonne velatae eadem penitentia conteneantur, et radantur omnes capilli capitis eius'.

33 *Die Admonitio generalis*, ed. by Mordek, Zechiel-Eckes, and Glatthaar, 70, p. 222: 'Sacerdotibus. Sed et hoc flagitamus vestram almitatem, ut ministri altaris Dei suum ministerium bonis moribus ornent, seu alii canonici observantiae ordines vel monachici propositi congregationes. Obsecramus, ut bonam et probabilem habeant conversationem, sicut ipse Dominus in euangelio praecepit: "Sic luceat lux vestra coram hominibus, ut videant opera vestra bona et glorificent patrem vestrum qui in celis est" [Matthew 5. 16], ut eorum bona conversatione multi protrahantur ad servitium Dei […]'.

secular business (*secularia negotia*), invoking the Council of Chalcedon and legislation by Pope Leo the Great.[34] Again, a concern for proper conduct, no matter the vocation, underlies this measure. The same can be said of Canon 26 of the Council of Reims in May 813, stipulating that monks and canons are not allowed to visit public houses,[35] and Canon 40 of the Council of Chalon-sur-Saône of the same year, which addresses the punishment of deposed priests: instead of living the life of a layman, they have to be sent 'in monasterio aut canonico aut regulari', in order to perform penance.[36] Both stipulations are clearly aimed at regulating the behaviour of the religious, while leaders of religious communities might rely on them when arbitrating the conduct of the inmates.

Tackling the Lack of Institutional Affiliation

Next to this preoccupation with the *bona conversatio* of the religious, and concurrently their reputation, another concern pops up when the two orders are put side by side, namely that of avoiding the phenomenon of vagrant clerics, monks, and nuns.[37] Wandering around implies that they lack an institutional affiliation and the appurtenant financial resources, again a situation hardly beneficial to the *fama* of these men and women. This is exactly the context in which the well-known Canon 11 of the Council of Ver from 755 has to be situated. This canon deals with

> those men who say that they have been tonsured to serve God but who only enjoy their own private goods and money and who are not placed under the authority of the bishop, nor do they live according to a rule in a monastery. These men have to reside in a monastery *sub ordine regulari* or they have to stay under episcopal authority and live *sub ordine canonica*, in a canonical fashion. If they do otherwise and they do not want to mend their ways when seized by the bishop, they will be excommunicated.[38]

---

34 *Die Admonitio generalis*, ed. by Mordek, Zechiel-Eckes, and Glatthaar, 23, p. 194: 'Omnibus. Item in eodem concilio infra duo capitula necnon et in decretis Leonis papae, ut nec monachus nec clericus in secularia negotia transeat. Et ut servum alterius nullus sollicitet ad clericalem vel monachicum ordinem sine voluntate et licentia domini sui'.

35 *Concilium Remense a. 813*, ed. by Werminghoff, 26, p. 256: 'Ut monachi et canonici tabernas ad edendum vel bibendum non ingrediantur, sicut in conciliis Laudocense et Affricano legitur esse interdictum'.

36 *Concilium Cabillonense a. 813*, ed. by Werminghoff, 40, pp. 281–82: 'Dictum nobis est presbyteros propter suam neglegentiam canonice degradatos seculariter gradu amisso vivere et paenitentiae agendae bonum neglegere. Unde statuimus, ut, gradu amisso, agendae paenitentiae gratia in monasterio aut canonico aut regulari mittantur'.

37 On these roaming clerics: De Jong, '*Imitatio morum*', p. 53; van Rhijn, *Shepherds of the Lord*, p. 43.

38 *Concilium Vernense a. 755*, ed. by Boretius, 11, p. 35: 'De illis hominibus, qui se dicunt propter Deum quod se tonsorassent, et modo res eorum vel pecunias habent et nec sub manu episcopi sunt nec in monasterium regulariter vivunt, placuit ut in monasterio sint sub

The same goes for nuns in a similar position. Canon 11 is traditionally interpreted as imposing a strict distinction between canons and monks. In this view, the canons have to live 'sub manu episcopi sub ordine canonica', whereas the monks are supposed to live *sub ordine regulari* in a monastery.[39] Recent scholarship, however, stresses that this canon is exclusively directed to clerics, who either need to stay under direct episcopal supervision in the bishop's household, or have to live together in (canonical) communities.[40] The preceding Canon 10 supports this interpretation because it deals with monks leading a truly regular life ('qui veraciter regulariter vivunt') who are prohibited from wandering around without abbatial authority.[41] Hence, after paying attention to the monks, it seems logical that in the next canon, Canon 11, another category of religious in the Church is addressed, namely the clerics. A similar sequence can be found in the Council of Aschheim (755–60), where Canon 8 admonishes the abbots and abbesses to live *regulariter* under the provision of the local bishop, and Canon 9 urges the clerics and the nuns (*nonnanes*) either to go to a monastery or to live under the supervision of the bishop *regulariter*.[42]

Notwithstanding the exact interpretation of this notorious canon, the problem addressed in Ver's Canon 11 concerns religious men without a proper institutional attachment, who are neither part of the episcopal clergy, nor reside in a religious community. As they do not belong to a community — regardless of its nature: the episcopal household, or a monastery — they are not entitled to an income from that community to allow them to maintain their religious vocation. Hence the stipulation: they only have their own financial means to rely on. The subsequent Canons 12 and 13 of the Council of Ver also concern religious without a proper affiliation. Canon 12 forbids clerics from another diocese to serve in an episcopal church or to work in the service of a lay lord without a letter of recommendation.[43] Canon 13 elaborates on the problem of bishops without an episcopal see (*de episcopis vagantibus*). They are not allowed to administer the sacraments without the approval of the local ordinary.[44]

---

ordine regulari aut sub manu episcopi sub ordine canonica; et si aliter fecerint, et correpti ab episcopi sue se emendare noluerint, excommunicentur. Et de ancillis Dei velatis eadem forma servetur'.

39 Cf. n. 30.
40 Van Rhijn, *Shepherds of the Lord*, pp. 40–41, and Ling in this volume.
41 *Concilium Vernense a. 755*, ed. by Boretius, 11, p. 35.
42 *Concilium Ascheimense a. 756/55–760*, ed. by Werminghoff, 8; 9, p. 58.
43 *Concilium Vernense a. 755*, ed. by Boretius, 12, p. 35: 'In canone Calcidonense capitulo XX. De non suscipiendis alterius aecclesiae clericos et de susceptoribus eorum absque litteris commendatitiis [...]'.
44 *Concilium Vernense a. 755*, ed. by Boretius, 13, pp. 35–36: 'De episcopis vagantibus qui parrochias non habent, nec scimus ordinationem eorum qualiter fuit, placuit iuxta instituta sanctorum patrum, ut in alterius parrochia ministrare nec ullam ordinationem facere non debeant sine iussione episcopi cuius parrochia est [...]'.

Concern for roaming clerics or clerics without institutional anchorage is also voiced by other capitularies and councils. Canon 22 of Charlemagne's *Capitulare missorum generale* from 802 dwells on the life of the canons and emphasizes that they should receive an education from the bishop or from a canonical community.[45] They are not allowed to wander outside (*foris vagari*), but have to remain *sub omni custodia*, by which the authority of the bishop or of the leader of a canonical community is meant. Then follows a detailed description of their regime. First, they have to refrain from profit, contact with women, theft, homicide, rape, and disputes. Second, a model behaviour is presented, including chastity, followed by the prohibition to wander around through towns and villages without licence or discipline, like the *sarabaiti*, who indulge in lust, fornication, and all other kinds of bad behaviour. This canon unambiguously links the lack of institutional affiliation and ensuing wandering lifestyle with the moral behaviour of these clerics, as wandering around is considered to be the source of many vices and denotes a lack of *disciplina*. The sarabaites are mentioned in the Rule of St Benedict (Chapter 1), where they are considered to be a 'very vile kind' of monks, living by no rule but their own desires.[46] The following canons continue along the same lines: Canon 23 stresses that priests should teach the clerics who stay with them how to live *canonice*, including a chaste existence; and Canon 24 prohibits the presence of women in the house of priests or deacons without canonical licence.[47]

The same connection between the insistence on a sober lifestyle, institutional anchorage under episcopal authority or that of a religious community, and the dangers of wandering around can be found in Canon 22 (*De clericis vagis*) of the Council of Mainz in 813.[48] This canon deals with clerics who are not

---

45 *Capitulare missorum generale* (802), ed. by Boretius, 22, pp. 95–96: 'Canonici autem pleniter vitam obserbent canonicam, et domo episcopali vel etiam monasteria cum omni diligentiam secundum canonica disciplina erudiantur. Nequaquam foris vagari sinantur, sed sub omnia custodia vibant, non turpis lucri dediti, non fornicarii, non fures, non homicides, non raptores, non litigiosi, non iracundi, non elati, non ebriosi, sed casti corde et corpore, humiles, modesti, sobrii, mansueti, pacifici ut filii Dei digni sint ad sacro ordine promovere. Non per vicos neque per villas ad ecclesiam vicinas vel terminantes sine magisterio vel disciplina, qui sarabaiti dicuntur, luxoriando vel fornicando vel etiam caetera iniqua operando, quae consentiri absordum est'. Cf. De Jong, '*Imitatio morum*', pp. 53–54.

46 *The Rule of Saint Benedict*, ed. by Venarde, 1, pp. 16–17; De Jong, 'Imitatio Morum', pp. 52–52; Kramer, 'The Exemption that Proves the Rule', pp. 245–46.

47 *Capitulare missorum generale* (802), ed. by Boretius, 23, p. 96: 'Presbiteri cleros quos secum habent sollicite praevideant, ut canonice vivant: non inanis lusibus vel conviviis secularibus vel canticis vel luxoriosis usum habeant, sed caste et salubre vivant', and p. 96 c. 24: 'Si quis autem presbiter sive diaconos, qui post hoc in domo sua secum mulieres extra canonicam licentiam habere presumpserit, honorem simul et hereditatem privetur usque ad nostram presentiam'.

48 *Concilium Moguntinense a. 813*, ed. by Werminghoff, 22, p. 267: 'De clericis vagis seu de acoephalis, id est de his, qui sunt sine capite neque in servitio domini nostri neque sub episcopo neque sub abbate, sed sine canonica vel regulari vita degentes, ut in libro officiorum II° cap. III° de eis dicitur, [quotation from Isidore's *De officiis ecclesiasticis*, II. 3].

placed under the authority of the king, a bishop, or an abbot, and who live 'sine canonica vel regulari vita'. Wherever they are found, bishops have to force them to live *sub custodia canonica* and to end their wandering days, under penalty of excommunication. Canon 20 of the same council discusses the maintenance of monasteries and religious buildings and provides information concerning inspection tours of houses of canons, monks, and nuns undertaken by the *missi*.[49] It quotes from Chapter 66 of the Rule of St Benedict: 'If possible, the monastery should be set up so that all necessities [...] are inside the monastic compound, so there is no need for monks to roam outside, which is not at all beneficial for their souls'.[50] However, the author of Canon 20 inserted *vel clericis* into the quotation from the Rule of St Benedict — there is no mention of clerics in the Rule — which shows that not just monks, but also clerics not connected to a particular religious institution were found roaming outside. In the following sentence, the two religious lifestyles are again juxtaposed when the *missi* are commissioned to inspect whether the religious houses have a *claustrum* where the souls of the inhabitants who live 'sub disciplina canonica vel regulari' can be saved. The message of this canon is that a sufficient material basis is needed for all religious communities to provide in the needs of the religious, so there is no reason to leave the monastery and roam outside. Canon 9, which is entirely dedicated to a description of the *vita canonicorum*, again clearly combines the sober lifestyle with institutional anchoring under the leadership of the bishop or a *magister*.[51] A similar description is given in

Tales omnino praecipimus ut, ubicumque inventi fuerint, episcopi sine ulla mora eos sub custodia constringant canonica et nullatenus eos amplius ita errabundos et vagos secundum desideria voluptatum suarum vivere permittant. Sin autem episcopis suis canonice oboedire noluerint, excommunicentur usque ad iuditium archiepiscopi regionis illius. Si autem nec ille eos corrigere valuerit, tunc omnino sub vinculis constringantur usque ad synodum, ut ibi eis iudicetur, utrum ad iuditium domini nostri aut ad istam magnam synodum adferantur sub custodia publica'. Cf. Picker, *Pastor Doctus*, p. 120.

49 *Concilium Moguntinense a. 813*, ed. by Werminghoff, 20, pp. 266–67: 'De locis monasteriorum vel aedificiis providendis. Deinde dignum ac necessarium est, ut missi per quaeque loca directi simul cum episcopis uniuscuiusque diocesis perspiciant loca monasteriorum canonicorum pariter et monachorum similiterque puellarum, si in apto et congruo loco sint posita, ubi commodum necessarium possit adquiri, quod ad utilitatem pertinent monasterii, sicut in sancta regula dicitur: Monasterium autem ita debet constitui, ut omnia necessaria infra monasterium excerceantur, ut non sit necessitas monachis vel clericis vagandis foras, quia omnino non expedit animabus eorum [Rule of St Benedict, Chapter 66]. Similiter quoque aedificia monasteriorum supradicti missi et cum eis episcopi per diversa loca praevideant, si apta sint et congruenter sanctae professioni composite, vel si claustrum firmum habeant, in quo salvari possint animae in eis commorantium sub disciplina canonica vel regulari. Ubi autem aliter inventum fuerit, hoc omnimodis episcopis loci ipsius faciat emendari, ita ut condignam professioni eorum custodiam habeant canonici vel monachi atque nonnanes, ne detur eis occasio male faciendi, quod absit'.

50 *The Rule of Saint Benedict*, ed. by Venarde, 66, pp. 214–15.

51 *Concilium Moguntinense a. 813*, ed. by Werminghoff, 9, pp. 262–63: 'De vita canonicorum. In omnibus igitur, quantum humana permittit fragilitas, decrevimus, ut canonici clerici canonice vivant, observantes divinae scripturae doctrinam et documenta sanctorum patrum,

Canon 23 of the Council of Tours in 813, destined to the canons of episcopal cities, but here the necessity to receive sufficient food and clothing from the bishop is stressed, 'so that they are not compelled for reasons of poverty to wander around and to become involved in scandalous activities and start living undisciplined lives, pursuing their own pleasures after abandoning the ecclesiastical office'.[52] Clearly, wandering was considered to result in a lifestyle unworthy of a canon and it led to scandalous behaviour outside the monastic or canonical compounds for all to see. But it could easily be avoided if the material resources of the canons were sufficiently taken care of.

'Everyone should remain in the State in which he was called'

Lastly, the juxtaposition of the two religious lifestyles turns up when the mission of each religious way of life is invoked. In Canon 6 of the Council of Arles in May of 813, the bishops are urged to see to the manner of life of canons and monks. They have to make efforts so that the religious live 'secundum ordinem canonicum vel regularem'.[53] This obligation is motivated by a quotation from Paul's First Epistle to the Corinthians, Chapter 7, verse 20, which immediately follows the directive: 'Unusquisque in qua vocatione vocatus est, in ea permaneat': 'Everyone should remain in the state in which he was called' (Revised Standard Version). Paul's Chapter 7 actually gives directions concerning marriage and the lines immediately preceding verse 20 deal with the change of status. Respect of and perseverance in a particular calling is also broached in the preamble of the *Capitulare missorum generale* from 802.[54] Here, laymen are included, as well. Charlemagne advises everyone to live according to the precepts of God and

---

et nihil sine licentia episcopi sui vel magistri eorum positi agere praesumant in unoquoque episcopatu et ut simul manducent et dormiant, ubi his facultas id faciendi suppetit vel qui de rebus ecclesiasticis stipendia accipiunt, et in suo claustro maneant et singulis diebus mane prima ad lectionem veniant et audient qui eis imperetur. Ad mensam vero similiter lectionem audient et oboedientiam secundum canones suis magistris exhibeant'.

52 *Concilium Turonense a. 813*, ed. by Werminghoff, 23, p. 289: 'Canonici clerici civitatum, qui in episcopiis conversantur, consideravimus, ut in claustris habitantes simul omnes in uno dormitorio dormiant simulque in uno reficiantur refectorio, quo facilius possint ad horas canonicas celebrandas occurrere ac de vita et conversatione sua admoneri et doceri. Victum et vestitum iuxta facultatem episcopi accipiant, ne paupertatis occasione compulsi per diversa vagari ac turpibus se implicare negotiis cogantur dimissoque eclesiastico officio incipiant indiscipline vivere et propriis deservire voluptatibus'.

53 *Concilium Arelatense a. 813*, ed. by Werminghoff, 6, p. 251: 'Providendum necesse est unicuique episcopo, qualiter canonici vivere debeant necnon et monachi, ut secundum ordinem canonicum vel regularem vivere studeant, ut ait apostolus: Unusquisque in qua vocatione vocatus est, in ea permaneat [1 Corinthians 7. 20]'.

54 *Capitulare missorum generale* (802), ed. by Boretius, 1, p. 92: 'Sed omnes omnino secundum Dei praeceptum iusta viverent rationem iusto iudicio, et unusquisque in suo proposito vel professione unanimiter permanere ammonere: canonici vita canonica absque turpis lucris

to remain wholly 'in suo proposito vel professione', in his purpose or calling: canons have to follow a *vita canonica* removed from profit, nuns have to live a carefully guarded life, lay men have to obey the law, and all have to live in charity and perfect peace. Finally, Canon 19 of the same council prohibits bishops, abbots, priests, deacons, and clerics to keep hunting dogs, falcons, and sparrowhawks, stipulating that 'each has to fully guard the order he is in, canonical or monastic' ('in ordine suo canonice vel regulariter').[55]

Taking together all these instances in Carolingian capitularies and conciliar legislation when the two religious lifestyles are explicitly put side by side, a rather surprising picture emerges. This is not so much a picture of confusion or rapprochement between religious lifestyles, but one of tackling very specific circumstances considered to be problematic by the legislators. First, in certain milieus, religious discipline is apparently not what it should be. Some clerics live together with women, while other clerics and monks are involved in secular business. In short, some religious seem to have forgotten about ecclesiastical law and display behaviour that is a far cry from what they are expected to do. Although not explicitly spelled out in these texts, it is obvious that their poor behaviour is thought to tarnish the good reputation of the religious. Secondly, the fact that some religious — no matter their way of life — are somehow too far removed from episcopal authority demands rectification. Some are living independent lives, they rely solely on their private financial means, and are not affiliated with a particular religious community. Therefore, they are believed to be evading episcopal or abbatial control and, hence, according to the mindset of the authors of these texts, could easily be led astray. Indeed, the lack of sufficient means might even force them to engage in all kinds of activities that do not suit their vocation. Consequently, to remedy these problems, stronger episcopal control and affiliation to a religious community are called for. A communal life under the direction of a bishop or an abbot guarantees the moral improvement of the religious and offers them a sufficient material basis. Only at this point does the specific religious regimen — canonical and monastic — enter the scene, not so much as a goal of its own, but as a means to attain a broader ambition: that of constructing a Christian society in which every man knows his place and behaves as he is supposed to, according to his particular status.[56]

---

negotio pleniter observassent, sanctemoniales sub diligenti custodia vitam suam custodirent, laici et saeculares recte legibus suis uterentur absque fraude maligno, omnem in invicem in caritate et pace perfecte viverent'.

55 *Capitulare missorum generale* (802), ed. by Boretius, 19, p. 95: 'Ut episcopi, abbates, presbiteri, diaconus nullusque ex omni clero canes ad venandum aut acceptores, falcones seu sparvarios habere presumant, sed pleniter se unusquisque in ordine suo canonice vel regulariter custodiant [...]'.

56 This idea is also very strong in the *Missi cuiusdam admonitio* (801–02), ed. by Boretius, pp. 238–40, especially p. 240, where the duties of successively women, men, children, 'clerici, canonici', monks, dukes, counts, and *iudices* are described. The clerics and canons have to

It is striking that from the early days of Carolingian legislation onwards monks and canons are systematically discussed in turn. At all times both orders in the Church are treated distinctly, very often in separate but adjoining canons. This may signify that at least in the mindset of the authors of capitularies and conciliar *acta* the two ways of religious life were considered to be fundamentally different from one another. What changes over the course of the second half of the eighth century is the fact that the regimen of each is more clearly circumscribed and defined: on the basis of ancient canon law, older normative texts, such as the Rule of St Benedict, and new texts specifically destined for life in canonical communities, first Chrodegang's Rule and, finally, the *Institutio canonicorum*.[57] Around the turn of the century, the reformers have produced sharper definitions of what each religious way of life entails, as becomes clear from the *Capitulare missorum generale* (802).[58] It is with this frame of mind that they examined what was happening in the many religious communities of their times.

Contemporary Religious Communities

The religious living under Alcuin's direction in the famous place of pilgrimage of Saint-Martin in Tours, do not fit the scheme of two distinct orders repeatedly articulated in the decade-long capitulary and conciliar tradition. The brethren's hesitation to categorize their specific calling — monks, canons, or neither (*neutrum*) — greatly displeases the emperor. To Alcuin, on the other hand, the 'third way', somewhere in between the canons and the monks, is all the more respectful. In Alcuin's words, we can find no trace of a Church in crisis, one of the tenets of the grand narrative of Carolingian reform. Quite the opposite, he strongly emphasizes the religious vigour of his brethren in Tours. Nor does he indicate a state of confusion or rapprochement between canons and monks. Apparently, outsiders, such as the emperor, may have struggled to define the religious of Saint-Martin and may have found the idiosyncratic lifestyle disturbing and troublesome. The religious themselves, and certainly their leader, on the other hand, did not perceive this state of affairs as problematic.

The difference of opinion between Charlemagne and Alcuin with regard to the nature of Saint-Martin may very well be the result of two different ways of looking at religious diversity: a theoretical approach which departs

---

obey their bishop, are not allowed to roam or to be involved in secular affairs. They have to stay chaste, pay attention to what is said in Holy Scriptures, and they have to diligently fulfil their ecclesiastical duties. Picker, *Pastor Doctus*, p. 120. On this insistence on the right order and the place each had to occupy within society: Smith, 'Emending Evil Ways', pp. 189–223; Kramer, 'Teaching Emperors', pp. 310–11; Kramer, *Rethinking Authority*, p. 60.

57 Van Rhijn, *Shepherds of the Lord*, pp. 39–46.
58 *Capitulare missorum generale* (802), ed. by Boretius, 10–22, pp. 91–96.

from fairly clearly delineated categories based on authoritative texts, and a pragmatic approach, which takes into account the complex realities in a place of worship that can look back on centuries of practical religious experience. Consequently, in the rare instances when confusion pops up, does it not merely lie in the eye of the beholder? Looking from the outside at religious life within the walls of certain communities the Carolingian rulers and some of their ecclesiastical advisers may have come across practices which they did not fully understand. Particular religious traditions upheld for decades by the inmates without further questioning might from the perspective of an outsider have looked puzzling. It is a small step from being considered awkward to being judged harmful for the good reputation of the religious, and, therefore, demanding intervention, adaptation, in other words, *correctio*. Moreover, in the case of Saint-Martin, as in many others, we should also consider the possibility that the rulers and their advisers may have used the notion of confusion, permeating the emperor's letter, as a stick to beat the inmates into complying with their vision of how religious life should appear.

 A complex, variegated, and localized make-up of religious life was probably to be found in other contemporary communities that served important saints' shrines.[59] However, it is often extremely difficult to gain insight into the exact way of life of these communities because of two reasons. Firstly, some religious houses simply do not possess sources that go back to the times before the Carolingian process of categorization; or if they do, the sources are either subject to suspicion with regard to their authenticity or, because of the literary genre, not very informative when it comes to defining the nature of the religious men or women.[60] In the case of the two important abbeys in Ghent, St Peter and St Baafs, contemporary and reliable information with regard to the history of both monasteries only goes back to the abbacy of Einhard (815–40).[61] This is because the extant Merovingian diplomatic sources related to the abbeys are only transmitted in ninth- or tenth-century texts and because contemporary hagiographical sources from the seventh and early eighth centuries focus primarily on the saints and are not interested in internal institutional matters. The available saints' lives hardly take the pains to define with any measure of precision the specific regimen in the communities.

 Secondly, we have to be extremely careful with sources from the second half of the eighth century onwards, especially if they are written under the influence of the ongoing 'reform'. Descriptions of particular situations risk

---

59 Fournier, *Nouvelles recherches*, pp. 50–51, speaks of the 'caractère composite de certaines associations religieuses' in the Carolingian period. Oexle, *Forschungen*, pp. 168–69; Noizet, 'Les basiliques martyriales', pp. 329–55. See contributions by Mériaux, Treffort, Ling, and Rembold in this volume.
60 Cf. the articles of Sebastian Folz and of Albrecht Diem in this volume.
61 Declercq, *Ganda & Blandinium*, pp. 17–19 and 23–25.

being couched by the reformers in specific reform language. Their vision then echoed down the centuries and ended up in modern scholarship, thus complicating even further our understanding of *what had actually happened*. Josef Semmler remarked in his 1980 article on monks and canons in Francia under the reign of Pippin III and Charlemagne that the internal situation in eighth-century communities is often depicted 'mit dem geschärften Blick und der präzisen Terminologie des neunten Jahrhunderts'.[62] The same goes for post-Carolingian sources, which very often take as their starting point an antagonism between canons and monks.[63] This holds true, for instance, for the mid-tenth-century *Deeds of the Abbots of Saint-Bertin*, written by the local monk Folcuin.[64] In Saint-Omer, an important restructuring of religious life took place under Abbot Fridugis around 820.[65] Since its foundation in the seventh century, the religious community comprised not one but two nuclei: one situated in the marshes with a church dedicated to St Bertin, and another a quarter of a mile further in what probably was the agricultural centre of the estate *Sithiu*. Here a basilica with the grave of Thérouanne's first bishop, St Omer or Audomarus, was built which developed into a place of pilgrimage around which a town grew. Both churches, Saint-Bertin in the marshes and Our Lady and Saint-Omer in the agglomeration, were served by religious who formed one and the same community, i.e. the abbey of *Sithiu*.

According to Folcuin, however, Abbot Fridugis destroyed the *regularis vita* of the place by installing canons in Our Lady's church where St Audomarus was venerated, and by drastically reducing the number of monks in the community around the church of Saint-Bertin. Folcuin thus imagines a Merovingian monastery exclusively peopled by Benedictine monks. But, what if the Merovingian community in Saint-Omer far more closely resembled other French basilical communities, such as Saint-Denis in Paris, Saint-Hilaire in Poitiers, or Saint-Martin in Tours, where monks and canons lived side by side? Seen from this perspective, all that Fridugis did was connect a particular lifestyle to a specific church. Frustratingly, we do not know for sure, because most information regarding the Merovingian history derives almost exclusively from Folcuin himself writing in the middle of the tenth century.

The example of ninth-century Saint-Omer should also make us aware of the importance of carefully analysing the position of a specific author or text.

---

62   Semmler, 'Pippin III.', p. 84.
63   Or later sources gloss over the presence in earlier times of female religious in a religious community, cf. Declercq, 'Un monastère double à Gand à l'époque mérovingienne', pp. 305–26, on how the monks of St Peter rewrote the origins of their community during the 'restoration' of the monastery around the middle of the tenth century, by omitting all references to the fact that St Peter was a double monastery in the Merovingian period.
64   Folcuin, *Gesta abbatum Lobbiensium*, ed. by Holder-Egger, 47, pp. 614–15.
65   Meijns, 'Chanoines et moines à Saint-Omer', pp. 691–706.

Contemporary texts produced by the religious communities themselves may use other, and possibly more accurate, terminology to designate the local way of life than narratives from outsiders, who did not come to grips with complex local varieties. Fortunately, many of the important French basilical communities have contemporary sources going back to Merovingian times. Some of these institutions have been the object of close study by, amongst others, Hélène Noizet, who investigated the situation in Saint-Martin in Tours.[66] She comes to the conclusion that in Saint-Martin monks and canons lived side by side before a reorientation took place in the early 800s. This resulted in a canonical way of life in the basilica in Tours, where *clerici* only are attested from 813 onwards. Those brethren who wanted to continue a stricter lifestyle would have found a shelter on one of the abbey's estates, namely that of Cormery. Here, Alcuin had founded a community of 20 monks living according to the Rule of St Benedict *c.* 800 with the help of Benedict of Aniane.[67] According to Ardo, Benedict's hagiographer, the community of Cormery expanded rapidly.

A similar situation of *cohabitation* or coexistence prior to the impact of Carolingian *correctio* can be observed in Saint-Hilaire in Poitiers.[68] All in all, this is not very surprising. These ancient basilical compounds, which stood under immediate episcopal supervision, comprised several churches and other buildings, such as a hospital for pilgrims. The accommodation of the pilgrims flocking towards the saint's shrine as well as the relic cult itself, activities implying daily involvement with the lay world, suited a clerical lifestyle very well, whereas a more monastic or ascetic regimen could be envisaged by other members of the community, living within the same walls of the abbey complex. Even after the Carolingian period, many Benedictine monasteries still housed, in one of their churches within the monastic compound, a community of canons, who cared for the relics of the patron saint and sang the office in a church which functioned as the burial place for the monastic community, and sometimes even as the parish church for the surrounding settlement.[69] While the Carolingian reformers may have restructured contemporary religious life along the lines of two distinct orders, the orders themselves, for diverse reasons, still found each other and, in some cases, continued living within each other's proximity for many centuries.

---

66 Noizet, *La fabrique de la ville*, pp. 29–36. Cf. also Farmer, *Communities of Saint-Martin*, pp. 189–94.
67 Ardo, *Vita Benedicti*, ed. by Waitz, 24, p. 210; Chupin, 'Alcuin et Cormery', pp. 103–12.
68 Levillain, 'Les origines du monastère de Nouaillé', pp. 267–73; Oexle, *Forschungen*, pp. 112–33; Trumbore Jones, '"The Most Blessed Hilary"', p. 4; Ling, 'The Cloister and Beyond', pp. 76–99.
69 Misonne, 'Chapitres séculiers', pp. 412–32 (for the diocese of Liège); Moraw, 'Über Typologie, Chronologie und Geographie', p. 17 (the German Empire); Meijns, 'Communautés de chanoines', pp. 90–123 (County of Flanders); Verdoot, 'Dans l'ombre des bénédictins', pp. 142–74 (Lobbes).

Conclusion

The sources allow us to imagine a much richer and more variegated way of life in the Merovingian period than that which the Carolingian reformers envisioned and subsequently attempted to establish in their own times. A dynamic but localized world in which the precise interpretation of the monastic and clerical calling underwent subtle changes, depending on chronological and geographical circumstances, specific traditions and fashions, resulting in eclectic, varied, and vibrant forms of religious life. Modern scholars have often framed the situation at the start of the Carolingian period in terms of confusion between the orders and rapprochement between clerics and monks. A more thorough study of the local circumstances in the period 750–800 is needed to check whether the local religious themselves perceived their reality as confusing. Alcuin, at least, did not associate religious life in Saint-Martin with confusion. He affirmed that the regime of his basilical community, which was somewhere in between monks and canons, was perfectly honourable and was present in many other places.

The ecclesiastical advisers of the Carolingian rulers who were responsible for the categorization process in the church were clearly of a different opinion from their patrons. Still, their ambitions and concrete measures were not so much framed in terms of ending confusion; even the obligation to make a choice is only implicitly formulated in their normative texts. This analysis of the most important councils and capitularies from the 740s until 813 uncovered first and foremost an ardent desire of the reformers to tackle particular problems: the wandering around of some religious, their lack of institutional anchoring, lax discipline, and low morals. These were all elements that jeopardized the good reputation of the religious, a source of grave concern to certain religious elites and the rulers. Hence the reformers' insistence on asserting episcopal authority and control over all clerics and religious communities.

The image that emerges from Carolingian capitularies and conciliar acts is not that of a Church in crisis and in urgent need of reform, nor does confusion or rapprochement between the different religious ways of life abound in these sources, as it does in traditional historical scholarship. The measures are first and foremost aimed at upholding religious discipline, at safeguarding the reputation of the religious men and women on whose prayers the well-being of the realm depended. They advise strong episcopal intervention when problems arise and they unequivocally emphasize the obligation of all religious to live a communal life under the direction of an abbot/abbess or a bishop. The ultimate goal seems to have been the creation of a society in which all, religious or laymen, had their proper place and perfectly knew the rules of conduct of their station in life.

Works Cited

Primary Sources

Die Admonitio Generalis Karls des Großen, ed. by Hubert Mordek, Klaus Zechiel-Eckes, and Michael Glatthaar, in *Monumenta Germaniae Historica: Fontes iuris germanici antiqui in usum scholarum separatim editi*, XVI (Hannover: Hahn, 2012)

Alcuin, *Epistolae*, ed. by Ernst Dümmler, in *Monumenta Germaniae Historica: Epistolae*, IV, *Epistolae Merowingici et Karolini aevi*, II (Berlin: Weidmann, 1895), pp. 1–481

Amalarius of Metz, *Missae expositionis geminus codex*, ed. by Joannes M. Hanssens, in *Amalarii Episcopi Opera Liturgica Omnia*, vol. 1 (Vatican City: Biblioteca apostolica vaticana, 1948), pp. 255–81

Ardo, *Vita Benedicti abbatis Anianensis et Indensis*, ed. by Georg Waitz, in *Monumenta Germaniae Historica: Scriptores*, XV.1 (Hannover: Hahn, 1887), pp. 198–220

Boniface of Mainz, *Epistolae*, ed. by Ernst Dümmler, in *Monumenta Germaniae Historica: Epistolae*, III, *Epistolae Merowingici et Karolini aevi*, I (Berlin: Weidmann, 1892), pp. 215–433; trans. by Ephraim Emerton, *The Letters of Saint Boniface* (New York, 1940)

Capitulare missorum generale, 802 initio, ed. by Alfred Boretius, in *Monumenta Germaniae Historica: Capitularia Regum Francorum*, I (Hannover: Hahn, 1883), no. 33, pp. 91–99

Capitularia Regum Francorum, ed. by Alfred Boretius and Victor Krause, in *Monumenta Germaniae Historica: Leges Sectio III*, 2 vols (Hannover: Hahn, 1883–1897)

Capitula de causis cum episcopis et abbatibus tractandis, 811, ed. by Alfred Boretius, in *Monumenta Germaniae Historica: Capitularia Regum Francorum*, I (Hannover: Hahn, 1883), no. 72, pp. 162–64

Capitula originis incertae, 813 vel post, ed. by Alfred Boretius, in *Monumenta Germaniae Historica: Capitularia Regum Francorum*, I (Hannover: Hahn, 1883), no. 79, p. 175

Concilium Arelatense a. 813, mensis Maii die 10 et 11, ed. by Albert Werminghoff, in *Monumenta Germaniae Historica: Concilia*, II. 1, *Concilia aevi Karolini*, I (Hannover: Hahn, 1906), no. 34, pp. 248–53

Concilium Ascheimense a. 756 vel 755–60, ed. by Albert Werminghoff, in *Monumenta Germaniae Historica: Concilia*, II. 1, *Concilia aevi Karolini*, I (Hannover: Hahn, 1906), pp. 56–58

Concilium in Austrasia habitum Q.D. Germanicum, 742, April 21, ed. by Albert Werminghoff, in *Monumenta Germaniae Historica: Concilia*, II. 1, *Concilia aevi Karolini*, I (Hannover: Hahn, 1906), pp. 1–4

Concilium Cabillonense a. 813, ed. by Albert Werminghoff, in *Monumenta Germaniae Historica: Concilia*, II. 1, *Concilia aevi Karolini*, I (Hannover: Hahn, 1906), no. 37, pp. 273–85

Concilium Liftinense a. 743, Mart., 1, ed. by Albert Werminghoff, in *Monumenta Germaniae Historica: Concilia*, II. 1, *Concilia aevi Karolini*, I (Hannover: Hahn, 1906), no. 2, pp. 5–7

Concilium Moguntinense a. 813, ed. by Albert Werminghoff, in *Monumenta Germaniae Historica: Concilia*, II. 1, *Concilia aevi Karolini*, I (Hannover: Hahn, 1906), no. 36, pp. 258–73

Concilium Remense a. 813, medio mense Maio, ed. by Albert Werminghoff, in *Monumenta Germaniae Historica: Concilia*, II. 1, *Concilia aevi Karolini*, I (Hannover: Hahn, 1906), no. 35, pp. 253–58

Concilium Turonense a. 813, ed. by Albert Werminghoff, in *Monumenta Germaniae Historica: Concilia*, II. 1, *Concilia aevi Karolini*, I (Hannover: Hahn, 1906), no. 38, pp. 286–93

Concilium Vernense a. 755. Jul. 11, ed. by Alfred Boretius, in *Monumenta Germaniae Historica: Capitularia Regum Francorum*, I (Hannover: Hahn, 1883), no. 14, pp. 32–37

Councils and Ecclesiastical Documents relating to Great Britain and Ireland, vol. 3, ed. by Arthur West Haddan and William Stubbs (Oxford: Clarendon Press, 1871)

Folcuin, *Gesta abbatum S. Bertini Sithiensium*, ed. by Oswald Holder-Egger, in *Monumenta Germaniae Historica: Scriptores*, XIII (Hannover: Hahn, 1881), pp. 600–35

Ionas ep. Aurelianensis, *Vita et translatio sancti Hucberti*, ed. by Charles De Smedt, *Acta Sanctorum, Novembris I* (Paris: Victor Palmé, 1887), pp. 806–18

Missi cuiusdam admonitio (801–02), ed. by Alfred Boretius, in *Monumenta Germaniae Historica: Capitularia Regum Francorum*, I (Hannover: Hahn, 1883), no. 121, pp. 238–40

The Rule of Saint Benedict, ed. by Bruce L. Venarde, Dumbarton Oaks Medieval Library, 6 (Cambridge, MA: Harvard University Press, 2011)

Secondary Works

Barrow, Julia, 'Ideas and Applications of Reform', in *The Cambridge History of Christianity*, vol. 3, *Early Medieval Christianities, c. 600–c. 1100*, ed. by Thomas F. X. Noble and Julia M. H. Smith, The Cambridge History of Christianity, 3 (Cambridge: Cambridge University Press, 2008), pp. 345–62

———, *The Clergy in the Medieval World: Secular Clerics, Their Families and Careers in North-Western Europe, c. 800–c. 1200* (Cambridge: Cambridge University Press, 2015)

Chupin, Annick, 'Alcuin et Cormery', *Annales de Bretagne et des pays de l'Ouest*, 111.3 (2004), 103–12

Claussen, Martin A., *Reform of the Frankish Church: Chrodegang of Metz and the Regula Canonicorum in the Eighth Century* (Cambridge: Cambridge University Press, 2005)

Constable, Giles, 'Renewal and Reform in Religious Life: Concepts and Realities', in *Renaissance and Renewal in the Twelfth Century*, ed. by Robert L. Benson, Giles Constable, and Carol D. Lanham (Oxford: Clarendon Press, 1982), pp. 37–67

―――, *The Reformation of the Twelfth Century* (Cambridge: Cambridge University Press, 1996)

Cubitt, Catherine, *Anglo-Saxon Church Councils, c. 650–c. 850* (London: Leicester University Press, 1995)

Cushing, Kathleen G., *Reform and the Papacy in the Eleventh Century: Spirituality and Social Change* (Manchester: Manchester University Press, 2005)

De Clercq, Carlo, *La législation religieuse franque de Clovis à Charlemagne: Étude sur les actes de conciles et les capitulaires, les statuts diocésains et les règles monastiques (507–814)*, Université de Louvain, Recueil de travaux publiés par les membres des Conférences d'Histoire et de Philologie, 2e série, 38 (Leuven/Paris: Librairie du Recueil Sirey/Bureau du recueil, Bibliothèque de l'Université, 1936)

Declercq, Georges, 'Heiligen, lekenabten en hervormers: De Gentse abdijen van Sint-Pieters en Sint-Baafs tijdens de Eerste Middeleeuwen (7de–12de Eeuw)', in *Ganda & Blandinium: De Gentse abdijen van Sint-Pieters en Sint-Baafs*, ed. by Georges Declercq (Gent: Snoeck-Ducaju & zoon, 1997), pp. 13–40

―――, 'Un monastère double à Gand à l'époque mérovingienne? L'abbesse Engelwara et la *congregatio seruorum et ancillarum Dei* de Saint-Pierre-au-Mont-Blandin', *Revue belge de Philologie et d'Histoire*, 95 (2018), 305–26

Dereine, Charles, 'Chanoines', in *Dictionnaire d'histoire et de géographie ecclésiastiques*, vol. 12 (Paris: Letouzey et Ané, 1953), cols 353–405

Dickinson, John Compton, *The Origins of the Austin Canons and their Introduction into England* (London: SPCK, 1950)

Diem, Albrecht, 'The Carolingians and the *Regula Benedicti*', in *Religious Franks: Religion and Power in the Frankish Kingdoms: Studies in Honour of Mayke de Jong*, ed. by Rob Meens, Dorine van Espelo, Bram van den Hoven van Genderen, Janneke Raaijmakers, Irene van Renswoude, and Carine van Rhijn (Manchester: Manchester University Press, 2016), pp. 243–61

Dierkens, Alain, 'La Christianisation des campagnes de l'Empire de Louis le Pieux: L'Exemple du diocèse de Liège sous l'épiscopat de Walcaud (*c.* 809–*c.* 831)', in *Charlemagne's Heir: New Perspectives on the Reign of Louis the Pious (814–840)*, ed. by Peter Godman and Roger Collins (Oxford: Clarendon Press, 1990), pp. 309–32

Dubreucq, Alain, 'La *vita secunda sancti Hucberti* de Jonas d'Orléans et sa tradition manuscrite', in *Religion, animaux et quotidien au Moyen Âge: Études offertes à Alain Dierkens*, ed. by Jean-Marie Duvosquel, Jean-Marie Sansterre, Nicolas Schroeder, Michel de Waha, and Alexis Wilkin, Revue belge de Philologie et d'Histoire/Belgisch Tijdschrift voor Filologie en Geschiedenis, 96 (Brussels: Le Livre Timperman, 2018), 305–26

Farmer, Sharon, *Communities of Saint-Martin: Legend and Ritual in Medieval Tours* (Ithaca: Cornell University Press, 1991)

Felten, Franz J., *Äbte und Laienäbte im Frankenreich: Studie zum Verhältnis von Staat und Kirche im früheren Mittelalter*, Monographien zur Geschichte des Mittelalters, 20 (Stuttgart: Anton Hiersemann, 1980)

Fournier, Edouard, *Nouvelles recherches sur les curies, chapitres et universités de l'ancienne église de France* (Paris: Nouvelle Soc. Anonyme du Pas-de-Calais, 1941/42)

Garver, Valerie L, '"Go humbly dressed as befits servants of God": Alcuin, Clerical Identity, and Sartorial Anxieties', *Early Medieval Europe*, 26.2 (2018), 203–30

Hartmann, Wilfried, *Die Synoden der Karolingerzeit im Frankenreich und in Italien* (Paderborn: F. Schöningh, 1989)

Howe, John, *Before the Gregorian Reform: The Latin Church at the Turn of the First Millennium* (Ithaca: Cornell University Press, 2016)

Jasper, Kathryn L., 'The Economics of Reform in the Middle Ages', *History Compass*, 10.6 (2012), 440–54

Innes, Matthew, *Introduction to Early Medieval Western Europe, 300–900: The Sword, the Plough and the Book* (London: Routledge, 2007)

Jong, Mayke de, '*Imitatio Morum*: The Cloister and Clerical Purity in the Carolingian World', in *Medieval Purity and Piety: Essays on Medieval Clerical Celibacy and Religious Reform*, ed. by Michael Frassetto (New York: Taylor & Francis, 1998), pp. 49–80

———, 'Carolingian Monasticism and the Power of Prayer', in *The Cambridge History of Christianity*, vol. 3: *Early Medieval Christianities, c. 600–c. 1100*, ed. by Thomas F. X. Noble and Julia M. H. Smith, The Cambridge History of Christianity, 3 (Cambridge: Cambridge University Press, 2008), pp. 622–53

Kramer, Rutger, 'Teaching Emperors: Transcending the Boundaries of Carolingian Monastic Communities', in *Meanings of Community across Medieval Eurasia: Comparative Approaches*, ed. by Eirik Hovden, Christina Lutter, and Walter Pohl, Brill's Series on the Early Middle Ages, 25 (Leiden: Brill, 2016), pp. 309–37 <https://brill.com/view/book/edcoll/9789004315693/B9789004315693-s015.xml> [accessed 8 September 2021]

———, 'The Exemption that Proves the Rule: Autonomy and Authority between Alcuin, Theodulf and Charlemagne (802)', *Religious Exemption in Pre-Modern Eurasia, c. 300–1300 CE, Medieval Worlds*, 6 (2017), 231–61 <https://www.medievalworlds.net/?arp=0x00372f2b> [accessed 8 September 2021]

———, *Rethinking Authority in the Carolingian Empire: Ideals and Expectations during the Reign of Louis the Pious (813–828)*, The Early Medieval North Atlantic, 6 (Amsterdam: Amsterdam University Press, 2019)

Levillain, Léon, 'Les origines du monastère de Nouaillé', *Bulletin de l'École des Chartes*, 71 (1910), 241–98

Leyser, Conrad, 'Review Article: Church Reform — Full of Sound and Fury, Signifying Nothing?', *Early Medieval Europe*, 24 (2016), 478–99

Ling, Stephen, 'The Cloister and Beyond: Regulating the Life of the Canonical Clergy in Francia, from Pippin III to Louis the Pious' (Unpublished doctoral thesis, University of Leicester, 2015)

Marchal, Guy P., 'Was war das weltliche Kanonikerinstitut im Mittelalter? Dom- und Kollegiatstifte: eine Einführung und eine neue Perspektive', *Revue d'histoire ecclésiastique*, 94 (1999), 761–807

McKitterick, Rosamond, *Charlemagne: The Formation of a European Identity* (Cambridge: Cambridge University Press, 2008)

Meens, Rob, 'Sanctuary, Penance, and Dispute Settlement under Charlemagne: The Conflict between Alcuin and Theodulf of Orléans over a Sinful Cleric', *Speculum*, 82 (2007), 277–300

Meijns, Brigitte, 'Chanoines et moines à Saint-Omer: Le dédoublement de l'abbaye de Sithiu par Fridogise (820–34) et l'interprétation de Folcuin (vers 962)', *Revue du Nord*, 83 (2001), 691–706

———, 'Communautés de chanoines dépendant d'abbayes bénédictines pendant le haut Moyen Âge: L'exemple du comté de Flandre', *Revue bénédictine*, 113 (2003), 90–123

Melve, Leidulf, 'Ecclesiastical Reform in Historiographical Context', *History Compass*, 13.5 (2015), 213–21

Miller, Maureen C., 'New Religious Movements and Reform', in *Companion to the Medieval World*, ed. by Carol Lansing and Edward D. English (Malden, MA: Wiley-Blackwell, 2009), pp. 211–29

Misonne, Daniel, 'Chapitres séculiers dépendant d'abbayes bénédictines au Moyen Âge dans l'ancien diocèse de Liège', in *La vita comune del clero nei secoli XI e XII: Atti della Settimana di Studio: Mendola, settembre 1959*, vol. 1, Pubblicazioni dell' Università cattolica del S. Cuore, Serie terza, Scienze storiche, 2, Miscellanea del centro di studi medioevali, 3 (Milan: Vita e Pensiero, 1962), pp. 412–32

Moraw, Peter, 'Über Typologie, Chronologie und Geographie der Stiftskirche im Deutschen Mittelalter', in *Untersuchungen zu Kloster und Stift*, Veröffentlichungen des Max-Planck-Instituts für Geschichte, 68, Studien zur Germania Sacra, 14 (Göttingen: Vandenhoeck & Ruprecht, 1980), pp. 9–37

Mordek, Hubert, *Studien zur fränkischen Herrschergesetzgebung: Aufsätze über Kapitularien und Kapitulariensammlungen ausgewählt zum 60. Geburtstag* (Frankfurt am Main: Peter Lang, 2000)

Nelson, Janet, 'Charlemagne and the Bishops', in *Religious Franks: Religion and Power in the Frankish Kingdoms: Studies in Honour of Mayke de Jong*, ed. by Rob Meens, Dorine van Espelo, Bram van den Hoven van Genderen, Janneke Raaijmakers, Irene van Renswoude, and Carine van Rhijn (Manchester: Manchester University Press, 2016), pp. 350–69

Noizet, Hélène, 'Les basiliques martyriales au VIe et au début du VIIe siècle', *Revue d'histoire de l'Église en France*, 87 (2001), 329–55

———, 'Alcuin contre Théodulphe: Un conflit producteur de normes', *Annales de Bretagne et des Pays de l'Ouest, Anjou, Maine, Poitou, Touraine*, 111 (2004), 113–29

———, *La fabrique de la ville: Espaces et sociétés à Tours (IXe-XIIIe siècles)*, Publications de la Sorbonne, Histoire ancienne et médiévale, 92 (Paris: Publications de la Sorbonne, 2007)

Oexle, Otto Gerhard, *Forschungen zu monastischen und geistlichen Gemeinschaften im westfränkischen Bereich*, Münstersche Mittelalter-Schriften, 31 (Munich: Wilhelm Fink, 1978)

Patzold, Steffen, *Episcopus: Wissen über Bischöfe im Frankenreich des späten 8. bis frühen 10. Jahrhunderts* (Ostfildern: Thorbecke, 2008)

Picker, Hanns-Christoph, *Pastor Doctus: Klerikerbild und Karolingische Reformen bei Hrabanus Maurus*, Veröffentlichungen des Instituts für Europäische Geschichte Mainz. Abteilung für Abendländische Religionsgeschichte, 186 (Mainz: Vandenhoeck & Ruprecht, 2001)

Reuter, Timothy, '"Kirchenreform" und "Kirchenpolitik" im Zeitalter Karl Martells: Begriffe und Wirklichkeit', in *Karl Martell in seiner Zeit*, ed. by Jörg Jarnut, Ulrich Nonn, Michael Richter, Matthias Becher, and Waltraud Reinsch, Beihefte der Francia, 37 (Sigmaringen: Jan Thorbecke, 1994), pp. 32–59

Rhijn, Carine van, *Shepherds of the Lord: Priests and Episcopal Statutes in the Carolingian Period* (Turnhout: Brepols, 2007)

Riché, Pierre, 'Le christianisme en occident', in *Histoire du christianisme des origines à nos jours, tome IV, Évêques, moines et empereurs (610–1054)*, ed. by Gilbert Dragon, Pierre Riché, and André Vauchez (Paris: Desclée, 1993), pp. 607–82

Rosé, Isabelle, 'Fondations et réformes à l'époque carolingienne', in *Monachesimi d'oriente e d'occidente nell'alto medioevo: Spoleto, 31 marzo–6 aprile 2016*, vol. 1, Settimane di studio della Fondazione Centro italiano di studi sull'alto medioevo, 64 (Spoleto: Fondazione CISAM, 2017), pp. 397–460

Schieffer, Rudolf, *Die Entstehung von Domkapiteln in Deutschland* (Bonn: Röhrscheid, 1976)

Scholz, Sebastian, 'Normierung durch Konzile: Die Reformsynoden von 813 und das Problem der Überscheidung von Geistlicher und Weltlicher Sphäre', in *Charlemagne: les temps, les espaces, les hommes; Construction et déconstruction d'un règne*, ed. by Rolf Große and Michel Sot, Collection Haut Moyen Âge, 34 (Turnhout: Brepols, 2018), pp. 271–80

Semmler, Josef, 'Reichsidee und kirchliche Gesetzgebung', *Zeitschrift für Kirchengeschichte*, 71 (1960), 37–65

——, 'Pippin III. und die fränkischen Klöster', *Francia*, 3 (1975), 88–146

——, 'Mönche und Kanoniker im Frankenreiche Pippins III. und Karls des Grossen', in *Untersuchungen zu Kloster und Stift*, Veröffentlichungen des Max-Planck-Instituts für Geschichte, 68, Studien zur Germania Sacra, 14 (Göttingen: Vandenhoeck & Ruprecht, 1980), pp. 78–111

——, 'Benedictus II: una regula — una consuetudo', in *Benedictine Culture, 750–1050*, ed. by Willy Lourdaux and Daniel Verhelst, Mediaevalia Lovaniensia, Series I, Studia, 11 (Leuven: Leuven University Press, 1983), pp. 1–49

——, 'Die Kanoniker und ihre Regel', in *Studien zum weltlichen Kollegiatstift in Deutschland*, ed. by Irene Crusius, Veröffentlichungen des Max-Planck-Instituts für Geschichte, 114, Studien zur Germania Sacra, 18 (Göttingen: Vandenhoeck & Ruprecht, 1995), pp. 62–109

——, 'Monachus — clericus — Canonicus: Zur Ausdifferenzierung geistlicher Institutionen im Frankenreich bis ca. 900', in *Frühformen von Stiftskirchen in Europa: Funktion und Wandel religiöser Gemeinschaften vom 6. bis zum Ende des 11. Jahrhunderts. Festgabe für Dieter Mertens zum 65. Geburtstag*, ed. by Sönke Lorenz and Thomas Zotz, Schriften zur südwestdeutschen Landeskunde, 54 (Leinfelden-Echterdingen: Thorbecke, 2005), pp. 1–18

Smith, Julia M. H., '"Emending Evil Ways and Praising God's Omnipotence": Einhard and the Uses of Roman Martyrs', in *Conversion in Late Antiquity and the Early Middle Ages: Seeing and Believing*, ed. by Kenneth Mills and Anthony Grafton, Studies in Comparative History, 4 (Rochester: University of Rochester Press, 2003), pp. 189–223

Trumbore Jones, Anna, '"The Most Blessed Hilary Held an Estate": Property, Reform, and the Canonical Life in Tenth-Century Aquitaine', *Church History*, 85 (2016), 1–39

Vanderputten, Steven, *Monastic Reform as Process: Realities and Representations in Medieval Flanders, 900–1100* (Ithaca: Cornell University Press, 2013)

Van Engen, John, 'The Future of Medieval Church History', *Church History*, 71 (2002), 492–522

Verdoot, Jérôme, 'Dans l'ombre des bénédictins: le chapitre canonial de Saint-Ursmer de Lobbes au Moyen Âge', *Revue Bénédictine*, 128 (2018), 142–74

Walsham, Alexandra, 'Migrations of the Holy: Explaining Religious Change in Medieval and Early Modern Europe', *Journal of Medieval and Early Modern Studies*, 44 (2014), 241–80 <https://read.dukeupress.edu/jmems/article/44/2/241/1186/Migrations-of-the-Holy-Explaining-Religious-Change> [accessed 8 September 2021]

Old Norms, New Boundaries

EMILIE KURDZIEL*

What is a *canonicus*?

The Carolingians and the Rethinking of Ecclesiastical ordines

At the end of the summer of 816, after several weeks of debate, the general council convened by Louis the Pious at the palace of Aachen promulgated two newly compiled texts regulating religious life: the *Institutio canonicorum* intended for *canonici* and the *Institutio sanctimoniales* intended for *canonicae* or *sanctimoniales*, that is women religious.[1] The main source we have at our disposal concerning the circumstances and motivations for their drafting is the prologue common to both texts. Evidently written at court after the council had met, it provides an official and authorized account of the assembly showing the ruler and the bishops acting hand in hand. It tells us that during the opening session the emperor 'carefully and attentively reviewed the long list of things necessary and suitable for the improvement (*emendatio*) of the holy Church of God' and among other things put on the agenda the drafting of the two 'canonical' norms of life.

> The norm of life of the *canonici* (*vita canonicorum*) was [indeed] scattered here and there in the sacred canons and the sayings of the Holy Fathers; for which reason he exhorted those present to extract from these same sacred canons and sayings of the Holy Fathers, by common will and accord, an archetype of the norm (*institutionis forma*) for the simple-minded and the less capable, in which the life of prelates and subordinates would be clearly set out, so that all those who belong to the canonical order (*canonica professio*) may shine brightly along the path they have embarked upon,

---

* I would like to thank Rutger Kramer, Graeme Ward, Marco Stoffella, and the anonymous reviewer of this book for their helpful suggestions and corrections.
1 *Institutio canonicorum Aquisgranense*, ed. by Werminghoff, pp. 307–420; *Institutio Sanctimonialum Aquisgranense*, ed. by Werminghoff, pp. 421–56 (from now on respectively IC and IS). About the council see Werminghoff, 'Die Beschlüsse'; Hartmann, *Die Synoden*, p. 4.

Emilie Kurdziel is *Maître de conférences* in Medieval History, Université de Poitiers / CESCM (Centre d'études supérieures de civilisation médiévale).

Monastic Communities and Canonical Clergy in the Carolingian World (780–840): Categorizing the Church, ed. by Rutger Kramer, Emilie Kurdziel, and Graeme Ward, MMS 8 (Turnhout: Brepols, 2022), pp. 131–178
PUBLISHERS ❦ PUBLISHERS   DOI 10.1484/M.MMS-EB.5.128531

without encountering any obstacles, and stand up with one voice and with devotion in Christ's army.[2]

The project, led by the court and the top echelon of its ecclesiastical counsellors, therefore consisted in the composition of a model norm or rule of life (*institutionis forma*), in the sense of an ideal model, almost archetypal, for the *canonici*. It is to the latter and to the manner in which it was elaborated that the prologue is essentially devoted. The last lines alone evoke its feminine counterpart, designated as *formula institutionis*, the diminutive being sufficient to indicate that the two texts had neither the same extent nor the same value in the eyes of the court.

At the end of the assembly, the male rule was acclaimed by the emperor and the council, after which it was decreed that all those who serve God in the canonical order (*canonica professio*) should, as far as their strength would permit, observe this model rule in all respects.[3] The *Institutio canonicorum* was therefore intended to apply to all *canonici*, in the same way that the *Regula Benedicti*, recognized at the same time as the single monastic rule, was to apply to all monks.[4] Yet at no time do the authors of the text take the trouble to clearly define who the *canonici* are, nor do the councils and capitulars which reiterate the order of a generalized observance of the new

---

2 *IC*, ed. by Werminghoff, Prologue, p. 312: 'Cum in nomine sanctae et individuae trinitatis christianissimus ac gloriosissimus Hludowicus superno munere victor augustus anno incarnationis domini nostri Iesu Christi DCCCXVI, indictione X, anno siquidem imperii sui tertio, Aquisgrani palatio generalem sanctumque convocasset conventum et coepisset secundum ardentissimam erga divinum cultum sibi caelitus inspiratam voluntatem multa congrua et necessaria de emendatione sanctae Dei ecclesiae [...] sollerter ac curiose pertractare, eo usque inter cetera perventum est, ut eundem sanctum et venerabilem Deo annuente adgregatum conventum consuleret, immo consulendo admoneret super quibusdam ecclesiarum praepositis, qui partim ignorantia, partim desidia subditorum curam parvipendebant et hospitalitatem minus iusto diligebant, quid facto opus est. Adiunxit etiam monendo, ut, quia canonicorum vita sparsim in sacris canonibus et in sanctorum patrum dictis erat indita, propter simplices quosque minusque capaces aliquam ex eisdem sacris canonibus et sanctorum patrum dictis institutionis formam pari voto parique consensu excerperent, per quam patenter praelatorum et subditorum vita monstraretur, quatenus omnes, qui canonica censentur professione, per viam propositi sui inoffenso gressu incederent et in Christi militia devotius unanimes atque concordes existerent'. Unless otherwise stated, all translations are my own.

3 *IC*, ed. by Werminghoff, Prologue, p. 312: 'Proinde omnium sententia statutum est ab omnibus, qui in canonica professione Domino militant, hanc institutionis formam, tot ecclesiasticorum virorum vigilanti studio congestam dignisque preconiis laudatam, iuxta virium possibilitatem modis omnibus observandam, quatenus hanc sive aliarum sanctarum scripturarum documenta sedula meditatione perlegentes et prelati et subditi vocatione, qua vocati sunt, ope divina adminiculati, infatigabiliter ambulent'. The idea is repeated in the 145th and concluding chapter of the rule, which summarizes the whole text in a brief and simple manner.

4 De Jong, *Carolingian Monasticism*; Diem, 'Inventing the Holy Rule'.

norm in the following years.[5] At most, they specify that *canonici* are those who are registered or serve God in the 'canonical' state or order (*canonica professio*), or those clerics who live *canonice*.[6] At the beginning of the ninth century, therefore, the meaning of the term *canonicus*, as well as the contours of the group it referred to, was apparently self-evident.

The same cannot be said of historians in the twentieth and twenty-first centuries. Historical scholarship, while it seems to have no difficulty in picturing what a monk was, often becomes hesitant or even ambiguous when it comes to defining precisely what a *canonicus* was or to whom exactly the rule of 816 was addressed. In many publications, the question of the identity of the addressees of the *Institutio canonicorum* is not asked, but merely settled by translation: the new norm of life was aimed at 'canons', the term conveying the idea of clerics living in communities, at the cathedral or in a collegiate church which one readily assumes to be quite important, since 'canon' also conveys the image of an elite distinct from the majority of clerics.[7] When an attempt is made to define more precisely the addressees of the rule, the majority of authors describe *canonici* as clerics of a particular kind, a sort of intermediary between monks and 'secular' clergy. For some, the rule of 816 was intended only or primarily for cathedral chapters, which the emperor and his advisors wanted to reform by systematizing the model proposed by Chrodegang;[8] for others, it was aimed at a wider audience, that of communities of clerics serving the cathedral chapter or a collegiate church, which could be either urban or rural, a basilica or a large 'parish' church.[9]

Special mention must be made here of the work of Josef Semmler, one of the foremost modern authorities on the reform of the monastic and canonical orders between Pippin III and Louis the Pious. Although he concentrated more on the monastic side of this reform effort, several of his articles return

---

[5] Cf. *Capitulare ecclesiasticum* (818–19), ed. by Boretius, 3, p. 276; *Episcoporum ad Hludowicum imperatorem relatio* (c. 820), ed. by Boretius, 9, pp. 367–68; *Episcoporum ad imperatorem de rebus ecclesiasticus relatio* (post. 821), ed. by Boretius, 7, p. 369; *Concilium Aquisgranense* (a. 836), ed. by Werminghoff, 39, p. 713; *Concilium Moguntinum* (847), ed. by Boretius and Krause, 13, pp. 179–80.

[6] In addition to the Prologue, see the short *Explicit* following c. 113, *IC*, ed. by Werminghoff, 113, p. 394, where *canonicus* (in the sense of an individual) is defined as 'quisquis canonicam professus est vitam'; and 117, pp. 398 and 134, pp. 410–12 where it appears that a *canonicus* is a cleric who lives *canonice*.

[7] See for example the very short passages devoted to the *canonici* and their rules, from Chrodegang to Louis the Pious, by Noble, 'The Christian Church' and Helvétius and Kaplan, 'Asceticism and its Institutions', respectively pp. 266 and 286.

[8] For instance Barrow, 'Ideas and Applications of Reform', p. 356; Barrow, *The Clergy*, pp. 81–85; Contreni, 'The Carolingian Renaissance', pp. 713–14.

[9] Marchal, 'Was War?'; Siegwart, *Die Chorherren- und Chorfrauengemeinschaften*; Meijns, 'L'ordre canonial'; Gaillard, *D'une réforme à l'autre*, pp. 126–27; Dereine, 'Chanoines' — who, while recognizing that originally every cleric was supposed to be *canonicus*, from the ninth century onwards draws a distinction between *canonici*, who lead the common life and devote themselves to the singing of the hours, and clerics who take on the pastoral ministry.

to the attempt made by Carolingian lawmakers to differentiate monks from canons, the drafting of rules for life peculiar to each group and the concrete reorganization that resulted in some ecclesiastical communities. Two articles, one from 1995 and the other from 2005, deal more directly with the question of the *Institutio canonicorum* and the differentiation between *monachi*, *clerici*, and *canonici*.[10] Semmler, however, never really tackles head-on the question of what exactly the category of *canonicus* encompasses. He defines *canonici* only indirectly, as opposed to monks, and on the basis of the picture given on the one hand by the *Institutio canonicorum* (and yet, by definition, the rule sets an ideal to be achieved more than it describes reality), and on the other hand by the examples of later communities designated in the sources as 'canonical', the most documented of which are those serving episcopal churches. Hence, he concludes quite logically that *canonicus* refers to a cleric belonging to a community that is not part of the *ordo monachorum*. The *ordo canonicorum* would thus have been added to the three orders recognized until then within imperial Frankish society: *laici*, *monachi*, and *clerici*. Common life, in one form or another, is always presupposed, with the underlying implication that when it does not exist, one cannot speak of *canonici*. In Semmler's eyes, *canonici* therefore represent a special group within the clergy, whose members lead a life close to that of monks and devoted themselves mainly, if not exclusively, to the chanting of the divine office. He acknowledges, however, that isolated clerics (i.e. clerics living and serving alone) must have been rare at the beginning of the ninth century.

His work, in many ways ground-breaking, has been very influential, and many if not most scholars still follow his view: the *canonici* represented only a sub-category within the clergy (its *sanior pars*), or a specific category, whose individual character became more distinct after the clarification made in 816 and essentially characterized by the fact of living the common life under the supervision of a superior and by the choral chant of the Liturgy of the Hours.[11] This is the consensus view. Yet, an alternative interpretation has been proposed, albeit more rarely, according to which *canonicus* made reference to any cleric who was not a monk, and the *Institutio canonicorum* therefore applied to all non-monastic clergy. This idea has been suggested a few times, in German historiography in particular, although without ever really being properly demonstrated, and always in a rather ambiguous way.[12]

In 1976, in his book on the origin and formation of cathedral chapters in Germany, Rudolf Schieffer wrote that the promulgation of the text 'aimed at nothing less than subjecting the entire non-monastic clergy of the Frankish

---

10 Semmler, 'Mönche und Kanoniker'; Semmler, 'Le monachisme occidental'; Semmler, 'Die Kanoniker und ihre Regel'; Semmler, '*Monachus — clericus — canonicus*'.
11 In addition to already mentioned works, see for instance Kramer, *Rethinking Authority*; *The Chrodegang Rules*, trans. by Bertram; and Ling in the present volume.
12 As for French research, Pierre Salmon is, to my knowledge, the only one who formulated the same idea, cf. Salmon, *L'office divin*, pp. 1–34.

Empire to a single standard in terms of liturgy and way of life'.[13] This is a strong assertion, but it is never substantiated in the few pages devoted to the rule and its ambitions. Further on, Schieffer adds that this norm was addressed to all clerics serving communally in non-monastic churches, this time apparently implying that it was aimed only at a certain category of clerics: those attached to a collegiate church. The ambiguity of his position is confirmed by the article 'Kanoniker' he wrote in 1991 for the *Lexikon des Mittelalters*.[14] He starts from the idea that, in the Merovingian councils of the sixth century, the term *canonicus* designates a cleric who celebrates liturgy communally under the direction of the bishop or an archpriest and who is, therefore, maintained by the property of the Church, still administered as a whole by the bishop. Such clerics organized themselves in the form of religious communities and, with the development of *Eigenkirchen* in the countryside, eventually became a minority among the clergy. Because of the growing confusion between these communities and monastic communities, Carolingian reformers felt the need to distinguish between the two orders and to submit *canonici* to their own rule. After the promulgation of the *Institutio canonicorum*, the *ordo canonicus* therefore included all the ecclesiastical communities of the Frankish Empire which were not subjected to the *Regula Benedicti*. In his mind, this excluded priests or clerics serving in small 'private' rural churches, that is those who would later be referred to as 'secular clergy'. Rudolf Schieffer thus takes here the counterpoint of the idea put forward in his 1976 book.

The latter idea subsequently circulated, mainly in German-language scholarship, without however being further demonstrated. Under the pen of the historians who have taken it up, one even notices a certain hesitation, if not a frank ambiguity.[15] These authors always seem to hesitate between two interpretations: the new rule was intended for all clergy, or its observance was limited to a certain number of established 'large communities', whose members alone were understood as *canonici*. Among this group of scholars, Egon Boshof has embraced the first option most explicitly. In his view, the *Institutio canonicorum* provides a norm of life for the cathedral clergy and existing non-monastic communities, but it also marks an important step in a process which increasingly obliges clergy to conform to the monastic model: it should not be thought, he writes, that the priests of the *Eigenkirchen* were excluded from the reform.[16]

The implicit background to such an assertion is the traditional opposition between public (or episcopal) and private churches, which has influenced

---

13 Schieffer, *Die Entstehung von Domkapiteln*, p. 232.
14 Schieffer, 'Kanoniker'.
15 For instance Hartmann, *Die Synoden*, pp. 155–60. And more recently Lorenz and Auge ed., *Die Stiftskirche in Südwestdeutschland*, pp. 1–6.
16 Boshof, *Ludwig der Fromme*, pp. 120–26.

historical research since the beginning of the twentieth century. This dualistic conception has led, among other things, to the early *canonici* being identified as clerics serving a large 'public' church directly submitted to episcopal authority, as opposed to the ecclesiastical staff of private oratories, in the hands of the lay elite. In line with recent research, which has quite strongly challenged this dualistic picture and the very concept of *Eigenkirche*,[17] the problem of the contours of the *ordo canonicorum* must be re-examined by breaking out of an overly systematic schematism between public and private churches. The interpretation of the political and institutional project that underpinned the drafting of the *Institutio canonicorum* in 816 and, more broadly, of the whole canonical side of the reform effort carried out between 816 (or even 813) and 819 entirely depends on a correct understanding of the meaning attributed to the terms *canonicus* and *ordo canonicorum* by the authors of the text and those, present at the assembly, who adopted it.

There is nothing obvious about these categories. On the contrary, they are constructions, and as such, they have a history. Their contours and content evolved over time, layers of significance having been superimposed on the words used to designate them. This is why the meaning of early medieval categories such as these is sometimes no longer immediately perceptible to us. Hence the necessity to recover this lost key, that is to exhume the conceptual categories specific to the Carolingian period. The most effective hermeneutical tool the historian can use to do this is lexicology. If we are to understand whom the council fathers of Aachen were addressing and what their aim was, it is therefore necessary to go back to the sources and words and, adopting a lexicological approach, to make a history of the category of *canonicus* and its associated notions, *ordo canonicus* or *canonicorum*, *canonice vivere*, *vita canonica*, all terms closely linked from a semantic and conceptual point of view. Now, precisely in the years leading up to the drafting of the *Institutio canonicorum*, these related notions underwent a legal and ethical redefinition. The aim of this contribution is to illuminate this process in order to gauge fully the significance of the action undertaken in 816 by the court and its ecclesiastical counsellors.

Such an attempt involves avoiding two common pitfalls which have contributed to muddying the waters so far. The first is the tendency to project into the eighth and ninth centuries a fact only later attested to: after the Gregorian period, it is clear that *canonici*, now divided into regulars and seculars, constitute a particular type of cleric (canons), and a minority within the clergy. But it wasn't necessarily so in the mind of the Carolingian rulers and high clergy. The second is the tendency to confuse the rules set out in normative texts with local institutional realities (that is churches described as being served by *canonici* or in which the mode of organization described by the *Institutio canonicorum* seems to have existed or to have been adopted).

---

17 Patzold and Van Rhijn ed., *Men in the Middle*, pp. 1–10; Patzold, *Presbyter*, pp. 25–28.

There is no denying that there is a back-and-forth link between written norms (from canon law to rules of life) and practices, bottom-up and top-down dynamics, nor that norms, especially in the ecclesiastical field, are inspired by pre-existing experimentations and institutional forms, which they seek to correct, clarify, institutionalize, or systematize. Nevertheless, the space of discourse constituted by normative writings ought to be considered for what it is, that is endowed with its own coherence and situated both above and outside practices. Norms do not describe reality, they seek to shape it. And evidently, local institutional realities do not necessarily conform to written norms. Put another way, if we are to clarify the significance attributed to the category of *canonicus* in the conciliar acts of 816, it is necessary to understand its meaning in equivalent contexts, that is normative texts, and therefore to track and analyse its occurrences in such writings, and in them only, without prejudging concrete achievements or practices on the ground.

This encompasses mainly two types of writings. Firstly, those emanating directly from the court and expressing the royal (then imperial) will or recapitulating the decisions taken during general councils and assemblies convened by the king (then the emperor) once or twice a year, these assemblies being the dominant legislative bodies at the time.[18] Those decisions were gathered and communicated through capitularies, more rarely through acts of councils in the strict sense[19] and comprised decrees and ordinances of a legal nature as well as regulations and provisions of an administrative, religious, or educational nature, and announcements of a religious-exhortative character.[20] For the most part they arose from dialogue with the bishops, abbots and counts, whose role it was to advise the lay ruler, but they all had the sovereign as their guarantor, even conciliar legislation.[21] Therefore, it can be assumed that the legal vocabulary used to characterize ecclesiastical institutional realities in this first ensemble of normative writings was the same, although it could evolve over time. A second group of writings includes the acts of regional councils of various importance held under the supervision of an archbishop or a group of bishops, and records of episcopal synods held by one bishop with the clergy of his diocese. These assemblies also acted as courts on matters of

---

18 Mordek, 'Fränkische Kapitularien und Kapitulariensammlungen'.
19 This is for example the case of the regional councils of 813, which are an exception for the Carolingian period. From the Mayors of the Palace Carloman and Pippin to Louis the Pious, conciliar decisions are indeed generally communicated and disseminated in the form of capitulars issued by the sovereign. There is however evidence of councils whose decisions have legal effects without being promulgated by the king or emperor in the form of a capitular. Cf. Hartmann, *Die Synoden*, p. 10.
20 Mordek, 'Leges und Kapitularien'. On capitulars in general, the history of capitulary scholarship and current debates, see the *Capitularia* project developed in Köln in close collaboration with the *Monumenta Germaniae Historica* (*MGH*) and the Cologne Center for eHumanities (CCeH): <https://capitularia.uni-koeln.de> [accessed 8 September 2021].
21 Isaïa, *Histoire des Carolingiens*, pp. 136–37.

ecclesiastical discipline, albeit at a lower level.[22] The way the participants in these assemblies perceived Church and the categories they used to express it could either diverge from the vision formulated at the central level or be similar to it (whether they inspired or, on the contrary, relayed this vision on the ground in the second case).

I have sought to identify in a systematic way all occurrences of *canonicus* in the sense of a cleric, that is of a person, but also of *ordo canonicorum*, *canonice vivere*, *vita canonica* and other related notions, present in these two types of normative writings, and I have charted this over the temporal arc that runs from the first occurrences of the use of *canonicus* in this sense, in the 530s, through to the years 816–19. I also took into consideration a series of more or less official documents relating to the preparation or the communication of legal and administrative action (capitularies in the broader sense), or documents that belong among the organizational tools: agendas for future assemblies, aide-memoires of decisions to be transmitted via *missi*, personal notes by royal agents about actions to be carried out, or lists of issues to be investigated. Generally taking the form of a succession of chapters like capitularies, they bear the imprint of ongoing debates; they are likely to use the same vocabulary as normative writing and to carry the same reading grids. In other words, for the Carolingian period, I have been systematically looking for occurrences in those documents edited as a whole and according to an often artificial distinction in the Concilia and Capitularia sections of the *Monumenta Germaniæ Historica*.[23] This leaves aside two types of normative documents which could in the future refine the conclusions reached here: royal and imperial diplomas intended for a particular church or monastery, which logically convey the same conceptual reading grid of the Church as capitularies; and contemporary hagiographical production, whose normative dimension is real but is played out on a very different level, and whose authors and audience are more difficult to identify.

It goes without saying that all the documents taken into account in this study and the decisions or reflections they bear the trace of have been elaborated in a particular context and for a specific purpose, and that their nature, aim and audience therefore need to be assessed on a case-by-case basis. But it is only by considering this material as a whole and by conducting a comparative lexicological study, that we can hope to bring out the logical meaning(s) of these categories and their evolution.

---

22   On the legal value of canonical legislation and the making of canon law in conciliar context, cf. Hartmann, *Die Synoden*; Hartmann, *Kirche und Kirchenrecht um 900*.

23   This includes the *Capitularia regum Francorum*, *Capitularia regum Francorum nova series*, and *Capitula episcoporum sections*, and the new edition of the *Admonitio generalis* of 789 by Mordek, Zechiel-Eckes, and Glatthaar published in a different section (*Die Admonitio Generalis Karls des Großen*, ed. by Mordek, Zechiel-Eckes, and Glatthaar). About the artificial distinction between capitularies and conciliar acts: Mordek, 'Fränkische Kapitularien und Kapitulariensammlungen'.

From these investigations, it appears that the wide range of people who can be labelled Carolingian lawmakers, that is key scholars of the court acting as authors of capitularies, as well as bishops, abbots, and clerics gathered in regional councils, but also court bureaucrats and *missi*, all made consistent use of the word *canonicus* (in the sense of a person) and related notions; and that this use underwent a semantic inflection from the 780s onwards. The present chapter intends to shed light on this process, that is to demonstrate how Carolingian rulers and their ecclesiastical counsellors, with the support of at least some of the magnates, attempted to rethink and recategorize the ecclesiastical orders, inventing a new category, the *ordo canonicorum*, to designate all clerics who had not taken a monastic vow and as such were destined to live according to the canons. This new category encompassed the whole non-monastic clergy, that is all those devoted to the active life, including local priests and clerics of lower grade serving small rural churches. It is to all of them and not simply to a small clerical elite, that the *institutio* of 816 was addressed, as Rudolf Schieffer and others after him had intuited. The implications of this largely remain to be explored. These will only be sketched here, and in some of the following chapters of this book.

The Eclipse of *canonici* between the Sixth and the Eighth Century

In the light of the occurrences of the word *canonicus* (to designate a cleric), a first striking fact appears: its disappearance from the Frankish sources for nearly two centuries.

As noted by Sebastian Scholz in this same volume, the first attestation of the word *canonicus* applied to a cleric in the Frankish world dates back to 535, and only four other attestations are known for the sixth century. In the conciliar legislation, it is used in three canons between 535 and 567, and there is no mention of it in later councils.[24] It seems to be just as rare in non-normative sources, where no other mentions seems to exist than those of Gregory of Tours attributing to one of his predecessors the institution in Tours of a *mensa canonicorum*, that is a common meal for his clerics, and evoking the existence of a similar institution in Bourges.[25] The canons of the Visigothic councils, to which reference is regularly made in the studies devoted to the origins of the canonical world, do not use the term.[26] Nor does it seem to have been in common use in Rome at the same time.

---

24 In the councils of Clermont (535) (*Concilium Claremontanum*, ed. by De Clercq, 15, p. 109); Orléans (538) (*Concilium Aurelianense*, ed. by De Clercq, 12, p. 119); Tours (567) (*Concilium Turonense*, ed. by De Clercq, 20, p. 183).
25 Gregory of Tours, *Libri Historiarum X*, ed. by Krusch, x. 31, p. 533; Gregory of Tours, *Liber vitae patrum*, ed. by Krusch, IX. 1, p. 253.
26 Cf. *Concilios visigótico*, ed. by Vivès.

Sebastian Scholz suggests understanding the *canonici* of the sixth century as 'those clerics of the episcopal churches and municipal parishes who were listed in the registers and were given sustenance by the bishop'.[27] While agreeing with him, I would add an additional nuance: *canonicus* in the sixth century referred to any cleric listed on the registers of a *particular* church, who was a member of its *own* clergy and therefore entitled to receive sustenance from its *own* property — and this regardless of the type of church. The appearance of the expression *clericus canonicus* accompanied the profound institutional changes which the Church in Gaul underwent in the sixth century, and more particularly the division of the episcopal patrimony and the recognition of a form of autonomy and legal personality for the various churches which now had not only their own resources but also their own clergy. Thus, the term would not refer to any cleric listed in the official catalogue of the clergy, in the broadest sense, but to the cleric listed on the *matricula* (the register) of a particular church. *Clerici canonici* thus referred not to all officially established clergy, but, in context, to the clergy of a particular church, the official clergy of such and such sanctuary in other words.[28]

It is, in any case, a rather rare word in the sixth-century Frankish sources. And contrary to what one sometimes reads, nothing indicates that it spread rapidly to become common use in the seventh century. The notion of *canonicus* in the sense inaugurated or at least first observable in 535 seems in fact to have been in use during a relatively short time span — the last two thirds of the sixth century — and in a confined space — the Merovingian kingdoms. After that, the word seems to vanish from the sources and to reappear only in the mid-eighth century.[29] At that time, it circulated in England and on the continent and perhaps it was re-imported into Carolingian circles from the Anglo-Saxon kingdoms. We encounter it in a letter addressed by Boniface of Mainz to the Angles in 737;[30] and a few years later, in the rule of life that Chrodegang intended for the clerics of his cathedral and more widely, it seems,

---

27 Cf. Scholz's contribution in the present volume.
28 I am currently preparing a paper on the subject.
29 A quick search in the sources of the Merovingian period edited in the *Monumenta Germaniae Historica*, once excluded the hagiographic material considered to have been written at the earliest in the ninth century by recent scholarship, did not allow me to identify other occurrences. Similarly, a search for all occurrences of words derived from the lemma *canonic** in the Library of Latin Texts database (<http://clt.brepolis.net/llta/Default.aspx> [accessed 8 September 2021]), taking into account not only normative but all types of texts between the fourth and the end of the eighth century, did not reveal any mention of *canonicus* being used to designate a cleric, either as an adjective or as a noun.
30 Boniface of Mainz, *Epistolae*, ed. by Dümmler, no. 46, p. 295. The letter is addressed to 'universis reverentissimis coepiscopis, venerabilibus presbiteratus candidatis gratia, diaconibus, canonicis clericis vero gregi Christi prelatis abbatibus seu abbatissis, humillimis et pro Deo subditis monachis consecratis et Deo devotis virginibus et cunctis consecratis ancillis Christi […]'. In his edition of the letter, Ernst Dümmler inserts a comma between *canonicis* and *clericis*, considering them to be two distinct categories. One might just as well

of the city of Metz.[31] In 775, Charlemagne received a letter from a certain Cathwulf, perhaps an Anglo-Saxon living in the Frankish realm and linked to Saint-Denis. Listing the king's duties, the latter mentions that of governing with his bishops the life of monks, *canonici*, and virgins.[32]

There is, however, no mention of *canonici* in the Frankish councils presided over by Boniface and Chrodegang in the 740s and 760s, which alongside monks and nuns mention only the clergy or clerics. On both sides of the English Channel, it was not until the 780s that the term appeared and came into common use in legislative or normative texts of general application. The report of the double council held in Northumbria and Mercia in 786, known as the 'Legatine Capitulary', mentions *canonici* along with monks. This is a priori the first occurrence in the Anglo-Saxon conciliar legislation. Attendees included Alcuin, who was about to join Charlemagne's court, and Abbot Wigbod as legate of the Frankish king.[33]

In the Carolingian realm, one of the first, if not the first mention of this kind appears in the *Admonitio generalis* of 789.[34] It is significant that the term *canonici* entered the royal legal vocabulary precisely in the text which, for the first time, formulated a general programme of reform for the Church and proposed concrete ways of building a Christian society through the education of the people.[35] Moreover, from this point on, the category of *canonicus* (in the sense of a cleric) as well as new associated notions such as *vita canonica*, seem to be omnipresent in those texts framing the reform of the Church, where instructions relating to *canonici* are multiplying. In the normative writings of the 780s to 820s and the associated administrative literature, about

---

admit that *canonicis* is used here as an adjective and that the expression 'canonicis clericis' is either an apposition referring to the senior grades mentioned just before, or the continuation of the enumeration then designating the lower clergy.

31   The majority of the chapters of the rule are unambiguously addressed to the cathedral clergy of Metz, but on two occasions mention is made of clerics residing in the city, outside the *claustrum*. In Chapter 2 they are designated as 'clerici canonici qui extra claustra canonica in civitate commanent', in Chapter 8 they are simply designated as 'omnis clerus qui foras claustra esse videtur et in ipsa civitate constitit'. In comparing the two chapters, however, it appears that it could be the same group. The rule is thus ambiguous as to the meaning of the term *canonicus*. Cf. Chrodegang, *Regula Canonicorum*; Claussen, *The Reform of the Frankish Church*.

32   Thought to be an Irishman for a long time, Cathwulf was probably an Anglo-Saxon, living on the continent and evolving in a milieu in contact with Boniface and Lull's circles. Cf. Garrison, 'The English and the Irish'; Garrison, 'Letters to a King'; Story, 'Cathwulf'.

33   Cf. Cubitt, *Anglo-Saxon Church Councils*, pp. 164–84.

34   There is a presumably earlier mention (779–80?) in a document mentioning masses and alms decreed for the king, the army, and because of the misfortunes of the time by bishops gathered in council. The responsibility was divided between the bishops (three masses and three psalters), the priests (three masses), the monks, the nuns and the *canonici* (three psalters). Cf. *Capitulare episcoporum* (780?), ed. by Boretius, p. 52.

35   Cf. McKitterick, *The Frankish Church*, pp. 1–40 and the introduction by Michael Glatthaar to the new edition of *Admonitio Generalis*.

fifty decisions concerning *canonici* and their obligations can be found, most of them concentrated in the second half of Charlemagne's reign. While this figure must be seen in the context of the normative fever and the consequent swelling of legislative and regulatory writings that characterized the reigns of Pippin III, Carloman, and, above all, Charlemagne, it nevertheless indicates the importance attached to *canonici*, their way of life and the obligations associated with their existence in the effort of *renovatio* of the realm carried out hand in hand by the court and part of the ecclesiastical hierarchy. The decisions taken in the 780s to 820s testify to an energetic will and a sustained effort to redefine the way of life of the *canonici*. A close analysis of these references shows, however, that the meaning of the word was no longer exactly that of the sixth century.

The State, the Life, and the Rule of Life

The first concern emerging from these instructions is the one which has been most underlined in the historiography, namely the will of the rulers and the ecclesiastical hierarchy to distinguish the way of life of the *canonici* from that of monks. Both groups are occasionally reminded that they are not supposed to live in the same way, but each according to the norms governing them.

A document of unknown origin, dating from the end of Charlemagne's reign and presumably recapitulating, for the benefit of some *missus*, the matters to be investigated and actions to be carried out after the regional councils of 813, stipulates for example:

> That care should be taken by all means and scrupulous inquiry be made on how *canonici* and monks live, so that each one of them may live according to his own rule, that is either according to the canons or according to the monastic rule, and not in the same way.[36]

In the same vein, the king stipulates in the *Admonitio generalis* of 789:

> Those clerics who claim to be monks by name or habit, but are not, that every effort be made to ensure that they are corrected and emended, so that they are either true monks, or true *canonici*.[37]

This general requirement is sometimes targeted at a particular community, for example in the sharp letter addressed by Charlemagne at the end of 801 or at the very beginning of 802 to the members of the congregation of

---

36 *Capitula originis incertae* (813?), ed. by Boretius, 3, p. 175: 'Providendum omnimodis ac diligenter exquirendum, qualiter canonici vivant necnon et monachi, ut unusquisque eorum secundum ordinem canonice ac regulariter vivant, et non similiter [...]'.
37 *Admonitio generalis* (789), ed. by Mordek, Zechiel-Eckes, and Glatthaar, 75, p. 228: 'Clericis. Ut illi clerici, qui se fingunt habitu vel nomine monachos esse et non sunt, omnimodis videtur corrigendos atque emendandos esse, ut vel veri monachi sint vel veri canonici'.

Saint-Martin of Tours, whom the emperor reproached for the vagueness of their state. 'You know', he writes to them, 'how much your way of life is already frequently criticized from all sides, and not without reason, since one day you call yourselves monks, the next *canonici* and the third not one, nor the other'.[38] His outburst, however, had much more to do with the enduring resistance of the clerics of Saint-Martin to their bishop and thus, indirectly, to Charlemagne's authority, and their meandering than with the actual indeterminacy of their status.[39]

As Brigitte Meijns points out in this volume, the primary purpose of the set of regulations regarding the life of monks and *canonici* was indeed not to encourage them to stand out from one another, as it is usually thought; rather, it was to remind each group to observe its own norm of life. To the *canonici* it is tirelessly repeated that they must live according to the canons (*canonice, iuxta canones*) or the canonical rule(s) (*sub ordine canonico* or *secundum ordinem canonicum*),[40] that is the provisions and regulations that form canon law and ecclesiastical discipline.[41] To the monks it is tirelessly repeated that they must live according to a — or the — monastic rule(s) ('*sub ordine regulari, secundum ordinem regularem, regulariter or monachice*')[42] and, in certain cases, according to one specific rule: the *Regula Benedicti*.[43]

---

38 Cf. Charlemagne's letter in Alcuin, *Epistolae*, ed. by Dümmler, no. 247, pp. 400–01.
39 Kramer, 'The Exemption'.
40 When referring to a norm and not to a social group, the expression 'ordo canonicus' has generally the meaning of 'canon law' or 'rule of church law' in the capitulars and councils of the eighth and ninth centuries. Cf. Niermeyer, '*ordo*', p. 746 and the examples he gives under Section 7.
41 Ecclesiastical discipline derived from the Tradition, embodied in the canon, the authoritative list of books accepted as Holy Scripture, which was progressively established between the sixth and eighth centuries. In the Carolingian period, it included a great variety of texts, comprising the Sacred Scripture, that is the Old and New Testaments, but also the rulings of ancient church councils (i.e. the canons in the strict sense), the writings of the Church fathers, the decretals of the popes, and even other materials, all charged with a sacrality and normative authority equivalent or almost equivalent to that of the Bible. To these should be added all the decisions taken by regional councils or episcopal synods, perceived as a continuation of Tradition. Cf. Congar, *La tradition et les traditions*; Munier, 'Les sources patristiques'; Gioanni, 'Les listes d'auteurs'.
42 'Ordo regularis' has been used since the seventh century in the Frankish realm in the sense of 'rule of monks' or at least of a set of written precepts that governs the life of monks in a monastery, hence as a synonym to '*regula*' (cf. Niermeyer, '*ordo*', p. 746). It should be kept in mind, however, that this did not necessarily refer to a rule in the narrow sense, as we think of it today, that is one specific prescriptive text. Cf. Diem and Rousseau, 'Monastic Rules'.
43 *Concilium Vernense* (755), ed. by Boretius, 11, p. 35: 'De illis hominibus, qui se dicunt propter Deum quod se tonsorassent, et modo res eorum vel pecunias habent et nec sub manu episcopi sunt nec in monasterium regulariter vivunt, placuit ut in monasterio sint sub ordine regulari aut sub manu episcopi sub ordine canonica; et si aliter fecerint, et correpti ab episcopo suo se emendare noluerint, excommunicentur. Et de ancillis Dei velatis eadem forma servetur'; *Admonitio generalis* (789), ed. by Mordek, Zechiel-Eckes, and Glatthaar, 71, p. 225: 'Sacerdotibus. Simul et hoc rogare curavimus, ut omnes ubicumque qui se voto

Besides, it is notable that whenever the term *canonici* appears in normative writings, it is almost systematically used in relation to their way of life and the precepts that govern it. The majority of occurrences link the state (*canonicus*), the life (*vita canonica*), and the norm or rule(s) that governs it (*ordo canonicus, regula, disciplina*, but most often simply *canones*).[44] In this case, life and norm

---

monachicae vitae constrinxerunt monachice et regulariter omnimodis secundum votum suum vivant [...]. Similiter qui ad clericatum accedunt, quod nos nominamus canonicam vitam, volumus ut illi canonice secundum suam regulam omnimodis vivant, et episcopus eorum regat vitam, sicut abbas monachorum'; *Interrogationes examinationis* (post 803?), ed. by Boretius, 9, p. 234: 'Canonicos interrogo, si secundum canones vivant an non'; *Capitula e canonibus excerpta* (813), ed. by Boretius, 4, p. 173: 'Providendum necesse est, qualiter canonici vivere debeant necnon et monachi, ut secundum ordinem canonicum vel regularem vivere studeant'; *Concilium Arelatense* (813), ed. by Werminghoff, 6, p. 251: 'Providendum necesse est unicuique episcopo, qualiter canonici vivere debeant necnon et monachi, ut secundum ordinem canonicum vel regularem vivere studeant, ut ait apostolus: Unusquisque in qua vocatione vocatus est, in ea permaneat'; *Concilium Moguntinense* (813), ed. by Werminghoff, 9, p. 262: 'De vita canonicorum. In omnibus igitur, quantum humana permittit fragilitas, decrevimus, ut canonici clerici canonice vivant [...]'; *Concilium Moguntinense* (813), ed. by Werminghoff, 11, p. 263: 'De vita monachorum. Abbates autem censuimus ita cum monachis suis pleniter vivere sicut ipsi, qui in presenti synodo aderant, palam nobis omnibus promiserunt, id est secundum doctrinam sanctae regulae Benedicti, quantum humana permittit fragilitas'; see also the account of the 802 assembly in the annals of Lorsch: '[...] iussio eius generaliter super omnes episcopos, abbates, presbyteros, diacones seu universo clero facta est, [...] ut canonici iuxta canones viverent [...] et quicquid in monasteriis seu in monachis contra regula sancti Benedicti factum fuisset, hoc ipsud iuxta ipsam regulam sancti Benedicti emendare fecissent'. (*Annales Laureshamenses*, ed. by Pertz, a. 802, p. 39). The same type of provisions can be found in Italian capitularies from the early 780s (under Pippin of Italy, Charlemagne's son), for instance in the *Capitulare cum episcopis langobardicis deliberatum* (c. 782), ed. and trans. by Azzara and Moro, 2, p. 57 (= ed. by Boretius, p. 189): 'Ut sacerdotes et clericos secundum normam priorum patrum vivant.'; 3, p. 57 (= ed. by Boretius, p. 189): 'Ut tam monachi quam monachas ubicumque fuerint, regulariter vitam degant'; *Pippini Italiae regis capitulare* (c. 782), ed. and trans. by Azzara and Moro, 2, p. 58 (= ed. by Boretius, p. 191): 'Ut pontifices ordinent et disponant unusquisque suas ecclesias canonico ordine, et sacerdotes suos vel clericos constringant canonice vivendo ordine. Et si quis pontifex cleros suos canonice ordine distringere noluerit et ad secularem pertraxerit habitum, quod canones cleros facere prohibent, comis qui in loco fuerit ordinatus distringat illos in omnibus ad suam partem sicut et alios exercitales'; ed. and trans. by Azzara and Moro, 2, p. 58 (= ed. by Boretius, 3, p. 192): 'Monasteria virorum et puellarum, tam que in mundio palatii esse noscuntur vel etiam in mundio episcopales seu de reliquis hominibus esse inveniuntur, distringat unusquisque in cuius mundio sunt, ut regulariter vivant; simul et senodochia, cuiuslibet sint, fratres in omnibus pascantur iuxta illorum possibilitatem'. About the Italian legislation of the Carolingian period, which is often overlooked in the studies questionning the reform/*correctio* of the Church, and the evolutions of the clerical organization which could have resulted from it in the Peninsula, see Kurdziel, 'Les "chapitres cathédraux italiens" du 9e siècle'.

44 In addition to the references cited in the previous note, cf. *Capitulare missorum generale* (802), ed. by Boretius, 22, p. 95: 'Canonici autem pleniter vitam obserbent canonicam'; *Capitula de examinandis ecclesiasticis* (oct. 802?), ed. by Boretius, 11, p. 110: 'Ut nullus tonsus sine canonica sit vita vel regulari [...]'; *Capitulare missorum generale* (802), ed. by Boretius, 1, p. 92: 'Sed omnes omnino secundum Dei praeceptum iusta viverent rationem iusto iudicio,

tend to merge, and for good reason: the 'life' in question here is nothing other than that described by the norm,[45] so that it can be prescribed to *canonici* to observe fully the *vita canonica*, that is, the 'canonical' life (in the sense of conforming to the canons), as described by the rule(s) that define(s) it — one feels the ambiguity of the formula.[46] On closer inspection, the *canonici* do not seem to define themselves other than in relation to these two realities: canonical life and canonical rule.

Most of the instructions prior to 816 remain, however, very vague as to the specific content of this *vita/regula*. The question is whether it differed, in the eyes of the Carolingian rulers, lawmakers, and bishops, from that of any cleric, who by the very fact of his state was bound to the respect of the canons. When they instruct *canonici* to live *secundum canones, secundum ordinem canonicum* or *sub vita canonica*, do they put under those terms something more than the general discipline to which any cleric was subjected? Or do they designate the same normative set, in which case *canonicus* more or less covers the same reality as *clericus*? On close examination, several clues point in the latter direction. One of the only definitions of the *vita canonica* provided by the normative sources can be found in the *Admonitio generalis* of 789. In a chapter addressed to priests (*sacerdotes*), the king demands that all those who have committed themselves by vow to monastic life (*monachica vita*) live according to the requirements of their state (*monachice*) and according to their rule (*regulariter*), in virtue of their own vows. He then adds:

> Similarly, those who embrace the clerical state (*clericatus*) which we call *vita canonica*, we want them to live 'canonically' (*canonice*) in all things, according to their rule (*regula*). And that the bishop should govern their life, as the abbot governs that of the monks.[47]

---

et unusquisque in suo proposito vel professione unanimiter permanere ammonere: canonici vita canonica absque turpis lucris negotio pleniter observassent [...]'; *Capitulare missorum item speciale* (802?), ed. by Boretius, 32, p. 103: 'Ut abbates canonici canones intelligant et canones observent, et clerici canonici secundum canones vivant'; ed. by Boretius, 34, p. 103: 'Ut abbatissae canonicae et sanctimoniales canonice secundum canones vivant, et claustra earum ordinabiliter composita sint'; *Concilium Remense* (813), ed. by Werminghoff, 8, p. 254: 'Lecti sunt sancti canones, ut quisque canonicus legem vitamque suam minime ignoraret, quod omnimodis non expedit, sicut in decretali legitur Innocentii'.

45 Coccia, 'Regula et Vita'; Agamben, *De la très haute pauvreté*.
46 *Capitulare missorum generale* (802), ed. by Boretius, 22, p. 95: 'Canonici autem pleniter vitam obserbent canonicam, et domo episcopali vel etiam monasteria cum omni diligentiam secundum canonica disciplina erudiantur'.
47 *Admonitio generalis* (789), ed. by Mordek, Zechiel-Eckes, and Glatthaar, 71, pp. 224, 226: 'Sacerdotibus. Simul et hoc rogare curavimus, ut omnes ubicumque qui se voto monachicae vitae constrinxerunt monachice et regulariter omnimodis secundum votum suum vivant [...]. **Similiter qui ad clericatum accedent, quod nos nominamus canonicam vitam, volumus ut illi canonice secundum suam regulam omnimodis vivant. Et episcopus illorum regat vitam, sicut abbas monachorum**'.

The wording is ambiguous and depends on the meaning of '*clericatus*', which could designate the condition of a cleric (as member of the sacred orders) or the act of ordination — in other words the clerical state in general — as well as the condition of a monk or a canon.[48] Is it to be understood that the king called *vita canonica* the condition of clerics in the broad sense, with the ordination entailing a commitment to this way of life just as the vow signalled for the monks the entry into the *vita monachica* mentioned a few lines above; or that the emperor thus designated a particular form of clerical state, which concerned only part of the clergy? The fact that the bishop had to govern the life of those engaged in *vita canonica* is not determinative: from a disciplinary point of view, he was the superior of all the clergy of the diocese, just as the abbot had the power of direction over the monks of his monastery. Therefore, one cannot conclude that the injunction only addressed those clerics serving the episcopal church.

A more conclusive argument resides in the fact that normative writings mentioning a norm of life to be followed by ecclesiastics contemplate only two options: either the monastic rule(s), or the canonical rule(s). The same goes for ways of life: either *vita monastica*, or *vita canonica* (but once again, life and rule tend to merge).[49] Most often, the canonical norm is associated with *canonici*. But on several occasions, it is clear that this norm concerned the whole non-monastic clergy. Among the most eloquent examples is an administrative document intended for a *missus*, dating perhaps from 802 and listing matters to be examined or made known during his next inspection. The eleventh entry stipulates that all clerics (*tonsus*) must be submitted either to the *vita canonica* or to the *vita regularis*, as well as to episcopal authority, because those who are without discipline and without a superior displease God.[50] This concerned all grades, from doorkeepers (*ostiarius*) to priests.

---

48 Cf. Niermeyer, 'Clericatus', although the example given to exemplify the second meaning 'the condition of a monk or a canon' is the very same Chapter 71 of the *Admonitio generalis*, which can be interpreted in another way as we shall see.

49 In addition to the references already cited in nn. 36, 43, 44, 46 and 47, cf. *Statuta Rhispacensia*, ed. by Boretius, 2, p. 226: 'Admonebant enim in ipso concilio, ut nullus eorum sive episcopus sive abbas vel presbiter aut monachus vel etiam ceteri ministri sanctae Dei eclesiae seu sanctaemoniales a recto tramite deviare praesummeret, et hic qui in canonica vita degere debuisset, recte et secundum ordinem absque ulla transgressione vitam conservasset canonicam, aut hi qui sub voto monachicam vitam observare vovissent'; *Capitulare missorum item speciale* (802?), ed. by Boretius, 19, 27, 32, 33, 34, 35, pp. 102–03; *Capitulare ecclesiasticum Caroli Magni* (a. 805–13), ed. by Mordek and Schmitz, 24, p. 408: 'Ut ministri altaris dei suum ministerium bonis moribus ornent observatione canonica seu monachi regulari disciplina […]'.

50 *Capitula de examinandis ecclesiasticis* (oct. 802?), ed. by Boretius, 11, pp. 110: 'Ut nullus tonsus sine canonica sit vita vel regulari, nullusque absolutus sine magisterio episcopali vel presbiter aut diaconus vel abbas; quia displicere Deo novimus eos qui sine disciplina vel magisterio sunt'.

The Council of Ver had already formulated the same requirement in very similar terms in 755:

> Of those men who claim to be devoted to God because they had themselves tonsured, provided that they have their goods and wealth at their disposal, and who are subjected neither to the authority of the bishop nor to a rule in a monastery, it is fitting that they should live either in a monastery according to a/the monastic rule(s) (*ordo regularis*), or under the authority of the bishop according to the canonical rule(s) (*ordo canonica*); and if they act differently and, having been punished by their bishop, refuse to make amends, they should be excommunicated.[51]

Every ecclesiastic thus had to be subjected either to the *vita canonica*, or to the *vita regularis*, as recalled again in the Bavarian council of Riesbach-Freising-Salzburg, held under the supervision of Arn of Salzburg in 799 or 800:

> Let no one among the *nobiles* dare to have himself tonsured to become abbot or priest before his case has been examined in the presence of the bishop of the diocese concerned. And if he has conceded any property to the monastery or church where he was tonsured, let him remain there either under canonical rule (*vita canonica*) or under monastic rule (*vita regularis*). But if afterwards he wishes to reside in his properties, let him participate in the host like other lay people.[52]

All those who had left the secular world for the service of God had therefore to choose between two possibilities: to live fully the *vita canonica* according to the canonical rule(s), or to live fully the *vita regularis* according to the monastic rule(s) (maybe already understood as the sole *Regula Benedicti*).[53] The *vita canonica* was not, therefore, understood as a specific way of life, embraced only by a limited portion of the clergy or by a particular type of cleric. It

---

51 *Concilium Vernense* (755), ed. by Boretius, 11, p. 35: 'De illis hominibus, qui se dicunt propter Deum quod se tonsorassent, et modo res eorum vel pecunias habent et nec sub manu episcopi sunt nec in monasterium regulariter vivunt, placuit ut in monasterio sint sub ordine regulari aut sub manu episcopi sub ordine canonica; et si aliter fecerint, et correpti ab episcopo suo se emendare noluerint, excommunicentur [...]'.
52 *Statuta Rhispacensia*, ed. by Boretius, 44, p. 230: 'Ut nullus de nobilibus neque abbas neque presbiter tonderi audeat, antequam in praesentia episcopi examinentur eius causa, ad cuius diocesim pertinet. Et si aliquas res vel ad monasterium vel ad ecclesiam tradiderit ubi tonsuratus est, **ibi sub canonica vel regulari maneat vita**. Si autem postea in propria sua residere vult, faciat hostem ut ceteri laici'. In the foreword, the council claims to follow the decisions of the Council of Frankfurt in 794 and of a Council of Aachen, the acts of which are not preserved.
53 *Capitulare missorum in Theodonis villa datum*, ed. by Boretius, 10, p. 122 preserved in two different versions: a. 'De his qui seculum relinquunt propter servicium dominicum impediendum et tunc neutrum faciunt, ut unum e duobus elegant: aut pleniter secundum canonicam aut secundum regularem institutionem vivere debeant'. b. 'De relinquentibus seculum ut unum e duobus eligant: aut pleniter secundum canonicam aut secundum regularem institutionem vivere debeant'.

concerned all clerics who were not subject to the only other alternative, the *vita regularis*, that is to say all clerics who had not taken monastic vows, including those whom we would designate today as members of the 'secular clergy'.[54] Those who followed neither of these were designated as wanderers (*vagi*) and headless (*acephali*) and regularly condemned by both conciliar and royal legislation, which took up again a commonplace of the councils of the first centuries. They had to be sanctioned and/or forced to submit to the authority of the bishop or an abbot and to respect a norm, whether canonical or monastic.[55]

Ordo canonicorum, ordo monachorum, and ordo laicorum

To these two ways of life, *vita canonica* and *vita regularis*, normative writings associate two categories of ecclesiastics. From Charlemagne's adoption of the title of emperor onwards, when it comes to all the *ordines* — in the sense of categories of ecclesiastics, not of grades of ordination — that constitute the Church, the extant documents always mention only two, the *ordo canonicorum* and the *ordo monachorum*, to which are added the laity when all the orders that made up Frankish (or Christian) society are taken into account. The clearest example comes from the general preamble to the four capitularies promulgated by Louis the Pious between December 818 and January 819.[56] These completed the effort of *renovatio* begun during the previous two years, which had led to the drafting of the *Institutio canonicorum* and the set of injunctions relating to a unified observance of the *Regula Benedicti* for monks. In this preamble, Louis the Pious specifies that he had convoked a general assembly of 'bishops, abbots, *canonici* and monks, along with some of his faithful *optimates*' in order to discuss the measures to be taken for 'each order, that is to say, that of the *canonici*, that of the monks and that of the laity'.[57]

---

54 On the formulation of the notion of 'secular clergy' in the twelfth century, cf. Barrow, *The Clergy*, p. 3 and n. 12.

55 *Capitulare missorum generale* (802), ed. by Boretius, 22, pp. 95–96: 'Canonici autem pleniter vitam obserbent canonicam, [...]. Nequaquam foris vagari sinantur, sed sub omni custodia vibant [...]; non per vicos neque per villas ad ecclesiam vicinas vel terminantes sine magisterio vel disciplina, qui sarabaiti dicuntur, luxoriando vel fornicando vel etiam caetera iniqua operando, quae consentiri absordum est.'; *Concilium Moguntinense* (813), ed. by Werminghoff, 22, p. 267: 'De clericis vagis. De clericis vagis seu acoephalis, id est de his, qui sunt sine capite neque in servitio domini nostri neque sub episcopo neque sub abbate, sed sine canonica vel regulari vita degente [...]'.

56 On these, cf. Ganshof, *Recherches sur les capitulaires*, pp. 13 and 44–45 and n. 169.

57 *Hludowici prooemium generale*, ed. by Boretius, p. 274: '[...] huius rei gratia quinto anno imperii nostri, accersitis **nonnullis episcopis, abbatibus, canonicis et monachis et fidelibus optimatibus nostris**, studuimus eorum consultu sagacissima investigare inquisitione, qualiter **unicuique ordini, canonicorum videlicet, monachorum et**

According to Carolingian imperial ideology, at least in the first decades of the ninth century, Frankish society thus comprised three orders: the *ordo canonicorum*, the *ordo monachorum*, and the *ordo laicorum*. This division of ecclesiastics into *canonici* and *monaci* and of society into *canonici*, *monachi*, and *laici* was not new. Several variations can be found in the normative writings from 800 onwards.[58] Two Italian manuscripts preserve for instance the text of a speech in the form of an *admonitio* intended to be pronounced publicly by a *missus*, perhaps in Italy.[59] In it, Charlemagne, already emperor, enjoins everyone to serve God in his own state or order, and then addressed each of these orders in turn to specify their own duties. He begins with women, men, and sons, then moves on to *clerici canonici*, then monks and finally dukes, counts, and judges. To the *clerici canonici* he orders that they obey their bishop, not move from place to place, not get involved in secular affairs, remain chaste, read the Holy Scriptures frequently, exercise their office with diligence: injunctions of a generic nature, that is, which do not seem to be addressed to a particular category of clerics but to all clergy. Besides, one would be surprised if in such an admonition, only part of the clergy was to be admonished. The discourse therefore distinguishes between two categories of ecclesiastics, monks and *clerici canonici*, who must be understood as all clerics who had not taken monastic vows.

Mention should also be made of a provincial council held in 805 in Bavaria, during which 'the bishops, abbots, and other ecclesiastics present' established a confraternity of prayer throughout the whole province and fixed the number of masses and psalms to be said, as well as the amount of alms to be given, on account of the death of a bishop, abbot or priest:

> […] for the death of a bishop or abbot of the province, that in every episcopal church and in every monastery of monks, one hundred masses be celebrated and one hundred psalms said; in addition, that all priests of the province, whether they are established in a rural church or as monk in a cellula, each celebrate three masses; and that every other ecclesiastic, *canonici* as well as monks, each recites one psalter. That bishops and abbots each give twenty *solidi* of silver in alms for the death of another; as for priests, that they give one *solidus* each for their bishop, one *tremissus* for

---

laicorum, iuxta quod ratio dictabat et facultas suppetebat, Deo opem ferente consuleremus'. The emperor also specifies that he organized his capitularies by subject matter, grouping in the first what among the measures taken during the assembly 'concerns the *canonici* and what must be observed by the monks'. The measures in question concern, in addition to monks, the clergy and ecclesiastical sanctuaries in the broadest sense, including small rural churches, to which nine chapters are devoted (cc. 6–14 and 19). Thus, the term *canonici* clearly covers here all non-monastic clergy, regardless of the type of church in which they officiated, including the most modest. See also Hartmann, *Die Synoden*, p. 163.

58 Contra: Ling (cf. his contribution in the present volume).
59 *Missi cuiusdam admonitio* (801–12), ed. by Boretius, p. 240; De Clercq, *La législation religieuse franque*, II, p. 226.

one of their fellow priests. For the death of a priest or any other ecclesiastic, whether *canonicus* or monk, that each of the priests, whether *canonicus* or monk, celebrate three masses, and in the same way, that every other ecclesiastic, *canonici* as well as monks, recite one psalm […].[60]

The bishops and other churchmen gathered in this council therefore divided the ecclesiastics of the province of Salzburg into two categories: *canonici* and *monachi*. Even in rural areas only two types of priests could be encountered, *canonici*-priests and monk-priests, depending on whether they were established in a church or in a *cellula*, that is a small monastery or the dependency of an abbey. Once again, the term *canonici* thus encompasses here all clerics who were not monks, regardless of their rank.

Examples could be multiplied, but the picture would remain the same: in the first years of the ninth century the term *canonici* was used in normative and administrative writings to designate all clerics, of all grades, regardless of the type of church they were serving, who had not taken monastic vows, as opposed to monks (the latter category including ordained monks or clerics who had chosen to live a monastic life).[61]

Canonicus = clericus?

In many cases the word *canonicus* thus replaces or is used as a quasi-synonym for *clericus*, although without systematically substituting for it. Several capitularies and councils alternate between measures aimed at clerics in general or clerics of a particular grade (most often priests), and others aimed at *canonici*. This explains the (apparent) ambiguity of the sources as well as the temptation of numerous scholars to identify in *canonici* a particular category within the clergy, distinct from the basic *clerici*.

---

60 *Concilium Baiuwaricum*, ed. by Werminghoff, p. 233: 'Anno natale Domini DCCCV., indictione XIII., mense Maio convenit sanctam synodum episcoporum atque abbatum ceterorumque ecclesiasticorum virorum de provintia Baioariorum de orationibus vel aelimosinis pro defunctis agendis, ut in unaquaque sede episcopali necnon per monasteria singula monachorum pro episcopo vel abbate conprovintiali defuncto fiant missae C celebratae, psalmi C. Super hoc autem omnes provintiales et parrochiales presbiteri et monachi per cellolas positi presbiteri, unusquisque missas III, ceteri autem ecclesiastici omnes, sive canonici sive monachi, unusquisque psalterium unum. Episcopi autem et abbates pro alio defuncto det unusquisque solidos XX aestimatione argenti in elimosinam eius, presbiteri autem pro episcopis suis det unusquisque solidum unum, pro presbitero autem conparrochiale tremissem unum; pro presbitero autem necnon et pro omnibus ecclesiasticis viris, sive canonicis sive monachis, defunctis singulus quisque presbiterorum, sive canonicus sit sive monachus, faciet missas III, similiter et omnes ceteri ecclesiastici, sive canonici sive monachi, psalmum I; quia convenit eos omnino ecclesiasticos, qui canonica voluerint esse content […]'; Hartmann, *Die Synoden*, pp. 148–49.

61 On priests-monks, see Cinzia Grifoni's contribution in the present volume.

The acts of the Council of Mainz of 813, one of the five regional councils convened simultaneously by Charlemagne in the spring, are a good example of this.[62] Canons 9, 10, and 11 are respectively entitled *De vita canonicorum*,[63] *De vita clericorum*,[64] and *De vita monachorum*,[65] from which one might deduce that they concern three different groups of ecclesiastics. The first canon enjoins *canonici* to live 'canonically' (*canonice*), to observe the teachings of the Divine Scriptures and the Holy Fathers, to obey their bishop or superior, and, where sufficient resources permit and for those who receive *stipendia* from ecclesiastical goods, to eat and sleep together, to remain in their *claustrum*, and to attend a reading every morning and during meals for edification purposes.[66] Canon 10, on the life of clerics, is concerned with those who falsely claim to have abandoned the secular world, and prescribes that they be clearly distinguished from the laity, as provided for in the 'clerical rule'

---

62 On these councils see Hartmann, *Konziliengeschichte*, p. 132; McKitterick, *The Frankish Church*, Chapter 1; Kramer, *Rethinking Authority*, pp. 70–91; Scholz, 'Normierung durch Konzile'.

63 This canon of the Council of Mainz, as well as Canons 10 and 11, is preserved in three tenth-century manuscripts, namely: 1) Munich, BSB, MS Clm 27246, saec. X (= M1); 2) Novara, ASDN, MS LXXI, saec. X (= N); 3) Vienna, ÖNB, MS 751, saec. X (= V1); in one twelfth-century manuscript, that is: 4) Munich, BSB, MS Clm 19414, saec. XII (= M2); and in one fifteenth-century manuscript: 5) Venice, BNM, MS Iur. can. 11, saec. XV (= V2). M1, N, and V1 contain the canons of the five regional councils of 813 (V1 containing lacunae). According to A. Werminghoff, who edited the council's acts in the *MGH*, M1, N, and V1 derive from the same original manuscript, X, now lost. M1 would be a direct copy of X, whereas N and V1 would both have been made from another copy of X, also lost. M1 would thus be the oldest version, and N and V1 would derive from a same manuscript. V1 and M2 do not give titles to the canons adopted by the Council of Mainz. M1 and N both entitle Canon 9 'De vita canonicorum'; V2 entitles it 'De vita clericorum capitula'. But in all manuscripts, the canon stipulates likewise 'ut canonici clerici canonice vivant [...]', so there is no variation of the content. Moreover, among the five regional councils copied in these different manuscripts, Mainz is the only one for which titles are systematically given to its canons in several manuscripts. In the acts of the council of Arles, titles remain an exception in all five manuscripts; in the acts of the councils of Chalon, Tours, and Reims, none of the tenth-century manuscripts give a title to any of their canons. Since Mainz's council canons are preceded by a title in M1 and N, and none of the other councils' canons copied in the same manuscripts, one can think that those titles were in the original document issued after the council. This is all the more likely if M1 and N derive from the canonical collection supposedly composed a few months after the five regional councils, which was to bring together their decisions (cf. *Annales regni francorum*, ed. Kurze, p. 138: 'constitutionum, quae in singulis factae sunt, collatio coram imperatore in illo conventu', i.e. during the assembly held in September 813).

64 This canon is entitled *De vita clericorum* in M1, N, and V2; it has no title in V1 and M2.

65 This canon is entitled *De vita monachorum* in M1, N, and V2; it has no title in V1 and M2.

66 *Concilium Moguntinense* (a. 813), ed. by Werminghoff, 9, pp. 262–63: 'De vita canonicorum. Cap. 9. In omnibus igitur, quantum humana permittit fragilitas, decrevimus, ut canonici clerici canonice vivant, observantes divinae scripturae doctrinam et documenta sanctorum patrum, et nihil sine licentia episcopi sui vel magistri eorum positi agere praesumant in unoquoque episcopatu et ut simul manducent et dormiant, ubi his facultas id faciendi suppetit vel qui de rebus ecclesiasticis stipendia accipiunt, et in suo claustro maneant

(*regula clericorum*). There follows a long list of prohibited feelings, behaviours, and activities outlining an ethic of clerical life.[67] Canon 11, finally, on the life of monks, essentially stipulates that abbots and monks should live according to the *Regula Benedicti*.[68]

This calls for several remarks. First of all, Canon 10 is in fact a long quotation from Isidore of Seville's *De ecclesiasticis officiis*, from which the council participants of 813 take up a chapter entitled *De regulis clericorum* (here significantly transformed in *regula clericorum* in the singular).[69] The prelates gathered in Mainz simply added two introductory sentences and inserted a short quotation from Jerome. Then, looking closely at the content of the prescriptions, it is not at all clear that what is set forth in canons 9 and 10 is aimed at two different groups of clerics. The first requirements of the canon *De vita canonicorum* are extremely generic and merely repeat commonplaces of conciliar legislation valid for the whole clergy (observe the canons, the

---

et singulis diebus mane prima ad lectionem veniant et audiant quid eis imperetur. Ad mensam vero similiter lectionem audiant et oboedientiam secundum canones suis magistris exhibeant'.

67 *Concilium Moguntinense* (a. 813), ed. by Werminghoff, 10, p. 263: 'De vita clericorum. Cap. 10. Discretionem igitur esse volumus atque decrevimus inter eos, qui dicunt se saeculum reliquisse, et adhuc saeculum sectantur. Placuit itaque sancto concilio, ut ita discernantur, sicut in regula clericorum dictum est. **His igitur lege patrum cavetur, ut a vulgari vita seclusi a mundi voluptatibus sese abstineant, non spectaculis, non pompis intersint, convivia inhonesta et turpia fugiant.** Tamen Hieronimus in epistola ad Nepotium dicit: Omnium Christianorum domos quasi proprias amare debemus, ut consolatores nos in meroribus suis potius quam convivas in prosperis noverint. Item Isidorus: **Clerici tamen convivia privata non tantum pudica, sed et sobria colant, usuris nequaquam incumbant neque turpium occupationes lucrorum fraudisque cuiusquam studium appetant. Amorem pecuniae quasi materiam cunctorum criminum fugiant, saecularia officia negotiaque abiciant, honorum gradus per ambitionem non subeant, pro beneficiis medicinae Dei munera non accipiant, dolos et coniurationes caveant, odium, æmulationem, obtrectationem atque invidiam fugiant. Non vagis oculis, non infreni lingua aut petulanti tumidoque gestu incedant, sed pudorem ac verecundiam mentis simplici habitu incessuque ostendant, obscenitatem etiam verborum sicut et operum penitus execrentur. Viduarum ac virginum visitationes frequentissimas fugiant, contubernia ferminarum nullatenus appetant, castimoniam quoque inviolati corporis perpetuo conservare studeant. Seniores quoque debitam preabeant oboedientiam nec ullo iactantiae studio se adtollant. Postremo in doctrina, in lectionibus, psalmis, ymnis et canticis exercitio iugi incumbant. Tales enim esse debent, qui divinis cultibus se mancipandos student exhibere, scilicet ut, dum scientiae operam dant, doctrinae gratiam populis administrent'.**
68 *Concilium Moguntinense* (a. 813), ed. by Werminghoff, 11, p. 263: 'De vita monachorum. 11. Abbates autem censuimus ita cum monachis suis pleniter vivere sicut ipsi, qui in presenti synodo aderant, palam nobis omnibus promiserunt, id est secundum doctrinam sanctae regulae Benedicti, quantum humana permittit fragilitas. Ac deinde decrevimus, sicut sancta regula dicit, ut monasterium, ubi fieri possit, per decanos ordinetur, quia illi praepositi saepe in elationem incidunt et in laqueum diaboli'.
69 The borrowed chapter is Chapter 3 of Book 2, the text of which is marked in bold in n. 68. Cf. Isidore of Seville, *De ecclesiasticis officiis*, ed. by Lawson.

Scriptures, and the teachings of the Fathers, obey their bishop and their superior). As for the prescriptions relating to communal life (to stay in the *claustrum*, to eat and sleep together, to hear edifying reading in the morning and during meals), it is specified that they concern only those churches where material conditions will make it possible and those clerics who receive *stipendia* (that is, who are fed and clothed directly from the *res ecclesiae*). These latter directives are therefore not meant to apply systematically nor uniformly to all the *canonici* referred to here.

The prescriptions of Canon 10 have a different, more moral character. They complement those of the preceding canon by reminding clerics of the rules of conduct implied by their state of separation from the world. It is therefore quite plausible that the two canons are in fact aimed at one and the same group of ecclesiastics: non-monastic clergy. That the bishops and other participants gathered in Mainz entitled the tenth canon *De vita clericorum* is easily explained by the borrowing from Isidore of the chapter *De regulis clericorum*, which, by his own admission, merely condenses the *lex patrum* on the life of clerics, listing a set of rules of conduct which are commonplace in the conciliar legislation and patristic literature of the first Christian centuries. Generally speaking, when quoting or mentioning older canons or patristic works, acts of early ninth-century councils tended to respect the letter of the received texts, at least to maintain the term *clericus* without replacing it with *canonicus* in canons which were nevertheless aimed at *canonici*. This is notably the case for the authors of the *Institutio canonicorum* in 816: the quotations of canons and patristic works in the florilegium which constitutes the first part of the rule (Chapters 1 to 113), systematically maintain the term *clericus* without replacing it with *canonicus*.[70] Another revealing example is the canon of the Council of Mainz of 847 entitled *De clericorum vita sive monachorum*, which enjoins bishops to ensure that *canonici* and monks live according to canonical or monastic rule(s) and refrain from any secular behaviour or activities, before drawing up a long list of them. Mentioning clerics in the title, the canon therefore addressed *canonici* and took up some of the standard themes of ecclesiastical discipline, without this seeming to pose any problem of understanding for a contemporary audience.[71]

A last clue indicates that *canonici* of Canon 9 and *clerici* of Canon 10 are to be understood as one and the same group. In several manuscripts containing the canons of the five regional councils of 813, an index can be found at the end of the acts. Intended to facilitate consultation, it is organized in the form of thematic entries listing the corresponding canons in the various councils.[72] Now, the tenth entry, entitled *De vita canonicorum*, refers to Canons 9 and 10

---

70 See for instance, *IC*, ed. by Werminghoff, 95, pp. 374, 97–102, pp. 375–78, or 112–13, pp. 384–95.
71 *Concilium Moguntinum* (847), ed. by Boretius and Krause, 13, pp. 179–80.
72 Cf. *Concilia* II. 1, ed. by Werminghoff, p. 301.

of the Council of Mainz (alongside Canon 8 of the Council of Rheims, Canon 23 of the Council of Tours and Canon 6 of the Council of Arles). Who created this index and when exactly (September 813?) is not known, but at least in his eyes there was no doubt that Canons 9 and 10 of the Council of Mainz concerned one and the same group of clerics and that the terms *canonici* and *clerici* were, in this case, equivalent.

Equivalent, but not strictly synonymous, however. And this is also the case on a more general level, for *canonicus* was not employed at the turn of the ninth century to designate any cleric, but any cleric who had not taken a monastic vow. The word and the category of ecclesiastic it encompasses does not cover therefore the meaning of the term in sixth-century Gaul, nor does it cover the meaning of 'canon' (*Kanoniker*, *chanoine*), at least in the sense in which 'canon' is usually understood, which reflects twelfth-century practice. One can even say that the very notion of 'canon' has not been formalized yet: there is no idea or concept of 'canon' in the first decades of the ninth century, even if contemporary actors are perfectly aware of the fact that some clerics do live a life closer to coenobitism than the rest of the clergy.[73] What is there, then?

Rethinking Ecclesiastical *ordines* (780s–820s)

What there is, is a new conceptual system, a new way of thinking about the Church and the groups that constitute it, which distinguishes four categories of individuals serving God (or two dual categories): *canonici* and *monaci* and their feminine counterparts, *canonicae* and 'Benedictine' nuns. This renewed reading grid of the *ecclesia* does not exactly replace the traditional clerics/monks dichotomy, but rather complements and clarifies it. In this recategorization of the ecclesiastical *ordines*, the differentiation between the constituent groups of the *ecclesia* is not based on their function but on their way of life. It is by their life and even more so by their norm of life that these *ordines* define themselves or ought to be defined.

Originally, what distinguished clerics from monks was essentially ordination and what it implied in terms of performance of the sacraments, in particular the Eucharist, and care of the faithful.[74] What we are witnessing from the 780s onwards is a shift, a redefinition of the criterion of discrimination between

---

73 This is how the following passage, often quoted, of a letter from Alcuin to Arn of Salzburg dated 802, should be interpreted: '[…] ut diligenter examinetur, quid cui conveniat personae, quid canonicis, quid monachis, quid tertio gradui, qui inter hos duos variatur; superiori gradu canonicis et inferiori monachis stantes'. (Alcuin, *Epistolae*, ed. by Dümmler, no. 258, p. 416). For a different interpretation of this 'third grade', 'superior to the *canonici* but inferior to the monks', see Ling's chapter in the present volume. The latter cites another very interesting passage of the *Missae expositionis geminus*, composed around 814, maybe by Amalarius of Metz, which to my opinion should be understood in the same way as Alcuin's.

74 About ordination, see Barrow, *The Clergy*, pp. 27–64.

the ecclesiastical *ordines*: in the new model elaborated during Charlemagne's reign, it is no longer ordination that differentiates one *ordo* from the other, but their respective way and norm of life. This renewed conception of the ecclesiastical *ordines* was not invented at the Carolingian court, since earlier mentions of *canonici* can be found on both sides of the Channel. It was rather adopted there, in 789 or shortly before that, but then pushed further and systematized. Alcuin, among others, may have played an influential role in this process. He attended the Northumbrian/Mercian council of 786, where bishops had been encouraged to 'watch with diligent care that all *canonici* live *canonice* and monks and nuns *regulariter* with regard to diet, dress and private property', and might even have participated in the drafting of its report.[75] Later that same year, he was brought to Charlemagne's court, presumably to implement religious change. Once there he probably played an active role in the creation and wording of the *Admonitio generalis*, and after 800 he participated in the ongoing reflection about the ways of life of the different categories of ecclesiastics, as indicated by the letter he wrote to Arn of Salzburg in 802.[76] In any case, it seems that the question of the categorization of the ecclesiastical orders has been the subject of simultaneous reflection in the Britain and in the Frankish kingdom, with potential unilateral or reciprocal influences that remain to be evaluated.

In the Frankish realm, the result of this rethinking, observable in a series of capitularies emanating from the court in the second part of Charlemagne's reign, as well as in several central or regional councils, is a system of absolute logical and conceptual coherence. It distinguishes, on the one hand, monks, living the regular life according to a regula — or *the regula* (i.e. the *Regula Benedicti*), and on the other hand, *canonici*, living the canonical life (*vita canonica*) according to the canons (*canonice, secundum canones*). Thus, it is their norm of life, the *canones* or the canonical discipline, which gives its name to the *canonici* of the ninth century. It would, incidentally, be more accurate to translate the term as 'canonical clerics' or 'canonicals' for this period rather than 'canons' in order to avoid any confusion (although the confusion is less

---

75 Alcuin, *Epistolae*, ed. by Dümmler, no. 3, 4, p. 22: 'Quartus sermo, ut episcopi diligenti cura prevideant, quo omnes canonici sui canonice vivant et monachi seu monachae regulariter conversentur, tam in cibis quam in vestibus seu peculiare, ut discretio sit inter canonicum et monachum vel secularem et illo habitu vivant, quo orientales monachi degunt et canonici exemplo orientalium et non tinctis Indie coloribus aut veste preciosa, sed episcopi, abbates et abbatisse subiectis sibi in omnibus exemplum bonum prebeant, ut Petrus ait: "Estote forma facti gregis secundum Deum" et cet. Qua de re suademus, ut synodalia edicta universalium sex conciliorum cum decretis pontificum Romanorum sepius lectitentur, observentur et iuxta eorum exemplar ecclesiae status corrigatur, ut nec quid novi ab aliquibus introduci permittatur, ne sit scisma in ecclesia Dei'. About his role in the composition of the so-called Legatine Capitulary of 786 and the debate it has raised, see Ling's chapter in the present volume, pp. 245–46.

76 See the introduction to the new edition of the *Admonitio Generalis*, ed. by Mordek, Zechiel-Eckes, and Glatthaar, pp. 47–63 and above, nn. 33 and 73.

important in English, German, or Italian for instance, where the semantic link with canonical legislation is preserved, than it is in the French 'chanoine'). We may note in passing the resemanticization of the noun '*canonicus*', conceived in the sixth century as deriving from *matricula* (list, register) rather than from *canones*.[77]

In this new conceptual system, male ecclesiastics were still divided into two categories and only two: those who were supposed to live according to the canons because they were simple clerics who had not professed monastic vows, and those who were supposed to live according to a monastic rule because they had made monastic vows, whether they were otherwise ordained, hence clerics or not. The same logic was applied to female religious, probably traced from the male model, *canonicae* or *sanctimoniales canonicae* responding to nuns or *sanctimoniales in monachico proposito existentes*, even though the differences between the two types of female life are in fact ambiguous and rather artificial.[78]

This recategorization of the ecclesiastical orders, carried out from the 780s onward by the court with the support of one part of the episcopate, did not fundamentally change institutional realities, but it proposed a reading grid, that is a way of conceptualizing and describing the Church more in tune with reality. At the beginning of the ninth century, ordination had indeed become more or less normal for a monk and, as the number of ordained monks continued to increase, this dividing line had lost its strength and obviousness, leading to a blurring of categories.[79] Ordination in itself was no longer a sufficient criterion for distinguishing between the different types of male ecclesiastics, and the very category of 'cleric' could lead to confusion. The importation into the legal vocabulary of the category of *canonicus* was therefore guided by a need for clarification. Carolingian legislators engaged in an exercise of redefining the categories, showing a concern for clarity and precision of legal language.

But clarification was not the sole motivation of this rethinking of the *ordines*, which is more than a mere renewed way of picturing the Church. Far from being content to take note of the institutional reality of the Frankish *ecclesia* at the beginning of the ninth century, this new conceptual grid formulated, indeed, a political agenda for the governance of the Church: to bring all men and women who had devoted their life to God to observe a well-identified set of written norms, in order to reform their life. *Correctio* went through written law and written norms.[80]

---

77 Most recently, Barrow, *The Clergy*, pp. 74–75. See also Scholz's contribution in the present volume.
78 Vanderputten, *Dark Age Nunneries*, Chapter 1, and Eber's contribution in the present volume.
79 About ordained monks, see most recently Barrow, *The Clergy*, p. 3 and n. 8.
80 On the importance of written law and more broadly written norms under Charlemagne's reign, cf. McKitterick, *The Carolingians and the Written World*, Chapter 2; McKitterick, *Charlemagne*, Chapter 4.

Choosing to emphasize the norm of life as the discriminating factor between the different orders was no coincidence. The reasons for the growing focus on the lives of clerics in the 780s–820s are well known. On their purity depended the performance of the Church's prayer and of the sacraments. Hence the necessity to make sure that they were free from the stain of sin and above all were chaste.[81] As for those with pastoral duties, starting with the bishops, it was up to them to guide the people on the way of salvation, preaching not only by word but also by example.[82] On their behaviour depended the adoption by the people of Christian morality and behaviour. This was the whole point of *correctio*. In the context of eschatological stress perceptible in the writings of Charlemagne's entourage from the 800s onwards, which emphasized the necessity to prepare for the coming end of the world, the need to exercise control over and to correct the life of clergy, monks, and nuns certainly appeared all the more pressing.[83] This goal was not incompatible with more political motivations, such as the will to strengthen the power of the bishops and the control of the Carolingian rulers over the Church.

That this could be achieved by subjecting every canonical cleric, monk, and woman religious to a precise and unique set of written norms, was, however, not obvious at all. As Albrecht Diem in particular has pointed out, the very idea that monastic life was necessarily guided by a written rule, not to mention a single rule, was by no means self-evident at the end of the eighth century.[84] With a few nuances, the same could be said of a unified normative corpus for the entire canonical clergy. How this idea gradually took hold during the reign of the first Carolingians, and what it meant from the point of view of the history of normative observance will be the subject of a later publication. Let us simply note here that the invention of the *ordo canonicorum* and the recategorization of ecclesiastical *ordines* are inextricably linked to the effort made during Charlemagne's reign to circumscribe, collect, emend, and make available the texts that were to serve as norms of clerical and monastic life.

From the Bonifatian Councils of the 740s onwards, kings and bishops had insisted that every cleric, monk, and woman religious should be subject to a superior and a norm of life.[85] Under Charlemagne, great attention was

---

81 Angenendt, 'Religiosität und Theologie'; Angenendt, 'Missa Specialis'; de Jong, 'Carolingian Monasticism'.
82 McKitterick, *The Frankish Church*; Mériaux, 'Ordre et hiérarchie'.
83 De Jong, 'Charlemagne's Church', p. 105; McKitterick, *The Frankish Church*.
84 Diem, 'Inventing the Holy Rule'; Rousseau and Diem, 'Monastic Rules'.
85 *Concilium germanicum* (742), ed. by Werminghoff, 7, p. 4; *Concilium Liftinense* (743), ed. by Werminghoff, 1, p. 7: 'Et omnis aecclesiastici ordinis clerus, episcopi et presbiteri et diaconi cum clericis, suscipientes antiquorum patrum canones, promiserunt se velle aecclesiastica iura moribus et doctrinis et ministerio recuperare. Abbates et monachi receperunt sancti patris Benedicti regulam ad restaurandum normam regularis vitae'; *Concilium Suessionense* (744), ed. by Werminghoff, 3, p. 34: 'Ut ordo monachorum vel ancillarum Dei secundum regula sancta stabiles permaneant'; *Concilium Vernense* (755), ed. by Boretius, 11, p. 35: 'De illis hominibus, qui se dicunt propter Deum quod se tonsorassent, et modo res

paid by the court to ensuring that everyone had a good knowledge of these norms, which required that they be properly disseminated. Bishops and priests were expected to know the canons and teach them to their inferiors. The same requirement applied to abbots regular and the *Regula Benedicti*. At the same time, the court made a major effort to delimit, collect, and revise the corpus of laws and norms proper to each of the three orders that made up Frankish society. Early in his reign, Charlemagne had acquired a copy of the *Regula Benedicti* from Montecassino and the canonical collection known as the Dionysio-Hadriana from the Pope, both of which were hallowed by the dual authority of the Roman see and the Roman Empire.[86] Several canons of the pontifical collection were published in the *Admonitio generalis*, and some excerpts were also included in subsequent capitularies and council acts.[87]

This endeavour at codification was taken further after the imperial coronation. At the general assembly of October 802, according to the account in the Annals of Lorsch, the emperor had the laws and norms concerning each order read aloud before their representatives, gathered in separate sessions. To the bishops, priests, and deacons, that is to the representatives of the *ordo canonicorum*, he had 'all the canons […] and pontifical decrees' read out, ordering that they be explained to them in detail. Among these texts was undoubtedly the Collectio Dionysio-Hadriana, but possibly also other canonical collections.[88] To the second group, abbots and monks, the *Regula Benedicti* was expounded and then explained by wise men (*sapientes*). In the last session, the emperor brought together the dukes, counts, and other lay representatives in the presence of specialists in law (*legislatores*), who read aloud the laws of the kingdom and explained to each one his own. After discussion, corrections were made wherever it was judged necessary and the amended laws were put in writing.[89] The court's objective was therefore threefold: to

---

eorum vel pecunias habent et nec sub manu episcopi sunt nec in monasterium regulariter vivunt, placuit **ut in monasterio sint sub ordine regulari aut sub manu episcopi sub ordine canonica**; et si aliter fecerint, et correpti ab episcopo suo se emendare noluerint, excommunicentur. Et de ancillis Dei velatis eadem forma servetur'.

86 Semmler, 'Die Beschlüsse des Aachener Konzils'; Wollasch, 'Benedictus Abbas Romensis'; McKitterick, *The Frankish Church*, Chapter 1.
87 For instance in 802, in the *Capitulare missorum generale*, ed. by Boretius, *Capitularia missorum speciale*, ed. by Boretius, and *Capitulare missorum item speciale*, ed. by Boretius.
88 Hartmann, *Die Synoden*, pp. 124–26, and n. 33.
89 *Annales Laureshamenses*, ed. by Pertz, a. 802, p. 39: 'Et mense Octimbrio congregavit universalem synodum in iam nominato loco (*the palace in Aachen*), et ibi fecit episcopos cum presbyteris seu diaconibus relegi universos canones, quas sanctus synoda recepit, et decreta pontificum, et pleniter iussit eos tradi coram omnibus episcopis, presbyteris et diaconibus. Similiter in ipso synodo congregavit universos abbates et monachos qui ibi aderant, et ipsi inter se conventum faciebant, et legerunt regulam sancti patris Benedicti, et eum tradiderunt sapientes in conspectu abbatum et monachorum; et tunc iussio eius generaliter super omnes episcopos, abbates, presbyteros, diacones seu universo clero facta est, ut unusquisque in loco suo iuxta constitutionem sanctorum patrum, sive in episcopatibus seu in monasteriis aut per universas sanctas ecclaesias, ut **canonici** iuxta

delimit a corpus of the texts that were to stand as law or as the official norm for each *ordo* and emend them; to make them known to the representatives of each order (at a time when the degree of knowledge of canon law and the *Regula Benedicti* undoubtedly varied from place to place); and thirdly to clarify their interpretation, through the voice of experts mandated by the court and charged with explaining before each group the ins and outs of these normative corpora.

The assembly of 802 thus constitutes an important stage in the process of reflection on the actual content of *vita canonica* and *vita monastica*. It is not known what practical implications the experts commissioned by the emperor deduced from the exposition of this normative corpus, nor on what points the discussions focused. The narrative emphasizes the court's leading role, but all this was evidently to be discussed and debated during the assembly, whose *raison d'être* it was. One should not imagine that a uniform line emerged concerning the life of *canonici*: some issues which were to be controversial in the following years, such as the generalization of common life or the renunciation of personal property, are likely to have already divided the assembly of 802. In a like manner, Adalard of Corbie and Benedict of Aniane disagreed over the length of the novitiate period during the monastic session, where the practical implications of the *Regula Benedicti* were being discussed.[90]

Only the laws of the kingdom, however, were corrected and put into writing. Bishops and abbots were perhaps too divided to come up with a unified text of general value at that time. Perhaps they judged that the reflection was simply not mature enough. Or perhaps the need for such a text was not felt yet, or this very idea was considered irrelevant and illegitimate by the majority.

The issue of the life of clerics, monks, and women religious was put back on the agenda about ten years later. The impetus came, once again, from the court as shown by two questionnaires drawn up in 811, probably in view of a future assembly.[91] With ferocious irony, Charlemagne directly addresses bishops and abbots, requesting them to enlighten him on several points. What, in their opinion, is and should be the life of bishops, abbots, and monks, and what still needs to be corrected on this point? What are the sacred texts that

---

canones viverent, et quicquid in clero aut in populo de culpis aut de negligentiis apparuerit, iuxta canonum auctoritate emendassent; et quicquid in monasteriis seu in monachis contra regula sancti Benedicti factum fuisset, hoc ipsud iuxta ipsam regulam sancti Benedicti emendare fecissent. Sed et ipse imperator, interim quod ipsum synodum factum est, congregavit duces, comites et reliquo christiano populo cum legislatoribus, et fecit omnes leges in regno suo legi, et tradi unicuique homini legem suam, et emendare ubicumque necesse fuit, et emendatum legem scribere, et ut iudices per scriptum iudicassent, et munera non accepissent; sed omnes homines, pauperes et divites, in regno suo iustitiam habuissent'.

90 Semmler, 'Reichsidee und kirchliche Gesetzgebung', p. 64.
91 *Capitula tractanda cum comitibus, episcopis et abbatibus* (811), ed. by Boretius, 9–13, pp. 161–62; *Capitula de causis cum episcopis et abbatibus tractandis* (811), ed. by Boretius, pp. 162–64. On these, cf. Ganshof, 'Note sur les "capitula" de 811'; Nelson, 'The Voice of Charlemagne'.

they should know and teach, including by their own conduct? And above all, what exactly does it mean to them to renounce the world? Would it be limited to not carrying arms and not being married, at least not publicly? The emperor also asks to be informed of the rules by which monks lived in Gaul before the *Regula Benedicti* was introduced and to reflect on the rule(s) of life of the nuns. Apart from their ironic charge, both questionnaires indicate that the emperor and his inner circle intended to reactivate and deepen reflection on the *vita canonica* and *monastica* and their practical meanings, involving bishops and abbots. Two major directions seem to have been contemplated by the court. Firstly, the identification of the texts, sacred or not, which were to serve as norms for clerical and monastic life was to be pursued. And secondly, emphasis was to be placed on the life of bishops and abbots, because it was up to them to teach all those who were subject to them, not only by voice but also by example.

The issues raised in 811 were submitted, among others, to the five regional councils convened by Charlemagne in the spring of 813. These assemblies were to serve as a large chamber of consultation for further *correctio* of the Empire and Church.[92] At the request of the court, the prelates who were gathered in Mainz, Rheims, Chalon, Arles, and Tours formulated prescriptions regarding the life of canonical clerics, some of which were taken up and generalized in 816. They also endeavoured to refine the list of the texts which were to be known and serve as a guide for bishops, abbots, and clerics, both in the fulfilment of their office and in their way of life, thus pursuing the process of collecting and sorting out the old norms initiated at the beginning of the reign.[93] In Rheims, Mainz, and Tours a set of texts were read and commented upon, namely the Gospel, the Acts of the Apostles, and the Letters of Saint Paul; the *sancti canones* to make sure that 'no one among the canonical clerics ignored the law governing his life'; the *Regula Benedicti* to remind the less learned abbots of its content; and Gregory the Great's *Regula pastoralis* so that bishops could 'understand how they should live themselves and how they should admonish their subjects'.[94] In Chalon and Tours, it was recommended that bishops should study assiduously the *scripturas canonicae* (i.e. the Gospels and letters of Paul), their exegesis by the Fathers and, again, the canons and Gregory's *Regula Pastoralis* and that they live and preach according to this

---

[92] Hartmann, *Konziliengeschichte*, p. 132; Kramer, *Rethinking Authority*, pp. 70–91.
[93] Ganshof, 'Note sur les "capitula" de 811'.
[94] *Concilium Remense*, ed. by Werminghoff, 3–11, pp. 254–55 (especially 8, p. 254: 'Lecti sunt sancti canones, ut quisque canonicus legem vitamque suam minime ignoraret, quod omnimodis non expedit, sicut in decretali legitur Innocentii'; and 10, p. 254: 'Lectae sunt sententiae libri pastoralis beati Gregorii, ut pastores eclesiae intellegerent, quomodo ipsi vivere et qualiter sibi subiectos deberent ammonere'); *Concilium Moguntinense*, ed. by Werminghoff, Prologue, pp. 259–60; *Concilium Turonense*, ed. by Werminghoff, 1–3, pp. 286–87.

model.[95] All these texts were intended to guide the life of clerics and their superiors, albeit in two different ways: as a source of teaching, therefore as a model, for some and as a binding norm in the strict sense for others. And several of them provided copious excerpts to the *Institutio canonicorum* three years later.[96] Written norms were however not the only point of reference in terms of ecclesiastical discipline: superiors were to embody the norm and to be themselves 'norma vivendi' for those subject to them as reminded in Chalon.[97] As for abbots and monks, according to the acts of the same council, almost all of them followed the *Regula Benedicti* in this part of the realm, which was a good thing since it explained in all points how they should live.[98]

Una regula, una institutio

Let us go back the *Institutio canonicorum* (*IC*) and its prologue. According to the account it gives of the assembly, Louis the Pious had entrusted the sacred council with the mission of extracting from the conciliar legislation and the writings of the holy fathers (the patristic corpus) the essence of canonical regulation concerning the life of clerics. They were to bring it all together in a concise text which would 'show the life of the prelates and their inferiors' and instruct them in how they should live, in other words a text which would constitute a norm of life for the canonical clerics.[99] To this anthology, which constitutes three quarters of the text (113 chapters), the council added, probably at the request of the court, thirty-one chapters providing a practical regulation for the organization of communities of canonical clerics, most of them written for the occasion (*c.* 114 to 144). As for the 145th and last chapter,

---

95 *Concilium Cabillonense*, ed. by Werminghoff, 1, p. 274: 'et secundum formam ibidem constitutam et vivant et praedicent'; *Concilium Turonense*, ed. by Werminghoff, 2, 3, p. 287.
96 This is the case, for example, of Gregory the Great's *Regula pastoralis*. On the sources of the *IC*, cf. van Waesberghe, *De Akense regels*, c. 3.
97 *Concilium Cabillonense*, ed. by Werminghoff, 2, p. 274: 'Et sint subditis norma vivendi, ita videlicet ut et verbis et exemplis populo ad aeternam patriam pergenti ducatum praebant', and 37, p. 281.
98 *Concilium Cabillonense*, ed. by Werminghoff, 22, p. 278. See also *Concilium Turonense*, ed. by Werminghoff, 25, p. 290.
99 *IC*, ed. by Werminghoff, Prologue, p. 312: 'aliquam ex eisdem sacris canonibus et sanctorum patrum dictis institutionis formam (excerpere), per quam patenter praelatorum et subditorum vita monstraretur'; *IC*, ed. by Werminghoff, 145, p. 419: 'qualiter clerici vivere debeant [...] ut [...] discant quid illis agendum quidve vitandum sit'; *IC*, ed. by Werminghoff, Prologue, p. 313: 'hanc institutionis formam excerperent et canonicis observandam conferrent, ut, quorum forte labore ob tarditatem ingenii seu inopiam librorum sparsim digesta difficile conprehendi posset, sollerti studio in eodem opere breviter congesta perfacile ab his repperiri posset, per quam, ut premissum est, et prelati recto tramite incedere et subditis normam vivendi absque ignorantiae obstaculo salubriter nossent praebere'.

entitled '*Epilogus breviter digestus*', it was intended to summarize briefly the whole, including the first part, for the simple and the less capable.

In 818/19, the emperor promulgated the observance of the *IC* by a capitulary, in the following words:

> Inasmuch as the canonical profession was dishonoured by many, partly through ignorance, partly through laziness, we have found it necessary, with the help of God, to gather together in one rule (***regula***) for the *canonici* and the *canonicae* certain sayings of the Holy Fathers, picked like some blossoming flowers in various meadows, and to give it to the *canonici* and the *sanctimoniales* to observe, so that through it the canonical regulation may be applied without ambiguity. And since the Holy Council has approved it with great praise and hence judged that it should be observed in every detail, we decree that it be clearly respected by all who live in this order and henceforth observed in all points by the *canonici* and *sanctimoniales* who live according to the canons.[100]

The drafting of the *IC* and the *IS* in 816 must therefore be interpreted as the culmination of the efforts made during Charlemagne's reign to circumscribe and redefine at once the ecclesiastical *ordines*, their norms of life in the broadest sense, and the written texts which were to regulate them. The elaboration of the *ordo canonicorum*, as a juridical category, is therefore to be understood as the product of the articulation, in the second half of the eighth century, of two principles:

1. The completion of a Christian society presupposed that each individual should live according to Christian principles and that each particular group (*ordo*) composing the *ecclesia* should respect the norms of life proper to its state, beginning with the clergy, who were to set an example for the rest of society.
2. This presupposed that the groups in question were clearly identified and delimited, as well as the norms of life and duties proper to each of them.

That is how society would be put in order(s) and hence corrected.

Subjecting every man and woman within the Church to one single norm of life was not the necessary outcome of this programme. And maybe was it not even the original plan. But, as it turned out, in 816–19,

---

100 *Capitulare ecclesiasticum* (818–19), ed. by Boretius, 3, p. 276: 'Quia vero canonica professio a multis partim ignorantia partim desidia dehonestabatur, operae pretium duximus, Deo annuente, apud sacrum conventum ut ex dictis sanctorum patrum, velut ex diversis pratis quosdam vernantes flosculos carpendo, in **unam regulam canonicorum et canonicarum congerere** et canonicis vel sanctimonialibus servandam contradere, ut per eam canonicus ordo absque ambiguitate possit servari. Et quoniam illam sacer conventus ita etiam laudibus extulit, ut usque ad unum iota observandam percenseret, statuimus ut ab omnibus in eadem professione degentibus indubitanter teneatur et modis omnibus sive a canonicis sive a sanctimonialibus canonice degentibus deinceps observetur'.

the *Regula Benedicti* was amended and promulgated as the single rule for monks and 'monastic nuns', while a single norm of life was composed and promulgated for the whole non-monastic clergy and 'canonical nuns': *una regula/una institutio*.

Fifteen years after the 'national' laws had been reviewed and emended (798–802/03), canonical and monastic orders were thus in turn offered a unified normative corpus. The extremely innovative nature of this proposal must be underlined: for the first time in the history of the Church and canon law a central power proposed to subject all clergy to a unified written rule of life. This unprecedented attempt at standardization is a small revolution which completes thirty or forty years of reflection on clerical and monastic orders and way of life.

There should be no misunderstanding as to what *regula*, to quote the designation used in the 818–19 capitular, means in this case. The last thirty-one chapters do provide a practical regulation for the internal organization of clerical communities, corresponding to the traditional (and partly erroneous) image one usually has of a rule. But this text is much more than that, and in this sense it is a continuation of old monastic norms.[101] A hybrid text, the *IC* is at the same time a *speculum episcoporum* (and more broadly a mirror for all superiors — *praepositi* — within the Church);[102] a treatise on vices and virtues (and, as such, an ethical programme for the whole clergy);[103] and an official handbook for the instruction of the clergy and future clerics. This last dimension is explicitly stated by the text, which was to be read aloud daily during the chapter, and by each cleric individually. Those who were not capable of doing so were to have it read aloud to them by someone else, and its 145th and final chapter had to be learned by heart by every canonical cleric.[104] In the minds of its authors, the *IC* was therefore intended to serve very concretely as a support for the instruction of clerics, from superiors to the youngest and the intellectually less well-endowed, by giving them knowledge of the essence of their life and missions.[105] It is probably not by chance, besides, that the text is designated in its prologue as an *institutio* (and not a *regula*): the authors were playing on the two meanings of *institutio*, 'rule' and 'instruction'. The insistence on the ethical dimension of the life of clerics, on the other hand, responded to the primary objective of the *IC*: to re-establish ecclesiastical discipline and raise the moral level of the *canonici* by providing them with a compendium of Christian ethics, which was to guide all their actions. As for the large number of chapters devoted to the bishops and other superiors, this is no surprise since these were to be living norms for those subject to them

---

101 Rousseau and Diem, 'Monastic Rules'.
102 Kramer, *Rethinking Authority*, pp. 96–106.
103 See also on this idea the chapter by Eber in this same volume.
104 *IC*, ed. by Werminghoff, 145, pp. 419–21.
105 Kramer, *Rethinking Authority*, pp. 94–96.

and for their flock. *Correctio* would take place by capillary action. Therefore, it was crucial that superiors be taught how to lead an irreproachable life, but also how to teach others, in turn, moral perfection and the body of knowledge required for the proper exercise of their office. Hence why the superior had to be a good connoisseur of Scriptures, doctrine, and canons, and should continuously train himself by reading the appropriate texts.[106]

Of a hybrid nature, this written norm of life was addressed as much to bishops as to young clerics in training, and was to be used by both the most learned and the less well accomplished. It was thus intended to be observed by all non-monastic clergy, but not in an absolutely uniform manner. Its authors themselves probably did not expect every *canonicus* in the empire to follow the text they had drafted to the letter, and the same has been argued for the *IS*.[107] This is particularly true for the practical regulation provided at the end of the text. Designed for a relatively large community, prescribing common life behind the walls of an enclosure, a common dormitory for the brothers, the singing of the seven offices of the hours, the presence of a school, it was perfectly adapted for a cathedral chapter. On the other hand, it is hard to see how it could have been applied in every detail in a small rural church. But the same was true, after all, for the *Regula Benedicti*: no one could expect it to be followed in the same way in a monastery of several hundred monks and in a small *cella*. The very nature of these rules for life was that they could be adapted to a certain extent to local conditions, and this was not contradictory with the demand for their generalized observance. The *IC* suggests it itself. Its prologue testifies to the fact that its promoters expected the new rule to be observed in all respects by every member of the canonical profession, 'as far as their strength would allow', which left de facto a certain margin of interpretation.[108] 'Nemo potest ad impossibile obligari', as stated the well-known legal maxim.[109] Regarding the food and drink to be distributed to the members of the congregation (the *stipendia*), the rule itself envisages variable rations according to local possibilities. Churches are classified into three groups, according to the amount of land they own and the rations calculated accordingly. Chapter 122 also specifies that in areas where wine is not produced, it will be replaced by beer.[110]

---

106 *IC*, ed. by Werminghoff, 9, 11, 12, 14, 16, 20, 23, 24, pp. 322–26, 328–30, 330–36, 338–40, 341, 343, 344–47.

107 Schilp, 'Die Wirkung der Aachener "Institutio Sanctimonialium"'.

108 *IC*, ed. by Werminghoff, Prologue, p. 313: 'statutum est ab omnibus, qui in canonica professione Domino militant, hanc institutionis formam […] **iuxta virium possibilitatem** modis omnibus observandam'.

109 Coined by a Roman jurist of the first century, Celsus, and known in several variants, this maxim is notably integrated in Justinian's *Digest* and in the *Corpus iuris canonici* in the thirteenth century (it constitutes the sixth *regula iuris* promulgated by Boniface VIII in 1298). Cf. Zimmermann, *The Law of Obligations*; Zorzetto, 'Thinking of Impossibility'.

110 *IC*, ed. by Werminghoff, 122, p. 401. On the issue of land fortunes assessment in the ninth century, cf. Devroey, *Puissants et misérables*, p. 438.

As others have argued recently, the aim was therefore not to uniformize at all costs the way of life of all clergy and the internal organization of every church and sanctuary served by canonical clerics.[111] This ambition would have been utopian in any case. The *IC* as a whole was primarily addressed to the bishops and their clerics, that is those of the *ecclesia mater* (the future cathedral). The provisions contained in its last thirty-one chapters were obviously intended to be adopted in those monasteries or collegiate churches opting for the *vita canonica* and in 'cathedral' churches. The latter even constituted a priority in the eyes of the high clergy and the court, which repeatedly demanded that bishops take the necessary steps to ensure that the institutional model drawn up in 816 was rapidly implemented in their own church.[112] Nevertheless, like the *Regula Benedicti*, the *IC* was now supposed to constitute a universal reference and, although with adaptations and compromises, to be adopted also in smaller churches, those *minora loca* mentioned in Chapter 122, for instance, which did not have a large patrimony, but sufficient to maintain a small community of clerics. This probably included modest basilicas dedicated to the veneration of some saint's relics as well as rather important parish churches served by a college of clerics headed by a priest or an archpriest (the superior), as could be found in market towns but sometimes also in more rural areas. Even rural priests serving smaller churches could theoretically observe, to a certain extent, the *vita canonica* as described in the norm of 816 with their household and/or the young clerics in formation at their side. And they were probably expected to do so by the sponsors of the text, and some other members of the higher clergy. Let's not forget either that even these modest rural churches were often served by a small group of clerics.[113]

Thus, even if the *IC* could not be followed everywhere to the letter, it nonetheless set an ideal, a horizon towards which the entire clergy were to strive, along with a reflection on what constituted its DNA, beyond differences. If canonical clerics defined themselves by their way and norm of life, then the norm's compendium drafted in 816 had to state explicitly what defined or should define them and what distinguished them from the other *ordines*. In this sense, the *IC* is in itself a rethinking of the ecclesiastical *ordines*, or one more step in that process. It formulates answers and proposals on several aspects already debated in the preceding years: the role of the superior, the relationship to property, the missions of the clergy, what separated them from monks and laity. I shall confine myself, in conclusion, to discussing two of these proposals, absolutely central though in terms of clerical identity.

---

111 Patzold, 'Prozesse der Vereinheitlichung?'; Kramer, *Rethinking Authority*.
112 *Concilium Turonense* (813), ed. by Werminghoff, 23, pp. 288–89; *Capitulare missorum* (819), ed. by Boretius, 7, p. 289; *Concilium Meldense-Parisiense* (845–46), ed. by Boretius and Krause, 53, p. 393.
113 Barrow, *The Clergy*, p. 270.

Divine Office and Common Life: Two Distinctive Features of the Canonical Clergy

First of all, the text presents the celebration of the Divine Office as the primary mission of the clergy, thus participating in defining its social function. Ten chapters are directly dedicated to the Office in the second part of the rule, the 145th chapter recalling that clerics 'are set aside for divine worship and as an exemplary model of virtue for others'.[114] *Canonici* are enjoined to devote themselves assiduously to the chant of the seven Offices of the Hours, and 'to implore, by their common praise, the forgiveness of God for their own sins and those of the people on whose offerings they live'. Following the words of the Apostle (Paul), they are to make, first and foremost, supplications, prayers, intercessions, and thanksgivings for all men, for kings, and for those in high station, so that 'we may live a quiet and peaceable life in all piety and chastity'.[115]

The clergy's social function within the *ecclesia* is thus clearly defined: maintained by the faithful, they are expected, in return, to intercede for everyone's salvation and for the good of the kingdom through continuous praise, complying with the celebration of the Liturgy of the Hours. Public prayer was not the prerogative of monks. Nor was it the prerogative of one specific type of cleric ('canons' as opposed to 'secular' clerics, themselves supposedly devoted to parochial duties in the world following the classical view).[116] This was not a novelty, but an essential reminder: the Divine Office, conceived as the prayer of the Church as an institution, was an obligation for all *canonici*, and even their main duty, as Visigothic and Merovingian councils of the fifth to seventh centuries already recalled regularly.[117] Every church and every canonical cleric as an individual had to take part (although not necessarily every day or for the complete cursus where conditions did not permit, i.e. in small churches).[118] The *IC* is not the only document formulating this requirement. In the 800s, Gherbald of Liège ordered the priests of his diocese

---

114 *IC*, ed. by Werminghoff, 126–33, pp. 406–09, 136, pp. 413–14, 137, p. 414, and 145, p. 419: 'Si igitur ab omnibus fidelibus his salutiferis praeceptis totis nisibus est favendum, quanto magis ab his, qui divinis cultibus mancipati sunt et aliis exemplo virtutum condimentum esse debent'.

115 *IC*, ed. by Werminghoff, 131, p. 408: 'laudes Deo in commune persolventes pro suis populorumque, quorum oblationibus vivunt, delictis Dominum exorent. Debent quoque iuxta apostolum "primo omnium ab his fieri obsecrationes, orationes, postulationes, gratiarum actiones pro omnibus hominibus, pro regibus et omnibus, qui in sublimate sunt constituti, ut quiaetam et tranquillam vitam agamus in omni piaetate et castitate"'. The quotation is from Paul, I Timothy 2. 1–3.

116 As suggested by Dereine, 'Chanoines'.

117 Billett, *The Divine Office*. See also the chapters of the last section of the present volume.

118 It seems that even in large communities such as cathedral chapters, it was common for the clerics to take turns in celebrating the Office, on a weekly basis. Cf. Kurdziel, 'Les formes de la vie commune'.

to sing the canonical hours, day and night, and to celebrate the Office.[119] In 813, the Council of Mainz suggested to extend this obligation to every priest within the empire.[120] Another contemporary document, in the form of an admonition to priests, ordered them to have pupils at their side, whom they would feed and instruct, so that if they were unable to re-join their church in time for the celebration of the Offices of terce, sext, none, and vespers, the *scholarii* in question could replace them.[121] The other duties of the clergy were addressed only incidentally in the *IC*, or left aside, including pastoral work and for good reason: not all clerics were in charge of souls after all.

The second proposal I would like to highlight here was much more innovative. By regulating, in the second part of the text, life in the *claustrum* without ever suggesting that this regulation concerned only a part of the canonical clergy, the *IC* suggested nothing other than to make common life the normal way of life for all clergy — although the term itself is hardly at all used in the text.[122] Life in common is indeed quite simply presented, right up to the 145th Chapter, as the norm (and hence its absence as the exception), in a very conscious attempt to generalize this way of life.

Admittedly, the practice of the common life among the clergy was in itself nothing new. Inspired by the apostolic community described in the Acts of the Apostles, it included such prestigious models as the communities established in their respective churches by Augustine in Hippo, Eusebius in Vercelli, and Gregory the Great in Rome. In the Frankish realm, indications of communal life have been observed in several episcopal churches and basilicas from the sixth century onwards.[123] And since the beginning of the eighth century, common life had been the object of new institutional experiments in the bishoprics instituted on the northern and eastern fronts of Christian expansion, under the influence of Anglo-Saxon missionaries, but also in Metz under Chrodegang and

---

119 Gherbald of Liège's, *Erstes Kapitular*, ed. by Brommer, 2, 7, 8, pp. 17–18.
120 *Concilium Moguntinense* (813), ed. by Werminghoff, 28, p. 268: 'Ut presbyteri utantur assidue orariis. Presbyteri sine intermissione utantur orariis propter differentiam sacerdotii dignitatis'.
121 'Quinto, ut ipsi presbyteri tales scholarios habeant, id est ita nutritos et insinuatos, ut si forte eis contingat non posse occurrere tempore competenti ad ecclesiam suam officii gratia persolvendi, id est tertiam, sextam, nonam et vesperas, ipsi scholarii et signum in tempore suo pulsent et officium honeste Deo persolvant'. (*Capitulare de presbyteris admonendis*, 809?, ed. by Boretius, 5, p. 238).
122 Barrow, 'Le terme "réforme"', underlines that the term only appears in the Augustine quotations of the first part of the *IC*, the florilegium.
123 Josef Semmler, for instance, spotted indications of communal life in Metz, Strasbourg, Paris, Autun, Lausanne, Saintes, Cahors, Uzès at the end of the eighth century; in Auxerre, Le Mans, Hildesheim before 816, according to narrative sources; and in Würzburg, Tournai, Nevers, Saint-Etienne, Dijon, and Mâcon. Cf. Semmler, 'Die Kanoniker und ihre Regel'. See also the earlier examples mentioned by Godding, *Prêtres*; Noizet, 'Les basiliques martyriales'; Dereine, 'Chanoines'; and Barrow, *The Clergy*, p. 285.

Lyon under Leidrad, in both cases with the support of Carolingian rulers.[124] The *IC* presumably drew on these recent local experiments, which its authors aimed to institutionalize and systematize on a wider scale. In this case, norms would have been formulated on the basis of local practices.

These blooming trees should not, however, hide the forest. We have no idea of the proportion of churches where clerics were actually living in community, and there is nothing to say that it constituted an obligation for all those serving the churches in question. Communal life could, besides, take various forms. It could be limited to sharing meals. It could also be intermittent (restricted for example to key periods of the liturgical year).[125] All things considered, life in common as envisaged by the *IC* may have existed in some places, and it certainly constituted an ideal in the eye of certain circles, but the impression emerging from the sources is rather that it remained most of the time a mere possibility, without any obligatory character (except maybe for the superior?), offered in particular to the poorest, the youngest, and those who aspired to a more ascetic life.[126] Frankish councils never made it an obligation.[127] The existence of a clerical community around the bishop, or in some other churches is sometimes assumed, at times encouraged, but never required.[128] Even in 813, such a requirement had nothing obvious: only two of the five regional councils spoke in favour of the institutionalization of common life, in one case limiting it to episcopal churches ('cathedrals') and monasteries of *canonici*.[129] If the measure had

---

124 Semmler, 'Mönche und Kanoniker'; Coville, *Recherches sur l'histoire de Lyon*, pp. 237–38; Claussen, *Chrodegang*.
125 Kurdziel, 'Les formes de la vie commune'.
126 Dereine, 'Chanoines'; Claussen, *Chrodegang*; Godding, *Prêtres*, pp. 223–27; Noizet, 'Les basiliques martyriales'. Contra: Pietri, *La ville de Tours*, p. 685; Pietri, 'Les abbés de basilique', who thinks that common life at the *episcopium* was the rule, and clerics not following it an exception.
127 The councils of the sixth and seventh centuries seem to be only concerned that bishops and other church superiors always be accompanied by at least one cleric who would guarantee their good morality (cf. the third chapter of the 567 council of Tours, *Concilium Turonense*, ed. by De Clercq, 3, p. 180, which is also the only known Frankish council of the sixth–seventh century evoking common life at the cathedral).
128 Visigothic councils had gone a little further, prescribing that clerics should be surrounded with brothers able to bear witness to their lives. A form of common life was therefore encouraged, both for bishops in their *domus* and for married clerics who lived in their own houses: the latter were supposed to welcome one or more of their co-religionists in their home to act as guarantors of the purity of their existence. Cf. councils of Gerona (a. 517), 6 and 7, p. 2; Toledo III (a. 589), 5, p. 21; Seville I (a. 590), 3, pp. 2–3; Toledo IV (a. 633), 42–44, p. 23; Toledo VIII (a. 653), 5, pp. 20–21, and Braga III (a. 675), 4, p. 7, in *Concilios visigoticos*, ed. by Vivès. The fourth council of Toledo (633) also stipulates that adolescents in formation were to live '*omnes in uno conclavi atrii*', under the care of an older cleric (Toledo IV (a. 633), 22–24, pp. 17–18).
129 *Concilium Turonense*, ed. by Werminghoff, 23, pp. 289: 'Canonici clerici civitatum, qui in episcopiis conversantur, consideravimus, ut in claustris habitantes simul omnes in uno dormitorio dormiant simulque in uno reficiantur refectorio, quo facilius possint ad horas canonicas celebrandas occurrere ac de vita et conversatione sua admoneri et doceri. Victum et vestitum iuxta facultatem episcopi accipiant, ne paupertatis occasione compulsi per diversa

been suggested by the court and its ecclesiastical counsellors, then it had met with some resistance.¹³⁰

The proposal indirectly formulated by the *IC* to generalize common life was therefore not self-evident at all, and was even all the more audacious since the form of life it prescribed was rather ascetic: canonical clerics were supposed to live in a *claustrum*, which they could only leave with the permission of the superior, and to share the refectory and dormitory, on the coenobitic model.¹³¹ No mention is made of the possibility of residing in individual houses within the *claustrum* or even outside it, as in Chrodegang's *Regula canonicorum* (except for the sick).¹³² The new rule of life, albeit with significant nuances, thus aligned the *vita canonica* with the *vita monastica*, imposing on clerics the expectation to adopt, wherever possible, a way of life that approached the life described by coenobitic rules.¹³³

This proposition constituted, undoubtedly, one of the greatest novelties of the norm of life drafted in 816 and implied a real upheaval in practices,

---

vagari ac turpibus se implicare negotiis cogantur dimissoque eclesiastico officio incipiant indisciplinate vivere et propriis deservire voluptatibus'; *Concilium Moguntinense a. 813*, ed. by Werminghoff, 9, p. 262: *De vita canonicorum*. 'Cap. 9. In omnibus igitur, quantum humana permittit fragilitas, decrevimus, ut canonici clerici canonice vivant, […] et ut simul manducent et dormiant, ubi his facultas id faciendi suppetit vel qui de rebus ecclesiasticis stipendia accipiunt, et in suo claustro maneant et singulis diebus mane prima ad lectionem veniant et audiant quid eis imperetur. Ad mensam vero similiter lectionem audiant et oboedientiam secundum canones suis magistris exhibeant'. See also c. 20 of the same Council of Mainz.

130 There are several indications that the suggestion may have come from the court: 1) the rather ascetic orientation of the 811 questionnaires; 2) the letter addressed by Leidrad to Charlemagne in 802, which stipulates that it was encouraged and supported by the court that he had carried out a profound reorganization of his clergy of Lyon, built a cloister where his 52 *canonici* now lived and imposed on his Church the adoption of the liturgical customs of Metz; and 3) the capitular of September 813 edited under the title *Concordia episcoporum*, which suggests that 'what was contained in the imperial capitular and what had been decided by the Council of Mainz' regarding the life of *canonici* be ratified (*Concordia episcoporum*, ed. by Werminghoff, 6, p. 298: 'De vita vero canonicorum, sicut in capitulare dominico continetur et in conventu Mogontiacensi constitutum est, observandum statuimus'). This document, drafted at the general assembly of September 813, was intended to synthesize the measures proposed by the five regional councils in the spring. The mention of a *capitulare dominicus* tends to indicate the existence of a working document, formulating propositions, provided by the court to these assemblies. De Clercq, *La législation religieuse franque*, I, pp. 248–49.

131 *IC* does however allow canonical clerics some leeway to have their own house, where they can reside or rest when ill (cf. *IC*, ed. by Werminghoff, 142, 143, and 144, pp. 417–18). On the replacement of individual cells by collective dormitories in coenobitic monasticism from the sixth century onwards, cf. Bauer, 'Monasticism after Dark'; Signori, 'Zelle oder Dormitorium?'.

132 Chrodegang, *Regula canonicorum*, ed. by Schmitz, 3, pp. 4–5.

133 On the variety of the actual forms of common life in cathedral chapters, cf. Kurdziel, 'Les formes de la vie commune', and the results of the second meeting of the *Categorizing the Church* programme, held in Poitiers in 2018, which will be published in 2022 in the form of a special issue of the *Cahiers de Civilisation Médiévale* under the title: *Ordonner l'Église II: Communautés cléricales et communautés monastiques dans le monde carolingien (8ᵉ–10ᵉ s.)*.

not to mention major architectural and even urban planning. Like the prescriptions relating to the Divine Office, it shows that the text had aimed to complete (and in the meantime to relaunch) the rethinking of the ecclesiastical *ordines* begun in the 740s. In this respect, the IC was a much deeper and bolder attempt at reform than is usually thought. Did it constitute a watershed for all that? The story of its effects remains largely to be written.

Works Cited

Manuscripts

Munich, Bayerische Staatsbibliothek, MS Clm 19414
———, Clm 27246
Novara, Archivio Storico Diocesano di Novara, MS LXXI
Venice, Biblioteca Nazionale Marciana, MS Iur. can. 11
Vienna, Österreichische Nationalbibliothek, MS Vindobonensis 751

Primary Sources

Alcuin, *Epistolae*, ed. by Ernst Dümmler, in *Monumenta Germaniae Historica: Epistolae Karolini aevi*, II, *Epistolae*, IV (Berlin: Weidmann, 1895), pp. 1–481

Annales Laureshamenses, ed. by Georg Heinrich Pertz, in *Annales et Chronica Aevi Carolini*, Monumenta Germaniae Historica: Scriptores, I (Hannover: Hahn, 1826), pp. 22–39

Die Admonitio generalis Karls des Großen, ed. by Hubert Mordek (†), Klaus Zechiel-Eckes (†), and Michael Glatthaar, in *Monumenta Germaniae Historica: Fontes iuris Germanici antiqui in usum scholarum separatim editi (Fontes iuris)*, XVI (Hannover: Hahn, 2012)

Astronomus, *Vita Hludowici Imperatoris*, ed. by Ernst Tremp, in *Monumenta Germaniae Historica: Scriptores rerum Germanicarum in usum scholarum separatim editi*, LXIV (Hannover: Hahn, 1995, pp. 279–558)

Boniface of Mainz, *Epistolae*, ed. by Ernst Dümmler, in *Monumenta Germaniae Historica: Epistolae*, III, *Epistolae Merowingici et Karolini aevi*, I (Berlin: Weidmann, 1892), pp. 215–433

Capitula de causis cum episcopis et abbatibus tractanda (811), ed. by Alfred Boretius, in *Monumenta Germaniae Historica: Capitularia Regum Francorum*, I (Hannover: Hahn, 1883), no. 63, pp. 162–64

Capitula de examinandis ecclesiasticis (oct. 802?), ed. by Alfred Boretius, in *Monumenta Germaniae Historica: Capitularia regum Francorum*, I (Hannover: Hahn, 1883), pp. 109–11

Capitula e canonibus excerpta a. 813, ed. by Alfred Boretius, *Monumenta Germaniae Historica: Capitularia regum Francorum*, I (Hannover: Hahn, 1883), no. 78, pp. 173–75

Capitula originis incertae 813 vel post, ed. by Alfred Boretius, in *Monumenta Germaniae Historica: Capitularia Regum Francorum*, I (Hannover: Hahn, 1883), no. 79, p. 175

Capitula Tractanda cum comitibus, episcopis et abbatibus 811, ed. by Alfred Boretius, in *Monumenta Germaniae Historica: Capitularia Regum Francorum*, I (Hannover: Hahn, 1883), no. 62, pp. 161–62

Capitulare cum episcopis langobardicis deliberatum (c. 782), ed. and trans. by Claudio Azzara and Pierandrea Moro, in *I capitolari italici: Storia e diritto della dominazione carolingia in Italia*, Altomedioevo, 1 (Rome: Viella, 1998), pp. 56–59; ed. by Alfred Boretius, in *Monumenta Germaniae Historica: Capitularia regum Francorum*, I (Hannover: Hahn, 1883), no. 89, pp. 188–89

Capitulare de presbyteris admonendis (809?), ed. by Alfred Boretius, in *Monumenta Germaniae Historica: Capitularia regum Francorum*, I (Hannover: Hahn, 1883), pp. 237–38

Capitulare ecclesiasticum (818–819), ed. by Alfred Boretius, in *Monumenta Germaniae Historica: Capitularia regum Francorum*, I (Hannover: Hahn, 1883), no. 138, pp. 275–80

Capitulare ecclesiasticum Caroli Magni (a. 805–13), ed. by Hubert Mordek and Gerhard Schmitz, 'Neue Kapitularien und Kapitulariensammlungen', *Deutsches Archiv Für Erforschung des Mittelalters*, 43 (1987), 361–439, 396–414

Capitulare episcoporum (780?), ed. by Alfred Boretius, in *Monumenta Germaniae Historica: Capitularia regum Francorum*, I (Hannover: Hahn, 1883), no. 21, p. 52

Capitulare missorum a. 819, ed. by Alfred Boretius, in *Monumenta Germaniae Historica: Capitularia Regum Francorum*, I (Hannover: Hahn, 1883), no. 141, pp. 288–91

Capitulare missorum generale, 802 initio, ed. by Alfred Boretius, in *Monumenta Germaniae Historica: Capitularia Regum Francorum*, I (Hannover: Hahn, 1883), no. 33, pp. 91–99

Capitulare missorum in Theodonis villa datum primum, mere ecclesiasticum (805 exeunte), ed. by Alfred Boretius, in *Monumenta Germaniae Historica: Capitularia Regum Francorum*, I (Hannover: Hahn, 1883), pp. 121–22

Capitulare missorum item speciale (802?), ed. by Alfred Boretius, in *Monumenta Germaniae Historica: Capitularia Regum Francorum*, I (Hannover: Hahn, 1883), no. 35, pp. 102–04

Chrodegang, *S. Chrodegangi, Metensis episcopi (742–66), regula canonicorum*, ed. by Wilhelm Schmitz (Hannover: Hahn, 1889)

Concilia II. 1, ed. by Albert Werminghoff, in *Monumenta Germaniae Historica: Concilia*, II. 1, *Concilia aevi Karolini*, I (Hannover: Hahn, 1906)

Concilios visigóticos e hispano-romanos, ed. by José Vivès (Barcelona, Madrid: Consejo superior de investigaciones científicas, Instituto Enrique Flórez, 1963)

Concilium Aquisgranense a. 836, ed. by Albert Werminghoff, *Monumenta Germaniae Historica: Concilia*, II. 2, *Concilia aevi Karolini*, II, 819–42 (Hannover: Hahn, 1908), no. 56, 704–67

Concilium Arelatense a. 813, ed. by Albert Werminghoff, in *Monumenta Germaniae Historica: Concilia*, II. 1, *Concilia aevi Karolini*, I (Hannover: Hahn, 1906), no. 34, pp. 248–53

Concilium Aurelianense a. 538, ed. by Charles De Clercq, in *Concilia Galliae: A. 511–A. 695*, Corpus Christianorum Series Latina, 148A (Turnhout: Brepols, 1963), pp. 4–14

Concilium Baiuwaricum, ed. by Albert Werminghoff, in *Monumenta Germaniae Historica: Concilia*, II. 1, *Concilia aevi Karolini*, I (Hannover: Hahn, 1906), no. 31, p. 233

Concilium Cabillonense a. 813, ed. by Albert Werminghoff, in *Monumenta Germaniae Historica: Concilia*, II. 1, *Concilia aevi Karolini*, I (Hannover: Hahn, 1906), no. 37, pp. 273–85

Concilium Claremontanum a. 535, ed. by Charles De Clercq, in *Concilia Galliae: A. 511–A. 695*, Corpus Christianorum Series Latina, 148A (Turnhout: Brepols, 1963), pp. 105–22

Concilium Germanicum a. 742, ed. by Albert Werminghoff, in *Monumenta Germaniae Historica: Concilia*, II. 1, *Concilia aevi Karolini*, I (Hannover: Hahn, 1906), no. 1, pp. 1–4

Concilium Liftinense a. 743, Mart., 1, ed. by Albert Werminghoff, in *Monumenta Germaniae Historica: Concilia*, II. 1, *Concilia aevi Karolini*, I (Hannover: Hahn, 1906), no. 2, pp. 5–7

Concilium Meldense-Parisiense (845–46), ed. by Alfred Boretius and Victor Krause, *Monumenta Germaniae Historica: Capitularia regum Francorum*, II (Hannover: Hahn, 1897), no. 293, pp. 388–421

Concilium Moguntinense a. 813, ed. by Albert Werminghoff, in *Monumenta Germaniae Historica: Concilia*, II. 1, *Concilia aevi Karolini*, I (Hannover: Hahn, 1906), no. 36, pp. 258–73

Concilium Moguntinum (847), ed. by Alfred Boretius and Victor Krause, *Monumenta Germaniae Historica: Capitularia regum Francorum*, II (Hannover: Hahn, 1897), no. 248, pp. 173–84

Concilium Remense a. 813, medio mense Maio, ed. by Albert Werminghoff, in *Monumenta Germaniae Historica: Concilia*, II. 1, *Concilia aevi Karolini*, I (Hannover: Hahn, 1906), no. 35, pp. 253–58

Concilium Suessionense (744), ed. by Albert Werminghoff, in *Monumenta Germaniae Historica: Concilia*, II. 1, *Concilia aevi Karolini*, I (Hannover: Hahn, 1906), no. 4, pp. 33–36

Concilium Turonense a. 567, ed. by Charles De Clercq, in Concilia *Galliae: A. 511–A. 695*, Corpus Christianorum Series Latina, 148A (Turnhout: Brepols, 1963), pp. 176–99

Concilium Turonense a. 813, ed. by Albert Werminghoff, in *Monumenta Germaniae Historica: Concilia*, II. 1, *Concilia aevi Karolini*, I (Hannover: Hahn, 1906), no. 38, pp. 286–93

Concilium Vernense a. 755. Jul. 11, ed. by Alfred Boretius, in *Monumenta Germaniae Historica: Capitularia regum Francorum*, I (Hannover: Hahn, 1883), no. 14, pp. 33–37

Concordia episcoporum, ed. by Albert Werminghoff, in *Monumenta Germaniae Historica: Concilia*, II. 1, *Concilia aevi Karolini*, I (Hannover: Hahn, 1906), pp. 297–301

Discipline générale antique: (IVe-IXe s.). I/2. Les canons des synodes particuliers, ed. by Périclès-Pierre Joannou, Pontificia commissio ad redigendum codicem iuris canonici orientalis, Fonti, 9 (Roma: Tipografia Italo-Orientale 'S. Nilo', 1962)

Episcoporum ad Hludowicum imperatorem relatio (c. 820), ed. by Alfred Boretius, *Monumenta Germaniae Historica: Capitularia regum Francorum*, I (Hannover: Hahn, 1883), no. 178, pp. 366–68

Episcoporum ad imperatorem de rebus ecclesiasticus relatio (post. 821), ed. by Alfred Boretius, *Monumenta Germaniae Historica: Capitularia regum Francorum*, I (Hannover: Hahn, 1883), no. 179, pp. 368–70

Gherbald of Liège, *Erstes Kapitular*, ed. by Peter Brommer, *Monumenta Germaniae Historica: Capitula episcoporum*, 1(Hannover: Hahn, 1984), pp. 3–21

Gregory of Tours, 'Liber vitae patrum', in *Gregorii episcopi Turonensis Miracula et opera minora*, ed. by Bruno Krusch, *Monumenta Germaniae Historica: Scriptores rerum Merovingicarum*, I. 2, Revidierter Nachdruck (Hannover: Hahn, 1969), pp. 211–83

——, 'Libri Historiarum X', in *Gregorii Turonensis Opera*, ed. by Bruno Krusch and Wilhelmus Levison, *Monumenta Germaniae Historica: Scriptores rerum Merovingicarum*, I. 1 (Hannover: Hahn, 1951)

Hludowici prooemium generale ad capitularia tam ecclesiastica quam mundana (818, 819), ed. by Alfred Boretius, in *Monumenta Germaniae Historica: Capitularia regum Francorum*, I (Hannover: Hahn, 1883), no. 137, pp. 273–75

IC = *Institutio canonicorum Aquisgranense*, ed. by Albert Werminghoff, in *Monumenta Germaniae Historica: Concilia*, II. 1, *Concilia aevi Karolini*, I (Hannover: Hahn, 1906), pp. 307–420

IS = *Institutio Sanctimonialium Aquisgranense*, ed. by Albert Werminghoff, in *Monumenta Germaniae Historica: Concilia*, II. 1, *Concilia aevi Karolini*, I (Hannover: Hahn, 1906), pp. 421–56

Interrogationes examinationis (post 803?), ed. by Alfred Boretius, in *Monumenta Germaniae Historica: Capitularia regum Francorum*, I (Hannover: Hahn, 1883), no. 116, pp. 235–36

Isidore of Seville, *Sancti Isidori Episcopi Hispalensis De Ecclesiasticis Officiis*, ed. by Christopher Lawson, Corpus Christianorum Series Latina, 113 (Turnhout: Brepols, 1989)

Missi cuiusdam admonitio (801–812), ed. by Alfred Boretius, in *Monumenta Germaniae Historica: Capitularia regum Francorum*, I (Hannover: Hahn, 1883), no. 121, pp. 238–40

Pippini Italiae regis capitulare (c. 782), ed. and trans. by Claudio Azzara and Pierandrea Moro, in *I capitolari italici: Storia e diritto della dominazione carolingia in Italia*, Altomedioevo, 1 (Rome: Viella, 1998), pp. 64–67; ed. by Alfred Boretius, in *Monumenta Germaniae Historica: Capitularia regum Francorum*, I (Hannover: Hahn, 1883), no. 91, pp. 191–93

Statuta Rhispacensia Frisigensia Salisburgensia (799–800), ed. by Alfred Boretius, in *Monumenta Germaniae Historica: Capitularia regum Francorum*, I (Hannover: Hahn, 1883), no. 112, pp. 226–30

Secondary Works

Agamben, Giorgio, *De la très haute pauvreté: règles et forme de vie. Homo Sacer IV, 1*, trans. by Joël Gayraud (Paris: Payot & Rivages, 2011)

Angenendt, Arnold, 'Religiosität und Theologie: Ein spannungsreiches Verhältnis im Mittelalter', *Archiv für Liturgiewissenschaft*, 20.21 (1978), 28–55

——, 'Missa Specialis: Zugleich ein Beitrag zur Entstehung der Privatmessen', *Frühmittelalterliche Studien*, 17 (1983), 153–221

Auge, Oliver, and Sönke Lorenz, eds, *Die Stiftskirche in Südwestdeutschland: Aufgaben und Perspektiven der Forschung. Erste wissenschaftliche Fachtagung zum Stiftskirchenprojekt des Instituts für Geschichtliche Landeskunde und Historische Hilfswissenschaften der Universität Tübingen (17.–19. März 2000, Weingarten)*, Schriften zur südwestdeutschen Landeskunde, 35 (Leinfelden-Echterdingen: DRW, 2003)

Barrow, Julia, 'Ideas and Applications of Reform', in *Early Medieval Christianities, c. 600–c. 1100*, ed. by Thomas F. X. Noble and Julia M. H. Smith, The Cambridge History of Christianity, vol. 3 (Cambridge: Cambridge University Press, 2008), pp. 345–62

——, *The Clergy in the Medieval World: Secular Clerics, their Families and Careers in North-Western Europe, c. 800–c. 1200* (Cambridge: Cambridge University Press, 2015)

——, 'Le terme "réforme" est-il adapté pour décrire les changements qui s'opèrent dans les communautés cléricales entre le IXe et le Xe siècle?', in *Ordonner l'Église II: Communautés cléricales et communautés monastiques dans le monde carolingien (8e–10e s.)*, special issue of the *Cahiers de Civilisation Médiévale*, ed. by Emilie Kurdziel, forthcoming

Bauer, Nancy, 'Monasticism after Dark: From Dormitory to Cell', *The American Benedictine Review*, 105.1 (1987), 95–114

Billett, Jesse, *The Divine Office in Anglo-Saxon England, 597–c. 1000*, Henry Bradshaw Society Subsidia, 7 (London: Boydell, 2014)

Boshof, Egon, *Ludwig der Fromme* (Darmstadt: Primus, 1996)

Claussen, Martin, *The Reform of the Frankish Church: Chrodegang of Metz and the 'Regula Canonicorum' in the Eighth Century*, Cambridge Studies in Medieval Life and Thought, 1 (Cambridge: Cambridge University Press, 2004)

Coccia, Emanuele, 'Regula et vita: Il diritto monastico e la regola francescana', *Medioevo e rinascimento*, 20, n.s., 17 (2006), 97–147

Congar, Yves, *La tradition et les traditions*, I (Paris: Fayard, 1960)

Contreni, John, 'The Carolingian Renaissance', in *The New Cambridge Medieval History*, vol. 2: *c. 700–c. 900*, ed. by Rosamond McKitterick (Cambridge: Cambridge University Press, 1995), pp. 709–57

Coville, Alfred, *Recherches sur l'histoire de Lyon du Vème siècle au IXème siècle (450–800)* (Paris: Picard, 1928)

Cubitt, Catherine, *Anglo-Saxon Church Councils: c. 650–c. 850*, Studies in the Early History of Britain Series (London: Leicester University Press, 1995)

De Clercq, Charles, *La législation religieuse franque de Clovis à Charlemagne*, vol. 1: *Étude sur les actes de conciles et les capitulaires, les statuts diocésains et les règles monastiques (507–814)* (Louvain: Bureau du Recueil, Bibliothèque de l'Université, 1936)

——, *La législation religieuse franque*, vol. 2: *De Louis le Pieux à la fin du IXe siècle, (814–900)* (Anvers: Centre de recherches historiques, 1958)

Dereine, Charles, 'Chanoines', in *Dictionnaire d'histoire et de Géographie Ecclésiastique* (Paris: Letouzey et Ané, 1953), cols 353–405

Devroey, Jean-Pierre, *Puissants et misérables: système social et monde paysan dans l'Europe des Francs (6e–9e siècles)* (Bruxelles: Palais des académies, 2006)

Diem, Albrecht, 'Inventing the Holy Rule: Some Observations on the History of Monastic Normative Observance in the Early Medieval West', in *Western Monasticism Ante Litteram: The Space of Monastic Observance*, ed. by Hendrick Dey and Elizabeth Fentress, Disciplina Monastica, 7 (Turnhout: Brepols, 2011), pp. 53–84

Gaillard, Michèle, *D'une réforme à l'autre (816–934): les communautés religieuses en Lorraine à l'époque carolingienne*, Publications de la Sorbonne Histoire ancienne et médiévale, 82 (Paris: Publication de la Sorbonne, 2006)

Ganshof, François Louis, *Recherches sur les capitulaires* (Paris: Sirey, 1958)

——, 'Note sur les "Capitula de causis cum episcopis et abbatibus tractandis" de 811', *Studia Gratiana*, 13 (1967), 1–25

Garrison, Mary, 'The English and the Irish at the Court of Charlemagne', in *Karl der Grosse und sein Nachwirken: 1200 Jahre Kultur und Wissenschaft in Europa*, vol. 1: *Wissen und Weltbild*, ed. by Paul Leo Butzer, Max Kerner, and Walter Oberschelp (Turnhout: Brepols, 1997), pp. 97–123

——, 'Letters to a King and Biblical Exempla: The Examples of Cathwulf and Clemens Peregrinus', *Early Medieval Europe*, 7 (1998), 305–28

Gioanni, Stéphane, 'Les listes d'auteurs "à recevoir" et "à ne pas recevoir" dans la formation du canon patristique: le *Decretum Gelasianum* et les origines de la "censure" ecclésiastique', in *Compétition et sacré au Haut Moyen Âge: Entre médiation et exclusion*, ed. by François Bougard, Philippe Depreux, and Regine Le Jan, Collection Haut Moyen Âge, 21 (Turnhout: Brepols, 2015), pp. 17–38

Godding, Robert, *Prêtres en Gaule mérovingienne* (Bruxelles: Soc. des Bollandistes, 2001)

Hartmann, Wilfried, *Die Synoden der Karolingerzeit im Frankenreich und in Italien*, Konziliengeschichte. Reihe A : Darstellungen (Paderborn: Schöningh, 1989)

——, *Kirche und Kirchenrecht um 900: die Bedeutung der spätkarolingischen Zeit für Tradition und Innovation im kirchlichen Recht* (Hannover: Hahn, 2008)

Helvétius, Anne-Marie, and Michel Kaplan, 'Asceticism and its Institutions', in *The Cambridge History of Christianity*, vol. 3: *Early Medieval Christianities, c. 600–c. 1100*, ed. by Thomas F. X. Noble and Julia M. H. Smith, The Cambridge History of Christianity, 3 (Cambridge: Cambridge University Press, 2008), pp. 275–98

Isaïa, Marie-Céline, *Histoire des Carolingiens: VIIIe–Xe siècle* (Paris: Points, 2014)

Jong, Mayke de, 'Carolingian Monasticism: The Power of Prayer', in *The New Cambridge Medieval History*, vol. 2: *c. 700–c. 900*, ed. by Rosamond McKitterick (Cambridge: Cambridge University Press, 1995), pp. 622–53

———, 'Charlemagne's Church', in *Charlemagne: Empire and Society* ed. by Joanna Story (Manchester: Manchester University Press, 2005), pp. 103–35

Kramer, Rutger, *Rethinking Authority in the Carolingian Empire: Ideals and Expectations during the Reign of Louis the Pious (813–828)*, The Early Medieval North Atlantic VI (Amsterdam: Amsterdam University Press, 2019)

Kurdziel, Emilie, 'Les formes de la vie commune dans les chapitres italiens de la première moitié du XIème siècle', in *La vie communautaire et le service à la communauté: l'exemple canonial et ses répercussions dans le monde laïc (Europe Occidentale, du XIe au XVe Siècle)*, ed. by Anne Massoni and Maria Amélia Campos (Évora: Publicações do Cidehus, 2020) <http://books.openedition.org/cidehus/11477>

———, 'Les "chapitres cathédraux italiens" du 9e siècle: quatre profils d'évolution', in *Ordonner l'Église II: Communautés cléricales et communautés monastiques dans le monde carolingien (8e–10e s.)*, special issue of the *Cahiers de Civilisation Médiévale*, ed. by Emilie Kurdziel, forthcoming

Marchal, Guy, 'Was war das weltliche Kanonikerinstitut im Mittelalter? Dom- und Kollegiatstifte: eine Einführung und neue Perspektive', *Revue d'histoire ecclésiastique*, 94 (1999), 761–807

McKitterick, Rosamond, *The Frankish Church and the Carolingian Reforms: 789–895* (London: Royal historical society, 1977)

———, *The Carolingians and the Written Word* (Cambridge: Cambridge University Press, 1989)

———, *Charlemagne: The Formation of a European Identity* (Cambridge: Cambridge University Press, 2011)

Meijns, Brigitte, 'L'ordre canonial dans le comté de Flandre depuis l'époque mérovingienne jusqu'à 1155: Typologie, chronologie et constantes de l'histoire de fondation et de réforme', *Revue d'histoire Ecclésiastique*, 97 (2002), 5–58

Mériaux, Charles, 'Ordre et hiérarchie au sein du clergé rural pendant le Haut Moyen-Âge', in *Hiérachie et stratification sociale dans l'Occident médiéval (400–1100)*, ed. by François Bougard, Dominique Iogna-Prat, and Regine Le Jan, Haut Moyen-Âge, 6 (Turnhout: Brepols, 2008), pp. 117–36

Mordek, Hubert, 'Leges und Kapitularien', in *Die Franken, Wegbereiter Europas: Vor 1500 Jahren; König Chlodwig und seine Erben*, 2 vols (Mainz: Reiss-Museum Mannheim, 1996), pp. 488–98

———, 'Fränkische Kapitularien und Kapitulariensammlungen: Eine Einführung', in *Studien zur Fränkischen Herrschergesetzgebung: Aufsätze über Kapitularien und Kapitulariensammlungen ausgewählt zum 60. Geburtstag*, ed. by Hubert Mordek (Frankfurt am Main: Peter Lang, 2000), pp. 1–53

Munier, Charles, 'Les sources patristiques du droit de l'Église du VIIIe au XIIIe siècle', *Revue de Droit Canonique*, 4 (1954), 184–92

Nelson, Janet, 'The Voice of Charlemagne', in *Courts, Elites, and Gendered Power in the Early Middle Ages*, ed. by Janet Nelson, Variorum Collected Studies Series, 878, Aldershot (London, 2007), pp. 76–88

Niermeyer, Jan Frederik, 'Clericatus', in *Mediae Latinitatis Lexicon minus* (Leiden: Brill, 1976), p. 190

Noble, Thomas F. X., 'The Christian Church', in *The Cambridge History of Christianity*, vol. 3: *Early Medieval Christianities, c. 600–c. 1100*, ed. by Thomas F. X. Noble and Julia M. H. Smith, The Cambridge History of Christianity, 3 (Cambridge: Cambridge University Press, 2008), pp. 249–74

Noizet, Hélène, 'Les basiliques martyriales au VIe et au début du VIIe siècle', *Revue d'Histoire de l'Église de France*, 87 (2001), 329–55

Patzold, Steffen, *Presbyter: Moral, Mobilität und die Kirchenorganisation im Karolingerreich* (Stuttgart: Hiersemann, 2020)

———, 'Prozesse der Vereinheitlichung? *Unitas, concordia* und *pax* in der karolingischen Welt', in *Entscheiden und Regieren: Konsens als Element vormoderner Entscheidungsfindung in transkultureller Perspektive*, ed. by Linda Dohmen and Tilmann Trausch, Macht und Herrschaft 9 (Bonn: Bonn University Press / Vandenhoeck & Ruprecht, 2020), pp. 197–219

Patzold, Steffen, and Carine van Rhijn, eds, *Men in the Middle: Local Priests in Early Medieval Europe*, Ergänzungsbände zum Reallexikon der Germanischen Altertumskunde, 93 (Berlin: De Gruyter, 2016)

Pietri, Luce, 'Les abbés de basilique dans la Gaule du VIe siècle', *Revue d'histoire de l'Église de France*, 69 (1983), 5–28

———, *La ville de Tours du IVe au VIe siècle: naissance d'une cité chrétienne*, Collection de l'EFR, 69 (Rome: École Française de Rome, 1983)

Rousseau, Philip, and Albrecht Diem, 'Monastic Rules (4th–9th c.)', in *The Cambridge History of Medieval Monasticism in the Latin West*, vol. 1: *Origins to the Eleventh Century*, ed. by Isabelle Cochelin and Alison Beach (Cambridge: Cambridge University Press, 2020), pp. 162–94

Salmon, Pierre, *L'office divin: histoire de la formation du bréviaire*, Lex orandi, 27 (Paris: Editions du Cerf, 1959)

Schieffer, Rudolf, *Die Entstehung von Domkapiteln in Deutschland*, Bonner Historische Forschungen, 43 (Bonn: Röhrscheid, 1976)

———, 'Kanoniker', in *Lexikon des Mittelalters*, vol. 5 (Munich: Artemis, 1991), cols 903–04

Schilp, Thomas, 'Die Wirkung der Aachener "Institutio Sanctimonialium" des Jahres 816', in *Frühformen von Stiftskirchen in Europa: Funktion und Wandel religiöser Gemeinschaften vom 6. bis zum Ende des 11. Jahrhunderts (Festgabe für Dieter Mertens)*, ed. by Sönke Lorenz and Thomas Zotz, Schriften zur Südwestdeutschen Landeskunde, 54 (Leinfelden-Echterdingen: Jan Thorbecke, 2005), pp. 163–84

Scholz, Sebastian, 'Normierung durch Konzile: die Reformsynoden von 813 und das Problem der Überschneidung von geistlicher und weltlicher Sphäre', in *Charlemagne: les temps, les espaces, les hommes. Construction et déconstruction d'un règne*, ed. by Michel Sot, Haut Moyen Âge, 34, (Turnhout: Brepols, 2018), pp. 271–79

Semmler, Josef, 'Reichsidee und kirchliche Gesetzgebung bei Ludwig dem Frommen', *Zeitschrift für Kirchengeschichte*, 71 (1960), 37–65

——, 'Die Beschlüsse des Aachener Konzils im Jahre 816', *Zeitschrift für Kirchengeschichte*, 74 (1963), 15–73

——, 'Mönche und Kanoniker im Frankenreiche Pippins III. und Karls des Großen', in *Untersuchungen zu Kloster und Stift*, ed. by Peter Moraw, Veröffentlichungen des Max-Planck-Instituts für Geschichte, 68 (Göttingen: Max-Planck-Institut für Geschichte, 1980), pp. 78–111

——, 'Le monachisme occidental du VIIIe au Xe siècle', *Revue Bénédictine*, 103 (1993), 68–89

——, 'Die Kanoniker und ihre Regel im 9. Jahrhundert', in *Studien zum weltlichen Kollegiatstift in Deutschland*, ed. by Irène Crusius, Veröffentlichungen des Max-Planck-Instituts für Geschichte, 114/Studien zur Germania Sacra, 18 (Göttingen: Max-Planck-Institut für Geschichte, 1995), pp. 61–109

——, 'Monachus — Clericus — Canonicus: Zur Ausdifferenzierung geistlicher Institutionen im Frankenreich bis ca. 900', in *Frühformen von Stiftskirchen in Europa: Funktion und Wandel religiöser Gemeinschaften vom 6. bis zum Ende des 11. Jahrhunderts*, ed. by Sönke Lorenz and Thomas Zotz, Schriften zur Südwestdeutschen Landeskunde, 54 (Leinfelden-Echterdingen: DRW-Verl., 2005), pp. 1–18

Siegwart, Josef, *Die Chorherren- und Chorfrauengemeinschaften in der Deutschsprachigen Schweiz vom 6. Jahrhundert bis 1160*, Studia Friburgensia, n.s., 30 (Freiburg: Universitätsverlag, 1962)

Signori, Gabriella, 'Cell or Dormitory? Monastic Visions of Space amist the Conflict of Ideals', *The Journal of Medieval Monastic Studies*, 3 (2014), 21–49

Story, Joanna, 'Cathwulf, Kingship, and the Royal Abbey of Saint-Denis', *Speculum*, 74.1 (1999), 1–21

Vanderputten, Steven, *Dark Age Nunneries: The Ambiguous Identity of Female Monasticism, 800–1050* (Ithaca: Cornell University Press, 2018)

Waesberghe, Joseph van, *De Akense regels voor canonici en canonicae uit 816: Een antwoord aan Hildebrand-Gregorius VII en zijn geestverwanten* (Assen: Van Gorcum, 1967)

Werminghoff, Albert, 'Die Beschlüsse des Aachener Concils im Jahre 816', *Neues Archiv für Ältere Deutsche Geschichtskunde*, 27 (1901), 605–75

Wollasch, Joachim, '"Benedictus Abbas Romensis": Das römische Element in der frühen benediktinischen Tradition', in *Tradition als historische Kraft: Interdisziplinäre Forschungen zur Geschichte des Früheren Mittelalters [Festschrift Karl Hauck]*, ed. by Manfred Balzer, Norbert Kamp, and Joachim Wollasch (Berlin: De Gruyter, 1982), pp. 119–37

Zimmermann, Reinhard, *The Law of Obligations: Roman Foundations of Civilian Tradition* (Oxford: Oxford University Press, 1996)

Zorzetto, Silvia, 'Thinking of Impossibility in Following Legal Norms: Some Brief Comments About Bartosz Brożek's Rule-Following (Cracow: Copernicus Press, 2013)', *Revus. Journal for Constitutional Theory and Philosophy of Law / Revija Za Ustavno Teorijo in Filozofijo Prava*, 20 (2013), 47–60

RUTGER KRAMER AND VERONIKA WIESER

Reduce, Reuse, Recycle

Episcopal Self-Reflection and the Use of Church Fathers in the Institutio canonicorum*

Sometime early in the ninth century, news reached the Carolingian court in Aachen that 'certain *praepositi* of churches, partly out of ignorance and partly out of laziness, were taking insufficient care of their subordinates, and esteemed hospitality less than was equitable'. This was apparently a big deal. Louis the Pious, who had just taken over the imperial throne from his father, reacted the way a proper emperor was supposed to, and immediately, 'inspired by Heaven', called together a 'holy and general council' which he admonished to take 'many useful and necessary measures for the improvement of the holy Church of God'.[1] To that end, he provided them with all the necessary assistance (mostly in the form of the many books he had at his disposal at the palace library), and the gathered prelates set to work, compiling a huge collection of patristic excerpts into a relatively coherent *florilegium* on the correct way of life of the clergy under their responsibility — 'as one might gather flowers from different meadows', as they put it. Read in its entirety, the text would provide its audience with a 'pattern for the education (*forma institutionis*) of the simple and less capable' members of the clergy. For good measure, the emperor and the synod also decided to add a 'brief but adequate' *libellus* 'intended for the observance of the holy women who live according to the canons'. With this *Institutio*

---

* Many thanks to Shari Boodts, Pietro Delcorno, Kati Ihnat, Emilie Kurdziel, Riccardo Macchioro, Bert Roest, and Graeme Ward for their helpful comments on earlier versions of this chapter.
1 The quotes in this paragraph all come from the prologue to the *Institutio canonicorum*, ed. by Werminghoff, pp. 312–13; ed. and trans. by Bertram, pp. 96–97.

Rutger Kramer currently works as Assistant Professor at the Radboud University Nijmegen and as Lecturer in Medieval History at Utrecht University.

Veronika Wieser works as a Postdoctoral Researcher at the Institute for Medieval Research at the Austrian Academy of Sciences and as Lecturer in Medieval History at the University of Vienna.

Monastic Communities and Canonical Clergy in the Carolingian World (780–840): Categorizing the Church, ed. by Rutger Kramer, Emilie Kurdziel, and Graeme Ward, MMS 8 (Turnhout: Brepols, 2022), pp. 179–215
PUBLISHERS ❧ PUBLISHERS   DOI 10.1484/M.MMS-EB.5.128532

sanctimonialium, these women, too, would have a 'model of living' (here the term used is *formula vivendi*), which, if carried out diligently, would enable them to become worthy brides of Christ by living up to venerable ideals of female chastity and virtuousness.[2]

This, in a nutshell, is the genesis of the text known as the *Institutio canonicorum*, as retold by the very people who had a hand in its compilation. The prologue to this monumental work paints the picture of an emperor who was concerned with the state of the Church under his responsibility, and who was then aided by a supporting staff of mostly bishops who would be glad to help him improve matters.[3] In the end, as they acclaim the results *consona voce*, divinely inspired unanimity and consensus reign supreme; everybody has done their job to help further the improvement of the Carolingian Church.[4] As such, this text fits perfectly within the context of the early years of Louis the Pious, Charlemagne's heir, who in 814 had inherited the Carolingian Empire and with it the optimistic zeal for harnessing the religious changes of the time that had characterized the last decades of his father's reign.[5] Taking particular advantage of the momentum gained by the organization of five large councils throughout the empire in 813 — in the wake of which Louis was also officially designated the heir to the empire — Louis had wasted no time continuing his father's efforts on that front.[6]

Together with his newly established court, Louis set himself up as a ruler in his own right, who took seriously the challenges laid before him. A series of councils were convoked at the palace in Aachen between 816 and 819. The lazy and inhospitable *praepositi* were used as a pretext for this, but it is important to remember that they were not a scapegoat. Fundamentally, these *praepositi* were 'provosts' or 'priors', assistants to the head of a community (i.e. the bishop or abbot) charged with anything from the regular day-to-day business of running the community to the treatment of guests and outsiders, specifically. It is a fuzzy and flexible term, which at the time could denote many things depending on the context, but most uses mark them out as being what John Howe has dubbed 'hinge persons': people in a position of authority, capable of existing both in the literate culture of the elite and in the everyday life of the laypersons dependent on the monastery or canonical

---

2 *Institutio Sanctimonialium Aquisgranensis*, ed. by Werminghoff, pp. 422–56; on this *Institutio sanctimonialium*, see the contribution by Michael Eber in this same volume, as well as Lifschitz, *Religious Women in Early Carolingian Francia*, pp. 12–13. The ideal of the virginal Bride of Christ is based to a large extent in the exact sources used in the *Institutio sanctiomonialium*: see Cooper, 'The Bride of Christ'.
3 De Jong, 'The State of the Church'; Kramer, *Rethinking Authority*, pp. 91–122.
4 Oehler, 'Der *Consensus omnium*'.
5 Nelson, 'How Carolingians Created Consensus'. For an overview of the early years of Louis the Pious's reign, see especially de Jong, *The Penitential State*, pp. 14–38.
6 Scholz, 'Normierung durch Konzile'; Nelson, 'Charlemagne and the Bishops'; Kramer, *Rethinking Authority*, pp. 59–90.

community.[7] As such, they could be teachers, deputies, advocates, preachers, or managers, but they would always be presented as the public face of a community — the human shield between the cloister and the world.[8] When the *praepositus* does not act as he should, the community cannot function in the world.

While the *praepositi* in the *Institutio canonicorum* thus come to embody the challenges facing the Church, they do so as a *pars pro toto*. Actually, the participants in the Council of Aachen cast their net much wider. Given their scope and overt ambition, these councils have even gone down in history as an attempt to completely overhaul — if not fully uniformize — the 'Carolingian Church', the *ecclesia* that provided a fabric for everybody partaking in the specific flavour of Christianity propagated from the Frankish court.[9] Specifically, life in the religious communities that dotted the Frankish imperial landscape would be affected, as it was the people living there who were tasked with the religious and indeed intellectual and cultural upkeep of the empire.[10] Recently, however, a lot of work has been done to nuance this monolithic interpretation of the reach of these councils and especially the impact the centralized attempts at *correctio* would have had on local

---

7   Howe, *Before the Gregorian Reform*, pp. 253–54. See Barrow, *The Clergy*, at pp. 81–85 for a more general overview of the many uses of *praepositi* in the Carolingian and post-Carolingian world; she also notes (with reference to Rudolf Schieffer's findings in *Die Entstehung von Domkapiteln in Deutschland*) that the adoption of the *Institutio canonicorum* as a veritable rule in the course of the tenth century led to a more precise definition of these *praepositi* and their functions within the organization of the Church.

8   Gregory the Great, for instance, uses the term to denote the 'one second in rank or the one charged with the care of business affairs': Kinnirey, *The Late Latin Vocabulary*, p. 81. Isidore of Seville, on the other hand, in his *Sententiae*, ed. by Cazier, 3.35–36, pp. 276–77), describes him as a cleric charged with preaching duties, whereas the *praepositus* appears in ninth-century charters from the monastery of Bobbio in a guise similar to the later *advocatus*, a legal representative of the monastery: Richter, *Bobbio in the Early Middle Ages*, pp. 107–26; on the *advocatus* in the same period see West, 'The Significance of the Carolingian Advocate'. Later, the term is also applied to anyone who acts as a deputy to someone else: Bisson, *The Crisis of the Twelfth Century*, p. 585, or indeed the de facto leader of a canonical community: Miller, 'Secular Clergy and Religious Life', p. 167, as well as the remarks by the same author in *The Formation of a Medieval Church*, p. 58 n. 65, which in turn respond to Venturini, *Vita ed Attività dello 'scriptorium'*. See also the overview given by Colish, 'Scholastic Theology at Paris', p. 33 n. 8. The fact that many of the discussions on the exact meaning of *praepositus* occur in footnotes seems to indicate that a more comprehensive study of the phenomenon remains a desideratum.

9   The main proponent of this top-down approach to these reforming efforts was Josef Semmler, whose work reverberates to this day. An overview of his work and influence is presented by Charles Mériaux in this volume, but in this context it is important to cite Semmler's influential articles, 'Die Beschlüsse des Aachener Konzils'; Semmler, 'Die Kanoniker und ihre Regel'; Semmler, 'Monachus — clericus — canonicus'; Semmler, 'Mönche und Kanoniker'. See, however, Geuenich, 'Kritische Anmerkungen', as well as Lifshitz, 'The Historiography of Central Medieval Western Monasticism', pp. 365–81.

10 De Jong, 'Carolingian Monasticism'; but see now also Choy, *Intercessory Prayer*, pp. 161–92.

customs (and *vice versa*). Still, the idealism and holism that pervaded works such as the *Institutio canonicorum* is undeniable. This text, and these councils, represented a view from the top. Regardless of their practical impact, their contents would be wholly in line with the ideas about *correctio* as seen from the court. These were the 'watchmen of the house of Israel' in action — the Carolingian bishops following the model provided by such Old Testament prophets as Ezekiel, who implored them to warn sinners whenever they could, lest their sins would be upon their heads, too.[11] This is why the text begins with the *praepositi*. They were the canaries in the coalmine. The bishops in Aachen had seen them falter, and drew their conclusions accordingly.

Given its scope, it should come as no surprise that the *Institutio canonicorum* (henceforth *IC*) is a substantial work, as far as conciliar acts go. The bulk of the text spans a full 115 pages in the *MGH* edition, and another forty-three pages are added for the part devoted to female communities exclusively. Going by its sheer volume, this work should be taken seriously — as indeed reflected in the large number of extant manuscripts (well over 150, including fragments and excerpts) identified by Hubert Mordek in his *Bibliotheca capitularium regum Francorum manuscripta* — and even so, it is noteworthy that he decided to add the laconic remark that 'doch bedürfte der vollständige Nachweis der Singulärrezeption [*of the IC*] eigener aufwendiger Recherchen' to his overview.[12] Similarly, the composition and reception of the *Institutio sanctimonialium*, while counting fewer extant manuscripts (a recent recount by Gerhard Schmitz raised the tally to nine), is also in need of a thorough re-appraisal.[13] For both texts, the sources, intentions, authors, and audiences remain elusive. Ostensibly aimed at canons, monks, and priests, the sheer volume and erudition that went into the *florilegium* alone indicates that this was a text by and for the elites of the empire. Taken as a whole, it seemed to mostly benefit the bishops and abbots who had a hand in composing it in the first place — not just the *praepositi* who were brought to task in the prologue.

This chapter aims to take a fresh look at the conceptual issues facing students of the canonical reforms under the Carolingians, and in the process cast the *IC* in a new light as well: not as a normative text *per se*, but as a reflection on what it meant to be a (male) leader within the church: abbots, priests, provosts, deacons — but especially bishops. Such leaders needed to be strict when necessary, flexible when needed, and always on the lookout to correct the sins of others and (in the process) themselves. We will start by presenting a brief summary of the *IC*, its structure and its possible intentions. Then, we will present three case studies of the way the compilers have treated their sources (in this case, Augustine and Jerome), so as to take a closer

---

11 De Jong, *The Penitential State*, pp. 114–18; on the persistence of this Carolingian interpretation of Ezekiel, see Gabriele, 'This Time'.
12 Mordek, *Bibliotheca*, pp. 1045–56 identified 136 full versions and twenty-two lost copies.
13 Schmitz, 'Aachen 816'.

look at how they attempted to recast venerable, centuries-old authorities in a new light and make them compatible with the challenges facing them in ninth-century Aachen.[14]

Rethinking the *Institutio canonicorum*

Thus far, the *IC* has been treated as either capitularies (as per Ganshof's assessment), or as a 'lex sui generis' (as Mordek refers to the text).[15] This latter interpretation also seems to have been behind the English translation by Jerome Bertram of parts of the *Institutio canonicorum*, in which the translator consistently refers to the text as a 'rule'. The implication throughout Bertram's introduction is that the goal behind the *IC* is similar to that behind Cassian's *Institutes Coenobiorum*, or, closer to home, the *Regula canonicorum* by Chrodegang, the eighth-century bishop of Metz, whose work is the true focus of Bertram's book.[16]

While there is every reason to think that the *IC* was intended to have a normative function, the work in its entirety tells a different story. Although it is highly probable that Chrodegang's *Rule* was among the many treatises that served as an inspiration to the bishops gathered in Aachen in 816, the part of the text that reads like a *regula* only comprises about thirty chapters, less than a quarter of the total, whereas the patristic *florilegium* makes up 113 chapters.[17] This part has long been neglected on the grounds that it comprises mere copies of older works, but, unsurprisingly, it is here that many of the mysteries within the text can be unlocked: the composers, in true Carolingian fashion, were content to merely copy their exemplars, but have rather re-compiled and re-composed these venerable texts into a new work that is as 'original' as the 'new' *regula* attached at the end.[18]

Significantly, the *IC* should thus not be seen as a monolithic text, but instead as a compromise — the result of lengthy deliberations on which passages to include, and which to leave out. Councils such as the series of deliberations that birthed the *IC* were forums for discussions, deliberations, and disagreements, and would be aimed at maintaining the unity of the *ecclesia* not by enforcing normative behaviour, but through the very expedient of

---

14 On this issue, see also now Moesch, *Augustine*.
15 Ganshof, *Was waren die Kapitularien?*, p. 104; Mordek, *Bibliotheca*, p. 1045.
16 Bertram, *Chrodegang Rules*, pp. 84–96 (cited under sources as the *IC*). On Chrodegang of Metz, his *Rule* and its impact, see especially Claussen, *The Reform of the Frankish Church*.
17 The *florilegium* is *IC*, ed. by Waitz, pp. 318–94, the *regula* is *IC*, ed. by Waitz, pp. 394–421.
18 This statement has become a trope over the past decades, but it nonetheless remains worth repeating. See, for similar methodological statements: Chazelle and van Name Edwards, 'Introduction', esp. p. 15, and, in the same volume, Heil, 'Labourers in the Lord's Quarry'; Levy, 'Commentaries on the Pauline Epistles', pp. 145–46.

having councils in and of themselves.[19] The discussions, in other words, were the point.[20] As shown by small remarks in subsequent works dealing with the adaptation of the input from Aachen at a local level, some disagreements had not actually ended when the council finished; rather than being seen as a problem, these instances would be explicated and seized as a moment to learn more about the issue at hand.[21] The *IC* should be seen as a reflection of that ideal — even if it was an ideal formulated 'against the background noise of axes being ground and teeth gritted'.[22] It was not meant to fully resolve tensions within the *ecclesia* per se, but to provide a space for these tensions to be resolved by the intended audience of the text — a jumping-off point for further deliberations (within the bandwidth defined by the text), but never as the final word on anything.

The breadth of topics covered by the *Institutio canonicorum* makes it a challenge to characterize the text according to any single genre. However, it seems reasonable to take its title at face value, and to see it as an 'Education in/for the Canons' rather than as a 'Rule for Canonical Clergy'. Taken as a whole, the patristic compilation is essentially a series of deliberations on the way those with a position of authority within the *ecclesia* ought to behave, as seen through the mirror held up by such venerable masters as Jerome, Augustine, Isidore of Seville, Julianus Pomerius, and Gregory the Great, to name but a few. In a nutshell, the text is not just aimed at the ignorant, lazy, and inhospitable *praepositi* from the prologue, but at anyone who held a position of leadership within the church, and who thus had a role in preserving the image of the institution.

Having a hand in composing a text like the *IC* is part of this role. It is difficult to gauge to what extent this text could be seen as being truly self-aware, but the amount of space devoted to the burdens of authority placed on bishops — and by extension, everybody who would have a pastoral or exemplary function — is undeniable. It reads like a *speculum episcoporum* more than anything else, as the text betrays an awareness of the fact that its compilers and its audience overlapped to some extent. In a tradition similar to the *speculum principum* written for worldly rulers, the *IC* became a moral treatise meant to hold a mirror up to its intended audience.[23]

---

19 Kramer, 'Order in the Church'.
20 De Jong and van Renswoude, 'Introduction'.
21 Specifically, these are references to councils in the commentaries on the *Regula Benedicti* composed by Smaragdus of Saint-Mihiel, *Expositio in Regulam Sancti Benedicti*, ed. by Spannagel and Engelbert, trans. by Barry, and by Hildemar of Corbie, *Commentarium in Regulam s. Benedicti*, ed. by Mittermüller (as well as a different recension of the same text: ed. by Hafner). A crowd-sourced translation of Hildemar's *Commentarium* may be found at <http://www.hildemar.org>. For a tentative answer as to why these authors chose to include references to disagreements in their works, see Kramer, 'Benedict of Aniane'.
22 Nelson, 'Revisiting the Carolingian Renaissance', p. 333.
23 On this genre, see Anton, *Fürstenspiegel*; Rouche, 'Miroirs des princes'; Vocino, 'Bishops in the Mirror'.

The entire first third of the *florilegium* consists of a series of descriptions of who bishops ought to be. It starts from a presentation of the various orders as described in Isidore's *De Ecclesiasticis officiis*, in which the order given by Isidore is reversed so that the text actually works its way 'to the top', from tonsured clergy to high priests.[24] Then, their role as pastors and teachers of their respective flocks is explained, based mostly on Gregory, Pomerius, and Isidore, the latter of whom reminds his audience that having the *nomen* of *episcopus* is 'a labor, not an honor'.[25] The middle part is devoted to early Christian canonical excerpts detailing *how* members of the clergy are supposed to behave, both within their parish and within the broader context of a Christian empire.[26] Finally, leading up to the 'actual' *regula*, the composers added another collection of patristic extracts, this time mostly dealing with the moral implications of having pastoral power — here we find, for example, letters by Jerome, as well as the sermons by Augustine *On the Way of Life of the Clergy* that will be one of the cases treated in this chapter.[27]

Only then do we get to the *Regula canonicorum* itself, which starts, noticeably, with two chapters describing, firstly, 'Which precepts are specifically to be applied to monks, and which to Christians in general' and secondly, 'How the canonical *institutio* [...] excels all other instruction'.[28] The first of the two explains that the essential difference between monks and Christians in general is the formers' insistence on poverty.[29] All the other virtues described in the preceding part, all further instructions given, should thus in theory be followed by everyone. The canonical clergy, the text continues, 'those who wish to be counted among those bearing the *nomen* of this profession', are to distinguish themselves predominantly by 'making themselves an example to others'.[30] In other words, the text touches upon the idea that, while monastic communities may be closest to the apostolic ideal of poverty, those opting for a canonical life retained an exemplary function in the secular world, preferably operating as part of a community under the supervision of their *praepositi*

---

24 *IC*, ed. by Waitz, 1–9, pp. 318–26; Isidore of Seville, *De Ecclesiasticis Officiis*, ed. by Lawson; trans. by Knoebel.
25 *IC*, ed. by Waitz, 9, p. 323; Isidorus, *De Ecclesiasticis Officiis*, ed. by Lawson, 2. 5.8, p. 59: 'Episcopus autem, ut quidam prudentiam ait, nomen est operis, non honoris'. Incidentally, Isidore has borrowed this quote from Augustine, *De Civitate Dei*, ed. by Dombart and Kalb, 19. 19, pp. 686–87.
26 *IC*, ed. by Waitz, 39–93, pp. 360–70.
27 *IC*, ed. by Waitz, 93–113, pp. 370–94.
28 *IC*, ed. by Waitz, 114–15, pp. 394–97.
29 On the significance of this, see Michael Eber's contribution in the present volume, as well as Kramer, 'Monasticism'; Nelson, 'Making Ends Meet'.
30 *IC*, ed. by Waitz, 115, p. 397; ed. by Bertram, p. 107: 'necesse est, qui huius professionis censentur nomine procurare, qualiter in semetipsis eandem institutionem vita et moribus exornent potius quam dehonestent, quoniam qui tantae auctoritatis instuitione pollent et se aliis imitabiles praebere debent. Verendum est, ne, si, quod absit, a proposito exorbitaverint, regno Dei indigni fiant'.

and living by a similar set of rules.[31] Thereby, they need to be supported by a thorough education so that they can actually continue to function without 'falling away from their position' because they had given in to temptation.[32]

Taken as a whole, therefore, the *IC* does not appear to be a text written for the canons who were supposed to live under this new rule, nor was it aimed squarely at the *praepositi* who acted as the middlemen between community and the outside. It was, instead, a composition for the bishops who would end up responsible for these communities. Throughout, the *florilegium* within the *IC* deals with establishing, consolidating, and living with authority. Unlike, for instance, Chrodegang's *Regula*, or the *Regula Benedicti* that came to provide the most widely agreed-upon template for rules for dedicated life in the Carolingian world, the *IC* was written by, and explicitly meant for, the leaders not the members of the community.[33] For instance, the *regulae* by Chrodegang and Benedict stipulated that regular recitation of the rules was required for members of the community, as a permanent reminder that they all lived with the same guidelines. The *IC*, on the other hand, never does this. It dwells on internalization of the rules, and on modes of convincing others to obey them. It also was consciously intended to be a text written for the here and now: respectful of the insights gleaned from patristic forebears, but always thinking about how these insights could be used going forward.

Reflections in a Two-Way Mirror: Beyond the Fathers

According to the *IC*, among the most important tools for maintaining authority over a group of believers was the ability to remain steadfast in the face of temptation and to maintain an appearance of incorruptibility at all times. Throughout the *florilegium*, it is constantly impressed upon the bishops who formed the target audience that they have been marked out as different and should behave accordingly.[34] As such, it continues to be important to remember that these same bishops had a hand in composing the work. They were reminding themselves that they were the leaders and the shepherds of the flock. They had to bear the heavy burden of authority, and act within

---

31 Choy, *Intercessory Prayer*, pp. 38–39.
32 The assumed diversity that is assumed to underpin the *IC*, as well as the idea that learning was a continuous process, was an integral part of Carolingian modes of teaching and learning: Contreni, 'Inharmonious Harmony', and, by the same author, Contreni 'Learning for God'.
33 See Diem, 'Inventing the Holy Rule'.
34 This is stated most clearly in *IC*, ed. by Waitz, 94, p. 370. This letter will be one of the case studies in this chapter: see below for more (bibliographical) information. On the origins and etymology of the term, see also Lienhard, 'Clergy'. Part of this section is a reworking of Kramer, *Rethinking Authority*, pp. 101–05.

the secular world but strive for holiness nonetheless — a combination that was difficult to achieve, but for which the reward would be all the greater.[35]

The sacrificial nature of the episcopacy did not mean they should let their status go to their heads nor that they should be burned by excessive zeal. Bishops needed discipline in all things. They could accomplish this, it is explained, by obtaining a proper education, which would shield their minds from the dangers of being burned. In a passage forming a bridge between the common vices of the clergy and the duties they have to fulfil, the bishops turned to a part of Gregory the Great's *Homeliae in Ezecheliem*, which had been reworked by the seventh-century bishop Taio of Zaragoza into a culinary metaphor explaining exactly that.[36] Knowledge, according to this passage, would be an 'iron wall' shielding the bishops, just like the *sartago* from Leviticus 6. 21–22, a cast-iron skillet used to offer the sacrifice up to the Lord, thoroughly cooked, but not burned, warmed by a love for God, but prevented from turning their zeal into anger or extreme strictness.[37]

Part of the reason that this was so heavily emphasized was that the dangers faced by bishops were not exclusively external, but could be generated by their own minds as well.[38] Against this, apart from the occasional synod, individual bishops had no mechanism of control other than their self-discipline. After all, those charged with the leadership of the church answered to no higher authority than God.[39] Although they would have to account for their deeds in the afterlife, those abusing their position in this world might actually harm

---

35 The most telling example of this occurs in *IC*, ed. by Waitz, 19, pp. 342–43, in a chapter called 'Prosperi, quod sacerdotes sancti contemplativae vitae fieri participes possunt', in which they explain that the two options are not mutually exclusive; see Pomerius, *De vita contemplativa*, ed. by Migne, 1.13, cols 415–520; trans. by Suelzer. On the Carolingian reception of Pomerius's work, see Timmermann, 'Sharers in the Contemplative Virtue'.

36 On the choice by the compilers to use Taio of Zaragoza's *Sententiarum Libri V*, ed. by Migne, rather than Gregory's originals, see Kramer, *Rethinking Authority*, pp. 97–100 and Aguilar Miquel, 'La primera tradición', pp. 207–23; generally, see also Leyser, 'The Memory of Gregory the Great'.

37 *IC*, ed. by Waitz, 34, p. 355: 'Quid est, quod Ezechihel propheta sartaginem inter se et civitatem murum ferreum ponit nisi quod isdem fortis zelus, qui nunc in mente doctoris agitur, in die extremi iudicii inter eum et animam, quam a vitiis zelatur, testis est, ut, etsi audire is, qui docetur, noluerit, doctor tamen pro zelo, quod exhibet, de auctoris neglegentia reus non sit? Murum ferreum propheta inter se et civitatem ponit, quia in ultionis tempore inde doctor a damnationis periculo munitur, unde nunc per zelum custodiae cordis frixuram patitur'; cf. Gregory the Great, *Homiliae in Hiezechihelem*, ed. by Adriaen, 1.12.29–30. *Doctor* should be seen here in the meaning of 'someone who teaches': Teeuwen, *Vocabulary of Intellectual Life*, pp. 76–79.

38 On Gregory the Great's views on how to internalize the burdens of power, see Leyser, 'Let Me Speak'.

39 Called *prepositi* in *IC*, ed. by Waitz, 22, p. 344, where it is also explained that: 'Aliquando etiam subditis nos oportet animo esse humiliores, quoniam facta subditorum iudicantur a nobis, nostra vero Deus iudicat'. See also the lengthy Chapter 12, ed. by Waitz, pp. 330–36, which consists of excerpts from Augustine, *Sermo de Pastoribus*, ed. by Lambot, sermo 46. This sermon will be a case study in this chapter as well.

their flock, the people who look up to their bishop, and who are bound to imitate his example. If one bishop was unworthy, the diocese would suffer. If the bishops faltered collectively, the entire *ecclesia* would eventually collapse.[40] The sins of their flock and their fellows would be visited upon him as well, the authors stressed, invoking Ezekiel's famous injunction that 'When [the Lord says] to the wicked: O wicked man, thou shalt surely die: if thou dost not speak to warn the wicked man from his way: that wicked man shall die in his iniquity, but I will require his blood at thy hand'.[41] Therefore, the *IC* emphasized time and again that everyone carrying the burden of authority was there to support everyone else. Over the course of various patristic excerpts, prelates were urged to act together as parts of the same episcopal body — or rather, as the head ruling over the body of Christianity, made up of the communities of the faithful under episcopal sway. After all, if the head was treated badly, its sickness would enter into that body as well.[42]

The way the bishops regarded themselves is not made visible in the *IC* through explicit self-reflection, or thinking about their office. Rather, they should see a reflection of their office in the behaviour of their peers and subordinates as they strove to live up to the admonitions contained within the text. They present a range of definitions and interpretations of clerical life covering all relevant aspects of the life and manners, virtues, and vices of the clergy. Thus, in their own way, the compilers adapted teachings from different contexts, periods, and authors into what they thought should constitute a tradition of clerical life, creating a historical dimension to the text and use the accumulation of authority to legitimate their Canonical Rule. There was, of course, a *regula* to be followed, but the teaching of the Church Fathers provided a moral and ethical framework around these prescriptions: a bandwidth of acceptable behaviour, and a set of guidelines for those tasked with enforcing the rules.[43]

Despite the compilers' efforts to present their readers with a singular understanding of clerical life, they were aware that this understanding needed to

---

40 Patzold, 'Bischöfe als Träger der politischen Ordnung'.
41 *IC*, ed. by Waitz, 26, p. 340: 'Sed iam quid adnuntiet, audiamus. "Si me dicente ad impium: Impie, morte morieris, non fueris locutus ut se custodiat impius a via sua, ipse impius in iniquitate sua morietur, sanguinem vero eius de manu tua requiram" [Ezekiel 33. 8, but cf. Ezekiel 3. 18]. Quid potuit expressius, quid apertius potest dici? "Si impio", inquid, "locutus non fueris, ut se ab impiaetate custodiat et ille perierit, sanguinem eius de manu tua requiram". Hoc est dicere: "Si ei peccata sua non adnuntiaveris, si eum non argueris, ut ab impiaetate sua convertatur et vivat, et te, qui non increpasti, et ipsum, qui te tacente peccavit, flammis perennibus perdant"'. On this key moral verse in the time of Louis the Pious, see de Jong, *The Penitential State*, pp. 114–15; Booker, *Past Convictions*, pp. 142ff; Kramer, 'Justified & Ancient'.
42 *IC*, ed. by Waitz, 30, p. 352: 'Caput enim languidum doctor est agens peccatum, cuius malum ad corpus pervenit, dum eo vel peccante vel prave docent e pestifer languor ad plebes subditas transit. Deteriores sunt qui sive doctrinis sive exemplis vitam moresque bonorum corrumpunt his, qui substantias aliorum praediaque diripiunt'.
43 See also Diem, 'The Carolingians and the *Regula Benedicti*' on the way the *Regula Benedicti* was also treated much more flexibly than might have been expected.

be multifocal — if they agreed with 'one voice' on the contents of the *IC*, they also would have agreed on the fact that these contents were polyphonous by nature and subject to many changes — many of them of their own making.[44] By choosing specific passages, the participants in the Aachen Council actually encouraged differentiation and variation by presenting different approaches to key topics such as episcopal authority, personal poverty, and the sustenance of the clergy.[45] Moreover, some of the texts incorporated also knowingly advocated a pragmatic approach to potential crises (within a community, or crises of conscience), rather than any single one-size-fits-all solution.

This multiplicity means that a full analysis of the *IC* and its adaptation of patristic thought falls well outside the scope of this chapter. The way these passages were adapted is best explored on a case-by-case basis, and even then, manifold interpretations are possible based on the same material, as shown by the chapters by Michael Eber and Emilie Kurdziel in this volume. For the remainder of this chapter, we will present three case studies which illustrate one possible interpretation of the *IC* as a whole. As we will argue, the *IC* was a text simultaneously by and for bishops, setting the rules while at the same time showing that keeping those rules required a flexible approach to the communities they were supposed to lead. The cases were chosen, in part, to highlight this aspect of the *IC*, even if it is but a single aspect of an otherwise much richer text.

Taken together, our cases also demonstrate how our Carolingian authors used and adapted even the most venerable patristic authors: which choices were made when excerpting the texts, and why some texts remained intact instead. All this will be shown based on, first of all, two texts that have been heavily excerpted and abbreviated: an extract from Augustine's Sermon 46, *On the Shepherds*, containing his interpretation of Ezekiel 34, and some of Jerome's best-known letters, especially the one he composed for Nepotian in 393 CE.[46] All these texts were known widely in the ninth century, meaning that, even if the *IC* was based on a pre-existing collection, the compilers would have known they were dealing with excerpted versions of the text, and decided that the version they had, corresponded to the choices that they would have otherwise made anyway.[47] We will, in either case, work from the assumption that these particular excerpts were decided upon in Aachen, as

---

44   See also, for a slightly later illustration of a similar phenomenon, West, 'Dissonance of Speech'.
45   Similar to the monastic precedent set by Benedict of Aniane: Claussen, 'Benedict of Aniane as Teacher'.
46   IC, ed. by Waitz, 12 and 94–98, pp. 330–36 and 370–77, respectively. For a discussion of the dating see Cain, *Jerome and the Monastic Clergy*, p. 2 with n. 10.
47   For more information on the manuscript transmission of Jerome's Letter to Nepotian, see Cain, *Jerome and the Monastic Clergy*, pp. 22–24, plus the additional bibliography provided in the footnotes. On the complex transmission and reception of Augustine in the Early Middle Ages, see Steinhauser, 'Manuscripts'; Weidmann, 'Augustine's Work in Circulation'.

the passages in question have been heavily edited to be integrated into the *IC*'s specific message. Our third case, also based on texts by Augustine, is interesting in that they have not been abbreviated at all. It concerns the two sermons *On the Way of Life of the Clergy* (355 and 356), which stand at the end of the *florilegium* proper and thus serve as a capstone to that part of the *IC*.[48]

These cases reveal how these texts were intended not just for the readers to reflect upon their own position within the *ecclesia*, but also how, behind the *speculum* created, the prelates in Aachen intended to keep a close eye not only on themselves, but also on each other and on the communities they represented.

Watchmen, Revisited: Augustine on Ezekiel

The observation that the compilers of the *IC* were aware that their audience could simultaneously think about themselves and about the communities under their sway may be demonstrated using a first, brief example, taken from Chapter 12 of the *IC*. This chapter consists of a long extract from Augustine's popular sermon *On the Shepherds*, in which he provides a theological perspective on bishops and their responsibilities in general. It is essentially an extensive exegesis on Chapter 34 from the Book of Ezekiel, one of the foundational Old Testament texts for the self-fashioning of the Carolingian episcopate.[49] Set against the background of the siege and destruction of Jerusalem in 589-7 BCE, the subsequent Babylonian captivity, and the hope for better times under the right leadership, this prophetical book provides fodder for a wide range of ideological discussions on good and bad leadership, all the while showing the devastating consequences of poor political decisions in the process. At the beginning of the book, God accuses Israel's shepherds of having abused their power, of not having taken care of their flock. Israel's bad shepherds had only sought their own advantage. They consumed the milk, clothed themselves in wool, did not tend the feeble sheep, and neglected to call back those who had gone astray. Because of their neglect and absence, the sheep had been scattered and lost. God pitied his people and intervened. He became the good shepherd, called his sheep, sought them out and led them back to their own land, to richer pastures. Upon their arrival, their leaders were once again reminded of their responsibilities, and given a stern admonition to do better this time around.

---

48 *IC*, ed. by Waitz, 112–13, pp. 385–94. On the reception of these sermons in the Carolingian world, see Leyser, 'Augustine in the Latin West', esp. pp. 458–60.

49 On the use of Ezekiel and the interpretation of watchman and doorkeeper as metaphors for bishops and their duties in the early Middle Ages see Toneatto, 'Lexiques', or, for a more extensive discussion of the use of the motif of the shepherd in general, see Suchan, *Mahnen und Regieren* and, from a more art historical point of view, Freeman, *The Good Shepherd*.

In the early fifth century, Ezekiel's prophecy about the lost sheep and the bad shepherds was a very useful metaphor for Augustine, who probably preached this lengthy sermon sometime between 405 and 414 as part of his efforts to defend orthodoxy during the Donatist controversy — an ongoing debate which also fuelled his sermons *On the Way of Life of the Clergy*, which we will return to later.[50] Echoing Ezekiel, Augustine's sermon was not primarily focused on the Donatists as lost sheep, but on the role played by bad shepherds in perpetuating the conflict; after all, they had failed to guide the community towards unity, in part by having erred themselves and thereby opening themselves up to criticism, and in part by not being able to deflect the criticism and stem the Donatist tide. His criticism was thus directed against the ineffective Catholic bishops who had enabled the Donatists to flourish. But it is important to note that he expressed this criticism not to the bishops exclusively, but aired his grievances publicly, to an audience of believers.

In the fifth century, this sermon was intended to form a pair with a second sermon on Ezekiel 34, *On the Sheep*, which Augustine composed and preached a short while afterward.[51] However, this one was not used in the IC, possibly because the topic of sheep was not of paramount importance to the compilers, but also because much of the input from that sermon was covered elsewhere. Seen on its own, the sermon *On the Shepherds* provided a reflection on the responsibilities and duties of good bishops that fit perfectly with the reforming zeal of the bishops in the ninth century. They, too, were greatly enamoured with Ezekiel's vision of authority, especially his image of the 'watchmen of the House of Israel', which became a shorthand for the proper functioning of the episcopate. It simultaneously served as a reminder of the responsibilities of the shepherd, and as a reflection of the Frankish/Carolingian Church as the 'new Israel', which in turn conferred a sense of responsibility on the flock as well — their Chosen status had to be earned, after all.

Both sermons contained plenty of obvious and polemical allusions to the Donatists, all of which were deleted in the IC. Essentially, this means that for instance the second part of Sermon 46 (Chapters 27 to 41), which directly engages with the teachings and practices of the Donatists, was not

---

50 Dating this sermon is notoriously difficult, as the internal evidence and the allusions to political events are not detailed enough to reach any clear conclusion. The most convincing arguments so far seem to place the sermon in the context of the preparations of the Conference in Carthage 411 and its aftermath, opening a time-frame for the sermon's composition sometime between 409 and 414. The conference was an official attempt to settle the conflict between the Donatist Church and the Catholic Church. See, on that topic, Frend, *The Donatist Church*, esp. pp. 275–89, McLynn, 'The Conference of Carthage Reconsidered', and Whelan, *Being Christian in Vandal Africa*.

51 While the two sermons show a close connection in their content, we cannot know the exact time span between their composition, although it is quite likely that *Sermo* 47 could have been composed within an interval of several weeks or a few months after *Sermo* 46: Augustine, *Sermo de Ovibus*, ed. by Lambot; Sermon 47, ed. and trans. by Hill and Rotelle, p. 323 with n. 1.

included, and many passages in the first half were abbreviated. To give one key example from Chapter 14: all the explicit references to the Donatists are excised here, but the key message of that section of the sermon remained.[52] It was a passionate plea spoken in the first person by Augustine:

> Yes of course, I'm unseasonable, I have the nerve to say, 'You want to go astray, you want to perish, I don't want it. I will call back the straying sheep, I will seek the lost one. Whether you like it, or whether you don't, that's what I'm going to do […]'.

Divorced from its context, the passage becomes a much more general reminder to the bishops that they are and remained the watchmen over the *ecclesia*, and should be ready to do the work even if their sheep — who could be headstrong (*contumaces*), Augustine reminded them — were resistant to their efforts.

Transplanted into the early ninth century, the *IC*'s adaptation of the sermon *On the Shepherds* thus becomes as close a statement about the reforming intentions of the council as possible. Almost paradoxically, the text states that such efforts would ensure continuity within the Church, as 'good shepherds are made from good sheep': the better they managed to keep the flock together and teach it properly, the better their successors would be.

Even more important for the community, however, was unity among bishops: 'They feed the sheep', this chapter finishes, 'and Christ feeds them'. Compared to Augustine's original, the *IC* is missing a long passage about the office of bishop and the supremacy of Peter here. These subjects were, in part, covered elsewhere in the *florilegium*, and, in part, not relevant to the point made by this chapter within the *IC*. In this new, ninth-century context, unity and harmony were key, so the text immediately continues: 'Let them all be in the one shepherd, and speak with the one voice of the shepherd which the sheep may hear and follow; not this or that shepherd, but the one shepherd. And in him let them all speak with one voice, not with conflicting voices'.

For both Augustine and Ezekiel, it was paramount to keep the flock together, to provide them with a proper pasture, and to take special care of the lost and weak members — which included arbitrating conflicts between rich and poor, and dispensing justice. Within the *IC*, it was thus Augustine's pastoral interpretation of Ezekiel's prophetic warnings that made this sermon especially valuable to its compilers. From his vantage point, and that of the Carolingian bishops, it was a reminder that their position between Christ and their flock might have been a reflection of their lot, a consequence of their upbringing and position. But this position only added to their responsibility: in order

---

52 The passage directly referring to Donatus, positioned in the middle of the chapter, was deleted: 'Non te timeo. Non enim potes evertere tribunal Christi et constituere tribunal Donati'. Augustine, *Sermo de Pastoribus*, ed. by Lambot, pp. 204–06. Cf. also Chapters 15, 17, and 18, where similar passages referring directly to Donatus and his teachings were not included into the *IC*.

for the Church to persist, they needed to be unified in their interpretation of their master's voice, and — for the purposes of the *IC* — agree how to teach this interpretation to the ones following them. Coming right at the start of the *IC*, after an introduction — based mostly on Isidore — on the function of the ecclesiastical hierarchy, giving direction to those in charge, this was a powerful statement about both the flexibility and the intransigence needed to be a good bishop.

Timeless Leadership: Jerome's Letter to Nepotian

Given their status as foundational documents for the design of the ecclesiastical hierarchy, it was an obvious choice for the composers of the *IC* to use Jerome's letters as a source for instructions on clerical life and authority throughout their work. A notable cluster of these occurs in the 'third part' of the compilation, on the behaviour of the clergy in general. In Chapters 94–98 of the *IC*, the compilers adapted Jerome's letters to Nepotian, Paulinus of Nola, Rusticus, Heliodorus, and Oceanus, respectively.[53] Originally written between 394 and 408, these letters address ideas about clerical life, the manners and training of the clergy, the difference between monks and clerics, and episcopal authority and the responsibilities that came with the office. The recipients of Jerome's letters were either, like Rusticus or Paulinus of Nola, in the process of abandoning their worldly life or, like Nepotian, monks wishing to convert to a priestly life. In this last case, Jerome even goes so far as to present Nepotian with a comprehensive guidebook on how to be an ideal priest, which is indicative of a more general trend at that time to compose small manuals to instruct especially newly converts about ascetic ideals and virtues. Jerome did so using a moralizing but also a satirical tone, using every rhetorical flourish at his disposal to make sure that Nepotian would not punch above his weight in his pursuit of a clerical career.[54]

Contrary to Jerome's other letters in the *IC*, of which only shorter passages were quoted, the compilers have taken longer passages from the letter to Nepotian.[55] The excerpts they chose provide basic guidelines for clerical life, including, most emphatically, the challenges and dangers of life within a community that extends beyond the walls of a monastery.[56] In fact, already before its use in the *IC* in 816, Jerome's letter to Nepotian was well known in the

---

53 Generally on the letters of Jerome, see Cain, *The Letters of Jerome*. The most widely used edition of Jerome's *corpus* of letters has been prepared by Hilberg.
54 Wiesen, *Saint Jerome*, pp. 65–112.
55 *IC*, ed. by Waitz, 94, pp. 370–73.
56 Cain, *Jerome and the Monastic Clergy*, on p. 1 states that this letter 'represents a major milestone in Jerome's career as a proponent of ascetic theory and practice for the simple reason that he fully articulates therein his grand ideal of the monastic clergy'. In subsequent footnotes, Cain's edition and translation will be used to refer to this letter (*To Nepotian*).

intellectual circles around the Carolingian court. As Maximilian Diesenberger has shown, Alcuin used it to discuss clerical preaching with Charlemagne.[57] It was also copied into the acts of the Council of Mainz in 813 and circulated among other letters of Jerome in Bavaria, albeit generally to emphasize different topics:[58] in Mainz, Jerome's deliberations were used to reflect on the practice of preaching, whereas the *IC* focused on the moral behaviour of the clergy and the tensions between internal fortitude and outward virtuousness.[59]

The version in the *IC* starts with an extremely shortened version of the letter's prologue, in which Jerome's elaborations on Old Testament passages and insights from Classical Antiquity are whittled down to a single sentence identifying the addressee and his desire to know 'how one who has renounced service to the world and has set out to be both a monk and a clergyman may keep to the straight path of Christ and not be dragged off onto all the different by-ways of vice'.[60] The parts skipped at the beginning mostly serve to emphasize Jerome's credibility as an adviser, pointing out that his old age makes up for the humility that is so often a trope in this genre. The moral lessons about continence, temperance, and prudence that come with age have been covered by other chapters in the *IC* already, meaning that the composers felt comfortable to assert that 'you (i.e. Nepotian) have learned and are daily learning all that is holy' from his uncle, the bishop Heliodorus. This is what is important: those holding the episcopal office are the *exemplum*, not necessarily the venerable statesmen like Themistocles or King David, philosophers like Pythagoras or orators like Cato, all of whom are mentioned by Jerome in the parts excised by the Carolingian bishops.[61]

The main part included in the *IC* starts with Jerome's explanations of the significance of the clerical office itself and its derivation from the Greek term *klèros* and the Latin term *sors*. As this means portion or inheritance, it would indicate, according to Jerome, that members of the clergy had the Lord as their portion and could thus possess nothing beside him. They should not hold any other property and in turn should be sustained by their church.[62] From there,

---

57 Diesenberger, *Predigt und Politik im frühmittelalterlichen Bayern*, pp. 154–56.
58 Diesenberger, *Predigt und Politik im frühmittelalterlichen Bayern*, pp. 155–56.
59 *Concilium Moguntinense*, ed. by Werminghoff, 10, p. 263.
60 Jerome, *To Nepotian*, ed. and trans. by Cain, pp. 32–33: 'Petis, Nepotiane carissime, litteris transmarinis et crebro petis ut tibi brevi volumine digeram praecepta vivendi et qua ratione is qui saeculi militia derelicta vel monachus coeperit esse vel clericus rectum Christi tramitem teneat ne ad diversa vitiorum diverticula rapiatur'.
61 See Rousseau, *Ascetics, Authority, and the Church*, pp. 126–29.
62 *IC*, ed. by Waitz, 94, p. 370: 'Igitur clericus, qui Christi servit ecclesiae, interpretetur primo vocabulum suum et nominis diffinitione prolata nitatur esse quod dicitur. Si enim cleros Grece, Latine sors appellatur, propterea vocantur clerici, quia de sorte sunt Domini vel quia Dominus ipse sors, id est pars, clericorum est. Et quia velut ipse pars Domini est vel Dominum partem habet, talem se exhibere debet, ut ipse possideat Dominum et ipse possideatur a Domino'. Trumbore Jones, 'The Most Blessed Hilary Held an Estate', p. 10 with n. 28, and Cain, *Jerome and the Monastic Clergy*.

this version of Jerome's letter gives all manner of advice on how to deal with being a (high-ranking) member of the clergy in the world. It warns against the temptation exerted by the riches necessary for the upkeep of his particular vision for the Church, telling the audience that their 'military experience' should not be seen as a 'standard for clerical obligations', because the gains they made as aristocrats were theirs but the tithes and alms they receive as bishops should be redistributed and used for the greater good.[63] The same warnings apply to the churches they may build, and the kind of flattery they may receive or indeed expect: richly decorated buildings and compliments are not the goal of being a cleric — malicious gossip, an 'itching tongue or ears',[64] should be avoided, and clerics should never fish for compliments or applause from the population attending their sermons.

Compared to Jerome's full letter, the Carolingian version has excised most parts that deal explicitly with the way the clergy should treat their flock: the emphasis is on how they should receive the treatment received in reaction to their demeanour. The one notable exception to this is the one danger that members of the secular clergy were far more likely than monks to encounter on a regular basis: women.[65] Here, Jerome's deliberations on such daily encounters, and the practical advice he gave about these, were especially relevant to the compilers. In case of illness, for instance, one of the brethren or his sister or mother or as a last resort an elderly woman should take care of the sick cleric; when entering a woman's house, he should always be accompanied by an acolyte or psalm-singer, for instance, and this companion should convey the same virtues and chastity to anyone who might be watching — which, according to Jerome, meant that this companion should present himself modestly, and not use tongs to curl his hair. After all, Jerome warned, any interaction with the opposite sex could turn into a fertile breeding ground for scandal, which not only ultimately harmed the plausibility of the prelate and would thus harm the Church at large, but which also endangered the recipient of such affections.

---

63 On Jerome's ambiguous attitudes towards wealth and poverty, see Brown, *Through the Eye of a Needle*, pp. 259–72. Jerome's allusion to the military experience of some members of the clergy refers directly to Nepotian, who, like his uncle, had exchanged his post in the imperial service for a church career, and to those who shared a similar background. This was a phenomenon that was quite common among Rome's aristocracy at that time, especially when imperial politics became unpredictable and dangerous. Paulinus of Nola resigned from his post too when confronted with the changing fortunes of politics in the 380s and 390s in Gaul and Italy, see Cain, *Jerome and the Monastic Clergy*, pp. 61–62; Vessey, 'Augustine among the Writers of the Church', p. 244; and for an overview, Salzman, *The Making of a Christian Aristocracy*.

64 Jerome, *To Nepotian*, ed. and trans. by Cain, 14, pp. 53–54.

65 IC, ed. by Waitz, 94, p. 371; Jerome, *To Nepotian*, ed. and trans. by Cain, 5. 4–8.15, pp. 40–43. On Jerome's cautioning towards women, which probably stemmed from the scandal he was involved in, see Andrew Cain, *The Letters of Jerome*, pp. 107–09, and Cooper, *Band of Angels*, pp. 191–218.

> Be on guard against everything that causes people to harbor suspicions about you. If any plausible-sounding rumour can be started about you, defuse it before it takes shape. A chaste love knows nothing of frequent trivial presents, handkerchiefs, garters, clothes spotted with kisses, food first tasted by the giver, and tender and sentimental notes.[66]

Following this passage, the original letter by Jerome continues listing ever more intimate ways in which women might tempt members of the clergy. The *IC*, however, shifts the emphasis. At the point where Jerome warns against people saying things like '"My honey, my darling, my heart's desire" and other absurd courtesies paid by lovers', the *IC* uses the same words abhorred by Jerome to simply remind the reader that 'My honey, my light and my desire is Christ'.[67]

It proves to be a key sentence in the Carolingian summary of this letter, as it turns the reflection inwards again. By deftly editing Jerome's original down to size, sinfulness is de-emphasized here. Instead, humility is glorified as the readers learn that they should direct their love towards Christ, and in doing so provide an example for their flock and make sure they are never in a position of being accused of hypocrisy — not just through their actions, but especially through the words they use to teach the people. In another subtle but meaningful edit, the most prevalent formulation in Jerome's letter, 'Let the mind and mouth of Christ's priest be in perfect harmony', in the *IC* turns into 'For a priest of Christ, let the mouth be in agreement with the mind'.[68] For Jerome, thoughts and prayers should function as one and the same thing, advocating for 'absolute moral transparency'.[69] For the Carolingian bishops, what is being spoken — made public — should follow what is being thought about internally, but the emphasis is on honesty, not on transparency.[70]

---

66 *IC*, ed. by Waitz, 94, p. 371; Jerome, *To Nepotian*, ed. and trans. by Cain, 5. 7, pp. 40–43: 'caveto omnes suspiciones et quidquid probabiliter fingi potest, ne fingatur, ante devita. crebra munuscula et orariola et fasciolas et vestes ori adplicatas et degustatos cibos blandasque et dulces litterulas sanctus amor non habet'. Cain, *Jerome and the Monastic Clergy*, pp. 148–49, connects this exhortation to Jerome's pessimistic nature as well as his personal experience with being accused of sexual impropriety some years prior to writing this letter.

67 Compare Jerome, *To Nepotian*, ed. and trans. by Cain, 5. 7, pp. 42–43: '"mel meum, lumen meum meumque desiderium" et ceteras ineptias amatorum, omnes delicias et lepores et risu dignas urbanitates in comoediis erubescimus, in saeculi hominibus detestamur' to *IC*, ed. by Waitz, 94, p. 371: 'Mel meum, lumen meum meumque desiderium Christus est'. On the use of 'honey' as a metaphor for Christ's teachings, see generally de Lubac, *Medieval Exegesis*, II, pp. 161–75.

68 Compare *IC*, ed. by Waitz, 94, p. 371: 'sacerdotis Christi os cum mente concordet' to Jerome, *To Nepotian*, ed. and trans. by Cain, 7. 2, pp. 44–45: 'sacerdotis Christi mens osque concordent'.

69 Cain, *Jerome and the Monastic Clergy*, p. 177.

70 Interestingly, of the eleven manuscripts used in the critical edition by Isidor Hilberg (pp. 413–41), no fewer than five follow the exact wording used in the *IC* (Zürich, Zentralbibl., MS Rh. 41, s. ix–x; Monte Cassino, Arch. dell'Abbazia, MS 295 MM, pp. 241–51, s. x; BAV, MS Vat. lat. 650, s. x; Berlin, Deutsche Staatsbibl., MS 18 (Phillips 1675), s. xii; and BAV, MS Vat. lat. 355+356, s. x, although that last one reads 'concordat' rather than

It falls beyond the scope of this chapter to fully delve into the intricacies of either Jerome's letter to Nepotian, its transmission, or the edits made to it by the Carolingian bishops in Aachen.[71] By and large, the remainder of the letter continues this concern for the intersection between appearance, the reaction of the public to this appearance, and the effect this reaction would have had on the mind of the clerics thus admonished.

The compilers even managed to turn this vicious circle into an act of self-reflection when they decided to leave Jerome's ending to the original letter mostly intact: 'For either I should have written nothing so as to avoid criticism, [...], or I write, knowing full well that the spears of all calumniators will be hurled at me', the Church Father writes, before finishing with 'Let he who feels inclined to be angry at me first admit that he is the sort of person being described'.[72] Originally intended to be a pre-emptive strike against his potential enemies who took issue with his views on virginity, in the context of the edited letter in the *IC* these statements become an invitation for the audience to indeed measure themselves against the Church Father's admonitions. In doing so, they turn Jerome's sarcasm into a passage reminiscent of a description in Cassian's *Institutes* of the path to perfection that monks should follow, during which they will be set upon by enemies throwing javelins at them — against which they should of course be shielded by their righteousness and steadfastness.[73]

Episcopal authority, as indeed Jerome's authority and that of the compilers of the *IC*, should come from their learning, their ability to 'learn what you may teach',[74] their experience, and their willingness to go against the flow when this is necessary to remain on the straight and narrow. After all, the one

---

'concordet'). Given that all these manuscripts postdate the *IC*, this most probably indicates the existence of another, earlier manuscript of Letter 52, which was used by the bishops — it probably gives no idea of the reception of the *IC*, given that all the manuscripts cited give the full text of the letter rather than the abridged version analysed here. Hilberg never finished the volume containing his stemmata and methodology, so we remain in the dark as to the rationale behind this editorial choice. Another manuscript, Le Mans, Bibl. mun., MS 126, s. ix, adds 'manusque' as well, highlighting the importance of deeds in addition to words even more emphatically.

71 It should be noted that Benedict of Aniane, in his *Concordia Regularum* uses the same letter to Nepotian to reach a wholly different conclusion about communal life and the role of bishops played in its upkeep: see Choy, *Intercessory Prayer*, p. 29.

72 *IC*, ed. by Waitz, 94, p. 373; Jerome, *To Nepotian*, ed. and trans. by Cain, 17, pp. 55–56: 'aut enim nihil scribendum fuit ne hominum iudicium subiremus, quod tu facere prohibuisti, aut scribentes nosse cunctorum adversum nos maledicorum tela torquenda' and 'qui mihi irasci voluerit, prius ipse de se quod talis sit confitetur'.

73 Stewart, *Cassian the Monk*, pp. 38–39. The use of javelins being thrown as a metaphor for unfair debates would be used in other Carolingian writings as well: see Kramer, *Rethinking Authority*, pp. 198–208.

74 The 'Hieronymian motto' *disce quod doceas*, from Jerome, *To Nepotian*, ed. and trans. by Cain, 7.1, pp. 45–46, had become a common phrase in the Carolingian ecclesiastical discourse: Cain, *Jerome's Epitaph on Paula*, p. 421; Steckel, *Kulturen des Lehrens*, p. 120.

way to remain free of the risk of being tempted by the prestige and luxuries of the outside world is to remember that they are being judged by Christ as well as by their flocks. The judgement of Christ was vital for their own salvation. The way their flocks assessed their prowess as a shepherd, however, was an indication for his ability to help them stay on the path to Heaven as well. This realization is the 'lot' of a good cleric, and the authors of the *IC* knew it.

The other letters of Jerome used in the *IC*, to Nepotian's uncle Heliodorus, Paulinus of Nola, Rusticus, and Oceanus, insist upon similar topics about the moral behaviour and the conduct of the clergy. To give one brief example: Paulinus, who, after having renounced his wealth, founded a monastic community alongside his wife at the shrine of Saint Felix in Cimitile/Nola, received his letter shortly after his arrival in Italy sometime in 395.[75] It was written shortly after Nepotian's, and indeed looks like an abbreviated version of that letter made by Jerome himself. This reminds us that such instructive letters were not only intended for private use but for a wider circulation.[76] The instructions chosen by the compilers (using only chapters 6 to 7 of the original text), dealing with food, prayer, reading, and worldly matters and powers, give the impression that this letter was used to give a 'best-of' of Jerome's admonitions. This, on a smaller scale than with the letter to Nepotian, gives a good idea of how the compilers worked (passages left out by the compilers of the IC are in italics).

> (6) *Since you are not wholly independent but are bound to a wife who is your sister in the Lord*, I entreat you — whether here or there — that you will avoid large gatherings, visits official and complimentary, and social parties, indulgences all of which tend to enchain the soul. Let your food be coarse — say cabbage and pulse — and do not take it until evening. Sometimes as a great delicacy you may have some small fish. He who longs for Christ and feeds upon the true bread cares little for dainties which must be transmuted into ordure. Food that you cannot taste when once it has passed your gullet might as well be — so far as you are concerned — bread and pulse. *You have my books against Jovinian which speak yet more largely of despising the appetite and the palate.* Let some holy volume be ever in your hand. Pray constantly, and bowing down your body lift up your mind to the Lord. Keep frequent vigils and sleep often on an empty stomach. Avoid tittle-tattle and all self-laudation. Flee from wheedling flatterers as from open enemies. Distribute with your own hand provisions to alleviate the miseries of the poor and of the brethren. *With your own hands, I say, for good faith is rare among men. You do not believe what I say? Think of Judas and his bag.* Seek not a lowly garb for a swelling soul. Avoid the society of men of

---

75 On Paulinus of Nola, the widely discussed renunciation of his wealth and his foundation of a monastic community see Brown, *Through the Eye of a Needle*, Trout, *Paulinus of Nola*, and, more specifically on his letter exchange, Mratschek, *Der Briefwechsel des Paulinus von Nola*.
76 On the topic of private and public letters in Antiquity see Ebbeler, 'Tradition', and specifically on Jerome see Cain, *Jerome and the Monastic Clergy*, pp. 1–24.

the world, especially if they are in power. *Why need you look again on things contempt for which has made you a monk? Above all let your sister hold aloof from married ladies. And, if women round her wear silk dresses and gems while she is meanly attired, let her neither fret nor congratulate herself. For by so doing she will either regret her resolution or sow the seeds of pride. If you are already famed as a faithful steward of your own substance, do not take other people's money to give away. You understand what I mean, for the Lord has given you understanding in all things.* Be simple as a dove and lay snares for no man: but be cunning as a serpent and let no man lay snares for you. For a Christian who allows others to deceive him is almost at much at fault as one who tries to deceive others. *If a man talks to you always or nearly always about money (except it be about almsgiving, a topic which is open to all) treat him as a broker rather than a monk. Besides food and clothing and things manifestly necessary give no man anything; for dogs must not eat the children's bread.*

(7) The true temple of Christ is the believer's soul; adorn this, clothe it, offer gifts to it, welcome Christ in it. *What use are walls blazing with jewels when Christ in His poor is in danger of perishing from hunger? Your possessions are no longer your own but a stewardship is entrusted to you. Remember Ananias and Sapphira who from fear of the future kept what was their own, and be careful for your part not rashly to squander what is Christ's. Do not, that is, by an error of judgment give the property of the poor to those who are not poor; lest, as a wise man has told us, charity prove the death of charity. Look not upon: Gay trappings or a Cato's empty name / In the words of Persius, God says: / I know your thoughts and read your inmost soul / To be a Christian is the great thing, not merely to seem one.* And somehow or other those please the world most who please Christ least.[77]

The compilers left out those passages containing Jerome's references to Paulinus's wife Therasia. Jerome's conflict with Jovinian — a monk who opposed Jerome's brand of asceticism — was similarly 'consigned to oblivion' by the compilers of the *IC*, as Carolingian scribes referring to Jerome were wont to do.[78]

In short, the Carolingian bishops not only got rid of passages already covered in other chapters, but also of those referring to the contemporary context. They had transformed the letter from a deeply contextual document into a text with altogether more abstract qualities. Highlighting that Jerome's advice had always been timeless, they made it very clear that it was thus ideally suited to the needs of ninth-century clerics as well.

---

77 *IC* c. 95; compare with Jerome, Letter 58, ed. by Hilberg, 6-7, pp. 535–537.
78 Leyser, 'Late Antiquity in the Medieval West', p. 33. Both examples, of the controversy between Jerome and Jovinian, and of Therasia's and Paulinus's joint ascetic endeavour are well known. For further reading see Hunter, 'Rereading the Jovinianist Controversy'. On the role of women for the ascetic movement in Late Antiquity see Cooper, *Band of Angels* and more specifically on Therasia, see Wieser, 'Like a safe tower on a steady rock'.

Community (In)Formation: Augustine's Sermons on the Way of Life of the Clergy

Besides Jerome's works, the compilers of the *IC* chose to give Augustine's voice a prominent position within their compilation. After all, the vast corpus of works of this Church Father make him not only one of the most prolific authors of Late Antiquity, but also an oft-consulted source of authority throughout the early Middle Ages.[79] Similar to this timelessness evinced in Jerome's letters, the two sermons by Augustine, *On the Way of Life of the Clergy*, which are quoted in full near the end of the patristic florilegium of the *IC*, conveyed the image of apostolic communities founded upon divine (and therefore unchanging) norms. Both Church Fathers had latched onto the idea of living together spiritually and materially as 'one heart and one soul' as quoted in Acts 4. 32 — an idea that dominated ascetic ideas in Late Antiquity and had a strong impact on Augustine's own clerical community in Hippo. The sermons, number 355 and 356, dating from around the turn of the year 425, were preached in reaction to a controversy over property and inheritance that threatened to harm the community's standing within the city. Augustine's defence of his clergy and the ensuing audit of the community's finances thus allows us to closely examine his ideal community. This provides detailed insights into Augustine's own motives for having founded the community in the first place and also into his vision of how it should deal with the question of church property and its challenges in the future. Thus, as we shall see, it was these specific topics and this mentality rather than the historical context which drew the interest of the Carolingian bishops in Aachen, as they plotted out the future of their own churches and the Church in general, and the roles bishops and clergy should have in it.

The background to conflict in Hippo is a complicated situation about a family heritage, which started with the complaint of a young nun, who claimed to have been defrauded from her expected inheritance.[80] Her father, Januarius, a *presbyter* in Augustine's household, had disinherited her and her brother in favour of the church of Hippo. The crux of the matter was not only the strained family relations or the complicated donation to the church, but also that Januarius had been a member of Augustine's clergy when he made his testament. When Januarius entered the community, he had seemed to act according to its rules and had bequeathed his property to his children. The remaining money would belong to his daughter, to be kept until she came of age. However, shortly before his death Januarius changed his mind, swore

---

79 Leyser, *Authority and Asceticism*, pp. 3–32.
80 For a more detailed discussion of the conflict and its context see Trumbore Jones, 'The Most Blessed Hilary Held an Estate', and, especially for an alternative interpretation of Augustine's public display of the conflict, see McLynn, 'Administrator', and Leyser, 'Augustine in the Latin West', pp. 450–64.

that it was his money, disinherited both his children and donated the money to the church. Although Augustine had declined the inheritance, a source 'of real pain',[81] he was nevertheless put in a difficult position by Januarius's behaviour. Besides having to appease the arguing siblings, he, in the first place, had to explain the rule violations in his clerical community — a position that was made all the more difficult since these violations would have technically benefited his community in a material sense and at the same time jeopardized its spiritual ideals. Augustine's solution to all this was a detailed and, more importantly, public examination of his clergy's finances and possessions. Those who retained possessions were expected to get rid of them, 'distribute the proceeds or donate them to the common fund'. He presented the results of his inquiry in the second sermon, giving a detailed examination of the possessions of each priest, deacon, and subdeacon:

> The deacon Faustinus, as almost all of you know, was converted to the monastery here from a military career in the world. He was baptized here, and then ordained deacon. But because what he possessed, *de jure*, not *de facto* as the lawyers say, was little enough, he just left it behind and it was held by his brothers. He has never given it a thought since his conversion, nor has he asked for anything from his brothers, nor has anything been asked of him. Now that it has come to this point of time, on my advice he has divided the property, and given half to his brothers, half to the poor Church that is established in the same place.[82]

Whereas the compilers of the *IC* were usually quick to excise information that could be used to localize and contextualize their sources, it is significant that in this case, they opted to keep the sermons intact. There is precedent for this: these two texts often circulated together as a reflection on life at the head of a religious community. Within the confines of the *IC*, staying loyal to this precedent and retaining the many local details offered by Augustine actually does make sense as well, especially given that these are the final chapters of the *florilegium* and thus form a 'bridge' between theory and practice. It is important to be aware of the local context, because this is a first-hand description of a real-life situation, as told by one of the most important bishops in the history of the Church. To be fully aware of the choices made by Augustine in resolving this crisis, and to learn how he used the controversy to teach the faithful of Hippo on clerical propriety and the function of the clergy within the city, was to be able to apply the teachings to one's own situation as well, should the need ever arise. It is, in short, important to historicize this diptych of sermons, because the ninth-century bishops choosing to include them in their text may have done so as well.

---

81 Augustine, *Sermo*, ed. and trans. by Hill and Rotelle, 355.3, pp. 166–67.
82 Augustine, *Sermo*, ed. and trans. by Hill and Rotelle, 356.4, p. 175.

Augustine started both these sermons by reminding his audience of the tension between internalized faith and the visibility of the clergy that also characterized Jerome's letters, focusing specifically on the widely discussed question of (church) property and spiritual purity.[83] Referring to his community, Augustine states that 'as far as we are concerned, our consciences are all that matters'; addressing the audience, however, he immediately follows this with an assurance that 'as far as you are concerned, our reputation among you ought not to be tarnished, but influential for good'.[84] From there, he continues with the values and principles upon which he had based his clerical community, namely the imitation of the Apostles. He emphasized that the requirement of apostolic poverty had been central from its very beginning, about three decades earlier, in 391, when he had arrived in Hippo seeking to establish a monastery.[85] Following his ordination as priest and later as bishop, he decided to found a clerical community instead, which centred on his episcopal duties and the necessity to welcome visitors. Augustine and his companions gave up their possessions, sold everything they had and distributed it to the poor so that they lived on what they had in common, following the communal spirit of the Apostles.[86] This addresses the conflict which had initiated his public re-evaluation of the clergy.

In laying out his clerics' past economic and social engagements, Augustine showed, on the one hand, that he fully embraced his own responsibilities for his clerical household: he knew everyone personally, exerted authority, and took measures to cleanse his clergy from any accusations. On the other hand, he cleverly reminded his audience how many formerly wealthy clerics had used their money to support the community and the church of Hippo. Doing this publicly, moreover, would have had the added advantage of consolidating the position of the clergy within the city — since every single priest had now been put on the spot for all to see — while also strengthening the inner fabric of the community by making sure its members knew that their flock knew they had been weighed and measured. In a city that still buckled under the pressure of the ongoing Donatist controversy, which questioned whether or not sinful priests were even able to perform their duties to the faithful, such an appeal to purity and responsibility would, Augustine seems to have thought, ultimately be more valuable than sweeping the affair under the rug.[87]

Augustine's reflections on inheritances and donations and how they should be used for the sustenance of the clergy and the church community

---

[83] For an overview on the discussion of the problem of the church's growing wealth in the fourth and fifth centuries see Brown, *Through the Eye of a Needle*, esp. pp. 481–502.

[84] Augustine, *Sermo*, ed. and trans. Hill and Rotelle, 355.1, p. 165.

[85] On Augustine's foundation of the 'garden monastery' in Hippo see Brown, *Augustine of Hippo*, pp. 142–45, 198–99.

[86] Augustine, *Sermo*, ed. and trans. Hill and Rotelle, 356.2, p. 174: 'All bishop Augustine's companions live with him exactly as it is written in the Acts of the Apostles'.

[87] Kondro, 'Clerical Misconduct'.

were certainly of interest to the compilers of the *Institutio*, who were faced with a similar challenge of balancing their budgets as well as their public standing.

However, whereas Augustine's sermons seem to have been originally intended as part of a public reckoning of this affair, of making sure the people in Hippo knew what they were up to, in the context of the *IC* the meaning of these texts alters ever so slightly. Chapter 115 of the *IC*, part of the segue between the *florilegium* and the *regula*, for example, stipulates that absolute apostolic poverty should be practised by monks only — canons were actually allowed to retain and donate private property.[88] In arguing that private property was a clear distinction maker between monks and canons, the *IC* thus went further than Augustine, who never mentioned monks *per se* and limited his comments to the people under him with a pastoral function. By stating that private property actually was important, the *IC* made it so that canons could rely on their own resources and not only on the benevolence of the Church. In a way, it gave them more responsibility to do good and to be good.

We find a similar discrepancy between formal demands and practical execution when we return to Augustine's sermons. Although the bishop stressed that nobody in his community was allowed to have private property, he admitted that some might still have some. He pointed out that he always refrained from making close inquiries as the community's principles were built upon mutual trust and the consent of its members to adhere to the rules: 'to make inquiries would, so it seemed to me, indicate I had a low opinion of them'.[89] All who were living with him knew about the laws governing their life together. A good bishop trusted his clergy to obey these laws without constant supervision.

It might seem that Augustine himself was not keen to observe if the rules he set were actually obeyed by his community. However, we probably should not attest his lack of strict observance only to his old age of eighty-four, as he himself claimed. Augustine was also very much — more than most — aware of the complexity of the situation as well as of possible consequences for his community, especially as this affair could have fuelled existing criticism against Augustine's strict no-property policy.[90]

In the first sermon, before the examination, Augustine claimed that he, contrary to his own policy, would be lenient towards those members of the clergy who had kept private property and would not deprive them of their clerical status.[91] He preferred this solution to hypocrisy and pretence, which would entail if someone would only claim to be poor but find other ways, like Januarius, to keep possessions. God would judge those clerics anyway,

---

88 Trumbore Jones, 'The Most Blessed Hilary Held an Estate'.
89 Augustine, *Sermo*, ed. and trans. by Hill and Rotelle, 355.2, p. 166.
90 McLynn, 'Administrator'.
91 Augustine, *Sermo*, ed. and trans. by Hill and Rotelle, 355.6, pp. 169–70.

so Augustine may have felt that pointing out the general lessons drawn from this situation would suffice to keep the community — and his own authority — plausible. In the subsequent sermon, however, he adjusted his attitude, explaining while expounding the examples of his community members, that most importantly it was the cleric's attitude towards property and how it was put to use that mattered.[92] Those clerics who still wanted to keep their property would have to leave his household and he would take more drastic measures towards those who lied about their possessions by not only expelling them but ending their career as a cleric ('so help me God, wherever I am bishop, that man cannot be a clergyman'[93]).

Between the two sermons, what the (Carolingian) reader sees is a bishop changing his mind, responding to a complicated situation that had become public and (apparently) increasingly controlled by public opinion. By including these sermons, it was implied that Augustine was worthy of emulation — not only his words mattered, but also his deeds and the (publicized) thought processes that explain why he did what he did. This made these texts such an interesting inclusion in the *IC*. Ending the *florilegium* with a case that highlights the difficulty of playing by the rules and of enforcing them provided a perfect segue to the part where the new rules for Carolingian bishops and their canons were explained. Augustine's example showed them what it took to take control of their own lives and times, within the bandwidth provided by the *regula* and under the watchful eye of God, their peers, and their flock. These two sermons, thus, show the difficult interaction between the people holding authority and those under their responsibility. Moreover, they also highlight the complex intersection between divinely approved apostolic norms and 'rules' written by humans.

It is this tension that forms the bedrock upon which the main argument of the *IC* is built: the sermons had been repurposed to become a reflection on the roles and responsibility of bishops, canons, and monks, not only to ensure their own salvation and that of their flock, but also to remind them that their authority depended on their credibility. Maintaining this could be a simple matter of following in Augustine's footsteps, and doing exactly as he did when encountering corruption in his community. These sermons, unabridged, provide a template on how to behave during a crisis of conscience, and how to present such a crisis to the inhabitants of a diocese. On the other hand, however, that very same blueprint provided by Augustine showed that such a resolution inadvertently required a certain degree of flexibility, both inwards, towards their own, defined, canonical communities, and outwards, towards the community of the faithful within their diocese.

---

92 Augustine, *Sermo*, ed. and trans. by Hill and Rotelle, 356.4–10, pp. 175–78; Trumbore Jones, 'The Most Blessed Hilary Held an Estate', pp. 13–14.

93 Augustine, *Sermo*, ed. and trans. by Hill and Rotelle, 356.14, p. 180.

To a Carolingian audience, far away from the hustle and bustle of life in fifth-century Hippo, Augustine's sermons were no longer about property. They were about propriety.

Reduce, Reuse, Recycle

The compilers of the *IC* had an abundance of texts at their disposal: by their own account, Louis the Pious had given them free use of the palace library to ensure they had the best sources for the occasion. In order to be able to make the most of that material, they had to make choices concerning the integration, abbreviation, or omission of passages and texts. These choices, as it turns out, could be practical, or ideological, or both — but they were mostly part of a conscious process of editing and reflecting upon the sources used.

Many studies have contributed to a deeper understanding of the *IC* and the choices made in the course of the editing process — the chapter by Michael Eber in this volume, a companion piece to this chapter, is one of these — and many more are still needed. To fully comprehend the making of the *IC* would require more time and space than this chapter or even this entire volume allows us. Nevertheless, this brief look at the use of several choice texts by hugely important Church Fathers does allow us a glimpse of the work in progress and the mindset of the people responsible for the final shape of the *IC*. While the text leans heavily on patristic authority, it does not necessarily fully adhere to all these teachings. When formulating solutions to complex problems, it was always worthwhile to permit a certain degree of complexity and variation. Thus, it seems that a more differentiated use of past authorities was thought to be helpful to get a better understanding of the ideal clerical life in the present, by encouraging reflection as well as discussion.

The passages from Jerome's letters and Augustine's sermons both contradict and complement each other: while Jerome, as an ascetic and a pastor, provides guidelines for the virtues and manners of the clergy, Augustine's writings, written from a self-consciously episcopal (albeit no less pastoral!) perspective, discuss more practical aspects of life in a clerical community and a bishop's role in it. While Augustine's works serve as a reminder that a bishop's work is never done, and his communities are in constant flux, Jerome provided a more timeless perspective, looking at the absolute truths behind what it meant to be a cleric.

Perhaps most importantly, our analysis of the use and redaction of Augustine and Jerome shows that the compilers managed to integrate different approaches to the kind of difficulties that might face bishops, who needed to be active in their own community and representative of an entire ecclesiastical province, taking care of all the priests and the laypeople in it as well. Some cases, like the two sermons of Augustine *On the Way of Life of the Clergy*, aimed to show the complexity of such situations, and implied that those willing to adapt to new developments or even respond to the feedback coming from their flock, were in very good company indeed. This may have contributed to an impression of inconsistency in the *IC*, but it certainly helped to give the audience — canons, bishops, abbots, priests, *praepositi* — a deeper understanding of their office and the issues they had to face, from general pastoral musings to ongoing debates on church property and its role in the categorization of certain types of communities.

On the other hand, the bishops authoring this *florilegium* were aware that what they were doing should supersede local contemporary politics as well. In the end, they were describing divine teachings, and reflecting on the responsibility that came with teaching the faithful the immutable truths of Christendom. There was plenty of wiggle room to do so, but in the end — literally — everything came down to the way their guidance led people toward salvation. These people could, in turn, be high-ranking church officials (including the authors of the *IC* themselves); they could be members of the monastic or canonical communities under the direct supervision of these prelates; or indeed the large groups of laypeople who depended on the piety and capabilities of the clergy as a whole (and on whose offerings the church depended). After all, it was they who were most directly affected by the 'insufficient care' and questionable hospitality of the *praepositi* whose misbehaviour was called out in the prologue to the *IC*, as a pretext for composing the *florilegium* in the first place.[94] More importantly, the bishop's ability to keep all those under their wings on the path to Heaven depended on their reputation as much as on their know-how and their pastoral prowess. One of the immutable truths they had to teach, as they were all too aware, was that nothing was as fickle as the will of the people — everything else could and should be doubted.[95]

The way the prelates in Aachen worked on the *IC* itself holds a mirror up to the Frankish episcopate. It was their way to resolve what would later be called the 'paradox of pastoral power' or the 'paradox of the shepherd': the problem of leading a community while being part of that same community and beholden to the same norms and rules.[96] How these bishops did so can be traced by explaining how and why they decided to reuse some nuggets of patristic wisdom, while reducing others to fit with the needs of the early ninth century, and recycling — or rather, upcycling — the ideas of the fathers into new content for the next generation. The process itself became a microcosm for the Carolingian treatment of Church authorities. The meta-narrative of the *IC*, a product of lengthy deliberations on how to keep venerable texts and ideas useful, seemed to have been that the Carolingian Church may have been built on a foundation of texts, but that in between these texts stood a group of people — *praepositi* — ready and willing to read them like they could

---

94 The representation of the relation between clerical communities and the laity in the *IC* is one avenue of research that needs to be developed further. See Ling, 'Interactions'.
95 Nelson, 'Carolingian Doubt?'.
96 Lynch, *Foucault's Critical Ethics*, pp. 120–21.

(hopefully) read a situation. As the *IC* explains, when it finally returns to the office of the *praepositus* near the end of the work in its entirety:

> Although they are given authority by others, they should never neglect the canonical rule, but the more concerned they are over the brethren, the more carefully they should observe the commands of Heaven. They should benefit the entire congregation, and faithfully fulfil the office laid upon them. They must provide what they are obliged to give the brethren promptly when it is due, and with charity. Thus, they will earn from the Lord the reward of a faithful steward.[97]

The chapter in question refers to the office of 'provost' (as translated by Bertram). This was the *de facto* leader of the community in a pragmatic sense, but the implications seem to apply to anyone who is put in charge of a community, through fate or by virtue of their authority. The lack of hospitality alluded to in the Prologue to the *IC* as a whole does not refer to material needs only: it also implies that *praepositi*, as indeed anyone in a position of authority, should meet the spiritual, intellectual and educational needs of a community as well, in accordance with the 'commands of Heaven'. Should they fail to do so, the chapter concludes, 'and fail to administer the authority committed to them properly, they should be corrected in the manner described above'.[98]

Works Cited

Manuscripts

Berlin, Deutsche Staatsbibliothek, MS 18 (Phillips 1675)
Le Mans, Bibliothèque municipale du Mans, MS 126
Monte Cassino, Archivio dell'Abbazia, 295 MM
Città della Vaticano, Biblioteca Apostolica Vaticana, Vat. lat. 355+356
———, MS Vat. lat. 650
Zurich, Zentralbibliothek, MS Rh. 41

---

[97] *IC*, ed. by Waitz, 139, p. 415; ed. and trans. by Bertram, pp. 123–24 and 165–66: 'Hi tamen, qui iuxta hunc morem praepositi vocantur, tales et tam strenui constituendi sunt, qui et vitae probabiles sint et ea, quae sibi iniuncta sunt, fideliter humiliterque expleant et pro eo, quod aliis praelati sunt, nequaquam parvipendant canonica instituta, sed, quanto plus implicantur in fratrum curis, tanto magis studeant caelestibus obtemperare monitis. Debent igitur cunctae congregationi utiles esse et de ministerio sibi commisso fideliter prodesse. Ea vero, quae fratribus dare debent, cum caritate tempore oportuno incunctanter praebeant, quatenus a Domino de fideli administratione gradum bonum adquirent'.

[98] *IC*, ed. by Waitz, 139, p. 415; ed. and trans. by Bertram, pp. 123–24 and 165–66: 'Erga huiuscemodi vero delinquentes et oboedientiam sibi commissam bene non administrantes modus superius comprehensus tenendus est'. Also, see above.

Primary Sources

Augustine, *De Civitate Dei*, ed. by Bernhard Dombart and Alfons Kalb, Corpus Christianorum Series Latina, 47–48 (Turnhout: Brepols, 1955)

——, *Sermo de Pastoribus*, ed. by Cyrille Lambot, Corpus Christianorum Series Latina, 41: Sermones de Vetere Testamento (Turnhout: Brepols, 1997), sermo 46, pp. 529–70

——, *Sermo de Ovibus*, ed. by Cyrille Lambot, Corpus Christianorum Series Latina, 41: Sermones de Vetere Testamento (Turnhout: Brepols, 1997), sermo 47, pp. 571–604

——, Sermo 355, in Augustine of Hippo, Sermons 341–400, ed. and trans. Edmund Hill and John Rotelle, *The Works of Saint Augustine* (Hyde Park: New City Press, 1995), pp. 165–72

——, Sermo 356, in Augustine of Hippo, *Sermons* 341–400, ed. and trans. Edmund Hill and John Rotelle, The Works of Saint Augustine (Hyde Park: New City Press, 1995), pp. 173–83

Concilium Moguntiense a. 813, ed. by Albert Werminghoff, in *Monumenta Germaniae Historica: Concilia*, II. 1, *Concilia aevi Karolini*, I (Hannover: Hahn, 1906), no. 36, pp. 258–73

Gregory the Great, *Homiliae in Hiezechihelem Prophetam*, ed. by Marcus Adriaen, Corpus Christianorum Series Latina, 142 (Turnhout: Brepols, 1971)

Hildemar of Corbie, *Commentarium in Regulam s. Benedicti*, ed. by Ruppert Mittermüller, *Expositio Regulae ab Hildemaro tradita* (Regensburg: Pustet, 1880); ed. by Wolfgang Hafner, *Der Basiliuskommentar zur Regula S. Benedicti*, Beiträge zur Geschichte des alten Mönchtums und des Benediktinerordens, 23 (Münster: Aschendorffsche Verlagbuchhandlung, 1959); http://www.hildemar.org [accessed 8 September 2021]

Institutio canonicorum, ed. by Albert Werminghoff, *Monumenta Germaniae Historica: Concilia*, II. 1, *Concilia aevi Karolini*, I (Hannover, 1906), pp. 312–421; ed. and trans. Jerome Bertram, *The Chrodegang Rules: The Rules for the Common Life of the Secular Clergy from the Eighth and Ninth Centuries* (Aldershot: Ashgate, 2005), pp. 96–131

Institutio Sanctimonialium Aquisgranensis, ed. by Albert Werminghoff, *Monumenta Germaniae Historica: Concilia*, II. 1, *Concilia aevi Karolini*, I (Hannover, 1906), pp. 422–56

Isidore of Seville, *De Ecclesiasticis Officiis*, ed. by Christopher Lawson, Corpus Christianorum Series Latina, 113 (Turnhout: Brepols, 1989); trans. by Thomas L. Knoebel, *Isidore of Seville: De Ecclesiasticis Officiis*, Ancient Christian Writers (New York: Newman Press, 2008)

——, *Sententiae*, ed. by Pierre Cazier, Corpus Christianorum Series Latina, 111 (Turnhout: Brepols, 1998)

Jerome, *Letters*, ed. by Isidor Hilberg, *Sancti Eusebii Hieronymi epistulae*, Corpus Scriptorum Ecclesiasticorum Latinorum, 54–56 (Vienna/Leipzig, 1910–1918)

Jerome, *To Nepotian*, ed. and trans. by Andrew Cain, *Jerome and the Monastic Clergy: A Commentary on Letter 52 to Nepotian, with an Introduction, Text and Translation* (Leiden: Brill 2013), pp. 31–58

Julianus Pomerius, *De vita contemplativa*, in *Patrologiae cursus completus: series latina*, ed. by Jacques-Paul Migne, LIX (Paris: Garnier, 1862), cols 415–520; trans. by Josephine Suelzer, *Julianus Pomerius: The Contemplative Life*, Ancient Christian Writers, 4 (London: Newman, 1947)

Smaragdus of Saint-Mihiel, *Expositio in Regulam S. Benedicti*, ed. by Alfred Spannagel and Pius Engelbert, *Corpus Consuetudinum Monasticarum*, vol. 8 (Siegburg: Schmitt, 1974), pp. 3–337; trans. by David Barry, *Smaragdus of Saint-Mihiel: Commentary on the Rule of Saint Benedict*, Cistercian Studies Series, 212 (Kalamazoo: Cistercian Studies, 2007)

Taio of Zaragoza, *Sententiarum Libri V*, in *Patrologiae cursus completus: series latina*, ed. by Jacques-Paul Migne, LXXX (Paris: Garnier, 1863), cols 727–990

Secondary Works

Aguilar Miquel, Julia, 'La primera tradición indirecta de las Sententiae de Tajón de Zaragoza (s. VII): un acercamiento a su difusión en época Carolingia', *Medium Aevum*, 89 (2020), 207–23

Anton, Hans Hubert, *Fürstenspiegel und Herrscherethos in der Karolingerzeit* (Bonn: Röhrscheid, 1968)

Barrow, Julia, *The Clergy in the Medieval World: Secular Clerics, their Families and Careers in North-Western Europe, c. 800–1200* (Cambridge: Cambridge University Press, 2015)

Bisson, Thomas N., *The Crisis of the Twelfth Century: Power, Lordship and the Origins of Government* (Princeton: Princeton University Press, 2009)

Booker, Courtney, *Past Convictions: The Penance of Louis the Pious and the Decline of the Carolingians* (Philadelphia: University of Pennsylvania Press, 2009)

Brown, Peter, *Augustine of Hippo: A Biography* (Berkeley: University of California Press, 1967)

——, *Through the Eye of a Needle: Wealth, the Fall of Rome, and the Making of Christianity in the West, 350–550 AD* (Princeton: Princeton University Press, 2012)

Cain, Andrew, *The Letters of Jerome: Asceticism, Biblical Exegesis, and the Construction of Christian Authority in Late Antiquity* (Oxford: Oxford University Press, 2009)

——, *Jerome and the Monastic Clergy: A Commentary on Letter 52 to Nepotian, with an Introduction, Text and Translation* (Leiden: Brill, 2013)

——, *Jerome's Epitaph on Paula: A Commentary on the Epitaphium Sanctae Paulae* (Oxford: Oxford University Press, 2013)

Chazelle, Celia, and Burton van Name Edwards, 'Introduction: The Study of the Bible and Carolingian Culture', in *The Study of the Bible in the Carolingian Era*, ed. by Celia Chazelle and Burton van Name Edwards, Medieval Church Studies, 3 (Turnhout: Brepols, 2003), pp. 1–16

Choy, Renie, *Intercessory Prayer and the Monastic Ideal in the Time of the Carolingian Reforms* (Oxford: Oxford University Press, 2017)

Claussen, Martin A., *The Reform of the Frankish Church: Chrodegang of Metz and the Regula canonicorum in the Eighth Century*, Cambridge Studies in Medieval Life and Thought Series, 4, vol. 61 (Cambridge: Cambridge University Press, 2004)

——, 'Benedict of Aniane as Teacher', in *Discovery and Distinction in the Early Middle Ages: Studies in Honor of John J. Contreni,* ed. by Cullen J. Chandler and Stephen A. Stofferahn (Kalamazoo, MI: Medieval Institute Publications, 2013), pp. 73–87

Colish, Marcia L., 'Scholastic Theology at Paris around 1200', in *Crossing Boundaries at Medieval Universities*, ed. by Spencer E. Young (Leiden: Brill, 2011), pp. 29–51

Contreni, John, 'Inharmonious Harmony: Education in the Carolingian World', *Annals of Scholarship*, 1 (1980), 81–96

——, 'Learning for God: Education in the Carolingian Age', *Journal of Medieval Latin*, 24 (2014), 89–129

Cooper, Kate, *Band of Angels: The Forgotten World of Early Christian Women* (London: Atlantic Books, 2013)

——, 'The Bride of Christ, the "Male Woman", and the Female Reader in Late Antiquity', in *The Oxford Handbook of Women and Gender in Medieval Europe*, ed. by Judith Bennett and Ruth Mazo Karras (Oxford: Oxford University Press, 2013), pp. 529–44

Diem, Albrecht, 'Inventing the Holy Rule: Some Observations on the History of Monastic Normative Observance in the Early Medieval West', in *Western Monasticism ante litteram: The Space of Monastic Observance in Late Antiquity and the Early Middle Ages*, ed. by Hendrik W. Dey and Elizabeth Fentress, Disciplina Monastica, 7 (Turnhout: Brepols, 2011), pp. 53–84

——, 'The Carolingians and the *Regula Benedicti*', in *Religious Franks: Religion and Power in the Frankish Kingdoms; Studies in Honour of Mayke de Jong*, ed. by Rob Meens, Dorine van Espelo, Bram van den Hoven van Genderen, Janneke Raaijmakers, Irene van Renswoude, and Carine van Rhijn (Manchester: Manchester University Press, 2016), pp. 243–61

Diesenberger, Maximilian, *Predigt und Politik im frühmittelalterlichen Bayern: Arn von Salzburg, Karl der Große und die Salzburger Sermones-Sammlung* (Berlin: De Gruyter, 2015)

Ebbeler, Jennifer, 'Tradition, Innovation and Epistolary Mores in Late Antiquity', in *Blackwell Companion to Late Antiquity*, ed. by Philipp Rousseau (Chichester, MA: Wiley-Blackwell, 2008), pp. 270–84

Freeman, Jennifer Awes, *The Good Shepherd: Image, Meaning and Power* (Waco, TX: Baylor University Press, 2021)

Frend, W. H. C., *The Donatist Church: A Movement of Protest in Roman North Africa* (Oxford: Oxford University Press, 1985)

Gabriele, Matthew, 'This Time. Maybe this Time: Biblical Commentary, Monastic Historiography, and Lost Cause-ism at the Turn of the first Millennium', in *Apocalypse and Reform from Late Antiquity to the Middle Ages*, ed. by Matthew Gabriele and James Palmer (Abingdon: Routledge, 2019), pp. 184–204

Ganshof, François Louis, *Was waren die Kapitularien?* (Darmstadt: Böhlau, 1961)
Geuenich, Dieter, 'Kritische Anmerkungen zur sogenannten "anianischen Reform"', in *Mönchtum — Kirche — Herrschaft 750-1000: Josef Semmler zum 65. Geburtstag*, ed. by Dieter R. Bauer, Rudolf Hiestand, Brigitte Kasten, and Sönke Lorenz (Sigmaringen: Thorbecke, 1998), pp. 99–112
Heil, Johannes, 'Labourers in the Lord's Quarry: Carolingian Exegetes, Patristic Authority, and Theological Innovation, a Case Study in the Representation of Jews in Commentaries on Paul', in *The Study of the Bible in the Carolingian Era*, ed. by Celia Chazelle and Burton van Name Edwards, Medieval Church Studies, 3 (Turnhout: Brepols, 2003), pp. 75–95
Howe, John, *Before the Gregorian Reform: The Latin Church at the Turn of the First Millennium* (Ithaca: Cornell University Press, 2016)
Hunter, David G., 'Rereading the Jovinianist Controversy: Asceticism and Clerical Authority in Late Ancient Christianity', *Journal of Medieval and Early Modern Studies*, 33.3 (2003), 453–70
Jong, Mayke de, 'Carolingian Monasticism: the Power of Prayer', in *The New Cambridge Medieval* History, vol. 2: *c. 700–c. 900*, ed. by Rosamond McKitterick (Cambridge: Cambridge University Press, 1995), pp. 622–53
——, *The Penitential State: Authority and Atonement in the Age of Louis the Pious, 814–40* (Cambridge: Cambridge University Press, 2009)
——, 'The State of the Church: *ecclesia* and Early Medieval State Formation', in *Der frühmittelalterliche Staat: europäische Perspektiven*, ed. by Walter Pohl and Veronika Wieser, Forschungen zur Geschichte des Mittelalters, 16 (Vienna: Akademie der Wissenschaften, 2009), pp. 241–54
Jong, Mayke de, and Irene van Renswoude, 'Introduction: Carolingian Cultures of Dialogue, Debate and Disputation', *Early Medieval Europe*, 25 (2017), 6–18
Kinnirey, Ann Julia, *The Late Latin Vocabulary of the Dialogues of St Gregory the Great* (Washington D.C.: Catholic University of America, 1935)
Kondro, Rachel Claire, 'Clerical Misconduct, Charity, and the Common Good: Saint Augustine's Sermons 355 & 356', *CONCEPT*, 34 (2011)
Kramer, Rutger, 'Order in the Church: Understanding Councils and Performing Ordines in the Carolingian World', *Early Medieval Europe*, 25 (2017), 54–69
——, 'Justified & Ancient: Bishops and the Bible in the *Relatio Compendiensis*', in *Politische Theologie und Geschichte unter Ludwig dem Frommen / Histoire et théologie politiques sous Louis le Pieux*, ed. by Sören Kaschke and Martin Gravel, Relectio: Karolingische Perspektiven — Perspectives Carolingiennes — Carolingian Perspectives, 2 (Ostfildern: Jan Thorbecke, 2019), pp. 181–96
——, *Rethinking Authority in the Carolingian Empire: Ideals and Expectations during the Reign of Louis the Pious (813–828)* (Amsterdam: Amsterdam University Press, 2019)
——, 'Monasticism, Reform and Authority in the Carolingian Era', in *The Cambridge History of Monasticism in the Latin West*, vol. 1: *Origins to the Eleventh Century*, ed. by Isabelle Cochelin and Alison Beach (Cambridge: Cambridge University Press, 2020), pp. 432–49

———, 'Benedict of Aniane, Adalhard of Corbie, and the Perils of Contentio', in *The Heroic Age* 20.1 (2021)

Levy, Ian Christopher, 'Commentaries on the Pauline Epistles in the Carolingian Era', in *A Companion to St Paul in the Middle Ages*, ed. by Steven Cartwright (Leiden: Brill, 2013), pp. 145–74

Leyser, Conrad, '"Let me speak, let me speak": Vulnerability and Authority in Gregory's Homilies on Ezekiel', in *Gregorio Magno e il suo Tempo: 19 Incontro di Studiosi dell'Antichità Cristiana in Collaborazione con l'Ecole Française de Rome, Roma, 9–12 maggio 1990*, vol. 2, Studia Ephemeridis Augustinianum 33–34, 2 vols (Rome: Institutum Patristicum Augustinianum, 1991), pp. 169–82

———, *Authority and Asceticism from Augustine to Gregory the Great* (Oxford: Oxford University Press, 2000)

———, 'Late Antiquity in the Medieval West', in *A Companion to Late Antiquity*, ed. by Philip Rousseau (Chichester: Wiley Blackwell, 2009), pp. 29–42

———, 'Augustine in the Latin West, 430–ca.900', in *A Companian to Augustine*, ed. by Mark Vessey (Chichester: Wiley Blackwell, 2012), pp. 450–64

———, 'The Memory of Gregory the Great and the Making of Latin Europe, 600–1000', in *Making Early Medieval Societies: Conflict and Belonging in the Latin West, 300–1200*, ed. by Kate Cooper and Conrad Leyser (Cambridge: Cambridge University Press, 2016), pp. 181–201

Lienhard, Joseph T., 'Clergy', in *Encyclopedia of Early Christianity* I, ed. by Everett Ferguson, Michael P. McHugh, and Frederick W. Norris, 2nd edn (New York: Garland Publishing, 1999), pp. 265–66

Lifschitz, Félice, *Religious Women in Early Carolingian Francia: A Study of Manuscript Transmission and Monastic Culture* (New York: Fordham University Press, 2014)

———, 'The Historiography of Central Medieval Western Monasticism', in *The Cambridge History of Monasticism in the Latin West*, vol. 1: *Origins to the Eleventh Century*, ed. by Isabelle Cochelin and Alison Beach (Cambridge: Cambridge University Press, 2020), pp. 365–81

Ling, Stephen, 'Interactions between the Clerical Enclosure and the Extra-claustral Clergy in Carolingian Francia: a Sacred Space with Porous Walls', in *Debating Religious Space and Place from Constantine to Cnut, AD 306–1035*, ed. by Chantal Bielmann and Brittany Thomas (Leiden: Sidestone Press, 2018), pp. 127–42

Lubac, Henri de, *Medieval Exegesis*, vol. 2: *The Four Senses Of Scripture*, trans. by Edward M. Macierowski (Grand Rapids: William B. Eerdmans, 2000)

Lynch, Richard A., *Foucault's Critical Ethics* (New York: Fordham University Press, 2016)

McLynn, Neil B., 'Administrator: Augustine and His Diocese', in *A Companian to Augustine*, ed. by Mark Vessey (Chichester: Wiley Blackwell, 2012), pp. 310–22

———, 'The Conference of Carthage Reconsidered', in *The Donastist Schism. Controversy and Contexts*, ed. by Richard Miles. Translated Texts for Historians, Contexts 2 (Liverpool: Liverpool University Press, 2016), pp. 220–48

Miller, Maureen C., *The Formation of a Medieval Church: Ecclesiastical Change in Verona, 950–1150* (Ithaca: Cornell University Press, 1993)

―――, 'Secular Clergy and Religious Life: Verona in the Age of Reform', in *Medieval Religion: New Approaches*, ed. by Constance H. Berman (New York: Routledge, 2005), pp. 156–82

Moesch, Sophia, *Augustine and the Art of Ruling in the Carolingian Imperial Period: Political Discourse in Alcuin of York and Hincmar of Rheims* (Abingdon: Routledge, 2020)

Mordek, Hubert, *Bibliotheca Capitularium Regum Francorum Manuscripta: Überlieferung und Traditionszusammenhang der fränkischen Herrschererlasse*, Monumenta Germaniae Historica Hilfsmittel, 15 (Munich: Monumenta Germaniae Historica, 1995)

Mratschek, Sigrid, *Der Briefwechsel des Paulinus von Nola: Kommunikation und soziale Kontakte zwischen christlichen Intellektuellen*, Hypomnemata, 134 (Göttingen: Vandenhoeck & Ruprecht, 2002)

Nelson, Janet L., 'Making Ends Meet: Wealth and Poverty in the Carolingian Church', *Studies in Church History*, 24 (1987), 25–35

―――, 'How Carolingians Created Consensus', in *Le monde carolingien: bilan, perspectives, champs de recherches: Actes du colloque international de Poitiers, Centre d'Études supérieures de Civilisation médiévale, 18–20 novembre 2004*, ed. by Wojciech Fałkowski and Yves Sassier (Turnhout: Brepols, 2009), pp. 67–81

―――, 'Carolingian Doubt?', *Studies in Church History*, 52 (2016), 65–86

―――, 'Charlemagne and the Bishops', in *Religious Franks: Religion and Power in the Frankish Kingdoms; Studies in Honour of Mayke de Jong*, ed. by Rob Meens, Dorine van Espelo, Bram van den Hoven van Genderen, Janneke Raaijmakers, Irene van Renswoude, and Carine van Rhijn (Manchester: Manchester University Press, 2016), pp. 350–69

―――, 'Revisiting the Carolingian Renaissance', in *Motions of Late Antiquity: Essays on Religion, Politics, and Society in Honour of Peter Brown*, ed. by Jamie Kreiner and Helmut Rcimitz, Cultural Encounters in Late Antiquity and the Middle Ages, 20 (Turnhout: Brepols, 2016), pp. 331–46

Oehler, Klaus, 'Der *Consensus omnium* als Kriterium der Wahrheit in der antiken Philosophie und der Patristik: eine Studie zur Geschichte des Begriffs der allgemeinen Meinung', *Antike und Abendland*, 10 (1961), 103–28

Patzold, Steffen, 'Bischöfe als Träger der politischen Ordnung des Frankenreichs im 8./9. Jahrhundert', in *Der frühmittelalterliche Staat: europäische Perspektiven*, ed. by Walter Pohl and Veronika Wieser, Forschungen zur Geschichte des Mittelalters, 16 (Vienna: Österreichische Akademie der Wissenschaften, 2009), pp. 255–68

Renswoude, Irene van, *The Rhetoric of Free Speech in Late Antiquity and the Early Middle Ages* (Cambridge: Cambridge University Press, 2019)

Richter, Michael, *Bobbio in the Early Middle Ages: The Abiding Legacy of Columbanus* (Dublin: Four Courts Press, 2008)

Rouche, Michel, 'Miroirs des princes ou miroir du clergé?', in *Committenti e produzione artistico-letteraria nell'alto medioevo occidentale*, vol. 1, Settimane di studio del Centro italiano di studi sull'alto medioevo, 39 (Spoleto: Presso la sede del Centro, 1992), pp. 341–64

Rousseau, Philip, *Ascetics, Authority, and the Church in the Age of Jerome and Cassian*, 2nd edn (Notre Dame: University of Notre Dame Press, 2010)

Salzman, Michele, *The Making of a Christian Aristocracy: Social and Religious Change in the Western Roman Empire* (Cambridge, MA: Harvard University Press, 2002)

Schmitz, Gerhard, 'Aachen 816: Zur Überlieferung und Edition der Kanonikergesetzgebung Ludwigs des Frommen', *Deutsches Archiv für Erforschung des Mittelalters*, 63 (2007), 497–533

Scholz, Sebastian, 'Normierung durch Konzile: Die Reformsynoden von 813 und das Problem der Überschneidung von geistlicher und weltlicher Sphäre', in *Charlemagne: les temps, les espaces, les hommes — Construction et déconstruction d'un règne*, ed. by Rolf Grosse and Michel Sot (Turnhout: Brepols, 2018), pp. 271–80

Semmler, Josef, 'Die Beschlüsse des Aachener Konzils im Jahre 816', *Zeitschrift für Kirchengeschichte*, 74 (1963), 15–73

——, 'Mönche und Kanoniker im Frankenreiche Pippins III. und Karls des Großen', in *Untersuchungen zu Kloster und Stift*, Veröffentlichungen des Max-Planck-Instituts für Geschichte, 68, Studien zur Germania Sacra, 14 (Göttingen: Vandenhoeck & Ruprecht, 1980), pp. 78–111

——, 'Die Kanoniker und ihre Regel im 9. Jahrhundert', in *Studien zum weltlichen Kollegiatstift in Deutschland*, ed. by Irene Crusius, Veröffentlichungen des Max-Planck-Instituts für Geschichte, 114 (Göttingen: Vandenhoeck & Ruprecht, 1995), pp. 62–109

——, 'Monachus — clericus — canonicus: zur Ausdifferenzierung geistlicher Institutionen im Frankenreich bis ca. 900', in *Frühformen von Stiftskirchen in Europa: Funktion und Wandel religiöser Gemeinschaften vom 6. bis zum Ende des 11. Jahrhunderts — Festgabe für Dieter Mertens zum 65. Geburtstag*, ed. by Sönke Lorenz and Thomas Zotz, Schriften zur südwestdeutschen Landeskunde, 54 (Leinfelden-Echterdingen: DRW, 2005), pp. 1–18

Steckel, Sita, *Kulturen des Lehrens im Früh- und Hochmittelalter: Autorität, Wissenskonzepte und Netzwerke von Gelehrten* (Cologne: Böhlau, 2011)

Steinhauser, Kenneth B., 'Manuscripts', in *Augustine Through the Ages: An Encyclopedia*, ed. by Allan D. Fitzgerald (Grand Rapids: William B. Eerdmans, 1999; paperback ed. 2009), pp. 525–33

Stewart, Columba, *Cassian the Monk* (Oxford: Oxford University Press, 1998)

Suchan, Monika, *Mahnen und Regieren: Die Metapher des Hirten im früheren Mittelalter*, Millennium-Studien, 56 (Berlin: De Gruyter, 2015)

Teeuwen, Mariken, *The Vocabulary of Intellectual Life in the Middle Ages* (Turnhout: Brepols, 2003)

Timmermann, Josh, 'Sharers in the Contemplative Virtue: Julianus Pomerius's Carolingian Audience', *Comitatus*, 45 (2014), 1–45

Toneatto, Valentina, 'Les lexiques du gouvernement ecclésiastique au haut Moyen Âge', in *Gouverner les hommes, gouverner les âmes*, ed. by Société des historiens médiévistes de l'Enseignement supérieur public (Paris: Publications de la Sorbonne, 2016), pp. 39–48

Trout, Dennis E., *Paulinus of Nola. Life, Letters, and Poems* (Berkeley: University of California Press, 1999)

Trumbore Jones, Anna, '"The Most Blessed Hilary Held an Estate": Property, Reform, and the Canonical Life in Tenth-Century Aquitaine', *Church History*, 85.01 (2016), 1–139

Venturini, Maria, *Vita ed Attività dello 'scriptorium' veronese nel secolo XI* (Verona: La Tipografica veronese, 1930)

Vessey, Mark, 'Augustine among the Writers of the Church', in *A Companion to Augustine*, ed. by Mark Vessey (Chichester: Wiley Blackwell, 2012), pp. 240–54

Vocino, Giorgia, 'Bishops in the Mirror: from Self-representation to Episcopal Model: The Case of the Eloquent Bishops Ambrose of Milan and Gregory the Great', in *Religious Franks: Religion and Power in the Frankish Kingdoms; Studies in Honour of Mayke de Jong*, ed. by Rob Meens, Dorine van Espelo, Bram van den Hoven van Genderen, Janneke Raaijmakers, Irene van Renswoude, and Carine van Rhijn (Manchester: Manchester University Press, 2016), pp. 331–49

Weidmann, Clemens, 'Augustine's Work in Circulation', in *A Companian to Augustine*, ed. by Mark Vessey (Chichester: Wiley Blackwell, 2012), pp. 431–49

West, Charles, 'The Significance of the Carolingian Advocate', *Early Medieval Europe*, 17 (2009), 186–206

——, '"Dissonance of Speech, Consonance of Meaning": The 862 Council of Aachen and the Transmission of Carolingian Conciliar Records', in *Writing the Early Medieval West: Studies in Honour of Rosamond McKitterick*, ed. by Charles West and Elina Screen (Cambridge: Cambridge University Press, 2018), pp. 169–82

Whelan, Robin, *Being Christian in Vandal Africa: The Politics of Orthodoxy in the Post-Imperial West* (Oakland: University of California Press, 2018)

Wiesen, David S., *Saint Jerome as a Satirist: A Study in Christian Latin Thought and Letters* (Ithaca: Cornell University Press, 1964)

Wieser, Veronika, '"Like a safe tower on a steady rock": Widows, Wives and Mothers in the Ascetic Elites of Late Antiquity', *Časopis Filozofskog Fakulteta, Sveučilište Jurja Dobrile U Puli*, 14 (2016), 4–21

MICHAEL EBER

Loose Canonesses?

(Non-)Gendered Aspects of the Aachen Institutiones

Introduction

In 816, Louis the Pious assembled a council in Aachen that made observance of the *Regula Benedicti* mandatory for monasteries. Additionally, his bishops wrote two texts intended to regulate those religious communities that were not subject to Benedict's rule: the *Institutio canonicorum* (*IC*) for male, the *Institutio sanctimonialium* (*IS*) for female communities. Due to a long tradition of 'disregard for female communities'[1] by modern researchers, the *IS* only really became the subject of sustained interest in the late 1980s. And even then, it was usually limited to those who were interested in what it could reveal about a specifically female form of communal religious life.[2] But there is reason to suppose that *IC* and *IS* initially had a closer relationship than their diverging research traditions would suggest: the prologue mentions both *institutiones* explicitly, suggesting they were understood as part of the same process of *emendatio* […] *sancta Dei ecclesiae*.[3] Louis the Pious, too, insisted to his bishops that exact copies of both were to be available in every diocese.[4] While their transmission is quite disparate,[5] there is some evidence that immediately after 816, both were in fact transmitted together. Gerhard Schmitz

---

1 Crusius, '*Sanctimoniales*', p. 11.
2 Crusius, '*Sanctimoniales*', p. 12.
3 *Institutio canonicorum Aquisgranensis* [henceforth *IC*], ed. by Werminghoff, Prologue, pp. 312–13.
4 *Hludowici imperatoris epistolae ad archiepiscopos missae*, ed. by Werminghoff, pp. 458–59; Schilp, 'Die Wirkung', p. 173.
5 Mordek, *Bibliotheca capitularium*, pp. 1045–58.

> **Michael Eber** has held posts as research assistant at Freie Universität Berlin and Leopold-Franzens-Universität Innsbruck. He has recently completed a PhD thesis on the reception of the Three Chapters Controversy in Merowingian Gaul as part of the DFG project 'Der Codex Remensis der Staatsbibliothek zu Berlin (Ms. Phill. 1743): Der gallische Episkopat als Mittler antiken Rechtswissens und Mitgestalter merowingischer Politik'.

Monastic Communities and Canonical Clergy in the Carolingian World (780–840): Categorizing the Church, ed. by Rutger Kramer, Emilie Kurdziel, and Graeme Ward, MMS 8 (Turnhout: Brepols, 2022), pp. 217–238

has recently rediscovered a manuscript in Rome that contains both *IC* and *IS*. It was most probably written in the monastery of St Silvester in Nonantola during the abbacy of Peter (814–25). As his embassy to Constantinople in 813 shows, Peter should be counted among the very elite of the Carolingian Empire. Thus, one would expect this manuscript to at least be very close to the 'official' Aachen version.[6]

Taking my cue from Albrecht Diem, who urged historians to take seriously the non-gendered aspects of the history of monasticism and the unisex potential of ostensibly gendered monastic models,[7] I will offer a reading of both *institutiones* in conjunction. In doing so, I intend to show the bishops assembled in Aachen as creating an at least somewhat unified normative framework, within which they believed it was possible to cultivate a religious life for those who could not rely on the *Regula Benedicti*. This is not to say that I read the *IS* as a simple 'translation [of the *IC*] to female'[8] — the respective patristic collections in particular (Chapters 1–113 of the *IC* and Chapters 1–6 of the *IS*) show the compilers' gender-specific considerations. For female communities, they were much more concerned with virginity, while male canons would have to contend with the expectation of living an ideal Christian life without the monastic 'luxury' of being entirely sequestered from the temptations of the secular world.[9] Still, in reflecting on the organization of religious communities, many issues overlapped, as did the solutions found by the compilers of *IC* and *IS*. The similarity is particularly evident in their treatment of private property: While they clearly took it seriously as a potential threat to a religious life, they created a framework within which it could be handled safely, independently of gender.

Pastoral Power and Property in the *Institutio canonicorum*

First, I will give a brief overview of what I perceive to be the salient features of the *IC*. The central issue is introduced by Augustine's *Sermo de pastoribus*, quoted at length in Chapter 12. Based on Ezekiel 34. 1–16, a passage on 'bad shepherds who feed themselves', he highlights the volatile position of those who wield pastoral power:[10] Since they are responsible for the salvation of others, they would be held accountable by God not only for their own life,

---

6 Schmitz, 'Aachen 816', pp. 500–09. The manuscript is Rome, BNCR, MS Vitt. Em. 1348 (available online, see Works Cited below); it was not used by Werminghoff in his 1906 edition.
7 Diem, 'Gender of the Religious', pp. 432–46.
8 Werminghoff, 'Die Beschlüsse', p. 634.
9 On the latter, see Kramer, *Rethinking Authority*, pp. 106–11.
10 On the concept of pastoral power, see Foucault, 'The Subject and Power', pp. 782–83. See also Suchan, *Mahnen und Regieren*, pp. 19–22.

but for that of their flock as well. In fact, even the herds of bad shepherds ultimately are safe, as God promises to gather them back together in Ezekiel 34. 12–16.[11] The shepherds themselves seem to be the only ones in actual peril; thus, Augustine's congregation could listen to the reading 'with intent' (*cum intentione*), while he and his clerics would have to listen 'with trembling' (*cum tremore*) in expectation of the Last Judgement.[12]

This is again taken up in Chapters 26 and 32, quotes from Chapters I. 20–21 of *De vita contemplativa*, the only extant work of Pomerius, a North African writer who emigrated to Southern Gaul in the late fifth century.[13] Misattributing it to Prosper of Aquitaine, the compilers used it extensively, but split it up in a way that obscured the fact that in Chapters I. 20–21, the speaker is not actually Pomerius, but rather his (possibly fictitious) interlocutor, a Bishop Julianus.[14] Quoting Ezekiel 33. 7–8 and 34. 1–10, Julianus stresses the terror he feels of being judged an inadequate 'watchman unto the house of Israel' or a 'bad shepherd',[15] culminating in his wish to leave the episcopacy and await God 'in solitude' (*in solitudine*).[16]

While the compilers of the *IC* did not use Pomerius's direct answer to Julianus's concerns,[17] they found one in Gregory the Great's *Regula Pastoralis* (*RP*), quoted by way of Taio of Saragossa's *Sententiae*, a systematic compilation of excerpts from Gregory's works.[18] The *RP* had already been recommended as a textual basis for clerical virtue in four out of the five reform councils of 813.[19] Gregory essentially argued that individual spiritual perfection was a prerequisite for effective spiritual leadership. Being a former monk, his definition of individual spiritual perfection was influenced by John Cassian's monastic writings. For example, in Chapter I. 11 of the *RP* (quoted in Chapter 27 of the *IC*),[20] he reframes a list of physical anomalies from Leviticus 21. 17–20, originally disqualifying criteria from the position of Levite, as spiritual anomalies disqualifying from a pastoral position, the spiritual norm being

---

11   *IC*, ed. by Werminghoff, 12, pp. 335–36.
12   *IC*, ed. by Werminghoff, 12, p. 330.
13   Timmermann, 'Sharers in the Contemplative Virtue', pp. 5–7.
14   Isidore of Seville called the author of *De vita contemplativa* 'Julianus Pomerius' in *De viris illustribus*. It is unclear whether he mistakenly combined the names or Julianus was in fact Pomerius's alter ego; see Timmermann, 'Sharers in the Contemplative Virtue', p. 17.
15   *IC*, ed. by Werminghoff, 26, pp. 347–48 and 32, pp. 353–54.
16   *IC*, ed. by Werminghoff, 32, p. 354.
17   The following chapter of *De vita contemplativa* is quoted in the *IC*, but only in Chapter 106 and in a completely different context: following several chapters concerning the obedience canons owed their bishops, the point seems to be that sinners (here: disobedient canons) would perish if they did not heed their bishops' exhortations, not that bishops would be saved if they exhorted them. See Pomerius, *De vita contemplativa*, I. 22, cols 437–38, trans. by Suelzer, pp. 47–48.
18   Werminghoff, 'Die Beschlüsse', pp. 616–18.
19   Floryszczak, *Die 'Regula Pastoralis'*, p. 310. Gregory may have been influenced by Pomerius's writings; see Timmermann, 'Sharers in the Contemplative Virtue', p. 25.
20   *IC*, ed. by Werminghoff, 27, pp. 349–51.

derived from a monastic tradition. Blindness, for instance, denotes a lack of contemplation (*contemplatio*), a small nose, an inadequate ability to discern between virtue and sin (*discretio*), both of which were key monastic virtues for Cassian. So to avoid being judged bad shepherds, priests would have to cultivate the same individual virtues as their monastic brethren.[21]

However, another quote from *RP* (combined with a thematically similar chapter from Isidore of Seville's *Sententiae*) points to an issue with an excessive focus on the priests' own (monastic) virtue. In Chapters 17/18, both the *RP* and the *Sententiae* are used to criticize those who, like Julianus, would eschew pastoral power for the sake of 'contemplation on its own' (*sola contemplatio*),[22] which, while a necessary condition for effectively wielding pastoral power, is obviously not the same as actually wielding it — that is, providing *correctio*, admonishing the flock and leading by example. In fact, by quoting the *RP* via the second book of Taio's *Sententiae*, largely concerned with the history of the institutional Church, the compilers may have deliberately used a 'clericalized' Gregory.[23]

But, as Gregory himself lamented upon his assumption of the papacy,[24] the many different concerns that came with a clerical position might well disturb one's *contemplatio*, thus jeopardizing both one's individual spiritual perfection and that of one's flock. How, then, can the individual perfection of *contemplatio* be reconciled with the fulfilment of pastoral duties? This is also the overarching question of *De vita contemplativa*. In Chapter 19 of the *IC*, 'Prosper' offers four possible definitions of *vita contemplativa*, two of which, knowledge of concealed and future things and the vision of God, are (only) attainable in the next life, the implication being that even solitary ascetics will not truly achieve them in this one. The other two, however, the study of scripture and freedom from secular occupations, should not present an obstacle to bishops.[25]

Of course, the last point might seem as if it only restates the problem: how can priests or bishops be truly free from secular occupations and still fulfil their pastoral (and administrative) duties? Pomerius's treatment of property is instructive in this regard. While he counts those who 'extend the boundaries of their estate without limiting their covetousness' among those who are 'entangled by worldly business',[26] he also praises Paulinus of Nola and Hilary of Arles for not only administering, but also increasing the property of the churches under their responsibility.[27] Buying and selling property thus was not necessarily a 'worldly business', but rather *could* be an

---

21   Demacopoulos, 'Gregory's Model of Spiritual Direction', pp. 205–09 and 211–16.
22   *IC*, ed. by Werminghoff, 17, p. 341.
23   Kramer, *Rethinking Authority*, pp. 97–99.
24   Leyser, *Authority and Asceticism*, p. 142.
25   *IC*, ed. by Werminghoff, 19, p. 342.
26   *IC*, ed. by Werminghoff, 19, p. 343.
27   *IC*, ed. by Werminghoff, 35, pp. 356–57.

activity directed towards God — depending on the intention of those doing it. Thus, attaining the *vita contemplativa* seems to be a matter of the correct mindset rather than the correct activity.[28] A mindset directed toward God was of course indispensable for priests, so that, in Pomerius's view, they are not only able, but obligated to live the contemplative life.[29]

Paulinus and Hilary had also renounced all their private property, from which Pomerius draws the seemingly simple conclusion that 'priests should have nothing of their own'. He also introduces the notion of Church property as 'vows of the faithful, ransom of sinners, and patrimony of the poor' (*vota fidelium, pretia peccatorum, patrimonium pauperum*).[30] While this formula would prove extremely influential as a justification for Church property, Jean Devisse has argued that 816 was the only occasion that it was quoted in its intended context: mandating individual poverty for clerics and explicitly tying the Church's property to its social responsibility.[31] It should be noted, however, that Pomerius also offers a way to deal with *private* property without being entangled in worldly business. Specifically because the Church had to sustain the poor with its property, using it to sustain clerics who are not 'poor by birth or by choice' would in essence be alienation. While he obviously prefers clerics to renounce their property, those who do not, can, in his view, 'keep [it] without sin' as long as they do not also receive the same support as those who do.[32]

Quoting the relevant passages from *De vita contemplativa* for a second time in Chapter 120, the compilers implement Pomerius's ideas, though arguably somewhat half-heartedly: those who possess both their own and Church property should receive food, drink, and a share of the donations to the congregations, while those who do not should receive clothing as well.[33] While they do not take personal wealth into account when it comes to the distribution of food, they are quite clearly concerned with ensuring equality within the congregation, stressing several times that all members have to accept the same rations, independent of their social status.[34] Additionally, the canons' private property also seems to have been considered *patrimonia pauperum* in some sense: the hospital connected to the community was to be supported not

---

28 Claussen, *Reform*, pp. 189–90.
29 IC, ed. by Werminghoff, 19, p. 342. Brown, *Through the Eye of a Needle*, pp. 485–86, sees the intended audience of *De vita contemplativa* in monks-turned-bishops like Caesarius of Arles, who, in this model, could retain the prestige gained by rejection of wealth while still administering the property of their diocese. In Aachen, it was used to hold all bishops to the standard set by previous monks (though, as Brown shows, monastic life had also always included multiple and complex ways to interact with property, rather than simple and full-throated rejection).
30 IC, ed. by Werminghoff, 35, pp. 356–57.
31 Devisse, 'L'influence de Julien Pomère', pp. 293–94.
32 IC, ed. by Werminghoff, 107–09, pp. 382–83.
33 IC, ed. by Werminghoff, 120, pp. 399–400.
34 IC, ed. by Werminghoff, 121–22, pp. 440–42.

only by the tithes of the ecclesiastical holdings, but by the tithes of the canons' property as well. Their private property thus contributed to the fulfilment of the canons' social duties, which were, in a sense, also devotional: The compilers quoted Matthew 25. 35 ('I was a stranger, and you took me in') to show that taking care of *pauperes* would almost literally bring the canons closer to Christ.[35] But private property also reduced the economic strain on the community as a whole, allowing canons to be less concerned with their livelihood and thus, somewhat paradoxically, supporting their ability to cultivate a religious life.

While Pomerius's reconciliation of handling property with *vita contemplativa* seems to have been highly influential on the bishops assembled in Aachen, it was not the only model of religious life they used. They also cited letters by Jerome (and one wrongly attributed to him) to spell out a programme of practices more conventionally associated with a monastic life. Recurring themes are rejection of property, fasts, and prayer, as well as avoiding contact with women as far as possible.[36] In Jerome's letter to the priest Nepotian (*Epistula* 52), quoted at length in Chapter 94, he suggests Nepotian read it together (*copulatum*) with that to the monk Heliodorus, his uncle.[37] Thus, Jerome himself did not see his instructions as applicable exclusively to monks, and the compilers of the *IC* seem to have quite deliberately clericalized the letters of the 'militant propagandist of monasticism'[38] even further. For instance, in *Epistula* 125, Jerome tried to convince Rusticus of a monastic life. While trying to pre-emptively refute the criticism of maligning clerics, Jerome also stressed the virtue of their profession, saying that Rusticus should 'live in the monastery so that [he would] deserve to become a cleric'.[39] With all references to Rusticus's monastic aspirations cut in the *IC*, this quote seems to suggest that not only monk-like virtues in general, but living in a monastery specifically was a prerequisite for a clerical career. Thus, the bishops in Aachen used Jerome's letters — sometimes with, sometimes against his apparent intention — to flesh out the idea that they had introduced via Taio-Gregory: as a precondition of wielding pastoral power, canons would both be held to the same standard of individual Christian perfection as monks, and have at their disposal a similar set of basic ascetic practices to achieve that perfection.[40]

---

35 *IC*, ed. by Werminghoff, 141, p. 416.
36 *IC*, ed. by Werminghoff, 94–98, pp. 370–77. The misattributed letter is Chapter 98 (*Epistula ad Oceanum de vita clericorum*). No hypotheses regarding its authentic author have been advanced, but it was one of a number of pseudonymous texts written against the practice of syneisactism (priests living in sexless marriage with virgins) using markedly misogynist language (see Elliott, *Spiritual Marriage*, p. 36). In the *IC*, it was used to reinforce that socializing with women was dangerous for clerics, a point also made in the (authentic) *Epistola ad Nepotianum* (Jerome, *Epistulae*, ed. by Hilberg, no. 52, 1, pp. 370–71).
37 *IC*, ed. by Werminghoff, 94, p. 370.
38 Fürst, *Hieronymus*, p. 43.
39 Jerome, *Epistulae*, ed. by Hilberg, no. 125, 17, III, p. 136; see *IC*, ed. by Werminghoff, 94, p. 374.
40 On the use of patristic texts in the *IC*, see also the contribution by Kramer and Wieser in this volume.

Just like in a monastery, the canons were, for instance, supposed to live surrounded by walls; the prelates were also told to control who entered and exited the *claustrum*.[41] As Jerome had suggested to a number of his correspondents, canons were only allowed to speak to women if there were witnesses present and under no circumstances enter their dwellings.[42] But if the church happened to be located within the walls of the *claustrum*, women were allowed to enter for service; conversely, canons seem to have been allowed to leave to 'attend to the divine duties' (*divinis obsequiis incubare*).[43] The compilers did not make explicit what exactly those duties included, but they were probably social as well as liturgical: the hospital and the church could be outside the walls of the *claustrum*. Explicitly pastoral duties like preaching and taking confession are, surprisingly, not mentioned, though that might be due to the different grades of ordination within the canonical community. Additionally, leaving the cloister might, like owning property, only have been seen as a danger to a religious life if approached with the wrong mindset; even if there was no specific 'divine duty' to fulfil, all canons could, as the *IC* frequently reminds them, contribute to an ideal Christian society by providing a good example to the laypeople they encountered.[44] At any rate, it is clear that the canons' communities had to be enclosed enough to protect them from secular entanglements, but open enough for them to contribute to the ideal Christian order in the secular world. The outcome of this balancing act was supported by a sophisticated patristic argument.

Volatility and Virginity in the *Institutio sanctimonialium*

In the case of the *IS*, however, it is not clear that the bishops were engaged in any balancing act, sophisticated or otherwise: even though both the *IC* and the *IS* arose from the same process of reflection, some have argued that the bishops put so little thought into their ideal of a female canonical community that a comparison between those two ideals might be futile. Franz Felten doubted that they had any intention beyond 'stowing away' religious women, as the *IS* is much shorter than the *IC*, less detailed and seemingly more confused both in content and vocabulary.[45] The patristic collection in particular is far less extensive, consisting only of more or less abridged versions of three of Jerome's letters (Chapters 1–3), Cyprian of Carthage's *De habitu virginum* (Chapter 4), Caesarius of Arles' *Vereor* (Chapter 5), and a text misattributed to Athanasius (or Anas[i]us, see below) (Chapter 6). Additionally, as Gerhard

---

41 *IC*, ed. by Werminghoff, 117, p. 398 and 143, p. 418.
42 *IC*, ed. by Werminghoff, 144–45, pp. 418–20.
43 *IC*, ed. by Werminghoff, 143–44, p. 418.
44 *IC*, ed. by Werminghoff, 123, pp. 404 and 145, p. 420.
45 Felten, 'Frauenklöster im Frankenreich', pp. 93–95.

Schmitz has shown, the compilers probably did not even assemble these few texts themselves, but rather copied them from a pre-existing collection: the same excerpts from these six texts — though not in the same order — appear in BnF, MS lat. 13440, fols 109^v–177^r.[46]

However, they also used other collections of patristic texts to and about religious women, as attested by the lengthy patristic quotes in Chapters 7 and 22. In fact, we may be able to pinpoint one — or at least a close relative: Lindsay Rudge has identified a 'Caesarian booklet', a collection of texts ascribed to Caesarius of Arles that contains the letters of which Chapters 5, 6, and 7 of the *IS* are excerpts (though only Chapters 5 and 7 are labelled 'Caesarian' in the *IS*).[47] The oldest manuscript witness of the 'booklet' also anonymously transmits a text entitled *Ad virgines*, a Latin prose translation of Evagrius Ponticus's Greek poem 'Προς την παρθένον'.[48] The Nonantola manuscript transmitting both *institutiones* uniquely adds this text to the *IS*, ascribing it to Augustine.[49] If some version of the 'Caesarian booklet' was available in Aachen, the compilers of the *IS* at least had to put enough thought into it to choose between different patristic collections. Additionally, the use of a pre-existing collection does not imply the absence of selective criteria, as Schmitz seems to suggest.[50] As with Taio's clericalized version of Gregory the Great's works in his *Sententiae*, the collection presumably was useful to the compilers of the *IS* because of its abbreviation *as well as* its interpretation of the texts.

Even if, then, the patristic collection of the *IS* is 'a rambling florilegium discussing the basic premises underlying the existence of women religious', as Steven Vanderputten recently stated,[51] it can still provide some insight into how the compilers framed their prescriptions.[52] A detailed analysis of the patristic texts quoted here — as well as, crucially, the sections cut in the process of excerption — will show that, in the first six chapters of the *IS*, its compilers neatly set up the issue that made regulating female religious communities necessary in their eyes, without having the patristic collection suggest any specific solution to that issue.

---

46 Schmitz, 'Zu den Quellen', pp. 23–52. The manuscript is available online, see Works Cited, below.

47 Chapter 7 is no longer part of the patristic collection, but its prescriptions on the desired qualities of abbesses are supplemented by a lengthy quote from a letter probably written by Caesarius's nephew Teridius to Caesaria the Younger, the second abbess of St Jean. The *IS* attributes it to Caesarius himself and calls the recipient 'Oratoria' (*IS*, ed. by Werminghoff, 7, p. 442), a corruption of the original title '*epistola hortatoria ad virginem deo dedicatam*'. See de Vogüé and Courreau, 'Lettre de Teridius à Césarie', pp. 398–405.

48 Rudge, 'Texts and Contexts', pp. 141–49. See BAV, MS Reg. lat. 140, fols 123^v–132^r and 139^v–150^v, available online, see Works Cited, below.

49 Schmitz, 'Aachen 816', pp. 517–22.

50 Schmitz, 'Zu den Quellen', p. 51 n. 105.

51 Vanderputten, *Dark Age Nunneries*, p. 16.

52 Schilp, *Norm und Wirklichkeit*, p. 62 n. 13 already called for an analysis of the patristic collection in his monographic treatment of the *IS* but could not supply it himself.

The first three chapters of the *IS* consist of excerpts from Jerome's letters to Eustochium (*Epistula* 22), Demetrias (*Epistula* 130), and Furia (*Epistula* 50). In Chapter 22, the compilers also quote from his letter to Laeta (*Epistula* 107, a text not found in either of the aforementioned patristic collections). Given Jerome's numerous contacts with devout women, the Carolingians seem to have seen his texts as uniquely suitable for instruction of female religious. In two manuscripts of the Vulgate from Tours, for example, he was depicted as preaching to women.[53] His letter to Eustochium is fittingly entitled *De virginitate servanda* in some manuscripts as it is a fundamental treatment of virginity in the context of female religious life.[54] Based on Psalm 45 (44). 11–12 ('Forget also thine own people, and thy father's house; so shall the king greatly desire thy beauty: for he is thy Lord'), he starts with a definition of female virginity as marriage to the divine king,[55] followed by a lengthy treatment of the danger the women and their virginity would be in: even God, Jerome warns, cannot raise up a fallen virgin.[56] The emphasis both on the superiority and volatility of female virginity will prove to be somewhat of a *leitmotif* in the patristic collection.

Jerome also gives quite specific instructions concerning Eustochium's lifestyle, admonishing her to only drink wine when medically necessary, eat moderately (as opposed both to eating excessively and fasting ostentatiously), pray at the canonical hours, and read holy scripture regularly.[57] These are essentially the same instructions Jerome gave in his letter to Nepotian cited in the *IC*, but in this case, the *ability* to control one's body through these practices is more explicitly linked to the *necessity* to control one's body in order to remain virginal.[58]

Also, again similar to Jerome's letters in the *IC*, these instructions are stripped of their explicitly monastic context. For example, the complete version contains a discussion of the differences between coenobite and anchorite monasticism,[59] arguably a panorama of — for Jerome — legitimate forms of monasticism.[60] Since a passage from the letter to Eustochium that is not transmitted in the *IS* is quoted in the *IC*,[61] the compilers presumably had access to an unabridged version but decided not to use it. Part of the reason the compilers of the *IS* chose the collection identified by Schmitz might have been that *its* compiler had already, in a sense, generalized the texts to define a generic form of female religious life, freed from their institutional

---

53 McKitterick, 'Women in the Ottonian Church', pp. 82–86.
54 Jerome, *Epistulae*, ed. by Hilberg, no. 22, I, p. 143 n. to l. 2.
55 *Institutio Sanctimonialium Aquisgranensis* [henceforth *IS*], ed. by Werminghoff, 1, pp. 423–24.
56 *IS*, ed. by Werminghoff, 1, pp. 424–25.
57 *IS*, ed. by Werminghoff, 1, pp. 425–28.
58 *IS*, ed. by Werminghoff, 1, pp. 426–27.
59 Jerome, *Epistulae*, ed. by Hilberg, no. 22, 35–36, I, pp. 197–201.
60 Driver, 'From Palestinian Ignorance to Egyptian Wisdom', pp. 296–300.
61 *IC*, ed. by Werminghoff, 124, p. 404.

and historic context. That way, it was easier for the bishops assembled in Aachen to confer the authority of Jerome's name on their own — and rather specific — institutional interpretation of female religious life.

The effect of this generalization is especially apparent in the following two chapters, excerpts from Jerome's letters to Demetrias, a fantastically rich member of the senatorial nobility (Chapter 2), and Furia, a widow (Chapter 3). One might have expected the compilers to use them to address issues relevant to specific subgroups of their audience,[62] but the excerpts mostly reiterate points already made in Chapter 1. The basic ascetic instructions are taken up again in both chapters;[63] the emphasis on the volatility of virginity only in Chapter 2 (to such an extent that it apparently seemed necessary to point out that the intention was not to make an ominous prophecy).[64] All references to Demetrias's nobility or wealth are cut, as are almost all references to Furia's widowhood. And even when Jerome cites 1 Timothy 5. 5–6 ('Now she that is a widow indeed, and desolate, trusteth in God, and continueth in supplications and prayers night and day. But she that liveth in pleasure is dead while she liveth'), it seems to be a general critique of women who dress provocatively.[65] In fact, he cites the same passage in his letter to Eustochium, here referring to a *puella*.[66]

Chapter 4 consists of excerpts from Cyprian of Carthage's *De habitu virginum*. Jerome referred Eustochium to this text, suggesting she read it if she wanted more information on virginity.[67] While this explicit citation did not make it into the abridged version, it might be one of the reasons why the compiler of the patristic collection of BnF, MS lat. 13440 found it fitting to combine these texts. They also continued their generalization and enhanced the similarity between the two: like Chapter 1, the abridged version begins with praise of female virginity — among other things as 'blossom of the ecclesiastical bud, [...] image of God [and] more illustrious part of Christ's herd'[68] — before treating at length the perils to which it was supposedly exposed.[69] Cyprian is particularly concerned with the outward signs of female virginity. From the biblical injunction that virgins be 'holy in body and spirit'

---

62 For proof that noble women were indeed only a subgroup of their audience, see Felten, 'Wie adelig waren Kanonissenstifte', pp. 85–88.
63 *IS*, ed. by Werminghoff, 2, pp. 429–30; 3, p. 431.
64 *IS*, ed. by Werminghoff, 2, p. 430.
65 *IS*, ed. by Werminghoff, 3, p. 431.
66 *IS*, ed. by Werminghoff, 1, p. 425.
67 On the relationship between these texts, see Adkin, 'Cyprian's *De habitu virginum*', pp. 237–54.
68 *IS*, ed. by Werminghoff, 4, p. 432.
69 Since Cyprian's text thus seems no more misogynistic than Jerome's letters, I am sceptical of Felice Lifshitz's suggestion that the absence of almost all of Chapter 4 in Würzburg, UB, MS M.p.th.q. 25 (break between fols 19ᵛ and 20ʳ; available online, see Works Cited, below) points to a female scribe consciously cutting a 'notoriously misogynistic diatribe' (Lifshitz, *Religious Women*, p. 14).

(1 Corinthians 7. 34) he draws the somewhat peculiar conclusion that their chastity would have to be visible in their clothing so as to avoid any doubt. *Habitus*/habit here carries the same double meaning as in English. Cyprian supplements this with short exegeses of 1 Peter 3. 1–4 and 1 Timothy 2. 9–10, both of which are concerned with the superiority of spiritual over worldly adornments. Specifically, he warns the women that dressing up in fine clothes and jewellery would make men lust after them, threatening their 'chastity of mind' even if no fornication occurred.[70] Thus, for Cyprian, female virginity was threatened both by the temptations the women were subject to and the temptations they caused in others.

While it is possible that Cyprian wrote *De habitu virginum* to religious women in *vita communis*,[71] explicit references to a community of women first appear in Chapter 5 of the *IS*, an excerpt of one of Caesarius of Arles' letters to the nuns of Saint-Jean (usually called *Vereor* after the first word of the complete version). Dedicated to fostering female religious life in Arles, he had founded Saint-Jean together with his sister Caesaria and written a *regula* for it. Thus, even more so than Jerome, whose texts were also quoted in the *IC*, Caesarius's name seems to have carried special authority in matters concerning religious women.[72] Caesarius himself, however, probably saw a lot of his thought as applicable independent of gender. He wrote a rule for male religious as well, but more importantly, *Vereor* is also transmitted in a version where the grammatical gender of the recipients was changed. In fact, there are more textual witnesses for the male than the female version.[73] Parts of the male *Vereor* already appeared in Caesarius's *Regula Monachorum*,[74] suggesting that he produced both versions himself. While the bishops in Aachen were probably unaware of this and certainly were not looking specifically for a unisex text, it can serve as a helpful reminder that religious men and women had to contend with many of the same problems.

Caesarius most probably wrote *Vereor* before the *Regula ad Virgines*, as one would expect him to reference a written rule in his exhortations had it existed already. In the intervening years, his views on enclosure seem to have radicalized, resulting in much stricter enclosure in the *Regula*.[75] Writing *Vereor*, he was already quite pessimistic about the women's ability to protect their virginity, telling them that '[w]e ought to resist the other vices with all our strength. Against sexual desire, however, it is proper not to fight but to flee'.[76] But he does not yet draw the conclusion that all connections to the

---

70 *IS*, ed. by Werminghoff, 4, pp. 432–33.
71 Dunn, 'Infected Sheep and Diseased Cattle', p. 11.
72 Klingshirn, *Caesarius of Arles*, pp. 29–32, 104–05 and 250–52.
73 Diem, 'Gender of the Religious', p. 440.
74 Rudge, 'Texts and Contexts', pp. 160–65.
75 Diem, *Das monastische Experiment*, pp. 168–93.
76 *IS*, ed. by Werminghoff, 5, p. 435; Caesarius of Arles, *Vereor*, ed. and trans. by de Vogüé and Courreau, 4, p. 312, trans. by Klingshirn, 21. 4, p. 133.

outside world would have to be cut. Instead, he tells the nuns never to leave the cloister, 'or only because of great and unavoidable need'. Familiarities with laymen are to be avoided 'to the extent that [they] can'.[77] Thus, Caesarius stresses the volatility of female virginity without prescribing any *specific* safeguards in *Vereor* — again leaving an opportunity for the compilers of the *IS* to insert their own institutional ideas.

Caesarius is also quite concerned with the ideal of equality within the walls of the cloister. Thus, he admonishes the nuns not to try to outdo each other in saintliness, but to support each other. No one should flaunt their noble birth or riches, be it in conduct or clothing.[78] But, as with the protection of virginity, no institutional safeguards against this are put in place. Not so in the complete version of *Vereor*, however: the excerpts in the *IS* leave out large parts concerned with monastic poverty in general and specifically the necessity to donate one's riches to the poor upon entering a monastery instead of leaving it to one's family.[79] While it is unclear whether the complete version was available in Aachen, criticizing religious women who attach importance to worldly riches *without* banning private property outright certainly fits well with the model for private property they developed for male communities. Here, the incentive to use the abridged version as it appears in the collection of BnF, MS lat. 13440 rather than the complete letter is most clear.

The patristic collection of the *IS* ends with a text entitled [*sermo*] *sancti Athanasii episcopi ad sponsas Christi* in Werminghoff's edition. However, aside from the Nonantola manuscript, only one twelfth-century manuscript gives this name, while all others transmit *Anas(i)i*, as does BnF, MS lat. 13440.[80] Even though Athanasius was seen as somewhat of an authority on ascetic matters since Evagrius of Antioch had translated his *Vita Antonii* into Latin,[81] his name does not seem to have been the main reason this text was included in the *IS*, or in Schmitz's collection. There seems to be agreement among modern scholars that the complete version was written by Pelagius;[82] like this condemned heretic, its author certainly stresses the role that individual agency plays in salvation, here exemplified by religious women's conscious choice of virginity: 'Like holier and purer offerings, they are elected by the Holy Spirit as merited by their choice (*pro voluntate suae meritis*)'.[83]

---

77 *IS*, ed. by Werminghoff, 5, p. 435.
78 *IS*, ed. by Werminghoff, 5, pp. 435–36.
79 Caesarius of Arles, *Vereor*, ed. and trans. by de Vogüé and Courreau, 6, pp. 316–19 and 8, pp. 324–27; trans. by Klingshirn, 21. 6 and 8, pp. 134–37.
80 *IS*, ed. by Werminghoff, p. 437, cf. Rome, BNCR, MS Vitt. Em. 1348, fol. 120^v and BnF, MS lat. 13440, fol. 122^r.
81 Müller, 'Das Phänomen des "lateinischen Athanasius"', p. 18.
82 Müller, 'Das Phänomen des "lateinischen Athanasius"', p. 24. See also Evans, *Four Letters of Pelagius*, pp. 20 and 41–51.
83 *IS*, ed. by Werminghoff, 6, p. 437.

While more than half of this text was cut, the excerpts retain the substance of the rather repetitive complete version:[84] while virgins, the 'brides of Christ', would earn a higher celestial reward than their counterparts bound in secular marriages, they could only do so if they also lived an ideal Christian life in all other respects. A large portion of this chapter is inspired by 1 Corinthians 7. 34 ('The unmarried woman careth for the things of the Lord, that she may be holy both in body and in spirit'), but the point here is that virginity is not enough to be 'holy in body'. Rather, the virgins would have to purify each body part *spiritually*; for example, they are told to cleanse their tongues of lies and their ears of worldly chatter.[85] As with Cyprian, the exegesis of 1 Corinthians 7. 34 is followed by one of 1 Peter 3. 1–4 and 1 Timothy 2. 9–10. But while Cyprian had used those bible passages to warn women of the desire they would cause in men, thus jeopardizing their virginity, 'Athanasius' lists general Christian virtues as 'spiritual adornments' the women should don to please their celestial husband.[86] In general, their virginity seems remarkably secure compared to the other texts. Beyond two passing calls to 'preserve [their] intention' (*[con]serva propositum*), the possibility that their virginity might be in danger is not entertained.[87] At the very end, they are even told to provide an imitable example of sanctity to a grammatically masculine 'someone' (*quisquis*).[88] Ending the patristic collection on such an 'optimistic' note might indicate a readiness to take the needs and input of religious women into account.[89]

Given the clear tendency to stress the volatility of female virginity in the preceding five chapters, the overarching message of the patristic collection still seems to be that virginity, while possible to safeguard, was in constant danger. Thus, one would expect the compilers of the *IS* to follow the general trend of prescribing strict enclosure[90] — sometimes seen as a necessary condition for the existence of female religious communities[91] — to minimize that danger. However, as with male canonical communities, their ideal of a community of canonesses does not seem to include radical enclosure or flight from the world but rather 'just' an ordered, communal religious life. They allowed the canonesses not only servants, but also private property,[92] the administration

---

84 Compare the edition of the full version: *Epistula S. Seueri*, ed. by Halm, pp. 225–50; for the transmission in the *IS*, see siglum A.
85 *IS*, ed. by Werminghoff, 6, pp. 438–39.
86 *IS*, ed. by Werminghoff, 6, pp. 439–40.
87 *IS*, ed. by Werminghoff, 6, pp. 439 and 441. In the complete version, the second call to perseverance is supplemented by a Cyprian-like reminder not to provide opportunities for lust to anyone else; see *Epistula S. Seueri*, ed. by Halm, p. 250.
88 *IS*, ed. by Werminghoff, 6, p. 441.
89 Cf. Felten, 'Frauenklöster im Frankenreich', p. 62.
90 On this trend, see Schulenburg, 'Strict Active Enclosure', esp. pp. 56–58.
91 Muschiol, *Famula Dei*, p. 74.
92 *IS*, ed. by Werminghoff, 21, p. 452; 9, pp. 444–45.

of which they obviously foresaw leading to contacts with male laypeople.[93] Schilp interpreted this as a transfer of (lay) elite lifestyles into religious communities,[94] but even if the relative leniency of IS was the product of a compromise between bishops and elite women, this compromise still would have had to be justified within the normative framework the compilers had designed themselves.

In the IC, it seems obvious why the compilers were not willing to take the 'easy route' and guarantee the canons' ordered life through radical enclosure: their 'divine duties' necessitated continued engagement outside the walls of the *claustrum*. But there is no indication that they ascribed similar duties to female canons. In fact, the Laodicean canon banning women from the altar was reiterated in the IC.[95] While there are some uses of pastoral imagery in the IS, they refer only to the abbess's role *within* the community.[96] On that issue, the IS echoes two concerns from the IC in a lengthy quote from a letter misattributed to Caesarius in Chapter 7: the dangers of leaving the safety of the community weighted against the dangers of neglecting one's duties, and a preoccupation with agreement of teaching and conduct.[97] In Chapter 14, the abbesses are also told to provide the same 'twofold nourishment' — i.e. edify by teaching and by example — that prefects of male canonical communities had to provide, as they, too, would have to account for the souls of their subjects.[98] But as far as the male compilers of the IS were concerned, the abbesses — and certainly not the simple canonesses — would not contribute to the salvation of Christians outside their community in a way that would necessarily bring them into direct contact with them.

Of course, they did take responsibility for the salvation of laypeople in a way that brought them into indirect contact with them. Monastic communities were bound to the wider *populus Christianus* in prayer — not, as Renie Choy has shown, by the simple reciprocity of praying for those who had donated to their community, but by tying their own salvation to that of others in perfect Christian *caritas* that was both cause and effect of intercessory prayer.[99] The preoccupation with virginity in particular probably stemmed, at least in part, from the desire to guarantee effective intercessory prayer: while the patristic authors quoted in the IS never link bodily purity with effective prayer, there

---

93   IS, ed. by Werminghoff, 20, p. 451. Contacts with secular women were not encouraged either, but clearly were not thought to pose the same danger to the canonesses' virginity. The compilers obviously did not consider same-sex attraction.

94   Schilp, *Norm und Wirklichkeit*, pp. 78–80 and 179–80. There is some evidence that landholding was in fact quite common for religious women; see Garver, *Women and Aristocratic Culture*, p. 111.

95   IC, ed. by Werminghoff, 82, p. 367.

96   IS, ed. by Werminghoff, 7, p. 442.

97   IS, ed. by Werminghoff, 7, p. 443. On this letter, see above, n. 47.

98   IS, ed. by Werminghoff, 14, p. 448; IC, ed. by Werminghoff, 123, p. 403.

99   Choy, *Intercessory Prayer*, passim, esp. pp. 48–75.

are at least indications that its compilers did just that. Women suffering from 'a certain bodily indisposition', for example, were forbidden from taking part in the canonical hours.[100] Gisela Muschiol has interpreted this as directed at menstruating women, who, in earlier penitentials and capitularies, had been excluded from the Eucharist or banned from entering churches; this, though, was the first time they were banned from the canonical hours, which were originally thought of as private liturgy.[101] The compilers also stressed the necessity of a correct frame of mind for effective prayer,[102] suggesting they were concerned with both the physical and spiritual preconditions for female intercessory prayer. If, then, intercessory prayer was central to the canonesses' own salvation and the only way for them to contribute to the salvation of those outside their community, it seems even more puzzling that the bishops designing these communities left open so many avenues for connections to the secular world which could potentially jeopardize its effectiveness.

Irene Crusius suggested that these connections could be explained by 'public functions' that communities of canonesses could carry out better than Benedictine nuns. Specifically, she hypothesized that this function was the education of laypeople, as Benedictine monasteries were — at least in principle — only supposed to educate *oblati*, that is children who would become Benedictine monks or nuns when their education was complete.[103] The chapter concerned with the education of girls is supplemented by a lengthy quote from Jerome's letter to Laeta, making it one of only two prescriptive chapters with long patristic quotes, suggesting that education was in fact a central part of the function of female canonical communities. However, I am not convinced it was 'public' in the way Crusius seems to imagine. There is no indication that canonesses were supposed to educate boys to prepare them for secular office — which is not to say that they definitely did not educate boys, only that it cannot serve as an explanatory model on the normative level.

Furthermore, the girls mentioned in Chapter 22 were probably seen as prospective canonesses. Concerning the education of Laeta's daughter Paula, Jerome gives the same basic ascetic instructions as in the three letters quoted in Chapters 1–3 and compares Paula to Samuel being raised in the temple.[104] As Mayke de Jong has shown, this biblical image was commonly used when describing child oblates, suggesting that the girls were also understood as having been given to the canonical community as a sacrificial offering; thus, they would — again, in principle — not have been allowed to leave the community after their education.[105] In fact, the compilers of the *IS* may have deliberately cut parts of Jerome's letter that suggested that Paula's education

---

100 *IS*, ed. by Werminghoff, 15, p. 448, l. 32/33.
101 Muschiol, 'Das "gebrechlichere Geschlecht"', p. 26.
102 *IS*, ed. by Werminghoff, 16, p. 449.
103 Crusius, '*Sanctimoniales*', pp. 16–18.
104 *IS*, ed. by Werminghoff, 22, pp. 452–54.
105 De Jong, *In Samuel's Image*, pp. 180–85.

would be different from the one she would have received in a monastery: In the original, Jerome's instructions are depicted as a clear second-best solution, the best being Paula's oblation to Jerome's monastery in Jerusalem.[106] Education, then, appears as an extension of the canonesses' responsibility for the salvation of those *within* the community.

I suggest that this riddle can only be solved by reading the IS not only through the lens of its own patristic collection, but that of the IC as well. The compilers of the IC seem to have considered the issues of enclosure and private property by asking which points of contact to the secular world they could *allow* without jeopardizing the canons' individual spiritual perfection. Similarly, reading the IS as an answer to that question — rather than the question of how canonesses could be *shut off* from the secular world — makes it possible to square the relative leniency of Chapters 7–28 with the constant anxiety around female virginity in the patristic collection without having to find a direct analogue to male canons' 'extramural' responsibilities in the IS.[107]

Again, the treatment of private property is instructive. Chapter 9 of the IS explicitly mentions three options for newly admitted canonesses: they can donate their property to the community with or without retaining the right to usufruct, or they can keep their property rights while publicly transferring the administration to a layperson of their choice. These options are bookended by references to the canonesses' mindset: they should be free from disturbance (*perturbatio*) and public occupations (*forensium rerum occupatio*). The chapter then ends with a reiteration of the prohibition to admit canonesses whose youth or lifestyle could cause scandals.[108] This might suggest that canonesses could only retain private property if they were judged to be able to deal with it in a way that would not disturb their or their sisters' religious life.[109] Thus, as for Pomerius, owning private property did not necessarily mean being entangled in secular occupations. If it was administered with the correct mindset and used to sustain a religious lifestyle, it was perfectly legitimate. Therefore, receiving the revenue of said property from the laymen who worked and administered it also had to be legitimate, which is why the bishops tried to create a controlled environment to do so instead of banning male guests outright: it had to be done at a certain time and place, and it had to be witnessed by other canonesses.[110]

---

106 De Jong, *In Samuel's Image*, p. 21. See Jerome, *Epistulae*, ed. by Hilberg, no. 107, 13, II, pp. 303–05.
107 Though not through comparison with the IC, Steven Vanderputten, *Dark Age Nunneries*, p. 20 recently came to a similar conclusion when he suggested that the IS was supposed to 'indicate a range of legitimate disciplinary and organizational possibilities'.
108 IS, ed. by Werminghoff, 9, pp. 444–45.
109 Schilp, *Norm und Wirklichkeit*, pp. 94–95 (though he stresses the impossibility of such a prediction).
110 IS, ed. by Werminghoff, 20, p. 451.

Pomerius's dictum of church property as '*vota* [here: *oblationes*] *fidelium, praetia peccatorum, patrimonia pauperum*' is also taken up again in the *IS* when mandating the construction of a hospital outside the cloister. While they only explicitly stress the spiritual consequences that alienating its property would have for the *male* cleric managing it, the compilers clearly saw canonical property through the same 'Pomerian' lens regardless of gender. The hospital thus would not only have to be sustained by the tithe of the community's property but also of the gifts the canonesses received.[111] Unlike in the *IC*, though, the canonesses' private property is not drawn on to support the hospital.[112] Writing from the perspective of male clerics, the bishops might simply have been more concerned with the salvation of the male clerics, and did not consider the same issues for canonesses at the same level of complexity.[113]

One might also speculate, though, that the canonesses were responsible for the support of the second hospital within the walls of the community to be used exclusively by widows and female paupers (*viduae et pauperculae*).[114] The structure within the *claustrum* is called *receptaculum* and the one outside *hospitale*, but the fact that both words are used interchangeably in the *IC* suggests that both served the same function as any early medieval hospital:[115] providing shelter and nourishment for a certain number of *pauperes*, as well as 'symbolic *caritas*' here represented by washing of the feet.[116] Clearly, care for *pauperes* was considered a central function of canonical communities.[117] But as it was also a central part of the canonesses' individual devotion, securing the provisioning of a hospital was not enough; the canonesses also needed to have access to the *pauperes*. While the bishops assembled in Aachen let male canons leave the community to 'attend to the divine duties', this was apparently seen as too risky for canonesses, which is not surprising, given that they used most of the patristic collection to demonstrate the volatility of female virginity. Ordering the construction of gender-specific hospitals might not have been an elegant solution, but it is one that clearly illustrates the bishops' willingness to weigh competing goals against each other and strike a balance between enclosure and engagement in the world.

---

111 *IS*, ed. by Werminghoff, 28, pp. 455–56.
112 *IC*, ed. by Werminghoff, 141, p. 416.
113 On the *IC* as self-reflection, see Kramer and Wieser's contribution in this volume.
114 *IS*, ed. by Werminghoff, 28, p. 455.
115 *IC*, ed. by Werminghoff, 141, p. 416.
116 Bodarwé, 'Pflege und Medizin', pp. 246–47.
117 Boshof, 'Untersuchungen zur Armenfürsorge', pp. 268–67 and 288–90, suggests that these *pauperes* were in fact poor, in the sense that they depended at least in part on donations for their livelihood (as opposed to *pauperes* as non-*potentes*: Bosl, 'Potens und Pauper', pp. 60–87). See also Claussen, *Reform*, pp. 192–200, who argues that Pomerius in *De vita contemplativa* might have limited charity to the 'holy poor', but that it was reinterpreted in Chrodegang of Metz's *Regula canonicorum* to apply to all the poor.

Conclusion

Whether the compilers of the Aachen *institutiones* were trying to protect their subjects against being judged a 'bad shepherd' or a 'fallen virgin', they did so with an acute understanding that individual spiritual perfection might be possible within communal religious life, but was always volatile. Independently of gender, it was to be shaped by the same basic repertoire of practices: prayer, fasts, and some form of enclosure. As the sources of the (perceived) volatility were gender-specific — the (arguably) logically necessary paradox of pastoral power on the one hand, simple misogyny on the other — the intended institutional implementation of those practices varied, but was determined by a somewhat unified normative logic: the bishops tended to regulate threats to the virtue of their rules' subjects instead of outright forbidding them.

This unified normative logic became apparent only by reading the *IS* through the lens of the *IC*. But doing so also necessarily meant taking on a male, clerical perspective on female canonical communities, in some ways obscuring the motives of the women in those communities, as well as those of their families. From their perspective, for example, private property might not have appeared as a threat to religious life as much as a right they were simply not willing to give up.[118] Additionally, while the men who wrote the *IS* clearly only ascribed the 'extramural' dimensions of pastoral responsibility — preaching and providing a positive example to laypeople — to male canons, the canonesses themselves may have been more confident in their ability to lead laypeople to salvation. One might even speculate that the compilers of the original patristic collection were women who cut all references to strict enclosure and total renunciation of wealth because they wanted to keep their religious communities in contact with the world around them; in typically Carolingian fashion, they sought to make 'mutually fruitful the inevitable encounter between the [terrestrial and spiritual] spheres'.[119] For the bishops to apply the same logic to male and female canonical communities could, then, have been nothing more than an *ex post* justification.

---

118 Garver, *Women and Aristocratic Culture*, pp. 113–14 and 191–92.
119 Sullivan, 'What was Carolingian Monasticism?', p. 283.

Works Cited

Manuscripts

Città del Vaticano, Biblioteca Apostolica Vaticana, MS Reg. lat. 140 <https://digi.vatlib.it/view/MSS_Reg.lat.140> [accessed 8 September 2021]

Paris, Bibliothèque national de France, MS fonds latin 13440 <https://gallica.bnf.fr/ark:/12148/btv1b100360354> [accessed 8 September 2021]

Rome, Biblioteca Nazionale Centrale di Roma, MS Vitt. Em. 1348 <http://digitale.bnc.roma.sbn.it/tecadigitale/manoscrittoantico/BNCR_Ms_VE_1348/BNCR_Ms_VE_1348/1> [accessed 8 September 2021]

Würzburg, Universitätsbibliothek, MS M.p.th.q. 25 <http://vb.uni-wuerzburg.de/ub/permalink/mpthq25> [accessed 8 September 2021]

Primary Sources

Caesarius of Arles, *Vereor*, in *Césaire d'Arles: Oeuvres Monastiques*, vol. 1: *Oeuvres pour les Moniales*, ed. and trans. by Adalbert de Vogüé and Joël Courreau, Sources Chrétiennes, 345 (Paris: Editions du Cerf, 1988), pp. 294–337; trans. by William E. Klingshirn, *Caesarius of Arles: Life, Testament, Letters*, Translated Texts for Historians, 19 (Liverpool: Liverpool University Press, 1994), pp. 131–39

Epistula S. Seueri ad Claudiam sororem de uirginitate, ed. by Karl Halm, in *Sulpicii Severi libri qui supersunt*, Corpus Scriptorum Ecclesiasticorum Latinorum, 1 (Vienna: Gerold, 1866), pp. 225–50

Hludowici imperatoris epistolae ad archiepiscopos missae, ed. by Albert Werminghoff, in *Monumenta Germaniae Historica: Concilia*, II. 1 (Hannover: Hahn, 1906), pp. 456–64

Institutio Canonicorum Aquisgranensis, ed. by Albert Werminghoff, in *Monumenta Germaniae Historica: Concilia*, II. 1 (Hannover: Hahn, 1906), pp. 307–421; trans. by Jerome Bertram, *The Chrodegang Rules: The Rules for the Common Life of the Secular Clergy form the Eighth and Ninth Centuries; Critical Texts with Translations and Commentary*, Church, Faith and Culture in the Medieval West (Aldershot: Ashgate, 2005), pp. 132–74

Institutio Sanctimonialium Aquisgranensis, ed. by Albert Werminghoff, in *Monumenta Germaniae Historica: Concilia*, II. 1 (Hannover: Hahn, 1906), pp. 421–65

Jerome, *Epistulae*, ed. by Isidor Hilberg, in *Sancti Eusebii Hieronymi Opera. Sect. 1: Epistulae*, Corpus Scriptorum Ecclesiasticorum Latinorum, 54–56, 3 vols (Vienna: Tempsky, 1910–1912)

Pomerius, *De vita contemplativa*, in *Patrologiae cursus completus: series latina*, ed. by Jacques-Paul Migne, LIX (Paris: Garnier, 1844–1864), cols 411–520; trans. by Mary Suelzer, *Julianus Pomerius: The Contemplative Life*, Ancient Christian Writers. The Works of the Fathers in Translation, 4 (Westminster: Newman, 1947)

Secondary Works

Adkin, Neil, 'Cyprian's *De habitu virginum* and Jerome's *Libellus de virginitate servanda (Epist. 22)*', *Classica et Mediaevalia*, 46 (1995), 237–54

Bodarwé, Katrinette, 'Pflege und Medizin in mittelalterlichen Frauenkonventen', *Medizinhistorisches Journal*, 37.3–4 (2002), 231–63

Boshof, Egon, 'Untersuchungen zur Armenfürsorge im fränkischen Reich des 9. Jahrhunderts', *Archiv für Kulturgeschichte*, 58.2 (1976), 265–339

Bosl, Karl, 'Potens und Pauper: Begriffsgeschichtliche Studien zur gesellschaftlichen Differenzierung im frühen Mittelalter und zum "Pauperismus" des Hochmittelalters', in *Alteuropa und die moderne Gesellschaft: Festschrift für Otto Brunner*, ed. by Alexander Bergengruen and Ludwig Deike (Göttingen: Vandenhoeck & Ruprecht, 1963), pp. 60–87

Brown, Peter, *Through the Eye of a Needle: Wealth, the Fall of Rome, and the Making of Christianity in the West, 350–550 AD* (Princeton: Princeton University Press, 2012)

Choy, Renie, *Intercessory Prayer and the Monastic Ideal in the Time of the Carolingian Reforms*, Oxford Theology and Religion Monographs (Oxford: Oxford University Press, 2016)

Claussen, Martin Allen, *The Reform of the Frankish Church: Chrodegang of Metz and the 'Regula Canonicorum' in the Eight Century*, Cambridge Studies in Medieval Life and Thought, 4.61 (Cambridge: Cambridge University Press, 2004)

Crusius, Irene, '*Sanctimoniales quae se canonicas vocant*: Das Kanonissenstift als Forschungsproblem', in *Studien zum Kanonissenstift*, ed. by Irene Crusius, Veröffentlichungen des Max-Planck-Instituts für Geschichte, 167/Studien zur Germania Sacra, 24 (Göttingen: Vandenhoeck & Ruprecht, 2001), pp. 9–38

Demacopoulos, George, 'Gregory's Model of Spiritual Direction in the *Liber Regulae Pastoralis*', in *A Companion to Gregory the Great*, ed. by Bronwen Neil and Matthew dal Santo, Brill's Companions to the Christian Tradition, 47 (Leiden: Brill, 2013), pp. 205–24

Devisse, Jean, 'L'influence de Julien Pomère sur les clercs carolingiens: De la pauvreté au ve et ixe siècles', *Revue d'histoire de l'Église de France*, 56 (1970), 285–95

Diem, Albrecht, *Das monastische Experiment: Die Rolle der Keuschheit bei der Entstehung des Klosterwesens*, Vita regularis, 24 (Münster: LIT, 2005)

——, 'The Gender of the Religious: Wo/Men and the Invention of Monasticism', in *The Oxford Handbook of Women and Gender in Medieval Europe*, ed. by Judith M. Bennett and Ruth Mazo Karras (Oxford: Oxford University Press, 2013), pp. 432–46

Driver, David, 'From Palestinian Ignorance to Egyptian Wisdom: Jerome and Cassian on the Monastic Life', *The American Benedictine Review*, 48 (1997), 293–315

Dunn, Geoffrey, 'Infected Sheep and Diseased Cattle, or the Pure and Holy Flock: Cyprian's Pastoral Care of Virgins', *Journal of Early Christian Studies*, 11.1 (2003), 1–20

Elliott, Dyan, *Spiritual Marriage: Sexual Abstinence in Medieval Wedlock* (Princeton: Princeton University Press, 1993)

Evans, Robert, *Four Letters of Pelagius* (London: Black, 1968)

Felten, Franz J., 'Wie adelig waren Kanonissenstifte (und andere weibliche Konvente) im (frühen und hohen) Mittelalter?', in *Studien zum Kanonissenstift*, ed. by Irene Crusius, Veröffentlichungen des Max-Planck-Instituts für Geschichte, 167/Studien zur Germania Sacra, 24 (Göttingen: Vandenhoeck & Ruprecht, 2001), pp. 39–128

——, 'Frauenklöster im Frankenreich: Entwicklungen und Probleme von den Anfängen bis zum frühen 9. Jahrhundert', in *Frühformen von Stiftskirchen in Europa: Funktion und Wandel religiöser Gemeinschaften vom 6. bis zum Ende des 11. Jahrhunderts; Festgabe für Dieter Mertens zum 65. Geburtstag*, ed. by Sönke Lorenz and Thomas Zotz, Schriften zur südwestdeutschen Landeskunde, 54 (Leinfelden-Echterdingen: DRW, 2005), pp. 31–95

Floryszczak, Silke, *Die 'Regula Pastoralis' Gregors des Großen: Studien zu Text, kirchenpolitischer Bedeutung und Rezeption in der Karolingerzeit*, Studien und Texte zu Antike und Christentum, 26 (Tübingen: Mohr Siebeck, 2005)

Foucault, Michel, 'The Subject and Power', *Critical Inquiry*, 8.4 (Summer 1982), 777–95

Fürst, Alfons, *Hieronymus: Askese und Wissenschaft in der Spätantike* (Freiburg: Herder, 2003)

Garver, Valerie, *Women and Aristocratic Culture in the Carolingian World* (Ithaca: Cornell University Press, 2009)

Jong, Mayke de, *In Samuel's Image: Child Oblation in the Early Medieval West*, Brill's Studies in Intellectual History, 12 (Leiden: Brill, 1996)

Klingshirn, William, *Caesarius of Arles: The Making of a Christian Community in Late Antique Gaul*, Cambridge Studies in Medieval Life and Thought, 4.22 (Cambridge: Cambridge University Press, 1994)

Kramer, Rutger, *Rethinking Authority in the Carolingian Empire. Ideals and Expectations during the Reign of Louis the Pious (813–828)*. The Early Medieval North Atlantic, 6 (Amsterdam: Amsterdam University Press, 2019)

Leyser, Conrad, *Authority and Asceticism from Augustine to Gregory the Great*, Oxford Historical Monographs (Oxford: Oxford University Press, 2000)

Lifshitz, Felice, *Religious Women in Early Carolingian Francia: A Study of Manuscript Transmission and Monastic Culture* (New York: Fordham University Press, 2014)

McKitterick, Rosamond, 'Women in the Ottonian Church: An Iconographic Perspective', in *The Frankish Kings and Culture in the Early Middle Ages*, ed. by Rosamond McKitterick, Variorum Collected Studies Series, 477 (Aldershot: Variorum, 1995), pp. 79–100

Mordek, Hubert, *Bibliotheca capitularium regum Francorum manuscripta: Überlieferung und Traditionszusammenhang der fränkischen Herrschererlasse*, Monumenta Germaniae Historica, Hilfsmittel, 15 (Munich: Monumenta Germaniae Historica, 1995)

Müller, Christian, 'Das Phänomen des "lateinischen Athanasius"', in *Von Arius zum Athanasianum: Studien zur Edition der 'Athanasius Werke'*, ed. by Annette von Stockhausen and Hanns Christof Brennecke, Texte und Untersuchungen zur Geschichte der altchristlichen Literatur, 164 (Berlin: De Gruyter, 2010), pp. 3–42

Muschiol, Gisela, *Famula Dei: Zur Liturgie in merowingischen Frauenklöstern*, Beiträge zur Geschichte des alten Mönchtums und des Benediktinertums, 41 (Münster: Aschendorff, 1994)

———, 'Das "gebrechlichere Geschlecht" und der Gottesdienst: Religiöser Alltag in Frauengemeinschaften des Mittelalters', in *Herrschaft, Bildung und Gebet: Gründung und Anfänge des Frauenstiftes Essen*, ed. by Günter Berghaus, Thomas Schilp, and Michael Schlagheck (Essen: Klartext, 2000), pp. 19–27

Rudge, Lindsay, 'Texts and Contexts: Women's Dedicated Life from Caesarius to Benedict' (doctoral thesis, University of St Andrews, 2007)

Schilp, Thomas, *Norm und Wirklichkeit religiöser Frauengemeinschaften im Frühmittelalter: Die 'Institutio sanctimonialium Aquisgranensis' des Jahres 816 und die Problematik der Verfassung von Frauenkommunitäten*, Veröffentlichungen des Max-Planck-Instituts für Geschichte, 137/Studien zur Germania Sacra, 21 (Göttingen: Vandenhoeck & Ruprecht, 1998)

———, 'Die Wirkung der Aachener "Institutio sanctimonialium" des Jahres 816', in *Frühformen von Stiftskirchen in Europa: Funktion und Wandel religiöser Gemeinschaften vom 6. bis zum Ende des 11. Jahrhunderts; Festgabe für Dieter Mertens zum 65. Geburtstag*, ed. by Sönke Lorenz and Thomas Zotz, Schriften zur südwestdeutschen Landeskunde, 54 (Leinfelden-Echterdingen: DRW, 2005), pp. 163–84

Schmitz, Gerhard, 'Aachen 816: Zu Überlieferung und Edition der Kanonikergesetzgebung Ludwigs des Frommen', *Deutsches Archiv für Erforschung des Mittelalters*, 63 (2007), 497–545

———, 'Zu den Quellen der Institutio Sanctimonialium Ludwigs des Frommen (a. 816): Die Homiliensammlung des Codex Paris lat. 13440', *Deutsches Archiv für Erforschung des Mittelalters*, 68 (2012), 23–52

Schulenburg, Jane T., 'Strict Active Enclosure and its Effects on the Female Monastic Experience (ca. 500–1100)', in *Medieval Religious Women*, vol. 1: *Distant Echoes*, ed. by John Nichols and Lillian Shank, Cistercian Studies, 71 (Kalamazoo: Cistercian Publications, 1984), pp. 51–86

Suchan, Monika, *Mahnen und Regieren: Die Metapher des Hirten im Frühen Mittelalter*, Millennium-Studies, 56 (Berlin: De Gruyter, 2015)

Sullivan, Richard, 'What was Carolingian Monasticism? The Plan of St Gall and the History of Monasticism', in *After Rome's Fall: Narrators and Sources of Early Medieval History. Essays presented to Walter Goffart*, ed. by Alexander Murray (Toronto: University of Toronto Press, 1998), pp. 251–87

Timmermann, Josh, 'Sharers in the Contemplative Virtue: Julianus Pomerius's Carolingian Audience', *Comitatus*, 45 (2014), 1–44

Vanderputten, Steven, *Dark Age Nunneries: The Ambiguous Identity of Female Monasticism, 800–1050* (Ithaca: Cornell University Press, 2018)

Vogüé, Adalbert de, and Joël Courreau, 'Lettre de Teridius à Césarie: Introduction', in *Césaire d'Arles: Oeuvres Monastiques*, vol. 1: *Oeuvres pour les Moniales*, trans. and ed. by Adalbert de Vogüé and Joël Courreau, Sources Chrétiennes, 345 (Paris: Editions du Cerf, 1988), pp. 398–417

Werminghoff, Albert, 'Die Beschlüsse des Aachener Concils im Jahre 816', *Neues Archiv für ältere deutsche Geschichtskunde*, 27 (1902), 605–75

Reception and Reflection

STEPHEN LING

'Superior to Canons, and Remaining Inferior to Monks'

Monks, Canons, and Alcuin's Third Order*

In 802 Alcuin, abbot of St Martin's, Tours, wrote to bishop Arn of Salzburg. Amongst other things Alcuin advised his friend to:

> Let those people who may congregate be diligently examined, any from the canons, any from the monks, and any who are given to the third grade, who fluctuate between the two, superior to canons and remaining inferior to monks.[1]

This statement has proved puzzling for scholars; to Bullough it represented an unusually 'conspicuous ambiguity' on the part of Alcuin,[2] whilst for de Jong it is seen as evidence that Alcuin did not conceive of a clear distinction between the monastic and canonical orders, as espoused by Chrodegang of Metz in his Canonical Rule (c. 755).[3] Through a close comparison of this letter to idealized texts such as Chrodegang's *Regula canonicorum*, the *Admonitio generalis*, and the *Institutio canonicorum*, this chapter will explore what Alcuin may have meant when he referred to this third grade and what this may tell us about Alcuin's understanding of the distinction between the canonical clergy and monks. It will demonstrate that while these comments were certainly unusual, Alcuin was not alone in discussing this ambiguous third grade. Such sentiments can also be found within the Rule of Chrodegang

---

* I would like to thank the editors and other contributors to this volume for their thoughts on this chapter.
1 'Ut diligenter examinetur, quid cui conveniat personae, quid canonicis, quid monachis, quid tertio gradui, qui inter hos duos variatur; superiori gradu canonicis et inferiori monachis stantes', Alcuin, *Epistolae*, ed. by Dümmler, no. 258, p. 416.
2 Bullough, 'What has Ingeld to do with Lindisfarne', pp. 100–01.
3 De Jong, 'From Scolastici to Scioli', p. 51.

> **Stephen Ling** currently is Researcher Development Officer at the University of Salford. His research interests focus on attempts to define and regulate the way of life practised by the canonical clergy in early medieval Europe.

(*c*. 755) and within the works of Amalarius of Metz, and as such were reflective of a wider school of thought within the Frankish Church, albeit one which was eventually rejected by both the court and condemned in the *Institutio canonicorum* of 816.

Alcuin and Eighth-Century Attempts to Define the Life of the Canonical Clergy

At first glance Alcuin's statements suggest that he had a fundamentally different understanding of the distinction between monks and canons than those of his contemporaries. It is perhaps telling that in 802 Charlemagne rebuked Alcuin and the community of St Martin's for the imprecision of their way of life, stating:

> How frequently your way of life has been criticised by many, and not without reason. **You sometimes called yourselves monks, sometimes canons and sometimes neither**. So, for your good, to do away with your bad reputation, we chose a suitable master and director for you, and invited him from a distant province. [Alcuin] could have taught you the right way of life by word of counsel and influenced you by the example of good conduct, for he was a religious man. But alas, all has turned out otherwise […] You who have shown contempt for our orders, whether you call yourselves canons or monks, must appear at our pleasure […].[4]

This certainly chimes with the opinions expressed by Alcuin in his letter to Arn of Salzburg. The exact nature of Alcuin's own way of life and the question of whether he saw any fundamental difference between canons and monks clearly vexed his Carolingian patron. Even after Alcuin's death in 804 there was tension about the way of life practised by the deacon during

---

4 'Ipsi quippe nostis, qui congregatio huius monasterii ac servi Dei — et utinam veri — dicimini, qualiter iam crebro vita vestra a multis diffamata est; et non absque re. Aliquando enim monachos, aliquando canonicos, aliquando neutrum vos esse dicebatis. Et nos, consulendo vobis, et ad malam famam abolendam, magistrum et rectorem idoneum vobis elegimus et de longinquis provintiis invitavimus, qui et verbis et admonitionibus vos rectam vitam instruere et, quia religiosus erat, bonae conversationis exemplo potuisset informare. Sed pro dolor aliorsum cuncta conversa sunt, et diabolus vos quasi ministros suos ad seminandam discordiam, inter quos minime decebat, invenit: scilicet inter sapientes et doctores ecclesiae. Et qui peccantes corrigere et castigare debuerunt, cogitis ad peccatum invidiae atque iracundiae pro rumpere. Sed illi Deo miserante nequaquam adsensum vestris malis suggestionibus praebituri sunt. Vos autem, qui contemptores nostrae iussionis extitistis, sive canonici sive monachi vocamini, ad placitum nostrum'. Alcuin, *Epistolae*, ed. by Dümmler, no. 247, pp. 400–01; trans. by Allot, no. 115, pp. 122–23. For details of the background to this letter, see Meens, 'Sanctuary'; Collins, *The Carolingian Debate*, pp. 91–121; Meens, 'Politics, Mirrors of Princes and the Bible'; Noizet, 'Alcuin Contre Theodulphe'; Kramer, 'The Exemption that Proves the Rule', pp. 231–51.

his lifetime. His hagiography, composed around 829 by an anonymous monk of Ferrières, claimed that he was 'a true monk without the monk's vow' and goes on to state that Alcuin wished to end his days at Fulda, living 'according to the rule of St Benedict', but was prevented from doing so by Charlemagne.[5] Despite these statements, the author described his subject entering heaven dressed correctly in the *dalmatica*, which was a sign of both his clerical office and his specific grade of deacon.[6] These statements reflect Alcuin's own interest in monasticism and in the 790s he recalled how he had greatly admired the 'way of life' practised at the monastery of Murbach and how he had considered joining their brethren.[7] Given this evidence it is easy to conclude, as some have, that Alcuin did not see a 'sharp' and substantive difference between the monastic and the canonical orders.[8] Alcuin's accepting attitude towards those who fluctuated between the monastic and canonical orders appears to be out of step with the wider attempts on both sides of the channel to distinguish between these two orders and to establish ecclesiastical discipline.

Here it is worth pausing to examine these efforts, particularly those which had occurred during Alcuin's lifetime. Although the terms *canonici* and *canonici clerici* had been used since at least the sixth century, denoting either those clerics who were entitled to take an income from ecclesiastical property or who lived according to the 'canons' of the Church, from the 740s onwards there was great interest in defining, regulating, and separating canons from the monastic order.[9] In 738 Boniface addressed both monks and the canonical clergy as separate orders in his letter to the Anglo-Saxons.[10] Around 747 Pippin III and the Frankish episcopate sought guidance from Pope Zacharias about the nature of life within episcopal households.[11] Likewise, in England both the 747 Council of Clofesho and the *Dialogues* of Archbishop Ecgberht of York sought to regulate the ecclesiastical order and addressed clerics separately to

---

5   *Vita Alcuini*, ed. by Arndt, 5, pp. 187–88 and 11, p. 191; de Jong, 'From Scolastici to Scioli', p. 50; Bullough, *Alcuin*, p. 166.
6   *Vita Alcuini*, ed. by Arndt, 27, p. 196; Bullough, 'What has Ingeld', p. 101 n. 27. For a discussion of the dalmatica see Miller, *Clothing the Clergy*, pp. 21–22, 28–29, and 249.
7   Alcuin, *Epistolae*, ed. by Dümmler, no. 271, pp. 429–30; Bullough, *Alcuin*, p. 166.
8   De Jong, 'From Scolastici to Scioli', p. 51.
9   While the origins of the term canonici are debated, it is clear that the name predates Chrodegang. It had been used from the fourth century onwards to describe clerics who had a right to claim financial support from the Church and from the sixth century onwards to describe those clerics who lived according to a rule or 'canon'. See Scholz's chapter in the present volume, 'The Organization of the Clergy and the *canonici* in the Sixth Century'. See also Barrow, *Clergy*, pp. 74–75; Schieffer, *Die Entstehung von Domkapiteln*, pp. 100–06; Picker, *Pastor Doctus*, pp. 118–19; Dereine, 'Chanoines', cols 354–64.
10 Cubitt, 'The Clergy in Early Anglo-Saxon England', p. 276; Boniface, *Epistolae*, ed. by Dümmler, no. 46, p. 74.
11 *Codex Carolinus*, ed. by Gundlach, no. 3, pp. 479–87.

monks.[12] The latter shows that the cathedral community of York was actively involved in discussions regarding the nature of monastic and clerical lives, and it was in this environment that Alcuin (b. c. 740) was raised.[13]

In Francia, the Synod of Ver, held in 755, continued to focus on the definition and regulation of monks and canons and Chapters 10 and 11 addressed these orders in turn. Monks were commanded to remain within the enclosure living a true regular life, while those tonsured who were permitted to own property, namely canons, were ordered to 'be in a monastery under a regular order or under a canonical order, at the hand of the bishop'.[14] In the wake of these developments Chrodegang, bishop of Metz, composed his rule, defining and regulating the life of the canonical clergy of his cathedral. In so doing he followed both the guidance of Pope Zacharias, by combining the precepts of the Benedictine Rule with 'the admirable traditions of the venerable fathers' and also enforced the findings of the Synod of Ver (755).[15] Chrodegang's *Regula canonicorum* is often seen as a landmark text and it represents the first extant and explicit rule for canons, defining their way of life as a distinct order within the Church.[16] The immediate influence of Chrodegang's text has often been overstated and whilst the document was circulated within Chrodegang's circle it is unlikely that his *Regula canonicorum* was known in York during Alcuin's childhood.[17]

Chrodegang's Rule was certainly of interest to Angilramn, archchaplain of the palace (784–91), and Chrodegang's successor as bishop of Metz.[18] Angilramn made some additions to the text and it is possible that he was the author of its final section (Chapters 30–34), which is different in tone to the main body of the rule.[19] Here there was a move away from normative texts and a focus on real world practical issues, including instructions on how one could join the order of canons. Angilramn made a concerted effort in the 780s

---

12 *Council of Clovesho (747)*, ed. by Hadden and Stubbs, pp. 362–76; *Dialogues Egberti*, ed. by Hadden and Stubbs, pp. 404–13; For discussions of these texts see Cubitt, 'Clergy in Early Anglo-Saxon England', pp. 273–87; Cubitt, *Anglo-Saxon Church Councils*, pp. 99–152; Ryan, 'Archbishop Ecgberht and his Dialogus', pp. 41–60.
13 For a discussion of Alcuin's early years see Dales, *Alcuin*, pp. 28–39, and Bullough, *Alcuin*, pp. 127–326.
14 *Concilium Vernense a. 755*, ed. by Boretius, 10, 11, p. 35.
15 Claussen, *Reform*, pp. 114–206; Bertram, *Chrodegang Rules*, pp. 12–26. For Zacharias's influence see Ling, 'The Cloister and Beyond', pp. 68–74.
16 Claussen, *Reform*, pp. 19–58.
17 For a close analysis of the immediate impact of Chrodegang's Rule within the Frankish Church see Ling, 'Analysing Attigny'.
18 For a synopsis of Angilramn's career see Kempf, in Paul the Deacon, *Liber de Episcopis*, ed. and trans. by Kempf, pp. 4–8.
19 Angilramn named himself as the author of an additional clause in Chapter 20 of the rule, 'Mihi autem Angilramn […]', *Regula Sancti Chrodegangi*, ed. and trans. by Bertram, 20, pp. 39, 67. For a discussion of the final section of the Rule see Claussen, *Reform*, pp. 92–113; Claussen, 'Practical Exegesis', pp. 119–46; the suggestion that Angilramn may be the author of the final section of the Rule is my own.

to enhance the reputation of the city of Metz and to promote Chrodegang's *Regula canonicorum*.[20] His commissioning of the *Liber de episcopis Mettensibus* was part of this process and its author, the Lombard intellectual Paul the Deacon, portrayed Chrodegang as the paragon of episcopal virtue calling him: 'a distinguished man worthy of all praises'; an eloquent writer 'fluent in Latin'; and a man who was a 'nourisher of the servants of God', who imbued his clergy 'with divine law'.[21] The *Liber* also summarized Chrodegang's renewal of the cathedral community stating:

> He brought the clergy together and **made them live within the confines of a cloister in the image of a monastery. He established for them a Rule of how they should soldier in the Church.** He provided them with provisions and living resource — enough that, not needing free time for perishable business, they might focus only on the Divine Office.[22]

Angilramn's amendments to, interest in, and promotion of Chrodegang's *Regula canonicorum* are significant given his influential position as archchaplain of the Aachen palace. In fulfilling this prominent office Angilramn came into contact with many of the new arrivals at court in the 780s. This included Alcuin who was resident in Francia by 786: a link between the two can be detected in Alcuin's letter collection and Letter 90 reports that the archchaplain had commended Alcuin to Abbot Usualdo of St Salvatore di Rieti.[23]

The 780s and early 790s were periods of great activity for the Carolingian court and beyond.[24] Documents produced there and by key Church councils provided further attempts to define and distinguish the canonical clergy from the monastic order. Crucially Alcuin was involved directly, or at least witnessed, the creation of many of these documents, including the report of the 786 Legatine Synod held in England, and the *Admonitio generalis* (789).[25] Both of these documents focused more concretely on the difference between monks and canons. Chapter 4 of the Legatine Capitulary commanded:

> that bishops watch with diligent care that all canons live by canon law and that monks and nuns abide by their rules, in diet and in dress and

---

20 Paul the Deacon, *Liber de Episcopis*, ed. and trans. by Kempf, pp. 86–89.
21 Paul the Deacon, *Liber de Episcopis*, ed. and trans. by Kempf, pp. 12–28 and 86–89; Kempf, 'Paul the Deacon's Liber', pp. 279–99.
22 'Hic clerum adunavit, et ad instar cenobii intra claustrorum septa conversari fecit, nomamque eis instituit, qualiter in Ecclesia militare deberent; quibus annonas viteque subsidia sufficienter largitus est, ut perituris vacare negociis non indigentes, divinis solummodo officiis excubarent'. Paul the Deacon, *Liber de Episcopis*, ed. and trans. by Kempf, pp. 86 and 87–88.
23 Alcuin, *Epistolae*, ed. by Dümmler, no. 90, pp. 134–35; Bullough, *Alcuin*, p. 365.
24 Bullough, 'Aula Renovata'.
25 For the authorship of the *Admonitio generalis* see Bullough, *Alcuin*, pp. 379–80; *Admonitio generalis*, ed. by Mordek, Zechiel-Eckes, and Glatthaar, pp. 47–63.

private property, so that there might be a distinction between a canon, a monk, and a secular person.[26]

While there has been much debate over the exact role of Alcuin in the composition of the Legatine Capitulary there is no doubt that he was present at the council, where he acted as a legate for the archbishop of York and the Northumbrian king.[27] It is likely that Alcuin brought a copy of this document to Tours and he certainly drew on this text when writing to the boys of St Martin's.[28] Chapter 17 of the 813 Council of Tours also quoted directly from Chapter 20 of the 786 document, requesting that sermons should be translated into the 'rustic Roman tongue, so that all may more easily understand things which are said'.[29]

The *Admonitio generalis* also focused on the need to separate the canonical clergy from the monastic order. Most significantly Chapter 71 commanded:

> that those who enter upon clerical status, which we call the canonical life, live in all respects as canons, in conformity with their rule; and the bishop is to rule their life, just as the abbot rules that of monks.[30]

Although this seminal text was a collaborative effort produced by the key scholars of the court, Alcuin was likely one of the major contributors to the capitulary.[31] It is notable that both of these provisions are similar to Chapter 4 of the 786 Legatine Capitulary and may well have drawn directly upon it.[32] Here then we may find an example of Alcuin's influence on the production of this text. In all of these provisions there is a clear focus on the binary nature of the enclosed life. The religious were to be either canons or monks, and any middle ground was unacceptable.

---

26 'Ut episcopi diligenti cura prevideant, quo omnes canonici sui canonice vivant et monachi seu monachae regulariter conversentur, tam in cibis quam in vestibus seu peculiare, ut discretio sit inter canonicum et monachum vel secularem et illo habitu vivant'. Alcuin, *Epistolae*, ed. by Dümmler, no. 3, p. 22; trans. by Carella, p. 104.

27 Cubitt, *Anglo-Saxon Church Councils*, pp. 164–71; Bullough, *Alcuin*, pp. 346–56; Story, *Carolingian Connections*, pp. 61–64; Wormald, 'In Search of King Offa's Law-Code'; Carella, 'Alcuin and the Legatine Capitulary of 786'.

28 Alcuin, *Epistolae*, ed. by Dümmler, no. 131, pp. 193–98; Dales, *Alcuin*, pp. 193–220.

29 'in rusticam Romanam linguam aut Thiotiscam, quo facilius cuncti possint intellegere quae dicuntur', *Concilium Turonense a. 813*, ed. by Werminghoff, 17, p. 288; Alcuin, *Epistolae*, ed. by Dümmler, no. 3, p. 22. Wright, 'Late Latin and Early Romance', pp. 353–59; McKitterick, *Frankish Church*, pp. 84–85.

30 'Similiter qui ad clericatum accedunt, quod nos nominamus canonicam vitam, volumus ut illi canonice secundum suam regulam omnimodis vivant, et episcopus eorum regat vitam, sicut abbas monachorum', *Die Admonitio generalis*, ed. by Mordek, Zechiel-Eckes, and Glatthaar, 71, pp. 224–27; trans. by King, p. 217.

31 *Admonitio generalis*, ed. by Mordek, Zechiel-Eckes, and Glatthaar, pp. 47–63; Bullough, *Alcuin*, pp. 379–80.

32 *Admonitio generalis*, ed. by Mordek, Zechiel-Eckes, and Glatthaar, pp. 47–63.

Alcuin must therefore have been aware of these admonitions which attempted to ensure that the religious communities of Francia and Anglo-Saxon England lived a more defined life, either as monks or canons. Yet, while there was a widely acknowledged consensus on the need to distinguish between the monastic and canonical forms of life, documents such as the *Admonitio generalis* provided little in the way of substantive guidance on this issue. The distinctions between the two orders primarily focused on dress and nomenclature rather than on the practical differences. A total of nine clauses of *Admonitio generalis* address both monks and canons, requesting the same behaviour of both groups, or in the case of Chapter 26 ordering in a vague manner that both 'clerics and monks were to persist in their way of life and the promise which they have pledged to God'.[33] The lack of detail is telling, and defining the practical difference between monks and canons seems to have been left up to the leaders of local communities, whether they were bishops or abbots. As van Rhijn has argued, the *Admonitio generalis* acted as a call to arms spurring bishops, such as Theodulf of Orléans, to write episcopal statutes containing both ideological and practical guidance for the priests subjected to their authority.[34] Likewise, addressing the practical issue of defining the difference between canons and monks attracted the attention of Alcuin and others in the 780s and 790s.

This would certainly have been one of Alcuin's concerns when he was appointed abbot of the community of St Martin's of Tours in 796, and Charlemagne's rebuke of 802 implies that upon his appointment Alcuin had been tasked with correcting the way of life practised within the Basilica.[35] As one of the ancient basilicas of Francia, the community had a mixed clerical and monastic history. In his *Historia francorum* and his *De virtutibus beati Martin episcopi* Gregory of Tours (d. 594) describes a clerical community who performed the divine office within the basilica, and there is little evidence of monks at St Martin's until the mid-seventh century when the community was renewed by Queen Bathild (d. 680).[36] It was then listed as one of six senior basilicas granted immunity from episcopal control and whose renewed 'brothers' were ordered to live *sub sancto regulari ordine*.[37] Although imprecise, the implementation of this regime had monastic overtones and

---

33 Chapters 14, 21, 23, 26, 27, 29, 70, 71, 73, all discuss clerics alongside monks: *Admonitio generalis*, ed. by Mordek, Zechiel-Eckes, and Glatthaar, pp. 179–243.
34 Van Rhijn, *Shepherds*, pp. 33–49.
35 Alcuin, *Epistolae*, ed. by Dümmler, no. 247, pp. 400–01; For a discussion of Alcuin's appointment to Tours see Chelini, 'Alcuin, Charlemagne et Saint-Martin de Tours', pp. 19–50.
36 Pietri, 'Les abbés de basilique', pp. 8–12, at p. 12.
37 *Vita Balthildis*, ed. by Krusch, 9, p. 488; trans. by Fouracre and Gerberding, pp. 109–10; Atsma, 'Les monastères urbains du Nord de la Gaule', p. 169; Fox, *Power and Religion*, pp. 39–43; Wood, *Merovingian Kingdoms*, pp. 197–200.

the community were likely inspired by the 'monastic' practices of Luxeuil.[38] Given this history it is no surprise that the community used both monastic and clerical language to describe themselves, as abbot Alcuin was placed in an awkward position trying to untangle this clerical and monastic heritage and mixed nomenclature.

Angilramn of Metz's Addition to Chrodegang's *Regula canonicorum*

To understand what Alcuin meant by his reference to a third order, his statements must be compared to those of his contemporaries who also addressed the practicalities of life within canonical communities, and here the final chapters of Chrodegang's Rule prove enlightening. As discussed above these four chapters are different in tone to the rest of the rule, they lack the clear structure of the earlier part of the text, are less dependent on the Rule of Benedict, and address ad hoc practical concerns which may have arisen due to the implementation of the main Rule.[39] For these reasons Claussen has argued that Chapters 30–34 were composed after the rest of the Rule of Chrodegang and form an addendum or epilogue to the Rule.[40] It seems likely that these chapters were written by Angilramn of Metz and the contents certainly have more in common with capitulary texts of the 780s and 790s than those produced in Chrodegang's day.[41] Chapter 31: 'How one who intends specifically to join this order of canons in this congregation, may make a solemn donation of his property in person to the Church while reserving use of it for the duration of his life', is particularly useful when considering Alcuin's third order. This chapter is one of the longest within the entire Rule and dealing correctly with the property of the canons was a key concern, not only because of the criticism that could be levelled at worldly priests who were concerned with 'filthy lucre', but also because receiving an income from Church property was a defining feature of the order of canons.[42] Monks, by comparison, took full vows of poverty.

As Claussen has argued, the chapter forms an exegesis on Acts of the Apostles and this idealized model of the Christian community living and

---

38 Fox, *Power and Religion*, p. 40.
39 Claussen, *Reform*, pp. 92–113.
40 Claussen, 'Practical Exegesis', pp. 124–25.
41 For instance, Chapter 34, which deals with the care of the *matricularii* who were cared for by the community, fulfilled the requirement of Chapter 73/75 of the *Admonitio generalis*, which required all houses of canons and monks to establish hostels for the care of the poor.
42 *Capitulare missorum generale a. 802*, ed. by Boretius, 22, pp. 95–96; Ling, 'The Cloister and Beyond', pp. 22–64.

dining together and sharing resources was to be implemented by the canonical clergy of Metz.[43] This image is invoked in the opening section of the chapter:

> We read that in the early Church, **at the time of the Apostles, they were so much of one mind, so united, that they left everything, and each one sold his lands and laid the price before the feet of the Apostles; that no one of them called anything his own, but they had 'all things in common', so that they were said to have 'but one heart and one soul'.** Every day, 'breaking bread from house to house', they shared what they held in common, men, women and children alike, and the whole crowd were fired with faith and driven by love for them to provide enough for everyone in thanksgiving.[44]

Despite this, the author acknowledges that such perfection lay beyond the ability of most canons and therefore explains the somewhat complex methods by which a canon's individual property would become communal assets, even while the canon was permitted to receive an income from their land. Firstly, upon a canon's death all their property would revert to the Church. Next the text outlines the precarial relationship between the canons and the bishop. A canon was permitted to receive income from anything produced on their former lands, which now technically belonged to the Church, having been donated upon the canon's entry into the cloister:

> The clerics shall have no power to diminish, sell or exchange any of the property which they hold *in precarias*, neither in land, vineyards or forests, meadows, houses, buildings, serfs or freemen, nor any other immovable property, except as we have said, **during their lifetime they may do as they please with the revenue or produce of their labour.**[45]

This precarial income would be received from the bishop who managed the communal assets of the community. Interestingly, the author permitted canons to receive different incomes, and there was no standardized stipend.

---

43 Acts 2. 45–47; 4. 32–34; 4. 42–47; Claussen, 'Practical Exegesis', pp. 124–25.
44 'Licet legamus antiquam ecclesiam sub tempore apostolorum ita unianimem concordemque extetisse et ita omnia reliquisse, ut singuli predia sua vendentes a pedibus apostolorum precaria poneret, ut nullus eorum sibi aliquid proprium dicere audere, sed erant illis "omnia communa", unde et habere dicebantur "cor unum et animam unam"; cotide enim circa domus panes frangentes, quod in commune accipiebant, tam viri quam femine seu parvuli, omniquae vulgus ardore fidei accensi atque in amore religionis provocati, cunctis cum gratiarum actione sufficientia erat'. *Regula Sancti Chrodegangi*, ed. and trans. by Bertram, 31, pp. 46, 76–77.
45 'Et ipsi clerici de ipsis rebus quas in precarias habent, neque de terris neque de vineis aut silvis, pratis, domibus, aedificiis, mancipiis, accolabus, vel quibuslibet rebus imobilibus minuandi aut vendendi aut commutandi potestam non habeant, excepto, ut diximus, de illa fructa vel quod ibidem laborare potuerint viventes faciant quod voluerint'. *Regula Sancti Chrodegangi*, ed. and trans. by Bertram, 31, pp. 48, 79.

Wealthy members of the community were even encouraged to live off the produce of their lands:

> In the same way it is determined that the clergy who have enough property of their own to be able to live on it should do so, if they are so weak that they are unwilling to give everything to the church of God where they serve; in this way they may minister in the church for the love of Christ, for they serve him at their own expense. **If the stipend they would have received for their ministry is left in the hands of the bursar, he can give it to those who have nothing, and they can possess their own property without blame; for they too have to some extent renounced their property in that they are content with their own without thinking that they are entitled to anything more.**[46]

By comparison to this muted acknowledgement of need for such practical arrangements, the final section of the chapter is full of praise for those who wished 'to join the congregation and to renounce all property for the sake of perfection'.[47] Those who made such vows of poverty were to be supported by the bishop, and perhaps also those rich canons who were permitted to receive precarial income from their lands. This chapter therefore begins and ends with an invocation for canons to take full vows of poverty, yet even if they did so they would still be members of the order of canons. Self-evidently this group would be superior to those who received precarial incomes, and inferior to those who took full monastic vows.

This is not the only place within the text where such an internal cleavage can be detected. In Chapter 20 Angilramn added a paragraph to the rule which permitted canons to consume meat between Pentecost and its Octave, stating:

> On these eight most holy days the clergy of St Stephen the Protomartyr, being our own, may have permission to eat meat, except for those who have decided to abstain for the good of their souls, or because penance has been laid on them.[48]

Here again an elite group of religious appear, canons who live more perfect lives than their carnivorous brethren, but who are not monks. As discussed above, Alcuin and Angilramn certainly knew of each other, and given the latter's key position as archchaplain, it is likely that he took part in the discussions leading to the issuing of the *Admonitio generalis*. Given the allusions to a third group within Chrodegang's *Regula canonicorum*, it seems that Angilramn and Alcuin shared this practical understanding of the workings of canonical communities.

---

46 *Regula Sancti Chrodegangi*, ed. and trans. by Bertram, 31, pp. 47, 77.
47 *Regula Sancti Chrodegangi*, ed. and trans. by Bertram, 31, pp. 47, 78–79.
48 […] ut his sacratissimis octavo diebus clerus santi Stephani protumartyris, vel noster, licentiam habeat carnem edendi, excepto illi qui pro conpendio animarum suarum et poenitencia indicta se abstinere voluerint'. *Regula Sancti Chrodegangi*, ed. and trans. by Bertram, 20, pp. 39, 67.

Amalarius of Metz and Early Ninth-Century Approaches to the Life of the Canonical Clergy

While Charlemagne's condemnation of 802 suggests that this tripartite understanding of the communal life was deemed unacceptable by the emperor and his ecclesiastical advisors, the issue was far from settled. The ill-defined nature of the order of canons continued to disturb Charlemagne and this subject was raised in the briefing papers issued in 811, perhaps as part of the preparations for the five regional Church Councils held in 813.[49] These documents were not conventional capitularies, if such a thing may be said to exist; rather they contain a list of questions for consideration of the key office holders of the kingdom. Significantly the capitularies were written in the first person and as such Nelson has argued we may be able to detect the voice and personal interests of Charlemagne within them.[50] Clauses 11 and 12 of the *Capitula tractanda cum comitibus, episcopis et abbatibus* are particularly salient to any discussion of the regulation of canons and monks. Here the emperor asked:

> 11. About the life of those who are called canons, what sort ought it to be?
> 12. About the *conversatio* of monks, and whether any can be monks except those who observe the Rule of Benedict. It must be asked if there were monks in Gaul before the tradition of the Rule of St Benedict reached these dioceses.[51]

These questions are symptomatic of the wider debate and discussion regarding the nature of the communal life at the start of the ninth century. As clause 12 illustrates, the difficulty in defining the precise nature of life within ancient and prestigious abbeys such as those of St Martin, St Denis, and St Maurice d'Aguane, was a continuing concern.[52] Likewise, there was clearly still support for Alcuin's interpretation of a tripartite split between monks and canons and those 'who fluctuate between the two'. Within the *Officio candelabrorum* of the *Missae expositionis geminus*, composed around 814, and usually attributed

---

49 *Capitula tractanda*, ed. by Boretius, no. 71, pp. 161–62; *Capitula de causis*, ed. by Boretius, no. 72, pp. 162–64; For a discussion and translation of these memoranda see Nelson, 'The Voice of Charlemagne', pp. 76–88.
50 Nelson, 'The Voice of Charlemagne', pp. 80–85.
51 11. 'De vita eorum qui dicuntur canonici, qualis esse debeat?' 12. 'De conversatione monachorum, et utrum aliqui monachi esse possint praeteros qui regulam sancti Benedicti observant. Inquirendum etiam, si in Gallia monachi fuissent, priusquam traditio regulae sancti Benedicti in has paroechias pervenisset'. *Capitula tractanda*, ed. by Boretius, no. 71, pp. 161–62.
52 For St Denis see Chapter 10 of the present volume by Rembold: 'The Apostates of Saint Denis'; for St Maurice see Helvétius, 'L'abbaye d'Agaune', pp. 126–30; Ripart, 'Les Temps Séculiers', pp. 135–49. For a wider discussion see Ling, 'The Cloister and Beyond', pp. 64–100; Ling, 'Analysing Attigny'.

to Amalarius of Metz, the following description of the different forms of communal life may be found:[53]

> Because our church has separate ways to live: there are monks living in accordance with the contemplative life, and living separately are those devoted to the active life, the canons, and there are those who mix these ways, living a contemplative and active life.[54]

This passage is all the more interesting given Amalarius's position in 814. Amalarius had been appointed Archbishop of Trier in 809 and as such was likely a recipient of Charlemagne's 811 memoranda; he certainly replied to other queries issued by the court, particularly those concerning baptism.[55] His statements within the *Missae expositionis geminus* may represent Amalarius's own answer to the king's queries on the nature of the communal life and are perhaps indicative of arrangements within the cathedral community of Trier.

The congruence between Amalarius's statements and Alcuin's is striking and they clearly shared the same tripartite understanding of the communal life. Tracing the details of Amalarius's life and career is problematic and despite the prolific nature of his work he provided little in the way of autobiographical detail. Nonetheless a link between the two men can be detected within Amalarius's *De ordine antiphonarii*, where the author added certain responsories because he had heard them: 'I was a mere boy in the presence of *Albinus* [Alcuin], the most learned teacher'.[56] Although it has been argued that this is a literary trope acknowledging the posthumous mastery and authority of Alcuin, when paired with Amalarius's further statement that he had heard antiphons and responsories used to dedicate a church to St Michael, 'sung by *Albinus*', it seems highly plausible that Amalarius was part of Alcuin's circle.[57] In any case, wherever he was raised Amalarius clearly respected the opinions of Alcuin and drew directly on the Englishman's

---

53 There has been debate over the authorship of this text. Steck has suggested that it has been misattributed: Steck, *Der Liturgiker Amalarius*, pp. 119–74. As Jones has recently pointed out, Steck's arguments downplay the manuscript evidence. The only complete MS of this work, Zürich, Zentralbibl., MS Car. C. 102, seems to descend from a file copy from the correspondence between Amalarius and Peter of Nonantola: Jones, 'A Lost Treatise by Amalarius', pp. 44–45. See also Graeme Ward's chapter in the present volume.

54 'Quia nostra ecclesia habet separatim degentes in contemplativa vita, ut sunt monachi, et habet separtim morantes in activa vita, ut sunt canonici, et habet mixtim hos qui in contemplativa vita degunt et qui in activa', Amalarius of Metz, *Missae expositionis geminus*, ed. by Hanssens, p. 273. My thanks to Graeme Ward for drawing this text to my attention.

55 Amalarius, *Epistula ad Carolum Imperatorum*, ed. by Hanssens, pp. 236–51; for a brief discussion of this text and its context see Cabaniss, *Amalarius of Metz*, p. 28.

56 'Quando videbar puer esse ante Albinum doctissimum magistrum', Amalarius, *Liber de ordine antiphonarii*, ed. by Hanssens, pp. 93–94; Ward, 'The Order of History', p. 99.

57 'Audivi illas in ea festivitate canere Albinum doctissimum magistrum nostrae regionis'. Amalarius, *Liber de Ordine Antiphonarii*, c. 67,2 ed. by Hanssens, p. 99; Ward, 'The Order of History', p. 99. Collins argues that these are literary tropes rather than biographical details see Collins, *The Carolingian Debate*, p. 11.

works and letters and shared an approach with Alcuin when considering the ordering of the cloister.[58]

Amalarius's statement in the *Missae expositionis geminus* may also reflect his experience of the communal life practised within the cathedral community at Trier, where he served as bishop from 809 until his removal *c.* 814.[59] Trier had close ties to Alcuin: Richbod (d. 804) who served as Archbishop of Trier between *c.* 792 and 804 was Alcuin's *discipulus* and corresponded with the deacon receiving the nickname Macarius.[60] More significantly Wizo (d. 809), who succeeded Richbod as Archbishop of Trier, was also one of Alcuin's pupils and he has been identified by both Morin and Marenbon as Candidus-Wizo.[61] Candidus-Wizo was heavily involved in the controversy over the fugitive cleric which led to the rebuke of the way of life practised at St Martin. Alcuin petitioned his old pupils Candidus-Wizo and Fredigius to intercede with the emperor and present Alcuin's case in defence of the venerable traditions of St Martin's.[62] These personal links present a conduit through which a tripartite understanding of the communal life could have been transmitted and spread.

Institutionally Trier was also closely tied to its suffragan see of Metz and the local synods held within the metropolitan diocese presented a prime opportunity for Chrodegang and Angilramn to promote the practices of their cathedral community through local networks, particularly given their elevated position as primate of the Frankish Church and archchaplain of the palace, respectively.[63] Certainly we know that Bishop Lull (d. 786) made use of Chrodegang's 'Institutes' at Mainz, and the cathedral community of Strasbourg also seems to have been influenced by the way of life practised at Metz.[64] Trier too may have drawn inspiration from the practical arrangements espoused in Chapter 31 of Chrodegang's *Regula canonicorum* and alluded to

---

58 The Metz association rests on rather ambiguous foundations and Duckett's confident argument that Amalarius was brought up in Metz under Chrodegang's Rule should now be viewed more cautiously, see Duckett, *Carolingian Portraits*, p. 93; Chazelle, 'Amalarius's "Liber Officialis"', p. 329; and Steck, *Der Liturgiker Amalarius*, pp. 7–11. For Amalarius's use of Alcuin's letters see Bullough, *Alcuin*, pp. 19–20 and 32–33.
59 It is likely that he lost his see and for a period was confined to his monastery at Hornbach. For Amalarius's fall from grace see Cabaniss, *Amalarius of Metz*, p. 40 and p. 48; Jones, *A Lost Work*, pp. 166–74; Collins, *Carolingian Debate*, pp. 44–45; Hanssens, 'Introductio', I, p. 67; Oexle, 'Die Karolinger', pp. 332–34.
60 Bullough, *Alcuin*, pp. 346 and 371.
61 Morin, 'Un Saint de Maestrict', pp. 176–83; J. Morenbon: *Logic, Theology and Philosophy*, pp. 57–58.
62 Kramer, 'The Exemption that Proves the Rule', pp. 235–39.
63 Although technically a suffragan see of Trier it is seems Chrodegang's and Angilramn's titles elevated them above the usual Metropolitan hierarchy.
64 Lull reports that he had used Chrodegang's 'canonical institute' to excommunicate the priest Willefrith; *Bonifatii et Lulli Epistolae*, ed. by Dümmler, no. 110, p. 237. For a full discussion of this reference and influence of Chrodegang's *Regula canonicorum* in Mainz and Strasbourg, see Ling, 'Analysing Attigny'.

by Alcuin and Amalarius. The commonalities between the scripts of Metz, Trier, and Echternach suggests that these foundations formed a distinct *atelier* perhaps associated with the palace of Thionville, and such palaeographic and art historical evidence illustrates the close ties between these sites and suggests an exchange of personnel and ideas. Richbod in particular has been associated with this *atelier* and his career provides a link with both Alcuin and Angilramn. It is via the Annals of Lorsch, likely composed by Richbod, that we learn of Angilramn's death in 791 whilst on campaign against the Avars, a fact omitted from the narrative in the Royal Frankish Annals.[65]

The Purpose of the Third Order

Whether the statements of the *Missae Expositionis Geminus* represent the well-established traditions of Trier, or an innovation introduced by Amalarius in 809, it is clear that this community and its leader shared the interpretations of Angilramn, Alcuin, and Arn of Salzburg. Amalarius's explanation of the different orders of the Church offer further details on this school of thought within the Frankish Church, one which conceived of the order of canons as consisting of two subgroups: those who lived a more disciplined and contemplative life, similar to that advocated in Chapter 31 of the Rule of Chrodegang; and those who were 'too weak' to fulfil these higher requirements and who discharged their vows through the provision of pastoral care.

The needs for both types of canon is made clear in a variety of texts produced in the second half of the eighth century. The Rule of Chrodegang clearly envisioned an active life beyond the cloister for most canons.[66] Chapter 6 states:

> At the time of the Divine Office at None, **as soon as the signal has been heard let them abandon what they have in hand, and those who are close enough to the Cathedral that they can get there quickly should go with the greatest speed.** If anyone should be far away from the church, so that he cannot be there for the work of God at the canonical hours, and the bishop and archdeacon agree that this is true, he should celebrate the Office where ever he may be, in fear of God. The archdeacon, primicerius or warden should see to it that the bells are rung at the proper times.[67]

---

65 *Annales Laureshamenses*, ed. by Pertz, a. 791, pp. 34–35; trans. by King, *Charlemagne*, p. 139. For Richbod's authorship of the Annals of Lorsch see Fichtenau, 'Abt Richbod', pp. 277–304.
66 Ling, 'Interactions', pp. 127–42.
67 'Ad oram nonam divini officii, mox ut auditum fuerit signum, relictis omnibus quaelibet fuerint in manibus, qui sic propinquo de illo domo sunt, ut ibidem occurrere possunt, cum summa festinatione veniant. Et si longe ab ipsa ecclesia episcopus vel arcidiaconus ita esse perpendit cogat opus Dei cum tremore divino ubi tunc fuerit. Et praevideat arcidiaconus vel primicerius seu custor ecclesie ut illa signa conpetentibus sonent'. *Regula Sancti Chrodegangi*, ed. and trans. by Bertram, 6, pp. 33, 59–60.

This chapter draws on the Rule of Benedict, with its provision for a monk to perform the office in the fields, but the isolated and rural monastic setting was replaced by the urban setting of the episcopal city.[68] While monks were too busy themselves with manual labour, canons were to see to the pastoral needs of the urban population.[69] Although some were employed in this pastoral work, a core 'contemplative' group remained within the cathedral close who were to give the signal for the Office and would lead liturgical services within the enclosure. They also likely helped the bishop and archdeacon in tasks such as compiling and composing the 'tracts and homilies' which were to be read at the Sunday chapter attended by the entire clergy of the city.[70] In some cases they may also have been tasked with translating such sermons into the vernacular, and as noted above this was a topic of great interest to Alcuin and his successors at Tours.[71]

From the late 780s onwards the need for such doctrinal and liturgical experts was emphasized in a series of texts and court edicts associated with Angilramn and Alcuin. In 786 in the letter to the lectors Charlemagne explained the need for such expertise within the Church:

> [...] Fired by the example of our father Pippin, of reverend memory, by whose zeal all the churches of the Gauls became graced by singing in the Roman tradition, we, with wise judgement, **are no less concerned to embellish them with a series of readings of great excellence. For we discovered that despite correct intentions the readings compiled for the night office by the fruitless toil of certain men were by no means suitable, inasmuch as they were set out without the names of their authors and abounded with the distortions of innumerable errors.**[72]

The letter to the lectors may well represent the opinions of Angilramn and the task of correcting and producing the new homiliary referred to in the letter was given to Paul the Deacon (d. 799), who at the time was composing his *Liber*

---

68 Rule of Benedict, Chapter 50.
69 For a discussion of the urban nature of Chrodegang's *Regula canonicorum* see Claussen, *Reform*, pp. 206–90, particularly pp. 206–21 and pp. 276–89.
70 *Regula Sancti Chrodegangi*, ed. and trans. by Bertram, 8, pp. 33–34, 60–61.
71 *Concilium Turonense a. 813*, ed. by Werminghoff, 17, p. 288.
72 'Accensi praeterea venerandae memoriae Pippini genitoris nostri exemplis, qui totas Galliarum ecclesias romanae traditionis suo studio cantibus decoravit, nos nihilominus solerti easdem curamus intuitu praecipuarum insignire serie lectionum. Denique quia ad nocturnale officium compilatas quo rundam casso labore, licet recto intuitu, minus tamen idonee repperimus lectiones, quippe quae et sine auctorum suorum vocabulis essent positae et infinitis vitiorum an fractibus scaterent, non sumus passi nostris in diebus in divinis lectionibus inter sacra officia inconsonantes perstrepere soloecismos, atque earundem lectionum in melius reformare tramitem mentem, intendimus'. Charlemagne, *Karoli Epistola Generalis*, ed. by Boretius, no. 30, pp. 80–81; trans. by King, p. 208.

de episcopis Mettensibus for the archchaplain.[73] There is certainly an interesting correlation between the letter and the *Liber de episcopis*, which states:

> He [Chrodegang] ordered that his clergy, abundantly imbued with divine law and the Roman liturgy, observe the customs and rite of the Roman Church which up to that time had hardly been done in the church of Metz.[74]

Chrodegang, Angilramn's forefather, and Pippin, Charlemagne's forefather, were both seen as bringing Roman liturgy to the Frankish Church. This theme crops up again in Chapter 78 of the *Admonitio generalis* which focused on the importance of clergy learning Roman chant:

> […] in conformity with what our father of blessed memory, King Pippin, strove to bring to pass when he abolished the Gallican chant for the sake of unanimity with the apostolic see.[75]

Within this important text also came the influential command: 'Let schools for teaching boys the psalms, musical notation, singing, computation and grammar be created in every monastery and episcopal residence'.[76] Masters were commanded to ensure their boys had access to uncorrupted 'correct catholic books'. Another letter of admonition, the *Epistolae de litteris colendis*, repeats much of this chapter of the *Admonitio* and it is likely that all three documents were drafted at the same time.[77] This drafting in the royal writing office has been associated with both Angilramn and Alcuin, and represents their shared interest in this subject.[78]

The tripartite understanding of the communal life expressed by Angilramn, Alcuin, and Amalarius was a logical response to these requirements and pressures — a way to ensure that the basic needs of the laity were met, while also promoting correct liturgical practices and interpretations of sacred texts. Bishops and their canonical clergy had to live both 'active' and 'contemplative' lives, as Chapter 10 of the Rule of Chrodegang makes clear:

> Any clergy who are setting out on a journey with a bishop to any destination, must not neglect to observe his way of life, in so far as the nature of the

---

73 Kempf, 'Liber de episcopis', p. 8.
74 'Ipsumque clerum abundanter lege divina Romanaque imbutum cantilena, morem atque ordinem Romane Ecclesiae servare precepit, quod usque ad id tempus in Mettensi Ecclesia factum minime fuit'. Paul the Deacon, *Liber de Episcopis*, ed. and trans. by Kempf, pp. 87, 89.
75 '[…] secundum quod beatae memoriae genitor noster Pippinus rex decertavit ut fieret, quando Gallicanum tulit ob unanimitatem apostolicae sedis et sanctae Dei aeclesiae pacificam concordiam'. *Die Admonitio generalis*, ed. by Mordek, Zechiel-Eckes, and Glatthaar, 78, pp. 230–31; trans. by King, p. 218.
76 'Et ut scolae legentium puerorum fiant. Psalmos, notas, cantus, compotum, grammaticam per singula monasteria vel episcopia'. *Admonitio generalis*, ed. by Mordek, Zechiel-Eckes, and Glatthaar 70, pp. 222–25; trans. by King, p. 217.
77 Bullough, *Alcuin*, pp. 384–85; Mostert, '"… but they pray badly"', pp. 112–14.
78 Martin, 'Bemerkungen', pp. 251–52 and 265; Bullough, *Alcuin*, p. 385.

journey permits it. Let them not miss the appointed hours, both for the divine office and for anything else.[79]

The career of Angilramn of Metz illustrates the diverse nature of such journeys. As noted above, he served as archchaplain of the Palace and with his entourage likely conducted services at the various sites used by the court during the late 780s. At the Synod of Frankfurt (794) the role of Angilramn during these years was fondly remembered:

> Our lord king informed the holy synod that he had permission of the holy see, that is of Pope Hadrian, to regularly have the archbishop Angilramn in his palace on account of ecclesiastical matters.[80]

It may have been Angilramn and his canons who baptized the Saxon chief, Widukind, at Attigny in 785.[81] More significantly we can be certain that Angilramn accompanied Charlemagne on his Avar campaign of 791, as the Annals of Lorsch record his death during the expedition.[82] The Avar campaign is well known for its liturgical significance and, perhaps in response to the pestilence which decimated the army's horses, the clergy led the army in litanies and fasts as recorded in Charlemagne's letter to Queen Fastrada:[83]

> We for our part with the Lord's help performed many litanies for three days [...] **Every priest was to offer a special mass, except where infirmity prevented it; and those clerics who knew the psalms were to sing fifty, and during the time that the litanies were being performed they were to go unshod. This our clergy thought proper, and we for our part applied ourselves and with the Lord's help carried it out.**[84]

---

79 'Quicunque ex clero in itinere cum episcopo vel aliubi proficiscuntur, ordinem suum, in quantum iter vel ratio permiserit, non necglegent; et non eo debent preterire orae constitutae, tam officiis divinis, quam aliude'. *Regula Sancti Chrodegangi*, ed. and trans. by Bertram, 10, pp. 34, p. 61.

80 'Dixit etiam domnus rex in eadem synodum, ut a sede apostolica, id est ab Adriano pontifici, licentiam habuisse, ut Angilramnum archiepiscopum in suo palatio assidue haberet propter utilitates ecclesiasticas'. *Concilium Francofurtense a. 794*, ed. by Werminghoff, 55, p. 171, trans. by Loyn and Percival, *Charlemagne*, pp. 62–63.

81 *Annales Regni Francorum*, ed. by Kurze, a. 785, pp. 69–72, trans. by Scholz, pp. 62–63; *Annales Laureshamenses*, ed. by Pertz, a. 785, p. 32, trans. by King, *Charlemagne*, p. 136.

82 *Annales Laureshamenses*, ed. by Pertz, a. 791, p. 34, trans. by King, *Charlemagne*, p. 139.

83 For the equine epidemic of 791 see *Annales qui dicuntur Einhardi*, ed. by Kurze, a. 791, p. 91; and Gillmor, 'The 791 Equine Epidemic', pp. 23–45. For a discussion of the litanies and their importance see McCormick, 'The Liturgy of War', pp. 1–23, particularly pp. 8–9.

84 'Nos autem, Domino adiuvante, tribus diebus letania fecimus [...] Et clerici, qui psalmos sciebant, unusquisque quinquaginta cantasset; et interim quod ipsas letanias faciebant, discaltiati am[bu]lassent. Sic consideraverunt sacerdotes nostri; et nos omnes ita aptificavimus [et] Domino adiuvante complevimus. Unde volumus, ut tu cum ill et ill vel ceteris fi[de]libus nostris considerare debeas, qualiter ipsas letanias ibidem factas fiant'. Charlemagne, *Epistolae variorum*, ed. by Dümmler, no. 20, pp. 528–29; trans. by Loyn and Percival, *Charlemagne*, pp. 135.

Given the presence of Angilramn on this campaign it seems likely that he organized these litanies which were then performed by his clerical entourage. Such liturgical experts were tasked with advising the army on the correct practices to perform and with singing the psalms. These clerics mixed the contemplative life, defined by study, prayer, and the performance of the Divine Office, with the active life beyond the cloister, seeing to the pastoral needs of the laity.[85]

Condemnation of the Tripartite Approach to the Communal Life

The two-tiered interpretation of the life of canons offered by Alcuin and Angilramn was undoubtedly a practical measure but this approach also caused its own problems. Most significantly having two ways of life for the order of canons was imprecise, complicated, and open to abuse; 'contemplative' canons could be seen as lax monks and some 'contemplative' communities, such as St Denis, were forced to adopt a more strenuous monastic form of life in the wake of the synods of Aachen held between 816 and 819. On the ground the complex arrangements of Chapter 31 of the Rule of Chrodegang, with its internal cleavage between those who copied 'the perfection' of the Apostles, and those who were too 'weak' to give up all property, was also unsatisfactory. A clue to the problems caused by the practice of canons receiving different levels of income was highlighted in Chapter 121 of the *Institutio canonicorum*:

> **It can happen that in a number of congregations of canons certain clerics who are well endowed with riches, and confer little or no benefit on the Church, receive a greater stipend than others, who are actively engaged in the work of God. This is quite unreasonable and unacceptable; it should never happen, and you can find no warrant whatsoever for it to be allowed, either in scripture or in the traditions of the holy fathers […]** Although it often happens elsewhere that subjects are honoured by their superiors with a greater allowance than others, on grounds of merit, in our institute we should exclude any consideration of persons, and the ration of food and drink should be the same for all.[86]

---

85 The Divine Office, particularly the secular *cursus* performed by canons within cathedrals, also served a pastoral function. However, while the laity may have attended some aspects of the Office, they could not be expected to participate in the full set of hours prescribed to the religious orders. For a discussion of the involvement of the laity in the Divine Office see Black, 'The Divine Office and Private Devotion', pp. 41–65, particularly pp. 55–59. For a discussion of the development of the secular *cursus* see Billet, *Divine Office*, pp. 13–77.

86 'Solet in plerisque canonicorum congregationibus inrationabiliter atque indiscrete fieri, ut nonnulli clerici, qui et divitiis affluunt et aut parum aut nihil utilitatis ecclesiae conferunt, maiorem caeteris divinum strenue peragentibus officium annonam accipiant, cum hoc

From 816 onwards all canons were to receive an equal income. The rejection of the practices advocated by Alcuin and Angilramn reflected the dominance at court of a new generation of churchmen, including Hildebald of Cologne, who served as archchaplain from the 790s until his death in 818; Helisachar, who was described as 'a loyal friend of canons'; Hilduin of St Denis; and of course Benedict of Aniane.[87] While many of this group had been educated by Alcuin, they rejected their former master's interpretation of the tripartite nature of the communal life. Amalarius, who fell from favour with the accession of Louis the Pious, was forced to accept the new interpretation of the canonical life offered in 816.[88] His lack of influence during the early years of Louis's reign is made clear in a poem he composed in either 814 or 815. By this point he had lost his position at Trier and perhaps had been sent into monastic confinement, where he lamented that 'now I reap sorrow; the heavens [are] bleak to [me], since I am undone by the death of Charles'.[89] The suppression of an internal cleavage within the canonical order is also clearly detected within the Enlarged Rule of Chrodegang (c. 830), which combined the precepts of Chrodegang's original text with those of the *Institutio canonicorum*.[90] When discussing the stipends and food allowance of canons, the compiler rejected Chapter 31 of the original rule and instead drew exclusively on Chapter 101 of the *Institutio canonicorum*.[91]

It is hoped that this analysis has demonstrated some of the complexities involved in Carolingian attempts to define and distinguish canons from monks. It cannot simply be assumed that Alcuin had little concept of the difference between these orders. Likewise we should not assume that Chrodegang's *Regula canonicorum* immediately and effectively created a clear distinction between monks and the canonical clergy. Rather, seen in context Alcuin's thoughts on this subject were part of a much wider school within the Frankish Church,

---

ita fieri debere nusquam, nec in auctoritate scripturarum nec in traditionibus sanctorum patrum [...] Quamquam enim plerique subditorum a praelatis rebus quibuslibet aliis plus caeteris merito soleant honorari, in hac tamen societate seclusa personarum acceptione una debet cibi et potus aequalitas esse'. *Institutio canonicorum*, ed. by Werminghoff, CXXI, p. 400, trans. by Bertram, *Chrodegang*, p. 149.

87 For the description of Helisachar see Ardo, *Vita Benedicti*, ed. by Waitz, 43, p. 220; trans. by Cabaniss, p. 107. Ardo also noted Benedict's interest in the way of life practised by canons: *Vita Benedicti*, ed. by Waitz, 42, p. 219; trans. by Cabaniss, p. 104. For a discussion of the impact of Louis's 'conquest of the palace' and his 'reform offensive' see amongst others: de Jong, *The Penitential State*, pp. 19–24; Innes, 'Charlemagne's Will', pp. 841–50.

88 For Amalarius's fall from grace see Cabaniss, *Amalarius of Metz*, p. 40 and p. 48; Jones, *A Lost Work*, pp. 166–74; Collins, *Carolingian Debate*, pp. 44–45; Hanssens, 'Introductio', I, p. 67; Oexle, 'Die Karolinger', pp. 332–34.

89 Amalarius, *Versus Marini*, ed. by Dümmler, 74–80, p. 428; trans. in Jones, *A Lost Work*, p. 168. I would like to thank Graeme Ward for his useful thoughts on the *Versus Marini*.

90 Barrow, *Clergy*, pp. 85–89; Barrow, 'Chrodegang, his Rule and its Successors', pp. 204–05; Langefeld, *The Old English Version*, pp. 11–15; Bertram, *Chrodegang Rules*, pp. 175–83.

91 *Regula S. Chrodegangi interpolata*, ed. and trans. by Bertram, 7, p. 191, p. 237.

one which sought to accommodate the needs for expertise within the cloister with the practicalities of pastoral care. However, the tripartite promoted by Angilramn, Alcuin, and Amalarius brought with it its own problems, which were addressed and corrected in the *Institutio canonicorum* of 816. To understand the process by which canons were defined as a group we must acknowledge the trial and error and discussion and debate which surrounded this difficult issue — a process involving innovation and experimentation, compromise and condemnation.

Works Cited

Manuscript

Zürich, Zentralbibliothek, MS Car. C. 102

Primary Sources

Die Admonitio generalis Karls des Großen, ed. by Hubert Mordek, Klaus Zechiel-Eckes, and Michael Glatthaar, in *Monumenta Germaniae Historica: Fontes iuris germanici antiqui in usum scholarum separatim editi*, XVI (Hannover: Hahn, 2012); trans. by P. D. King, *Charlemagne: Translated Sources* (Kendal: University of Lancaster, 1987), pp. 209–20

Alcuin, *Epistolae*, ed. by Ernst Dümmler, in *Monumenta Germaniae Historica: Epistolae*, IV, *Epistolae Merowingici et Karolini aevi*, II (Berlin: Weidmann, 1895), pp. 1–481; trans. by Stephen Allott, *Alcuin of York, c. A.D. 732 to 804: His Life and Letters* (York: William Sessions, 1974)

——, *Epistolae*, ed. by Ernst Dümmler, in *Monumenta Germaniae Historica: Epistolae*, IV, *Epistolae Merowingici et Karolini aevi*, II (Berlin: Weidmann, 1895), no. 3, pp. 19–29; trans. by Bryan Carella, 'Alcuin and Alfred: Two Anglo-Saxon Legal Reformers' (unpublished PhD thesis, University of North Carolina, 2006), pp. 99–120

Amalarius of Metz, *Epistula ad Carolum Imperatorum*, ed. by Joannes M. Hanssens, in *Amalarii Episcopi Opera Liturgica Omnia*, vol. 1: *Introductio: Opera Minora* (Vatican City: Biblioteca apostolica vaticana, 1948), pp. 236–51

——, *Liber de Ordine Antiphonarii*, ed. by Joannes M. Hanssens, in *Amalarii Episcopi Opera Liturgica Omnia*, vol. 3: *Liber de ordine Antiphonarii-Eclogae de ordine Romano-Appendix tomi I et II — Indices* (Vatican City: Biblioteca apostolica vaticana, 1950), pp. 110–224

——, *Missae expositionis geminus codex*, ed. by Joannes M. Hanssens, in *Amalarii Episcopi Opera Liturgica Omnia*, vol. 1: *Introductio: Opera Minora* (Vatican City: Biblioteca apostolica vaticana, 1948), pp. 255–81

——, *Versus Marini*, ed. by Ernst Dümmler, in *Monumenta Germaniae Historica: Poetae*, I (Berlin: Weidmann, 1878), pp. 426–28

Annales Laureshamenses, ed. by Georg Heinrich Pertz, in *Monumenta Germaniae Historica: Scriptores*, I (Hannover: Hahn, 1826) pp. 22–39; partially trans. by P. D. King, *Charlemagne: Translated Sources* (Kendal: University of Lancaster, 1987), pp. 137–45

Annales qui dicuntur Einhardi, ed. by Friedrich Kurze, in *Monumenta Germaniae Historica: Scriptores Rerum Germanicarum in usum scholarum separatim editi*, VI (Hannover: Hahn, 1895)

Annales Regni Francorum, ed. by Friedrich Kurze, in *Monumenta Germaniae Historica: Scriptores Rerum Germanicarum in usum scholarum separatim editi*, VI (Hannover: Hahn, 1895); trans. by Bernhard Walter Scholz with Barbara Rogers, *Carolingian Chronicles:* Royal Frankish Annals and Nithard's Histories (Ann Arbor: University of Michigan Press, 1970), pp. 37–125

Ardo, *Vita Benedicti abbatis Anianensis et Indensis*, ed. by Georg Waitz, in *Monumenta Germaniae Historica: Scriptores*, XV.1 (Hannover: Hahn, 1887), pp. 198–220; trans. by Allen Cabaniss, *Benedict of Aniane: The Emperor's Monk: Ardo's Life*, Cistercian Studies Series, 220 (Kalamazoo: Cistercian Publications, 2008)

Bonifatii et Lulli Epistolae, ed. by Ernst Dümmler, in *Monumenta Germaniae Historica: Epistolae*, III, *Epistolae Merowingici et Karolini aevi*, I (Berlin: Weidmann, 1892), pp. 215–433

Capitulare missorum generale, 802 initio, ed. by Alfred Boretius, in *Monumenta Germaniae Historica: Capitularia Regum Francorum*, I (Hannover: Hahn, 1883), no. 33, pp. 91–99

Capitula Tractanda cum comitibus, episcopis et abbatibus, ed. by Alfred Boretius, in *Monumenta Germaniae Historica: Capitularia Regum Francorum*, I (Hannover: Hahn, 1883), no. 62, pp. 161–62

Capitula de causis cum episcopis et abbatibus tractanda, ed. by Alfred Boretius, in *Monumenta Germaniae Historica: Capitularia Regum Francorum*, I (Hannover: Hahn, 1883), no. 63, pp. 162–64

Charlemagne, *Epistolae Variorum*, ed. by Ernst Dümmler, in *Monumenta Germaniae Historica: Epistolae*, IV, *Epistolae Merowingici et Karolini aevi*, II (Berlin: Weidmann, 1895), no. 20, pp. 528–29

——, *Karoli epistola generalis*, ed. by Alfred Boretius, in *Monumenta Germaniae Historica: Capitularia Regum Francorum*, I (Hannover: Hahn, 1883), no. 30, pp. 80–81; trans. by P. D. King, *Charlemagne: Translated Sources* (Kendal: University of Lancaster, 1987), p. 208

Codex Carolinus, ed. by Wilhelm Gundlach, in *Monumenta Germaniae Historica: Epistolae*, III, *Epistolae Merowingici et Karolini aevi*, I (Berlin: Weidmann, 1891), pp. 476–657

Concilium Francofurtnese a. 794, ed. by Albert Werminghoff, in *Monumenta Germaniae Historica: Concilia*, II. 1, *Concilia aevi Karolini*, I (Hannover: Hahn, 1906), no. 19, pp. 110–71

Concilium Turonense a. 813, ed. by Albert Werminghoff, in *Monumenta Germaniae Historica: Concilia*, II. 1, *Concilia aevi Karolini*, I (Hannover: Hahn, 1906), no. 38, pp. 286–93

Concilium Vernense, 755. Jul. 11, ed. by Alfred Boretius, in *Monumenta Germaniae Historica: Capitularia Regum Francorum*, I (Hannover: Hahn, 1883), no. 14, pp. 32–37

Council of Clovesho, 747, ed. by Arthur W. Hadden and William Stubbs, *Councils and Ecclesiastical Documents Relating to Great Britain and Ireland*, vol. 3 (Oxford: Clarendon Press, 1871), pp. 360–83

Dialogues Egberti, ed. by Arthur W. Hadden and William Stubbs, *Councils and Ecclesiastical Documents Relating to Great Britain and Ireland*, vol. 3 (Oxford: Clarendon Press, 1871), pp. 404–13

Institutio canonicorum, ed. by Albert Werminghoff, in *Monumenta Germaniae Historica: Concilia*, II. 1, *Concilia aevi Karolini*, I (Hannover: Hahn, 1906), pp. 308–421; ed. and trans. by Jerome Bertram, in The Chrodegang Rules: The Rules for the Common Life of the Secular Clergy from the Eighth and Ninth Centuries; Critical Texts with Translations and *Commentary* (Aldershot: Ashgate, 2005), pp. 96–174

Loyn, Henry Royston, and John Percival, ed. and trans., *The Reign of Charlemagne: Documents on Carolingian Government and Administration* (London: Edward Arnold, 1975)

Paul the Deacon, *Liber de Episcopis Mettensibus*, ed. and trans. by Damien Kempf, Dallas Medieval Texts and Translations, 19 (Leuven: Peeters, 2013)

Regula longior canonicorum Seu Regula S. Chrodegangi interpolata, ed. and trans. by Jerome Bertram, in The Chrodegang Rules: The Rules for the Common Life of the Secular Clergy from the Eighth and Ninth Centuries; Critical Texts with Translations and Commentary (Aldershot: Ashgate, 2005), pp. 184–285

Regula Sancti Chrodegangi, ed. and trans. by Jerome Bertram, in *The Chrodegang Rules: The Rules for the Common Life of the Secular Clergy from the Eighth and Ninth Centuries*; Critical Texts with Translations and Commentary (Aldershot: Ashgate, 2005), pp. 27–83

Vita Alcuini, ed. by Wilhelm Arndt in *Monumenta Germaniae Historica:* Scriptores, XV.1 (Hannover: Hahn, 1887), pp. 182–97

Vita Balthildis, ed. by Bruno Krusch, in *Monumenta Germaniae Historica: Scriptores Rerum Merovingicarum*, II (Hannover: Hahn, 1888), pp. 483–85; trans. by Paul Fouracre and Richard A. Gerberding, *Late Merovingian France: History and Hagiography 640–720*, Manchester Medieval Sources Series (Manchester: Manchester University Press, 1996), pp. 97–110

Secondary Works

Atsma, Hartmut, 'Les monastères urbains du Nord de la Gaule', *Revue d'histoire de l'Eglise de France*, 62 (1976), 163–87

Barrow, Julia, 'Chrodegang, his Rule and its Successors', *Early Medieval Europe*, 26 (2006), 201–12

——, *The Clergy in the Medieval World: Secular Clerics, Their Families and Careers in North-Western Europe, c. 800–c. 1200* (Cambridge: Cambridge University Press, 2015)

Bertram, Jerome, *The Chrodegang Rules: The Rules for the Common Life of the Secular Clergy from the Eighth and Ninth Centuries* (Aldershot: Ashgate, 2005)

Billet, Jesse, *The Divine Office in Anglo-Saxon England, 597–c. 1000* (London: Boydell, 2014)

Bischoff, Bernhard, *Die Abtei Lorsch im Spiegel ihrer Handschriften*, 2nd edn, Geschichtsblätter Kreis Bergstraße, Sonderband, 10 (Lorsch: Laurissa, 1989)

Black, Jonathan, 'The Divine Office and Private Devotion in the Latin West', in *The Liturgy of the Medieval Church*, ed. by Thomas J. Heffernan and E. Ann Matter (Kalamazoo: Western Michigan University, 2001), pp. 45–71

Bullough, Donald A., 'Aula Renovata: The Carolingian Court before the Aachen Palace', *Proceedings of the British Academy*, 71 (1985), 267–301

―――, 'What Has Ingeld to Do with Lindisfarne?', *Anglo-Saxon England*, 22 (1993), 93–125

―――, *Alcuin: Achievement and Reputation; Being Part of the Ford Lectures Delivered in Oxford in Hilary Term 1980*, Education and Society in the Middle Ages and Renaissance, 16 (Leiden: Brill, 2004)

Cabaniss, Allen, *Amalarius of Metz* (Amsterdam: North-Holland Publishing Company, 1954)

Carella, Bryan, 'Alcuin and the Legatine Capitulary of 786: The Evidence of Scriptural Citations', *Journal of Medieval Latin*, 22 (2012), pp. 221–56

Chazelle, Celia, 'Amalarius's "Liber Officialis": Spirit and Vision in Carolingian Liturgical Thought', in *Seeing the Invisible in Late Antiquity and the Early Middle Ages: Papers from 'Verbal and Pictorial Imaging: Representing and Accessing Experience of the Invisible, 400–1000': (Utrecht, 11–13 December 2003)*, ed. by Giselle de Nie, Karl Frederick Morrison, and Marco Mostert, Utrecht Studies in Medieval Literacy, 14 (Turnhout: Brepols, 2005), pp. 327–57

Claussen, Martin A., *Reform of the Frankish Church: Chrodegang of Metz and the Regula Canonicorum in the Eighth Century* (Cambridge: Cambridge University Press, 2005)

―――, 'Practical Exegesis: The Acts of the Apostles, Chrodegang's "Regula Canonicorum" and Early Carolingian Reform', in *Medieval Monks and their World: Ideas and Realities*, ed. by David Blanks, Michael Frassetto, and Amy Livingstone (Leiden: Brill, 2006), pp. 119–47

Collins, Samuel W., *The Carolingian Debate over Sacred Space* (New York: Palgrave Macmillan, 2012)

Cubitt, Catherine, *Anglo-Saxon Church Councils, c. 650–c. 850* (Leicester: Leicester University Press, 1995)

―――, 'The Clergy in Early Anglo-Saxon England', *Historical Research*, 78 (2005), 273–87

Dales, Douglas, *Alcuin: His Life and Legacy* (Cambridge: James Clarke & Co, 2012)

Dereine, Charles, 'Chanoines', in *Dictionnaire d'histoire et de géographie ecclésiastiques*, vol. 12 (Paris: Letouzey et Ané, 1953), cols 353–405

Duckett, Eleanor Shipley, *Carolingian Portraits: A Study in the Ninth Century* (Ann Arbor: University of Michigan Press, 1962)

Fichtenau, Heinrich, 'Abt Richbod und die Annales Laureshamenses', in *Beitrage zur Geschichte des Klosters Lorsch, Geschichtsblätter für den Kreis Bergstraße*, 4, 2nd edn (Lorsch: Laurissa, 1980), pp. 277–304

Fox, Yaniv, *Power and Religion in Merovingian Gaul: Columbanian Monasticism and the Frankish Elites* (Cambridge: Cambridge University Press, 2014)

Innes, Matthew, 'Charlemagne's Will: Piety, Politics and the Imperial Succession', *English Historical Review*, 112.448 (1997), 833–55

Jones, Christopher A., *A Lost Work by Amalarius of Metz: Interpolations in Salisbury, Cathedral Library, MS. 154*, Henry Bradshaw Society Subsidia, 2 (London: Boydell Press for the Henry Bradshaw Society, 2001)

——, 'A Lost Treatise by *Amalarius*: New Evidence from the Twelfth Century', in *The Study of Medieval Manuscripts of England: Festschrift in Honor of Richard W. Pfaff*, ed. by George Hardin Brown and Linda E. Voigts, Arizona studies in the Middle Ages and the Renaissance, 35 (Tempe: Arizona Center for Medieval and Renaissance Studies, 2010), pp. 41–68

Jong, Mayke de, 'From Scolastici to Scioli: Alcuin and the Formation of an Intellectual Elite', in *Alcuin of York: Scholar at the Carolingian Court — Proceedings of the Third Germania Latina Conference held at the University of Groningen, May 1995*, ed. by Luuk Houwen and Alasdair A. MacDonald, Mediaevalia Groningana, 22 (Groningen: Egbert Forsten, 1998), pp. 45–58

——, *The Penitential State: Authority and Atonement in the Age of Louis the Pious, 814–40* (Cambridge: Cambridge University Press, 2009)

Hanssens, Joannes M., 'Introductio', in *Amalarii Episcopi Opera Liturgica Omnia*, vol. 1: *Introductio: Opera Minora*, ed. by Joannes M. Hanssens (Vatican City: Biblioteca apostolica vaticana, 1948), pp. 39–224

Kempf, Damien, 'Paul the Deacon's Liber de episcopis Mettensibus and the Role of Metz in the Carolingian Realm', *Journal of Medieval History*, 30.3 (2004), 279–99

Kramer, Rutger, 'The Exemption that Proves the Rule: Autonomy and Authority between Alcuin, Theodulf and Charlemagne (802)', *Religious Exemption in Pre-Modern Eurasia, c. 300–1300 CE, Medieval Worlds*, 6 (2017), 231–61 <https://www.medievalworlds.net/?arp=0x00372f2b> [accessed 8 September 2021]

Langefeld, Brigitte, *The Old English Version of the Enlarged Rule of Chrodegang* (Frankfurt am Main: Peter Lang, 2003)

Ling, Stephen, 'The Cloister and Beyond: Regulating the Life of the Canonical Clergy in Francia, from Pippin III to Louis the Pious' (unpublished doctoral thesis, University of Leicester, 2015)

——, 'Interactions Between the Clerical Enclosure and the Extra-Claustral Clergy in Carolingian Francia: A Sacred Space with Porous Walls', in *Debating Religious Space and Place in the Early Medieval World (c. AD 300–1000)*, ed. by Chantal Bielmann and Brittany Thomas (Leiden: Sidestone Press Academics, 2018), pp. 127–42

——, 'Analysing Attigny: Contextualising Chrodegang of Metz's Influence on the Life of Canons', in *Rethinking the Carolingian Reforms*, ed. by Arthur Westwell, Ingrid Rembold and Carine van Rhijn (Manchester: Manchester University Press, forthcoming)

Marenbon, John, *From the Circle of Alcuin to the School of Auxerre: Logic, Theology and Philosophy in the Early Middle Ages*, Cambridge Studies in Medieval Life and Thought, 3rd series, 15 (Cambridge: Cambridge University Press, 2006)

Martin, Thomas, 'Bemerkungen zur Epistola de litteris colendis', *Archiv für Diplomatik*, 31 (1985), 227–72

McKitterick, Rosamond, *The Frankish Church and the Carolingian Reforms, 789–895* (London: Royal Historical Society, 1977)

——, *Charlemagne: The Formation of a European Identity* (Cambridge: Cambridge University Press, 2008)

Meens, Rob, 'Politics, Mirrors of Princes and the Bible: Sins, Kings and the Well-being of the Realm', *Early Medieval Europe*, 7.3 (1998), 345–57

——, 'Sanctuary, Penance, and Dispute Settlement under Charlemagne: The Conflict between Alcuin and Theodulf of Orléans over a Sinful Cleric', *Speculum*, 82 (2007), 277–300

Miller, Maureen C., *Clothing the Clergy: Virtue and Power in Medieval Europe, c. 800–1200* (Ithaca: Cornell University Press, 2014)

Morin, Germain, 'Un saint de Maestricht rendu à l'histoire', *Revue Bénédictine*, 8 (1891), 176–83

Mostert, Marco: '"… but they pray badly using corrected books": Errors in Early Carolingian Copies of the Admonitio generalis', in *Religious Franks — Religion and Power in the Frankish Kingdoms: Studies in Honour of Mayke de Jong*, ed. by Rob Meens, Dorine van Espelo, Bram van den Hoven van Genderen, Janneke Raaijmakers, Irene van Renswoude, and Carine van Rhijn (Manchester: Manchester University Press, 2016), pp. 112–27

Nees, Lawrence, 'Godescalc's Career and the Problem of Influence', in *Under the Influence: The Concept of Influence and the Study of Illuminated Manuscripts*, ed. by John Lowden and Alixe Bovey, Publications of the Research Centre for Illuminated Manuscripts, 1 (Turnhout: Brepols, 2007), pp. 21–43

Nelson, Janet L., 'The Voice of Charlemagne', in *Belief and Culture in the Middle Ages: Studies Presented to Henry Mayr-Harting*, ed. by Richard Gameson and Henrietta Leyser (Oxford: Oxford University Press, 2001), pp. 76–90

Noizet, Hélène, 'Alcuin contre Théodulphe: Un conflit producteur de normes', *Annales de Bretagne et des Pays de l'Ouest, Anjou, Maine, Poitou, Touraine*, 111 (2004), 113–29

Oexle, Otto Gerhard, 'Die Karolinger und die Stadt des heiligen Arnulf', *Frühmittelalterliche Studien*, 1 (1967), 250–365

Picker, Hanns-Christoph, *Pastor Doctus: Klerikerbild und Karolingische Reformen bei Hrabanus Maurus*, Veröffentlichungen des Instituts für Europäische Geschichte Mainz. Abteilung für Abendländische Religionsgeschichte, 186 (Mainz: Vandenhoeck & Ruprecht, 2001)

Pietri, Luce, 'Les Abbés de basilique dans la Gaule au VIe Siècle', *Revue d'Histoire de l'Eglise de France*, 69.182 (1983), 5–28

Rhijn, Carine van, *Shepherds of the Lord: Priests and Episcopal Statutes in the Carolingian Period* (Turnhout: Brepols, 2007)

Ripart, Laurent, 'Les temps séculiers (IXe–Xe siècles)', in *L'abbaye de Saint-Maurice*, vol. 1: *Histoire et archéologie*, ed. by Bernard Andenmatten and Lurent Ripart (Gollion: Infolio, 2015), pp. 135–49

Ryan, Martin J., 'Archbishop Ecgberht and His Dialogus', in *Leaders of the Anglo-Saxon Church: From Bede to Stigand*, ed. by Alexander R. Rumble, Publications of the Manchester Centre for Anglo-Saxon Studies, 12 (Manchester: Boydell, 2012), pp. 41–60

Schieffer, Rudolf, *Die Entstehung von Domkapiteln in Deutschland* (Bonn: Röhrscheid, 1976)

Steck, Wolfgang, *Der Liturgiker Amalarius — eine quellenkritische Untersuchung zu Leben und Werk eines Theologen der Karolingerzeit*, Münchner Theologische Studien, Historische Abteilung, 35 (St Ottilien: EOS, 2000)

Story, Joanna, *Carolingian Connections: Anglo-Saxon England and Carolingian Francia, c. 750–870*, Studies in Early Medieval Britain, 2 (Aldershot: Ashgate, 2003)

Ward, Graeme, 'The Order of History: Liturgical Time and the Rhythems of the Past in Amalarius of Metz's De Ordine Antiphonarii', in *Writing the Early Medieval West*, ed. by Elina Screen and Charles West (Cambridge: Cambridge University Press, 2018), pp. 98–112

Wood, Ian N., *The Merovingian Kingdoms 450–751* (Abingdon: Routledge, 1994)

Wormald, Patrick, 'In Search of King Offa's Law-Code', in *People and Places in Northern Europe, 500–1600: Essays in Honour of Peter Hayes Sawyer*, ed. by Ian N. Wood and Niels Lund (Woodbridge: Boydell & Brewer, 1991), pp. 25–45

Wright, Roger, 'Late Latin and Early Romance: Alcuin's De Orthographia and the Council of Tours (AD 813)', in *Papers of the Liverpool Latin Seminar*, vol. 3, ed. by Francis Cairns (Liverpool: F. Cairns, 1983), pp. 343–63

CINZIA GRIFONI

This is a Cleric

Hrabanus Maurus's De institutione clericorum, Clerical Monks, and the Carolingian Church*

For Janneke

> 'Cernite quid velit, fratres, sententia legis, | Quae mandat rite noscere verba dei' (Understand, brethren, what the dictate of the law requests, | Which orders that God's words be known properly).[1]

These two verses open a brief poem, with which Hrabanus Maurus (d. 856) introduced his 'Instruction for Clerics' (*De institutione clericorum*, hereafter *DIC*) and dedicated it to his confreres at Fulda ('Ad fratres Fuldensis monasterii'). In the ensuing verses he stated more precisely which dictate and which law he had in mind with the poem's opening. He meant the precepts contained in the Bible and, in particular, in both Apocalypse 2. 7, where the Apostle John encourages the community of Ephesus to understand properly the words the Holy Spirit dictated to him, and in Psalm 77. 1, where God exhorts His people to lend an ear to His law. The three books forming the *DIC* — the poem sets forth — aim to support Hrabanus's brethren in the endeavour of attaining the correct knowledge of God's precepts, especially those pertaining to the clergy.

---

* The research for this article was funded by the Austrian Science Fund (FWF): SFB F42-G18 Visions of Community. I am deeply indebted to Owen Phelan for his generosity in reviewing both content and form of my contribution. I wish to thank Graeme Ward for his valued comments and suggestions as well as Rutger Kramer, who discussed drafts of this article with me.
1 Hrabanus Maurus, *De institutione clericorum, Prooemium ad fratres Fuldensis monasterii*, ed. by Zimpel, p. 290, ll. 2–3.

> **Cinzia Grifoni** works as a Postdoctoral Researcher at the Institute for Medieval Research of the Austrian Academy of Sciences and as a Lecturer at the University of Vienna. She currently runs a project on Carolingian practices of annotation called 'Margins at the Centre'.

Monastic Communities and Canonical Clergy in the Carolingian World (780–840): Categorizing the Church, ed. by Rutger Kramer, Emilie Kurdziel, and Graeme Ward, MMS 8 (Turnhout: Brepols, 2022), pp. 267–300

In Hrabanus's time a further set of instructions recommended to clerics the proper knowledge and fulfilment of God's words, the *Institutio canonicorum*. This text consists of an extensive florilegium of patristic teachings concerning clerics in general followed by instructions addressed to canons, i.e. those clerics who lived a communal life in a cloister under the supervision of a bishop.[2] As its prologue states, the *Institutio canonicorum* recorded the work of a council summoned and overseen by Emperor Louis the Pious at Aachen in 816.[3] Soon after, with the *Capitulare ecclesiasticum*, the emperor took care to declare the advice and regulations gathered in the *Institutio canonicorum* mandatory for all canons.[4] The short lapse of time separating the Council of Aachen and the ensuing publication of the *Institutio canonicorum* from the completion of the *DIC* in 819 led modern scholars to see Hrabanus's treatise as a direct reaction to that set of instructions. The modern editor of the *DIC*, Detlev Zimpel, interpreted, for instance, the introductory poem with which we began as the first of several statements of conformity to court-led reforms, which Hrabanus would express repeatedly throughout his work.[5] More precisely, Zimpel regarded the *DIC* in its entirety as a work written to

---

[2] On nature and purposes of the *Institutio canonicorum* see Rutger Kramer, *Rethinking Authority*, pp. 96–122 as well as his and Veronika Wieser's contribution to the present book.

[3] The *Institutio canonicorum*, as well as the advice concerning nuns issued during the same Council (*Institutio sanctimonialium*) are published in *Concilium Aquisgranense a. 816*, ed. by Werminghoff. Both in 816 and 817 the Aachen Councils engaged also with regulating monastic life: see *Synodi primae Aquisgranensis (a. 816)*, ed. by Semmler, and *Synodi secundae Aquisgranensis (a. 817)*, ed. by Semmler.

[4] See *Capitulare ecclesiasticum*, ed. by Boretius, 3, p. 276, ll. 11–19: 'Quia vero canonica professio a multis […] dehonestabatur, operae pretium duximus, Deo annuente, apud sacrum conventum ut ex dictis sanctorum patrum […] in unam regulam canonicorum et canonicarum congerere et canonicis vel sanctimonialibus servandam contradere, ut per eam canonicus ordo absque ambiguitate possit servari. Et […] statuimus ut ab omnibus in eadem professione degentibus indubitanter teneatur et modis omnibus sive a canonicis sive a sanctimonialibus canonice degentibus deinceps observetur'. The dating of the *Capitulare ecclesiasticum* oscillates between 816 and 818/19 depending on the editors; see 'Capitulare ecclesiasticum' (online). Extant letters, which Louis sent to several archbishops, also testify to his intention to disseminate the contents of the *Institutio canonicorum*. These are published in *Concilium Aquisgranense a. 816*, ed. by Werminghoff, pp. 458–64. The recent volume, Grosse and Sot ed., *Charlemagne: les temps, les espaces, les hommes*, engages with the dissemination and reception of capitularies; see, in particular, Depreux, 'Charlemagne et les capitulaires' and van Rhijn, 'Charlemagne's *correctio*', p. 48. On the diverse nature of what we call 'Carolingian Capitularies' see McKitterick, *Charlemagne*, pp. 233–63, and, most recently, Patzold, 'Capitularies', and Patzold, *Karl der Große*.

[5] Detlev Zimpel produced both an edition and a German translation of Hrabanus's *De institutione clericorum*, both preceded by detailed introductions. See respectively: Hrabanus Maurus, *De institutione clericorum*, ed. by Zimpel and Hrabanus Maurus, *Über die Unterweisung*, ed. and trans. by Zimpel. Here on p. 126 n. 13 Zimpel states that the introductory poem mirrors the general attitude characterizing the *DIC*, i.e. Hrabanus's purpose of promoting and enforcing Louis's attempts at reform.

support the results of the Aachen Councils, and in particular the *Institutio canonicorum*.

Hrabanus's activity as scholar, preacher, and exegete has attracted the attention of scholarship increasingly in the past decades.[6] The *DIC* in particular formed the subject of several scholarly works. Beside the edition and the comprehensive study published by Zimpel in 1996, the two monographs published by Maria Rissel and Hanns-Christoph Picker respectively examined its contents, sources, and purposes.[7] Furthermore, the *DIC* was made available to a larger audience through translations into both German and Italian.[8] Finally, three articles have dealt with the educational programme contained in its third book. These are the two contributions by Armando Bisanti from the 1980s[9] and the recent article by Owen Phelan, which concentrated on the interaction between education, righteous moral conduct, and pastoral practice as depicted by Hrabanus both in the *DIC* and in several other works.[10]

One of the major issues of scholarly debate on the *DIC* consists of establishing its degree of dependence from the *Institutio canonicorum* given that both works addressed a clerical audience and were composed within a narrow time-frame. Most scholars considered Hrabanus's treatise as a loudspeaker of the Carolingian interventions on clerical life and education. In particular, Zimpel regarded it as a 'Kampfschrift zur Durchsetzung der Beschlüsse von 816 bis 819', i.e. as a polemic tool for supporting the dissemination of the Aachen directives.[11] In his view, a substantial part of the *DIC* aimed at re-issuing a relevant bulk of them in a new narrative structure and in a more intelligible order. On a similar note, Phelan stressed how 'Hrabanus worked very consciously to amplify education and pastoral efforts at reform outlined in conciliar decrees and royal or imperial instructions from the end of the eighth and beginning of the ninth century'.[12]

In contrast, Picker interpreted the *DIC* as a 'Gegenentwurf', i.e. as an alternative draft to the *Institutio canonicorum*, since the two writings endorsed different ideas of the clergy.[13] In his opinion, the *DIC* originated, on the one hand, as an enthusiastic reception of Charlemagne's concerns for a uniform liturgy, a well-defined ecclesiastical hierarchy, and an improved level of literacy among the clergy.[14] On the other hand, it represented a rather critical response

---

6   For a bibliography concerning Hrabanus until 2009, see Bullido del Barrio, 'Hrabanus Maurus-Bibliographie'.
7   See Rissel, *Rezeption*, pp. 163–293; Picker, *Pastor Doctus*.
8   For the German translation by Zimpel see above n. 5. Luigi Samarati translated the *DIC* into Italian in 2002.
9   Bisanti, 'Il capitolo' and Bisanti, 'Struttura compositiva'.
10 Phelan, 'New Insights'.
11 Hrabanus Maurus, *De institutione clericorum*, ed. by Zimpel, pp. 13–14. Similarly, Zimpel speaks of *DIC* as a 'Beitrag zur Durchsetzung dieser [...] Bestimmungen' on p. 33.
12 Phelan, 'New Insights', p. 64.
13 Picker, *Pastor Doctus*, pp. 125–26.
14 Picker, *Pastor Doctus*, pp. 41–52.

to the attempts made by Louis the Pious and his advisers — Benedict of Aniane *in primis* — to promote the category of canons and to distinguish sharply clerics from monks. In Picker's opinion, the clergy Hrabanus had in mind was formed by the ordained monks of his community, who were responsible for encouraging Christian values and practices amongst local communities beyond the walls of the cloister.[15]

What is certain is that both the *Institutio canonicorum* and Hrabanus's *DIC* aimed to frame and depict a particular category within the Church: the clergy. In so doing, they both took their position within a long debate on the nature and tasks of the clerical office, in which the intellectual elites of Carolingian Europe had been involved since the middle of the eighth century.[16] Both the information contained in the prologue and the very contents of the *DIC* suggest that Hrabanus had begun to work on such themes already before 816, as we will see below. It seems probable that, inspired by the issue of the *Institutio canonicorum*, Hrabanus gathered in the *DIC* the results of his long engagement with defining the essence of the clerical condition. His vision of what makes a cleric perfect was different from that elaborated at Aachen, at least as some relevant aspects are concerned.

Resting on a comparison between the two texts, the present contribution investigates the ideal picture of clergy they promoted. I will describe, firstly, the intended audience of Hrabanus's treatise and the context in which it originated. Secondly, I will summarize the structure and contents of the *Institutio canonicorum* and of the *DIC* respectively, stressing both the points of contact and the major differences. Finally, I will present the *DIC* as an instruction for clerical life complementary to that issued at Aachen, which Hrabanus conceived originally for the ordained monks of his community and disseminated further, in the course of his ecclesiastical career, by adapting its contents to the needs of new audiences.

De institutione clericorum (*DIC*): Audience and Context of Origin

As is typical for all of his writings, Hrabanus framed the *DIC* with paratexts, in which he delivered precious information about his work. These are, firstly, a prologue in prose; secondly, the opening poem mentioned above; thirdly, a further poem which closes the treatise.[17] In these texts, Hrabanus expressed his concerns and purposes, explained the structure and contents of the work,

---

15 Picker, *Pastor Doctus*, pp. 249–50: '*De institutione clericorum* zielt auf ein weltoffenes, klerikales Mönchtum, das sich gesamtkirchlichen Aufgaben nicht verschließt, sondern aktiv an der pastoralen Versorgung der Bevölkerung, an der Christianisierung und am kulturellen Leben mitwirkt'.

16 See the contributions by Brigitte Meijns and Stephen Ling in the present volume.

17 Hrabanus Maurus, *De institutione clericorum*, ed. by Zimpel, pp. 281–83, 290–91, 520–21.

and mentioned the sources at his disposal as well as the way he had compiled them. Furthermore, he stated the reasons that had led him to compose the *DIC* and described the audience he was addressing with his work.

The opening poem addresses Hrabanus's confreres at the monastery of Fulda and consists of fifteen elegiac couplets. After the initial admonition to pay attention to God's precepts, Hrabanus outlined succinctly the contents of the three books that comprise the *DIC* and stated explicitly that he had written them at his brethren's request.[18] Concluding, he named himself as the author (*ego peccator Hrabanus*) and asked for prayers.

As for the other paratexts, both the prologue in prose and the closing poem are addressed to Haistulf, archbishop of Mainz (d. 825).[19] This dedication is not surprising if we recall the tight connection binding Fulda to the see of Mainz ever since the beginning of Fulda's history, and in particular since Boniface (d. 754) was appointed as archbishop soon after having promoted the foundation of the monastery in 742.[20] Many of Hrabanus's works attest to his special ties to the see of Mainz. He dedicated to Archbishop Haistulf not only the *DIC* in 819, but also his Commentary on the Gospel of Matthew, which he finished between 821 and 822, and a collection of sermons issued around 825.[21] Furthermore, Hrabanus offered to Archbishop Otgar (d. 847), Haistulf's successor, his Commentaries on the Book of Wisdom and on the Heptateuch and presented both archbishops with a copy of his *De laudibus sanctae crucis*.[22] Finally, he wrote epitaphs for both prelates, which were transmitted along with his poetry.[23] Also Hrabanus's own ecclesiastical career testifies to the persistence of this connection, since he himself was appointed as Archbishop of Mainz after Otgar's death in 847.

The prologue to the *DIC* is particularly relevant for our purposes. Here Hrabanus expressed his personal connection to Haistulf, who had ordained him as a priest in 814.[24] Moreover, he described the contents of the three books, asking the archbishop to verify their accuracy and to correct them, if needed. As a guarantee for the orthodoxy of his work, he took care to name

---

18 Hrabanus Maurus, *De institutione clericorum*, ed. by Zimpel, p. 290, ll. 14–15: 'Nam quia poscistis haec vobis reddere scriptis, \ Exhibui parvis haec tribus ipse libris'.
19 For Haistulf see Schmid ed., *Die Klostergemeinschaft von Fulda*, p. 323.
20 It is still a matter of debate whether Fulda belonged to the diocese of Mainz, since several scholars consider the monastery as being rather under the oversight of Würzburg. For a summary of the debate see Patzold, 'Konflikte', p. 109 n. 148–49, who supports Würzburg, and Picker, *Pastor Doctus*, pp. 144–45, who argues for Mainz. For a detailed history of the monastery see Hussong, 'Studien', esp. Part 1, pp. 54–61.
21 See Cantelli Berarducci, *Opera Exegetica*, I, p. 347; Phelan, 'New Insights', pp. 78–80; and Phelan, 'Carolingian Renewal'.
22 Hrabanus Maurus, *Carmina*, ed. by Dümmler, I. 5, p. 162; Berggötz, 'Hrabanus Maurus und seine Bedeutung', pp. 8–9.
23 For the two epitaphs, see Hrabanus Maurus, *Carmina*, ed. by Dümmler, no. 84, p. 237, and no. 87, pp. 238–39.
24 See *Chronicon Laurissense breve*, ed. by Schnorr von Carolsfeld, s. 1, p. 38.

the authorities he had relied upon. Along with Augustine and Cassiodorus, he mentioned by name Isidore, Gregory the Great, and a further six late antique Fathers, while he left some other models (*ceteros nonnullos*) unspecified. He stressed also that he had written some passages in his own words, when it was necessary.[25] Finally, Hrabanus mentioned in the prologue his reasons for writing the *DIC*: the work had been conceived as a response to the frequent questions posed by his confreres at Fulda (*Quaestionibus* [...] *fratrum nostrorum*), and particularly by the priests among them, whom Hrabanus described as 'those who were worthy because of their holy rank' (*qui sacris ordinibus pollebant*).[26]

As we will see below analysing the first book of the *DIC*, Hrabanus regarded as clerics (*clerici*) all ordained males holding one of the ecclesiastical positions, from bishop to doorkeeper. Among them, he considered as members of the 'holy rank' (*ordo sacer*) only priests, whom he called *sacerdotes* or *presbiteri*, and bishops, whom he mostly addressed as *episcopi* or *(summi) sacerdotes*.[27] His brethren's questions concerned, in Hrabanus's words, both the nature of their office and the ecclesiastical prescriptions they were expected to follow.[28] We can assume, therefore, that Hrabanus had written the *DIC* to support those fellow-monks who either already had been ordained as priests or were progressing along the path towards priesthood.[29] The *DIC* deals also with clerical duties which concern bishops alone, thus not excluding the possibility that monks be appointed as bishops (Hrabanus himself became a monk-bishop in 847).[30]

---

25 See Hrabanus Maurus, *De institutione clericorum*, ed. by Zimpel, *Prologus*, p. 283, ll. 50–56: 'Cyprianum dico atque Hilarium, Ambrosium, Hieronimum, Augustinum, Gregorium, Iohannes, Damasum, Cassiodorum atque Isidorum et ceteros nonnullos [...] interdum vero, ubi necesse fuit, secundum exemplar eorum quaedam sensu meo protuli'. The study of the sources conducted by Zimpel confirms this picture: indeed, on the one hand Isidore's *De ecclesiasticis officiis* and *Etymologies*, Gregory's *Regula Pastoralis*, Cassiodorus's *Institutiones*, and Augustine's *De doctrina Christiana* provided Hrabanus with the most reference material. On the other, several passages lacking a known source can be ascribed to Hrabanus's pen (see Hrabanus Maurus, *De institutione clericorum*, ed. by Zimpel, pp. 37–61 and 75–94).

26 Hrabanus Maurus, *De institutione clericorum*, ed. by Zimpel, *Prologus*, p. 281, ll. 13–15. The *Institutio canonicorum* describes the pre-eminent position of canons with very similar words: see *Institutio canonicorum*, ed. by Werminghoff, 115, p. 397, ll. 17–18: 'qui tantae auctoritatis institutione pollent'. I will return to this point below.

27 See Chapter 5 (*de ordine tripertito episcoporum*) and 6 (*de presbiteris*) of the first book, as well as Chapter 13, in which Hrabanus described the steps in the career of a cleric leading to the *sacrum ordinem*, i.e. to the position of priest or bishop. For the definition of the term *sacerdos* see Hrabanus Maurus, *De institutione clericorum*, ed. by Zimpel, I. 5, p. 299, ll. 34–35: 'Sacerdos autem vocari potest sive episcopus sit sive presbiter'.

28 Hrabanus Maurus, *De institutione clericorum*, ed. by Zimpel, *Prologus*, p. 281, ll. 15–17: 'qui me de officio suo et variis observationibus, quae in ecclesia dei decentissime observantur, saepissime interrogabant [...]'.

29 Sandmann, 'Wirkungsbereiche', pp. 739–45 surveys the evidence concerning Fulda's monks operating as priests both inside and outside the monastic walls.

30 But see Sandmann, 'Wirkungsbereiche', pp. 745–51 for the limited number of monk-bishops originating from the Fulda community.

Fulda's ordained monks recur a further time in the course of the prologue as the intended audience of the *DIC*. Hrabanus first states that he gave his book the title *De institutione clericorum* because of its contents.[31] In fact, these concern exclusively the duties of clerics, whom he defines as those 'who hold a leading position in the Church and are expected to teach God's people about His precepts'. He then affirms that the purpose of his treatise is that 'they [i.e. Fulda's *fratres*] instruct themselves, or those under their tuition, in divine service'.[32] Thus, the *DIC* addresses explicitly monks who are expected to carry out clerical functions by virtue of their ordination. They can use the *DIC* in order both to learn how to perform their task properly and to teach those brethren who are less proficient in their clerical formation.

How did Hrabanus categorize ordained monks, or clerical monks,[33] within the Church? Were they monks, clerics, or both? The terms Hrabanus used to address them do not help to answer this question. Indeed, he called them exclusively by the generic appellation of *fratres*, both in the prologue and in the introductory poem. In the body of the *DIC* he never addressed his readers directly, but it is reasonable to argue from the very contents of the treatise that he regarded them as members of the clergy. At the same time, however, Hrabanus considered his readers as monks in all respects, as we will see below concerning the topic of property and the eating prescriptions. For sure, he never called them canons (*canonici*). The term *canonicus* occurs only seventeen times within the *DIC* and always with the meaning 'authoritative' or 'orthodox', as in the expressions *canonici libri* (three times), *canonicae horae* (four times) and *canonicae scripturae* (six times).[34] Significantly, when he distinguished the constitutive orders of the Church at the beginning of the first book, he listed only three categories: the laity, the monks, and the clerics. As for the monks he defined them succinctly as 'those who live

---

31 Zimpel stresses that the title *De institutione clericorum* occurs already in Chapter 95 of the *Institutio canonicorum*. Here it introduces an excerpt from Jerome's *Epistle to Paulinus* on clerical virtues. See Hrabanus Maurus, *Über die Unterweisung*, ed. and trans. by Zimpel, p. 19. Perhaps Hrabanus derived his title from this passage.

32 Hrabanus Maurus, *De institutione clericorum*, ed. by Zimpel, *Prologus*, p. 282, ll. 37–41: 'Et quia haec omnia, quae diximus, ad clericorum officium maxime pertinent, qui locum regiminis in ecclesia tenent et de universis legitimis dei populum dei instruere debent, placuit ipsos libros "de institutione clericorum" nuncupari, id est, cum qua se vel sibi subditos ad servitium divinum instituere debent'.

33 The modern designations 'ordained monks' and 'clerical monks', as well as their German equivalent 'Klerikermönche', apply to those monks who exhibit some sort of clerical grade (see Picker, *Pastor Doctus*, pp. 115–18). The priests among them are called by modern scholarship 'priest-monks', for instance in Raaijmakers, *The Making of the Monastic Community*, p. 187. Hildebrandt, *External School*, pp. 115–18 speaks both of 'priest-monks' and 'monk-priests'. German-speaking scholarship uses mostly the terms 'Priestermönche' following Nussbaum, *Kloster, Priestermönch*. See for instance: Sandmann, 'Wirkungsbereiche', pp. 739–45 and Häussling, *Mönchskonvent*, who also stresses at p. 150 that a history of the 'Klerikalisierung des Mönchtums' still needs to be written.

34 See Picker, *Pastor Doctus*, p. 123.

secluded from worldly contact', i.e. he limited himself to reproducing the etymological meaning of the word *monachus* found in Isidore. Then he moved straightaway to depict the characteristics of clerical life, according to the focus of the treatise. Evidently, the ordained monks whom he addressed could not be represented through the definition of monks he had provided, since their pastoral office required interaction with the world. Should we conclude that Hrabanus regarded ordained monks as clerics only?

If the designations occurring in the *DIC* are not useful in solving the dilemma, two authoritative texts could provide the solution. They are, firstly, the *Regula Benedicti*, which allowed monks to be ordained but required them to keep living according to the monastic rule (Chapter 62). Secondly, a chapter of the *Admonitio generalis*, which prompted monks who had moved up into the clerical rank not to drop the fulfilment of their monastic vows.[35] The two texts address ordained monks as monks (*monachi*) and require from them to remain monks. Despite the definition of *monachi* occurring in the *DIC*, I would argue that Hrabanus similarly regarded his ordained brethren as monks in the first instance, because of their regular observance, and secondarily as clerics by reason of their office. With his treatise Hrabanus aimed to provide them with adequate clerical training; he did not engage with their monastic education, which rested upon other texts. Furthermore, like the *Regula Benedicti* and the *Admonitio generalis* before him, Hrabanus did not take the trouble to create a new category within the Church, which would better describe his own and his brethren's complex ecclesiastical status.

It is important to note that neither the *Institutio canonicorum* nor previously the *Admonitio generalis*, despite the sharp distinction between monks and canons they urged, prohibited the existence, or rather the persistence, of clerical monks. Indeed, these continued to constitute a significant part of the Carolingian clergy also after the issue of the *Institutio canonicorum*. In particular, clerical monks formed a substantial part of the community of Fulda in Hrabanus's time. It has been reckoned that about a third of Fulda's monks (*c*. 200 people), including Hrabanus himself, had been ordained as priests in the first half of the ninth century. A further third of the community held the position of deacon or subdeacon.[36] Lists of monks belonging to Fulda or to its dependent monasteries confirm that clerical monks formed the majority of the respective communities.[37] As such, they could not only perform liturgical

---

35 Quoting a letter by the fifth-century pope Innocentius I, Chapter 27 of the *Admonitio generalis* says explicitly that if 'a monk rises to the rank of cleric he should not withdraw the resolutions of his monastic vows' ('[...] ut monachus, si ad clericatum provehatur, propositum monachicae professionis non amittat'), which means that a clerical monk was expected to live according to the monastic rule he had first embraced.

36 Raaijmakers, *The Making of the Monastic Community*, pp. 187–88; de Jong, 'Carolingian Monasticism', p. 647: 'If one includes subdeacons, 70% of the monks during the abbacy of Hraban were of clerical rank'.

37 Picker, *Pastor Doctus*, p. 88.

duties in their own cloister, but also support the laity living in the proximity of the monastery or its direct dependences with pastoral care.

The questions which Fulda's ordained monks, according to the prologue of the *DIC*, addressed to Hrabanus could be interpreted as evidence of a local debate on the nature of the clerical office that had been triggered by the deliberations of the Aachen Councils. Indeed, the vision of the clergy conveyed by the *Institutio canonicorum* and promoted by the court depicted non-monastic clergy, specifically the communities of canons, as the most accomplished form of clerical life. It thus probably provoked discussions among Fulda's ordained monks. As far as monastic observance is concerned, clear evidence survives of the debate raised among Fulda's monks by the decisions of the Aachen Councils on this matter, as we will see below discussing the *Supplex Libellus*. These had been met with caution rather than with passive acceptance.[38] When mentioning in the prologue the many questions posed by his brethren, Hrabanus alluded perhaps to similar discussions, this time on clerical issues, that arose in the wake of the Aachen Councils. Tasked with providing answers, the priest-monk Hrabanus composed his treatise.

The *DIC* took shape — Hrabanus reports in the prologue — when he gathered in a single volume all the specific replies he had offered to his fellow-monks individually, either in oral or in written form. Indeed, his brethren had urged him to put his answers together and produce a comprehensive treatise, which they could consult at any time they needed.[39] Hrabanus describes the *DIC* as a systematic explanation of clerical life based upon his extensive study of the Bible and of the patristic tradition. Considering both the size of the treatise and the material work needed to produce a final version of it in the form of a book, it seems plausible that Hrabanus had started engaging with such topics already before 816. The *DIC* could therefore be regarded not only as a reaction to the *Institutio canonicorum* in particular, but also as Hrabanus's contribution to a continuing reflection on the ideal form of clerical life, which had its roots in late antique literature, and particularly in Augustine's and Jerome's writings. In this, he took the instances of his brethren into account and provided them with a picture of the perfect cleric, which, in contrast to that contained in the *Institutio canonicorum*, was perfectly compatible with their monastic observance. The request for correction and approval Hrabanus made to Haistulf in closing the prologue was not necessarily a formality.[40] He needed the actual support of a friendly-minded bishop to lend credibility and legitimization to his own vision.

---

38 On this debate see the introduction to Hrabanus Maurus, *Über die Unterweisung*, ed. and trans. by Zimpel, pp. 16–22 and 56–58; Picker, *Pastor Doctus*, pp. 63–67; Phelan, 'New Insights', p. 68.
39 Hrabanus Maurus, *De institutione clericorum*, ed. by Zimpel, Prologus, p. 281, ll. 13–24.
40 *Pastor Doctus*, pp. 30–31.

Concluding the survey of the paratexts framing the *DIC*, the poem transmitted at the end of the third book confirms the authoritative position bestowed on Haistulf. It is a short panegyric, in which Hrabanus described the archbishop as the guide of the Fulda community in a spiritual, a doctrinal, and a moral sense. Haistulf is acclaimed as *doctor, summusque sacerdos, | dux sacer et princeps, lux, via, pastor, honor* (a teacher, a bishop, | a holy guide and a leader, a light, a way, a shepherd, an honour).[41] Moreover, Hrabanus mentioned the occasion on which Haistulf received the *DIC* as a present. It was the consecration of the new abbey church of Fulda in 819, which the Archbishop of Mainz personally attended.

This very event put an end to a quite turbulent period in the history of the monastery. Indeed, the beginning of the ninth century had been marked by epidemics and, most of all, by the quarrels between the monks and the Abbot Ratger (r. 802–17), which had led to Ratger's deposition in 817. As one of his poems reveals, Hrabanus was among those who had openly criticized the abbot's governance.[42] Fulda's monks had gathered their complaints in a petition known as the *Supplex Libellus* and had submitted it twice, the first time to Charlemagne, and the second to Louis the Pious.[43]

According to Steffen Patzold, the *Supplex Libellus* should be considered as a witness to the heated conflicts arising among Fulda's community when Abbot Ratger tried to reform the local practices of monastic observance according to the contents of various councils held from the beginning of the ninth century.[44] The modification of the local monastic practices, which Ratger had attempted to introduce in response to imperial decrees, caused troubles among the community and was met with general defiance. Indeed, Chapter 18 of the *Libellus* requests Ratger's opinion to be corrected (*corrigatur*): he would have undermined the worth of the local practices (*instituta sancti Bonifatii*) by claiming that these had been condemned by the prescriptions of a synod (*decreta eius synodus*).[45] According to Josef Semmler, the monks referred to the directives for monastic observance issued by the Council held at Aachen from 816 to 817.[46] The passage is significant for our purposes since

---

41 Hrabanus Maurus, *De institutione clericorum*, ed. by Zimpel, p. 520, ll. 3–4.
42 Hrabanus Maurus, *Carmina*, pp. 204–05, no. 40. See also: Picker, *Pastor Doctus*. p. 67 and Raaijmakers, *The Making of the Monastic Community*, pp. 119–31.
43 *Supplex Libellus*, ed. by Semmler.
44 The innovations Ratger tried to introduce concerned: a) the local forms of liturgy, in conformity with the *ordo benedictinum* sponsored by the court; b) limitation of the working activities of the monks outside the *claustrum*, in the dependent *villae* or *cellae*; c) the comforts concerning clothing. See Patzold, 'Konflikte', pp. 113–16 and 131–38; de Jong, 'Carolingian Monasticism', pp. 646–48; Raaijmakers, *The Making of the Monastic Community*, pp. 126–29.
45 *Supplex Libellus*, ed. by Semmler, 18, p. 326, ll. 11–12: 'Quod ipse abbas corrigatur, ne instituta sancti Bonifatii detrahat dicens, quod decreta eius synodus damnaverit'. See also Picker, *Pastor doctus*, pp. 64–67.
46 Semmler, 'Studien zum Supplex Libellus', pp. 286–88.

it records a divergence of opinions between Fulda's abbot and his monks with regard to the regulations coming from court. In other words, it provides us with evidence of the fact that conciliar acts and capitularies formed a subject of discussion at Fulda right after their promulgation. Candidus's *Vita Aegil* bears a further witness to this local debate. Indeed, the text reports the visit paid to the monastic community by west Frankish *missi* sent by Louis the Pious between 817 and 818.[47] The *missi* had the task of restoring harmony among the monks after Ratger's deposition and measuring their adherence to the regulations issued at Aachen.[48]

Precisely during this exciting time of confrontation Hrabanus wrote in Fulda his instruction for clerical life, which he dedicated to his fellow clerical monks and presented to the Archbishop of Mainz for approval. As we have seen, modern scholarship assumes unanimously that Hrabanus knew the contents of the *Institutio canonicorum* before completing his treatise. In order to better appreciate the relationship between the two texts, in what follows I will compare the structure and the contents of the *DIC* with those of the *Institutio canonicorum*; I will then summarize and discuss the major differences between them in the conclusions.

Institutio canonicorum vs. *DIC*: Structure, Sources, and Contents

As Table 9.1 shows, the topics shared by the *Institutio canonicorum* and the *DIC* are very limited in number (they are underlined for the sake of clarity). The two texts have in common, firstly, the definition of what a cleric is, which they obtained by drawing on the same source (the *De ecclesiasticis officiis* of Isidore, the seventh-century bishop of Seville) but placed at very different points. While the *DIC* featured it right at the beginning of Book 1, as one would expect, the *Institutio canonicorum* dealt with this issue only in the final chapters of the patristic florilegium. Secondly, tonsure and clerical grades occupied a pre-eminent position in both works and were explained by building upon a very similar Isidorian background.[49] Nevertheless, the organization of the material followed different criteria. While the *Institutio canonicorum* opened straightaway with these topics, the *DIC* introduced them after a more general description of the structure of the Christian society. Thirdly, both texts engaged with the Liturgy of the Hours drawing again on Isidore.

---

47 See Kramer, 'Teaching Emperors', pp. 318–22.
48 Candidus, *Vita Aegil*, ed. by Becht-Jördens, 3.4.36–40, p. 5. See Raaijmakers, *The Making of the Monastic Community*, pp. 130–31 and Semmler, 'Instituta sancti Bonifatii', p. 101.
49 See, respectively, *Concilium Aquisgranense a. 816*, *Institutio canonicorum*, ed. by Werminghoff, 1–9, pp. 318–26, and Hrabanus Maurus, *De institutione clericorum*, ed. by Zimpel, I. 3–12, pp. 293–308. Both passages drew mainly on Isidore, *De ecclesiasticis officiis*, ed. by Lawson, II. 4–14, pp. 55–73.

Table 9.1. *Institutio canonicorum* and *DIC*: Structure, contents, and sources (shared topics are underlined).

Institutio canonicorum	
Ch.1	<u>Tonsure</u> (from Isidore's *De eccl. officiis*)
1–9	<u>Clerical Grades</u> (from Isidore's *De eccl. officiis*)
10–38	Virtues and Vices of Prelates (various patristic sources, among them <u>Gregory's *Regula Pastoralis*</u>)
39–93	Various prescriptions for clerics drawn from ecclesiastical councils or papal legislation
94–113	Advice for clerical life drawn from various Church Fathers (Jerome, Gregory, Augustine, and others). In particular: Ch. 99–101: Definition of clerical status from Isidore's *De eccl. officiis* (<u>*De clericis*</u>, *De regulis clericorum*, *De generibus clericorum*)
114–45	Regula canonicorum: instructions for coenobitic life in a cloister
	In particular: Ch. 126–30: <u>Liturgy of the Hours</u> (from Isidore's *De eccl. officiis* = 7 Hours)

Hrabanus's *De Institutione Clericorum*	
Book 1	(main source: Isidore's *De eccl. officiis*) Definition of 'Ecclesia' Three Orders (*Laici, Monachi, Clerici*) <u>Tonsure</u> <u>Clerical Grades</u> Clerical Clothing Sacraments: Baptism, Chrism, and Eucharist The Mass
Book 2	(main source: Isidore's *De eccl. officiis*) <u>Liturgy of the Hours</u> (8 Hours, including Prime) Other Prayers Penance, Fasting, Almsgiving Ecclesiastical Feasts, Chant, Lectures, Creed, History of Heresies
Book 3	(main sources: Augustine's *De Doctr. Christiana*; <u>Gregory's *Regula Pastoralis*</u>) The good cleric: learned, virtuous, skilled in communicating The aim of learning: the achievement of wisdom and love of God Peculiarities of the biblical language The liberal arts and their usefulness for biblical studies Guidelines for speaking and writing well

However, their explanation differed for the hour of Prime. Finally, both the *Institutio canonicorum* and the *DIC* included advice concerning moral life as well as the preparation and the performance of sermons, which derived from Gregory's *Regula Pastoralis*. But while Hrabanus only touched upon these matters, and mostly in Chapter 37 of his third book, the *Institutio canonicorum* returned to the topics several times.[50] Zimpel regarded these shared contents as evidence of the dependence of the *DIC* on the *Institutio canonicorum*, which Hrabanus would have used as a model. In Zimpel's view, the consonances between the two works would demonstrate Hrabanus's intention to divulge the imperial regulations.[51] However, the discrepancies are significantly more numerous than the few similarities recorded by Zimpel. Indeed, the majority of the themes occurring in the one text are absent from the other. Moreover, the inner structure of the two texts diverges, which is the consequence of the different purposes they pursued. This leads me to reconsider Zimpel's position. Beginning with the *Institutio canonicorum*, let us take a closer look at contents and purposes of the two works.

a) The Institutio canonicorum

The prologue introducing the *Institutio canonicorum* states that the document aimed at creating a compendium of various authoritative passages to support those prelates who lacked either intellectual skills or reference books in the task of living righteously and guiding properly their flock.[52] The resulting arrangement of the topics dealt with is rather loose and moves from the general to the specific as in a funnel. Indeed, the *Institutio canonicorum* can be divided into two sections.[53] The first, containing the Prologue, the *Capitulatio*, and Chapters 1 to 113, takes the form of a collection of patristic passages of mostly moral content, which regulate the life of all sorts of clerics. This group of more than one hundred chapters, among which orientation is not always easy, functions as a general introduction to the second section, which comprises just over thirty chapters and addresses a specific group of clerics, the canons.

As for the first part, the various segments were assembled one after the other according to the criterion of either juxtaposing excerpts from different works dealing with the same topic or reproducing only one source in its treatment

---

50   See Picker, *Pastor Doctus*, pp. 56–58.
51   See the introduction to Hrabanus Maurus, *De institutione clericorum*, ed. by Zimpel, pp. 56–58. Here Zimpel considered the *Institutio canonicorum* as the very source Hrabanus employed to write some passages of his treatise.
52   See *Concilium Aquisgranense a. 816, Institutio canonicorum*, ed. by Werminghoff, *Prologus*, p. 313, ll. 1–13.
53   For a detailed analysis of the *Institutio canonicorum* see the chapter in the present volume by Rutger Kramer and Veronika Wieser.

of several aspects of clerical life.⁵⁴ The section opens with a description of the meaning and shape of the tonsure, which was the most immediate mark of identification for clerics. This chapter reproduces verbatim a passage of Isidore's *De ecclesiasticis officiis* and occupies a pre-eminent position, which it did not have in the Isidorian model.⁵⁵ The ensuing chapters deal with the clerical grades (Chapters 2–9), once more drawing primarily on Isidore's *De ecclesiasticis officiis*, but inverting the order of presentation of the single items. Isidore had arranged his material beginning with the bishops and including every group of people forming the Church, in particular also the monks and the laity. The *Institutio canonicorum* selected only Isidore's chapters dealing with specifically clerical positions, but reproduced them in the opposite order. As a result, the exposition contained in the *Institutio canonicorum* begins with the lowest grade of the *ostiarius* (doorkeeper) and reaches up to the bishops.⁵⁶ It skips the figures of the *psalmistae*, *custodes sanctorum*, and *corepiscopi*, despite their presence in the model,⁵⁷ and inserts the description of the *acolythi* (candle-bearers) instead. In so doing, the compiler of the *Institutio canonicorum* adapts the contents of Isidore's *De Ecclesiasticis officiis* to those of Isidore's *Etymologies* and uses both works as a source. Indeed, the *Etymologies* do not deal with *psalmistae*, *custodes sanctorum*, and *corepiscopi* either, while they contain a short description of the *acolythi*, which the *Institutio canonicorum* reproduces.⁵⁸ Also the inversion of the order of presentation of the Isidorian model responds to a plan. By ending his account of the clerical grades with the bishops, the compiler of the *Institutio canonicorum* obtained a neat conjunction to the next section of the work.

Indeed, Chapters 10 to 113 are concerned with describing virtues and vices of the clerical status with an initial focus on bishops (Chapters 10–38), as well as with fixing rules of correct behaviour for all sorts of clerics. Moral issues form the predominant focus of this bulky section of the *Institutio canonicorum*. Conversely, these topics recur in the *DIC* only to a minimal extent. It is remarkable that the *Institutio canonicorum* did not pay any particular attention

---

54 See, for instance, Chapters 27–30 of the *Institutio canonicorum*, which deal with the topic of negligent priests by juxtaposing passages drawn from Gregory, Prosper of Aquitaine, and Isidore respectively; and Chapters 94–98, which consist of a florilegium of various passages drawn from Jerome's epistles describing clerical life in general.
55 Isidore dealt with tonsure in the fourth chapter of the second book (see Isidore, *De ecclesiasticis officiis*, ed. by Lawson, 2. 4, pp. 55–56).
56 In presenting the clerical grades from the lowest to the highest position, the *Institutio canonicorum* might have been inspired by the list contained in Isidore's *Etymologiae* VII. 12. 3, which names the several grades in bottom-up succession. However, the list is followed by a description of each clerical grade arranged in a top-down order, like in Isidore's *De ecclesiasticis officiis* (see *Etymologiae*, ed. by Lindsay, VII. 12. 4–33).
57 Isidore deals with these categories in *De ecclesiasticis officiis*, ed. by Lawson, II. 12; II. 9; II. 6 respectively.
58 Isidore, *Etymologiae*, ed. by Lindsay, VII. 12. 29–30.

to the definition of what a cleric is. Only towards the end of the first section is the reader provided with two very similar definitions of cleric, i.e. firstly in Chapter 94, with a long excerpt from Jerome's *Letter to Nepotianus*,[59] and again in Chapter 99, with a passage drawn from Isidore's *De ecclesiasticis officiis*.[60] Both definitions depict the cleric as God's lot and God's heir by referring to the Greek meaning of the word *cleros* and to a few biblical quotations. On both occasions, however, the definitions are hidden in the body of the respective chapters and were not given the prominent position one would expect in an instructional text dedicated precisely to this category.

The second section of the *Institutio canonicorum*, the so-called *Regula canonicorum* (Chapters 114–45), contains a corpus of specific prescriptions concerning one well-defined group of clerics, i.e. the *clerici canonici*, whom modern scholarship regards as a creation of Carolingian ecclesiastical policy.[61] In particular, Chapter 113 serves as a conjunction between the two sections of the *Institutio* and introduces the focus of the ensuing chapters, which regulate the coenobitic form of life of those clerics who lived in a cloister under the supervision of a bishop. Starting with Chapter 115, these clerics are addressed by the name of canons (*canonici*).[62] Conversely, the more general designation of *clerici* occurs only fifteen times in the second section of the *Institutio canonicorum*, either within passages derived from patristic sources or to indicate those members of the clergy who were expected to enter a given community of canons.[63]

The purposes of the present chapter do not require a complete review of this section. For the sake of comparison with the *DIC* it suffices to make the following three points. Firstly, Chapter 115 regards canonical life to be the highest form of life (*institutio*) within the Church. However, it does not explain the reason for the supremacy of canons. The text simply relies upon

---

59 *Concilium Aquisgranense a. 816, Institutio canonicorum*, ed. by Werminghoff, 94, pp. 370, 12–18 and Jerome, *Epistulae*, ed. by Hilberg, 52, p. 421, ll. 10–15.
60 See *Concilium Aquisgranense a. 816, Institutio canonicorum*, ed. by Werminghoff, 99, p. 377 and Isidore, *De ecclesiasticis officiis*, ed. by Lawson, II. 1, p. 53. Isidore's source for this passage is Augustine's *Enarrationes in Psalmos*, ed. by Dekkers and Fraipont, 67. 19, p. 882.
61 For the promotion of a communal and regular life for clerics after the model of monastic coenobitism in Carolingian legislation before the *Institutio canonicorum* see *Admonitio generalis*, ed. by Mordek, Zechiel-Eckes, and Glatthaar, 71 and 75, pp. 226, 336–38 and pp. 228, 354–56; Semmler, 'Die Reform'; Semmler, 'Monachus'; Picker, *Pastor Doctus*, pp. 118–23; the chapter by Stephen Ling in the present volume. For the Carolingian creation of the *clericus canonicus* as opposed to the monk see de Jong, 'Carolingian Monasticism', p. 629. For the late antique and early medieval use of the term *canonicus* applied to the clergy see furthermore Barrow, *The Clergy*, p. 74.
62 *Concilium Aquisgranense a. 816, Institutio canonicorum*, ed. by Werminghoff, 115, p. 397, ll. 13–31.
63 For example, the term *clerici* is used to designate the clerics who are not yet members of a community of canons in Chapters 118 and 119, whereas it recurs within patristic quotations in Chapter 124 (see *Concilium Aquisgranense a. 816, Institutio canonicorum*, ed. by Werminghoff, p. 399 and p. 404, l. 24 respectively).

an unspecified 'manifest authority' (*evidenti auctoritate*).⁶⁴ As a matter of fact, the *Institutio canonicorum* introduced here an innovation, which could hardly be grounded in traditional sources. Patristic authorities (Jerome, Gregory, Isidore) had reserved the highest position within the Church for clerics in general by reason of their pastoral duties and their handling of the sacraments. In contrast to the *Institutio canonicorum*, the prologue of the *DIC* conformed to the tradition in this regard, since it guaranteed to all sorts of clerics a leading position in the Church.

Secondly, the same Chapter 115 addresses briefly the issue of property, recalling that canons, in contrast to monks, are allowed to dress in linen clothes, eat flesh, have possessions, and make use of them, as well as all things belonging to the Church.⁶⁵ In asserting this, Chapter 115 contradicts the advice contained in previous segments of the *Institutio canonicorum* itself, which cited patristic authorities on clerics renouncing possessions and income.⁶⁶ By contrast, the issue of property is completely absent from the *DIC*. This is crucial evidence of the fact that Hrabanus regarded the clerical monks of Fulda, whom he originally addressed with his work, primarily as monks, who were expected to live without personal possessions.

Thirdly, Chapters 126 to 130 contain instructions regarding the Liturgy of the Hours. They reproduce verbatim the corresponding section of Isidore's *De ecclesiasticis officiis* and illustrate both the biblical models and the spiritual meaning of the Hours that canons were expected to pray. These comprise seven Hours, from the Terce to Matins, and do not include Prime.⁶⁷ Conversely, the *DIC* envisaged the singing of Prime, as it was typical for the monastic Office.⁶⁸

---

64 *Concilium Aquisgranense a. 816, Institutio canonicorum*, ed. by Werminghoff, 115, p. 397, ll. 14–15: 'evidenti auctoritate liquet canonicam institutionem caeteris praestare institutionibus'.

65 *Concilium Aquisgranense a. 816, Institutio canonicorum*, ed. by Werminghoff, 115, p. 397, ll. 19–21: 'Quamquam enim canonicis […] liceat linum induere, carnibus vesci, dare et accipere proprias res […]'; 115, p. 397, ll. 29–30: '[…] et quia [monachi] nihil sibi proprium reliquerunt, manifestum est illis copiosioribus ecclesiae sumptibus quam canonicis, qui suis et ecclesiae licite utuntur rebus, indigere'.

66 See in particular Chapters 35 and 108 of the *Institutio canonicorum*, which reproduce Chapters 9 and 11 of the second book of Julianus Pomerius's *De vita contemplativa* respectively (cols 453B–454A and 455C). The same request for clerics to renounce possessions recurs in Chapters 110–13 of the *Institutio canonicorum*. Conversely, Chapter 88 assumes that bishops have their own belongings.

67 See Isidore, *De ecclesiasticis officiis*, ed. by Lawson, I. 19–23, pp. 23–27.

68 Billet, *Divine Office*, p. 14, recalls that both the secular and the monastic forms of the Office in the early medieval Latin West envisaged eight Hours. He notes at p. 33 that Prime was absent from the *cursus* described by Cassiodorus in his *Expositio Psalmorum*. However, he does not discuss the absence of Prime in Isidore's *De ecclesiasticis officiis* and in the *Institutio canonicorum* (at p. 65).

b) The DIC

The structure Hrabanus planned for the *DIC* follows a well-thought-out design, which reflects the author's intent to produce an exhaustive and user-friendly reference tool. Hrabanus divided the *DIC* into three clearly outlined blocks which correspond to the three books of the treatise. He facilitated the orientation within them by explaining structure, contents, and purposes twice in the paratexts. Furthermore, he enhanced the readability of his work by inserting small summaries of the topics dealt with and previews of ensuing subjects. We find them both at key turning points of the treatise, as for instance at the end of the first book and at the beginning of the second, and amid groups of chapters, as at the end of Chapters 10 and 15 of the third book, to mark the passage from one topic to another.

As for the contents, the first book is concerned with clerical grades, the liturgical clothing of priests, the sacraments (i.e. Baptism, Chrismal Unction, and Eucharist) and finally the Mass, in which the sacrament of Eucharist is celebrated. The book opens with a general definition of *ecclesia*, which Hrabanus derived only in part from short passages of Isidore's *Etymologies*.[69] In his own words, *ecclesia* is the worldwide community of baptized people, Christ's spouse and body. Three orders can be distinguished within the *ecclesia*, namely the laity, the monks, and the clerics (Chapter 2).[70] Neither the laity nor the monks are paid much attention. With regard to monks, Hrabanus limited himself to recalling the meaning of the term *monachus*, i.e. 'living alone', relying upon the Greek etymology of the name. He specified briefly that this implies that monks live secluded from any worldly contact.[71] As this scant definition testifies, it was not the purpose of the *DIC* to describe the essence and tasks of the monastic vocation. The third order, the clerics, clearly form the focus of the chapter. First of all, Hrabanus provided a definition of what a cleric is. To this end, he employed the same Isidorian passage used in Chapter 99 of the *Institutio canonicorum*.[72] Thus, he too presented the clerics as God's lot and heirs, who are expected to serve Him with all their energy and commitment. Furthermore, Hrabanus stressed with his own words the leading position of this group within the ecclesiastical hierarchy. Clerics occupy the top grade of the social scale since they deal with the holy and are allowed to administer the sacraments to other people.[73] In so doing, Hrabanus preferred to stick

---

69 See Hrabanus Maurus, *De institutione clericorum*, ed. by Zimpel, I. 1, p. 291 with *apparatus fontium*.
70 See Picker, *Pastor Doctus*, pp. 98–100 for origin and currency of the three-orders model.
71 Hrabanus Maurus, *De institutione clericorum*, ed. by Zimpel, I. 1, p. 292, ll. 4–5: 'Secundus est monachicus, id est singulariter conversans, hoc est a saeculari conversatione remotus'.
72 See above n. 60.
73 Hrabanus Maurus, *De institutione clericorum*, ed. by Zimpel, I. 2, pp. 292–93, ll. 16–17: 'Iste autem ordo iure praeponitur in ecclesia, quia in sanctis deservit et sacramenta populis dispensat'. In his appraisal Hrabanus shared arguments made already by Jerome and Bede,

to the patristic tradition which granted this privilege to all sorts of clerics, without differentiation. In contrast, as seen above, Chapter 115 of the *Institutio canonicorum* saw canons alone at the top of Christian society.

In Chapter 3 Hrabanus described tonsure.[74] He reproduced the same Isidorian chapter employed also by the *Institutio canonicorum*, which explains the apostolic origin of the practice and confers to tonsure the symbolic value of a tiara.[75] Moreover, he enriched the information delivered both by Isidore and the *Institutio canonicorum* by adding a passage from a letter of Aldhelm of Malmesbury, though omitting to mention the new source explicitly.[76] Via Aldhelm, Hrabanus reinforced the apostolic origin of tonsure and provided his readers with further symbolic meanings for this particular haircut. Tonsure was thought to have been introduced by the apostle Peter himself in order to recall both the crown of thorns worn by Christ during His Passion and the haircut inflicted by the Romans on their slaves before selling them. After tonsure the first book of the *DIC* deals with the clerical grades (Chapters 4–13), which Hrabanus examined in descending order, beginning with the three sorts of bishops (patriarchs, archbishops, and bishops, including the *corepiscopi* as their deputies) and ending with the doorkeeper (*ostiarius*). In this, he reproduced the contents of his main source, Isidore's *De ecclesiasticis officiis*, more faithfully than the *Institutio canonicorum* had done. Hrabanus skipped only Isidore's chapter on the *custodes sacrorum*, retaining both the *corepiscopi* and the psalmists of Isidore's scheme. In comparison to the *Institutio canonicorum*, Hrabanus drew from Isidore's *Etymologies* not only the passage on the candle-bearers, but also the description of the various sorts of bishops, as well as some integrative information concerning the other positions.[77] He closed this section with a chapter (Chapter 13) dedicated to summarizing the steps of the clerical career from the lowest positions to the sacred rank (*ordo sacer*) of priests and bishops. In particular, Hrabanus took care to mention the years of service envisaged for each clerical grade as well as the minimal age required for becoming a deacon (twenty-five years) and priest (thirty

---

although he did not quote them directly. See, for instance, Jerome, *Epistulae*, ed. by Hilberg, 14, p. 55, ll. 3–9. Parallels with Bede's work are stressed by Picker, *Pastor Doctus*, p. 111 n. 139.

74 For a thorough analysis of the meaning Hrabanus conferred to tonsure see Picker, *Pastor Doctus*, pp. 101–06.

75 Isidore, *De ecclesiasticis officiis*, ed. by Lawson, II. 4, pp. 55–56.

76 Hrabanus introduced Aldhelm's passage through a generic reference: 'Moreover, there are some scholars who affirm' ('Sunt quoque quidam doctorum, qui adserunt'), probably because Aldhelm did not count as an established authority in ecclesiastical matters. At the end of the passage Hrabanus left the decision about whether to trust his opinion to the judgement of the reader ('Sed de his quid suscipiat, iudicio lectoris derelinquimus'); see Hrabanus Maurus, *De institutione clericorum*, ed. by Zimpel, I. 2, pp. 294–95, ll. 35–36 and 43–44. Picker, *Pastor Doctus*, p. 102 with n. 86 records a further quotation of this letter in Amalarius's *Liber officialis* II. 5. 8.

77 See Picker, *Pastor Doctus*, pp. 134–35.

years). Again, neither Isidore nor the *Institutio canonicorum* included such regulations, which Hrabanus elaborated building upon papal legislation.[78]

The rest of the first book concerns primarily priests and bishops. In Chapters 14 to 23 Hrabanus addressed the topic of priestly and episcopal vestments with the purpose of comparing the garments of the Old Testament with those of his time and explaining their mystical significance. His systematic exposition of this matter constituted a novelty if compared to previous instructions for clerics and especially to the *Institutio canonicorum*.[79] This latter was concerned with the general issue of clothing only so far as to prohibit canons from wearing monastic cowls, and, more generally, from dressing extravagantly (Chapters 124–25). Isidore, in turn, had not discussed the issue of clothing in his *De ecclesiasticis officiis*. Since he lacked a specific model, Hrabanus selected pieces of information from several sources which dealt with the topic in passing. However, these cover only a limited part of the section, which Hrabanus had to write mostly in his own words.[80] He listed nine garments, from the *superhumerale* to the *pallium*. For each of them he provided an explanation featuring the etymological analysis of their name, their spiritual value, and an interpretation of the biblical verses in which the respective items occur.

The meaning of the sacraments (Baptism, Chrismal Unction, and Eucharist), the importance of a proper instruction for catechumens before Baptism, the biblical roots of the accompanying rites and the origin of the order of the Mass close the first book (Chapters 24–33). In this part, Hrabanus touched upon crucial duties of priests and bishops, which the *Institutio canonicorum* had not mentioned at all. His engagement with these topics was probably inspired by the efforts Charlemagne and Alcuin had made in order to achieve a correct execution of the liturgy, and of the baptismal rite in particular, to mention but one well-known example.[81] Hrabanus's aim was to support bishops and priests in understanding the roots and theological value of the rites they were expected to celebrate. To accomplish his task he relied on various sources — Cyprian, Jerome,

---

[78] See Hrabanus Maurus, *De institutione clericorum*, ed. by Zimpel, I. 13, pp. 308–09 with the reference to Pope Zosimus's letter to Esychius of Salona. The *Institutio canonicorum* mentioned the minimal age of thirty years for priests in a line of Chapter 9 (see *Concilium Aquisgranense a. 816, Institutio canonicorum*, ed. by Werminghoff, p. 324, l. 11).

[79] Zimpel stresses that Hrabanus's chapters on clerical garments were the most excerpted and copied by following scholars, since they filled a gap in the traditional sources dealing with clerical life: see Hrabanus Maurus, *Über die Unterweisung*, ed. and trans. by Zimpel, p. 28.

[80] The *apparatus fontium* of Zimpel's edition lists Bede's *De Tabernaculo* and *In Marci evangelium expositio*, Isidore's *Etymologies*, and Jerome's *Epistle* 64 as the sources on which Hrabanus occasionally drew for this section (Hrabanus Maurus, *De institutione clericorum*, ed. by Zimpel, I. 14–23, pp. 309–15).

[81] For Charlemagne's and Alcuin's interest on the regulation of the baptismal rite see Phelan, *The Formation of Christian Europe*, esp. pp. 94–206; for an edition on the numerous contemporary texts written to this task, see Keefe, *Water and the Word*, II.

Isidore, Bede, and Alcuin's letters[82] — but wrote again a relevant part of the contents on his own.[83] Only occasionally did Hrabanus provide his readers with information concerning the correct performance of specific rites from a practical point of view, as for instance when he listed which questions are to be asked of the catechumens (Chapter 27), when he differentiated the duties of the priest from those of the bishop during Baptism (Chapters 28 and 30), and finally when he described the correct order of the various liturgical parts of the Mass (Chapter 33). All in all, however, the *DIC* was not designed to function as a liturgical handbook or as an instruction-reader for priests.[84] Rather, it aimed at presenting the theological and liturgical knowledge considered essential for being (or becoming) a priest. In this regard, Hrabanus's educational plan was very ambitious and by far outdid the expectations of priests expressed both by the court and by contemporary episcopal statutes.[85]

The second book of the *DIC* is mainly devoted to the prayers, actions, and liturgical feasts, which all grades of clerics, not only priests and bishops, were expected to perform. The main source for the treatment of such topics was again Isidore's *De ecclesiasticis officiis*, which Hrabanus adapted and enriched according to his purposes. The first section of the book (Chapters 1–16) describes various types of prayers, both mandatory and optional. Isidore had engaged with this theme only with regard to the Liturgy of the Hours, which he had divided into seven offices, from the Terce to Matins. The substantial additions to the Isidorian model made by Hrabanus in this part reveal his monastic formation and suggest that he had a monastic audience in mind. He envisaged, for instance, eight offices for the Liturgy of the Hours, from Matins to night Vigils including Prime, in accordance with the monastic model fixed by the *Regula Benedicti*. Given the absence of Prime in the Isidorian scheme, Hrabanus had to legitimize the adherence to this liturgical duty and

---

82 Particularly interesting are Hrabanus's borrowings from Alcuin's *Letter* 134 to the priest Oduin on Baptism, which had a huge impact at court and across the realm. See Phelan, *The Formation of Christian Europe*, pp. 121–28; Keefe, *Water and the Word*, II, no. 9, pp. 239–45; Van Rhijn, *Shepherds*, pp. 115–19.

83 For a detailed survey of the sources Hrabanus employed I refer to the *apparatus fontium* of Zimpel's edition as well as to the additional information provided by Picker, *Pastor Doctus*, pp. 31–37.

84 For the notion of 'instruction-reader' see Keefe, *Water and the Word*, vol. 1, pp. 23–26.

85 See in particular *Admonitio generalis*, ed. by Mordek, Zechiel-Eckes, and Glatthaar, 68, pp. 220, ll. 292–96, which requires from priests: 'ut fidem rectam teneant et baptisma catholicum observent et missarum preces bene intellegant. Et ut psalmi digne [...] modulentur et dominicam orationem ipsi intellegant et omnibus praedicent intellegendam, ut quisque sciat, quid petat a deo'. The *Institutio canonicorum* did not pay particular attention to a well-defined educational programme, as we will see below. For the requests contained in episcopal statutes until 820 see Van Rhijn, *Shepherds*, pp. 107–24 and Van Rhijn, 'Charlemagne's *correctio*', pp. 49–51. To my knowledge, the relationship in terms of shared contents between the *DIC* and contemporary episcopal statutes is still unexplored.

produce his own original explanation of its meaning.[86] Moreover, he included some verbatim quotations from the *Regula Benedicti* and several excerpts from Cassian's *Conlationes*, a text frequently read by monks, to describe the various sorts of prayers which are not mandatory, but should nevertheless be performed by all Christians, be they clerics or not, in order to express gratitude or contrition towards God.[87] In contrast to this broad overview, as already mentioned above, the *Institutio canonicorum* was interested in the issue of prayers only so far as to prescribe to canons the singing of seven Hours, Prime excluded, according to the Isidorian model.

A quote from Isidore's *Etymologies* at the end of Chapter 16 — recalling that fasting and alms bestow wings onto human prayers and bring them faster to God's ears — enables Hrabanus to introduce the following section of Book Two. Here he produced firstly a detailed survey of the different sorts of fasting (optional and mandatory, private and public, Chapters 17–27)[88] and dealt secondly with almsgiving (Chapter 28), which he presented as the deeds resulting from one's spiritual and material mercy not only towards others but also towards oneself. A monastic perspective can be noticed in this section too. Concluding his treatment of fasting, Hrabanus added an explanation as to why the consumption of poultry and other birds was allowed, whereas eating the meat of quadrupeds was forbidden. In doing so, he made no direct use of intermediary sources and rather relied on the *Regula Benedicti* to underpin his arguments.[89] This provides us with further evidence of the fact that Hrabanus's work addressed specifically those clerics who lived under a monastic rule.[90] Moreover, as Picker has shown, Hrabanus allowed the eating of poultry in line with his personal (or perhaps the local?) interpretation of the Rule. In doing so, he went against the prescriptions for monks issued at Aachen between 816 and 819.[91]

---

86 See Hrabanus Maurus, *De institutione clericorum*, ed. by Zimpel, II. 3, pp. 346–47. It is important to recall that Prime is included in Chrodegang's *Regula canonicorum* and in Amalarius's *Liber officialis*. I thank Graeme Ward for this caveat. Therefore, its absence from the *Institutio canonicorum* does not necessarily mean that the singing of Prime was reserved to monks. See Billet, *Divine Office*, p. 14.
87 See in particular Chapter 12 and 13 reproducing extensive passages from the ninth Book of Cassianus's *Conlationes*.
88 The *Institutio canonicorum* dealt with the significance of fasting for clerics only to record the punishments required for those who contravene the usual conventions, the knowledge of which is simply implied (see Chapters 68–69).
89 As both Zimpel and Picker stress, Hrabanus quoted or alluded to the Rule of Benedict only three times within the *DIC*: see Hrabanus Maurus, *Über die Unterweisung*, ed. and trans. by Zimpel, pp. 58–59 and Picker, *Pastor Doctus*, p. 36.
90 Hrabanus Maurus, *De institutione clericorum*, ed. by Zimpel, II. 27, p. 371, ll. 14–17: 'Avium quoque esum credo inde a patribus permissum esse, eo quod ex eodem elemento, de quo et pisces creatae sunt. Nam in regula monachorum non invenimus aliarum carnium esum eis contradictum esse, nisi quadrupedum', with reference to Chapters 37 and 39 of the *Regula Benedicti*; see also Zimpel's comments on pp. 23–24.
91 Picker, *Pastor Doctus*, pp. 67–70.

After having engaged shortly with penance and reconciliation (Chapters 29–30) Hrabanus moved to a survey of the major feasts of the liturgical calendar (Chapters 31–46). He described origin and theological meaning of each of them drawing mostly on the corresponding chapters in the first book of Isidore's *De ecclesiasticis officiis*. He devoted particular attention to the rites connected to Easter, trying to make sense of the various practices in use and stressing the provisional nature of his results.[92] Moreover, he enriched the Isidorian elements of his explanation with passages drawn from Bede's *De temporum ratione* in order to provide his audience with an authoritative reference point for the challenging issue of calculating the date of Easter Sunday. The second book of the *DIC* closes illustrating 'the origin of chant, lectures, and the authority of the Creed', as Hrabanus outlined in own words at the end of Chapter 46.[93] He described, firstly, the liturgical chants (i.e. canticles, psalms, hymns, antiphons, and responsories). Then he moved to the readings, fixing both the rules for a good performance and the canon of the orthodox biblical books. Finally, he treated the contents of the Apostles' Creed and added a detailed list of heresies, which reproduces verbatim the corresponding chapters of the eighth book of Isidore's *Etymologies*.

The third book of the *DIC* represents an absolute novelty among instructions concerning early medieval clergy. Hrabanus developed and described carefully an ambitious educational programme for priests and priests to-be, which builds upon the double assumption he expressed in his own words in Chapter 1. First, only those clerics who have prepared themselves properly to lead the Christian people, that is to teach God's flock in example and word, can be regarded as good. Accordingly, good clerics are expected to understand correctly God's dictates as contained in the Bible, live a righteous life, and be able to communicate what they know in an effective way. Second, their preparation should consist primarily in the study of the Bible and of the liberal arts as presented in the body of the third book. These are the weapons that a future leader of a Christian community (*futurus populi rector*) ought to acquire both for his own and for his flock's benefit.[94] Taking his words from Gregory's *Regula Pastoralis*, Hrabanus underpinned these concepts by stressing that priests' ignorance and bad moral behaviour have noticeable repercussions

---

92 Summing up, for instance, the information on the different fasting practices before Easter, Hrabanus underlined that he had gathered what others had said or written on the topic, leaving it to his readers to find more precise and sensible answers. See Hrabanus Maurus, *De institutione clericorum*, ed. by Zimpel, II. 34, pp. 383, 27–29: 'Sed haec omnia nos ita hic posuimus, sicut in aliorum dictis vel scriptis comperimus, lectori viam dantes, si quae veracius et rationabilius exquisita invenerit obtinere'.

93 Hrabanus Maurus, *De institutione clericorum*, ed. by Zimpel, II. 46, p. 407, ll. 45–49: 'Sed quia de festivitatibus celebrioribus ad instructionem eorum, qui in ecclesia deo serviunt et populo praesunt, secundum sensum maiorum iam supra diximus, de origine quoque cantus et lectionum et auctoritate symboli adhuc in prasenti libro dicamus'.

94 Hrabanus Maurus, *De institutione clericorum*, ed. by Zimpel, III. 1, p. 435, ll. 1–19.

on society: bad priests are responsible for the sins of all Christians and, consequently, for God's disapproval of the Christian people. He concluded the first chapter by declaring the intentions of the third book of the *DIC*. This aims to show both to those who already serve God within the holy ranks of the Church (*in sacris ordinibus*, that is priests and bishops), and to those who will do it, the level of erudition, good conduct, and ability to teach that are necessary for their way of life to match their prudence (*prudentia*) and for their words to conform to what they have learnt.[95]

Prudence, in turn, is equated to wisdom (*sapientia*) in Chapter 2, which Hrabanus wrote entirely in his own words. Here he presented the achievement of wisdom and the acknowledgment of truth as the most important goal for clerics, since they both constitute an indispensable means to experience the highest good (*summum bonum*). In other words, a linear progression leads the cleric from the study of the Bible first to the achievement of wisdom and then to the perception of the nature of the highest good. Wisdom can be achieved through the study of the salvific contents of the Bible and of those results of pagan scholarship which can be regarded as useful. Hrabanus's educational programme legitimizes fully the study of the liberal arts and presents the deep knowledge of the Bible as a necessary step to achieving wisdom. Wisdom, in turn, is regarded as the precondition not only for good moral conduct but also for the ability to communicate God's message effectively.

In the ensuing chapters (3–5) Hrabanus added a final point to his theoretical framework by explaining the nature of the highest good (*summum bonum*), which can be experienced once one has reached the perfection of wisdom. To this purpose he first recalled in Chapter 3, with the help of Augustine, that the task of understanding the true meaning of the Bible requires serious engagement given the obscure and ambiguous nature of its language. Then he moved to a short description of the seven grades of wisdom (*timor dei, pietas, scientia, fortitudo, consilium, intellectus, sapientia*), that is of the spiritual gifts one needs in order to attain wisdom and approach the Bible successfully (Chapter 4).[96] In this section he reproduced mostly extracts of Augustine's *De doctrina Christiana* but added also original considerations, especially when he described the features and goals of *scientia*, i.e. of learning. In particular, Hrabanus linked *scientia* to the study of the Bible and anticipated that this would

---

95 Hrabanus Maurus, *De institutione clericorum*, ed. by Zimpel, III. 1, p. 438, ll. 69–75: 'Sed quia utrumque necesse est, et ut bonam vitam sapientia inlustret et sapientiam bona vita commendet, utrumque in hoc libro, si dominus annuerit, digeremus, id est, ut sciant hi, qui in sacris ordinibus ecclesiae aut iam domino deserviunt, aut deservituri erunt, quantae eruditionis eis opus sit in animo, et quam sobriae vitae in exemplo, quantaeque virtutis et discretionis in docendo, ut nec discordet vita prudentiae neque sermo dissentiat disciplinae'. A translation of this passage, with a different rendering of the last sentence, can be found in Phelan, 'New Insights', p. 75.
96 See Phelan, 'New Insights', pp. 75–76.

form the main subject of the book.[97] Quoting Augustine, but also writing some passages in his own words, he stated that the study of the Bible has its main support in the theological virtues of faith, hope, and charity and that the fruit of learning should comprise charity alone, i.e. love.[98] He returned to this specific point in Chapter 5 — which he wrote entirely in his own words — where he underlined that the achievement of perfect wisdom, i.e. of the full knowledge of God, leads necessarily to the perfect love of God. This is the highest good: the achievement of wisdom joined to the love of God,[99] which implies necessarily the love of the neighbour, as Hrabanus had explained in Chapter 4.[100] Wisdom and love form a unity in Hrabanus's scheme in the sense that intellectual engagement with the Bible should immediately inform the moral behaviour of those striving to understand God's word. The activity of learning, which is necessary to attain wisdom, and wisdom itself are useless if they are not followed by the love of God and of others.

In the next section Hrabanus turned to his actual intention of explaining the nature and contents of learning (*scientia*), as he had anticipated previously in Chapter 4. From Chapter 6 to Chapter 15 he focused on the structure and linguistic particularities of the Bible. Combining extracts from Augustine's *De doctrina Christiana* and Isidore's *Etymologies*, he explained the differences between the Christian and the Hebrew canon of the books contained in the Bible and gave methodological suggestions for approaching the study of its contents. Then he concentrated on the difficulties of the biblical language, and in particular on both the unknown and the ambiguous terms as explained by Augustine in the second and third book of his *De doctrina Christiana*. With Chapter 16 Hrabanus introduced the study of the liberal arts specifying, in this and in the following chapter, which aspects of secular teaching are to be rejected (as, for instance, the disciplines connected to the production of horoscopes, amulets, and enchantments) and which, on the contrary, are

---

[97] Hrabanus Maurus, *De institutione clericorum*, ed. by Zimpel, III. 4, pp. 441–42, pp. 10–12: 'Post istos duos gradus timoris atque pietatis ad tertium venitur scientiae gradum, de quo nunc agere institui'.

[98] Hrabanus Maurus, *De institutione clericorum*, ed. by Zimpel, III. 4, p. 443, ll. 39–30: 'solummodo scientiae fructus in caritate consistit'.

[99] Hrabanus Maurus, *De institutione clericorum*, ed. by Zimpel, III. 5, p. 445, ll. 14–21: 'Nam salvator in evangelio sapientiam et caritatem unum esse intelligi volens ad patrem dixit: "Pater iuste, mundus te non cognovit; ego autem te cognovi, et hi cognoverunt, quia tu me misisti, et notum feci eis nomen tuum, et notum faciam, ut dilectio, qua dilexisti me, in ipsis sit, et ego in ipsis". Quisquis ergo percipit plenam notitiam dei, simul habet in se perfectam dilectionem dei et his ambobus fruens aeternam beatitudinem adepto summo bono tenebit'.

[100] Hrabanus Maurus, *De institutione clericorum*, ed. by Zimpel, III. 4, p. 442, ll. 12–14: 'Nam in eo se exercet omnis divinarum scripturarum studiosus, nihil in eis aliud inventurus, quam diligendum esse deum propter deum et proximum propter deum'. Phelan, 'New Insights', pp. 72–78 analyses these and further passages of the *DIC* in which Hrabanus stressed the unity between learning, or wisdom, and love in priestly formation. Phelan also provided an English translation of the relevant sections.

worthy of being cultivated in order to approach the study of the Holy Writ (as, for instance, the study of history and computus). Beginning with Chapter 18, he then turned to a systematic exposition of the contents and aims of the liberal arts, resting mainly upon Cassiodorus's *Institutiones*, Augustine's *De doctrina Christiana*, and Isidore's *Etymologies*. He dedicated one chapter to each of the seven disciplines, taking care to explain the origin of their respective names, their contents and purposes, as well as their relevance either for the study of the Bible or in the formation of future leaders of the Christian flock.

The chapter devoted to grammar (Chapter 18), for instance, opens explaining the derivation of the name from the Greek word 'gramma' meaning 'letter'. Then it provides the reader with a multi-layered explanation of the aims of the discipline, which Hrabanus obtained by combining the information contained in several sources. Grammar is not only 'the science of correct speaking' (as it is for Jerome, Isidore, the *Anonymus ad Cuimnanum*), but also 'the science of correct writing' (as in Quintilian, the *Ars Laureshamensis*, and Alcuin). With the almost contemporary commentary known as *Donatus Ortigraphus* Hrabanus shared, moreover, the concept of grammar as 'the science providing tools for interpreting poets and historians' ('scientia interpretandi poetas atque historicos'), which derives ultimately from late antique education (Diomedes, Marius Victorinus).[101] Finally, grammar is, in Hrabanus's own words, 'the judge of all writers' (*iudex omnium librariorum*), since only those who master grammatical rules will be able to write flawless books.[102] Both in the case of grammar and of most of the other secular arts, Hrabanus took care to stress the particular usefulness of the discipline either for the study of the Bible or for clerical duties in general. A firm command of grammar enables a scholar to recognize and interpret the figures of speech occurring in the Bible properly. Moreover, the knowledge of the metric rules regulating the composition of verses allows clerics to fully understand the metric parts of the Bible as well as the work of authoritative Christian poets such as Sedulius, Juvencus, Venantius Fortunatus, and the like. Similarly, in Chapter 20 Hrabanus stressed the importance of mastering dialectic for clerics who ought to recognize and rebut heretical thoughts; at the end of Chapter 22 he recalled the value of arithmetic for understanding the mystical meaning of the numbers contained in the Bible; at the end of Chapter 25 he

---

101 See Bisanti, 'Il capitolo', esp. pp. 9–12.
102 Hrabanus Maurus, *De institutione clericorum*, ed. by Zimpel, III. 18, ll. 5–6 and 17–19, pp. 468–69. The definition of grammar as the 'judge of all writers' recalls the concern expressed in Chapter 70 of the *Admonitio generalis* that books be written with deep care ('omni diligentia'). The word *librarius* meant 'scribe' in Classical Latin but acquired gradually also the meaning of 'author' in medieval Latin (see the *Thesaurus Linguae Latinae Online* and Niermeyer's *Mediae Latinitatis Lexicon Minus Online* s. v. respectively). I chose to translate *librarius* with the similarly ambivalent term 'writer' since I think that Hrabanus had both scribes and authors in mind.

declared astronomy as very useful for clerics who were to calculate Easter correctly.

Concluding his survey of the liberal arts as applied to biblical study Hrabanus reminded his readers that although it is useful for a Christian scholar to bend a part of pagan teachings to the righteous use of understanding and disseminating God's word, knowledge has no value in itself (Chapter 26). Picking up the line of thoughts he had developed at the beginning of the Third Book, Hrabanus stressed in Chapter 27 that the intellectual efforts leading to wisdom should be accompanied by similar efforts to live according to Christian virtues, so that the moral life of a cleric does not contradict the contents of his study or of his teaching.[103] The ideal man of God (*homo Dei*) corresponds, in Hrabanus's view, to the ideal orator of the Classic tradition. He should be a *vir bonus dicendi peritus* ('a good man, who knows how to speak'), i.e. a man who can guide the others both through the example of his own virtuous life and through his words.[104]

While he dedicated only a few lines of Chapter 27 to recall briefly which Christian virtues should inform a cleric's life, Hrabanus dealt in the last twelve chapters of the Third Book with the skills a priest, or a priest to-be, must necessarily learn in order to spread the Christian message effectively, be it through sermons, teachings, or admonitions (Chapters 28–39). The main source he employed to this task was the fourth book of Augustine's *De doctrina Christiana*, to which he added several passages from Gregory's *Regula Pastoralis*. As a result, the *DIC* transmitted a concept of eloquence which consists of the capacity to communicate the same true contents in different ways according to the different audiences attending one's performance.

As I hope to have shown with this survey of the contents of the *DIC*, the ambitious vision of a clerical training that it laid out, which involved a comprehensive education and the achievement of moral perfection and rhetorical proficiency, is unique for the early Middle Ages. Hrabanus found his main model in the ideals expressed by patristic authorities, particularly Augustine and Gregory the Great. The general educational concerns contained both in Alcuin's works as well as in the *Epistola de litteris colendis* and the *Admonitio generalis* surely inspired the development of his handbook. Contemporary court-sponsored instructions for monks may also have influenced his work, although these texts paid attention to educational aspects only so far as to

---

103 On Chapter 27 see Phelan, 'New Insights', pp. 77–78.
104 Hrabanus Maurus, *De institutione clericorum*, ed. by Zimpel, III. 27, pp. 488–89, ll. 39–46: 'His autem speciebus virtutum perfecte adornatus, et sapientiae lumine illustratus homo dei rite ac congrue servitium eius potest agere atque oratoris officium digne potest in ecclesia implere, quem antiqua definitio adfirmat, virum bonum et dicendi peritum esse debere. Si ergo haec definitio in oratoribus gentilium observabatur, multo magis in oratoribus Christi observari convenit, quorum non solum sermo, immo etiam tota vita doctrina virtutum debet esse'. The definition of the ideal orator as *vir bonus dicendi peritus* occurs in Cato (fragment 14 of his *Libri ad Marcum filium*) and in Quintilian's *Ars Oratoria* (XII. 1).

make general requests, leaving their implementation to the skills and the possibilities of individual teachers.[105]

Similarly, the *Institutio canonicorum* did not engage with the issue of clerical education specifically, as Picker and Phelan stressed in their respective studies.[106] The text contains only random assumptions of literacy on the part of the clerics motivated by their duty to instruct others and to argue against dissenting opinions. So, for instance, Chapter 9 presents the *scientia scripturarum* (the knowledge of the Scriptures) as necessary for bishops in order both to instruct their flock and to cast their opponents back; both Chapter 94 and 96 address clerics with the admonition: *disce, quod doceas* (learn first what you can then teach), which Jerome had expressed in two of his letters; half a line of Chapter 123 promotes the education of canons both in the sacred and in the secular disciplines ('doctrinis sanis et diversarum artium disciplinis erudiantur').[107] What the *Institutio* expressly required from its canons was the mastery of liturgical performance, i.e. the capacity to sing and read aloud correctly. Indeed, two entire chapters are dedicated to this issue.[108]

With his plan for an all-round education Hrabanus took the concerns expressed by the intellectual elites of his time very seriously. He developed and systematized their requirements according to his own vision. He completed an exhaustive handbook on all aspects of clerical life which has no parallels in the early Middle Ages. In this he promoted an ideal of learned clergy, which was destined for great success in the centuries to come.

Although its original target group consisted of clerical monks,[109] the contents of the *DIC* could easily respond to the needs of a more general clerical audience. The adaptations of the treatise produced by Hrabanus himself show that the task of defining what a cleric is accompanied him throughout his entire ecclesiastical career and that he took care to promote its dissemination outside of monastic circles. Between 842 and 847 he used the *DIC* as a basis for the composition of the three books of his *De ecclesiastica*

---

105 Picker, *Pastor Doctus*, p. 225 n. 94 recalls the few requests contained in Chapter 5 of the so-called *Capitulare Monasticum* as well as to Chapter 36 of Benedict of Aniane's *Collectio capitularis*.
106 See Picker, *Pastor Doctus*, pp. 220–22, who detects only a few occurrences of an educational concern in Chapters 122 (to be corrected to 123), 133, 137, and in the *Epilogus* of the *Institutio anonicorum*; Phelan, 'New Insights', pp. 66–68.
107 See *Concilium Aquisgranense a. 816, Institutio canonicorum*, ed. by Werminghoff, 9, p. 325, ll. 15–19; 94, p. 371, ll. 18–19; 96, p. 374, l. 32; 123, p. 403, ll. 24–25 respectively.
108 *Concilium Aquisgranense a. 816, Institutio canonicorum*, ed. by Werminghoff, 133 and 137, pp. 409 and 414.
109 Almost one third of the ninth-century manuscripts of the *DIC* listed in Hrabanus Maurus, *De institutione clericorum*, ed. by Zimpel, pp. 161–230 originated within a monastic scriptorium probably for the education of local clerical monks. See also Picker, *Pastor Doctus*, pp. 110–11.

disciplina, which he dedicated to the Mainz *chorepiscopus* Reginbald.[110] The new treatise was planned as a companion for clerics involved in missionary activities, as Reginbald was. It consists of a selection and new arrangement of most chapters of Books Three and One of the *DIC*, which focus on the education of clerics, preaching, the catechumenate, and Baptism. When he himself had become Archbishop of Mainz and was no longer healthy enough as to instruct in person the young priests under his care, Hrabanus produced a further adaptation of the *DIC* and dedicated it to his auxiliary bishop Thiotmar. The work, which circulated under the title of *De sacris ordinibus*, reproduced the contents of Book One, changing the order of some of its chapters.[111] Moreover, it contained supplementary chapters on the preparation of catechumens and the rite of Baptism, with which Hrabanus addressed concerns expressed by both Alcuin and Charlemagne around forty years earlier.[112]

Apart from Hrabanus's re-use of his own work, the *DIC* enjoyed a very broad reception until the twelfth century at least, with *c.* sixty extant manuscripts from all over western Europe. It circulated in three differing recensions which rearranged, abridged, or expanded its contents.[113] Hrabanus's ambitious vision of a learned and morally irreproachable clergy, competent in liturgical as well as in educational matters, elaborated and epitomized the main concerns of his time, thus providing late medieval reflections on the ideal cleric with an essential point of reference.

Conclusions

It is not always easy to measure the degree of implementation on a local or individual level of directives coming from the political centre. The evidence analysed above shows that what conciliar acts and capitularies achieved was to bring to the attention of local communities concerns which the Carolingian rulers deemed to be relevant.[114] These documents triggered debate, raised

---

110 *De ecclesiastica disciplina* is available in *Patrologia Latina*, CXII, cols 1191–262. Phelan, 'New Insights', pp. 85–87, describes the contents and sources of the work.
111 Hrabanus Maurus, *De sacris ordinibus* can be read in *Patrologia Latina*, CXII, cols 1165–92. The dedicatory letter to Thiothmar is published also in Hrabanus Maurus, *Epistolae*, ed. by Dümmler, no. 55, pp. 508–09. Zimpel provided a description of the contents of the work (see Hrabanus Maurus, *De institutione clericorum*, ed. by Zimpel, Introduction, pp. 259–60).
112 Hrabanus enriched his *De sacris ordinibus* with chapters entitled: Quae sit interpretatio symboli secundum Latinos; De credulitate in deum; De scrutinio; Quid sit abrenuntiatio; De abrenuntiatione satanae; De ordine sacri baptismatis (8–13, cols 1170–75). A study of the sources Hrabanus employed for these chapters, as well as a comparison with contemporary instruction-readers for priests, remains a desideratum. For Alcuin's and Charlemagne's requests concerning the catechumenate see Phelan, *The Formation of Christian Europe*, pp. 75–81 and 102–28.
113 Hrabanus Maurus, *De institutione clericorum*, ed. by Zimpel, Introduction, pp. 231–70.
114 See Patzold, 'Capitularies', pp. 112–16.

different interpretations, provoked adherence, but also motivated those involved to find creative ways of claiming conformity while maintaining their diversity, as happened in the case of the *Supplex Libellus*. The investigation of Hrabanus's *DIC* in the context of the Carolingian Church leads us to similar conclusions. The treatise did not originate from the passive absorption and reproduction of Carolingian prescriptions about the clergy, but rather from the critical engagement of a local teacher, as Hrabanus was at that time, with them. The comparison with the *Institutio canonicorum* has proved particularly telling in this respect.

The *Institutio canonicorum* tackled the question of what makes a cleric perfect. The answer it produced consisted in the promotion of a coenobitic and regular life for clerics under the supervision of a bishop. In its vision, the new status of the *clerici canonici* embodied the most accomplished way of life for clerics. The document provided this particular group with teachings of a predominantly moral nature and with a limited set of practical instructions. Although neither the *Institutio canonicorum* nor Chapter 3 of the *Capitulare ecclesiasticum* — which made its contents mandatory — prescribed that all clerics, and in particular the clerical monks, become canons, the *Institutio* did reserve to canons the honour of occupying the highest position in the Church. This marked a significant innovation with regard to the patristic tradition, which had granted such privilege to all sort of clerics. In other words, the *Institutio canonicorum* suggested that clerics could be sure to live their vocation and carry out their duties in the most accomplished way only by entering a community of canons.[115]

More generally, it can be observed that Carolingian ecclesiastical policy envisaged all clerics as opting for a regular form of life, either according to the Benedictine or to the canonical rule.[116] Either group was expected to live a coenobitic life in a cloister: the clerical monks under the supervision of an abbot, the canons under the supervision of a bishop. Accordingly, the documents issued in the aftermath of the Aachen Councils of 816/19 addressed either monks or canons, while further forms of observance were not contemplated.

The dissemination of such documents triggered reflection on the essence of clerical observance on the local level. Inspired, we can assume, by these documents, Hrabanus too developed his concept of the ideal cleric. He

---

115 As Rudolf Schieffer put it, the *Institutio canonicorum* created a normative basis for the further development of the non-monastic clergy ('außermonastischer Klerus'), which aimed at organizing clerical life in a communal way following monastic models. See Schieffer, *Entstehung*, p. 240.

116 See, for instance, *Admonitio generalis*, ed. by Mordek, Zechiel-Eckes, and Glatthaar, 75, p. 228, ll. 354–56, which asks those clerics, who merely pretend to be monks, to choose their main form of observance and become either real monks (*veri monachi*) or real canons (*veri canonici*). This does not prohibit clerics from living according to a monastic rule. Rather, it urges them to live according to a rule (either monastic or canonical) and in a *coenobium*.

addressed exactly that group of clerics (i.e. clerical monks), who had received no mention in the *Institutio canonicorum* but formed a substantial group within (not only) his own cloister. Around 819 he completed his systematization and exhaustive explanation of all markers of clerical life. The comparison of structure and topics conducted above has shown that the *DIC* is a carefully planned, all-round companion of theological, liturgical, and exegetical knowledge which complemented, and only to a remarkably small extent repeated, the contents of the *Institutio canonicorum*. Hrabanus's depiction of the ideal cleric was tailored for clerical monks in the first instance. The complete absence of norms concerning property and the typically monastic eating prescriptions presented in Book Two support this conclusion. Hrabanus thought of Fulda's clerical monks as monks in every respect, who, like canons, had been entrusted with liturgical and pastoral care. In contrast to canons however, they were bound to poverty and to the observance of (the local interpretation of) the *Regula Benedicti*. When writing the *DIC* Hrabanus was not concerned with providing his readers with a monastic education, since they already possessed it. Rather, he aimed to produce an all-round companion which could support them in the fulfilment of their clerical duties.

The *DIC* was neither a 'Kampfschrift' nor a 'Gegenentwurf' in relation to the *Institutio canonicorum*, i.e. it neither aimed at disseminating its contents nor at polemically contrasting them, as Zimpel and Picker argued respectively. The issue of the *Institutio canonicorum* probably pushed Hrabanus to develop and make public his own position within the heated debate on clerical life, of which the *Institutio canonicorum* itself was both a result and a further trigger.

Both texts urged a change for the better.[117] The *Institutio canonicorum* saw as a priority the promotion of a regular life for clerics, as well as the fixation of norms of moral conduct. Hrabanus regarded clerical education as the crucial issue at stake. He required of clerics the cultivation of secular and biblical learning, the mastery of rhetoric skills, the exercise of Christian virtues, the manifestation of love both towards God and neighbour. His programme guided the action of clerics within society and aimed ultimately at the improvement of the entire *populus Christianus*.

---

117 I thank Carine van Rhijn and my colleagues within the research group 'Rethinking Carolingian *correctio*' for having shown me that the widespread attempts to realize cultural and moral improvement in the Carolingian period do not always need to be interpreted as the results of a top-down reform.

Works Cited

Digital Resources

'Capitulare ecclesiasticum' [BK 138], in *Capitularia: Edition der fränkischen Herrschererlasse*, ed. by Karl Ubl and collaborators (Cologne, 2014–) <https://capitularia.uni-koeln.de/capit/ldf/bk-nr-138/> [accessed 8 September 2021]

Thesaurus Linguae Latinae (TLL) <https://www.degruyter.com/view/db/tll> [accessed 8 September 2021]

Niermeyer's *Mediae Latinitatis Lexicon Minus Online* <https://dictionaries.brillonline.com/niermeyer> [accessed 8 September 2021]

Primary Sources

Die Admonitio Generalis Karls des Großen, ed. by Hubert Mordek (†), Klaus Zechiel-Eckes (†), and Michael Glatthaar, in *Monumenta Germaniae Historica: Fontes Iuris Germanici Antiqui in usum scholarum separatim editi*, XVI (Wiesbaden: Harrassowitz, 2013)

Augustine of Hippo, *Enarrationes in Psalmos*, ed. by Eligius Dekkers and Jean Fraipont, Corpus Christianorum Series Latina, 38–40 (Turnhout: Brepols, 1956)

Candidus, *Vita Aegil*, ed. by Gereon Becht-Jördens, *Vita Aegil abbatis Fuldensis a Candido ad Modestum edita prosa et versibus: Ein Opus Geminum des IX. Jahrhunderts; Einleitung und kritische Edition* (Marburg: Selbstverlag, 1994)

Capitulare ecclesiasticum, ed. by Alfred Boretius, in *Monumenta Germaniae Historica: Capitularia regum Francorum*, I (Hannover: Hahn, 1883), no. 138, pp. 275–80

Chronicon Laurissense breve, ed. by Hans Schnorr von Carolsfeld, *Neues Archiv der Gesellschaft für ältere deutsche Geschichtskunde*, 36 (1911), 13–39

Concilium Aquisgranense a. 816: Institutio Canonicorum Aquisgranensis, ed. by Albert Werminghoff, in *Monumenta Germaniae Historica: Concilia*, II. 1, *Concilia Aevi Karolini*, I (Hannover: Hahn, 1906), pp. 307–421

Concilium Aquisgranense a. 816: Institutio Sanctimonialium Aquisgranensis, ed. by Albert Werminghoff, in *Monumenta Germaniae Historica: Concilia*, II. 1, *Concilia Aevi Karolini*, I (Hannover: Hahn, 1906), pp. 421–56

Hrabanus Maurus, *De ecclesiastica disciplina*, in *Patrologiae cursus completus: series latina*, ed. by Jacques-Paul Migne, CXII (Paris: Garnier, 1844–1864), cols 1191–262

——, *Carmina*, ed. by Ernst Dümmler, in *Monumenta Germaniae Historica: Poetae Latini Aevi Carolini*, II (Berlin: Weidmann, 1884), pp. 154–258

——, *Epistolae*, ed. by Ernst Dümmler, in *Monumenta Germaniae Historica: Epistolae*, V, *Epistolae Karolini Aevi*, III (Berlin: Weidmann, 1899), pp. 379–516

——, *De institutione clericorum libri tres*, ed. by Alois Knöpfler, Veröffentlichungen aus dem Kirchenhistorischen Seminar München, 5 (Munich: Lentner, 1900)

——, *De institutione clericorum libri tres*, ed. by Detlev Zimpel, Freiburger Beiträge zur mittelalterlichen Geschichte, 7 (Frankfurt am Main: Peter Lang, 1996)

——, *De institutione clericorum/Über die Unterweisung der Geistlichen*, ed. and trans. by Detlev Zimpel, Fontes Christiani, 61, 2 vols (Turnhout: Brepols, 2006)

——, *La formazione dei chierici: Introduzione, traduzione e note*, trans. with an introduction by Luigi Samarati (Roma: Città Nuova Editrice, 2002)

——, *De sacris ordinibus*, in *Patrologiae cursus completus: series latina*, ed. by Jacques-Paul Migne, CXII (Paris: Garnier, 1844–1864), cols 1165–92

Isidore of Seville, *De ecclesiasticis officiis*, ed. by Christopher M. Lawson, Corpus Christianorum Series Latina, 113 (Turnhout: Brepols, 1989)

Isidore of Seville, *Etymologiarum sive Originum libri XX*, ed. by Wallace Martin Lindsay, 2 vols (Oxford: Clarendon Press, 1911)

Iulianus Pomerius, *De vita contemplativa libri tres*, in *Patrologiae cursus completus: series latina*, ed. by Jacques-Paul Migne, LIX (Paris: Garnier, 1844–1864), cols 415–52

Jerome, *Epistulae*, vol. 1: *1–70*, ed. by Isidor Hilberg, Corpus Scriptorum Ecclesiasticorum Latinorum, 54 (Vienna: Tempsky, 1910)

Synodi primae Aquisgranensis decreta authentica (a. 816), ed. by Josef Semmler, in *Corpus Consuetudinum Monasticarum*, vol. 1: *Initia Consuetudinis Benedictinae: Consuetudines saeculi octavi et noni* (Siegburg: Schmitt, 1963), pp. 451–68

Synodi secundae Aquisgranensis decreta authentica (a. 817), ed. by Josef Semmler, in *Corpus Consuetudinum Monasticarum*, vol. 1: *Initia Consuetudinis Benedictinae: Consuetudines saeculi octavi et noni* (Siegburg: Schmitt, 1963), pp. 469–81

Supplex Libellus monachorum Fuldensium Carolo imperatori porrectus, ed. by Josef Semmler, in *Corpus Consuetudinum Monasticarum*, vol. 1: *Initia Consuetudinis Benedictinae: Consuetudines saeculi octavi et noni* (Siegburg: Schmitt, 1963), pp. 321–27; ed. by Ernst Dümmler, in *Monumenta Germaniae Historica: Epistolae*, IV, *Epistolae Karolini Aevi*, II (Berlin: Weidmann, 1894), pp. 548–55

Secondary Works

Barrow, Julia, *The Clergy in the Medieval World, c. 800–c. 1200* (Cambridge: Cambridge University Press, 2015)

Berggötz, Oliver, 'Hrabanus Maurus und seine Bedeutung für das Bibliothekswesen der Karolingerzeit. Zugleich ein Beitrag zur Geschichte der Klosterbibliothek Fulda', *Bibliothek und Wissenschaft*, 27 (1994), 1–48

Billett, Jesse D., *The Divine Office in Anglo-Saxon England, 597–c. 1000* (Woodbridge: Boydell, 2014)

Bisanti, Armando, 'Il capitolo "De arte grammatica et speciebus eius" di Rabano Mauro (*De inst. cler.* III, 18)', *Schede Medievali: Rassegna dell'officina di studi medievali*, 4 (1983), 5–18

——, 'Struttura compositiva e tecnica compilatoria nel libro III del *De institutione clericorum* di Rabano Mauro', *Schede Medievali. Rassegna dell'officina di studi medievali*, 8 (1985), 5–17

Bullido del Barrio, Susana, 'Hrabanus Maurus-Bibliographie 1979–2009', in *Hrabanus Maurus in Fulda*, ed. by Marc-Aeilko Aris and S. Bullido del Barrio, Fuldaer Studien, 13 (Frankfurt am Main: Josef Knecht, 2010), pp. 255–332

Cantelli Berarducci, Silvia, *Hrabani Mauri Opera Exegetica*, Instrumenta Patristica et Mediaevalia, 38, 3 vols (Turnhout: Brepols, 2006)

Depreux, Philippe, 'Charlemagne et les capitulaires: formation et reception d'un corpus normatif', in *Charlemagne: les temps, les espaces, les hommes; Construction et déconstruction d'un règne*, ed. by Rolf Grosse and Michel Sot (Turnhout: Brepols, 2018), pp. 19–41

Grosse, Rolf, and Michel Sot, ed., *Charlemagne: les temps, les espaces, les hommes; Construction et déconstruction d'un règne* (Turnhout: Brepols, 2018)

Häussling, Angelus Albert, *Mönchskonvent und Eucharistiefeier: Eine Studie über die Messe in der abendländischen Klosterliturgie des frühen Mittelalters und zur Geschichte der Meßhäufigkeit* (Münster: Aschendorff, 1973)

Hildebrandt, Madge M., *The External School in Carolingian Society*, Education and Society in the Middle Ages and Renaissance, 1 (Leiden: Brill, 1992)

Hussong, Ulrich, 'Studien zur Geschichte der Reichsabtei Fulda bis zur Jahrtausendwende', *Archiv für Diplomatik*, 31 (1985), 1–225 and 32 (1986), 129–304

Jong, Mayke de, 'Carolingian Monasticism: The Power of Prayer', in *The New Cambridge Medieval History*, vol. 2: *c. 700–c. 900*, ed. by Rosamond McKitterick (Cambridge: Cambridge University Press, 1995), pp. 622–53

Keefe, Susan A., *Water and the Word: Baptism and the Education of the Clergy in the Carolingian Empire*, 2 vols (Notre Dame: University of Notre Dame Press, 2002)

Kramer, Rutger, 'Teaching Emperors: Transcending the Boundaries of Carolingian Monastic Communities', in *Meanings of Community across Medieval Eurasia: Comparative Approaches*, ed. by Eirik Hovden, Christina Lutter, and Walter Pohl (Leiden: Brill, 2016), pp. 309–37

——, *Rethinking Authority in the Carolingian Empire: Ideals and Expectations during the Reign of Louis the Pious (813–828)* (Amsterdam: Amsterdam University Press, 2019)

McKitterick, Rosamond, *Charlemagne: The Formation of a European Identity* (Cambridge: Cambridge University Press, 2008)

Nussbaum, Otto, *Kloster, Priestermönch und Privatmesse: Ihr Verhältnis im Westen von den Anfängen bis zum hohen Mittelalter*, Theophaneia: Beiträge zur Religions- und Kirchengeschichte des Altertums, 14 (Bonn: Hanstein, 1961)

Patzold, Steffen, 'Konflikte im Kloster Fulda zur Zeit der Karolinger', *Fuldaer Geschichtsblätter*, 76 (2000), 69–162

——, 'Capitularies in the Ottonian realm', *Early Medieval Europe*, 27.1 (2019), 112–32

——, *Wie regierte Karl der Große?* (Köln: Greven, 2020)

Phelan, Owen M., *The Formation of Christian Europe: The Carolingians, Baptism and the Imperium Christianum* (Oxford: Oxford University Press, 2014)

——, 'New Insights, Old Texts. Clerical Formation and the Carolingian Renewal in Hrabanus Maurus', *Traditio*, 71 (2016), 63–89

———, 'The Carolingian Renewal in Early Medieval Europe Through Hrabanus Maurus's *Commentary on Matthew*', *Traditio*, 75 (2020), 143–75

Picker, Hanns-Christoph, *Pastor Doctus: Klerikerbild und karolingische Reformen bei Hrabanus Maurus* (Mainz: Philipp von Zabern, 2001)

Raaijmakers, Janneke, *The Making of the Monastic Community of Fulda, c. 744–c. 900* (Cambridge: Cambridge University Press, 2012)

Rhijn, Carine van, *Shepherds of the Lord: Priests and Episcopal Statutes in the Carolingian Period* (Turnhout: Brepols, 2007)

———, 'Charlemagne's *correctio*: A Local Perspective', in *Charlemagne: les temps, les espaces, les hommes. Construction et déconstruction d'un règne*, ed. by Rolf Grosse and Michel Sot (Turnhout: Brepols, 2018), pp. 43–59

Rissel, Maria, *Rezeption antiker und patristischer Wissenschaft bei Hrabanus Maurus*, Lateinische Sprache und Literatur des Mittelalters, 7 (Frankfurt am Main: Peter Lang, 1976)

Sandmann, Mechthild, 'Wirkungsbereiche fuldischer Mönche', in *Die Klostergemeinschaft von Fulda im früheren Mittelalter*, ed. by Karl Schmid, vol. 8/2.2 (Munich: Wilhelm Fink, 1978), pp. 692–791

Schieffer, Rudolf, *Die Entstehung von Domkapiteln in Deutschland*, Bonner Historische Forschungen, 43 (Bonn: Ludwig Röhrscheid, 1982)

Schmid, Karl, ed., *Die Klostergemeinschaft von Fulda im früheren Mittelalter*, vol. 8/2.1–3: *Kommentiertes Parallelregister und Untersuchungen* (Munich: Wilhelm Fink, 1978)

Semmler, Josef, 'Studien zum Supplex Libellus und zur anianischen Reform in Fulda', *Zeitschrift für Kirchengeschichte*, 69 (1958), 268–98

———, 'Instituta Sancti Bonifatii: Fulda im Widerstreit der Observanzen', in *Kloster Fulda in der Welt der Karolinger und Ottonen*, ed. by Gangolf Schrimpf, Fuldaer Studien, 7 (Frankfurt am Main: Josef Knecht, 1996), pp. 79–103

———, 'Die Reform geistlicher Gemeinschaften in der ersten Hälfte des 9. Jahrhunderts und der Klosterplan von St Gallen', in *Studien zum St Galler Klosterplan*, vol. 2, ed. by Peter Ochsenbein und Karl Schmuki, Mitteilungen zur vaterländischen Geschichte, 52 (Sankt Gallen: Historischer Verein des Kantons St Gallen, 2002), pp. 87–105

———, 'Monachus — clericus — canonicus: Zur Ausdifferenzierung geistlicher Institutionen im Frankenreich bis ca. 900', in *Frühformen von Stiftskirchen in Europa: Funktion und Wandel religiöser Gemeinschaften vom 6. bis zum Ende des 11. Jahrhunderts*, ed. by Sönke Lorenz und Thomas Zotz, Festgabe für Dieter Mertens zum 65. Geburtstag, Schriften zur südwestdeutschen Landeskunde, 54 (Leinfelden-Echterdingen: DRW, 2005), pp. 1–18

INGRID REMBOLD

The 'Apostates' of Saint-Denis

*Reforms, Dissent, and Carolingian Monasticism**

A group of monks of Saint-Denis 'in apostasiam prolapsi fuerant' (had fallen into apostasy): such was the verdict of a council of bishops convened at the monastery in the second half of 829 or early 830.[1] Having been thus charged, and thus convicted, those who had abandoned the rule made a public confession of their sins; they were reclothed in the monastic cowl and made to undergo penance for the remission of sin. Their repentance did not last long. Rebellious monks soon formed a conspiracy and presumed to petition the emperor directly. In 832, a second council was convened, the matter re-examined, and the monks re-condemned.[2] No further resistance was forthcoming.

In contrast to much of the (admittedly slight) evidence for Carolingian monastic reform, what stands apart in this episode is the apparent belligerence of the conflict, as recorded — often after the fact — by reformers. The rhetoric of apostasy, as employed in the 829/30 conciliar source, is highly unusual in the comparatively placid framework of Carolingian monastic discourse. This rhetorical register may be seen to relate both to the particular context in which the dispute took place, in the worsening crisis of the late 820s, and to the very tenuousness of the reformers' positions. For these councils did not represent the delayed implementation of the Aachen monastic reforms of 816/17, as many have argued. Rather, these councils constituted a departure from — or, at the very least, a significantly different interpretation of — the earlier Aachen reforms. Following the Aachen councils, the reformer Benedict

---

* I would especially like to thank Rutger Kramer, Graeme Ward, and Robin Whelan for their helpful suggestions. At a late stage of this article's production, I learned that Todd Mattingly was also working on this topic. For his sophisticated analysis, which I have not been able to incorporate into this article due to time constraints, see Todd Mattingly, 'A Crisis of Identity: Monks, Canons and the Ninth-Century Reform of Saint-Denis' a paper presented at the Leeds International Medieval Congress in July 2018. A modified version of this presentation will appear in his forthcoming University of Toronto PhD thesis.

1 *Praeceptum Synodale a. 829–830*, ed. by Werminghoff, p. 685.
2 *DD Kar.* 2, II, nos 315–16, pp. 774–85.

Ingrid Rembold is Lecturer in Medieval History at the University of Manchester.

of Aniane (d. 821) visited the community and determined that the majority of its denizens (apart from those who chose to pursue Benedictine observance) should live as canons. Now, just over a decade later, his express arrangements were disregarded and overturned; the canonical community he had created was transformed into a monastery of monks. Even the community's newly professed observance of the Benedictine rule differed from that set out in the earlier Aachen councils. Both a charter of Abbot Hilduin (d. *c.* 855–60) and a contemporary historiographical work, the *Gesta Dagoberti*, point specifically to the promotion of perpetual psalmody, or *laus perennis*, at Saint-Denis in this period, which flew in the face of earlier interpretations of the *Regula Benedicti* put forward at the Aachen councils.[3] The point of all of this is not to argue that what happened at Saint-Denis in 829/30 and 832 was not reform; on the contrary, it was certainly understood as reform by all who were present, and was even expressly referred to as such ('reformata statuit') in a charter granted by Louis the Pious.[4] Rather, the reforms of Saint-Denis draw attention to the interplay between local, particular interests and empire-wide discourses; to the contestation and re-interpretation of established conciliar norms; and to ongoing debates around — and the shifting terrain of — monastic reforms. In short, they underscore the competing and evolving visions of reform which were operative in the Carolingian world, and in so doing, revisit the role of the Aachen reforms themselves.

In the late 820s, as military crises and factional upheavals led inexorably towards rebellion and civil war, a moral reassessment was underway. The penitential state (to borrow a coinage of Mayke de Jong) was in full operation by the Paris Council of 829, at which bishops pledged to extirpate all scandals within the church.[5] Gone was the triumphalism of 816/17; fading, too, were some of the principles which had animated reformers at the earlier councils. Attitudes towards monastic observance were shifting. The supposed equality of the canonical and Benedictine orders, as expressed in the Aachen reforms, was slowly being replaced by a sense of monastic superiority; at the same time, Merovingian, pre-Benedictine precedent was increasingly employed to

---

3 See below. *Gesta Dagoberti*, ed. by Krusch, pp. 396–425; for the Hilduin charter, see Felibien ed., *Histoire de l'abbaye royale de Saint-Denys*, no. 75, pp. lv–lvi. For the extent to which the Aachen Councils were actively interpreting, rather than passively implementing, the *Regula Benedicti*, see especially Diem, 'Review of *St Galler Klosterplan*'; see also Diem, 'The Carolingians and the *Regula Benedicti*', here especially pp. 251–53. Note that *laus perennis* is itself an anachronistic term: see here the comment of Diem, 'Who is Allowed to Pray for the King?', p. 70.

4 For a more general problematization of modern historiography on 'reform', see the important contribution of Barrow, 'Ideas and Applications of Reform', especially pp. 356–57. For the reference to reform in Louis's charter, see *DD Kar.* 2, II, no. 315, p. 776: *reformata statuit*; see here especially Patzold, *Episcopus*, pp. 250–51 n. 448. See further the use of 'reform' at the similar case study of Montier-en-Der: *DD Kar.* 2, II, no. 309, p. 763: *monasticam vitam reformari*.

5 De Jong, *The Penitential State*, pp. 170–84, here especially p. 182.

justify the imposition of 'regular' Benedictine observance. The use of such precedent, however, entailed a restructuring of priorities: hence the frequent stress laid upon the age-old tradition of *laus perennis* in sources from the late 820s, in contrast to earlier injunctions to observe the Benedictine *cursus*. As Benedictine norms were projected into the distant past, those norms were themselves transformed, refracted through the lens of accumulated local traditions, histories, and practices. At Saint-Denis we have an unparalleled vantage point from which to view these developments.

***

It is with the Aachen reform councils of 816/17 that we will begin. In many ways, these councils simply amplified existing trends in Frankish monasticism. They did, however, diverge in advocating a strict division — or indeed, refining an existing, if exceedingly inexact division — between canonical and monastic forms of life; in the case of the latter, they mandated observance of *their* interpretation of the Benedictine rule. Naturally, this bifurcate categorization created issues for monasteries with their own ancient observances, observances which differed from the new, imperially promulgated norms.[6] Such institutions were confronted by a stark dilemma: Benedictine or canonical? There was no middle ground.

Saint-Denis was one such institution. An old, basilical monastery, its origins stretched back to the fifth century, when a basilica was founded on what became a thriving cult site; a religious community is clearly attested from c. 620.[7] The community did not observe either the Benedictine or canonical rule, either of which would have been anachronistic in seventh-century Francia; rather, by the mid-seventh century they adopted a non-Benedictine, and presumably non-rule-based, monastic observance distinguished by the demanding liturgy of perpetual psalmody, or *laus perennis*.[8] Their holy and exalted reputation may be judged by the many privileges granted to them, and by the designation of Saint-Denis as a royal burial place. This extraordinary

---

6 Semmler, 'Mönche und Kanoniker'.
7 For the early history of Saint-Denis, see especially Levillain, 'Études sur l'abbaye de Saint-Denis II'; Semmler, 'Saint-Denis', here pp. 75–105; see also Brown, 'Politics and Patronage', pp. 1–4.
8 For the flexibility of Merovingian approaches to monastic rules, see especially Diem, 'Inventing the Holy Rule'; Dierkens, 'Prolégomènes'. For the anachronism inherent in characterizing Saint-Denis as either Benedictine or canonical before 816/17, see Oexle, *Forschungen*, p. 112; see also Semmler, 'Pippin III.', pp. 143–45. On a different note, it should be observed that *laus perennis* was not observed continuously at Saint-Denis: while Dagobert attempted to establish it, Clovis II/Balthild was obliged to re-establish the practice in 654; for this, and for the observance of *laus perennis* at Saint-Denis more generally, see Fox, *Power and Religion*, pp. 40, 235; Hen, *The Royal Patronage of Liturgy*, pp. 35–37; Robertson, *The Service-Books*, pp. 13–18; Rosenwein, 'One Site', pp. 281, 283; Semmler, 'Pippin III.', 139–40; Semmler, 'Saint-Denis', pp. 83, 100–03.

prominence continued into the Carolingian period, as kings and emperors continued to shower favours upon the community and mark it out as a place of special significance. Pippin III was raised at Saint-Denis and later died and was buried there; his son, Charlemagne, granted his first surviving charter to the institution.[9] Clearly, Saint-Denis was still viewed as a holy place, a site of legitimation and divine favour for Frankish kings.

Nonetheless, from the early ninth century on, attempts were made to reform Saint-Denis in accordance with contemporary norms.[10] The *Translatio sanguinis Domini*, a tenth-century text from Reichenau, records one such attempt by Abbot Waldo, previously abbot of Reichenau, following his appointment to Saint-Denis in 806:

> Discovering that the rule of monastic life was exceedingly distorted and that the brothers followed a mode of life that was more secular than spiritual, Waldo attempted many things to convert the rebels to the standard of rectitude, inflamed with the very great zeal of divine fervour. He even entered the chapter house with armed soldiers that he had assembled and, so they say, crushed the insolence of those who were making a disturbance, as it were, by fighting back. […] He recalled those who had deserted to the discipline of a regular life, and thus he transformed deformed brothers into modest followers of obedience.[11]

Such an account is undoubtedly influenced by contemporary tenth-century currents of reform, and its historicity may be called into question. It remains probable, however, that some reforming activity was undertaken; the very appointment of Waldo from distant, Benedictine Reichenau signals an interest in regularizing the institution's observance, in a manner akin to Charlemagne's (in this case unsuccessful) attempt to enact reform at Saint-Martin of Tours through the appointment of Alcuin.[12] While no contemporary witnesses to Waldo's reform survive, Louis the Pious, looking back on this episode, wrote that the monks 'promissionem fecerant et regulariter, licet minus perfecte,

---

9 *DD Kar.* 1, no. 55, pp. 81–82; Brown, 'Politics and Patronage', pp. 3–7; Ling, 'The Cloister and Beyond', p. 91; Semmler, 'Saint-Denis', p. 93.

10 The best accounts of these reforms are to be found in Oexle, *Forschungen*, pp. 112–19; Semmler, 'Saint-Denis', pp. 105–11. What follows is deeply indebted to both.

11 *Ex translatione sanguinis Domini*, ed. by Waitz, 12, p. 447*: 'Ubi monasticae vitae regulam admodum distortam, fratresque secularis potius quam spiritalis vitae sequaces inveniens, nimio divini fervoris zelo succensus, ad rectitudinis normam multum rebelles convertere conatus est, adeo ut, conductis secum militibus armatis, capitulum illorum, ceu fertur, ingressus, insolentiam tumultuantium quasi repugnando perdomuisset […] ad regularis eos vitae quam deseruerant disciplinam revocaret, sicque ex discolis fratribus modestos oboedientiae sectatores commutaret'. Oexle, *Forschungen*, pp. 112–13; Semmler, 'Saint-Denis', p. 105.

12 For Alcuin's tenure at Saint-Martin of Tours, cf. Hosoe, '*Regulae* and Reform', pp. 265–77; for the appointment of abbots and the pursuance of reform, cf. Geuenich, 'Zur Stellung und Wahl', p. 174.

vixerant' (had made a promise and lived regularly, if less perfectly).[13] Such a qualification may be taken to denote that the monks did not yet live according to the *Regula Benedicti*.

In the aftermath of the Aachen reform councils of 816/17, the calculus shifted: such a compromise was no longer possible, and the bifurcate choice between Benedictine and canonical monasticism beckoned. Accordingly, at Louis the Pious's behest, and with the consent and approval of the community's abbot, Hilduin, who had been appointed in 814, efforts were once again undertaken to reform Saint-Denis. This reform can only be reconstructed from a later, hostile perspective: that of Louis himself, reflecting on the experience in a confirmation charter of 832. In this charter, Louis first describes his general policy:

> In order to correct the standard of the monastic institution, we appointed two religious men, venerable in life, the Abbots Benedict [of Aniane] and Arnulf [of Noirmoutier], who attentively and zealously pursued this matter throughout our empire.[14]

Yet at Saint-Denis their enterprise had gone awry: the community had been pulled asunder. Or, as Louis put it, 'Idem vero boni et devoti, sed simplicissimi patres supramemoratorum fratrum calliditate et duritia suaque simplicitate abducti' (these good and devoted, but most simple fathers were led astray by the shrewdness and rigour of the aforementioned brothers — and likewise, by their own simplicity).[15] Benedict and Arnulf failed, 'non studio, sed minus subtili et necessaria investigatione et providentia' (not in their zeal, but in their less thorough and critical investigation and in their foresight); in short, they neglected to uncover whether the brothers had made a monastic profession, and in so doing paved the way towards the desertion of their promise.[16] The former monks, now apostates, were allowed to live as canons.

Such was the perspective of 832. Yet if one reads against the anachronistic invective of Louis's narration, the results of the earlier reform seem clear. Forced to choose between the binary options of Benedictine and canonical observance, the reformers Benedict and Arnulf found the community at Saint-Denis better suited to, and more receptive to, the latter. The community may have made a monastic profession, to be sure, but it was not a *Benedictine* profession, and the difference mattered.[17] Reformers understood that previous

---

13 DD Kar. 2, II, no. 315, p. 777; Berkhofer, *Day of Reckoning*, p. 13; Oexle, *Forschungen*, p. 113; Semmler, 'Saint-Denis', pp. 105–06.
14 DD Kar. 2, II, no. 315, p. 777: 'Unde ad monasticae institutionis normam corrigendam duos religiosos et venerabilis vitae viros Benedictum et Arnulfum abbates constituimus, qui per nostrum [...] imperium seduli huic negotio studiose insisterent'. Levillain, 'Études sur l'abbaye de Saint-Denis II', pp. 36–37; Oexle, *Forschungen*, p. 113.
15 DD Kar. 2, II, no. 315, p. 777.
16 DD Kar. 2, II, no. 315, p. 777.
17 See here especially Semmler, 'Pippin III.', pp. 134–36; see also Semmler, 'Mönche und Kanoniker', pp. 85–86, n. 40.

categories did not map exactly onto the newly established norms; accordingly, individuals appear to have been afforded a limited degree of agency to move between orders.[18] At Saint-Denis, the majority of the community adopted canonical observance and was permitted to do so.[19] A significant minority, however, chose to observe the *Regula Benedicti*, and so, in order to appease all factions, Benedict and Arnulf decided to relocate those who wished to observe the *Regula Benedicti* to a dependent cell, the *cella sancti Dionysii*.[20]

This was not a surprising or unusual decision. Other major basilical communities, notably Saint-Martin of Tours and Saint-Maurice d'Agaune, also opted for canonical observance, which was by no means adjudged to be an inferior form of devotion.[21] The division of the original community was likewise a tried-and-true solution, as similar divisions were enacted at both Saint-Hilaire and Saint-Martin.[22] At the time, such an arrangement was presumably accepted both by Abbot Hilduin and by Louis the Pious: certainly, the latter was kept well informed about affairs at Saint-Denis, as attested by the ten to twelve charters (largely confirmations of exchanges) which he granted to its abbot in the years between 817 and 829.[23] While not ideal, it represented a necessary compromise, and there is no evidence to suggest that it was contested in its first ten years.

It was only in the late 820s that a dispute first arose — or, at the very least, that Abbot Hilduin first proved receptive to the demands of the dissenting community.[24] Both he and his protégé Hincmar, later of Reims fame, raised the matter before Louis the Pious, bringing with them particular highlights from the institution's archives, including — for these are expressly mentioned in a

---

18 For this, see Semmler, 'Mönche und Kanoniker', pp. 98–99.
19 Oexle, *Forschungen*, p. 114; Semmler, 'Mönche und Kanoniker', pp. 85–86; Semmler, 'Saint-Denis', p. 107. See also de Jong, 'Carolingian Monasticism', p. 632 (though note that de Jong confuses Saint-Martin with Saint-Denis); Levillain, 'Études sur l'abbaye de Saint-Denis II', pp. 36–37.
20 Berkhofer, *Day of Reckoning*, pp. 13–14; Levillain, 'Études sur l'abbaye de Saint-Denis II', pp. 36–37; Oexle, *Forschungen*, pp. 112–14, here especially p. 112 n. 45; Semmler, 'Saint-Denis', p. 107. Some of the above argue that the community of Saint-Denis had been composed of monks and canons before 817 and only thereafter split into separate communities; by contrast, Oexle argues, in my mind persuasively, for a non-Benedictine monastic observance prior to 817.
21 For Saint-Martin of Tours, see Oexle, *Forschungen*, pp. 132–33; Semmler, 'Mönche und Kanoniker', pp. 85–86; for Agaune, see Rosenwein, 'One Site', p. 273; see further Semmler, 'Pippin III.', 138–39. For the equality of monastic and canonical observance, see Rutger Kramer, 'Great Expectations', p. 263; Oexle, *Forschungen*, p. 133.
22 Semmler, 'Mönche und Kanoniker', pp. 85–86, 100.
23 *DD Kar.* 2, I–II, nos 158, 187, 190, 201–02, 236, 247–48, 267, 269, pp. 394–95, 462–64, 469–71, 497–501, 585–87, 617–19, 667–69, 671–73; nos 270–71, pp. 673–78, are dated in the period 825–30, and thus may pre- or postdate the community's 829/30 reform. This should, however, be viewed in the context of Saint-Denis's extensive diplomatic survivals, as noted by Brown, 'Politics and Patronage', pp. 5–7. See also Lapidge, *Hilduin*, pp. 15–16, 27.
24 Oexle, *Forschungen*, p. 115.

later charter — a 654 privilege of Bishop Landeric of Paris and confirmation charter of Clovis II.[25] Louis in turn referred the matter back for conciliar adjudication, resulting in the 829/30 council with which we began.[26] This council determined that Saint-Denis was, and had always been, a monastic institution; following an examination of witnesses, it further established that the members of its community had made a regular profession, the desertion of which constituted apostasy. Those who, having fallen, had since died would be consigned to eternal perdition; those who still lived retained the chance of redemption though penance and the observance of a regular life.[27]

This was in no way a straightforward enactment of monastic reform, as represented by the 816/17 Aachen councils; rather, it expressly overturned the earlier reform of Benedict of Aniane and Arnulf of Noirmoutier. Several aspects of this affair stand out as noteworthy: the extent to which this represented a *volte-face* of monastic policy on the part of both Hilduin and Louis, paired with the refusal of all those involved to acknowledge it as such; the use of Merovingian precedent to justify the enactment of Benedictine observance; and finally the register of the language employed, and in particular, the accusation of apostasy.

As discussed above, the 816/17 reforms had confirmed the equality of the Benedictine and canonical orders; likewise, reformers had accepted a degree of flexibility in determining the order(s) to be observed at non-binary institutions. Yet since the 816/17 reforms, attitudes had hardened; a sense of Benedictine superiority had begun to emerge. This may be detected, for example, in the reform of Montier-en-Der, which was transformed from a canonical to a Benedictine monastery in 827.[28] Here too, age-old precedent proved decisive: as Louis's 827 charter for the institution reports, Abbot Haudo 'privilegia [...] nobis ostendit, ubi liquido apparuit, quod antiquitus regulare monasterium fuisset' (showed us privileges [...] whence it was clearly apparent, that in former times it had been a regular monastery).[29] Whether the monastery was Benedictine or non-Benedictine seems to have been beside the point: the monks would be Benedictine henceforth. In a later confirmation charter from 832, Louis ventures into a value judgement of the pre-reform community: he declares that 'monastica vita penitus in eodem

---

25 *Constitutio de partitione*, ed. by Werminghoff, p. 689; see also Tardif ed., *Monuments historiques*, no. 10, pp. 8–9; *DD Mer. 1*, no. 85, pp. 216–20. Semmler, 'Saint-Denis', p. 108.
26 For Hincmar's involvement, see Flodoard, *Historia Remensis ecclesiae*, ed. by Stratmann, III. 1, pp. 190–91; for this reference, see Berkhofer, *Day of Reckoning*, pp. 201–02 n. 16. See also Ling, 'The Cloister and Beyond', pp. 97–98; Oexle, *Forschungen*, pp. 32–33; Stone, 'Introduction', p. 4.
27 *Praeceptum Synodale a. 829–830*, ed. by Werminghoff, pp. 683–87. Levillain, 'Études sur l'abbaye de Saint-Denis II', pp. 39–40; Oexle, *Forschungen*, p. 115; Semmler, 'Saint-Denis', pp. 108–09.
28 For this, see Semmler, 'Montier-en-Der', here especially pp. 88–89; see also Hosoe, 'Regulae and Reform', pp. 37, 65–66.
29 *DD Kar. 2*, II, no. 261, pp. 652–54, here p. 653.

loco abolita esset et in canonicum ordinem transierat' (monastic life had been thoroughly obliterated in that place, and it had passed into the canonical order).[30] The restoration of Benedictine observance at Montier-en-Der, achieved by imperial, abbatial, and conciliar cooperation, was lauded as an act of great piety and religious observance.

The reform of Montier-en-Der may appear, in retrospect, as a dress rehearsal for that of Saint-Denis. Saint-Denis, too, saw a considerable degree of cooperation between emperor, abbot, and council, and its reform once again entailed a moral assessment of the canons, whose way of life, once thought to be equal in virtue, was dismissed as 'voluptuosa' (voluptuous).[31] Most significantly, the reform was justified by Merovingian precedent, which, if vague about the type of rule, did at least stipulate the institutions' monastic observance. At Montier-en-Der, the foundation charter of Childeric II was brandished as precedent for Benedictine reform; while the charter is no longer extant, its contents may be guessed at by a charter of Theuderic III, which merely referred to the establishment of a monastery and confirmed its immunity, without any indication of the way of life it observed.[32] Somewhat more detail was given in the charters of Saint-Denis: the charter of Bishop Landeric gestures to monks who live 'saecundum sanctum ordinem' (according to the sacred order), while the charter of Clovis II, while containing no mentions of rules, lays out instructions for the observance of *laus perennis*, a form of liturgical observance which ran counter to the Benedictine liturgy.[33] Further use of such age-old precedent may be seen at the 830 Council of Langres, where precedent from the time of Clothar II (584–629) was marshalled to reform (or rather *reaedificare*, 'rebuild') the community at Saint-Pierre de Bèze along Benedictine lines.[34] None of this Merovingian precedent served as proof of previous Benedictine observance, as that would have been grossly anachronistic: the emphasis laid on rule-based monasticism, and specifically Benedictine monasticism, was itself a Carolingian innovation.[35] Nevertheless, by the late 820s, the very fact of previous monastic observance was taken as justification for the enforcement of Benedictine monasticism.[36]

---

30 *DD Kar. 2*, II, no. 309, pp. 762–64, here p. 763; see also Hosoe, '*Regulae* and Reform', p. 37.
31 For the designation 'voluptuous', see Flodoard, *Historia Remensis ecclesiae*, ed. by Stratmann, III. 1, p. 190.
32 *DD Mer. 1*, no. 128, pp. 324–27. Note that Constance Bouchard argues for the authenticity of Childeric II's charter, which others, including Theo Kölzer, in his MGH edition, have classified as a forgery: Bouchard, *The Cartulary of Montier-en-Der*, pp. 12–15. I have followed Kölzer here, but either way, the point remains the same: Childeric II's charter, whether simply reworked, or Bouchard argues, or forged whole cloth, does not stipulate the monastery's way of life.
33 Tardif ed., *Monuments historiques*, no. 10, pp. 8–9; *DD Mer. 1*, no. 85, p. 219.
34 *Concilium Lingonense a. 830*, ed. by Werminghoff, pp. 681–82.
35 For this, see especially Diem, 'Inventing the Holy Rule', pp. 53–84; Dierkens, 'Prolégomènes', pp. 371–94.
36 Compare to Diem, 'The Carolingians', pp. 258–60.

In several ways, then, the reform at Saint-Denis, while necessarily shaped by local interests and pressures, was paralleled by similar cases where Merovingian 'precedent' was reshaped to the demands of the present. One significant area of divergence, however, was in the rhetorical register of the reformers, who pronounced moral judgements against individuals — and specifically, in the accusation of apostasy made against the then canons at Saint-Denis. Here, the difference may be partly attributed to the receptiveness of the community to reform: while those at Montier-en-Der allegedly made their profession voluntarily, no such claim is made for the denizens of Saint-Denis, whose continued resistance after 829/30 makes clear the strength of their opposition. The seeming legitimacy of the intransigent Saint-Denis canons, who had the authority of Benedict of Aniane behind them, may have convinced the reformers of the necessity of engaging in smear tactics. Such accusations may further reflect the contemporary political climate, the gathering winds and thunderclouds of 829. Finally, and perhaps most significantly, one may point to the very prominence of the community, as explicitly stated in an 829/30 conciliar source: Saint-Denis is described as '[monasteri]um praeclarissimi et eximii martyris beati Dionysii […] a regibus Francorum progenitoribusque eiusdem gloriosissimi imperatoris amplissimis rebus d[itatum]' (the monastery of the most famous and special martyr, the blessed Dionysius […] enriched with most ample possessions by the kings of the Franks and the ancestors of the most glorious emperor).[37] Scandal at any monastery was bad enough, but at Saint-Denis, with all its longstanding connections to Frankish royal power, the stakes were heightened. And apostasy, taken here to denote the renunciation of the monastic profession, was a high-stakes accusation: it was not a charge to be levelled lightly.[38]

Indeed, there are only a handful of occasions where apostasy was invoked, all cases of the utmost political necessity. Thus Pippin II of Aquitaine, ever the adversary of his uncle, King Charles the Bald, was denounced as an apostate after leaving his monastery in 864 to pursue his own royal ambitions; so too Carloman, son of Charles the Bald, was condemned for apostasy in 871 after he too quit his profession in the hope of political glory.[39] In 869 Carolingian forces captured and executed one further anonymous 'apostatam monachum' ('apostate monk') who had allegedly cooperated with Northmen.[40] These are hardly standard cases, and all postdate the reforms of Saint-Denis. Yet one could argue that 829, too, was characterized

---

37 *Praeceptum Synodale a. 829–830*, ed. by Werminghoff, p. 684. I am grateful to Rutger Kramer for this suggestion.
38 *Annales Bertiniani*, trans. by Nelson, p. 111 n. 3.
39 *Annales Bertiniani*, ed. by Grat, Vielliard, and Clémencet, 864, p. 105; trans. by Nelson, 864, p. 111. *Council of Compiègne a. 871*, ed. by Hartmann, p. 407. One may note that Hincmar was involved in all of these accusations (with the possible exception of the anonymous monk): his participation appears to have been a common denominator.
40 *Annales Bertiniani*, ed. by Grat, Vielliard, and Clémencet, 869, p. 166, trans. by Nelson, p. 163.

by the heightened political stakes experienced in these cases. Military defeats and palace upheavals had led the Carolingian apparatus to a state of existential crisis. This is perhaps best exemplified by the Paris Council of 829, which exhorted bishops and kings alike to purge all scandal from the church.[41] The Saint-Denis council, which followed closely on its heels, appears to be coloured both by its general approach and its heightened moral frenzy: Steffen Patzold has noted the extent to which Louis the Pious's 832 confirmation charter, in particular, was influenced by its precepts.[42] As de Jong notes, identifying the sins of the church was necessary in order to make atonement, and in so doing, to win back God's favour.[43] Accordingly, the canons, at one time endorsed in their position, became apostates in this new and punitive political landscape.

Of course, if the political climate was responsible for their conviction, it also offered the former canons, now penitent monks, a chance to revisit the council's judgement. For the clouds of 829 had, by 830, become a veritable storm: Pippin of Aquitaine went into open rebellion, with his brothers soon to follow. This rebellion was short-lived; before the end of 830, Louis the Pious successfully reasserted his authority. Hilduin, who had declared support for the rebellion, fell into disgrace; he was (temporarily) deprived of his abbacies and sent into exile in Saxony, accompanied by Hincmar.[44] Taking advantage of their absence, a faction of the newly re-invested monks formed what Louis would later refer to as a *coniuratio*, or conspiracy; either before or shortly after Hilduin's 831 reinstatement as abbot, they brought a petition to Louis's ears. Interestingly, just as the bishops had engaged in smear tactics against the former canons, so too now they turned the tables: Louis records that the faction brought

> a tome of accusations and blasphemies against the bishops who, with our authority and paternal solicitude, had corrected them from the apostasy in which they had lived and persuaded them to return to the profession which they had renounced. They even added other charges to that document which are not worthy to be inserted into our imperial writings.[45]

---

41 De Jong, *The Penitential State*, pp. 148–84; see further Patzold, *Episcopus*, pp. 149–68.
42 Patzold, *Episcopus*, pp. 250–51 n. 448.
43 De Jong, *The Penitential State*, pp. 156, 182.
44 Flodoard, *Historia Remensis ecclesiae*, ed. by Stratmann, III. 1, p. 191; *Translatio sancti Viti*, ed. and trans. by Schmale-Ott, IV, pp. 46–47; Brown, 'Politics and Patronage', p. 33; Berkhofer, *Day of Reckoning*, p. 14; Lapidge, *Hilduin*, p. 17; Levillain, 'Études sur l'abbaye de Saint-Denis II', p. 40; Oexle, *Forschungen*, pp. 32–33; Stone, 'Introduction', pp. 3–4.
45 *DD Kar.* 2, II, no. 315, p. 778: 'thomum in accusationem et blasfemiam episcoporum, qui se de apostasia, in qua versabantur, paterna sollicitudine nostra auctoritate correxerant, et ad propositum, quod abdicaverant, redire suaserant, addentes etiam in eadem scedula alia, quae digna non sunt imperialibus nostris scriptis interseri'. Levillain, 'Études sur l'abbaye de Saint-Denis II', p. 40; Oexle, *Forschungen*, p. 116; Semmler, 'Saint-Denis', pp. 109–10. For the role of rumour in politics more generally, see especially Gravel, *Distances*, pp. 96–108.

Scandal in the church was a moving target. Louis duly convened a second council, to be staffed not only by 'eosdem episcopos, contra quos querebatur, necnon et alios ab ac[c]usatione inmunes' (those bishops, against whom complaints had been made, but also others immune from that accusation).[46] The matter was retried; the former canons were again defeated. This time, however, further care was taken to ensure Benedictine observance: a division of goods was effected to ensure the continuity of the community.[47] The reform of Saint-Denis had been definitively accomplished — at least until the next round.

***

After the 832 reform, Saint-Denis remained a monastic, and specifically Benedictine, community. Yet just as the precedent used to mandate Benedictine observance had widened, so too did the definition of that observance. If Benedictine monasticism could be projected deep into the Merovingian past, so too elements of Merovingian-era monastic observance could be brought forward and accommodated under the ever-expanding Benedictine umbrella. Accordingly, after its reform, the observance of the *Regula Benedicti* at Saint-Denis differed significantly from the interpretation of the Rule advanced at the Aachen reform councils of 816/17, and particularly in regard to the liturgy. For, soon after the monastery's reform, Hilduin sought to revive and reinstate the community's traditional liturgy of perpetual psalmody, the so-called *laus perennis*.[48]

Instructions for the arrangement and performance of the Benedictine *cursus* were laid out in Chapters 8–20 of the Rule; according to Chapter 18, which dealt with the singing of psalms, the entire psalter was to be performed in the course of a week.[49] The Aachen reforms had already diverged from this, advocating 138 psalms each day, in itself a significant increase in liturgical duties, but such psalmody was still moderate when compared to the 450 psalms performed each day by those practising *laus perennis*.[50] *Laus perennis* was not inherently incompatible with Benedictine monasticism — at least, not according to the Carolingians' pick-and-choose approach to the rule. They were very happy, for example, to disregard its chapter on abbatial election,

---

46 *DD Kar.* 2, II, no. 315, p. 778.
47 *DD Kar.* 2, II, no. 316, pp. 779–85; *Constitutio de partitione*, ed. by Werminghoff, pp. 688–94. Oexle, *Forschungen*, pp. 116–17; see also Berkhofer, *Day of Reckoning*, pp. 13–18; Lapidge, *Hilduin*, pp. 40–41; Robertson, *The Service-Books*, pp. 35–36.
48 It is assumed that this traditional liturgy had been supplanted by the Roman rite under Abbot Fulrad in the mid-eighth century: see Robertson, *The Service-Books*, p. 33; Semmler, 'Saint-Denis', p. 103.
49 Robertson, *The Service-Books*, pp. 20–21.
50 For these figures, see de Jong, 'Carolingian Monasticism', pp. 632–33; de Jong, *In Samuel's Image*, p. 249; contrast to Robertson, *The Service-Books*, p. 16; Semmler, 'Saint-Denis', pp. 106–07.

as Albrecht Diem has noted.[51] Yet *laus perennis* was incompatible with the interpretation of the rule advanced at the councils of 816/17, which advocated strict adherence to the Benedictine *cursus*: Chapter 3 of the 816 synod instructed, 'Ut officium iuxta quod in regula sancti Benedicti continentur celebrent' (that the office should be celebrated just as it is preserved in the rule of the blessed Benedict).[52] While such an injunction could apply *stricto sensu* to all other forms of non-Benedictine liturgical observances, including the Roman and Gallican rites, *laus perennis* may well have been another target: its rigour in this matter differentiated it from all other known observances.

Nevertheless, monastic observance at Saint-Denis went hand in hand with *laus perennis*, in accordance with earlier Merovingian practice. Two contemporary sources document the community's return to *laus perennis*: Hilduin's foundation charter for his new crypt-chapel, and a historiographical work known as the *Gesta Dagoberti*.[53] To turn briefly to the former: several months after the 832 council, Hilduin dedicated a new crypt-chapel to the Virgin Mary. In his foundation charter, Hilduin set out his arrangements for its liturgical observance in a passage which today, unfortunately, is fragmentary. Namely, he stipulated that,

> with eight of those monks of the blessed congregation succeeding each other in turn, let them for all time perform their office both day and night in that place according to the Roman custom, and let them celebrate every day in constant attendance the established offices and antiph…[54]

A significant lacuna interrupts his narration, thereby precluding any definitive reconstruction. While the *more Romano* points in a different direction — *laus perennis* was traditionally associated with the older Gallican rite, although the schema could be (and indeed was) adapted to Roman practice — the instruction for the monks to attend to the chapel *per vices* clearly indicates *laus perennis*; so too the stress laid upon monks' continued presence ('omni tempore […] tam diurnum quam nocturnum […] cotidiana assiduitate')

---

51 Diem, 'The Carolingians', pp. 244, 252–53; see also Diem, 'Inventing the Holy Rule', p. 71.
52 *Synodi primae decreta authentica*, ed. by Semmler, 3, p. 458. For the 816 Aachen reforms' attitude to *laus perennis*, see de Jong, *In Samuel's Image*, p. 59; de Jong, 'Carolingian Monasticism', pp. 632–33. See further the discussions of Diem, 'Inventing the Holy Rule', p. 55 n. 13; Hosoe, '*Regulae* and Reform', pp. 40–42; Semmler, 139–40; Robertson, *The Service-Books*, p. 35.
53 Buchner, 'Zur Entstehung', pp. 263–64.
54 Felibien ed., *Histoire de l'abbaye royale de Saint-Denys*, no. 75, p. lvi: 'ut octo ex Monachis hujus sanctae Congregationis succedentes sibi per vices; omni tempore in ea tam diurnum quam nocturnum more Romano officium faciant & constituta officia vel antiph……… . cotidiana assiduitate concelebrant'; Buchner, 'Zur Entstehung', pp. 263–64. Contrast to Robertson, *The Service-Books*, p. 224 n. 21, who argues that this charter did not institute *laus perennis*; I should note, however, that I have drawn on elements of her translation of this passage. Contrast also to Semmler, 'Pippin III.', p. 141. See further Lapidge, *Hilduin*, pp. 41–44; Semmler, 'Saint-Denis', p. 111.

suggests perpetual service.[55] I would suggest, then, that these instructions were for *laus perennis*: on a smaller scale and Romanized, certainly, but *laus perennis* all the same.

The *Gesta Dagoberti*, meanwhile, may be dated *c.* 835, following on the heels of yet another (unsuccessful) rebellion against Louis the Pious.[56] Abbot Hilduin, who had presumably learned his lesson in the aftermath of the first rebellion, remained loyal, and when Louis the Pious was eventually reinstated as emperor in 834, the ceremony was staged at Saint-Denis, once again rendered a site of legitimation for Frankish kings.[57] The *Gesta* explicitly addresses such cooperation between ruler and monastery: it recounts the life of the Merovingian king Dagobert (d. 639), with particular attention paid to his alleged refoundation of, and subsequent patronage of, the monastery of Saint-Denis.[58] In so doing, it draws on earlier texts, chiefly Fredegar's *Chronicle* (from which many chapters are borrowed almost verbatim), with further borrowings from the *Liber Historiae Francorum*, the *Vita Amandi*, the *Passio SS Dionysii, Rustici et Eleutherii*, and, more questionably, the *Inventio sancti Dionysii* (although in this case the dependence may well be the other way around).[59] But the *Gesta Dagoberti* also introduce a significant amount of new material, as well as reconfiguring existing material in line with contemporary priorities. The resulting historicity of the text need not concern us. Instead, the text offers a privileged window onto the community's self-perception — or indeed, onto its anonymous author's attempts to re-establish cohesion within a shaken community. By concentrating on Dagobert and his interactions with the community — a subject offering the safety of the distant past — the author could conjure a sense of pride in the community's triumphant, exulted origins. Notably, the *Gesta* avoid any hint of recent controversies. Benedictine monasticism is entirely absent; instead, the *Gesta* advocate a nonspecific monastic observance, characterized in particular by the practice of *laus perennis*.[60]

This perpetual singing of psalms forms a recurring theme throughout the *Gesta*. Already in Chapter 20, the *Gesta* attribute Dagobert's lavish generosity

---

55 Contrast to Robertson, *The Service-Books*, p. 224 n. 21.
56 I have adopted the dating of Levillain, 'Études sur l'abbaye de Saint-Denis I', p. 115.
57 See here Booker, *Past Convictions*, pp. 204, 238, 251.
58 In contrast to the argument put forward by Constance Bouchard, such a choice of subject need not imply criticism of contemporary Carolingian rulers: see Bouchard, *Rewriting Saints and Ancestors*, pp. 148–49.
59 For these references and the question of dependences, see the MGH edition of the text; for the relation of the *Gesta* to the *Inventio*, see especially Lapidge, *Hilduin*, pp. 103–06; see also Buchner, 'Zur Entstehung', pp. 254–55; Levillain, 'Études sur l'abbaye de Saint-Denis I', pp. 71–88; Tessier, 'Les derniers travaux', pp. 48–51.
60 Cf. Levillain, 'Études sur l'abbaye de Saint-Denis I', pp. 80–81; Levillain, 'Études sur l'abbaye de Saint-Denis II', pp. 35, 42–43. Contrast to Wallace-Hadrill, who argues that this work makes a clear argument for Benedictine monastic reform at Saint-Denis: Wallace-Hadrill, 'Archbishop Hincmar', pp. 4–7.

towards the community to his desire for 'laus perpetuo' ('perpetual praise'), which may be taken to refer to psalmody.[61] In Chapter 35, this is made explicit: Dagobert gave generously to the community, and 'eos turmatim ad instar monasterii Acaunensium sive sancti Martini Turonis psallere instituit' (established them [the brothers serving God there] to sing psalms in turn according to the model of the monasteries of Agaune and Saint-Martin of Tours); his institution of this practice is again confirmed in a summary of his achievements in Chapter 43.[62] Most importantly, Chapter 51 of the *Gesta* includes verbatim the confirmation charter of Clovis II — the same privilege discussed above in the lead-up to the 829/30 council — albeit with some additions and embellishments:

> Because of our love of God and our reverence of his blessed martyrs and in order to attain eternal life, we wish to present this benefit to that blessed place, [...] namely to this order, that, just as the singing of psalms in columns was established in the time of our lord and father, and just as it is preserved day and night in the monasteries of Saint-Maurice d'Agaune and Saint-Martin of Tours, let it be thus celebrated in this place throughout all future times.[63]

One could argue that this simply reflected the history of Saint-Denis, which was indeed non-Benedictine. But such an argument would be disingenuous: writing history is, after all, a series of choices about the present. Many institutions had non-Benedictine pasts which were made over in the Benedictine model: institutional histories could be rewritten, and founding saints could be rebranded as the personification of Benedictine virtues.[64] Even short of such revisionism, the author could simply have focused on other aspects of Saint-Denis's history. Instead the *Gesta* positively emphasized the observance of *laus perennis* at Saint-Denis at four separate points.[65]

---

61 *Gesta Dagoberti*, ed. by Krusch, 20, p. 407.
62 *Gesta Dagoberti*, ed. by Krusch, 35, 43, pp. 413–14, 421; the latter reference derives from Fredegar, *Chronicon*, ed. and trans. by Wallace-Hadrill, IV. 79, p. 68. See also Rosenwein, 'One Site', p. 288. For the reference to Agaune, see also Diem, 'Who is Allowed to Pray for the King?', p. 80.
63 *Gesta Dagoberti*, ed. by Krusch, 51, pp. 423–25, here pp. 424–25: 'Nos enim propter Dei amorem et reventiam ipsorum sanctorum martyrum atque adipiscendam vitam aeternam hoc benificium ad ipsum locum sanctum [...] volumus prestare; eo scilicet ordine, ut, sicut ibidem tempore domni et genitoris nostri psallentium ordo per turmas fuit institutus, vel sicut in monasterio sancti Mauricii Agaunis et sancti Martini Turonis die noctuque tenetur, ita in loco ipso per omnia futura tempora celebretur'. See also *DD Mer. 1*, no. 85, pp. 216–20. Note that I have followed previous scholars in interpreting 'monasterio [...] sancti Martini Turonis' as 'Saint-Martin of Tours', as opposed to Marmoutier, as Saint-Martin of Tours was a basilical community which observed *laus perennis* at the time of the text's composition, and thus offered the author of the *Gesta* a useful and well-known point of comparison.
64 See, for example, the comments of Angenendt, *Liudger*, p. 120; Diem, 'The Carolingians', pp. 258–60.
65 *Gesta Dagoberti*, ed. by Krusch, 20, 35, 43, 51, pp. 407, 414, 421, 425; compare to *DD Mer. 1*, no. 85, pp. 216–20; Fredegar, *Chronicon*, ed. and trans. by Wallace-Hadrill, IV. 79, p. 68.

One of these points — the confirmation charter of Clovis II — is made to serve as the culmination of the work. Here, the *Gesta* underscored the legitimacy of Clovis's privilege and its conciliar subscription still further, stating that:

> Among them there were several bishops present, whom today the blessed church does not doubt to be most blessed, at whose most venerated tombs the Lord works many miracles even up to the present day.[66]

Thereafter, the author named ten saints who allegedly subscribed to the privilege, at least three of whom are notably absent in the original charter.[67] The proven sanctity of the bishops who confirmed Clovis's privilege vouched for the authority of their arrangements — here, specifically, the institution of *laus perennis* at Saint-Denis.

Finally, it should be noted that the *Gesta* anachronistically cited the basilical community of Saint-Martin at Tours as a model for *laus perennis* at three separate points (the observance of *laus perennis* at Saint-Martin's was only instituted in the early ninth century).[68] This, I would argue, was a deliberate choice on the part of the author, who attempted to create an imagined *laus perennis* interest group encompassing the old and venerable basilical monasteries of Saint-Denis, Saint-Martin, and Saint-Maurice. In addition to naming the monasteries of Saint-Martin and Saint-Maurice as models for the institution of *laus perennis*, the author moreover posited cooperation between these three institutions' patron saints in a chapter unique to the text.[69] In this chapter, the *Gesta*'s author recounts how an isolated holy man, who had been praying for King Dagobert on the day of his death, was suddenly confronted by a vision, in which a 'teterrimos spiritus' (foul spirit) rocked the boat of a chained and tormented Dagobert, but, upon his invocation of Saints Denis, Maurice, and Martin — to whom he called perpetually, unceasingly (!) for aid — this

---

66 *Gesta Dagoberti*, ed. by Krusch, 51, pp. 423–25, here p. 425: 'Inter quos nonnulli pontifices extiterunt, quos hodie sancta ecclesia sanctissimos esse non dubitat, eo quod ad eorum venerabilia sepulchra virtutes non modicas usque in praesens Dominus operetur'.

67 *Gesta Dagoberti*, ed. by Krusch, 51, pp. 423–25, here p. 425; compare to *DD Mer. 1*, no. 85, pp. 219–20. The saints listed in the *Gesta* are as follows: Audoenus, Rado, Palladius, Clarus, Eligius, Sulpicius, Autbertus, Castadius, Etherius, and Landericus; of these, Audoenus, Sulpicius, and Otbert are absent in Clovis II's charter. Some, but not all, of these 'absent' saints may be listed with alternative spellings in Bishop Landeric's 654 charter, which formed the basis for Clovis II's confirmation: see Tardif ed., *Monuments historiques*, no. 10, pp. 8–9. For the addition of names, see Buchner, 'Zur Entstehung', p. 267 n. 70.

68 *Gesta Dagoberti*, ed. by Krusch, 35, 43, 51, pp. 414, 421, 425. For the anachronistic introduction of Saint-Martin into this source, see Buchner, 'Zur Entstehung', p. 263; Levillain, 'Études sur l'abbaye de Saint-Denis I', pp. 72–73; Robertson, *The Service-Books*, p. 14.

69 Note, however, that the author claims to have read the story in a charter: Buchner, 'Zur Entstehung', p. 267; Tessier, 'Les derniers travaux', p. 48. Buchner moreover points out that parts of this chapter are adapted from a story about King Theodoric in the *Dialogues* of Gregory the Great: Buchner, 'Zur Entstehung', pp. 267–68.

saintly dream team swooped down to his rescue, conducting him safely to the Patriarch Abraham himself.[70] A quotation from Psalm 64 follows.[71] Dagobert was thus saved as a result not only of his own perpetual prayer, but also of his patronage of holy places — and in particular, his patronage of the liturgy of perpetual psalmody at the shrines of saints Denis, Martin, and Maurice.

Such a concerted interest group was not simply the invention of the author. All three institutions — all ancient, basilical monasteries which served as thriving cult sites — had independently vouched their commitment to *laus perennis*: Saint-Martin of Tours, through its new observance of the liturgy; Saint-Maurice d'Agaune, through its renewed focus on this legacy in its recently forged foundation charter; and Saint-Denis, through the arrangement of its new crypt liturgy and the *Gesta Dagoberti*.[72] Even as the Aachen reforms sought to promote a modified Benedictine *cursus*, dissonant voices were raised. And, as more reformers took recourse to decontextualized Merovingian-era precedent, so too older, non-Benedictine practices became incorporated into supposedly normative practices. The use of precedent cut both ways.

***

Past scholarship on Carolingian monasticism tended to attribute a certain coherence to the monastic reform movement. The Aachen councils of 816/17 were regarded — often, if by no means always — as the culmination of Carolingian monastic policy, to which all pre-816 policy ineluctably led, and from which all further policy followed. Recent reappraisals have done much to counteract such narratives, in large part through pointing out the sheer extent of post-816 diversity. The Aachen councils remain significant, but are recontextualized: historians increasingly seek to reconstruct not *the* 'Carolingian monastic reform', but rather Carolingian monastic reforms.[73] Indeed, as Diem writes, the *Regula Benedicti* which the councils so actively promoted 'could mean everything to everyone' and so 'could easily be used to support different, sometimes even incompatible reform agendas'.[74]

Certainly, by the late 820s at Saint-Denis, reformers had a different vision from that of the earlier Aachen councils. The arrangements of Benedict of

---

70 *Gesta Dagoberti*, ed. by Krusch, 44, pp. 421–22, here p. 421. For the reception of this story in a letter of Louis the Pious from *c*. 835, see *Epistolae variorum*, ed. by Dümmler, no. 19, p. 326; for this, see Buchner, 'Zur Entstehung', pp. 268–69; cf. Tessier, 'Les derniers travaux', pp. 48–49.
71 *Gesta Dagoberti*, ed. by Krusch, 44, p. 422; Psalm 64. 5–6. Note that the *Gesta Dagoberti* diverges slightly from the Vulgate: 'Beatus quem elegisti et assumsisti, Domine; inhabitabit in atriis tuis. Replebimur in bonis domus tuae, sanctum est templum tuum, mirabile in equitate'.
72 See here also Rosenwein, 'One Site', pp. 285–90.
73 See here especially Kramer, 'Great Expectations', p. 297.
74 Diem, 'The Carolingians', p. 251.

Aniane were expressly overturned; while thereafter the community followed the *Regula Benedicti*, they did so in a manner which departed significantly from the interpretations of the 816/17 councils, specifically in regard to their liturgical practices. Moreover, this difference in liturgical practice was accentuated and given a significant role in the community's self-definition, a choice which almost certainly related more to local pride and particularized traditions than to any self-conscious engagement with, or contestation of, the earlier Aachen councils. The reforms of 816/17, far from having a delayed implementation, were thus reversed at Saint-Denis within a period of some fifteen years, and with all the trappings of legitimacy. This reversal was accomplished by men such as Hilduin and Hincmar, acting with both imperial and conciliar support. The events at Saint-Denis should not be dismissed as an exception or an aberration: the very movers and shakers of Carolingian reforms were behind it.

Charlemagne's reign did not commence with him endorsing the *Regula Benedicti* as the gold standard of monasticism. Rather, as Jinty Nelson has highlighted, the earliest surviving text from his reign was his gift of a dependent cell to the monastery of Saint-Denis, on the condition that the monks observe *laus perennis* on behalf of himself and his father.[75] Some sixty-five years later, those who sought to reform the monastery looked not to the Aachen councils, but rather to the monastery's own illustrious history of patronage from, and cooperation with, Frankish kings. The reformed Benedictine monks chose to identify not with the *Regula Benedicti*, nor with any other written rule for that matter, but rather with their own distinguished traditions. In so doing, they laid out their own vision of reform.

Works Cited

Primary Sources

Annales Bertiniani, ed. by Félix Grat, Jeanne Vielliard, and Suzanne Clémencet, *Annales de Saint-Bertin* (Paris: C. Klincksieck, 1964); trans. by Janet L. Nelson, *The Annals of St-Bertin*, Ninth-century Histories, 1 (Manchester: Manchester University Press, 1991)

Concilium Lingonense a. 830, ed. by Albert Werminghoff, in *Monumenta Germaniae Historica: Concilia*, II. 2, *Concilia aevi Karolini*, II (Hannover: Hahn, 1908), no. 51, pp. 681–82

Constitutio de partitione bonorum monasterii S. Dyonisii a. 832, ed. by Albert Werminghoff, in *Monumenta Germaniae Historica: Concilia*, II. 2, *Concilia aevi Karolini*, II (Hannover: Hahn, 1908), no. 53, pp. 688–94

---

75 *DD Kar. 1*, no. 55, pp. 81–82; Nelson, 'Charlemagne's Charter D. 55'.

Council of Compiègne a. 871, ed. by Wilfried Hartmann, in *Monumenta Germaniae Historica: Concilia aevi Karolini*, IV (Hannover: Hahn, 1998), no. 36, pp. 407–09

DD Kar. 1, ed. by Engelbert Mühlbacher, in *Monumenta Germaniae Historica: Die Urkunden Pippins, Karlmanns, und Karls des Grossen* (Hannover: Hahn, 1906)

DD Kar. 2, ed. by Theo Kölzer, in *Monumenta Germaniae Historica: Die Urkunden Ludwigs des Frommen*, 3 vols (Wiesbaden: Harrassowitz, 2016)

DD Mer. 1, ed. by Theo Kölzer, in *Monumenta Germaniae Historica: Die Urkunden der Merowinger* (Hannover: Hahn, 2001)

Epistolae variorum inde a morte Caroli Magni usque ad divisionem imperii collectae, ed. by Ernst Dümmler, in *Monumenta Germaniae Historica: Epistolae Karolini aevi*, III (Berlin: Weidmann, 1899)

Ex translatione sanguinis Domini, ed. by Georg Waitz, in *Monumenta Germaniae Historica: Scriptores*, IV (Hannover: Hahn, 1841), pp. 445–49

Felibien, Michel, ed., *Histoire de l'abbaye royale de Saint-Denys en France (Recueil de pieces justificatives pour l'histoire de l'abbaye royale de Saint Denys en France)* (Paris: Frederic Leonard, 1706)

Flodoard, *Historia Remensis ecclesiae*, ed. by Martina Stratmann, in *Monumenta Germaniae Historica: Scriptores*, XXXVI (Hannover: Hahn, 1998)

Fredegar, *Chronicon*, ed. and trans. by John M. Wallace-Hadrill, *The Fourth Book of the Chronicle of Fredegar with its Continuations* (London: Nelson, 1960)

Gesta Dagoberti, ed. by Bruno Krusch, in *Monumenta Germaniae Historica: Scriptores* rerum Merovingicarum, II (Hannover: Hahn, 1888), pp. 396–425

Praeceptum Synodale a. 829–830, ed. by Albert Werminghoff, in *Monumenta Germaniae Historica: Concilia*, II. 2, *Concilia aevi Karolini*, II (Hannover: Hahn, 1908), no. 52, pp. 683–87

Synodi primae decreta authentica, ed. by Josef Semmler, in *Corpus Consuetudinum Monasticarum*, vol. 1: *Initia Consuetudinis Benedictinae: Consuetudines saeculi octavi et noni* (Siegburg: Franciscus Schmitt, 1963), pp. 451–67

Tardif, Jules, ed., *Monuments historiques: cartons de rois* (Paris: J. Claye, 1866)

Translatio sancti Viti, ed. and trans. by Irene Schmale-Ott, *Übertragung des hl. Märtyrers Vitus* (Münster: Aschendorff, 1979)

Secondary Works

Angenendt, Arnold, *Liudger: Missionar, Abt, Bischof im frühen Mittelalter* (Münster: Aschendorff, 2005)

Barrow, Julia, 'Ideas and Applications of Reform', in *The Cambridge History of Christianity*, vol. 3: *Early Medieval Christianities, c. 600–c. 1100*, ed. by Thomas F. X. Noble and Julia M. H. Smith (Cambridge: Cambridge University Press, 2008), pp. 345–62

Berkhofer, Robert F., *Day of Reckoning: Power and Accountability in Medieval France*, Middle Ages Series (Philadelphia: University of Pennsylvania Press, 2004)

Bouchard, Constance, *The Cartulary of Montier-en-Der, 666–1129*, Medieval Academy Books, 108 (Toronto: University of Toronto Press, 2004)

——, *Rewriting Saints and Ancestors: Memory and Forgetting in France, 500–1200* (Philadelphia: University of Pennsylvania Press, 2015)

Booker, Courtney, *Past Convictions: The Penance of Louis the Pious and the Decline of the Carolingians* (Philadelphia: University of Pennsylvania Press, 2009)

Brown, Giles P. A., 'Politics and Patronage at the Abbey of Saint-Denis (814–98): The Rise of a Royal Patron Saint' (unpublished doctoral dissertation, University of Oxford, 1989)

Buchner, Max, 'Zur Entstehung und zur Tendenz der "Gesta Dagoberti": Zugleich ein Beitrag zum Eigenkirchenwesen im Frankenreiche', *Historisches Jahrbuch*, 47 (1927), 252–74

Diem, Albrecht, 'Inventing the Holy Rule: Some Observations on the History of Monastic Normative Observance in the Early Medieval West', in *Western Monasticism ante litteram: The Spaces of Monastic Observance in Late Antiquity and the Early Middle Ages*, ed. by Hendrik Dey and Elizabeth Fentress, Disciplina Monastica, 7 (Turnhout: Brepols, 2011), pp. 53–84

——, 'Who is Allowed to Pray for the King? Saint-Maurice d'Agaune and the Creation of a Burgundian Identity', in *Post-Roman Transitions: Christian and Barbarian Identities in the Early Medieval West*, ed. by Gerda Heydemann and Walter Pohl, Cultural Encounters in Late Antiquity and the Middle Ages, 14 (Turnhout: Brepols, 2013), pp. 47–88

——, 'Review of *St Galler Klosterplan: Faksimile, Begleittext, Beischriften und Übersetzung*, ed. by Ernst Tremp and the Stiftsbibliothek St Gall (Sankt Gallen: Verlag am Klosterhof, 2014)', *The Medieval Review*, 15.11.21, <https://scholarworks.iu.edu/journals/index.php/tmr/article/view/20408> [accessed 4 February 2022]

——, 'The Carolingians and the *Regula Benedicti*', in *Religious Franks: Religion and Power in the Frankish Kingdoms; Studies in Honour of Mayke de Jong*, ed. by Rob Meens, Dorine van Espelo, Bram van den Hoven van Genderen, Janneke Raaijmakers, Irene van Renswoude, and Carine van Rhijn (Manchester: Manchester University Press, 2016), pp. 243–61

Dierkens, Alain, 'Prolégomènes à une histoire des relations culturelles entre les îles britanniques et le continent pendant le Haut Moyen Âge: La diffusion du monachisme dit colombanien ou iro-franc dans quelques monastères de la région parisienne au VIIe siècle et la politique religieuse de la reine Bathilde', in *La Neustrie: Les pays au nord de la Loire de 650 à 850; Colloque historique international*, ed. by Helmut Atsma, Beihefte der Francia, 16.2 (Sigmaringen: Thorbecke, 1989), pp. 371–94

Fox, Yaniv, *Power and Religion in Merovingian Gaul: Columbanian Monasticism and the Frankish Elites* (Cambridge: Cambridge University Press, 2014)

Geuenich, Dieter, 'Zur Stellung und Wahl des Abtes in der Karolingerzeit', in *Person und Gemeinschaft im Mittelalter: Karl Schmid zum fünfundsechzigsten Geburtstage*, ed. by Gerd Althoff, Dieter Geuenich, Otto Gerhard Oexle, and Joachim Wollasch (Sigmaringen: Thorbecke, 1988), pp. 171–86

Gravel, Martin, *Distances, rencontres, communications: réaliser l'Empire sous Charlemagne et Louis le Pieux* (Turnhout: Brepols, 2012)

Hen, Yitzhak, *The Royal Patronage of Liturgy in Frankish Gaul to the Death of Charles the Bald*, Henry Bradshaw Society, Subsidia, 3 (London: Boydell, 2001)

Hosoe, Kristina M., '*Regulae* and Reform in Carolingian Monastic Hagiography' (unpublished doctoral dissertation, Yale University, 2014)

Jong, Mayke de, 'Carolingian Monasticism: The Power of Prayer', in *The New Cambridge Medieval History*, vol. 2: *c. 700–c. 900*, ed. by Rosamond McKitterick (Cambridge: Cambridge University Press, 1995), pp. 622–53

——, *In Samuel's Image: Child Oblation in the Early Medieval West*, Brill's Studies in Intellectual History, 12 (Leiden: Brill, 1996)

——, *The Penitential State: Authority and Atonement in the Age of Louis the Pious, 814–40* (Cambridge: Cambridge University Press, 2009)

Kramer, Rutger, 'Great Expectations: Imperial Ideologies and Ecclesiastical Reforms from Charlemagne to Louis the Pious (813–822)' (unpublished doctoral dissertation, Freie Universität Berlin, 2014)

Lapidge, Michael, *Hilduin of Saint-Denis: The Passio S. Dionysii in Prose and Verse*, Mittellateinische Studien und Texte, 51 (Leiden: Brill, 2017)

Levillain, Léon, 'Études sur l'abbaye de Saint-Denis à l'époque mérovingienne I', *Bibliothèque de l'école des chartes*, 82 (1921), 5–116

——, 'Études sur l'abbaye de Saint-Denis à l'époque mérovingienne II', *Bibliothèque de l'école des chartes*, 86 (1925), 5–99

Ling, Stephen, 'The Cloister and Beyond: Regulating the Life of the Canonical Clergy in Francia, from Pippin III to Louis the Pious' (unpublished doctoral dissertation, University of Leicester, 2015)

Nelson, Janet L., 'Charlemagne's Charter D. 55 (dated 13 January 769)', blog post published 7 July 2014 <http://www.charlemagneseurope.ac.uk/blog/charlemagnes-charter-d-55-13-january-769> [accessed 8 September 2021]

Oexle, Otto G., *Forschungen zu monastischen und geistlichen Gemeinschaften im westfränkischen Bereich*, Münstersche Mittelalter-Schriften, 31 (Munich: Wilhelm Fink, 1978)

Patzold, Steffen, *Episcopus: Wissen über Bischöfe im Frankenreich des späten 8. bis frühen 10. Jahrhunderts*, Mittelalter-Forschungen, 25 (Ostfildern: Thorbecke, 2008)

Robertson, Anne W., *The Service-Books of the Royal Abbey of Saint-Denis: Images of Ritual and Music in the Middle Ages* (Oxford: Oxford University Press, 1991)

Rosenwein, Barbara H., 'One Site, Many Meanings: Saint-Maurice d'Agaune as a Place of Power in the Early Middle Ages', in *Topographies of Power in the Early Middle Ages*, ed. by Mayke de Jong, Frans Theuws, and Carine van Rhijn, The Transformation of the Roman World, 6 (Leiden: Brill, 2001), pp. 271–90

Semmler, Josef, 'Pippin III. und die fränkischen Klöster', *Francia: Forschungen zur Westeuropäischen Geschichte*, 3 (1975), 88–146

——, 'Mönche und Kanoniker im Frankenreiche Pippins III. und Karl des Großen', in *Untersuchungen zu Kloster und Stift*, ed. by Max-Planck Institut für Geschichte, Studien zur Germania Sacra, 14 (Göttingen: Vandenhoeck & Ruprecht, 1980), pp. 78–111

———, 'Saint-Denis: Von der bischöflichen Coemeterialbasilika zur königlichen Benediktinerabtei', in *La Neustrie: Les pays au nord de la Loire de 650 à 850; Colloque historique international*, ed. by Helmut Atsma, Beihefte der Francia, 16.2 (Sigmaringen: Thorbecke, 1989), pp. 75–123

———, 'Montier-en-Der au IXe siècle: une abbaye royale et bénédictine', in *Les Moines du Der, 673–1790: Actes du colloque international d'histoire, Joinville — Montier-en-Der, 1er–3 octobre 1998*, ed. by Patrick Corbet with Jackie Lusse and Georges Viard (Langres: Dominique Guéniot, 2000), pp. 83–93

Stone, Rachel, 'Introduction: Hincmar's World', in *Hincmar of Rheims: Life and Work*, ed. by Rachel Stone and Charles West (Manchester: Manchester University Press, 2015), pp. 1–43

Tessier, Georges, 'Les derniers travaux de M. Levillain sur l'abbaye de Saint-Denis a l'époque mérovingienne', *Le Moyen âge: revue d'histoire et de philologie*, 39 (1929), 36–77

Wallace-Hadrill, John M., 'Archbishop Hincmar and the Authorship of the *Lex Salica*', *The Legal History Review*, 21.1 (1953), 1–29

JOHANNA JEBE

Debating the *una regula*

Reflections on Monastic Life in Ninth-Century Manuscripts from St Gall

Introduction: Approaching Debates on the *una regula**

Under the shelfmark Sang. 914, the Stiftsbibliothek of St Gall holds a codex written by the ninth-century monastic scriptorium *in situ*, one well known today as the *Leithandschrift* for modern critical editions of the *Regula Benedicti*. Two stories have been told in relation to the manuscript — one from the ninth, the other from the twentieth century — which enlarge upon its origins and further establish its significance. The first is transmitted by the manuscript itself in the copy of a letter which compilers added some thirty-five years later to their text of the Rule.[1] In this letter, two monks from the monastery at Reichenau, Grimald and Tatto, report how they were sent, presumably to the court at Aachen, with instructions to copy meticulously the very special version of the *Regula Benedicti* sent to Charlemagne from Montecassino — a version which was regarded as the direct copy of the presumed autograph of Benedict of Nursia himself.[2] The letter thus serves in a sense as a proof of authenticity, attesting to the provenance of the Reichenau copy from the

---

* I wish to express my sincere thanks to Anne Davidson Lund as well as to Jamie Page, Fraser McNair, Graeme Ward, and Heike Garbe who kindly helped me to improve this chapter by correcting and improving its English at different stages. I am also very grateful to Rutger Kramer for our valuable discussions on the issues of monasticism and reforms since I gave the first outline of my argument at the IMC in Leeds.

1 St Gall, Stibi, Cod. Sang. 914, pp. 202–03, also ed. by Dümmler, Grimaldus et Tatto, *Epistula*, pp. 301–02. In order to authenticate the copy, the manuscript also adds a second letter (pp. 173–79), written by Abbot Theodemar of Montecassino to Charlemagne and concerning the template for St Gall's copy.

2 See Traube, *Textgeschichte der Regula S. Benedicti*, pp. 31–34, 51–55, 63–79, who established the interpretation of Charlemagne's copy as the court's official norm text, the so-called *Aachener Normalexemplar*. It should be noted, though, that the precise location of this

> **Johanna Jebe** is an akademische Mitarbeiterin at the University of Tübingen, where she specializes in Carolingian monasticism.

Monastic Communities and Canonical Clergy in the Carolingian World (780–840): Categorizing the Church, ed. by Rutger Kramer, Emilie Kurdziel, and Graeme Ward, MMS 8 (Turnhout: Brepols, 2022), pp. 323–352
DOI 10.1484/M.MMS-EB.5.128537

authoritative version of the monastic father himself. And it closely links St Gall's codex 914 to this venerable strand of transmission, as the manuscript is judged to be a direct copy of Grimald's and Tatto's Reichenau manuscript, itself now unfortunately lost.[3]

The second, twentieth-century story takes up the report of Grimald and Tatto and embeds it within the narrative of a court-driven reform of monastic life in the 800s. According to this narrative, the manuscript is emblematic of the so-called 'Anianische Reform' (Hallinger/Semmler). Since the 1960s, Carolingian monasticism has been predominantly perceived in light of a top-down initiative of *unificatio*, which aimed to have all monasteries submit to the *Regula Benedicti* as the sole and binding norm for monastic life and to guarantee its uniform observance. In a local context, determining how strictly this Rule was observed in individual monasteries could thus act as an indicator of the extent to which a community adhered to the court's programme of monastic reform.[4] It is here that the story of Grimald and Tatto fits putatively into the scheme. For Josef Semmler and his successors, codex Sang. 914 served as a prime witness for the success of those reform efforts. Its existence made clear that the monasteries of Reichenau and St Gall considered it useful — even essential — for their particular form of monastic life to have available the most authentic copy possible of the *Regula Benedicti* as a code of instruction. And through the lens of normative depictions of 'reform', the story given by the letter also came very close to the court's ideal of it. It seemed thus clear that the Reichenau monks looked to the court as a source of authoritative texts, and the court provided them reliably with an official *Normalexemplar*.[5] For contemporary scholarship, the mere presence of codex 914 in the holdings of St Gall is still sufficient to rank the monastery among those institutions in favour of the *Anianische Reform*.[6]

---

manuscript (whether in Aachen or in any particular reform monastery) remains unknown, even if most publications proclaim otherwise without the authority of evidence, see already Semmler, 'Karl der Große und das fränkische Mönchtum', pp. 221–22.

3   This identification as a copy of the original made by Grimald and Tatto has been decisively argued by Rudolf Hanslik in 'Praefatio', pp. xxiv–xxvi and 'Die Benediktinerregel im Wiener Kirchenvätercorpus', pp. 166–68; it was commonly accepted by the time Bernhard Bischoff agreed on its provenance, see Bischoff, 'Die Handschrift', p. xiv.

4   As Charles Mériaux's chapter in the present volume offers a comprehensive overview of the scholarship about the reforms of 816/17 and of Josef Semmler's research, I limit the references by pointing to his paper; I should only highlight Semmler's seminal article on the spread of the reforms at local level: 'Benedictus II' (1983).

5   See esp. Masser, *Regula Benedicti des Cod. 915*, pp. 18–19; Semmler, 'Benedictus II', pp. 19 with n. 47 (referring to the Reichenau).

6   Duft, Gössi, and Vogler, *Die Abtei St Gallen*, p. 22; McKitterick, *The Frankish Kingdoms*, pp. 119–20; Schaab, *Mönch in Sankt Gallen*, p. 14. Many scholars nevertheless consider St Gall as a rather passive participant in the reforms, developing only in the shadow of the Reichenau abbey, see among others Zettler, 'Der St Galler Klosterplan', p. 660.

The second story surrounding codex 914 nevertheless brings with it a host of problematic implications and presuppositions. These derive from the twentieth century's particular image of Carolingian monasticism as described above, one which emerged primarily at a time when new editions of the first volume of the *Corpus Consuetudinum Monasticarum* (1963) provided a fruitful and highly stimulating access to a new set of sources, specifically, normative texts associated with the Aachen synods. The influence of these norm-focused narratives can still be felt when it comes to questions of monastic practice and identity at local levels, as seen for Sang. 914. Even if critical appraisal from the 1990s onwards has called into question the many simplifications inherent in the model of a court-driven top-down enterprise of reform, and even if scholarship today draws a much more nuanced picture of what it meant to be a Carolingian monk than just being 'Benedictine', earlier models of thinking still lead historians studying local monastic developments into a search for the 'impact on the ground' of court initiatives.[7] This focus on discrepancies between norm and practice threatens to limit our understanding severely. It implicitly reproduces these norms as channels for modern research, and thus continues to see ninth-century monasticism mainly through the eyes of the court. Questions about the development of monastic ideas within local communities and their relation to court discourses, which I want to treat in this chapter, tend therefore to be narrowed by an understanding which sees them in terms of acceptance, refusal, adaptation, or simple disregard of the famous reformers' initiatives.

By contrast, my chapter seeks to avoid viewing debates about 'good' monastic life in the cloister of St Gall in terms of a relationship between court-imposed norm and local practice. In my analysis of Rule codices from that monastery, I intend to pay less attention to an historiographical narrative of court-driven reform — the second story sketched out above — and instead take seriously the stories of Grimald and Tatto, as well as the later St Gall copyists of Sang. 914, and above all the manuscripts themselves, to ask what these reveal about the ambitions and thoughts of these protagonists in dealing

---

7 For the former interpretation of the Carolingian era as the cradle of Benedictine monasticism see e.g. Frank, 'Die Benediktusregel und ihre Auslegung bis Benedikt von Aniane', esp. p. 27 or Semmler, 'Benedictus II', pp. 5–6, 18, 47; for the most incisive criticism of the model of *Anianische Reform* see Geuenich, 'Kritische Anmerkungen zur sogenannten "anianischen Reform"' and the overview by Kettemann, 'Subsidia Anianensia', pp. 1–21; on a much livelier picture of the controversial debates in the context of Aachen, involving several different actors and interconnections of court and monasteries, see e.g. de Jong, 'Monastic Writing and Carolingian Court Audiences', esp. p. 180 and Kramer, *Rethinking Authority in the Carolingian Empire*; out of the many new approaches to Carolingian monasticism, I can pick only a very few with a close connection to the questions discussed in this chapter: Gaillard, *D'une réforme à l'autre*; Choy, 'The Deposit of Monastic Faith'; Sullivan, 'What Was Carolingian Monasticism?'; Coon, 'Collecting the Desert in the Carolingian West'; Diem, 'The Carolingians and the "Regula Benedicti"'; Raaijmakers, *The Making of the Monastic Community of Fulda*.

with a more than two hundred-year-old tradition.[8] In choosing to focus on the *Regula Benedicti*, I thus do not seek to develop a narrative of the success or failure of the Aachen synods. Rather, I focus on the text because of its uncontested importance in contemporary discourses on monasticism at all levels, as visible from local manuscript production in Sang. 914 up to synodal decisions. As many of this book's contributions highlight, the Rule gained a significant new status in this period as it was established for the first time as the exclusive criterion for defining monks and nuns.[9] Nevertheless, we know comparatively little about the attitude that monks themselves adopted towards this crucial marker of their status, primarily because of the lack of sources beyond individual commentaries on this text (most notably those of Smaragdus of St Mihiel and Hildemar of Civate). Following the impetus of research over the last twenty-five years which has convincingly revealed how deeply Carolingian manuscript culture affected ninth-century monastic life, I will make a case for tackling the tricky question of how we might apprehend local ideas about monastic life by focusing upon the manuscripts the monks themselves produced and used.[10] As I intend to argue, the process of copying and compiling the *Regula Benedicti* says much about local protagonists' attitudes and expectations towards the text.

My chapter therefore pursues two aims. Firstly, I seek to show how lively and independently local discussions and practices of monastic life in the ninth century could be when examined on their own terms. This will also reveal how the Rule itself, established so firmly as the distinctive criterion defining monastic life, remained a matter of discussion in religious communities, especially with regard to the question of what it meant to observe it correctly, or what 'observance' meant at all. My title, 'Debating the *una regula*', thus seeks not just to trace discussions carried out within monasteries, but to call into question whether the paradigm of the *una regula* itself — i.e. the Benedictine Rule as sole binding norm — offers an adequate description of ninth-century monasticism, or if we should be more sensitive towards contemporary perceptions of normativity. Secondly, my chapter intends to

---

8 This approach and the spectrum of questions raised here also provide the basis of my recently submitted PhD thesis, which deals with discussions about monasticism in the light of libraries and book production in the monasteries of Fulda and St Gall ('Regeln, Schrift, Correctio: Karolingerzeitliche Entwürfe von Mönchtum im Spiegel der Schriftproduktion aus St. Gallen und Fulda', University of Tübingen, December 2021).

9 See e.g. the councils of 813 (*Concilium Arelatense*, ed. by Werminghoff, 6, p. 251; *Concilium Cabillonense*, ed. by Werminghoff, 23, p. 278) or 802 (*Annales Laureshamenses*, ed. by Pertz, a 802, p. 39, printed also in Werminghoff, a. 802, p. 230), and, on the changing claims about monastic rules, the research of Albrecht Diem, e.g. 'The Carolingians and the "Regula Benedicti"', pp. 243–44; Diem and Rousseau, 'Monastic Rules', esp. pp. 184–86.

10 See Nichols, 'What is a Manuscript Culture?' and esp. the research of R. McKitterick, D. Ganz, W. Pohl, and M. de Jong, united e.g. in: de Rubeis and Pohl ed., *Le scritture dai monasteri*; with broad temporal discussion of medieval monasticism Heinzer, '"Exercitium scribendi"', pp. 107–15.

contribute to recent discourses of the intertwining of ideas between court and monasteries, even if it rejects a basic structure of norm versus practice. It argues, rather, for a more nuanced handling of different notions of reform.[11] In making my argument I will therefore highlight three distinct connotations of the latter term. (1) In making explicit mention of reform, its impacts, or of reform narratives, I refer to the problematic twentieth-century *Leitmotiv* of the *Anianische Reform* and its notion of monastic developments on the ground as a response to top-down initiatives. These scholarly interpretations are to be distinguished from (2) the documented initiatives of Carolingian rulers and elites to correct and improve all aspects of life in order to restore the *ordines* within the Christian *ecclesia*, and in so doing create a godly society. Incontestably, these plans entailed visions of a preferably uniform monastic way of life, which, however, did not necessarily represent Carolingian monasticism *per se*. (3) I will extrapolate from the manuscripts a picture of local actors who show a highly considered and self-conscious involvement with the *Regula Benedicti* and other traditions as a means of obtaining reliable guidance for the best possible monastic life. Their response to these demands is, however, evidently influenced by particular patterns of thinking which circulated among Carolingian elites. I refer to these as leading convictions of *correctio*, such as a shared trust in the written word to guarantee reliable codes of instruction. I will argue that tracing the independent ways in which local actors drew on concepts of *correctio* to tackle challenges associated with their own daily guidance offers a fruitful means not just to examine the interrelationship of court and monasteries from a fresh perspective, but also to apprehend distinctly Carolingian ways of being a monk.

Tracing the *Regula* in the Manuscript Production of the St Gall Scriptorium

The *Regula Benedicti* had already been introduced in St Gall in 747, according to the monastery's own ninth-century hagiographic tradition.[12] Even if this information is very suspect, thanks to the community's efforts to invent a pro-Carolingian past *post factum*, it was obviously possible during our investigation period to conceive of the monastery's identity in that way, while at the same time also acknowledging an Irish-Columbanian heritage, derived from its founder Gallus, a companion of the esteemed monastic father.[13] The abbey library still holds three of the monastery's manuscripts of the *Regula*

---

11 See recently on this widely debated problem Barrow, 'Definitions of Reform in the Church'; Howe, 'Reforming Reform' (with a focus on the work of Steven Vanderputten).
12 *Vita sancti Galli* (833–34) by Walahfrid Strabo, ed. by Krusch, II. 10, p. 320, ll. 1–15.
13 See Duft, 'Irische Einflüsse auf St Gallen und Alemannien', pp. 19–35; Meeder, *The Irish Scholarly Presence at St Gall*, esp. pp. 37–38, 110–11.

Benedicti written in the eighth and ninth centuries (St Gall, Stiftsbibliothek, cods. Sang. 916, Sang. 914, Sang. 915). The oldest, Cod. Sang. 916, dates from the turn of the ninth century and was most probably used for teaching and study, as it offers a parallel vernacular version between the lines, along with many physical traces of its having been used right from the start.[14] However, this chapter will focus mainly on the two later copies from the beginning and the middle of the ninth century. The community produced both for its own use, and thus they offer a chance to examine St Gall's attitude towards this central source of instruction from two manuscripts produced within thirty-five years of each other. This makes it possible to shine a spotlight on the monastery's interpretation of monastic life at two different periods and to compare the differences over time.

Cod. Sang. 914 and the Dilemma of the Correct Copy — Rethinking the Meaning of 'Impact of Reform'

The decision at St Gall to produce this copy of the *Regula Benedicti* dates to a period when monastic life was not only discussed prominently in the Aachen Reform Synods, but was also very much on the local agenda because of developments within the monastery. The abbey was at that time within the midst of upheaval on its way to becoming an independent monastic community. Particularly under Abbot Gozbert (816–37), freely elected after a long period of abbatial appointments by external institutions, St Gall was making increasing efforts to gain an independent profile and status separate from the bishopric of Constance. St Gall accordingly sought out closer contact with the court, finally putting its house under royal protection in 818 and gaining yet more independence from the episcopal claims on taxes and on the abbacy through the confirmation and re-issuing of enlarged royal charters in 833 and 854 respectively.[15] Undertaking to write a new copy of the Rule was one initiative among many that reflected the monastery's endeavour in these years to review the main aspects of monastic life — its constitution, its culture, its worship, and its economy. It is noteworthy within this spirit that the new manuscript Sang. 914 even embodied a different textual tradition from that of Sang. 916. Since the latter represents, as mentioned above, an intensely used manuscript for basic monastic teaching and learning, the wording of the new manuscript presumably even differed from the habitually internalized version known by St Gall's inhabitants.

---

14 Masser, *Regula Benedicti des Cod. 915*, pp. 19–20.
15 *Chartularium Sangallense*, ed. by Erhart, Heidecker, and Zeller, no. 219; no. 359, I, pp. 208–09, 334–35; *Urkundenbuch*, ed. by Wartmann, no. 434, II, pp. 52–54. See further Zettler, 'St Gallen als Bischofs- und als Königskloster', pp. 35–37; Duft, Gössi, and Vogler, *Die Abtei St Gallen*, pp. 22–23, 102–03.

In the following, I will show that it is possible to gain a nuanced understanding of the community's attributions to the *Regula Benedicti* at this decisive period of the monastery's development, if one analyses the actual procedures involved in the scriptorium's copying of the new version of the Rule (A), and of the texts with which it was combined (B).

(A) Copying Procedures — Discussing the Essence of a 'Correct' Written Code of Instruction

As set out in the introduction, the text of the Rule in Sang. 914 derives from Charlemagne's model text, supposedly a direct copy of the presumed autograph of Benedict of Nursia. When looking at the way this master copy is reproduced in the St Gall-Reichenau chain,[16] one can discover a lively contemporary debate on what precisely Carolingian monks understood to be a 'correct' code of instruction and on the role played by the fact that this was written down. Remarkably, the model is not simply copied, but Sang. 914 provides a meticulously exact text-critical apparatus which is so closely integrated into the text that it cannot be a later addition.[17] In the letter highlighted above, Tatto and Grimald explain the working processes on the apparatus in detail. Their remarks at this point serve as a kind of 'user manual', not only for the copy they made, but also for Sang. 914. Accordingly, as the first copyists in this transmission chain, both monks not only reproduced the the copy from Montecassino without the slightest divergence from its sense, syllables, or even individual letters of the alphabet ('sensibus et sillabis necnon etiam litteris [...] minime carentem'[18]), but they also compared it with every copy of the Rule they could get hold of. Then they marked with an *obelus* (÷) each word they were only able to find in the presumed autograph of Benedict of Nursia. Furthermore, they added in the margin those variants which they tracked down in other versions of the Rule, painstakingly indicating by a colon the word referred to in the text.[19] Comparing this description with the manuscript Sang. 914, the work seems perfectly executed in similar fashion, noting the minutest differences — even if they are only minor orthographical details, like substituting i/e or u/b.[20]

---

16 The codex is fully digitized, see the Manuscripts section of the Works Cited. Gilissen, 'Observations codicologiques' gives the most detailed codicological description.
17 Hanslik, 'Die Benediktinerregel im Wiener Kirchenvätercorpus', pp. 167–68; Bischoff, 'Die Handschrift', p. xiv.
18 Grimaldus et Tatto, *Epistula*, ed. by Dümmler, p. 302, ll. 8–9.
19 The *obelus* is normally combined with a colon/duo puncta/*metobelus* as a closing parenthesis; a typical passage looks as follows (St Gall, Stibi, Cod. Sang. 914, p. 6, l. 6): 'qui audit uerba mea ÷hęc: et facit ea:similabo' with the reference in the margin ':ad:', referring to the variant reading 'adsimilabo'. See also Figure 12.1.
20 A list of some variant readings can be found in Traube, *Textgeschichte der Regula S. Benedicti*, pp. 51–52, see also Note 28 of this chapter. From about halfway through the text the copyists become increasingly negligent about integrating the technical signs correctly.

Figure 12.1. *Regula Benedicti*, prologus with text-critical apparatus (ll. 6, 11, 13); St Gall, Stiftsbibliothek, Cod. Sang. 914, p. 6. Around 820. Reproduced with the permission of the Sankt Gallen Stiftsbibliothek.

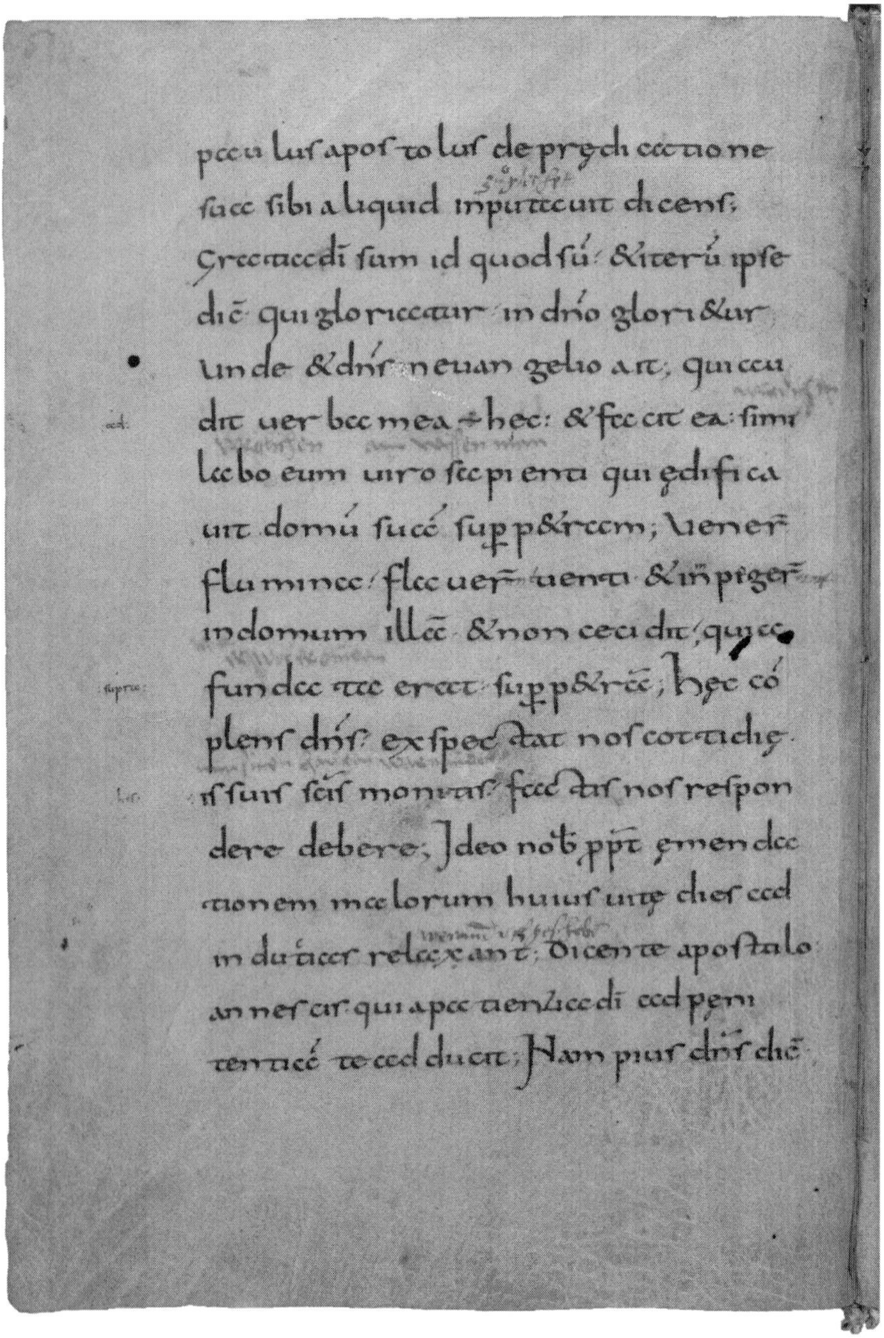

This eighty-folio work is therefore an exceptional example of the extreme precision with which Carolingian monastic scholars autonomously struggled to determine what the correct text was and how to transfer it into a reliable form for their respective audience. This is a testament to their trust in — and concern for — correct texts as codes of instruction for their lives. But what conclusions can be drawn from this about the understanding of monasticism at St Gall?

Where the text-critical apparatus of Sang. 914 has been taken into consideration by modern scholars, it has been understood in the mindset of *Anianische Reform* as a subversion of the court's intentions concerning monastic reform. The apparatus's critical approach towards the *Normalexemplar* would, it is maintained, have run contrary to the central efforts towards *unificatio*.[21] However, I would suggest rethinking this conclusion as a revealing example of how a narrow understanding of 'reform' in terms of court-driven initiative and their impact risks leading to a dead end. Further analysis can show instead that the copyists' implementation of that apparatus in Sang. 914 reveals, on the contrary, a complex, multi-layered, and carefully considered interweaving of ideas from both court and cloister, a picture which emerges if one re-interprets their attitude towards the text of the Benedictine Rule in the light of broader convictions about *correctio*.

Indeed, it is both the actual technical process of critical textual comparison, as well as careful consideration of the reliability of texts related to this work, which together reveal the sound grasp that the codex's creators had upon the intellectual developments of their time. The signs they use to annotate the text are not entirely of their own invention. Rather, they point to a familiarity with comparable examples of textual criticism circulating amongst the Carolingian elite. The particular technical signs originate in the scholarly practice of Alexandrine philological criticism and were most probably transferred to the Carolingian world via late antique Christian writings, particularly through Jerome's example of textual comparison in the Gallican Psalter and the related explanatory preface which he wrote.[22] In the libraries at Reichenau and St Gall it is possible to find individual examples from the ninth century of this chain of transmission, some containing explanatory texts about the technical signs, and others demonstrating their practical use in Bible manuscripts.[23] Recently Eva Steinová has also been able to point out other contemporary examples

---

21   For a prominent exponent of this view see Masser, *Kommentar zur lateinisch-althochdeutschen Benediktinerregel*, p. 39.

22   Bischoff, 'Die Handschrift', p. xiii; Traube, *Textgeschichte der Regula S. Benedicti*, pp. 65–66; Steinová, 'Notam superponere studui', pp. 122–26, 134–35; for Alexandrine textual criticism Jacob, 'Lire pour écrire', pp. 64–65.

23   Examples testifying to the local availability of knowledge about textual criticism are — for Reichenau — e.g. Karlsruhe, BLB, MS Aug. Perg. 38, fol. 11ᵛ (s. IX 2/4, Jerome's preface) and for St Gall the Alcuin-Bible: Stibi, Cod. Sang. 75, e.g. p. 463, further the florilegium about critical symbols, Stibi, Cod. Sang. 261, p. 155 and the *Psalterium Gallicanum*, Stibi,

which prove that textual comparisons similar to those made in Sang. 914 were common knowledge in ninth-century discourse communities — albeit not concerning the *Regula Benedicti* and seldom with a consistency comparable to that of our codex from the Lake Constance region.[24] This bigger picture confirms, therefore, the high-level participation of monks from Reichenau in this movement.

But it is not enough to interpret these annotations of the Rule merely in the light of a widespread *zeitgeist* which occasioned scholarly interest in the history of texts or monastic traditions.[25] The involvement with the written word goes deeper and shows a very complex interaction of different motifs of *correctio*. It is significant that all the other cases of sustained, systematized textual criticism presented by Steinová, and comparable in quality to Sang. 914, relate to revisions of the Bible. The Bible not only represented the most highly esteemed blueprint for all aspects of life at that time, but the meticulous revision of its spelling and grammar was also one of the chief concerns of Carolingian *correctio*. The reformers essentially linked the linguistic accuracy of 'correct' texts to their trustworthiness in ensuring a 'correct' *cultus divinus*.[26] In this context, the diligent and labour-intensive work on the Rule in Sang. 914 demonstrates more than just the fundamental importance which ninth-century monks attributed to reliable texts to use for their instruction. It also reveals a deep concern on the part of its scribes, and a genuine struggle to work out exactly what the 'correct' text might be. Sang. 914's illustration of the two competing influences throws up a striking tension, one which derives from the particular character of the Rule's textual tradition. Textual criticism led to contradictions between different and, in this case, competing key concepts about *correctio*. On the one hand, the whole history of Grimald and Tatto's mission illustrates how those in charge of a Rule codex placed their trust in a standard and in the authority they felt was best offered by the oldest and thus most authentic version of a text.[27] On the other hand, it turned out that this original version was written in the

---

Cod. Sang. 20, p. 4 with its practical application of the signs all over the codex, e.g. p. 32. Kaczynski, 'The Authority of the Fathers', p. 11 also underlines a particular interest in Jerome and the text of the Bible at St Gall.

24 Steinová, 'Notam superponere studui', pp. 126–38, esp. 135–38 for examples of minor revisions to Isidore, Gregory the Great, church law, and liturgy; similarly Traube, *Textgeschichte der Regula S. Benedicti*, pp. 65, 77.

25 E.g. Traube, *Textgeschichte der Regula S. Benedicti*, p. 76, who interprets the apparatus as a philological curiosity without any concrete purpose or consequences for practical living.

26 Key texts for that idea are the *Epistola de litteris colendis*, ed. by Stengel, pp. 246–54 or the *Admonitio generalis*, ed. by Mordek, Zechiel-Eckes, and Glatthaar, LXX, pp. 224; see further Angenendt, 'Libelli bene correcti', pp. 118, 129–35; Mostert, '…but they pray badly', esp. pp. 112–14, 122, 124; Steinová, 'Notam superponere studui', pp. 122–24.

27 A key principle, which was also revealed, e.g., when Charlemagne asked in Rome for an authoritative text of the *Sacramentarium Gregorianum*, cf. Mordek, 'Kirchenrechtliche Autoritäten', pp. 239–43.

colloquial Latin of the sixth century, which must have been rather unfamiliar or even disconcerting to Carolingian ears and eyes.[28] The text in the margins, by contrast, derives mostly from the so-called 'Gebrauchstext'/*textus receptus*, the grammatically normalized version of the *Regula Benedicti*, most widely used in eighth- and ninth-century monasteries.[29] It seems therefore that the monks were concerned at one and the same time about, firstly, the claim to authority of a text by virtue of its age and origins, and secondly, whether such a misspelled and grammatically peculiar text could really provide a trustworthy code of instruction for their lives.[30] The text-critical apparatus is in a sense a written manifestation of that uncertainty, and of the tension between competing rationales for authority.[31]

The recourse to an old system of technical signs which enables a simultaneous visualization of two diverging versions of a text was therefore an ingenious solution. Clearly, the copyist of Sang. 914 and its predecessors interpreted contemporary intellectual modes of thinking in an independent, productive, and self-confident manner, and used them in a highly skilled way both to tackle the problem they were confronted with and to reflect carefully on the best guidance for their monastic lives.

---

28 Disturbing examples are easy to figure out in comparison with later normalizations made in Carolingian Cod. Sang. 915: These are e.g. orthographical incongruences like the frequent interchanging of u/b, deriving from phonetic habits of late Latin, but sometimes giving rise to a divergent grammatical meaning, cf. Cod. Sang. 914, p. 4: 'Domine quis habitavit in tavernaculo tuo' (instead of 'Domine, quis habitabit in tabernaculo tuo'). On occasion grammar and syntax seem inadequate for ninth-century systematizations, cf. Cod. Sang. 914, p. 1 'ad te ergo nunc mihi sermo dirigitur', which Carolingian codices correct into 'meus sermo'. Other particularities are the use of 'de'+accusative or 'ci' instead of 'ti'. For more examples cf. Mohrmann, 'La latinité de saint Benoît', who also discusses the former controversy about the originality of the Rule's Latin, contradicting Paringer, 'Le manuscrit de Saint-Gall 914'.

29 Zelzer, 'Regulae monachorum', pp. 376–77, 379–81; Zelzer, 'Zur Stellung des Textus Receptus', pp. 205–18, 242–46. Zelzer's theory on the 'monastische Gebrauchstext' replaces Traube's older model of the *textus receptus* and its 'contaminations'.

30 Similarly (but on the question of the minor dissemination of Charlemagne's copy from Montecassino) Zelzer, 'Zur Stellung des Textus Receptus', pp. 214–15 and Traube, *Textgeschichte der Regula S. Benedicti*, pp. 73, 75–77. The hypothesis that the foreign Latin was a source of frustration or objections on the part of Carolingian monks is supported by Smaragdus of St Mihiel, who often feels the necessity to reconcile the readers of his commentary with the inconsistencies of the language offered by the *Normaltext*, see Smaragdus, *Expositio in regulam s. Benedicti*, ed. by Spannagel and Engelbert, I, p. 7 and Ponesse, 'Editorial Practice', pp. 78–84.

31 That the copyist of Sang. 914 kept visible the tension between the versions of the text seems even more curious when one bears in mind that earlier scholars like Chrodegang of Metz (and later generations of monks, see pp. 339–40) had no similar objections while working on the text of the Rule. Instead they compiled different variants to a completely new text which they esteemed the best, see e.g. Claussen, *The Reform of the Frankish Church*, pp. 156–57 and on Latin normalizations as 'emendation' by Carolingian scholars Ponesse, 'Editorial Practice', pp. 66–70; Mostert, '…but they pray badly', pp. 120–27.

As far as codex Sang. 914 is concerned, debates about monastic orientation vary in focus between the initiatives taken by the monks at Reichenau and their further development at St Gall. Concerning our local protagonists, it is regrettably impossible to say with certainty whether Grimald and Tatto themselves decided to make the complex collation of texts, or whether the initiative originated with the *bibliothecarius* of Reichenau, Reginbert. I tend to give the monks the credit for this decision, though: their letter shows repeatedly their eagerness to honour the librarian and to give him a most careful account of their working practices, yet they never give the slightest hint of any prior instruction from Reginbert about implementing a text-critical apparatus of any kind.[32] Furthermore, Tatto could easily be thought capable of such a demanding enterprise, as we can surmise from other sources. He ranked among the leading intellectuals of Reichenau, was educated and well connected at the court and to episcopal sees, and later became abbot of Kempten with the support of Louis the Pious. By contrast, we lack detailed information about Grimald, though we do know that he cannot be identified with Abbot Grimald of St Gall.[33]

However, while such thoughts about Reichenau must remain speculation, there are good reasons to think that the monastery of St Gall was sensitive to the different interpretations of a 'correct' code of instruction being presented side by side when it made its own copy of Reichenau's text. Examining the compilation of Sang. 914 allows us to see this more precisely.

(B) Compilation Procedures — Traces of the Rule's Integration into the Monastic Life at St Gall

The *Regula Benedicti* is not the only text in Sang. 914, but it forms the core of the manuscript's oldest part. The texts which the monks combined with the Rule in the first stage of their work provide particular insights into the original function of the new copy and its role in the monastic life of St Gall monastery. Thus the compilation proves that the brethren integrated their new manuscript into the very heart of the documentary corpus used for the community's guidance and the consolidation of its specific identity, instead of copying it merely out of scholarly concern and critical interest in the text of the Rule. The Rule was most probably first combined with an abbreviated

---

32 This silence about the apparatus also stands in contrast to Grimald and Tatto's emphasis — as seen in two separate mentions — of their understanding of Reginbert's wish to possess a copy of the supposed autograph, see Grimaldus et Tatto, *Epistula*, ed. by Dümmler, p. 302, ll. 7–9 and 21–22. Other scholars have attributed the initiative to Reginbert (e.g. Traube, *Textgeschichte der Regula S. Benedicti*, p. 77) or to Paulus Diaconus and the *Normalexemplar* itself (Mundó, 'Corrections "anciennes" et "modernes"', pp. 427–31; Vogüé and Neufville, 'Introduction', pp. 323–24).

33 See Geuenich, 'Beobachtungen zu Grimald von St Gallen', pp. 60–61; Schwarzmaier, 'Zur Frühgeschichte des Klosters Kempten', pp. 332–34.

martyrologium Hieronymianum, a version frequently ascribed for liturgical use,[34] and an early necrological list (Cod. Sang. 914, pp. 234–85), both written by the same hand as the *Regula Benedicti*.[35] It is a combination which usually indicates that a codex was intended for practical use in the *capitulum officii*, the main daily meeting of the whole community. There, the monks would listen to a corpus of texts designed to guide their moral development and reinforce the identity of their monastery, while also taking into account the affairs of the community and daily commemorating the saints as well as — increasingly during the ninth century — their deceased brethren.[36] The traces of such a practical application are even stronger for Sang. 914, in that the *martyrologium* and the calendar list contain entries of the names of deceased brothers, without doubt former monks from St Gall and dateable paleographically to the first half of the century. It was Joachim Wollasch who first pointed out that the Sang. 914 is consequently one of the earliest medieval proofs of a common monastic *memoria* and of a community's search for an appropriate way to conduct a regular corporate act of remembrance.[37]

The earliest stage of compilation therefore leads to two conclusions. Firstly, it shows that the monks of St Gall cared considerably about the version of the Rule produced by Grimald and Tatto, holding it in such high esteem that they integrated it into the heart of the community's daily assertion of its own identity. And it was this particular interpretation they chose, one which simultaneously depicts two concepts of authority about the best text by balancing the authority of the most original version with the authority of the correct text. Secondly, this seems to have been a conscious choice, and not simply a passive or unreflecting imitation of Reichenau's example. A comparative view of the three other codices still extant from Reichenau and St Gall, which also derive from the Grimald–Tatto version or Sang. 914, shows that only Sang. 914 copied the *Regula Benedicti* together with its text-critical

---

34 The martyrology belongs to the so-called group of the *Martyrologia Hieronymiana breviaria*, which Dubois, *Les martyrologes du moyen âge latin*, pp. 60–61 connects with high probability to liturgical usage. Its text is very similar to the martyrologies from Gellone (BNF, MS lat. 12048) and from Autun (Berlin, Staatsbibl., MS Phill. 1667), which Felice Lifshitz ascribes to the closer circles around Benedict of Aniane, cf. *Name of the Saint*, pp. 61–72, 121–22, 124–25; De Rossi and Duchesne, in *Martyrologium Hieronymianum*, AA SS Nov. II/1, p. xxx; Nov. II/2, p. xii.

35 Gilissen, 'Observations codicologiques', pp. 56–57, 67 and Bischoff, 'Die Handschrift', p. xii. The manuscript also contains other texts, some of them even from the context of the Aachen synods, but they cannot be assigned to the first phase of compilation with the same certainty as the martyrology. I reconsider the unity of this codex in much greater detail in my forthcoming PhD thesis (see Note 8).

36 *Regula sancti Benedicti abbatis Anianensis sive Collectio Capitularis*, ed. by Semmler, pp. 532–33 and St Gall, Stibi, Cod. Sang. 914, p. 189: 'LXVI. Ut ad capitulum primitus martyrologium legatur et dicatur uersus, deinde regula aut omelia qualibet legatur, deinde Tu autem domine dicatur'.

37 See Wollasch, 'Zu den Anfängen liturgischen Gedenkens', pp. 69–78.

apparatus.[38] This should not be taken for granted: the transmission of the manuscript reveals that ninth-century codices which combine the *Regula Benedicti* and martyrologies are quite flexible in their form. The two contemporary codices Karlsruhe, MS Aug. perg. 128 and Zürich, MS Rh. Hist. 28, both from Reichenau, are both linked, like Sang. 914, to the Grimald–Tatto text, but each is combined with a different martyrology. A similar picture arises from the general transmission of manuscripts containing copies of the court's Rule from Montecassino, where only three of seven manuscripts are bound together with martyrologies, whilst none of these comes from the same textual family as Sang. 914.[39] Apparently, these codices could be shaped within a general framework to meet the individual needs and tastes of a monastery. It is therefore not possible to show evidence for any automatic copying procedures, in respect of any supposed authority of the court's template, which may have influenced St Gall's reception of the *Regula* as presented in the Sang. 914.[40]

The testimony of the manuscript therefore also makes a case for a more nuanced understanding of the circulation of texts, formerly understood as a clear result of the court's reform initiatives. St Gall was certainly keen to show an openness to the ideas about monastic life pronounced at the court, since this would have been vital while trying to obtain royal protection during the decisive years of the community's aspirations towards independence from the bishopric of Constance. But the profound and unique processing of the text in Sang. 914 suggests first and foremost that the community acted out of concern for its content rather than merely as a reaction to external reform activities. St Gall (like the other monasteries represented by the textual witnesses of the court's Rule from Montecassino) critically examined how best to adapt the general stock of authoritative texts on guidance to produce the community's own best interpretation of what a godly life should be.

Cod. Sang. 915 and the *una regula* — Bringing Multiple Voices to the Fore

Looking at the second manuscript of the *Regula Benedicti*, it is possible to gain a comparative perspective over time on the arguments and concerns

---

38 St Gall, Stibi, Cod. Sang. 915 (St Gall, approximately 850); Karlsruhe, BLB, MS Aug. perg. 128 (Reichenau/St Gall, s. ɪx/2); Zürich, Zentralbibl., MS Rh. Hist. 28 (Reichenau, s. ɪx end), cf. Hanslik, 'Praefatio', pp. xxxiii–xxxiv.

39 Setting aside the tradition of Benedict's *Codex Regularum* and Smaragdus's *Commentary on the Rule*, these are: Munich, BSB, MS Clm 19408; Vienna, ÖNB, MS 2232; Augsburg, Ordinariatsbibl., MS 1; Montecassino, Archivio dell'Abbazia, MS Cass. 175 and the Reichenau manuscripts Zürich, Zentralbibl., MS Rh. Hist. 28 and Karlsruhe, BLB, MS Aug. Perg. 128, both of which are nonetheless closely related to Sang. 914.

40 Felix Heinzer has come to a similar conclusion concerning sacramentaries, see 'Exercitium scribendi', pp. 112–13.

raised in local debates about monastic life. With Sang. 915 (around 850), the scriptorium decided to create a new Rule copy approximately a generation apart, apparently with a similar purpose to Sang. 914.

(A) Copying Procedures — A Monastery's Needs for Readability and Understanding

The *Regula Benedicti* of Sang. 915 now forms the central part of a chapter book from the eleventh century, but its ancient core around the Rule can be dated reliably back to the Carolingian monastery.[41] In comparison to Sang. 914, one notices immediately the careful and clear layout of the text. The codex is written in a pure Caroline minuscule with very few abbreviations. It is characterized by wide spacings and clear capital letters used in the body of the text to mark new sentences and units of meaning.[42] It further shows efforts towards systematic punctuation, partly using *positurae* symbols, which are, according to Parkes, often indicators of a rule's being used for readings in Chapter.[43]

The editor of the codex's version of the *Regula Benedicti*, Achim Masser, has argued in a similar vein that, in view of its overall layout, Sang. 915 must originally have been written for oral presentation.[44] The point is significant, because the context in which rules were read out would have been the assembly at *capitulum officii*. If one accepts Masser's argument, then codex 915 would represent a substitution or at least a substantial complement to Sang. 914, a new text which the community saw as necessary.[45] It is difficult to prove with certainty, though, that St Gall intended this new copy for use in that way. The alternating punctuation was added by multiple hands, almost impossible to date, and only a few can be traced back with certainty to the first copyist.[46]

---

41 A detailed description of the manuscript is offered by Autenrieth, 'Der Codex Sangallensis 915'. The precise dating of the copy to between 846 and 865, given by Schaab, *Mönch in Sankt Gallen*, p. 26, is not convincing. Palaeographical arguments point to the beginning of the second half of the century.

42 See e.g. St Gall, Stibi, Cod. Sang. 915, pp. 42 or 60.

43 Parkes, *Pause and Effect*, pp. 37–38, 193, 301–07; Masser, *Regula Benedicti des Cod. 915*, p. 26.

44 See Masser, *Regula Benedicti des Cod. 915*, pp. 17–21, 26.

45 The codicological evidence supports the idea of a substitution: St Gall, Stibi, Cod. Sang. 914 has been intensively reworked around the middle of the ninth century, i.e. at the time when the Rule of Sang. 915 was presumably produced, see Gilissen, 'Observations codicologiques', pp. 62–64 and Bischoff, 'Die Handschrift', p. xii (dating the supplements earlier than Gilissen does). Since the scriptorium only added texts related to the Aachen reforms (St Gall, Stibi, Cod. Sang. 914, pp. 197–202/33) at this stage, it seems to have transformed the manuscript from the former chapter book into a predominantly historical reform compendium.

46 See e.g. St Gall, Stibi, Cod. Sang. 915, p. 95 where some of the *punctus* marking the end of a *sententia* (ll. 13, 15, 20) or minor pauses (ll. 18, 21) might be by the first hand, while older points placed as media distinction at a midway height are later corrected into *punctus elevatus* (ll. 10, 12). Dating is especially complicated: Bruckner emphasizes that a simpler system scaling back on points for minor pauses gained fashion again in St Gall in the second half of

Figure 12.2. *Regula Benedicti*, first page of the prestigious new copy for the community; St Gall, Stiftsbibliothek, Cod. Sang. 915, p. 27. Middle of the ninth century. Reproduced with the permission of the Sankt Gallen Stiftsbibliothek.

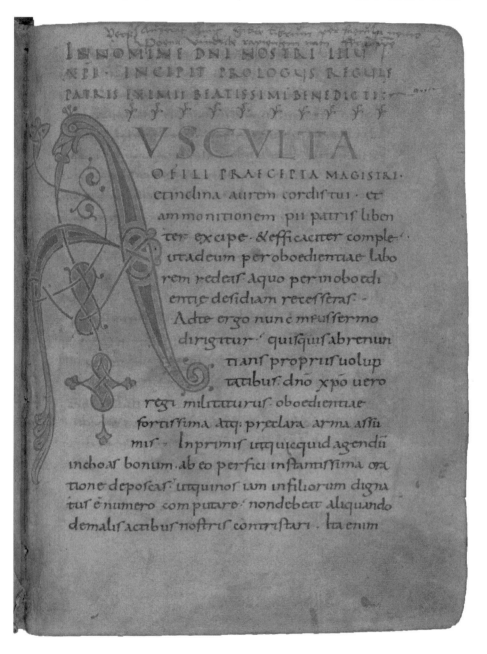

The style is nevertheless similar to, for example, the so-called Hartmut Bibles, a series of ambitious new manuscripts of the entire text of the Bible, which were most certainly meant to be read out in a liturgical context.[47] At the very least, the remarkable decoration of the codex in form of elaborate initial letters suggests that this copy was intended to occupy an esteemed position in the textual corpus of the monastery.[48] Its prominence is further confirmed by historic developments, since in the eleventh century it was this version of the *Regula Benedicti* which was accorded the status of forming the nucleus of St Gall's chapter book.[49]

Thus the scriptorium once again produced a manuscript with strategic aspirations, suitable to serve as a prestigious daily reference text for a flourishing monastic community. And for a new generation of St Gall monks accustomed to the standards of an advanced Caroline minuscule, the new text was presumably easier to decipher than the heavily abbreviated version of the Sang. 914 codex, written in Alemannic minuscule and interrupted by its distracting apparatus. A further observation is even more remarkable. In codex 915, the community no longer opted for a version of the authoritative autograph presumed to be that of Benedict of Nursia. Instead the monks chose to have a text in the contemporary Latin of the ninth century, by compiling it themselves from the marginal variants found in Sang. 914.[50] It seems that by the time of Sang. 915 the need for an understandable and readable version of the Rule for the monastery's daily service had gained supremacy over earlier considerations about fidelity to the letter of the text and the reliability of the *urtext* as setting a standard. I suggest that this allows at least a small glimpse of the negotiation process and of the different characters participating in that negotiation, one which goes beyond the narrow boundaries of intellectual discourse and ideologies of improvement. The modernized Latin of the chosen text and the manuscript's clear layout seem to derive from the very practical needs, experiences, and demands of the wider collective. The requirement for an up-to-date text suitable for

---

the ninth century, which is around the period of interest concerning Sang. 915, cf. Bruckner, *Scriptoria medii aevi Helvetica*, III/2, p. 27; however, he can also date the first systematic revisions of several St Gall manuscripts concerning accentuation to between the middle and the second half of the ninth century (*Scriptoria medii aevi Helvetica*, III/1, p. 52) — the monastery was therefore at least aware of debate around accents and oral presentation at the time the codex was created.

47 See Schaab, 'Bibeltext und Schriftstudium in St Gallen', pp. 123–24 and from the volumes of the Hartmut Bible especially the manuscripts St Gall, Stibi, Cod. Sang. 81 and Cod. Sang. 83, in which the *positurae* symbols already replace in part the former system of scaled points.
48 See St Gall, Stibi, Cod. Sang. 915, p. 27 (Figure 12.2, also fully digitized, see the Manuscripts section of the Works Cited); Euw, *Die St Galler Buchkunst*, I, pp. 354–55. Cohen, 'Book Production' also interprets the illuminations of Sang. 915 as evidence for the enhancement of the text's status.
49 See Authenrieth, 'Der Codex Sangallensis 915', esp. pp. 42–43, 46–47, 50.
50 Hanslik, 'Praefatio', p. xxxiii and Vogüé and Neufville, 'Introduction', p. 341 n. 75.

use as a daily guide for monastic life seems to reflect a concern of the whole community beyond merely the elite, i.e. beyond the views of the group whose direct influence on the shape of a monastery's identity are those most predominantly accessible through most the sources.

The manuscripts of the Rule in St Gall turn out to be an object of study in which very practical claims compete with carefully elaborated reflections on the normative power of the correct text, as seen in Sang. 914. The everyday needs and habits of the community come to light and gain weight as an autonomous element influencing St Gall's particular understanding of monasticism. This is further reflected in the continued engagement in the monastery with the text of the *Regula Benedicti*. It is possible to trace some hands from the following decades which systematically correct parts of the Latin text of the Rule's interlinear version, in the oldest codex 916, mentioned earlier. Interestingly, they do not adjust it according to the wording of the authoritative Benedict autograph of Sang. 914, but according to the new copy of Sang. 915.[51] It seems therefore that in the monastery a certain interpretation of the text of the Rule had gained supremacy, underpinned by an authority deriving mainly from habit — something of which the monks might not even have been aware, since this convention was probably formed by listening day in, day out to the particular version of the Rule used for the *capitulum officii*.

(B) Compilation Procedures — Tracing the una regula *and Tracing a* Corpus regularum

The combination of texts added to the *Regula Benedicti* in the ninth-century layer of Sang. 915 reveals one further insight. The manuscript's oldest section around the Rule already has added to it, in a contemporary hand and in a very similar style, five other monastic rules: the 'Regula Augustini' (i.e. the *Praeceptum*), the *Regula Pauli et Stephani* and three from the Columbanian tradition, the *Regula Columbani*, his *Sermo V* (p. 167 'epistula sancti Columbani'), and the *Regula coenobialis*.[52] The *Regula Benedicti* thus forms part of a broader collection of monastic texts from which the community seems to have drawn inspiration for its understanding of what it meant to be a monk.

Hence, codex 915 offers a different picture of Carolingian monasticism from that depicted by the normative sources. The *Regula Benedicti* plays a prominent role in the manuscript, but its role differs from that proclaimed by the Aachen synods which emphasized its exclusive status as the *una regula*, the *sole* norm for monastic life.

---

51 At length: Masser, *Die lateinisch-althochdeutsche Benediktinerregel*, pp. 51–60.
52 St Gall, Stibi, Cod. Sang. 915, pp. 111–76; the *Regula coenobialis* is not completely transmitted, as a tenth-century hand finishes the text from page 176 onwards. As this change coincides with a change of quire, it is possible that the last quire of the ninth-century copy was lost or damaged and substituted in the tenth century. We cannot therefore exclude with certainty the notion that the ninth-century corpus of rules was once even more comprehensive.

I find it inadequate, however, to explain this phenomenon primarily as resulting from a discrepancy between norms and practice, and thus as a 'relapse' to pre-reform practices, as norm-centred reform narratives do.[53] Viewing the phenomenon instead from the local perspective and reading it as autonomous evidence for a form of Carolingian monasticism, codex Sang. 915 reveals a monastery at the pinnacle of the intellectual developments of its time. Apparently, collections of older monastic rules very similar to Sang. 915 were circulating more and more in this period — St Gall was thus neither refusing to reform, nor taking its own path.[54] It thus took part in a seemingly normal phenomenon and was perhaps even one of its driving forces, as the manuscript dissemination suggests. This shows that there are at least twenty-three textual witnesses from the ninth to the fifteenth centuries (though predominantly prior to the thirteenth century), arranged around a stable body of exactly the same rules partly found in Sang. 915, often in company with the *Regula Basilii* and the *Regula quattuor patrum*.[55] The evidence suggests that this corpus (or parts of it) have at least three different strands of circulation: one strand around Tours and Angers (possibly deriving from reform circles at the court); one highly influential strand around St Gall, Reichenau, and Münsterschwarzach; and an Italian strand which probably shares its archetype with the East Frankish strand, but which is only traceable in manuscripts from the eleventh century onwards. The five witnesses from the ninth century belong to the first two groups.[56] St Gall can therefore be shown to be playing an integral part in a communications network through which Carolingian monasteries participated in an active and multi-centred exchange of monastic traditions throughout the whole of the ninth century.[57] Since the network in this case relied fundamentally on texts as the medium for this transfer of knowledge, I would argue in favour of an explanation which understands this recourse to the potential of the written word as the real key to understanding the very

---

[53] For interpretations in the light of a 'failure' of reform see e.g. Hosoe, 'Regulae and Reform', pp. 55–59 and (with a broader openness to intrinsic achievements) 308–10. Emphasizing more nuance on the phenomenon: Kottje, 'Einheit und Vielfalt', pp. 341, 331–35; McKitterick, *The Frankish Kingdoms*, pp. 117–24.

[54] The coherence of these rules as a stable corpus was first described in detail by Mundó, 'I "Corpora" e i "Codices regularum"', pp. 487–88, 493–99 and Vilanova, *Regula Pauli et Stephani*, pp. 34–45; now: Engelbert, *Der Codex regularum des Benedikt von Aniane*, pp. 18–20.

[55] See especially the valuable table at Vilanova, *Regula Pauli et Stephani*, pp. 34, further 20–45 (s. VIII/IX: five MSS including Benedict's *Codex Regularum*; s. XI: one MSS; s. XII: eight MSS; later: nine MSS); Verheijen, *La règle de saint Augustin*, I, pp. 183–85 and II, pp. 214–15; Walker, *Sancti Columbani Opera*, pp. xxxix–lii, lxxv–lxxviii; Lapidge, 'Columbanus Luxoviensis et Bobbiensis Abb.', pp. 212–20.

[56] See Vilanova, *Regula Pauli et Stephani*, pp. 38–45, 51, 27–28; Verheijen, *La règle de saint Augustin*, I, pp. 183–95, 136, 153.

[57] Engelbert also labels the Lake Constance monasteries as 'Relaisstationen' ('radio repeaters', p. 337) for early traditions concerning rules, see 'Die Lambacher Handschrift CmL XXXI', pp. 337–39; Mundó, 'I "Corpora" e i "Codices regularum"', pp. 494, 501.

Carolingian way of being a monk.[58] Although scholarship on rule collections has tried to describe them as an overarching phenomenon dating back to the origins of the first of the rules concerned, i.e. the sixth and seventh centuries,[59] the evidence from manuscript transmission suggests a different scenario. It is only around 800 that the respective corpus of rules is traceable in codices, and its increasing diffusion at that time, which has to be amplified by at least four more similar collections (evidenced by contemporaneous library catalogues), speaks for a new and genuinely self-propelling dynamic.[60] Since so many monastic centres copied rules, and since they also judged written texts to be the most appropriate way to rework their heritage in order to secure guidance for their monastic way of life, it seems reasonable to consider this phenomenon as a distinct expression of ninth-century monasticism, born out of a close intertwining with the overarching (and thus also local) discourses of *correctio*, rather than a renegade process undertaken by monks opposed to the key principles of contemporary monasticism — the latter a view central to earlier historiographical notions of reform.

As far as St Gall is concerned, the corpus of rules has been shown above to be more than simple reading material or a study tool for the monastery's elite.[61] Consideration of layout has pointed to the integration of codex 915 into the very heart of the monastery's body of texts which was intended to underpin the monks' daily way of life and to maintain the community's identity. Each of the five texts around the Rule is prepared in that same way, with clearly discernible units and alternating punctuation as described for the *Regula Benedicti*. Seen in this context, the manuscript reveals expectations of the texts different from those at comparable monastic centres. Scholarship

---

58 With a similar emphasis, Raaijmakers, *The Making of the Monastic Community of Fulda*, pp. 197–98; Diem and Rousseau, 'Monastic Rules', pp. 163, 180–81, 184–88.
59 Mundó, 'I "Corpora" e i "Codices regularum"', pp. 478–79, 487–88, 493–94 and Engelbert, *Der Codex Regularum des Benedikt von Aniane*, p. 18. There are indeed two rule collections at Corbie with integral parts dated to the sixth and seventh centuries, but Mundó's other ascriptions only build on his very singular theory which is weakly founded on the core text of each collection and outdated ideas about a 'century of mixed rules'.
60 The oldest witness is Lambach, Benediktinerstift, MS Cml XXXI (s. IX in.). Vilanova also tends to date the major archetypes of Sang. 915's rule collection 'a finals des s. viii', see *Regula Pauli et Stephani*, pp. 44–45, 32–33; Engelbert, 'Die Lambacher Handschrift Cml XXXI', pp. 336–39; Lehmann ed., *Mittelalterliche Bibliothekskataloge*, I, pp. 77, 84, 251. Other ascetic collections are traceable in like fashion in Carolingian libraries, cf. e.g. McKitterick, *The Frankish Kingdoms*, pp. 121 and of course the *Codex Regularum* of Benedict of Aniane, which might, however, when faced with the spread of the phenomenon, not be as singular and innovative as Ardo's *Vita Benedicti Anianensis* emphasizes, see among others Engelbert, *Der Codex Regularum des Benedikt von Aniane*, pp. 22–24.
61 Scholarship often opts for that explanation to reconcile evidence from the Carolingian libraries with ideas about *una regula*, see e.g. McKitterick, *The Frankish Kingdoms*, pp. 121–22; Choy, 'The Deposit of Monastic Faith', p. 78, who interprets the purpose of the collection Lambach, Benediktinerstift, MS Cml XXXI (see Note 60 above) as 'primarily concerned with the textual transmission of monastic rules' and Hosoe, 'Regulae and Reform', pp. 56–58.

about the community at Fulda, for example, tends to emphasize that the community aimed to accumulate all the accessible written knowledge at the time about monasticism in order to provide a comprehensive library as an ideal source of study.[62] The compilation chosen for Sang. 915 not only fulfils a purpose beyond this sort of scholarly interest, in its use for official readings to the community. It also bears traces of a deliberate and considered choice of rules, even if they were taken from one fixed corpus. In contrast to any other documents in its particular strand of transmission, and to other possible models available according to St Gall's library catalogue, the codex *directly* places the *Praeceptum* and the *Regula Pauli et Stephani* after the *Regula Benedicti* and therefore relegates the Columbanian tradition down from second position after the *Regula Benedicti* or Basil, the position it usually holds among the collections.[63] Taking into account that no other document known from the ninth century changed that order of the rules, one should consider that there was a deliberate decision behind this arrangement. Perhaps St Gall perceived the additional moral and spiritual foundation which both rules from the Roman church tradition offered, concerning personal relations within the community (*Praeceptum*) and inner dispositions during the divine offices (*Regula Pauli et Stephani*), as the first complements needed to perfect the *Regula Benedicti*'s instructions about behaviour.[64] The rearrangement might also have been aimed at bundling up the Columban tradition within the collection, uniting the *Rule* with the *Sermo* and the *Regula coenobialis*. It is nevertheless remarkable that only the monastery named after Gallus, of all possible monasteries, does not seem to prioritize the Columbanian tradition as a matter of principle — a tradition to which it is always thought to adhere naturally as a consequence of its founder's Columbanian roots.

Debating the Rule and Debating the *una regula* — Conclusions

I would like to conclude with three observations which link the considerations gained from local debates back to this volume's key questions of what monks are, and how they perceived and engaged with the *Regula Benedicti*, seen as the pivotal criterion of distinction between monks and canons.

First, we should stress that the example of St Gall in fact indicates a fundamental consideration for the *Regula Benedicti* in the actual conduct

---

62 Schrimpf ed., *Mittelalterliche Bücherverzeichnisse des Klosters Fulda*, pp. 57–75; Raaijmakers, *The Making of the Monastic Community of Fulda*, pp. 195–98.

63 See Vilanova, *Regula Pauli et Stephani*, table p. 34 and Lehmann ed., *Mittelalterliche Bibliothekskataloge*, I, pp. 77, 251.

64 *Praeceptum*, ed. by Verheijen, I. 1–II. 4, III. 2–4, V. 1–2, VI, pp. 417–22, 428–30, 433–35 [chapter numbers according to the edition, which differ from those of Sang. 915]; *Regula Pauli et Stephani*, ed. by Vilanova, V–IX, XII–XIV, XXXVII, XLI, pp. 110–14.

of Carolingian monasteries, and not only in the normative discussions distinguishing religious *ordines*. St Gall granted the Rule a prominent role for its daily interpretation of godly life and for the community's central knowledge on which it based its monastic identity. The very considered and sophisticated struggle for the correct template, mirrored in Sang. 914, has shown that local actors reflected independently and with a deep commitment to the *Regula Benedicti*. They showed great expertise in elucidating its 'correct version', which was supposed to guarantee the best instructive qualities for being a good monk. The motivations behind these efforts, however, have revealed themselves as more complex than a simple adaptation to the reform initiatives being discussed at the court. Aiming for royal protection, St Gall also had its own political reasons for expressing an openness to the court's ideas about monastic life; in addition, the monastery's attitude towards the rule manuscripts mirrors a true concern for the *Regula Benedicti* arising out of spiritual conviction.

Second, the focus on how monasteries worked concretely with core text of their time allows remarkable insights into the fact that the Rule itself — and thus the fundamental distinction between monks and canons both in seminal sources and in this volume — remained a matter of discussion in monastic communities, particularly with regard to the question of what it meant to observe it correctly or what 'observance' itself meant. Sang. 914 and 915 presented a selection of competing and partly contradicting rationales and requirements to consider concerning the Rule's qualities as a measure of monastic life, such as the claims of authority by age, and therefore the implied authenticity of a text or the extent to which its language was correct and could be understood by the majority of the monks. The monastery's decision about which of these claims guaranteed the most reliable version of the *Regula* was crucial, as a misdemeanour provoked by a misunderstanding of a text might endanger the community's progress in its pursuit of a life pleasing to God. This multiplicity of arguments and their re-evaluation made visible in the new creation of Sang. 915 also prove that St Gall monks understood their *vita secundum regulam* as more than a simple 'metaphor'.[65] On the contrary, as never before in the history of monasticism, the very concrete textual manifestation of the Rule gained an importance as a factor of trust and as a guarantee of securing the pursuit of an exemplary monastic life.[66] These expectations towards written codes of conduct should therefore be considered as one of the most fundamental features of the specific manifestations of monasticisms in Carolingian times.[67]

---

65 An interpretation brought forward by Semmler, 'Karl der Große und das fränkische Mönchtum', p. 220; also discussed critically by Diem, 'The Carolingians and the "Regula Benedicti"', p. 246.
66 See also Diem, 'Inventing the Holy Rule', pp. 53–58, 65–72.
67 Cf. Vanderputten, *Medieval Monasticisms*, esp. pp. 3–4; Choy, 'The Deposit of Monastic Faith', esp. pp. 74–75; Sullivan, 'What Was Carolingian Monasticism?', pp. 251–55, 285–87.

Thirdly, this peek into the scriptorium has once more underlined the necessity to revisit the normative assumptions which modern scholarship has projected onto ninth-century monasticism with regard to the idea of the *una regula*. The dynamic production of rule collections, as has been shown for Sang. 915, directly links this issue to the attributions of authority which Carolingian monks ascribed to individual monastic rules. On that front, my chapter can of course only contribute the limited perspective of its sources to this long-running debate about the development of normative observance in monasticism, though the sources in question are certainly central for that period.[68] With regard to the manuscript evidence of Sang. 915, living according to the Rule obviously did not mean understanding the *Regula Benedicti* in modern legalistic terms as an exclusive law, nor did it mean understanding monastic existence in terms of being Benedictine. If monasteries actively produced rule collections as a genuine Carolingian phenomenon and inserted them into the heart of their normative repertoire for readings in Chapter, the contemporary notion of normative observance towards the Benedictine Rule might never have implied claiming it as exclusive (neither does the Rule itself[69]). A quick examination of St Gall's library catalogue, contemporary with the copy of the rules in Sang. 915, is helpful in approaching these notions of normativity: when the monks of St Gall organized their knowledge, they defined *regul[ae] sanctorum patrum* as a literary group in its own right, but placed it directly next to the categories 'De vita [...]' and 'De virtutibus seu passionibus' of monastic fathers and holy people, and at a junction between exegetical literature concerning the Bible and a later part of the catalogue about administrative texts, liturgy, and schoolbooks.[70] Rules rank therefore among the texts which offer spiritual instruction by embodying, just like the saints, role models that interpreted God's will for their life in an exemplary manner. With these godly interpretations, the texts are comparable to the exegetical literature which was meant to explain the Bible as the most important source of instruction. Again, it is significant that Carolingian monks judged the medium of texts as the most appropriate way to give these excellent interpretations of godly life an unambiguous and reliably accessible form for daily instruction by collective or individual reading, and to maintain them for posterity. Other rules could therefore complement the *Regula Benedicti* in a community's individual

---

68 In Carolingian scholarship, the question has recently been brought up again by Albrecht Diem ('The Carolingians and the "Regula Benedicti"', esp. p. 245; Diem and Rousseau, 'The Development of Monastic Rules') and Christoph Dartmann (among others, 'Normative Schriftlichkeit im früheren Mittelalter', pp. 26–46), but is discussed similarly for other medieval centuries as well as for Carolingian norms in general, see among others Andenna and Melville ed., *Regulae — Consuetudines — Statuta*; Althoff, 'Geltungsansprüche schriftlich fixierter Normen'; Patzold, 'Normen im Buch'.
69 *Regula Benedicti*, ed. by Hanslik, 73, pp. 179–81.
70 Lehmann ed., *Mittelalterliche Bibliothekskataloge*, I, pp. 75–80; St Gall, Stibi, Cod. Sang. 728, pp. 13–16.

selection of exemplary codes of conduct without any implementation of a *legal* observance according to ninth-century mindsets. Compared to other conceptions of monasticism, the Carolingian idea of being a monk is therefore less that of a 'Benedictine monasticism' than a monasticism orientated towards written rules, which Carolingian monks trusted to guide their spiritual growth, of which the *Regula Benedicti* seemed the most perfect example.

Works Cited

Manuscripts

Augsburg, Ordinariatsbibliothek, MS 1
Berlin, Staatsbibliothek, MS Phill. 1667
Karlsruhe, Badische Landesbibliothek, MS Aug. perg. 38
———, MS Aug. perg. 128
Lambach, Benediktinerstift, MS Cml XXXI
Montecassino, Archivio dell'Abbazia, MS Cass. 175
Munich, Bayerische Staatsbibliothek, MS Clm 19408
———, MS Clm 28118
Paris, Bibliothèque nationale de France, MS fonds latin 12048
St Gall, Stiftsbibliothek, Cod. Sang. 20
———, Cod. Sang. 75
———, Cod. Sang. 81
———, Cod. Sang. 83
———, Cod. Sang. 261
———, Cod. Sang. 728
———, Cod. Sang. 914 <http://www.e-codices.unifr.ch/de/list/one/csg/0914> [accessed 8 September 2021]
———, Cod. Sang. 915 <http://www.e-codices.unifr.ch/de/csg/0915/27> [accessed 8 September 2021]
———, Cod. Sang. 916
Vienna, Österreichische Nationalbibliothek, MS 2232
Zürich, Zentralbibliothek, MS Rh. Hist. 28

Primary Sources

Die Admonitio Generalis Karls des Großen, ed. by Hubert Mordek, Klaus Zechiel-Eckes, and Michael Glatthaar, in *Monumenta Germaniae Historica: Fontes iuris germanici antiqui in usum scholarum separatim editi*, XVI (Hannover: Hahn, 2012)

Annales Laureshamenses, ed. by Georg Heinrich Pertz, in *Annales et Chronica Aevi Carolini*, Monumenta Germaniae Historica: Scriptores, I (Hannover: Hahn, 1826), pp. 22–39

Benedicti Regula, ed. by Rudolf Hanslik, Corpus Scriptorum Ecclesiasticorum Latinorum, 75, 2nd rev. edn (Leipzig: Hoelder-Pichler-Tempsky, 1977)

Chartularium Sangallense, vol. 1: *700–840*, ed. by Peter Erhart in cooperation with Karl Heidecker and Bernhard Zeller (St Gall: Herausgeber- und Verlagsgemeinschaft Chartularium Sangallense, 2013)

Concilium Arelatense a. 813, ed. by Albert Werminghoff, in *Monumenta Germaniae Historica: Concilia*, II. 1, *Concilia aevi Karolini*, 1 (Hannover: Hahn, 1906), no. 34, pp. 248–53

Concilium Cabillonense a. 813, ed. by Albert Werminghoff, in *Monumenta Germaniae Historica: Concilia*, II. 1, *Concilia aevi Karolini*, 1 (Hannover: Hahn, 1906), no. 37, pp. 273–85

Epistola de litteris colendis, ed. by Edmund E. Stengel, in *Urkundenbuch des Klosters Fulda*, vol. 1: *Die Zeit der Äbte Sturmi und Baugulf*, Veröffentlichungen der Historischen Kommission für Hessen und Waldeck, 10 (Marburg: Elwert, 1958), pp. 246–54

Grimaldus et Tatto, *Epistula*, ed. by Ernst Dümmler, *Monumenta Germaniae Historica: Epistolae*, V (Berlin: Weidmann, 1899), pp. 301–02

Lehmann, Paul, ed., *Mittelalterliche Bibliothekskataloge Deutschlands und der Schweiz*, vol. 1: *Die Bistümer Konstanz und Chur*, 2nd edn (Munich: Beck, 1969)

Martyrologium Hieronymianum et commentarius, in *Acta Sanctorum, Nov II/1–II/2*, ed. by Giovanni Battista de Rossi and Louis Duchesne (Brussels: Apud Socios Bollandianos, 1894, 1931)

Praeceptum/Regula Augustini, ed. by Luc Verheijen, in *La règle de saint Augustin*, vol. 1 (Paris: Etudes Augustiniennes, 1967), pp. 417–37

Regula sancti Benedicti abbatis Anianensis sive Collectio Capitularis, ed. by Josef Semmler, in *Corpus Consuetudinum Monasticarum*, vol. 1: *Initia Consuetudinis Benedictinae: Consuetudines saeculi octavi et noni* (Siegburg: Schmitt, 1963), pp. 502–36

Regula Pauli et Stephani: Edició crítica i comentari, ed. by Dom J. Evangelista M. Vilanova, Scripta et documenta, 11 (Monteserrat: Abadia de Monteserrat, 1959)

Smaragdus of Saint-Mihiel, *Expositio in regulam s. Benedicti*, ed. by Alfred Spannagel and Pius Engelbert, *Corpus Consuetudinum Monasticarum*, vol. 8 (Siegburg: Respublica, 1974)

Urkundenbuch der Abtei Sanct Gallen, vol. 2: *840–920*, ed. by Hermann Wartmann (Zürich: Antiquarische Gesellschaft/S. Höhr 1866)

Walahfrid Strabo, *Vita sancti Galli*, ed. by Bruno Krusch, in *Monumenta Germaniae Historica: Scriptores rerum Merovingicarum*, IV, *Passiones vitaeque sanctorum aevi Merovingici*, II (Hannover: Hahn, 1902), pp. 280–337

Secondary Works

Althoff, Gerd, 'Geltungsansprüche schriftlich fixierter Normen und "ungeschriebener Gesetze" im Mittelalter', *Frühmittelalterliche Studien*, 41 (2007), 277–79

Andenna, Cristina, and Gert Melville, *Regulae — Consuetudines — Statuta: Studi sulle fonti normative degli ordini religiosi nei secoli centrali del Medioevo; Atti del [...] Seminario Internazionale di Studio (26–27 ottobre 2002, 23–24 maggio 2003)*, Vita religiosa, 12 (Münster: LIT, 2005)

Angenendt, Arnold, '"Libelli bene correcti": Der richtige Kult als ein Motiv der karolingischen Reform', in *Das Buch als magisches und als Repräsentationsobjekt*, ed. by Peter Ganz, Wolfenbütteler Mittelalter-Studien, 5 (Wiesbaden: Harrassowitz, 1992), pp. 117–36

Autenrieth, Johanne, 'Der Codex Sangallensis 915: Ein Beitrag zur Erforschung der Kapitelofiziumsbücher', in *Landesgeschichte und Geistesgeschichte: Festschrift für Otto Herding zum 65. Geburtstag*, ed. by Kaspar Elm, Eberhard Gönner, and Eugen Hillenbrand (Stuttgart: Kohlhammer, 1977), pp. 42–55

Barrow, Julia, 'Developing Definitions of Reform in the Church in the Ninth and Tenth Centuries', in *Italy and Early Medieval Europe: Papers for Chris Wickham*, ed. by Ross Balzaretti, Julia Barrow, and Patricia Skinner (Oxford: Oxford University Press, 2018), pp. 501–11

Bischoff, Bernhard, 'Die Handschrift', in *Regula Benedicti de codice 914 in bibliotheca monasterii S. Galli servato [...] quam simillime expressa*, ed. by Benedikt Probst (St Ottilien: EOS, 1983), pp. viii–xiv

Bruckner, Albert, *Scriptoria medii aevi Helvetica: Denkmäler schweizerischer Schreibkunst des Mittelalters*, vol. 3/1–2: *Schreibschulen der Diözese Konstanz: St Gallen* (Geneva: Roto-Sadag, 1936–1938)

Choy, Renie S., 'The Deposit of Monastic Faith: The Carolingians on the Essence of Monasticism', *Studies in Church History*, 49 (2013), 74–86

Claussen, Martin A., *The Reform of the Frankish Church: Chrodegang of Metz and the 'Regula canonicorum' in the Eighth Century*, Cambridge Studies in Medieval Life and Thought, 4th ser., 61 (Cambridge: Cambridge University Press, 2004)

Cohen, Adam, 'Book Production and Illumination from Reichenau and St Gall', in *Carolingian Culture at Reichenau & St Gall: The Carolingian Libraries of St Gall and Reichenau*, respons. coordination Patrick J. Geary and others (UCLA Digital Library © 2012 by University of California Los Angeles, University of Virginia, and University of Vienna) <http://www.stgallplan.org/en/tours_book.html> [accessed 8 September 2021]

Coon, Lynda L., 'Collecting the Desert in the Carolingian West', *Church History and Religious Culture*, 86 (2006), 135–62

Dartmann, Christoph, 'Normative Schriftlichkeit im früheren Mittelalter: Das benediktinische Mönchtum', *Zeitschrift der Savigny-Stiftung für Rechtsgeschichte: Kanonistische Abteilung*, 131 (2014), 1–61

Jong, Mayke de, 'Monastic Writing and Carolingian Court Audiences: Some Evidence from Biblical Commentary', in *Le scritture dai monasteri. Atti del IIo Seminario Internazionale di Studio 'I Monasteri nell'Alto Medioevo', Roma, 9–10 maggio 2002*, ed. by Flavia de Rubeis and Walter Pohl (Rome: Inst. Romanum Finlandiae, 2003), pp. 179–95

Diem, Albrecht, 'Inventing the Holy Rule: Some Observations on the History of Monastic Normative Observance in the Early Medieval West', in *Western Monasticism ante litteram: The Spaces of Monastic Observance in Late Antiquity and the Early Middle Ages*, ed. by Hendrik W. Dey and Elizabeth Fentress, Disciplina monastica, 7 (Turnhout: Brepols, 2011), pp. 53–84

———, 'The Carolingians and the "Regula Benedicti"', in *Religious Franks — Religion and Power in the Frankish Kingdoms: Studies in Honour of Mayke de Jong*, ed. by Rob Meens, Dorine van Espelo, Bram van den Hoven van Genderen, Janneke Raaijmakers, Irene van Renswoude, and Carine van Rhijn (Manchester: Manchester University Press, 2016), pp. 243–61

Diem, Albrecht, and Philippe Rousseau, 'Monastic Rules (4th–9th Centuries)', in *The Cambridge History of Medieval Monasticism in the Latin West*, vol. 1: Origins to the Eleventh Century, ed. by Alison I. Beach and Isabelle Cochelin (Cambridge: Cambridge University Press, 2020), pp. 162–94

Dubois, Jacques, *Les martyrologes du moyen âge latin*, Typologie des sources du moyen âge occidental, 26 (Turnhout: Brepols, 1978)

Duft, Johannes, Anton Gössi, and Werner Vogler, *Die Abtei St Gallen: Abriß der Geschichte, Kurzbiographien der Äbte, das stift-sanktgallische Offizialat* (Sankt Gallen: Verlag am Klosterhof, 1986)

Duft, Johannes, 'Irische Einflüsse auf St Gallen und Alemannien', in *Mönchtum, Episkopat und Adel zur Gründungszeit des Klosters Reichenau*, ed. by Arno Borst, Vorträge und Forschungen, 20 (Sigmaringen: Thorbecke, 1974), pp. 9–35

Engelbert, Pius, 'Die Lambacher Handschrift Cml XXXI aus dem neunten Jahrhundert und ihr Codex Regularum', *Revue Bénédictine*, 124 (2014), 325–47

———, *Der Codex Regularum des Benedikt von Aniane: Faksimile der Handschrift Clm 28118 der Bayerischen Staatsbibliothek München* (Sankt Ottilien: EOS, 2016)

Euw, Anton von, *Die St Galler Buchkunst vom 8. bis zum Ende des 11. Jahrhunderts*, vol. 1 (Sankt Gallen: Verlag am Klosterhof, 2008)

Frank, Karl Suso, 'Die Benediktusregel und ihre Auslegung bis Benedikt von Aniane', *Rottenburger Jahrbuch für Kirchengeschichte*, 9 (1990), 11–27

Gaillard, Michèle, *D'une réforme à l'autre (816–934): Les communautés religieuses en Lorraine à l'époque carolingienne* (Paris: Publications de la Sorbonne, 2006)

Geuenich, Dieter, 'Beobachtungen zu Grimald von St Gallen, Erzkapellan und Oberkanzler Ludwigs des Deutschen', in *Litterae medii aevi: Festschrift für Johanne Autenrieth zu ihrem 65. Geburtstag*, ed. by Michael Borgolte and Herrad Spilling (Sigmaringen: Thorbecke, 1988), pp. 55–68

———, 'Kritische Anmerkungen zur sogenannten "anianischen Reform"', in *Mönchtum — Kirche — Herrschaft 750–1000: Josef Semmler zum 65. Geburtstag*, ed. by Dieter R. Bauer, Rudolf Hiestand, Brigitte Kasten, and Sönke Lorenz (Sigmaringen: Thorbecke, 1998), pp. 99–112

Gilissen, Léon, 'Observations codicologiques sur le codex Sangallensis 914', in *Miscellanea codicologica F. Masai dicata*, vol. 1, ed. by Pierre Cockshaw, Monique-Cécile Garand, and Pierre Jodogne, Les Publications de Scriptorium, 8 (Gent: Story-Scientia, 1979), pp. 1–70

Hanslik, Rudolf, 'Die Benediktinerregel im Wiener Kirchenvätercorpus', in *Commentationes in regulam S. Benedicti*, ed. by Basilius Steidle, Studia Anselmiana, 42 (Rom: Herder, 1957), pp. 159–69

———, 'Praefatio', in *Benedicti Regula*, ed. by Rudolf Hanslik, 2nd rev. edn, Corpus Scriptorum Ecclesiasticorum Latinorum, 75 (Leipzig: Hoelder-Pichler-Tempsky, 1977), pp. xi–lxxiv

Heinzer, Felix, '"Exercitium scribendi": Überlegungen zur Frage einer Korrelation zwischen geistlicher Reform und Schriftlichkeit im Mittelalter', in *Die Präsenz des Mittelalters in seinen Handschriften*, ed. by Hans-Jochen Schiewer and Karl Stackmann (Tübingen: Niemeyer, 2002), pp. 107–29

Hosoe, Kristina M., '*Regulae* and Reform in Carolingian Monastic Hagiography' (doctoral dissertation, Yale University, 2014) <https://pqdtopen.proquest.com/pubnum/3580711.html> [accessed 8 September 2021]

Howe, John, 'Reforming Reform: Steven Vanderputten's Monastic Histories', *The Catholic Historical Review*, 102 (2016), 814–19

Jacob, Christian, 'Lire pour écrire: Navigations alexandrines', in *Le pouvoir des bibliothèques: La mémoire des livres en Occident*, ed. by Marc Baratin and Christian Jacob (Paris: Albin Michel, 1996), pp. 47–83

Kaczynski, Bernice M., 'The Authority of the Fathers: Patristic Texts in Early Medieval Libraries and Scriptoria', *The Journal of Medieval Latin*, 16 (2006), 1–27

Kettemann, Walter, '"Subsidia Anianensia": Überlieferungs- und textgeschichtliche Untersuchungen zur Geschichte Witiza-Benedikts, seines Klosters Aniane und zur sogenannten "anianischen Reform"' (doctoral thesis, University of Duisburg/Essen, 2000/2008) <urn:nbn:de:hbz:464-20080509-172902-8> [last accessed 8 September 2021]

Kottje, Raymund, 'Einheit und Vielfalt des kirchlichen Lebens in der Karolingerzeit', *Zeitschrift für Kirchengeschichte*, 76 (1965), 323–42

Kramer, Rutger, *Rethinking Authority in the Carolingian Empire: Ideals and Expectations during the Reign of Louis the Pious (813–828)* (Amsterdam: Amsterdam University Press, 2019)

Lapidge, Michael, 'Columbanus Luxoviensis et Bobbiensis Abb.', in *La trasmissione dei testi latini del Medioevo: Mediaeval Latin Texts and their Transmission*, vol. 4, ed. by Paolo Chiesa and Lucia Castaldi (Florence: SISMEL, Ed. del Galluzzo, 2012), pp. 208–22

Lifshitz, Felice, *The Name of the Saint: The Martyrology of Jerome and Access to the Sacred in Francia, 627–827* (Notre Dame: University of Notre Dame Press, 2006)

Masser, Achim, *Die lateinisch-althochdeutsche Benediktinerregel Stiftsbibliothek St Gallen Cod. 916*, Studien zum Althochdeutschen, 33 (Göttingen: Vandenhoeck & Ruprecht, 1997)

———, *Regula Benedicti des Cod. 915 der Stiftsbibliothek von St Gallen: Die Korrekturvorlage der lateinisch-althochdeutschen Benediktinerregel* (Göttingen: Vandenhoeck & Ruprecht, 2000)

———, *Kommentar zur lateinisch-althochdeutschen Benediktinerregel des Cod. 916 der Stiftsbibliothek St Gallen* (Göttingen: Vandenhoeck & Ruprecht, 2002)

McKitterick, Rosamond, *The Frankish Kingdoms under the Carolingians 751–987* (London: Longman, 1983)

Meeder, Sven, *The Irish Scholarly Presence at St Gall: Networks of Knowledge in the Early Middle Ages*, Studies in Early Medieval History (London: Bloomsbury, 2018)

Mohrmann, Christine, 'La latinité de saint Benoît: Étude linguistique sur la tradition manuscrite de la règle', *Revue Bénédictine*, 62 (1952), 108–39

Mordek, Hubert, 'Kirchenrechtliche Autoritäten im Frühmittelalter', in *Recht und Schrift im Mittelalter*, ed. by Peter Classen, Vorträge und Forschungen, 23 (Sigmaringen: Thorbecke, 1977), pp. 237–55

Mostert, Marco: '"... but they pray badly using corrected books": Errors in Early Carolingian Copies of the Admonitio generalis', in *Religious Franks — Religion and Power in the Frankish Kingdoms: Studies in Honour of Mayke de Jong*, ed. by Rob Meens, Dorine van Espelo, Bram van den Hoven van Genderen, Janneke Raaijmakers, Irene van Renswoude, and Carine van Rhijn (Manchester: Manchester University Press, 2016), pp. 112–27

Mundó, Anscari M., 'I "Corpora" e i "Codices regularum" nella tradizione codicologica delle regole monastiche', in *Atti del 70 Congresso internazionale di studi sull'alto medioevo*, vol. 2 (Spoleto: Sede del centro studi, 1982), pp. 477–520

——, 'Corrections "anciennes" et "modernes" dans le Sanctgall. 914 de la règle de Saint Benoît', in *Studia Patristica*, vol. 8: *Papers presented to the Fourth International Conference on Patristic Studies held at Christ Church, Oxford, 1963*, part 2: *Patres Apostolici, Historica, Liturgica, Ascetica et Monastica*, ed. by Frank L. Cross (Berlin: Akademie, 1966), pp. 424–35

Nichols, Stephen G., 'What is a Manuscript Culture? Technologies of the Manuscript Matrix', in *The Medieval Manuscript Book: Cultural Approaches*, ed. by Michael Johnston and Michael van Dussen (Cambridge: Cambridge University Press, 2015), pp. 34–59

Parkes, Malcolm B., *Pause and Effect: An Introduction to the History of Punctuation in the West* (Aldershot: Scolar Press, 1992)

Paringer, Benedikt, 'Le manuscrit de Saint-Gall 914 représente-t-il le latin original de la règle de Saint Benoît', *Revue Bénédictine*, 61 (1951), 81–140

Patzold, Steffen, 'Normen im Buch: Überlegungen zu Geltungsansprüchen so genannter "Kapitularien"', *Frühmittelalterliche Studien*, 41 (2007), 331–50

Ponesse, Matthew D., 'Editorial Practice in Smaragdus of St Mihiel's Commentary on the Rule of St Benedict', *Early Medieval Europe*, 18 (2010), 61–91

Raaijmakers, Janneke E., *The Making of the Monastic Community of Fulda, c. 744–c. 900*, Cambridge Studies in Medieval Life and Thought, 4th ser., 83 (Cambridge: Cambridge University Press, 2012)

Rubeis, Flavia de, and Walter Pohl, *Le scritture dai monasteri: Atti del II° Seminario Internazionale di Studio 'I Monasteri nell'Alto Medioevo', Roma, 9–10 maggio 2002* (Rome: Inst. Romanum Finlandiae, 2003)

Schaab, Rupert, 'Bibeltext und Schriftstudium in St Gallen', in *Das Kloster St Gallen im Mittelalter: Die kulturelle Blüte vom 8. bis zum 12. Jahrhundert*, ed. by Peter Ochsenbein (Darmstadt: Wissenschaftliche Buchgesellschaft, 1999), pp. 119–36

——, *Mönch in Sankt Gallen: Zur inneren Geschichte eines frühmittelalterlichen Klosters*, Vorträge und Forschungen Sonderband, 47 (Ostfildern: Thorbecke, 2003)

Schrimpf, Gangolf, with Josef Leinweber and Thomas Martin, ed., *Mittelalterliche Bücherverzeichnisse des Klosters Fulda und andere Beiträge zur Geschichte der Bibliothek des Klosters Fulda im Mittelalter*, Fuldaer Studien, 4 (Frankfurt am Main: Knecht, 1992)

Schwarzmaier, Hansmartin, 'Zur Frühgeschichte des Klosters Kempten: Eine Untersuchung zu den Konventslisten des Klosters unter Abt Tatto', in *Nomen et fraternitas: Festschrift für Dieter Geuenich zum 65. Geburtstag*, ed. by Uwe Ludwig and Thomas Schilp (Berlin: De Gruyter, 2008), pp. 317–42

Semmler, Josef, 'Karl der Große und das fränkische Mönchtum', in *Mönchtum und Gesellschaft im Frühmittelalter*, ed. by Friedrich Prinz, Wege der Forschung, 312 (Darmstadt: Wissenschaftliche Buchgesellschaft, 1976), pp. 204–64

——, 'Benedictus II: Una regula — una consuetudo', in *Benedictine Culture 750–1050*, ed. by Willem Lourdaux and Daniel Verhelst, Mediaevalia Lovaniensia, Ser. 1, Studia, 11 (Leuven: Leuven University Press, 1983), pp. 1–49

Steinová, Eva, '"Notam superponere studui": The Use of Technical Signs in the Early Middle Ages' (doctoral thesis, University of Utrecht, 2016) <https://dspace.library.uu.nl/handle/1874/331044> [accessed 8 September 2021]

Sullivan, Richard E., 'What Was Carolingian Monasticism? The Plan of St Gall and the History of Monasticism', in *After Rome's Fall: Narrators and Sources of Early Medieval History. Essays presented to Walter Goffart*, ed. by Alexander C. Murray (Toronto: University of Toronto Press, 1998), pp. 251–87

Traube, Ludwig, *Textgeschichte der Regula S. Benedicti*, ed. by Heribert Plenkers, Abhandlungen der Bayerischen Akademie der Wissenschaften, Philos.-Philolog. und Hist. Klasse, 25.2, 2nd edn (Munich: Bayer. Akademie der Wissenschaften, 1910)

Vanderputten, Steven, *Medieval Monasticisms: Forms and Experiences of the Monastic Life in the Latin West*, Oldenbourg Grundriss der Geschichte, 47 (Berlin: De Gruyter, 2020)

Verheijen, Luc, *La règle de Saint Augustin*, 2 vols (Paris: Etudes Augustiniennes, 1967)

Vogüé, Adalbert de, and Jean Neufville, 'Introduction', in *La Règle de Saint Benoît*, vol. 1, Sources chrétiennes, 183 (Paris: Ed. du Cerf, 1972), pp. 30–410

Walker, G. S. M., ed., *Sancti Columbani Opera*, Scriptores Latini Hiberniae, 2 (Dublin: Institute for advanced studies, 1957)

Wollasch, Joachim, 'Zu den Anfängen liturgischen Gedenkens an Personen und Personengruppen in den Bodenseeklöstern', *Freiburger Diözesanarchiv*, 100 (1980), 59–78

Zelzer, Klaus, 'Zur Stellung des Textus Receptus und des interpolierten Textes in der Textgeschichte der Regula S. Benedicti', *Revue Bénédictine*, 88 (1978), 205–46

——, 'Regulae Monachorum: Regula Magistri, Regula Eugippi, Regula Benedicti', in *La trasmissione dei testi latini del Medioevo: Mediaeval Latin Texts and Their Transmission*, vol. 1, ed. by Paolo Chiesa and Lucia Castaldi (Florence: SISMEL, Edizioni del Galluzzo, 2004), pp. 364–93

Zettler, Alfons, 'Der St Galler Klosterplan: Überlegungen zu seiner Herkunft und Entstehung', in *Charlemagne's Heir: New Perspectives on the Reign of Louis the Pious (814–840)*, ed. by Peter Godman and Roger Collins (Oxford: Clarendon Press, 1990), pp. 655–87

——, 'St Gallen als Bischofs- und als Königskloster', *Alemannisches Jahrbuch* (2001/2002), 23–38

Reform in Practice

MIRIAM CZOCK †

Monks Pray, Priests Teach, Canons Sing, and the Laity Listens

The Regula Benedicti *and Conceptual Diversity of Sacred Space in Carolingian Discourse*

It has long been held that there were efforts in the Carolingian period to bind all monks and nuns in the empire to the monastic rule of Benedict of Nursia as part of an ongoing project to create religious unity — a *populus christianus* — through correcting Christian life.[1] Although correction seems to have been a process that was not always as straightforward as once believed, there seems no doubt that the attempt at regulating monastic practice further expanded and deepened under Louis the Pious with the councils of Aachen of 816 and 817.[2] One feature of the monastic programme rolled out in these years was a heightened differentiation between the monks, clergy, and laity. Scholarship sees the differentiation primarily as a manifestation of the immense importance of Carolingian monastic prayer. It was monastic prayer that kept the empire going. To ensure its power, the spiritual purity of monks was needed. In order to perform their duty to pray without any disrupting interference from the outside world, monks needed spatial separation from it.[3] Within the Carolingian imagination, the cloister's confines were a place where monks, closed off from all worldly interference, were living a life of ascetic practice that differentiated them from everybody

---

1 Discussion on how to label the cultural endeavour undertaken in Carolingian times is still ongoing. For an introduction to the phenomena and further reading, see McKitterick, *The Frankish Church*; Brown, 'Introduction'; Depreux, 'Ambitions et limites'; Staubach, '*Cultus divinus*'; de Jong, 'Charlemagne's Church'; de Jong, '*Ecclesia*'; Phelan, *The Formation*.
2 Semmler, 'Benedictus II'; Semmler, 'Die Beschlüsse'. For a general overview of the developments see de Jong, 'Carolingian Monasticism'; Kramer, *Rethinking Authority*; Diem, 'The Carolingians'.
3 De Jong, 'Carolingian Monasticism'; de Jong, 'Imitatio morum'; Diem, *Das monastische Experiment*, pp. 228–39, pp. 332–34; Choy, *Intercessory Prayer*, Coon, *Dark Age Bodies*.

Miriam Czock was Senior Lecturer in Medieval History at the Historisches Institut of the Universität Duisburg-Essen.

Monastic Communities and Canonical Clergy in the Carolingian World (780–840): Categorizing the Church, ed. by Rutger Kramer, Emilie Kurdziel, and Graeme Ward, MMS 8 (Turnhout: Brepols, 2022), pp. 355–380

living outside of these confines. In the early medieval imagination, monastic identity was thus constructed by the delineation of monks from the outside world, whatever the relation between the secular world and the monastery in reality looked like.

Accordingly, monastic life has been described by modern scholars as a spatial praxis.[4] Not only was the monastery separated from the outside world, there was also an inner spatial hierarchy within it: some areas were more important than others.[5] The complex structuring and polarization of *exteriora* (outside) and *interiora* (inside) shaped monastic life as practice. Moreover, monastic discourse made frequent use of spatial images as metaphors and virtual representations of the spiritual requirements of monastic life.[6] Monastic spiritual praxis itself thus became envisaged in spatial terms. Despite emphasis on spatiality, the monastery seldom was imagined as a tangible, physical place. Rather than mapping an actual material, visible place, the spatial formation of the monastery, imagined as sacred space, was a virtual concept deeply intertwined with the implementation of the *Regula Benedicti* and the observance of discipline.[7] Until now, scholarship on Carolingian conceptions of sacred space has focused on imagining the monastery as a whole, overlooking Chapter 52 of the *Regula Benedicti*, which was explicitly concerned with the status of a physical tangible place: the oratory. Given the fundamental changes in monasticism and in the ways sacred space was imagined in the Carolingian period, it is curious that analyses of the discourse of monastic space seem to have overlooked the oratory's special status in the *Regula Benedicti* and consequently in Carolingian thought. This is despite the fact that scholars have underlined the special status ascribed to prayer, not only in Carolingian theology and politics but also in monastic practice. In focusing on the oratory, this study shifts the existing perspective of research, which currently emphasizes the separateness of the whole monastery as a sacred place to ensure the power of prayer, to the sacredness of the place of prayer itself.

---

[4] On space in the *Regula Benedicti* and monasticism up to the Carolingian age: Noisette, 'Usages et représentations'; Penco, 'Un elemento'; Bonnerue, 'Elements de topographie'; Dey, 'Building Worlds Apart'; Destefanis, 'Ad portam monasterii'. On monastic space in the Carolingian empire: Maganou-Nortier, 'L'espace monastique'; Uggè, 'Lieux, espaces et topographie'; Zettler, 'Public, Collective'.

[5] For the idea of different layers of *interioria et exteriora* see Lauwers, '*Circuitus* et *figura*'; Lauwers, '"Interiora" et "exteriora"'. For an archaeological overview see Sennhauser, 'Klostermauern', who discusses the role which walls played in the delimitation of the claustrum in both the written sources and the archaeological material.

[6] Collins, *The Carolingian Debate*, pp. 67–90; Lauwers, '*Circuitus* et *figura*'; Lauwers, '"Interiora" et "exteriora"'. On the relation of the monastic body to place and space, see Coon, *Dark Age Bodies*. For a non-Carolingian perspective and on the question of monastic ideas, see O'Brien, 'The Cleansing of the Temple'; O'Brien, *Bede's Temple*.

[7] De Jong, 'Imitatio morum'; Lauwers, '"Interiora" et "exteriora"'. For the normativity of the *Regula Benedicti* see Dartmann, 'Normative Schriftlichkeit'.

Carolingian emphasis on the spatiality of the spiritual was, moreover, not only felt in the perceptions of the monastery as sacred space,[8] but also beyond the monastic world. The Carolingian period proved to be a decisive turning point in the definition of Christian sacred space.[9] While in the patristic period there was no concept of sacred space that was rooted in the materiality of place, that had changed by Carolingian times. The slow development and adaptation of a concept of sacred space was due to an exegetical problem. Arguments about sacred space had to work around the fact that the Old Testament reports numerous instances of the manifestation of God in certain places, while the New Testament conveys the idea that God does not live in any localizable place on earth. Carolingian discourse embraced the Old Testament concept through a New Testament lens, fundamentally changing how sacred space was envisaged.[10] The new approach is perhaps best reflected in the uniquely Carolingian invention of a church consecration ordo in the second half of the eighth century.[11] Church consecration through its very logic to sanctify the church building expressed a previously unthinkable concept: a limited, locatable sanctified place. Church consecration no longer only imagined the church related to a more or less abstract spiritualized concept of sacred space, but also saw it as materialized in a sanctified place. This shift in paradigm resulted in two different, but sometimes intertwined approaches in Carolingian discourse, which drew on the same concept of spiritualized ideas of space and its sacredness: one focusing essentially on place as physical, visible space in connection to its spiritual function, the other on spatial formations of spiritual habitus that were imaginary and not necessarily bound to physical place as such.

By focusing on Chapter 52 of the *Regula Benedicti* this study sheds light not on how sacred space was envisaged as a virtual representation of spiritual

---

8   There is a plethora of definitions of sacrality. The fact that sacrality is a category not definable by one-dimensional definitions has been underlined in recent years, thus leaving behind models formed mainly in the nineteenth and beginning of the twentieth centuries, which envisaged the sacred to be suprahistorical and objective: see for example Eliade, *The Sacred*, who claimed it either to be numinous or a counterpart to the profane. These one-dimensional definitions are now replaced by theories which tend to be discursive and rely on a phenomenological approach. See for example: Hamm, 'Heiligkeit im Mittelalter'; Auffarth, 'Wie kann man von Heiligkeit'. This new approach historicizes concepts of sacrality and reveals the contradictions, metamorphoses, and the abandonment of ideas. Following these recent approaches instead of defining sacred space by measures derived from any theory of sacrality, here Carolingian concepts of space used for religious purposes are assessed by reading them in a phenomenological way.
9   Repsher, *The Rite*; Forneck, *Die Feier der Dedicatio*; Iogna-Prat, *Lieu de culte*; Iogna-Prat, *La maison dieu*; Jäggi, 'Die Kirche als heiliger Raum'; Lauwers, 'De l'Église primitive'; Méhu, 'Historiae et imagines'; de Blaauwe, 'Die Kirchweihe'; Collins, *The Carolingian Debate*; Polanichka, 'Transforming Space'; Czock, *Gottes Haus*; Czock, 'Early Medieval Churches'; Czock, 'Kirchenräume schaffen'; Bruun and Hamilton, 'Rites for Dedicating Churches'.
10 Collins, *The Carolingian Debate*; Czock, *Gottes Haus*, esp. pp. 244–83.
11 Repsher, *The Rite*; Forneck, *Die Feier der Dedicatio*; Czock, *Gottes Haus*, pp. 147–73.

habitus, but on how a physical visible place got encoded as sacred by relating it to the spiritual. It uses Chapter 52 of the *Regula Benedicti* as a starting point to understand how physical space, the spiritual habitus, and spiritual function of monks became intertwined in a single concept that imagined space as sacred. Although there never was one 'norm' or a universal practice of all monks, we will see that the discourse around Chapter 52 of the *Regula Benedicti* projects a model of sacred space that underscores the singularity of monastic practice. I determine how the increased emphasis on the *Regula Benedicti* as the rule which all monks should follow influenced a discursive framework that consciously built different normative models of sacred space for the different *ordines* — monks, clerics, and the laity. The particular ways in which sacred space was constructed discloses that, whatever forms Christian worship and the arrangements of liturgical ritual actually took in the Carolingian Empire,[12] ideas about sacred space mirrored the fact that in the medieval imagination the different *ordines* had distinctive roles in the liturgy.

Rather than providing a detailed discussion of the sources connected to the Aachen councils of 816/17,[13] this study will look instead mainly at those sources which are concerned with the observance of the *Regula Benedicti*. The focus will be on the commentaries on the *Regula Benedicti*,[14] which offer vital clues as to how the *Rule* was read and ultimately interwoven into a wider normative framework. I will also explore Walahfrid Strabo's exposition of the liturgy, another text that indicates how discourse encoded the church as sacred space in a normative arrangement that was influenced by the *Regula Benedicti*.[15] Drawing on these sources, I will review the application of the *Regula Benedicti* in the Carolingian period to show how attitudes shifted, how place and prayer became increasingly connected, and how different perspectives on sacred space were created for the different *ordines* of Christian society. This study, moreover, contributes to the understanding of how the adoption and the dissemination of the *Regula Benedicti* shaped the normative discourse around sacred space.

Remarkably, Chapter 52 of the *Regula Benedicti* is the only chapter in the whole *Regula* that is explicitly devoted to the status of place. It defines the oratory as a place of prayer and it demands that nothing else should be done or kept there.[16] After underscoring the importance of prayer, the text goes

---

12 There was a great local diversity of liturgical ritual. For an overview of the medieval liturgy still see Vogel, *Medieval Liturgy*. For a critique and for a new approach see Parkes, 'Questioning'; Parkes, *The Making*. For liturgical practice, see Harper, *The Forms and Orders*.
13 For a short overview, see Diem, 'The Carolingians'.
14 Diem, 'The Carolingians', pp. 246–51; Dartmann, 'Die Konstruktion'.
15 For Walahfrid see also Choy's chapter in the present volume.
16 *Benedicti Regula*, ed. by Hanslik, LII, pp. 122–23: 'De Oratorio Monasterii. Oratorium hoc sit, quod dicitur, nec ibi quidquam aliud geratur aut condatur. Expleto opere dei omnes cum summo silentio exeant et habeatur reuerentia deo, ut frater, qui forte sibi peculiariter uult orare, non inpediatur alterius improbitate. Sed et si aliter uult sibi forte secretius orare,

on to describe the correct execution of prayer and mandates that no one is to be disturbed during it. Benedict demands that after the liturgy everyone has to leave the oratory in a silent reverent manner, and that no brother who stays behind to pray alone is impeded by another. In case someone wants to enter and pray alone, he should do so not with a clamorous voice, but in tears and with an attentive heart. Everyone who does not act according to these rules should not be permitted to stay behind after the liturgy. Rather than underscoring the importance of physical place, this chapter gives us insight into a preoccupation with prayer. Forgoing other possible terms like *ecclesia*, *basilica*, or *templum* for the place of worship, Benedict chose to call it the *oratorium* (house of prayer), thereby projecting the idea that prayer was at the centre of monastic worship.

This is characteristic of Benedict's approach to space: rather than describing the spatial separation between monastery and world in terms of physical place, the Rule reflects a spatial logic connected to the life of the community.

The deep-seated intertwining of spiritual habitus and spatial practice is attested by the principal rejection of the idea of sacred space in Chapter 19, which covers discipline while singing the psalms and reminds the reader that God is everywhere and that in every place he looks upon good and evil.[17] Even chapters dealing with the construction of the monastery argue from the point of view of communal life. There is no specific chapter on how the monastery's layout should look in spatial terms, although the chapter on the porter of the monastery does include some thoughts on the monastery as place.[18] It sets down that, if possible, all essentials should be stored within the enclosure so the monks need not endanger their souls by wandering outside of the monastery.[19] Therefore all necessities must be provided for inside of the monastery. This is a key passage for unpacking how Benedict used spatial figurations in his rule. In Benedict's thinking, space is not simply a tangible, physical place; rather, his approach connects space with the habitus of the monks as well as the functional hierarchy inside the monastery. Moreover, the morality of the monks relies on their separateness from the world. Benedict's conception of the monastery — which links an institutional framework,

---

simpliciter intret et oret, non in clamosa uoce, sed in lacrimis et intentione cordis. Ergo qui simile opus non facit, non permittatur explicito opere dei remorari in oratorio, sicut dictum est, ne alius impedimentum patiatur'.

17 *Benedicti Regula*, ed. by Hanslik, XIX, pp. 74–75: 'De disciplina psallendi. Ubique credimus diuinam esse praesentiam et oculos Domini in omni loco speculari bonos et malos, maxime tamen hoc sine aliqua dubitatione credamus cum ad opus diuinum adsistimus. Ideo semper memores simus, quod ait propheta: Servite Domino in timore; et iterum: Psallite sapienter; et: In conspectu angelorum psallam tibi. Ergo consideremus, qualiter oporteat in conspectu diuinitatis et angelorum eius esse, et sic stemus ad psallendum, ut mens nostra concordet uoci nostrae'.

18 *Benedicti Regula*, ed. by Hanslik, LXVI, pp. 155–57.

19 De Jong, 'Imitatio morum'; see also Matthew Gillis, 'Headless and on the Road', which the author kindly let me read in advance of publication.

functional uses, and moral behaviour together in a logic of separation from the world — formed the spiritual habitus of the monks. This spiritual habitus was a model Carolingian intellectuals followed. At the same time, they had to adapt it to a monasticism that was different from Benedict's model in that it specifically separated monks not only by their spiritual habitus, but physically and therefore spatially from the laity to validate their prayers.[20]

While the *Regula Benedicti* was a yardstick for a Carolingian monastic regime,[21] the normative ideal of the oratory it sets out seems not have to become part of the mainstream set of monastic norms pronounced in the capitularies and canons. These pronouncements — just like the Rule — mostly avoid discussing the spatial aspects of monastic life as spatial praxis unless in its most broad definition as space, and instead follow the model in which monastic habitus, spirituality, and separateness from the world become intertwined.[22] There is, however, one exception to this: the Frankfurt Council of 794, which clearly states that there should be an oratory in the claustrum where the important offices should take place.[23] This apparent lack of interest in the oratory outside the *Regula* reflects the general lack of systematization regarding the labelling of the different kinds of churches in the eighth and ninth centuries. The sources for example use oratory to denote anything from a small village church to a place of prayer a rich man had in his house.[24] It is often only from context that we can glean what kind of church is actually meant.[25] Moreover, like the Rule, the Carolingian discussion of it does not provide us with any indicators concerning the specifics of what the oratory was in architectural or monumental terms. It is telling then that in spite of the oratory's importance as a place of monastic practice,[26] discussion of it seems mainly to have been limited to the flurry of interpretive works that sprang up as a result of the desire to make the Rule compatible with Carolingian monastic practice.[27] It is striking that although these texts come in different forms, the emphasis on prayer seems to have remained the determining factor.

---

20 De Jong, 'Carolingian Monasticism'; Choy, *Intercessory Prayer*.
21 De Jong, 'Carolingian Monasticism'; Dartmann, 'Normative Schriftlichkeit'.
22 De Jong, 'Carolingian Monasticism'; Kramer, *Rethinking Authority*, pp. 59–90. See for example the legislation of the Councils before Aachen 816 that also provisioned the *Regula Benedicti* as the one rule to live by for monks: *Concilium Rispacense, Frisingense, Salisburgensia a. 800*, ed. by Werminghoff, pp. 210–13; *Concilium Remense a. 813*, ed. Werminghoff, p. 256; *Concilium Turonense a. 813*, ed. by Werminghoff, p. 290.
23 *Concilium Francfurtense a. 794*, ed. by Werminghoff, xv, p. 168: 'De monasterio, ubi corpora sanctorum sunt: ut habeat oratorium intra claustra, ubi peculiare officium et diuturnum fiat'. For an idea of how the liturgical order could have looked like, see Rabe, *Faith*, pp. 122–37.
24 Harro, 'Landkirche und Landklerus'; Wood, *The Proprietary Church*, pp. 11–12, 66, 69.
25 Harro, 'Landkirche und Landklerus'; Wood, *The Proprietary Church*.
26 Rabe, *Faith*, pp. 122–37.
27 Diem, 'The Carolingians'; for another very short overview, see *Glosae in Regula Sancti Benedicti*, ed. by Van der Meer, pp. vii–xii.

The first of these texts, the *Concordia Regularum*, was written by Benedict of Aniane, who is often portrayed as the central figure within the reform associated with the early years of Louis the Pious.[28] The text's dating is debated. It may have been written in the late eighth century, or perhaps around the years 816/17.[29] In this work, Benedict applied a florilegium of quotes from other monastic rules in textual parallel to the *Regula Benedicti* as a tool of normative exegesis. His interpretative readings of Chapter 52 do not include its original opening line, which deals with the oratory as physical place. The difference in perspective is already apparent in the heading Benedict gave Chapter 52. Instead of being called 'About the oratory', its caption reads 'About those who arrive tardy to the Work of God or to the table'.[30] In this way, he changed the perspective from place to time. By eschewing any references to place, and instead emphasizing the Work of God and collating only the elements concerned with the exercise and discipline of prayer,[31] the *Concordia Regularum* encapsulates a discussion of Chapter 52 that is entirely spiritual in character.

While the *Concordia Regularum* wholly precluded the discussion of physical sacred space by omitting the first sentence of Chapter 52, Smaragdus of Saint-Mihiel gave the original text in whole and remained faithful to it in his interpretation. Like Benedict of Aniane, Smaragdus had a central place in the early ninth-century discussions about the organization of church and empire.[32] Conceived with the council of 816/17 in mind,[33] his work is a line-by-line commentary on the *Regula Benedicti*. The organizing principle of the commentary is to gloss certain words and clarify their meaning. In addition, Benedict assessed the rule through theological clarifications that frequently rested on patristic or biblical citations. The last third of the work, however, reads the Rule through the lens of selected quotations from previous monastic rules. Although these are taken from the *Concordia Regularum*,[34] his explanation of Chapter 52 does not follow the content of this source. Rather,

---

28 For Benedict of Aniane, see Kettemann, 'Subsidia Anianensia'. For his influence on the Rule, see Diem, 'Inventing the Holy Rule'.

29 Benedict of Aniane, *Concordia Regularum*, ed. by Bonnerue, Praefatio, pp. 48–53; see also Claussen, 'Benedict of Aniane'.

30 Benedict of Aniane, *Concordia Regularum*, ed. by Bonnerue, 52, pp. 444–61: 'LII. De his qui ad opus Dei uel ad mensam tarde occurrunt. 52,1 — Ex Regula sancti Benedicti. Ad horam diuini officii, mox auditum fuerit signum, relictis omnibus currantur, cum grauitate tamen, ut non scurrilitas inueniat fomitem. […]'.

31 For the exercise of prayer, see Choy 'The Brother Who May Wish'.

32 Kramer, *Rethinking Authority*, pp. 123–68; Ponesse, 'Smaragdus of Saint-Mihiel'; Ponesse, 'Editorial Practice'. For a more general introduction to his image of monastic space, see Collins, *The Carolingian Debate*, pp. 81–84.

33 Smaragdus of Saint-Mihiel, *Expositio in Regulam S. Benedicti*, ed. by Spannagel and Engelbert, pp. xxix–xxx.

34 Smaragdus of Saint-Mihiel, *Expositio in Regulam S. Benedicti*, ed. by Spannagel and Engelbert, pp. xxxi–xxxiv.

he cites the first line of Chapter 52 and glosses it with other quotations that emphasize the oratory's function as a place of prayer. The arguments of both of the rules which he used to interpret the chapter depend on the relation of the word oratory to the word *orare* ('to pray'). They thus infer that the name of the place represents its function: prayer. In Smaragdus's perspective the oratory thus was a special place defined by the function it served.[35] He thus attributed some meaning to physical place, but by staying within the bounds of the *Regula Benedicti*, he cast the space in the spiritual use that ultimately defined it.

A different approach can be found in the *Glosae in Regula Sancti Benedicti Abbatis ad Usum Smaragdi Abbatis Sancti Michaelis*, which can be dated to the time between the last decade of the eighth century and 817.[36] The *Glosae* began life as interlinear or marginal glosses, which were later put together as a stand-alone text that reproduced the text of the *Regula Benedicti* in an abridged or paraphrased manner. The *Glosae*'s interpretation of Chapter 52 thus is significantly different to Smaragdus's *Expositio*, which the *Glosae* pre-date.[37] Yet although Smaragdus relied heavily on it for his first two books, he did not draw on the *Glosae*'s distinctly and significantly different reading of Chapter 52.

The compiler of the *Glosae* echoed the text of Chapter 52 in his own words, carefully maintaining the chain of arguments set out in the *Regula Benedicti*. In explaining the oratory, however, the text deviates from the Rule in one crucial point. After defining the oratory as a place that should be 'what it is called', it goes on to say that the oratory is consecrated for prayer and that 'nobody should do anything else there except that for which it is made and from which it received its name'.[38] In imagining the oratory as physical space, the slightly nuanced wording, which included consecration to define the place of prayer, signifies an important change from the *Regula*, the *Concordia Regularum*, and Smaragdus's *Expositio*. The integral sanctifying relationship was no longer between place and prayer;

---

35 Smaragdus of Saint-Mihiel, *Expositio in Regulam S. Benedicti*, ed. by Spannagel and Engelbert, 52, pp. 278–79: 'Oratorium hoc sit quod dicitur, nec ibi quicquam aliud aut condatur. Expleto opere dei omnes cum summo silentio exeant et habeatur reverentia deo, ut frater qui forte sibi peculariter vult orare, non inepediatur improbitate. [...] Hinc beatus Agustinus ait "In oratorio nemo aliquid agat nisi ad quod est factum fiat, unde nomen accepit. [...]" Item alibi "In oratorio praeter orandi et psallendi dei cultum penitus nihil agatur, ut nomini huic et opera iugiter iugiter inpensa concordent [...]"'. For a translation see trans. by Barry, pp. 445–46.
36 *Glosae in Regula Sancti Benedicti*, ed. by Van der Meer, pp. xviii–xx.
37 *Glosae in Regula Sancti Benedicti*, ed. by Van der Meer, pp. xli–lvi.
38 *Glosae in Regula Sancti Benedicti*, ed. by Van der Meer, 52, p. 81: 'LII. De Oratorio. Oratorim hoc sit, quod dicitur. Oratorium orationi tantum est consecratum, in quo nemo aliquid agere debet nisi ad quod est factum, unde et nomen accepit. Omnes cum summo silentio exeant et habeatur reverentia deo, id est honorificentia, ut frater non inpediatur alterius improbitate, id est inportunitate'.

here, the place became consecrated for the purpose of prayer. The *Glosae* thus invoked a unique Carolingian approach to places of worship: they were consecrated to fulfil their function.

The *Glosae*'s changes imply a shift in discourse that did not register in Benedict's and Smaragdus's work, but which another contemporary source sheds fuller light on: Walahfrid Strabo's explanation of the liturgy, his *Libellus de Exordiis*.[39] Walahfrid wrote his treatise sometime between 840 and 842 in exile from his abbacy of the Reichenau in order to lay out a history of the liturgy.[40] However, his book is not only a historical account of and commentary on the development of the liturgy: he also simultaneously considered the practical and spiritual implications of the liturgy. The commentary's translator, Alice Harting-Correa, thought that Walahfrid's work was not so much a monastic treatise as one composed for priests.[41] To pin down Walahfrid's target audience precisely is impossible, as in the context of the Carolingian monastery a substantial number of monks could also be priests.[42] Indeed an excerpt of his work found its way into a book dating to the late ninth century that was intended to train priests.[43] Whoever his target audience might have been, judging from Walahfrid's monastic upbringing on the Reichenau and his background as abbot we can assume that he was deeply influenced by monastic ideas. Those for example get mirrored in his line of arguments about sacred space, which hark back to the *Regula Benedicti*.

The first chapters of his work are chiefly concerned with the material objects of the liturgy, such as church bells. In particular, church buildings feature prominently in his reasoning about the material objects of faith. His explanations consider the origin of churches, which he calls temples,[44] the names of certain sacred objects and how other languages refer to the church,[45] and why both temples and altars have to be consecrated.[46] He also contemplates the church's role as a place of prayer. It is in this context that Walahfrid unfolds a programme of what to do and what not to do in the temple.

Walahfrid's structural principle of argumentation is to take quotes from scripture on which he bases his subsequent thoughts and reflections. This is a technique he also uses to introduce his chapter (Chapter 10) about what ought to be done in places consecrated to God. He starts this section by recounting

---

39 Pössel, 'Appropriate to the Religion'. See also the contribution by Renie Choy in the present volume.
40 Walahfrid Strabo, *Libellus de Exordiis*, ed. and trans. by Harting-Correa, pp. 21–22.
41 Walahfrid Strabo, *Libellus de Exordiis*, ed. and trans. by Harting-Correa, pp. 12–21, esp. p. 15.
42 De Jong, *In Samuel's Image*, pp. 138–39. Pössel, 'Appropriate to the Religion', p. 84 assumes his audience to be the monks of Reichenau.
43 Pössel, 'Appropriate to the Religion', p. 82, based on an assessment of Van Rhijn, 'Royal Politics in Small Worlds'.
44 Walahfrid Strabo, *Libellus de Exordiis*, ed. and trans. by Harting-Correa, 1, pp. 50–53.
45 Walahfrid Strabo, *Libellus de Exordiis*, ed. and trans. by Harting-Correa, 6 and 7, pp. 62–73.
46 Walahfrid Strabo, *Libellus de Exordiis*, ed. and trans. by Harting-Correa, 9, pp. 80–85.

two passages from scripture. Both govern the arguments he subsequently unfolds. He introduces his tenth chapter thus:

> What ought to be done in places consecrated to God, the Lord makes plain by the words of the Prophet and by His own words: 'My house shall be called the house of prayer for all nations', the psalmist says, 'I will enter Thy house; I will worship at Thy holy Temple, in fear of Thee'.[47]

By using these passages of scripture, Walahfrid created a model of space which integrated the relationship of place, prayer, and worship. In order to outline the particularities of the place of worship Walahfrid then turned to the Old Testament story of Jacob. Jacob had recognized the presence of the angels in consecrated places, for he had seen them ascending and descending the heavenly ladder. Walahfrid's evocation of the story of Jacob emphasizes the proximity of sanctified places to God, embodied in his angels.[48] Affirming this motif with more biblical passages, he then says that David, worshipping at the holy temple, sang the praise of God in the presence of angels. He also states that the law of Moses demonstrates that vows and sacrifices should happen only in consecrated places. These images also offer Walahfrid an occasion to again underline the fact that the place of worship was to be consecrated. He imagined the church as a holy place, ultimately defined as where heaven and earth met. In this section of his text, he shines a light on another aspect of the intertwining of function and space, by placing not prayer, but the liturgy and worship at the heart of the matter.

However, Walahfrid not only presents the Church as a place where God is encountered in prayer and worship, but also as a place of teaching. Using a series of biblical examples, he explains that Moses already taught at the tabernacle's door; Christ taught in the temple, where subsequently the apostle Peter prayed with John; and at the temple, Paul later fulfilled his vows and all the other apostles taught.[49] Clearly, he imagined the church building as a place of prayer and instruction. In addition to the biblical model, he gives an etymological explanation of *oratorio*, which serves to support his interpretation

---

47 Walahfrid Strabo, *Libellus de Exordiis*, ed. and trans. by Harting-Correa, 10, p. 84: 'Quid autem fieri debeat in locis Deo consecratis, Dominus per prophetam et per se ipsum manifestat dicens: "Domus mea domus orationis vocabitur cunctis gentibus", et psalmista: "Introibo in domum tuam, adorabo ad templum sanctum tuum in timore tuo", et multa his similia'.

48 Walahfrid Strabo, *Libellus de Exordiis*, ed. and trans. by Harting-Correa, 10, p. 84: 'Angelorum etiam praesentiam in locis talibus haberi et Jacob agnovit, quando scala in Bethel erecta vidit angelos ascendentes et descendentes, et David testatur dicens: "In conspectu angelorum psallam tibi et adorabo ad templum sanctum tuum". Vota enim et sacrificia in his Deo offerri debere et lex Moysi pleniter docet […]'. The presence of the angels at the altar or at the liturgy was an often-invoked theme of the early Middle Ages: see Note 71 in this chapter.

49 Walahfrid Strabo, *Libellus de Exordiis*, ed. and trans. by Harting-Correa, 10, p. 84: 'Doctrinae quoque verbum populo in ecclesia dispensari et Moyses ostendit, cum ad ostium tabernaculi mandata Domini populo exposuit, et ipse Dominus "in templo duodennis inventus est

of the biblical passages. Again, he was underlining the idea that the church was a place of prayer and of instruction. Accordingly, Walahfrid declares that the house of God is not only called *oratorium* because it is a place of prayer, but also because it is a place of teaching.[50] Honouring both of these facets, he puts forward the idea that *oratio* is a term for a humble request as well as for rational discourse. He concludes this thought with the idea that the major orders of the church wear a stole as they teach in the *oratorium* and that wise composers of speeches are called orators.[51] This small passage alone is enough to reveal that Walahfrid, however tentatively, discerned different orders within the church by dividing them by their performative function, since there are those who teach in church, priests.[52] What Walahfrid imagines is the function of the priest to teach the faith in church. Having priests singled out as teachers, Walahfrid implicitly includes those who are instructed: the congregation. It in turn is implicitly envisaged as passive listener to the teachers. Since he emphasizes not only prayer, but teaching too, he reveals his target audience as priests, as only they would have to know about the church as a place of teaching.

Having made this distinction on the level of performative function, Walahfrid moves his discussion to the topic of unity in the last section of the chapter, which characterizes the church as the place of baptism.[53] By evoking the church as the place of baptism, Walahfrid invites his reader to think about the common ritual and spiritual denominator of all Christians. In Walahfrid's vision, sacred space's function was related to the spiritual and ritual habitus of those who used it, which simultaneously distinguished the performative roles of priest and congregation, while also projecting a sense of unity and uniformity.

The conception of the church as a place of prayer and instruction is accompanied by some behavioural measures which Walahfrid discusses in his next chapter. He begins it by stating that no secular business, even if it is considered legal, is allowed in the church. He underlines this argument first with a biblical reference to the expulsion of the traders from the temple,[54]

---

in medio doctorum sedens" et creberrime in evangelio repperitur in templo sermonem fecisse [...]. Sed et Petrus cum Iohanne in templo oravit, et Paulus vota persolvit, et omnes apostoli docuerunt'.

50 Walahfrid Strabo, *Libellus de Exordiis*, ed. and trans. by Harting-Correa, 10, p. 84: 'Unde cum eadem domus Dei oratorium doctrinae ita dicta putari, quia oratio est oris ratio et non tantum humilis postulatio, verum etiam rationabilis intellegitur hoc nomine locutio'.

51 Walahfrid Strabo, *Libellus de Exordiis*, ed. and trans. by Harting-Correa, 10, pp. 84–86: 'Inde est, quod primi ordines in ecclesia utuntur orariis, quia ad ipsos pertinet docendi offitium, et publici declamatores ac sapientes dictionum compositores oratores vocantur'.

52 For the interaction of clerical enclosure and extra-claustral clergy see Ling, 'Interactions'.

53 Walahfrid Strabo, *Libellus de Exordiis*, ed. and trans. by Harting-Correa, 10, p. 86.

54 Walahfrid Strabo, *Libellus de Exordiis*, ed. and trans. by Harting-Correa, 11, p. 86: 'Alia vero negociorum carnalium in Deo consecratis aedifitiis opera fieri non debere, ut non dicam, quae nusquam licent, sed quaedam alia, quae alibi interdum veniabiliter execrentur, inde

thus establishing that in a building consecrated to God no secular dealings ought to take place. To further his argument, he draws on the second epistle of Paul to the Corinthians, in which the apostle had asked the Corinthians not to hold any dispute or banquets in the church.[55] Walahfrid also reminds his readers that in the same letter, Paul reported on the disorderly behaviour of people who pray. He also quotes Paul's warning that those who behave inappropriately while attending church, do more harm than good. By quoting these passages from scripture, Walahfrid established two issues he discusses further: banqueting and praying in church.

Paul's warning is in Walahfrid's eyes the reason why Benedict instructed in his Rule that the *oratorium* (prayer house) was there only for prayer, and that nothing else should be done or kept there. Significantly, Walahfrid not only used scripture to exhort his readers but also the *Regula Benedicti*, explicitly stating that it was a rule for monks. Integrating the *Regula* into a wider context, Walahfrid tapped into the normative tradition of monasticism, thereby revealing the importance the Rule could be given in discussions about sacred space.

Nevertheless, Walahfrid's borrowing from Chapter 52 of the *Regula Benedicti* seems to be singular. Walahfrid's unique addition no doubt stemmed from his upbringing as a monk, his role as court tutor in the years 829–38, and his position as abbot of Reichenau from 838 to his death, which he only had to give up for two years of exile in 840–42.[56] All this implies that his thoughts reflected a monastic discourse, although he might have not been writing specifically for monks. In short, Walahfrid's use of the *Regula* shows that the efforts of the court to make it the most important monastic rule in the Frankish realm made an impact on the ways sacred space was imagined.

Walahfrid does not end by citing the *Regula Benedicti* on the oratory. Rather he concludes that the *Regula* demonstrates how it is sinful to gather in church without necessity, or to transform sacred places into barns or warehouses, adding that this is 'why the canons, too, have frequently forbidden banqueting and dining in churches, unless the needs of travelling compel it'.[57] In conclusion of

---

semovenda ipse Dominus ostendit, cum zelo domus Dei ductus vendentes et ementes eiecit de templo et per prophetam quodam loco queritur dicens: "Dilectus meus in domo mea fecit scelera multa"'.

55 Walahfrid Strabo, *Libellus de Exordiis*, ed. and trans. by Harting-Correa, 11, p. 86: 'Apostolus quoque Corinthios in ecclesia dissentiones habentes itemque convivantes increpat dicens: "Primum quidem convenientibus vobis audio scissuras esse", [...]. Et superius de inordinatis orantium gestibus praemittit: "Hoc autem precipio non laudans, quod non in melius, sed in deterius convenitis". Unde beatus pater Benedictus in Regula monachorum praecipit, ut "oratiorum hoc sit, quod dicitur, nec ibi quicquam aliud geratur aut condatur"'.

56 Walahfrid Strabo, *Libellus de Exordiis*, ed. and trans. by Harting-Correa, pp. 6–12. For Walahfrid see Berschin, *Walahfrid Strabo*. For his years as tutor, see Fees, 'War Walahfrid'.

57 Walahfrid Strabo, *Libellus de Exordiis*, ed. and trans. by Harting-Correa, 11, p. 88: 'Ubi ostenditur culpabiles eos esse, qui nulla necessitate coacti indigna ibi committunt vel loca sancta in horrea et apothecas convertunt, cum in canonibus quoque saepius sit interdictum, ne in ecclesiis convivia vel prandia fiant, nisi quis itineris necessitate cogatur'.

his argument Walahfrid employs not only the *Regula* to establish the authority of his findings, but also the tradition of ecclesiastical law. He relates ideas of monastic discipline voiced in the Rule to the wider normative framework of rules on behaviour in church pronounced by late antique church councils, which had gained authority by his time.[58] Walahfrid thus fuses two different kinds of normative tradition to underline his argument. Here the intricacy of his argument really comes to the fore, since he now joins the argumentative strands regarding banqueting and prayer he unfolded in relation to Paul's letter to the Corinthians.

Walahfrid made his point about consecrated space by manufacturing an intricate chain of associations centring on the Bible, which established a matrix of the Church's function as a place of prayer, worship, and teaching. Moreover, his turn to the canons illustrates that there was another normative tradition on the church as sacred space on which Carolingian thinkers could draw.

These kinds of discursive patterns also colour and shape the deliberations of the last text I will consider, which puts the two normative traditions squarely in the Carolingian discourse of the church as sacred space: Hildemar of Corbie's commentary on the *Regula Benedicti*. If Walahfrid's rhetorical strategy was to weave a complex chain of biblical examples and normative prescriptions, it is Hildemar's text that provides us with the full panorama of how differentiating discourses and images of sacred space could come together.[59] Hildemar's commentary on Chapter 52 is therefore perfect for understanding how the *Regula Benedicti* provided the framework for the discussion of Carolingian theorists about sacred space, while these same theorists — in the context of the Carolingian reforms — framed its ideas in new ways. Hildemar's line-by-line commentary written around 845 has been described as a handbook for monks.[60] His text features interpretations that either stick very closely to the original wording of the Rule or at times give meandering explanations. Hildemar's comment on Benedict's teachings on the oratory reflects an interpretative reading and reverberates with normative tropes. Framing Benedict's ruling on the oratory he says:

> Since [Benedict] spoke above about how men who either are [engaged] in work or on a journey render their duty to almighty God, consequentially the opportunity arose from that for him to speak now about **the oratory.** That is [just as he spoke] about the brothers assigned work or sent on a journey, he now directs those who are in the monastery

---

58 It cannot be determined for sure which tradition Walahfrid used, see Walahfrid Strabo, *Libellus de Exordiis*, ed. and trans. Harting-Correa, p. 239 n. 468.8. For the use of a similar tradition see Hildemar's comment on the *Regula*, cited on pp. 10–11 and esp. n. 63 below.
59 For a more general overview of Hildmar's concept of monastic space, see Hafner, 'Der St Galler Klosterplan'; Collins, *Debate on Sacred Space*, pp. 84–90; Lauwers, '*Circuitus* et *figura*', pp. 67–72.
60 On the quality of the text as a handbook see de Jong, 'Growing up'.

about how they should pray. Therefore he added this chapter about **the oratory.** Next: **Let the oratory of the monastery be what it is called: a place where nothing else is done or kept**. […] St Benedict teaches honesty, […], according to canonical authority, since the canons of the Council of Laodicea, chapter 28, of which the heading is *Meals ought not to be prepared in churches*, command it. For thus the canons say that it is not fitting for feasts that are called agapae to take place in churches on Sundays, that is in the churches of the Lord, nor to eat within the house of the God or to set up dining couches. It is well that he [Benedict] says Let the oratory be what it is called. The oratory is so named because it is dedicated only to prayer [orationi] and in which no one ought to do anything except that for which it was made and whence takes its name. And the Lord says: *My house is a house of prayer.* [Matthew 21. 13] […] thus also he names the oratory of the monastery, and through this, when he said **of the monastery**, he reveals that he included all **oratories.** But if according to canonical instruction the laity ought not to do anything in other **oratories,** it is much more fitting that monks guard [oratories for this one purpose]. Whence it is not fitting that a monk goes to any **oratory** unless it is for the sake of obedience or necessity. For **is done** is tied to action, but **is kept** is tied to placement.[61]

Hildemar here distils Carolingian ideas about sacred space. It is delineated from other places by its use and its use relates it to the divine, making it a place that belongs to God. Spatial sacredness was rooted in God's relation to a place. Sacred space was thus imagined from its connection or relation

---

61 Hildemar of Corbie, *Commentary on the Rule of Benedict*, trans. by Prior, 52: 'Quia superius dixit, qualiter illi, qui in opere sunt vel in via, suum officium reddant Deo omnipotenti, nacta ex hoc occasione consequens erat, ut nunc etiam diceret de **oratorio**, i.e. dispositis fratribus in labore vel in via directis, disponit etiam illos, qui in monasterio sunt, qualiter **orent.** Ideo subjunxit hoc capitulum de **oratorio**. Sequitur: **Oratorium monasterii hoc sit, quod dicitur, nec ibi quidquam aliud geratur aut condatur. Expleto opere Dei omnes cum summo silentio exeant, et agatur reverentia Deo, ut frater, qui forte sibi peculiariter vult orare, non impediatur alterius improbitate**. Honestatem, […], docet B. Benedictus, sequens auctoritatem canonicam; praecipiunt enim canones in concilio Laodicensi cap. 28, cujus titulus iste est: *In ecclesiis prandia fieri non debeant*. [*Council of Laodicea* (363/64), Canon 28, part of numerous collections] Sic enim dicunt canones, quod non oporteat in dominicis, i.e. in Domini ecclesiis, convivia, quae vocantur agapae, fieri, nec intra domum Dei comedere vel accubitos sternere. Bene dixit **oratorium hoc sit, quod dicitur. Oratorium** dicitur, quia **orationi** tantum est consecratum, in quo nemo aliquid **agere** debet, nisi id, ad quod est factum, unde et nomen accepit. Et Dominus dicit: *Domus mea domus orationis est.* [Matthew 21. 13]. Quia propositum fuit B. Benedicto, sicut dicit **cellerarius monasterii et decanus monasterii,** ita etiam dixit **oratorium monasterii,** ac per hoc, cum dixit **monasterii,** ostendit, omnia **oratoria** comprehendere. Verum si in aliis **oratoriis** non debent quidquam laici agere secundum institutionem canonicam, multo magis monachos oportet custodire. Unde non oportet monachum ad aliqua oratoria ire, nisi causa obedientiae vel necessitatis. **Agatur** enim attinet ad actionem, **condere** vero ad positionem'.

to the divine. This underscores the sophisticated way in which thoughts on sacred space were expressed and how intricate the concept was. Since it is God's house, the underlying assumption is that it is already sacred: by nature of it being a place of prayer, it should be used for prayer.

While the delineation of the oratory from other spaces as a place dedicated to prayer follows the Rule, Hildemar's interpretation features important conceptual principles for the definition of sacred space that the Rule lacks, since he associates Benedict's definition of the function of the oratory as a place of prayer first with the canons of Laodicea and then to a quotation from the Gospel of Matthew. He also points out that there was a certain tradition for the laity which monks had to surpass. In keeping with this, he connects the normative tradition for monks to that of the laity. Hildemar's interpretation thus develops a matrix of ideas shaped by different kinds of norms, of which the *Regula Benedicti* is only one, a matrix that is deeply influenced by wider Carolingian reflections on sacred space and monasticism.

Moreover, although at first glance Hildemar seems to present a coherent normative concept, he draws a boundary, however indistinctly, between the laity and monks. In comparison to the laity, monks were expected to live more virtuous lives. Hildemar's interpretation thus is a testament to the fact that norms, however nuanced, distinguished and differentiated between categories of Christians. He intellectually separated monks and laity, while simultaneously subsuming them under the same norm (i.e. sacred space). So while differentiation seems to be a minor point in Hildemar's text, it acquires major significance when we consider why Hildemar associated these texts. The way he connects excerpts from different sources tells us that arguments could shift focus and nuance norms in specific ways to accommodate a nevertheless unifying discourse of sacred space. These shifts reflect the emergence of a new understanding of the different *ordines*, pushed not least by ideas about the function that sacred space served for them. To understand the gradual changes in the concepts developed we now need to have a closer look at why Hildemar chose the canon of Laodicea and Matthew 21. 13 as references to explain Chapter 52.

Hildemar's choice of Canon 28 of the Council of Laodicea chimes with Walahfrid's choice to close his arguments with a canon banning banqueting in church. Both his choice and Hildemar's draw on an antique tradition, which was well known in Carolingian times as it was included in various canonical collections.[62] Why they chose this thematic strand can only be speculated. However, the canon of Laodicea was also geared towards the behaviour of the clergy and laity. Its concern was to prohibit bishops and the clergy from having banquets in church, unless necessitated by hospitality. Moreover, it demanded that the laity must not participate in such feasts. By citing the Council of Laodicea directly, Hildemar was using a canon that was also selected by the Council of Aachen of 816 as

---

62 Czock, *Gottes Haus*, pp. 38–39.

authoritative and included in its acts.[63] In Hildemar's commentary thus emerged a normative horizon, which might have been influenced by the normative output of the reform council. This points to the close connection between the Council of Aachen's impetus for reforming the clergy and the reform of monasticism.

While there is a connection between Hildemar's text and the list of canons for clerical life drawn up by the Council of Aachen, the Aachen council also provided a rule for the canons, which again offers a slightly different frame to the idea of sacred space and what should and should not be done within it.[64] The rule sought to regulate canonical life. In one of its canons it demands that the house of God shall be a house of prayer, so there should be no idle chatter, but everyone shall be standing in church with reverence and awe, whether they pray, sing, read, or listen. In this way, it added again to the list of things that should be done in church in a significant way, by including singing. Considering the issue from the perspective now of the canons, it gave centrality to singing the psalms in the place of worship.[65] This is a further example that shows how the issue of sacred space could be treated differently, depending on perspective. This becomes even more apparent, when compared

---

63 *Concilium Aquisgranense a. 816*, ed. by Werminghoff, 59, p. 364: 'LVIIII. In Africano concilio, ut in ecclesiis convivia minime celebrentur, t. VIII. Ut nulli episcopi vel clerici in ecclesia conviventur, nisi forte transeuntes hospitiorum necessitate illic reficiant. Populi etiam ab huiusmodi conviviis, quantum fieri potest, prohibeantur'. For the council and its influence, see Hartmann, *Die Synoden*, pp. 155–61. However what Hildemar and some of the Carolingian tradition took for a canon of the Council of Laodicea is actually a canon of the Council of Carthage 419. For the antique tradition, see Stutzmann, *Recovering*, pp. 119–20.

64 For a commentary and translation, see *Institutio canonicorum*, ed. and trans. by Bertram, pp. 84–96, 132–74. From a legislative perspective, see Semmler, 'Die Kanoniker und ihre Regel'; Schilp, 'Die Wirkung'. For the development of canonical life in Francia, see Ling, 'The Cloister and Beyond', esp. pp. 159–99; Gaillard, *D'une réforme à l'autre (816–934)*, pp. 124–47; Kramer, *Rethinking Authority*, pp. 91–122. See also the chapters by Eber and by Kramer and Wieser in the present volume.

65 *Concilium Aquisgranense a. 816*, ed. by Werminghoff, 131, p. 408: 'CXXXI. Ut horas canonicas canonici religiose observent. Studeant summopere canonici praedictas horas vigilantissima cura custodire et in his divinum officium humiliter ac devote persolvere. Mox enim ut datum fuerit signum, festinato omnes ad ecclesiam conveniant, quam non pompatice aut inhoneste vel inconposite, sed cum reverentia et Dei timore ingrediantur. […] Sunt etenim quidam clericorum, qui in secularibus negotiis et disceptationibus pene totum infatigabiliter deducunt diem et, mox ut ecclesiam ad divinum officium peragendum intraverint, ita fatigati videntur, ut nec orationi vacare nec ad psallendum stare queant, sed potius sedentes non divinis, sed vanis solent instare loquelis ac saecularia verba et, quod dictu nefas est, turpia et obscena invicem proferunt. Oportet namque, ut ab his, qui id faciunt, et ab illis, qui eos forte imitari volunt, iste execrabilis usus radicitus evellatur, quia secundum Domini sententiam domus eius domus orationis vocanda est. Omnes igitur ab otiosis sermocinationibus auditum pariter castigent et linguam et in ecclesia cum timore et veneratione stantes aut orent aut cantent aut legant aut audiant. Verba vero turpia et livida ac secularia nec ipsi proferant nec alios proferre sinant, quin immo laudes Deo in commune persolventes pro suis populorumque, quorum oblationibus vivunt, delictis Dominum exorent. […]'. And also Canon 132 about the presence of angels for those who sing and psalmodize to the Lord, p. 409. For spatial concepts in the *Institutio* see Ellger, 'Das "Raumkonzept"'.

to Chapter 19 of the *Regula*, which also was concerned with singing the psalms. In Chapter 19 of the *Regula* and in its subsequent Carolingian interpretations, singing the psalms is specifically not associated with any space, as God is everywhere.[66] This once again sheds light on the fact that worship was not always imagined as a spatial practice. Moreover, it reminds us that a variety of approaches was to be accommodated in the norms. Indeed, this is plain from the acts of the Council of Aachen of 816. Even if we understand the list of canons and the rule included in the *Institutio* as two different genres of normative texts coupled together as one and we can therefore assume that they were complementary, they nonetheless emphasize one perspective or the other. Hildemar, by contrast, brought different perspectives together as one.

While Hildemar's use of the canon of the Council of Laodicea might be connected to its inclusion in the acts of Aachen 816, his citation of Matthew 21. 13 reveals another facet of Carolingian discourse on how to behave in churches. A typical example for its employment is found in the *Admonitio generalis* of 789. The *Admonitio* is a key document of Carolingian *correctio*, in which many of the basic ideas about Christian society are articulated in a programmatic way. It paved the way for the normative framing of many ideas in Charlemagne's and his successors' reigns. It is often represented as the real beginning of the programmatic legislation that Charlemagne undertook to correct and emend his people.[67] This work includes a chapter that instructs priests (and by extension the laity) about the character of the church as holy space, which called for certain behaviour. The text admonishes the priests to see that the churches in their parish are properly honoured. Likewise, the altars of God are to be venerated according to their dignity, the house of God and the sanctified altars should not be a thoroughfare for dogs, and the sanctified sacrifices are to be collected with great diligence by those worthy to do so and stored with honour. Furthermore, the chapter forbids controversies, tumults, vain speaking, and other such things, citing Matthew 21. 13 and saying that the house of God should be a house of prayer and not a robber's den. Lastly, the congregation coming to mass should have its spirit aimed at God and stay for the whole of the liturgy.[68] Although Matthew 21. 13 is cited where the house of God is connected to prayer, the overall emphasis is not on prayer, but on the

---

66 *Benedicti Regula*, ed. by Hanslik, XIX, pp. 74–75; Benedict of Aniane, *Concordia Regularum*, ed. by Bonnerue, 25, pp. 192–206 except for the gloss relying on the *Tractatus Augustini*, 25. 11 see p. 197; *Glosae in Regula Sancti Benedicti*, ed. by Van der Meer, 19, pp. 207–09; Smaragdus of Saint-Mihiel, *Expositio in Regulam S. Benedicti*, ed. by Spannagel and Engelbert, pp. 208–09; Hildemar of Corbie, *Commentary on the Rule of Benedict*, trans. by Hosoe, 19.

67 Edition with comprehensive introduction: *Die Admonitio Generalis*, ed. by Mordek, Zechiel-Eckes, and Glatthaar. English translation: trans. by King. For a thorough reading of the Admonitio see Buck, *Admonitio und Praedicatio*, pp. 67–156.

68 *Die Admonitio Generalis*, ed. by Mordek, Zechiel-Eckes, and Glatthaar, 69, p. 222: 'Aliquid sacerdotibus, aliquid populo. Item placuit nobis ammonere reverentiam vestram, ut unusquisque vestrum videat per suam parrochiam, ut ecclesia dei suum habeat honorem. Simul altaria secundum suam dignitatem venerentur, et non sit domus dei et altaria sacrata pervia canibus,

Eucharist. The importance of the Eucharist is given even more prominence in the later subtle additions to the paradigm made by Theodulf of Orleans. As much as he draws in principle on the thoughts formulated in the *Admonitio generalis*, Theodulf adds to the provision in a very specific way.[69] He offers a warning to those who congregate at church for any other reason than to praise God and do his service. He prohibits debates, tumult, and idle chatter in the holy place, proceeding to say that where the name of the Lord is invoked and where God's sacrifices are offered, the angels are undoubtedly present.[70] It is perilous to say or act in a way that does not conform with the expectations and demands of the place. For his deliberations he offers a different rationale from the *Admonitio*, referencing instead the cleansing of the temple: Theodulf noted that if the Lord ejected those from the temple who offered sacrificial animals, how much more will dishonesty, vain speaking, mockery, and such jests evoke God's wrath. Theodulf's normative contribution to the discussion not only affirms the emphasis on the Eucharist, but also explicitly connects heavenly and earthly liturgies through the angels' presence at the altar.[71] The scriptural models which pervade this motif were frequently invoked in the early Middle Ages and were years later discussed by Walahfrid in his explanation of the liturgy.[72] But if we read Theodulf's reasoning only as one of tradition we risk overlooking that there is a reason why he incorporated this idea into

---

[...]. Et ut secularia negotia vel vaniloquia in ecclesiis non agantur, quia domus dei domus orationis debet esse, non spelunca latronum. Et ut intentos habeat animos ad deum, quando veniunt ad missarum sollempnia, et non exeant ante conpletionem benedictionis sacerdotalis'.

69 Theodulf of Orleans, *Erstes Kapitular*, ed. by Brommer, x, p. 110: 'Non debere ad ecclesiam ob aliam causam convenire nisis [*sic*!] ad laudandum deum et eius servitium faciendum. Disceptationes vero et tumultus et vaniloquia et ceteras actiones ab eodem sancto loco penitus prohibenda sunt. Ubi enim dei nomen invocatur, deo sacrificium offertur, angelorum frequentia inesse non dubitatur. Periculosum est tale aliquid dicere vel agere, quod loco non convenit. Si enim dominus illos de templo eiecit, qui victimas, quae sibi offerentur, emebant vel vendebant, quanto magis illos iratus inde abiciat, qui mendaciis, vaniloquiis, risibus et huiuscemodi nugis locum divino cultui mancipatum foedant?' (Matthew 21. 12 / John 2. 14–15). For parallels and the reception of Theodulf's capitulary see Czock, *Gottes Haus*, pp. 220–21.

70 The background for Theodulf's evocation of the presence of the angels can be deduced from one of his other works, the so-called *Libri Carolini*. For Theodulf as author of the *Libri Carolini* see Dahlhaus-Berg, *Nova antiquitas*; *Opus Caroli regis*, ed. by Freeman and Meyvaert, pp. 12–23.

71 *Opus Caroli regis*, ed. by Freeman and Meyvaert, IV. 3, p. 494: 'Multis namque honoribus locus ille sublimandus est, ubi a fidelibus populis undique convenitur et eorum supplicationes Deo miserante exaudiuntur et nostrę salutis mysteria celebrantur et Deo sacrificium laudis offertur, ubi ad perferenda Deo sacrificia a fidelibus populis per manus sacerdotum inlata angelicus fit concursus, ubi crebro suavisonus psallentium reboat concentus, ubi divinę lectionis arentia corda inrigantes personant fluctus'. For how the *Libri Carolini* imagined sacred space see Payet, 'L'image des lieux'. It is already Gregory the Great who puts forward the idea that the angels participate in the Eucharist, see Gregory the Great, *Dialogi*, ed. by de Vogüé, IV. 58, p. 195. This idea is also to be found in Chapter 19 of the *Regula Benedicti* but again does not relate to space, but only to the signing of the psalms: *Benedicti Regula*, ed. by Hanslik, XIX, pp. 74–75.

72 *Concilium Aquisgranense a. 816*, ed. by Werminghoff, p. 409.

his normative approach. Theodulf, in typical Carolingian manner, imagined the church as space in a matrix of function, habitus, and sacrality. He clearly emphasizes the role of the church as the space for worship which was pervaded by sacrality centred on the Eucharist. This is in marked contrast to the monastic perspective, which stressed prayer. The slight difference in detail again indicates that categories had to be employed in connection to the function of the place it served, the different *ordines*, and the role each played in liturgy.

By concentrating on Chapter 52 of the *Regula Benedicti* and its influence on Carolingian debate on the church as sacred space, it has been possible to shed light on how elements of one discourse were transformed and assimilated for different audiences. At the core, the church was imagined as a place in which idle chatter or comparable things were forbidden, because it was a sacred space. The church served as place of worship, offering the Eucharist, prayer, singing, teaching, and listening. Since the liturgy could encompass all of these spiritual functions, each had to be included in how the space was imagined. Nevertheless, authors could shift the emphasis on the different functions by including only some or by stressing just one in their norms. As the spiritual habitus of the monks put prayer at the centre, prayer was paramount to the monastic discourse on the church as sacred space as the commentaries on the *Regula Benedicti* demonstrated. Since hearing the word of God in church as well as worship centring on the Eucharist was a key theme for the laity, it was emphasized in the normative output of kings and bishops on the theme of sacred space. Walahfrid, writing for priests from a monastic perspective, centres his model on prayer and teaching, while the *Institutio canonicorum* clearly focuses on singing and liturgy. Although the issue is always considered in a matrix of spirituality, habitus, and place, the particular spiritual demands made on the different *ordines* were reflected in the thinking about sacred space crafted for them. This again goes to show that Carolingian discourse could accommodate different ideas for different purposes, without losing touch with a unifying concept.[73]

Works Cited

Primary Sources

Die Admonitio Generalis Karls des Großen, ed. by Hubert Mordek, Klaus Zechiel-Eckes, and Michael Glatthaar, in *Monumenta Germaniae Historica: Fontes iuris germanici antiqui in usum scholarum separatim editi*, XVI (Hannover: Hahn, 2012); trans. by P. D. King, *Charlemagne: Translated Sources* (Kendal: University of Lancaster, 1987), pp. 209–20

Benedict of Aniane, *Concordia Regularum*, ed. by Pierre Bonnerue, Corpus Christianorum Continuatio Medievalis, 168 (Turnhout: Brepols, 1999)

---

[73] On debate see now de Jong and van Renswoude, 'Introduction'.

Benedicti Regula, ed. by Rudolf Hanslik (Vienna: Hoelder-Pichler-Tempsky, 1960)

Concilium Aquisgranense a. 816, ed. by Albert Werminghoff, in *Monumenta Germaniae Historica: Concilia*, II. 1, *Concilia aevi Karolini (742–842)*, I (Hannover: Hahn, 1906), no. 39, pp. 307–464

Concilium Francfurtense a. 794, ed. by Albert Werminghoff, in *Monumenta Germaniae Historica: Concilia*, II. 1, *Concilia aevi Karolini (742–842)*, I (Hannover: Hahn, 1906), no. 19, pp. 110–71

Concilium Remense a. 813, ed. by Albert Werminghoff, in *Monumenta Germaniae Historica: Concilia*, II. 1, *Concilia aevi Karolini (742–842)*, I (Hannover: Hahn, 1906), no. 35, pp. 253–58

Concilium Rispacense, Frisingense, Salisburgensia a. 800, ed. by Albert Werminghoff, in *Monumenta Germaniae Historica: Concilia*, II. 1, *Concilia aevi Karolini (742–842)*, I (Hannover: Hahn, 1906), no. 24, pp. 205–15

Concilium Turonense a. 813, ed. by Albert Werminghoff, in *Monumenta Germaniae Historica: Concilia*, II. 1, *Concilia aevi Karolini (742–842)*, I (Hannover: Hahn, 1906), no. 38, pp. 286–94

Glosae in Regula Sancti Benedicti abbati sas usum Smaragdi Sancti Michaelis abbatis, ed. by Matthieu van der Meer, Corpus Christianorum Continuatio Medievalis, 282 (Turnhout: Brepols, 2017)

Gregory the Great, *Dialogi*, ed. and trans. by Adalbert de Vogüé and Paul Antin, *Grégoire le Grand, Dialogues*, vol. 3: *(Livre IV)*, Sources Chrétiennes, 265 (Paris: Éd. du Cerf, 1980), pp. 8–206

Hildemar of Corbie, *Commentary on the Rule of Benedict*, trans. by Albrecht Diem, Kristina Hosoe, Corinna Prior, and others <http://hildemar.org/index.php?option=com_content&view=article&id=9&Itemid=115> [accessed 8 September 2021]

Institutio Canonicorum concilii Aquisgranensis, ed. and trans. by Jerome Bertram, in *The Chrodegang Rules: The Rules for the Common Life of the Secular Clergy from the Eighth and Ninth Centuries; Critical Texts with Translations and Commentary* (Aldershot: Ashgate, 2005), pp. 96–174

Opus Caroli regis contra synodum (Libri Carolini), ed. by Ann Freeman and Paul Meyvaert, in *Monumenta Germaniae Historica: Concilia*, II, Suppl. 1 (Hannover: Hahn, 1998)

Smaragdus of Saint-Mihiel, *Expositio in Regulam S. Benedicti*, ed. by Alfred Spannagel and Pius Engelbert, *Corpus Consuetudinum Monasticarum*, vol. 8 (Siegburg: Schmitt, 1974); trans. by David Barry, *Commentary on the Rule of Saint Benedict* (Kalamazoo: Cistercian Publications, 2007)

Theodulf of Orleans, *Erstes Kapitular*, ed. by Peter Brommer, *Monumenta Germaniae Historica: Capitula Episcoporum*, I (Hannover: Hahn, 1984), pp. 73–142

Walahfrid Strabo, *Libellus de exordiis et incrementis quarundam in observationibus ecclesiasticis rerum*, ed. and trans. by Alice L. Harting-Correa (Leiden: Brill, 1996)

Secondary Works

Auffarth, Christoph, 'Wie kann man von Heiligkeit in der Antike sprechen? Heiligkeit in religionswissenschaftlicher Perspektive', in *Communio Sanctorum: Heilige, Heiliges und Heiligkeit in spätantiken Religionskulturen*, ed. by Peter Gemeinhardt and Katharina Heyden, Religionsgeschichtliche Versuche und Vorarbeiten, 61 (Berlin: De Gruyter, 2012), pp. 1–33

Berschin, Walter, *Walahfrid Strabo und die Reichenau: 'Augia felix'* (Marbach: Deutsche Schillergesellschaft, 2000)

Blaauw, Sible de, 'Die Kirchweihe im mittelalterlichen Rom: Ritual als Instrument der Sakralisierung eines Ortes', in *Sakralität zwischen Antike und Neuzeit*, ed. by Berndt Hamm, Klaus Herbers, and Heidrun Stein-Kecks (Stuttgart: Steiner, 2007), pp. 91–99

Bonnerue, Pierre, 'Eléments de topographie historique dans les règles monastiques occidentales', *Studia monastica*, 37 (1995), 57–77

Brown, Giles, 'Introduction: The Carolingian Renaissance', in *Carolingian Culture: Emulation and Innovation*, ed. by Rosamond McKitterick (Cambridge: Cambridge University Press, 1994), pp. 1–52

Bruun, Mette Birkedal, and Louis I. Hamilton, 'Rites for Dedicating Churches', in *Understanding Medieval Liturgy: Essays in Interpretation*, ed. by Helen Gittos and Sarah Hamilton (Farnham: Routledge, 2016), pp. 177–204

Buck, Thomas M., *Admonitio und Praedicatio: Zur religiös-pastoralen Dimension von Kapitularien und kapitulariennahen Texten (507–814)* (Frankfurt am Main: Lang, 1997)

Choy, Renie, '"The Brother Who May Wish to Pray by Himself": Sense of Self in Carolingian Prayers of Private Devotion', in *Prayer and Thought in Monastic Tradition: Essays in Honour of Benedicta Ward, SLG*, ed. by Santha Bhattacharji, Rowan Williams, and Dominic Mattos (London: Bloomsbury, 2014), pp. 101–20

——, *Intercessory Prayer and the Monastic Ideal in the Time of the Carolingian Reforms* (Oxford: Oxford University Press, 2016)

Claussen, Martin, 'Benedict of Aniane as Teacher', in *Discovery and Distinction in the Early Middle Ages: Studies in Honor of John J. Contreni*, ed. by Cullen J. Chandler and Steven A. Stofferahn (Kalamazoo: Medieval Institute Publications, 2013), pp. 73–88

Coon, Lynda L., *Dark Age Bodies: Gender and Monastic Practice in the Early Medieval West* (Philadelphia: University of Pennsylvania Press, 2013)

Collins, Samuel W., *The Carolingian Debate over Sacred Space* (New York: Palgrave Macmillan, 2012)

Czock, Miriam, 'Kirchenräume schaffen, Kirchenräume erhalten — Kirchengebäude als heilige Räume in der Karolingerzeit', in *Visibilität des Unsichtbaren: Sehen und Verstehen in Mittelalter und Früher Neuzeit*, ed. by Anja Rathmann-Lutz (Zürich: Chronos, 2011), pp. 53–67

——, *Gottes Haus: Untersuchungen zur Kirche als heiligem Raum von der Spätantike bis ins Frühmittelalter* (Berlin: De Gruyter, 2012)

———, 'Early Medieval Churches as Cultic Space between Material and Ethical Purity', in *Discourses of Purity in Transcultural Perspective (300–1600)*, ed. by Matthias Bley, Nikolas Jaspert, and Stefan Köck (Leiden: Brill, 2015), pp. 21–41

Dahlhaus-Berg, Elisabeth, *Nova Antiquitas et Antiqua Novitas: Typologische Exegese und isidorianisches Geschichtsbild bei Theodulf von Orléans* (Vienna: Böhlau, 1975)

Dartmann, Christoph, 'Normative Schriftlichkeit im früheren Mittelalter: das benediktinische Mönchtum', *Zeitschrift der Savigny-Stiftung für Rechtsgeschichte Kanonische Abteilung*, 100 (2014), 1–61

———, 'Die Konstruktion monastischer Identitäten in karolingerzeitlichen Kommentaren', in *Identität und Gemeinschaft: vier Zugänge zu Eigengeschichten und Selbstbildern institutioneller Ordnungen*, ed. by Mirko Breitenstein, Julia Burkhardt, Stefan Burkhardt, and Jörg Sonntag (Berlin: LIT, 2015), pp. 13–30

Jong, Mayke de, 'Growing up in a Carolingian Monastery: Magister Hildemar and his Oblates', *Journal of Medieval History*, 9 (1983), 99–128

———, 'Carolingian Monasticism: The Power of Prayer', in *The New Cambridge Medieval History*, vol. 2: *c. 750–900*, ed. by Rosamond McKitterick (Cambridge: Cambridge University Press, 1995), pp. 622–53

———, *In Samuel's Image: Child Oblation in the Early Medieval West*, Brill's Studies in Intellectual History, 12 (Leiden: Brill, 1996)

———, 'Imitatio morum: The Cloister and Clerical Purity in the Carolingian World', in *Medieval Purity and Piety: Essays on Medieval Clerical Celibacy and Religious Reform*, ed. by Michael Frassetto (New York: Garland Publishing, 1998), pp. 49–80

———, 'Charlemagne's Church', in *Charlemagne: Empire and Society*, ed. by Joanna E. Story (Manchester: Manchester University Press, 2006), pp. 103–35

———, '*Ecclesia* and the Early Medieval Polity', in *Staat im frühen Mittelalter*, ed. by Stuart Airlie, Walter Pohl, and Helmut Reimitz, Forschungen zur Geschichte des Mittelalters, 11 (Vienna: Österreichische Akademie der Wissenschaften, 2006) pp. 113–32

Jong, Mayke de, and Irene van Renswoude, 'Introduction Carolingian Cultures of Dialogue, Debate and Disputation', *Early Medieval Europe*, 25.1: *Themed Issue, Cultures of Dialogue and Debate in Late Antiquity and the Early Medieval West* (2017), pp. 6–18

Depreux, Philippe, 'Ambitions et limites des réformes culturelles à l'époque carolingienne', *Revue historique*, 304 (2002), 721–53

Destefanis, Eleonora, 'Ad portam monasterii: Accessi e spazi liminari nei monasteri dell'Occidente altomedievale (secoli VI–IX)', in *Per diversa temporum spatia: Scritti in onore di Gisella Cantino Wataghin*, ed. by Eleonora Destefanis and Chiara Maria Lambert (Vercelli: Mercurio, 2011), pp. 51–84

Diem, Albrecht, *Das Monastische Experiment: Die Rolle der Keuschheit bei der Entstehung des westlichen Klosterwesens* (Münster: LIT, 2005)

——, 'Inventing the Holy Rule: Some Observations on the History of Monastic Normative Observance in the Early Medieval West', in *Western Monasticism ante litteram: The Spaces of Monastic Observance in Late Antiquity and the Early Middle Ages*, ed. by Hendrik Dey and Elizabeth Fentress (Turnhout: Brepols, 2011), pp. 53–84

——, 'The Carolingians and the *Regula Benedicti*', in *Religious Franks: Religion and Power in the Frankish Kingdoms; Studies in Honour of Mayke de Jong*, ed. by Rob Meens, Dorine van Espelo, Bram van den Hoven van Genderen, Janneke Raaijmakers, Irene van Renswoude, and Carine van Rhijn (Manchester: Manchester University Press, 2016), pp. 243–61

Eliade, Mircea, *The Sacred and the Profane: The Nature of Religion* (New York: Harper Torchbooks, 1961)

Ellger, Otfried, 'Das "Raumkonzept" der Aachener Institutio sanctimonialium von 816 und die Topographie sächsischer Frauenstifte im früheren Mittelalter: Eine Problemübersicht', in *Essen und die sächsischen Frauenstifte im frühen Mittelalter*, ed. by Jan Gerchow and Thomas Schilp (Essen: Klartext, 2003), pp. 129–59

Fees, Irmgard, 'War Walahfrid Strabo der Lehrer und Erzieher Karls des Kahlen?', in *Studien zur Geschichte des Mittelalters: Jürgen Petersohn zum 65. Geburtstag*, ed. by Matthias Thumser, Annegret Wenz-Haubfleisch, and Peter Wiegand (Stuttgart: Theiss, 2000)

Forneck, Torsten-Christian, *Die Feier der Dedicatio ecclesiae im Römischen Ritus: Die Feier der Dedikation einer Kirche nach dem deutschen Pontifikale und dem Meßbuch vor dem Hintergrund ihrer Geschichte und im Vergleich zum Ordo dedicationis ecclesiae und zu einigen ausgewählten landessprachlichen Dedikationsordines* (Aachen: Shaker, 1999)

Gaillard, Michèle, *D'une réforme à l'autre (816–934): les communautés religieuses en Lorraine à l'époque carolingienne* (Paris: Edition de la Sorbonne, 2006)

Gillis, Matthew, '"Headless and on the Road": Troublesome Monks in the Carolingian Era', in *Nach Rom gehen: Monastische Reisekultur im Mittelalter*, ed. by Peter Erhart (Vienna: Böhlau, 2021), pp. 121–34

Hamm, Berndt, 'Heiligkeit im Mittelalter: Theoretische Annäherungen an ein interdisziplinäres Forschungsvorhaben', in *Literatur — Geschichte — Literaturgeschichte: Beiträge zur mediävistischen Literaturwissenschaft; Festschrift für Volker Honemann zum 60. Geburtstag*, ed. by Nine Robijntje Miedema and Rudolf Suntrup (Frankfurt am Main: Peter Lang, 2003), pp. 627–46

Hafner, Wolfgang, 'Der St Galler Klosterplan im Licht von Hildemars Regelkommentar', in *Studien zum St Galler Klosterplan*, ed. by Johannes Duft (Sankt Gallen: Fehr'sche Buchhandlung, 1962), pp. 177–92

Harper, John, *The Forms and Orders of Western Liturgy: From the Tenth to the Eighteenth Century; A Historical Introduction and Guide for Students and Musicians* (Oxford: Clarendon Press, 1991)

Harro, Julius, 'Landkirche und Landklerus im Bistum Konstanz' (doctoral thesis, Universität Konstanz, 2003) <https://www.ub.uni-konstanz.de/kops/volltexte/2003/1051/> [accessed 8 September 2021]

Hartmann, Wilfried, *Die Synoden der Karolingerzeit in Frankreich und in Italien* (Zurich: Ferdinand Schöningh, 1989)

Iogna-Prat, Dominique, 'Lieu de culte et exégèse liturgique à l'époque carolingienne', in *The Study of the Bible in the Carolingian Era*, ed. by Celia M. Chazelle and Burton van Name Edwards (Turnhout: Brepols, 2003), pp. 215–44

——, *La maison dieu: Une histoire monumentale de l'Église au Moyen Âge* (Paris: Edition du Seuil, 2006)

Jäggi, Carola, 'Die Kirche als heiliger Raum: Zur Geschichte eines Paradoxons', in *Sakralität zwischen Antike und Neuzeit*, ed. by Berndt Hamm, Klaus Herbers, and Heidrun Stein-Kecks (Stuttgart: Steiner, 2007), pp. 75–89

Kettemann, Walter, 'Subsidia Anianensia: Überlieferungs- und textgeschichtliche Untersuchungen zur Geschichte Witiza-Benedikts, seines Klosters Aniane und zur sogenannten "anianischen Reform"; mit kommentierten Editionen der "Vita Benedicti Anianensis", "Notitia e servitio monasteriorum" des "Chronicon Moissiacense, Anianense" sowie zweier Lokaltraditionen aus Aniane' (doctoral thesis, Universität Duisburg, 2000) <https://duepublico.uni-duisburg-essen.de/servlets/DocumentServlet?id=18245> [accessed 8 September 2021]

Kramer, Rutger, *Rethinking Authority in the Carolingian Empire: Ideals and Expectations during the Reign of Louis the Pious (813–828)* (Amsterdam: Amsterdam University Press, 2019)

Lauwers, Michel, 'De l'Église primitive aux lieux de culte. Autorité, lectures et usages du passé de l'église dans l'occident médiéval (IXe–XIIIe siècle)', in *L'autorité du passé dans les sociétés médiévales*, ed. by Jean-Marie Sansterre (Rome: Institut historique belge de Rome, 2004), pp. 297–323

——, '*Circuitus* et *figura*: Exégèse, images et structuration des complexes monastiques dans l'Occident médiéval (IXe–XIIe siècle)', in *Monastères et espace social: Genèse et transformation d'un système de lieux dans l'Occident médiéval*, ed. by Michel Lauwers (Turnhout: Brepols Publishers, 2014), pp. 43–109

——, '"Interiora" et "exteriora", ou la construction monastique d'un espace social en Occident entre le Ve et le XIIe siècle', in *La società monastica nei secoli VI–XII: Sentieri di ricerca*, ed. by Marialuisa Bottazzi, Paolo Buffo, Caterina Ciccopiedi, Luciana Furbetta, and Thomas Granier (Rome: Centre Europeo Ricerche Medievali/Ecole française de Rome, 2016), pp. 59–88

Ling, Stephen, 'The Cloister and Beyond: Regulating the Life of the Canonical Clergy in Francia from Pippin III to Louis the Pius' (unpublished dissertation, University of Leicester, 2015)

——, 'Interactions Between the Clerical Enclosure and the Extra-Claustral Clergy in Carolingian Francia: A Sacred Space with Porous Walls', in *Debating Religious Space and Place in the Early Medieval World (c. AD 300–1000)*, ed. by Chantal Bielmann and Brittany Thomas (Leiden: Sidestone Press Academics, 2018), pp. 127–42

Magnou-Nortier, Elisabeth, 'L'espace monastique vu par Adalhard, abbé de Corbie, d'après ses Statuts', in *Pratique et sacré dans les espaces monastiques au Moyen Âge et à l'époque moderne*, ed. by Robert-Henri Bautier, Henri Platelle, and Philippe Racinet (Amiens: C.A.H.M.E.R., 1998), pp. 51–71

McKitterick, Rosamond, *The Frankish Church and the Carolingian Reforms, 789–895* (London: Royal Historical Society, 1977)

Méhu, Didier, '*Historiae et imagines*: De la consécration de l'église au moyen âge dans l'Occident médiéval', in *Mises en scène et mémoires de la consécration de l'église dans l'occident médiéval*, ed. by Didier Méhu (Turnhout: Brepols, 2007), pp. 15–48

Noisette, Patrice, 'Usages et représentations de l'espace dans la Regula Benedicti: Une nouvelle approche des significations historiques de la Régle', *Regulae Benedicti Studia*, 14.15 (1985/1986), 69–80

O'Brien, Conor, *Bede's Temple: An Image and Its Interpretation* (Oxford: Oxford University Press, 2015)

——, 'The Cleansing of the Temple in Early Medieval Northumbria', *Anglo-Saxon England*, 44 (2015), 201–20

Parkes, Henry, *The Making of Liturgy in the Ottonian Church: Books, Music and Ritual in Mainz, 950–1050* (Cambridge: Cambridge University Press, 2015)

——, 'Questioning the Authority of Vogel and Elze's *Pontifical romano-germanique*', in *Understanding Medieval Liturgy: Essays in Interpretation*, ed. by Helen Gittos and Sarah Hamilton (Farnham: Ashgate, 2016), pp. 75–103

Payet, Xavier, 'L'image des lieux de culte dans les Livres carolins: La question des idées directrices à travers la "Renaissance carolingienne en architecture"', in *Texte et archéologie monumentale: Approches de l'architecture médiévale*, ed. by Philippe Bernardi, Andreas Hartmann Virnich, and Dominique Vingtain (Montagnac: éditions Mergoil, 2005), pp. 82–92

Penco, Gregorio, 'Un elemento della mentalità monastica medievale: la concezione dello spazio', *Benedictina*, 35 (1988), 53–71

Phelan, Owen M., *The Formation of Christian Europe: The Carolingians, Baptism and the Imperium Christianum* (Oxford: Oxford University Press, 2014)

Pössel, Christina, 'Appropriate to the Religion of their Time': Walahfrid's Historicisation of the Liturgy', in *Writing in the Early Medieval West: Studies in Honour of Rosamond McKitterick*, ed. by Elina Screen and Charles West (Cambridge: Cambridge University Press, 2018), pp. 80–97

Polanichka, Dana, 'Transforming Space, (per)forming Community: Church Consecration in Carolingian Europe', *Viator*, 43 (2012), 79–98

Ponesse, Matthew, 'Editorial Practice in Smaragdus of St Mihiel's Commentary on the Rule of St Benedict', *Early Medieval Europe*, 18 (2010), 61–91

——, 'Smaragdus of Saint-Mihiel and the Carolingian Monastic Reform', *Revue bénédictine*, 116 (2016), 367–92

Rabe, Susan A., *Faith, Art, and Politics at Saint-Riquier: The Symbolic Vision of Angilbert* (Philadelphia: University of Pennsylvania Press, 1995)

Repsher, Brian, *The Rite of Church Dedication in the Early Medieval Era* (Lewiston: Edward Mellen Press, 1998)

Schilp, Thomas, 'Die Wirkung der Aachener "Institutio sanctimonialium" des Jahres 816', in *Frühformen von Stiftskirchen in Europa: Funktion und Wandel religiöser Gemeinschaften vom 6. bis zum Ende des 11. Jahrhunderts; Festgabe für Dieter Mertens zum 65. Geburtstag*, ed. by Sönke Lorenz and Thomas Zotz (Leinfelden-Echterdingen: DRW, 2005), pp. 163–84

Schmitz, Gerhard, 'Zu den Quellen der Institutio Sanctimonialium Ludwigs des Frommen (a. 816): Die Homiliensammlung des Codex Paris lat. 1344', *Deutsches Archiv für Erforschung des Mittelalters*, 68 (2012), 23–52

Semmler, Josef, 'Die Beschlüsse des Aachener Konzils im Jahre 816', *Zeitschrift für Kirchengeschichte*, 74 (1963), 15–73

——, 'Benedictus II.: *una regula — una consuetudo*', in *Benedictine Culture 750–1050*, ed. by Willem Laourdaux and Daniel Verhelst (Leuven: Leuven University Press, 1983), pp. 1–49

——, 'Die Kanoniker und ihre Regel im 9. Jahrhundert', in *Studien zum weltlichen Kollegiatstift in Deutschland*, ed. by Irene Crusius (Göttingen: Vandenhoeck & Ruprecht, 1995), pp. 62–109

Sennhauser, Hans Rudolf, 'Klostermauern und Klostertürme', in *Wohn- und Wirtschaftsbauten frühmittelalterlicher Klöster: Internationales Symposium, 26.9.–1.10.1995 in Zurzach und Müstair, im Zusammenhang mit den Untersuchungen im Kloster St Johann zu Müstair*, ed. by Hans Rudolf Sennhauser (Zürich: Veröffentlichungen des Instituts für Denkmalpflege an der ETH, 1996), pp. 195–218

Staubach, Nikolaus, '*Cultus divinus* und karolingische Reform', *Frühmittelalterliche Studien*, 18 (1984), 546–81

——, '*Populum Dei ad pascua vitae aeternae ducere studeatis*: Aspekte der karolingischen Pastoralreform', in *La pastorale della Chiesa in occidente dall' età ottoniana al Concilio Lateranense IV: atti della Quindicesima Settimana Internazionale di Studio Mendola, 27–31 agosto 2001* (Milan: Vita e pensiero università, 2004), pp. 27–54

Uggè, Sofia, 'Lieux, espaces et topographie des monastères de l'Antiquité tardive et du haut Moyen Âge: réflexions à propos des règles monastiques', in *Monastères et espace social: Genèse et transformation d'un système de lieux dans l'Occident médiéval*, ed. by Michel Lauwers (Turnhout: Brepols, 2014), pp. 15–42

Rhijn, Carine van, 'Royal Politics in Small Worlds: Local Priests and the Implementation of Carolingian Correctio', in *Kleine Welten: Ländliche Gesellschaften im Karolingerreich*, ed. by Thomas Kohl, Steffen Patzold and Bernhard Zeller (Ostfildern: Jan Thorbecke, 2019), pp. 237–52

Vogel, Cyrille, *Medieval Liturgy: An Introduction to the Sources*, trans. by William George Story and Niels Krogh Rasmussen (Washington: Pastoral Press, 1986)

Zettler, Alfons, 'Public, Collective and Communal Spaces in Early Medieval Monasteries: San Vincenzo and the Plan of Saint Gall', in *Monasteri in Europa occidentale (secoli VIII–XI): Topografia e strutture, atti del convegno internazionale. Museo Archeologico di Castel San Vincenzo, 23–26 settembre 2004*, ed. by Flavia de Rubeis and Federico Marazzi (Rome: Viella, 2008), pp. 259–73

RENIE CHOY

Cathedral and Monastic

*Applying Baumstark's Categories to the Carolingian Divine Office**

In the discipline of liturgical studies, the Carolingian reforms occupy a prominent place: one can be nearly certain that any given account of the history of the Divine Office will mention the long-term significance of the eighth to early ninth centuries in the development of daily prayer in the Western tradition. Modern liturgical historians have consistently evaluated the legacy of the Carolingian reforms using the vocabulary of the 'monastic office' and 'cathedral office', conventionally used with reference to Late Antiquity to distinguish the rigorous all-day psalmody of the desert monks from the morning and evening services of ceremonial prayer celebrated by bishops and clerics with the Christian assembly. The 'cathedral office' adopted by the Carolingians is understood to have nothing in common with this late antique 'cathedral office', for the office which Pippin III, Chrodegang, and Charlemagne imposed upon secular clergy was a heavily monasticized cursus borrowed from monastic communities in Rome. To twentieth-century Catholic liturgists wishing to restore Lauds and Vespers as the public prayer of the assembled faithful, this obligatory expansion of the secular office over the course of the eighth and ninth centuries represented an obfuscation of two traditions which should have remained distinct: the Liturgy of Hours ceased 'to be of the people'.[1] But is it appropriate to evaluate the Carolingian changes to the Divine Office against the late antique cathedral tradition? And had the Carolingians even been aware of such a standard?

---

* The author wishes to thank the editors and Jesse Billett for offering their insight, and Christina Pössel for sharing her work prior to publication.
1 Taft, *Liturgy of the Hours*, p. 180, but a similar pronouncement is ubiquitous: for example, Martimort, Dalmais, and Jounel, *Liturgy and Time*; Guiver, *Company of Voices*; and Bradshaw, *Daily Prayer in the Early Church* ('the effect of monasticism was to spell the end of the cathedral office as the prayer of the people', at p. 123).

Renie Choy is Lecturer in Church History at St Mellitus College.

Monastic Communities and Canonical Clergy in the Carolingian World (780–840): Categorizing the Church, ed. by Rutger Kramer, Emilie Kurdziel, and Graeme Ward, MMS 8 (Turnhout: Brepols, 2022), pp. 381–401

Any discussion about the monastic-cathedral distinction of the Divine Office must of course make reference to Anton Baumstark, whose observations in the early twentieth century launched continuous scholarship into the two contrasting tendencies in the church's daily prayer.[2] The accuracy of his distinction has been subjected to much discussion.[3] Yet Baumstark's twin categories have proven so helpful a way of penetrating the complex evolution of the canonical hours — and so effective an 'interpretative tool of liturgical history'[4] — that surveys of the Divine Office will inevitably begin there, and scholars have substantiated this distinction by identifying the classic features of both. The 'monastic office' of the desert in Egypt and the Thebaid focused on the continual recitation of the entire Psalter, largely in numerical order.[5] The 'cathedral office', by contrast, focused on the principal hours of the morning and evening and featured ceremony (e.g. lamp lighting at vespers), selective psalmody appropriate for the time of day (e.g. Psalms 62 and 148-50 for the morning; Psalm 140 for the evening), and an episcopal blessing. In its basic terminology, the cathedral-monastic distinction remains in use as a way of categorizing the Divine Office of the Western Middle Ages, celebrated according to either the monastic cursus (Benedictine cursus), or the cathedral cursus (Roman or secular cursus).[6] Technically, however, the cathedral cursus of the Latin Middle Ages is understood to have little to do with that of Late Antiquity.[7] What we today call the 'cathedral office' originated during the reigns of Pippin III and Charlemagne when, under the influence of Chrodegang, the pattern of prayer used by the monastic communities serving the greater basilicas of Rome was adopted as the sole form of the Divine Office for use by Frankish canonical clergy.[8] For Pierre Salmon, Chrodegang's *Regula canonicorum* represents a document of fundamental importance to the history of the Divine Office and particularly

---

2 Baumstark, 'Kathedrale und Kloster'; Baumstark, *Liturgie Comparée*; Mateos, 'The Origins of the Divine Office'; Bradshaw, *Daily Prayer in the Early Church*; Taft, *Liturgy of the Hours*.
3 A scepticism explicitly presented in Knowles, 'A Renaissance in the Study of Byzantine Liturgy?'; see also Guiver, *Company of Voices*, p. 53; Bradshaw, 'Cathedral and Monastic'; Frøyshov, 'The Cathedral-Monastic Distinction Revisited'. For a response to the criticism of Baumstark's categories, see Taft, 'Cathedral vs Monastic Liturgy in the Christian East'.
4 Taft, 'Eastern Saints' Lives and Liturgy', p. 40.
5 The 'pure' monastic psalmody of the Egyptian desert is contrasted with the hybrid office of urban monasticism, a third category added by Mateos, 'The Origins of the Divine Office'.
6 Collamore, 'Prelude', p. 3.
7 Jesse Billett writes that the 'Roman' or 'cathedral' *cursus* is 'not to be confused with the "cathedral Office" of late antiquity, which was something altogether different'. See his lucid overview in *The Divine Office in Anglo-Saxon England*, pp. 13–77. The rest of this section owes much to Billett's summary.
8 Charlemagne's *Admonitio generalis* of 789 (Chapter 80); the *Institutio canonicorum* at the Council of Aachen 816. Amalarius of Metz's *Liber officialis*, 4. 1–2 and *Liber de ordine antiphonarii*, 1–7 is the earliest witness to the Frankish reception and modification of this office which had been used by monks in the Roman basilicas.

for the invention of the breviary.[9] For up until the beginning of the ninth century, the complete office of daily prayer had only been celebrated in the Roman basilicas which had monasteries attached to them, and in the monasteries which followed the *Regula Columbani*, the *Regula Benedicti*, or another monastic programme; secular clergy, on the other hand, shared the duty of praying the hours between their churches and according to their different ecclesiastical ranks.[10] The Carolingian innovation of enormous consequence was thus the obligation for clergy to each pray daily, in their own churches, all the Hours; even more decisively, those who were unable to celebrate all the Hours chorally with the community of clerics had to make up for it in private.[11] The adoption of the complete cursus and, by possible consequence, of private recitation by secular clerics led to the alienation of 'the people' from the Divine Office.[12] Since singing the hours would take at least eight hours daily, the Divine Office as celebrated by clerics by Chrodegang's time was clearly not intended for the laity, even if they might personally benefit from hearing the chant in the background.[13] This situation, in broad strokes, is why the 'cathedral office' of the Carolingian period and subsequent Western Middle Ages is said to be something entirely different from the 'cathedral office' of Late Antiquity. Owing to the 'breakup of the system of cathedral liturgy' and the 'monasticization and privatization of the office',[14] the distinction between cathedral and monastic offices had become so minor by the Carolingian period that, today, only a student of liturgy would

---

9   Salmon, *Breviary through the Centuries*, pp. 8–11, with details about the relevant conciliar decrees. He notes, though, that in this immensely important reform, Chrodegang was only bringing 'to a logical outcome, to completion, the earlier reform movement' which Boniface had already begun in the 740s in Francia, and which had also influenced Anglo-Saxon practice, notably at the Synod of Clofesho.
10 Salmon, *Breviary through the Centuries*, pp. 28–41.
11 Salmon's argument is based on an interpretation of the *Rule of Chrodegang*'s Chapter 6, titled 'That all should attend the Divine Office at the Canonical Hours', trans. by Bertram, *Chrodegang Rules*, p. 59: 'At the time for the Divine Office of None, as soon as the signal has been heard, let them abandon what they have in hand, and those who are close enough to the cathedral that they can get there quickly should go with the greatest speed. If anyone should be far away from the church, so that he cannot be there for the Work of God at the canonical hours, and the bishop or archdeacon agree that this is true, he should celebrate the Office wherever he be, in the fear of God'. Salmon himself quotes from later manuscripts which omit the specification of the hour of 'None' in order that the instruction may apply generally to all the hours (Bertram, *Chrodegang Rules*, p. 59 n. 43, and Salmon, *Breviary through the Centuries*, p. 9). It is therefore debatable whether this rule represents sufficient proof that Chrodegang indeed supported 'private recitation' of the hours. Nevertheless, this phrase has achieved a certain notoriety, signalling something rather ominous. Taft describes it as 'an innovation that will […] have far-reaching effects […] This was an unheard-of novelty for the secular clergy, though it was common practice in monastic circles […]'.
12 Martimort, Dalmais, and Jounel, *Liturgy and Time*, p. 180; Taft, *Liturgy of the Hours*, pp. 297–300. See also Guiver, *Company of Voices*, p. 94.
13 Bertram, *Chrodegang Rules*, p. 15.
14 Taft, *Liturgy of the Hours*, pp. 297 and 299.

be able to discern the differences in their respective *cursus*.[15] For modern-day liturgical commentators and scholars of the twentieth-century liturgical movement, this radical departure of the early medieval cathedral office from the cathedral office of Late Antiquity is precisely the problem. In the period of the Second Vatican Council, experts familiar with the history of the Divine Office strongly called for the restoration of the late antique 'cathedral tradition', pointing to its demise in the early Middle Ages; those disappointed with the conservatism of the liturgical reforms lamented that the church then (as in their own time during the twentieth century) did not appreciate the monastic-cathedral distinction.[16] The twin categories which Baumstark observed regarding the Divine Office in Late Antiquity are relevant to our discussion about the Divine Office in Carolingian Francia, because they have coloured the way we interpret the Carolingian reforms. To the logistical and pastoral problems posed by the monasticization of the cathedral office, the 'intelligent solution', Taft comments, 'would have been to return the parochial celebration of the hours *to its original cathedral dimensions*, but intelligence has been only rarely an operative force in the development of the liturgy'.[17]

With this sense of regret at the Carolingian negligence of the authentic cathedral tradition, we might therefore be surprised to note that the methodology by which Baumstark first observed the cathedral-monastic distinction was, in fact, long ago predicted by a Carolingian scholar himself. Walahfrid Strabo's *Libellus de exordiis et incrementis quarundam in observationibus ecclesiasticis rerum* — completed between 840 and 842 and described as 'the first handbook of liturgical history' or the 'first history of the liturgy' — bears an intriguing resemblance to the *Comparative Liturgy* of his German descendant Anton Baumstark, first published in 1939 and similarly described as a pathbreaking work which gives theoretical formulation to liturgical history.[18] This is not the place to rehearse the method and significance of *Comparative Liturgy* (the subject of much analysis and debate), but the resemblance between *Comparative*

---

15 For a technical explanation of how to identify the differences between the two *cursus*, see Billett, *The Divine Office in Anglo-Saxon England*, pp. 13–23.
16 See the overview and analysis provided by Campbell, *From Breviary to the Liturgy of the Hours*, throughout but especially pp. 1–8 and Chapters 4–6. See also Taft, *Liturgy of the Hours*, pp. 314–16, and see Bradshaw's analysis of this desire for the restoration of a cathedral pattern and his contribution to the discussion in 'Cathedral vs. Monastery: The Only Alternatives for the Liturgy of the Hours?'.
17 Taft, *Liturgy of the Hours*, p. 299, emphasis mine.
18 Harting-Correa, *Walahfrid Strabo's 'Libellus de exordiis…'*, p. 1, quoting Bischoff, 'Eine Sammelhandschrift Walahfrid Strabos', p. 47 and Cattin, *Music of the Middle Ages*, p. 20. And the title of Walahfrid's book ('about the origins and development of some aspects of the liturgy' when translated into English) equally resembles Baumstark's *Vom geschichtlichen Werden der Liturgie* ('On the Historical Development of the Liturgy'). On Baumstark, see Taft and Winkler ed., *Comparative Liturgy Fifty Years after Anton Baumstark*, and West, *On the Historical Development of the Liturgy*. On Walahfrid's historical method on display in *De exordiis*, see Pössel's '"Appropriate to the Religion of their Time"'.

Liturgy and what for us is the highly relevant Chapter 26 ('About the canonical hours, kneeling, hymns, chants and their development') of Walahfrid's *De exordiis* is noteworthy.[19] The two main 'laws on liturgical evolution' which Baumstark identified were already noticed by Walahfrid in the early ninth century. The first principle, the evolution of liturgical rites from diversity to uniformity, had been suggested by Walahfrid when he stated that 'the complete arrangement of the liturgy, which is now observed throughout the Roman world, was established long after antiquity had elapsed'.[20] Likewise, Walahfrid had also already noticed Baumstark's second law, that liturgy 'proceeds from simplicity and brevity towards every greater richness and prolixity':

> For when the faithful grew in numbers and the pestilence of heresies stained the orthodox peace in a greater variety of ways, the liturgy of true observance had to be enlarged: a more intelligible religion might attract the souls of those approaching the faith, and a more enhanced liturgy of Truth might show the consistency of the catholics against the foes.[21]

For Baumstark, these principles illustrated how, though the substance of the liturgy remains unaltered by time, their forms are 'subject by their very nature to a process of continuous evolution', the variations of which are shaped by 'differences of race and language and the peculiar genius of each people'.[22] Indeed, Walahfrid had earlier made the same observation: there is a 'great diversity in the liturgy not only in racial and linguistic variety but also in just one race and language because of change over the years or the teachers' zealous instruction', he noted.[23] Liturgy has changed, and this fact invites the liturgical historian's investigations. The urge to uncover how the liturgy has developed — to discover the 'laws of liturgical evolution' (to use Baumstark's language derived from nineteenth-century science) or the process by which the liturgy was 'perfected for many reasons' (to adopt the less scientific vocabulary of Walahfrid's premodern context) — explains Walahfrid's entire approach to Chapter 26 on the development of the canonical

---

19 Walahfrid, *De exordiis*, ed. and trans. by Harting-Correa, 26, pp. 154–69.
20 Baumstark, *Comparative Liturgy*, p. 16 ('Let us first consider again the hypothesis that an authoritative body of rules, whether ordered by Our Lord or the Apostles, served as the norm for further development. If such were the case, [...] liturgical evolution would have proceeded from unity to multiplicity, from uniformity to variety. But such is the exact opposite of what we find. The final result of liturgical evolution is in the Catholic West the almost unlimited predominance of the Roman Rite. [...] It is as we go back through the course of time that liturgical variety increases'); referred to as General Principle 1 in Taft, 'Comparative Liturgy', p. 525. Walahfrid, *De exordiis*, ed. and trans. by Harting-Correa, 26, p. 165.
21 Baumstark, *Comparative Liturgy*, p. 19, referred to as General Principle 2 in Taft, 'Comparative Liturgy', p. 525. Walahfrid, *De exordiis*, ed. and trans. by Harting-Correa, 26, p. 165.
22 Baumstark, *Comparative Liturgy*, p. 1.
23 Walahfrid, *De exordiis*, ed. and trans. by Harting-Correa, 26, pp. 163–64.

hours.²⁴ The basic premise of the chapter, as Walahfrid insists several times, is that the liturgy changes and develops over time: 'We must realize that it was long after the Gospel's unfolding that the celebration of some of the day- and night-time hours was arranged the way it is performed now'.²⁵ For Walahfrid, as for Baumstark, the reason for narrating the history of the Divine Office is to understand how and why the liturgy evolved from diversity to unity, and from simplicity to prolixity.

Baumstark saw these laws at work in the distinction between a cathedral office of the people and a monastic office for a separate class of ascetics, a phenomenon common to both East and West. Walahfrid, too, suggests that he was at least aware that, historically, there had been an office for the people characterized by its simplicity and accessibility. Quoting the Council of Toledo (633), he refers to the doxological *Gloria Patri* sung at the end of all the psalms which he notes people 'sing daily in the public and private liturgy'.²⁶ 'Public' in this quotation refers to an earlier canon itemizing the 'celebration of mass, vespers, and mattins', which itself was based on the earlier Council of Braga (561) decreeing uniformity of practice in the morning and evening offices, and prohibiting the adoption of individual or monastic uses in ecclesiastical practice.²⁷ 'Alas', Taft writes about this latter canon, 'as we know from the later history of the Liturgy of the Hours in the West, this pastorally wise resistance to the monasticization of the cathedral hours did not win the day'. He continues, 'The very notion that there was ever any such thing as a cathedral office was eventually lost in the mists of history [...]'.²⁸

---

24 Baumstark, *Comparative Liturgy*, p. 15; Walahfrid, *De exordiis*, ed. and trans. by Harting-Correa, 26, p. 157. Pössel's '"Appropriate to the Religion of their Time"' offers a clear and comprehensive analysis about Walahfrid's conception of the liturgy's incremental growth over time.

25 Walahfrid, *De exordiis*, ed. and trans. by Harting-Correa, 26, p. 155: 'Sciendum est multa post revelationem evangelii tempora transisse, antequam ita ordinarentur quarundam per diem et noctem horarum solemnia, sicuti nunc habentur'.

26 Walahfrid, *De exordiis*, ed. and trans. by Harting-Correa, 26, p. 160 ('quem cotidie publico privatoque officio in fine omnium psalmorum dicimus'), quoting the *Concilium Toletanum* IV (633), ed. by Vives, 13, p. 196.

27 *Concilium Toletanum* IV (633), ed. by Vives, 2, p. 188: 'Unus igitur ordo orandi atque sallendi a nobis per omenem Spaniam atque Galliam conservetur, unus modus in missarum sollemnitatibus, unus in vespertinis matutinisque officiis [...]'; *Concilium Bracarense* (561), ed. by Vives, 1, p. 71: 'De uno ordine sallendi. Placuit omnibus communi consensu ut unus atque idem psallendi ordo in matutinis vel vespertinis officiis teneatur et non diverse ac private neque monasteriorum consuetudines cum ecclesiastica regula sint permixtae'. Bradshaw, *Daily Prayer in the Early Church*, p. 115. The liturgical instructions promulgated at the Council of Braga of 561 were known to Walahfrid, because Canon 12, forbidding the singing of poetical compositions in church, provoked much debate in the ninth century concerning the use of hymns. Addleshaw also notes that the Council of Tarragona (516) mentions only two offices, Vespers and Matins, as obligatory for clergy in parish churches, and that it was 'forbidden to mix up the monastic with the secular scheme of offices' under Spanish legislation. See his *The Early Parochial System and the Divine Office*, p. 13.

28 Taft, *Liturgy of the Hours*, p. 158.

Here at least, however, Walahfrid acknowledges the existence of a public, ecclesiastical office. And this office, he suggests, had once been accessible and simple: bells in his time sound the hours for celebrating the liturgy, but their use is not recorded in the early church 'because meetings were not held as frequently then as they are now. Devotion simply compelled some of the faithful to assemble at prescribed hours […]'.[29]

Perhaps because of this fact, made equally by Walahfrid as by modern commentators, of an earlier simplicity giving way to the eventual accretion of canonical hours, liturgists have had to content themselves with discerning the remnants of the late antique cathedral office in the heavily monasticized Roman cursus that ultimately 'won the day', remnants which show some last, desperate signs of the public assembly which had once been so important in the cathedral tradition.[30] For example, the third nocturn of Sunday Vigils appears to be based on the ancient weekly cathedral Vigil; psalmody for Lauds may represent that of Roman Lauds in the cathedral tradition; intercessions, the gospel canticle, hymns, and the responsory and verse at Lauds and Vespers (e.g. Psalm 140. 2) may all derive from the ancient cathedral tradition; Amalarius's reference to the offering of incense at Vespers may be a witness to the ancient cathedral Vespers.[31] For our purpose here, of course, this search for 'remnants' of the ancient cathedral office is a pointless way to approach the question of the Carolingian reception of the monastic-cathedral distinction. Some of their chief witnesses for the liturgical code of the Roman office (in which these 'remnants' of the ancient cathedral office appear) may be found in monastic rules (*Regula Magistri* and *Regula Benedicti*); in turn, the rule which Chrodegang imposed on his cathedral clerics relies heavily on the *Regula*

---

29 Walahfrid, *De exordiis*, ed. and trans. by Harting-Correa, 5, p. 63. Addressing the question of what contrasts Walahfrid might have drawn between the Gallican office of the past and the Roman Office of his day presents a notoriously difficult problem due to the scarcity of evidence. A reconstruction of the Gallican office in use by Frankish clergy before its replacement by the Roman Office is outside the scope of this chapter, but the point which can be raised is that, despite 'monastic' influences on Gallic cathedral worship since at least the sixth century (best seen in the examples of Caesarius in Arles and Gregory in Tours), the hours of early morning and evening prayer enjoyed special regard by virtue of their antiquity (e.g. Canon 30 of the Council of Agde in 506 which emphasized Matins and Vespers held daily by the bishop and his presbyters for the people). Taft, *Liturgy of the Hours*, pp. 93–163; Bradshaw, *Daily Prayer*, pp. 111–23; Woolfenden, *Daily Liturgical Prayer*, pp. 47 and 270–72.

30 To understand why artefacts of the cathedral office can be discerned in the 'Roman office' used by monastic communities serving greater basilicas in Rome, one must return to the ancient 'cathedral office' in Rome. In the *tituli*, the presbyteral churches of Rome, probably only the two Hours of Lauds and Vespers were celebrated daily. The series of prayers for the morning and evening in the so-called Verona Sacramentary (BAV, MS Vat. Reg. lat. 316) and in the seventh-century Gelasian Sacramentary bear witness to the probable existence of this office. It was up to liturgical scholars to trace how its structure might have left its mark on the office of the basilicas served by the monastic communities. See Campbell, *From Breviary to the Liturgy of the Hours*, pp. 1–5 and nn. 1–6.

31 Campbell, From Breviary to the Liturgy of the Hours, pp. 1–5.

Benedicti.[32] Both secular and monastic usage in Carolingian Divine Office had a public component by nature of its common origins. Likewise, responsories, plural forms, or even overt references to the gathering of people may refer to a community of clerics, monks, and/or lay people without clarity, because the language comes from the ancient period. These 'public' components had ceased to hold any real meaning by the early medieval period and are useless for identifying the distinction between a cathedral or monastic use.

The limited effectiveness of the 'public assembly' as a factor for distinguishing 'canonical' from 'monastic' in the Carolingian period applies not just to the liturgical code, but also to other types of evidence. In legislation, there was a general requirement — repeated at different points in different collections — that the laity should observe Sundays and all feast days by attending at least Vespers and Night Vigils in addition to Mass.[33] The legislation does not specify where the faithful are to attend these services, and the prominence given to feast days along with the ever-increasing importance of saints' shrines associated with monasteries obliterates any assumption that the 'Vespers and Night Vigils' refer only to non-monastic churches.[34] Indeed, the architecture of Carolingian abbeys shows clear accommodation of the laity as pilgrims, who would have, by virtue of visiting the shrines, heard the celebration of the canonical hours.[35] And while Hildemar asserts that during the sacred Triduum, canons may legitimately shorten their Office because of the 'crowd of people, including women and children' and that 'monks are free from these impediments', the great monastic reformer Benedict of Aniane by contrast rather presumes

---

32 For a brief explanation, Hiley, *Western Plainchant*, p. 493 is helpful. See also the comments in McKinnon, 'The Origins of the Western Office', p. 70 on the pointlessness of searching for 'borrowed' material.

33 E.g. *Capitula a sacerdotibus proposita* (c. 802), ed. by Boretius, 8, p. 106: 'Ut omnes sacerdotes horis conpetentibus diei et noctis suarum sonent aecclesiarum signa et sacra tunc Deo celebrent officia et populos erudiant, quomodo aut quibus Deus adorandus est horis' (that all priests must ring the bells of their churches at the appropriate hours of the day and night, and they must both celebrate these sacred hours and teach the people how and at which hours God is to be worshipped); Theodulf of Orléans, *Erstes Kapitular* (First episcopal statute) (c. 802), ed. by Brommer, 24, p. 121: 'Conveniendum est sabbato die cum luminaribus cuilibet christiano ad ecclesiam. Conveniendum est ad vigilias sive ad matutinum officium' (Each Christian must come to church with lights on the Sabbath Day. He must come to the office of Vigils or to Matins); Regino of Prüm in his questions for bishops to ask lay representatives, *Libri duo de Synodalibus Causis*, ed. by Wasserschleben, II. 5, p. 246: question 57 'Est aliquis, qui in die dominica vel in praecipuis festivitatibus quidquam operis faciat, et si ad matutinas et ad missam et vesperas his diebus impraetermisse omnes occurrant?' (Whether there is any man who has done work on Sunday or on special feast days, and whether all have come without fail to Matins and to Mass and to Vespers on these days?). On the first of these capitularies listed and its status as an episcopal statute intended for diocesan priests, see van Rhijn, *Shepherds of the Lord*, pp. 219–28. On Regino of Prüm and lay attendance at church services, see Hamilton, *Church and People in the Medieval West*, p. 168.

34 For the development of feast days of obligation, see Thompson, 'The Carolingian *De Festiuitatibus* and the Blickling Book'.

35 Crook, *Architectural Setting of the Cult of Saints*.

the presence of the public at his monastery.[36] Either way, there was certainly no focused attention on cultivating the Divine Office as a public assembly in non-monastic churches distinct from the celebration of the canonical hours in monastic churches. In fact, one of the major pieces of work produced for the improvement of the Divine Liturgy in this period — the compilation of a lectionary of patristic readings to be read at the Night Office during the seasons and festivals of the year — presents a most striking example of how the 'crowd of people', even if present, were not an object of particular attention. Three factors could have given this new homiliary an orientation toward the laity: that a layperson (Charlemagne) commissioned it, that legislation instructed the laity to attend the Night Office on festal occasions, and that the compiler was familiar with Caesarius, an expert on preaching *ad populos* who had himself treated Night Vigils as a public office for the instruction of the laity.[37] Yet McCune categorically denies that this homiliary should be considered an aid for popular preaching, concluding that this significant product of the Carolingian reforms to the Divine Office was intended for use by monks at their night Offices.[38] On the basis of these types of evidence, then, it does appear that the Carolingians dismissed the concept of the public congregation as a way of distinguishing the cathedral from the monastic office.

The populace, however, do make a clear appearance in Walahfrid's account of the evolution of the Divine Office, not by way of distinguishing the cathedral (Roman) from the monastic (Benedictine) cursus of his time, but by way of explaining the very origins of the Divine Office. Harting-Correa, in her introduction and commentary to *De exordiis*, regularly notes Walahfrid's extraordinary mastery of liturgical history, accurate by any measure but all the more extraordinary for how comparable his work is to present-day scholarship. On this chapter, however, Harting-Correa observes that though Walahfrid is remarkably well-informed about the topic, his chapter appears less to be about the Divine Office than about hymnography.[39] Given the apparent digressionary and even undisciplined way that Walahfrid has constructed this chapter, we must try to understand the logic behind this, the first extant explanation of the historical evolution of the Divine Office.

Walahfrid opens with the assertion we have already noted: that the Divine Office did not suddenly appear in fixed form, but that it acquired its present

---

36 Hildemar, *Expositio*, ed. by Mittermüller, 18, pp. 29–31 (and see Billett, *Divine Office in Anglo-Saxon England*, pp. 70–71); Ardo, *Vita Benedicti abbatis*, trans. by Cabaniss, 38. 1, p. 98: 'First, how the bell was to be run for the night hours. [...] Benedict ordered that a small bell in the brothers' dormitory be tapped, so that the gathering of monks deep in prayer might first occupy their own places and then later, when the doors of the church were opened, entry might be permitted to guests'.
37 Smetana, 'Paul the Deacon's Patristic Anthology'; Taft, *Liturgy of the Hours*, pp. 150–54 and 180–82.
38 McCune, 'An Edition and Study of Select Sermons'.
39 Harting-Correa, *Walahfrid Strabo's 'Libellus de exordiis...'*, p. 288.

shape only long after the birth of Christianity. So he begins with some brief examples about the private observation of prayer at specific hours in the New Testament.[40] Next follows an apparent digression about kneeling. But Walahfrid's purpose here is to show how a private practice undertaken by individuals was eventually regulated by the Church: the Irish kneel in prayer to satisfy their own devotion, but the canons indicate which hours and seasons in public prayer one should or should not kneel. With this statement, Walahfrid introduces the crucial distinction between a private practice for personal devotion and a public prayer episcopally regulated — and thus the digression about kneeling.[41] Next, Walahfrid returns to his subject by offering more examples of private prayer: Jesus praying in the night, Paul and Silas praying in prison, and even Philo's evidence about Jewish practice. Next follows a curiously bold claim, that though individuals had observed the Hours from an early period, the 'distribution of psalms or prayers' in the fixed pattern now used 'was begun in the time of the elder Theodosius and thereafter perfected for many reasons'.[42] So the private and varied celebration of the Hours leads only to its formal beginning with Theodosius. This claim about Theodosius I's place in the history of the Divine Office is as perplexing as it is fascinating, for unlike Constantine, Theodosius is not associated with significant acts of liturgical patronage or legislation.[43]

One may conjecture that Walahfrid had in mind the contribution of Pope Damasus whom he mentions several lines down, who during the reign of Theodosius 'established "that psalms should be chanted day and night in all the churches" and monasteries, and "he decreed this for bishops and priests"'.[44] As we have come to expect, Walahfrid's knowledge here is precise and accurate, anticipating what McKinnon identified as the 'later fourth-century psalmodic movement', the popularization of the psalms as a way of praying the canonical hours.[45] But this 'psalmodic movement' and Pope Damasus alone do not exhaust the significance of Theodosius. For it was in the time of Theodosius that two figures of great interest to Walahfrid made their key contributions to the history of the Divine Office. First, Ambrose:

---

40 Walahfrid, *De exordiis*, ed. and trans. by Harting-Correa, 26, p. 154.
41 Walahfrid, *De exordiis*, ed. and trans. by Harting-Correa, 26, p. 154.
42 Walahfrid, *De exordiis*, ed. and trans. by Harting-Correa, 26, pp. 156–57: 'Ex his itaque et similibus intellegimus apud multos horas, quae et nunc celeberrimae sunt, observatas, sed non ea distributione psalmorum vel orationum, qua nunc utimur, quam et circa tempora Theodosii senioris inchoatam ac deinceps expletam multis animadvertimus causis'.
43 Harting-Correa, whose excellent commentary is consistently helpful by way of explaining Walahfrid's meanings and references, is silent here, only mentioning the years of Theodosius's reign (379–95 AD): *Walahfrid Strabo's 'Libellus de exordiis…'*, p. 291.
44 Walahfrid, *De exordiis*, ed. and trans. by Harting-Correa, 26, p. 157 quoting the *Liber Pontificalis*, trans. by Davis, 39. 5, p. 31 for Damasus: the *Liber Pontificalis* puts his dates to 1 October 366–11 December 384 (trans. by Davis, 39. 1, p. 30).
45 McKinnon, 'Desert Monasticism'.

For Ambrose of Milan composed hymns of divine praise for the people, as blessed Augustine shows in his *Confessiones*, and alleviated the persecution of the Empress Justina by their novelty. It is also written in the life of the same Ambrose: 'That is when antiphons, hymns and vigils began to be used in the church of Milan'.[46]

What Walahfrid refers to as 'for the people' points both to a social and liturgical context. It refers to Justina's demand that the Basilica Portiana (ascribed in Milanese tradition to the church now known as San Vittore al Corpo), and later the New Basilica (most probably the cathedral, known in the Middle Ages as S. Tecla), be surrendered to the Arians. The people responded by organizing a sit-in inside the besieged basilica to protect their bishop, and as a way to keep his people's spirits up, Ambrose wrote hymns specifically for congregational singing at the hours of Matins, Vespers, and Vigils.[47] Walahfrid sustains and reiterates this focus on the cathedral hours as a gathering of the people by a second example, this time John Chrysostom: for John of Constantinople was

> the first to enrich prayers with evening hymns for this particular reason. The Arians used to hold services outside the city. However, on Saturday and Sunday they gathered inside the gates and along the porticos and sang hymns and antiphons composed according to the Arian doctrine; and doing this for the greatest part of the night, at dawn they went out singing these antiphons through the middle of the city to the gate, and assembled at their church. They kept on doing this repeatedly, however, as if to spite the orthodox Christians. [...]; then, lest the simple folk be attracted by songs of this kind, John instructed his people so that they, too, should be occupied with night-time hymns, and in this way the Arians' activity be obscured and the faithful's profession of faith be strengthened. John's zeal had its effect on the crowd, and all the dangers ceased.[48]

This example draws attention once more to the crowds of people, for whom John Chrysostom composed hymns for the Night Vigils. As with Ambrose in Milan, the setting for John Chrysostom's interventions is the public, congregational, 'cathedral' prayer in Constantinople. Both churchmen used popular hymns to combat the popular attraction to Arianism, and in both cases, it was an urban space of civic importance that had come under threat.[49]

---

46 Walahfrid, *De exordiis*, ed. and trans. by Harting-Correa, 26, p. 157. Walahfrid quotes Augustine, *Confessiones*, ed. by Verheijen, IX. 7, pp. 141–42.
47 Liebeschuetz, *Ambrose of Milan*, pp. 124 and 133–34; Taft, *Liturgy of the Hours*, pp. 141–43; Dunkle, *Enchantment and Creed*, p. 90.
48 Walahfrid, *De exordiis*, ed. and trans. by Harting-Correa, 26, pp. 157–59, quoting Cassiodorus, *Historia Ecclesiastica Tripartita*, ed. by Jacob and Hanslik, X. viii. 1–4, p. 595.
49 On both events discussed alongside each other and in the context of cathedral vigils, see Taft, *Liturgy of the Hours*, pp. 171–76. For an insightful read about these two figures discussed in tandem, see Liebeschuetz, *Ambrose and John Chrysostom*.

Thus, Walahfrid's decision to give Theodosius such a central place in the history of the Divine Office shows intentionality beyond simply employing a shorthand for dating.[50] With the *Liber Pontificalis* and Cassiodorus's *Historia Ecclesiastica*, both sources on which Walahfrid depends, ignoring Theodosius's role in liturgical developments but emphasizing that of Constantine, the latter emperor would have been the more logical one to name had Walahfrid's aim been simply to identify the moment when Christianity became legalized.[51] The principle attracting the attention of Walahfrid is therefore not the 'emancipation of the Divine Office', consistently identified by prominent scholars as the most significant moment for the development of the Liturgy of the Hours.[52] Rather, Walahfrid's focus is on the liturgical productivity which marks the generation following Constantine. In recognizing the importance of the later fourth century specifically, Walahfrid shows remarkable foresight, anticipating once again with precision the conclusions of modern liturgical historians that while the services of Lauds and Vespers began to be publicly observed with Constantine's toleration of Christianity, it was only later in the same century that the Divine Office took on a stable shape which we would recognize today. For in the late fourth century, the Divine Office underwent a significant moderation, a blending together of the monastic-cathedral offices. At this point, under the influence of urban monastic communities, the 'cathedral core' was 'enveloped by services that consisted almost entirely of continuous monastic psalmody': this development is clearly seen in the psalmodic services of Vigils preceding Lauds, the addition of the hours of Terce, Sext, and None, the psalmody preceding Vespers, and the Vigil beginning in the early hours of Saturday morning into Sunday Mass, all of which were added to the cathedral *horarium*.[53] These points of structural detail are probably unknown to Walahfrid, but what he does note with reference to the later fourth century is the concept of the 'True Faith', which he insists is the reason for the admissibility of liturgical developments (the 'many new compositions for the Church').[54] Theodosius, of course, has his place in religious history, if not for liturgical innovation,

---

50 Nelson, 'Translating Images of Authority'; Anton, *Fürstenspiegel*.
51 McKinnon, 'Desert Monasticism', p. 520, where he argues that monastic psalmody made an essential contribution to the psalmodic movement but that an equally important causal factor was the 'emancipation of the Church in 313'.
52 Baumstark, *On the Historical Development of the Liturgy*, p. 57; McKinnon, *The Advent Project*, pp. 35–38. Of note is that in all histories of the Divine Office, the birth of the 'cathedral office' is assigned to Constantine in 312/13, *not* to Theodosius.
53 McKinnon, *The Advent Project*, p. 38, and see Bradshaw, *Daily Prayer in the Early Church*, Chapter 4. Egeria's description of the Jerusalem liturgy is our best extant witness to these liturgical developments. Her description makes explicit how the monastic and cathedral portions of the daily office are distinguished by the absence or presence of a bishop.
54 Walahfrid, *De exordiis*, ed. and trans. by Harting-Correa, 26, pp. 160–61: 'His verbis ostenditur multa in ecclesia noviter componi, quae non sint, si a fide veritatis non abhorreant, abicienda'.

then for his Edict of Thessalonica, which declared all heterodox beliefs anathema and thereby instituted the concept of a distinctively Catholic Christian people.[55] The Edict legislates as orthodox the belief 'in one deity of Father and Son and Holy Spirit, equal in majesty and in the form of the Holy Trinity'. Crucially, only those adhering to this law can embrace the name of 'Catholic Christians'; the meeting places of all others will not even deserve the name 'church'.[56] Walahfrid places much attention on the Nicean and anti-Arian emphases in the development of the Divine Office: 'Nevertheless', he writes, 'we know that we are not mistaken in believing in the co-eternity of the glory of the Father and of the Son and of the Holy Spirit', and the *Gloria Patri* is admitted in the church's prayers because 'it would teach the belief in the co-eternal Trinity [...]'.[57] For Walahfrid, the critical factor in shaping the Divine Office was not the legalization of Christianity, but the emergence of orthodoxy, and more particularly, of an orthodox, Catholic Christian people.

Let us notice, then, which components Walahfrid uses to build his early history of the Divine Office: the origins of the *cursus* we recognize today, he suggests, coincides with the time when the name of 'Catholic Christians' and a clear definition of 'church' first properly emerges under the legislation of an emperor, with the creative input of bishops. So Walahfrid's examples are of what we would now identify as the late antique 'cathedral office'. The absence of the 'monastic office' is noticeable: missing from his narrative of the origins of the Divine Office is the part played by ascetics in Egypt, despite the Carolingian fascination with them.[58] Benedict of Nursia appears twice in Walahfrid's history, not by way of illustrating an entirely separate, monastic impulse in the evolution of the Divine Office, but only to offer an example of the diversity of possible arrangements alongside the Gallican and Roman.[59] Furthermore, Walahfrid's approach to narrating the history of hymnography is especially peculiar because, until his time, hymns in the context of the Liturgy of the Hours would have been exclusively associated

---

55 This edict was likely known to Walahfrid through the *Lex Romana Visigothorum*, or the Breviarium *Alarici*, which most scholars believe was the principal source of Roman law within the Carolingian empire. McKitterick, 'Some Carolingian Law-Books and their Function', p. 15; Wood, *Theodosian Code*, pp. 159 and 165–66.
56 *Codex Theodosianus*, ed. by Mommsen and Meyer, XVI. 1.2, p. 834, trans. in Lee, *Pagans and Christians in Late Antiquity*, p. 136: 'Hanc legem sequentes Christianorum catholicorum nomen iubemus amplecti, reliquos vero dementes vesanosque iudicantes haeretici dogmatis infamiam sustinere nec conciliabula eorum ecclesiarum nomen accipere, divina primum vindicta, post etiam motus nostri, quem ex caelesti arbitrio sumpserimus, ultione plectendos'.
57 Walahfrid, *De exordiis*, ed. and trans. by Harting-Correa, 26, p. 163.
58 Coon, 'Collecting the Desert in the Carolingian West'.
59 Walahfrid, *De exordiis*, ed. and trans. by Harting-Correa, 26, pp. 162–63 and 166–67.

with the monastic cursus.[60] What was adopted as the secular office in Francia did not, in its original context of the greater basilicas of Rome, include the singing of hymns; hymns in the Carolingian office for canonical clergy were a novelty.[61] Naturally, without a model from Rome, Walahfrid's explanation of the origins of hymnody could have started with the monastic cursus, the *Regula Benedicti*, which did order that one hymn should be sung at each of the eight canonical hours.[62] But rather than asserting the influence of the monastic on the secular office, Walahfrid only mentions Benedict to make the rather tangential point that the Benedictine *cursus* instructs the *Gloria Patri* be said after all psalms but to fewer responsories compared to the Roman *cursus*. Here, once more, we note Walahfrid's silence on the question of the 'monasticization' of the Divine Office. At heart, this is due to the fact that Walahfrid's *De exordiis* cannot be definitively classified as a treatise intended for a monastic audience — Harting-Correa notes that the word 'monasteries' occurs only a single time in this work — and though Walahfrid had been abbot of Reichenau, his duties at the Aachen court also demanded attention to the interests of the secular clergy.[63] Yet the one place that the words 'monasteries' and 'monks' do appear in *De exordiis* is in this chapter on the Divine Office, and Walahfrid must have known how much the *Institutio canonicorum* depended on a monastic rule, the *Regula Benedicti*.[64] But Walahfrid does not recognize the 'monasticization' of the cathedral office, neither in terms of its *horarium* nor the obligation to say all the hours. Walahfrid simply makes a single point: the Office is a creation of the late fourth century.[65] With the conception of a Catholic Christian people whose orthodoxy and whose churches must be protected, the Divine Office was formally born. Here, there is no office of the Egyptian desert, just the

---

60 Other than processional ones, such as 'Gloria, laus, et honor' attributed to Theodulf of Orléans for Palm Sunday or 'In adventu Caroli, filii Augustorum' which Walahfrid himself wrote for Charles the Bald, hymns were used only in the monastic cursus. For an analysis of Walahfrid's discussion on hymnography in Walahfrid's *De exordiis*, see Harting-Correa, *Walahfrid Strabo's 'De Exordiis…'*, pp. 288–89; Harting-Correa, 'Make a Merry Noise!'; Bullough and Harting-Correa, 'Texts, Chant and the Chapel of Louis the Pious'.

61 Billett, *Divine Office in Anglo-Saxon England*, p. 107; Batiffol, *History of the Roman Breviary*, pp. 139–40.

62 Wieland ed., *The Canterbury Hymnal*, p. 1: 'In any examination of the history of hymns a central place must be given to St Benedict of Nursia […]'.

63 Harting-Correa, *Walahfrid Strabo's 'De exordiis…'*, pp. 1 and 291. But see Pössel, '"Appropriate to the Religion of their Time"', p. 80.

64 In fact, a strong candidate for authorship of the *Institutio canonicorum* is the monastic reformer Benedict of Aniane himself: Bertram, *Chrodegang Rules*, p. 94.

65 In this conclusion, he once again anticipates a modern-day liturgical scholar: 'The Office is a creation of the fourth century; it came about by a merger of the morning and evening services of the urban cathedral with the daily round of monastic offices to create a *horarium* roughly commensurate with the medieval Western Office' (McKinnon, 'The Origins of the Western Office', p. 63).

office of the cathedral. On his part, Walahfrid has *not* apparently forgotten that 'there was ever any such thing as a cathedral office'.[66]

Baumstark's two categories — and more significantly how they have been employed to analyse the evolution of the Divine Office through time — have affected our reading of the ninth-century reforms. The concerns of the twentieth-century liturgical movement have prompted us to assume an intentional 'monasticization' of the Divine Office for a class of people who ought really to be celebrating it publicly, for the gathered assembly. Thus McKinnon has observed that the monastic office is 'something of an embarrassment to modern liturgical scholars'. For the monastic commitment to the weekly recitation of the Psalter decisively shaped the character of the Western Office, exerting its influence upon secular clerics who should have been celebrating the office in an entirely different manner: this is 'precisely the sort of thing that so disturbs contemporary liturgical historians'.[67] Yet this particular sense of embarrassment comes from a disproportionate focus on the arrangement of the monastic office: the weekly recitation of the psalter, the complete *horarium*. As implied throughout this chapter, however, the distinctions between 'the pure monastic prayer of the desert monks and the popular offices of the cathedral churches are more than structural'.[68] Rather, they reflect two entirely separate concepts and mentalities about the nature of daily prayer. One key difference commonly observed is the cathedral office's ecclesial dimension in contrast with the monastic emphasis on silent meditation and individual spiritual formation.[69] But De Vogüé identified a much more subtle but crucial distinction:

> The canons' office and the monks' prayer by no means fall *under the sanction of ecclesiastical authority* by the same title or in the same degree. In the first case, it is normal that the hierarchy *control* a form of worship which it has taken on. In the second, a *great freedom* belongs to societies whose true end is not to celebrate public worship before men in the name of the Church, but to lead their members to the *secret and personal* realization of 'Pray without ceasing' by means of a communitarian pedagogy.[70]

---

66 See Note 27, above.
67 McKinnon, 'The Origins of the Western Office', pp. 66 and 72. The 'embarrassment' comes from the fact that because monks felt the need to recite the entire Psalter weekly, the office was clearly shaped by arithmetic rather than the selection of thematically appropriate psalms. Bradshaw, 'Cathedral and Monastic', p. 347, also observes that liturgical scholars have often held the view of 'cathedral office — good, monastic office — bad'. Billett offers an insightful response to this sense of embarrassment by demonstrating the possibilities for a deepening liturgical spirituality which the psalmodic movement generated: 'A Spirituality of the Word'.
68 Taft, 'Eastern Saints' Lives and Liturgy', p. 41.
69 Bradshaw, *The Search for the Origins of Christian Worship*, p. 174, and Bradshaw, 'Cathedral and Monastic' where he proposes the terms 'city' and 'desert' as more effective terms for characterizing the distinction between the two approaches to daily prayer (the former concerned with engagement with the external world; the latter withdrawn and inward-looking).
70 De Vogüé, *The Rule of St Benedict*, pp. 132–33, quoted in Campbell, *From Breviary to Liturgy of the Hours*, p. 289 n. 4 (emphasis mine).

De Vogüé, of course, inevitably, continues: 'Admittedly these distinctions were soon more or less effaced to the extent that a type of monastery centered on serving the sanctuary and the task of worship grew up, especially in frankish, anglo-saxon, and germanic countries [*sic*]'. This is perhaps Walahfrid's point exactly: the practice of celebrating the canonical hours 'grew up' when everything came under the sanction of ecclesiastical authority — when everything, in other words, came under the 'cathedral' tradition. Critically, to Walahfrid it was not the cathedral core which had become enveloped by monastic services, but the other way around. The Divine Office reached its formal stature only when it acquired an ecclesiastical responsibility for guardianship over the Catholic people.

We return to the idea of the evolution of the liturgy and Baumstark's 'laws' which he saw at work in the history of the Divine Office. From Walahfrid's vantagepoint in the ninth century, the liturgy had attained a 'perfection' which permits him to write the first history about its development. Looking back over the eight centuries of change since earliest Christianity, Walahfrid can conclude (with Baumstark, it seems) about the principles discernible in the evolution of the canonical hours: the movement from diversity to unity, and from simplicity to prolixity. In Walahfrid's view, there was only one reason for these two movements: the church's acceptance of its ecclesial responsibility, reflecting a 'cathedral style of liturgy'.[71] It is the cathedral impulse — pastoral, ecclesial, public, rather than the focus on individual spiritual pursuit — which formally produced the Divine Office in the late fourth century. The 'spiritual administration of the Universal Church' accounts for the origins and perfection of the liturgy, and the final chapter of *De exordiis* on clerical orders displays Walahfrid's view on the absolute importance of liturgical presidency.[72] If liturgical reformers have tended to uphold the cathedral tradition of the late fourth century as the 'gold standard' for the authentic expression of 'the people's' prayer, then Walahfrid's conviction that the Divine Office in his time stood in direct succession to this institution might perhaps offer some comfort.[73] Given Walahfrid's narrative of the origins and development of the Divine Office, the more interesting question to ask now seems to be *not* whether the ninth-century reformers cared that there had ever been such a thing as a 'popular cathedral office', but how they

---

[71] Taft, 'Eastern Saints' Lives and Liturgy', p. 41.

[72] Walahfrid, *De exordiis*, ed. and trans. by Harting-Correa, 32, pp. 188–97. Walahfrid's conviction about priestly duty and its relationship to the Divine Office is equally expressed by Hrabanus Maurus, who draws attention to the prophet David's prayer at Terce, Sext, and None as an act of intercession to God for himself and for the people (*pro populo*) of Israel: *De Institutione Clericorum*, ed. by Zimpel, II. 1, II, p. 250.

[73] Bradshaw, 'Cathedral vs. Monastery', p. 123. Again, Hrabanus Maurus' *De Institutione Clericorum* offers an interesting parallel, defining the canonical hours as the prayer of the whole church (*preces et orationes generaliter sine differentia universae domino offere decet ecclesiae*): *De Institutione Clericorum*, ed. by Zimpel, II, p. 248.

thought the rather 'cathedralized' monastic office of their day related to the 'pure monastic prayer' of the desert ascetics.

Works Cited

Manuscript

Città della Vaticano, Biblioteca Apostolica Vaticana, MS Vat. Reg. lat. 316

Primary Sources

Ardo, *Vita Benedicti abbatis Anianensis et Indensis*, ed. by Georg Waitz, in *Monumenta Germaniae Historica: Scriptores*, xv.1 (Hannover: Hahn, 1887), pp. 198–220; trans. by Allen Cabaniss, *Benedict of Aniane: The Emperor's Monk; Ardo's Life*, Cistercian Studies Series, 220 (Kalamazoo: Cistercian Publications, 2008)

Augustine, *Confessiones*, ed. by Luc Verheijen, Corpus Christianorum Series Latina, 27 (Turnhout: Brepols, 1981)

Capitula a sacerdotibus proposita, ed. by Alfred Boretius, in *Monumenta Germaniae Historica: Capitularia Regum Francorum*, 1 (Hannover: Hahn, 1883), no. 36, pp. 105–07

Cassiodorus-Epiphanius, *Historia ecclesiastica tripartita*, ed. by Walter Jacob and Rudolf Hanslik, Corpus Christianorum Series Latina, 71 (Vienna: Hölder-Pichler-Tempsky, 1952)

Concilium Toletanum IV, ed. by José Vives Gatell, *Concilios Visigóticos e Hispano-Romanos* (Barcelona: Consejo Superior de Investigaciones Científicas, 1963), pp. 186–225

Concilium Bracarense, ed. by José Vives Gatell, *Concilios Visigóticos e Hispano-Romanos* (Barcelona: Consejo Superior de Investigaciones Científicas, 1963), pp. 65–77

Hildemar of Corbie, *Expositio Regulae Sancti Benedicti*, ed. by Ruppert Mittermüller, *Vita et regula SS. P. Benedicti una cum expositione regulae a Hildemaro tradita* (Regensburg: Pustet, 1880)

Hrabanus Maurus, *De Institutione Clericorum*, ed. by Detlev Zimpel, Fontes Christiani, 61.1–2 (Turnhout: Brepols, 2006)

Liber Pontificalis, trans. by Raymond Davis, *The Book of Pontiffs (Liber Pontificalis): The Ancient Biographies of First Ninety Roman Bishops to AD 715*, Translated Texts for Historians, 6 (Liverpool: Liverpool University Press, 1989)

Regino of Prüm, *Libri duo de Synodalibus Causis et Disciplinis Ecclesiasticis*, ed. by Friedrich G. A. Wasserschleben, rev. and ed. by Wilfried Hartmann, *Das Sendhandbuch des Regino von Prüm* (Darmstadt: Wissenschaftliche Buchgesellschaft, 2004)

Codex Theodosianus, ed. by Theodor Mommsen and Paul Martin Meyer, *Theodosiani libri XVI cum Constivtionibvs Sirmondianis et Leges novellae ad Theodosianvm pertinentes*, vol. I. 2 (Berlin: Weidmann, 1905)

Theodulf of Orléans, *Erstes Kapitular*, ed. by Peter Brommer, *Monumenta Germaniae Historica: Capitula Episcoporum*, I (Hannover: Hahn, 1984), pp. 103–42

Walahfrid Strabo, *Libellus de exordiis et incrementis quarundam in observationibus ecclesiasticis rerum*, ed. and trans. by Alice L. Harting-Correa, *Walahfrid Strabo's 'Libellus de exordiis et incrementis quarundam in observationibus ecclesiasticis rerum': A Translation and Liturgical Commentary*, Mittellateinische Studien und Texte, 19 (Leiden: Brill, 1996)

Secondary Works

Addleshaw, G. W. O., *The Early Parochial System and the Divine Office*, Alcuin Club, Prayer Book Revision Pamphlets, 15 (London: Mowbray, 1957)

Anton, Hans Hubert, *Fürstenspiegel und Herrscherethos in der Karolingerzeit*, Bonner historische Forschungen, 32 (Bonn: L. Röhrscheid, 1968)

Batiffol, Pierre, *Histoire du Bréviaire Romain*, 3rd edn (Paris: A. Picard, 1911); trans. by A. M. Y. Baylay, *History of the Roman Breviary* (London: Longmans Green, 1912)

Baumstark, Anton, *Liturgie Comparée* (Chevetogne: Éditions de Chevetogne, 1939); *Comparative Liturgy*, trans. by Bernard Botte (London: Mowbray, 1958)

―――, 'Kathedrale und Kloster', in *Vom geschichtlichen Werden der Liturgie* (Freiburg: Herder, 1923), pp. 64–70; *On the Historical Development of the Liturgy*, trans. by Fritz West (Collegeville: Liturgical Press, 2011)

―――, *Vom geschichtlichen Werden der Liturgie*, Ecclesia orans (Freiburg im Breisgau: Herder, 1923); *On the Historical Development of the Liturgy*, trans. by Fritz West, (Collegeville: Liturgical Press, 2011)

Bertram, Jerome, *The Chrodegang Rules: The Rules for the Common Life of the Secular Clergy from the Eighth and Ninth Centuries; Critical Texts with Translations and Commentary* (Aldershot: Ashgate, 2005)

Billett, Jesse, 'Chanting the "Roman" Office in England from the Conversion to the Conquest', in *Rome Across Time and Space*, ed. by Claudia Bolgia, Rosamond McKitterick, and John Osborne (Cambridge: Cambridge University Press, 2011), pp. 84–110

―――, *The Divine Office in Anglo-Saxon England, 597–c. 1000* (London: Boydell, 2014)

―――, 'A Spirituality of the Word: The Medieval Roots of Traditional Anglican Worship', *Pro Ecclesia: A Journal of Catholic and Evangelical Theology* 27.2 (Spring 2018), 157–79

Bischoff, Bernhard, 'Eine Sammelhandschrift Walahfrid Strabos (Cod. Sangall. 878)', in *Aus der Welt des Buches: Festgabe zum 70. Geburtstag von Georg Leyh dargebracht von Freunden und Fachgenossen*, Zentralblatt für Bibliothekswesen. Beiheft, 75 (Leipzig: Harrassowitz, 1950), pp. 30–48

Bradshaw, Paul, *Daily Prayer in the Early Church*, Alcuin Club Collections, 63 (London: Alcuin/SPCK, 1981)

———, 'Cathedral vs. Monastery: The Only Alternatives for the Liturgy of the Hours?', in *Time and Community: In Honor of Thomas J. Talley*, ed. by J. Neil Alexander (Washington, D.C.: Pastoral Press, 1990), pp. 123–36

———, *The Search for the Origins of Christian Worship: Sources and Methods for the Study of Early Liturgy*, 2nd edn (London: SPCK, 2002)

———, 'Cathedral and Monastic: What's in a Name?', *Worship* 77.4 (2003), 341–53

Bullough, Donald, and Alice L. Harting-Correa, 'Texts, Chant and the Chapel of Louis the Pious', in *Carolingian Renewal: Sources and Heritage*, ed. by Donald Bullough (Manchester: Manchester University Press, 1991), pp. 241–71

Campbell, Stanislaus, *From Breviary to Liturgy of the Hours: The Structural Reform of the Roman Office, 1964–1971* (Collegeville: Liturgical Press, 1986)

Cattin, Giulio, *Music of the Middle Ages*, vol. 1, trans. by Steven Botterill (Cambridge: Cambridge University Press, 1984)

Collamore, Lila, 'Prelude: Charting the Divine Office', in *The Divine Office in the Latin Middle Ages: Methodology and Source Studies, Regional Developments, Hagiography Written in Honor of Professor Ruth Steiner*, ed. by Margot Fassler and Rebecca Baltzer (Oxford: Oxford University Press, 2000), pp. 3–11

Coon, Lynda, 'Collecting the Desert in the Carolingian West', in *The Encroaching Desert: Egyptian Hagiography and the Medieval West*, ed. by Jitse Dijkstra and Mathilde van Dijk, Church History and Religious Culture, 86 (Leiden: Brill, 2006)

Crook, John, *The Architectural Setting of the Cult of Saints in the Early Christian West, c. 300–1200* (Oxford: Clarendon Press, 2000)

Dunkle, Brian, *Enchantment and Creed in the Hymns of Ambrose of Milan* (Oxford: Oxford University Press, 2016)

Frøyshov, Stig S. R., 'The Cathedral-Monastic Distinction Revisited, Part I: Was Egyptian Desert Liturgy a Pure Monastic Office?', *Studia Liturgica*, 37 (2007), 198–216

Guiver, George, *Company of Voices: Daily Prayer and the People of God* (New York: Pueblo, 1988)

Hamilton, Sarah, *Church and People in the Medieval West: 900–1200* (Harlow: Pearson, 2013)

Harting-Correa, Alice L., 'Make a Merry Noise! A Ninth-Century Teacher Looks at Hymns', in *The Church and the Arts*, ed. by Diana Wood, Studies in Church History, 28 (Oxford: Blackwell, 1992), pp. 79–86

———, *Walahfrid Strabo's 'Libellus de exordiis et incrementis quarundam in observationibus ecclesiasticis rerum': A Translation and Liturgical Commentary*, Mittellateinische Studien und Texte, 19 (Leiden: Brill, 1996)

Hiley, David, *Western Plainchant: A Handbook* (Oxford: Clarendon Press, 1993)

Knowles, Peter, 'A Renaissance in the Study of Byzantine Liturgy?', *Worship*, 68 (1994), 232–41

Lee, A. D., *Pagans and Christians in Late Antiquity: A Sourcebook*, 2nd edn (New York: Routledge, 2015)

Liebeschuetz, J. H. W. G., *Ambrose of Milan: Political Letters and Speeches*, Translated Texts for Historians, 43 (Liverpool: Liverpool University Press, 2005)

———, *Ambrose and John Chrysostom: Clerics Between Desert and Empire* (Oxford: Oxford University Press, 2011)

McCune, James C., 'An Edition and Study of Select Sermons from the Carolingian Sermonary of Salzburg' (unpublished doctoral thesis, King's College London, 2006)

McKinnon, James, 'Desert Monasticism and the Late Fourth-Century Psalmodic Movement', *Music and Letters*, 75 (1994), 505–21

———, 'The Origins of the Western Office', in *The Divine Office in the Latin Middle Ages: Methodology and Source Studies, Regional Developments, Hagiography, Written in Honor of Professor Ruth Steiner*, ed. by Margot Fassler and Rebecca Baltzer (New York: Oxford University Press, 2000), pp. 63–73

McKitterick, Rosamond, 'Some Carolingian Law-Books and their Function', in *Authority and Power: Studies on Medieval Law and Government presented to Walter Ullmann*, ed. by Peter Linehan (Cambridge: Cambridge University Press, 1980), pp. 13–27

Martimort, Aimé Georges, Irénée Henri Dalmais, and Pierre Jounel, *The Church at Prayer*, vol. 4: *The Liturgy and Time*, trans. from the French by Matthew J. O'Connell (Collegeville: Liturgical Press, 1986)

Mateos, Juan, 'The Origins of the Divine Office', *Worship*, 41 (1967), 477–85

Nelson, Janet, 'Translating Images of Authority: The Christian Roman Emperors in the Carolingian World', in Janet Nelson, *The Frankish World, 750–900* (London: Hambledon, 1996), pp. 89–98

Pössel, Christina, 'Appropriate to the Religion of their Time': Walahfrid's Historicisation of the Liturgy', in *Writing the Early Medieval West*, ed. by Elina Screen and Charles West (Cambridge: Cambridge University Press, 2018), pp. 80–97

Rhijn, Carine van, *Shepherds of the Lord: Priests and Episcopal Statutes in the Carolingian Period* (Turnhout: Brepols, 2007)

Salmon, Pierre, *The Breviary through the Centuries*, trans. from the French by Sister David Mary (Collegeville: Liturgical Press, 1986)

Smetana, Cyril L., 'Paul the Deacon's Patristic Anthology', in *The Old English Homily and its Backgrounds*, ed. by Paul E. Szarmach and Bernard Felix Huppé (Albany: SUNY Press, 1978), pp. 75–97

Taft, Robert, *The Liturgy of the Hours in East and West: The Origins of the Divine Office and its Meaning for Today* (Collegeville: Liturgical Press, 1986)

———, 'Comparative Liturgy: Fifty Years after Anton Baumstark (d. 1948); A Reply to Recent Critics', *Worship*, 73.6 (1999), 521–40

———, 'Cathedral vs Monastic Liturgy in the Christian East: Vindicating a Distinction', *Bollettino della Badia Greca di Grottaferrata*, 3rd ser., 2 (2005), 173–219

———, 'Eastern Saints' Lives and Liturgy: Hagiography and New Perspectives in Liturgiology', in *In God's Hands: Essays on the Church and Ecumenism in Honour of Michael A. Fahey, S. J.*, ed. by Jaroslav Z. Skira and Michael S. Attridge (Leuven: Leuven University Press, 2006), pp. 33–54

Taft, Robert, and Gabriele Winkler, ed., *Comparative Liturgy Fifty Years after Anton Baumstark (1872-1948): Acts of the International Congress, Rome, 25-29 September 1998*, Orientalia Christiana Analecta, 265 (Rome: Pontificio Istitutio Orientale, 2001)

Thompson, Nancy M., 'The Carolingian *De Festiuitatibus* and the Blickling Book', in *The Old English Homily: Precedent, Practice and Appropriation*, ed. by Aaron J. Kleist (Turnhout: Brepols, 2007), pp. 97-119

Vogüé, Adalbert de, *The Rule of St Benedict: A Doctrinal and Spiritual Commentary*, trans. by John B. Hasbrouch, Cicstercian Studies Series, 54 (Kalamazoo: Cistercian Publications, 1983)

Wieland, Gernot R., ed., *The Canterbury Hymnal*, Toronto Medieval Latin Texts, 12 (Toronto: Pontifical Institute of Medieval Studies, 1982)

Wood, Ian, *The Theodosian Code: Studies in the Imperial Law of Late Antiquity*, ed. by Jill Harries and Ian Wood, 2nd edn (London: Duckworth, 2010)

Woolfenden, Gregory, *Daily Liturgical Prayer: Origins and Theology* (Aldershot: Ashgate, 2004)

GRAEME WARD

Implementing Liturgical Change in Ninth-Century Lyon

*Authority, Antiphoners, and Aachen 816**

At a synod convened at Thionville on 2 February 835, Archbishop Agobard of Lyon was deposed as a result of his role in the rebellion against Louis the Pious in 833.[1] To oversee the *ecclesia lugdunensis* in his stead, the emperor installed Amalarius, erstwhile Archbishop of Trier (*c.* 809–14) and renowned liturgical exegete. At the age of around 60, Amalarius was presumably selected because he was a seasoned ecclesiastical administrator and imperial envoy (he travelled both to Constantinople in 813 and Rome in 831), who was both known to the court and at that time did not hold episcopal office.[2] His appointment, however, was met with fierce resistance at Lyon, not least by those members of the local clergy who remained loyal to their ousted archbishop. Chief amongst them was Florus, a deacon of the cathedral church who, from 835 onwards, produced a series of seven polemical texts designed to challenge and undermine the legitimacy, authority, and orthodoxy of Amalarius's leadership.[3] His efforts

---

* I wish to thank Julia Smith, Jesse Billett, Emilie Kurdziel, and Rutger Kramer for their critical help and guidance with this chapter; all remaining errors are my own. It was written with the financial support of a British Academy Postdoctoral Fellowship.

1 Astronomer, *Vita Hludowici imperatoris*, ed. by Tremp, 54, pp. 500–03 and 57, pp. 516–17. On 833 and its significance, see De Jong, *The Penitential State* and Booker, *Past Convictions*. The classic study of Agobard is Boshof, *Erzbischof Agobard*; more recently, see Rubellin, 'Introduction' and the essays in Bougard, Charansonnet, and Isaïa ed., *Lyon dans l'Europe carolingienne*.

2 Amalarius is considered to have been born *c.* 775 in the vicinity of Metz. Helpful overviews of Amalarius's life can be found in Hanssens, 'Amalarii vita'; Steck, *Der Liturgiker Amalarius*, esp. pp. 7–11, 197–200; Jones, *A Lost Work by Amalarius of Metz*, esp. pp. 1–14 and 140–74; Bobrycki, 'A Hypothetical Slave'; Knibbs, 'Introduction'; Cabaniss, *Amalarius of Metz*, is enjoyable although less reliable.

3 Texts edited in Florus of Lyon, *Opera polemica*, ed. by Zechiel-Eckes and Frauenknecht, pp. 1–90, where they are labelled AM I–VII; for analysis, Zechiel-Eckes, *Florus*, pp. 21–76. See also Zechiel-Eckes, 'Florus von Lyon'.

Graeme Ward is a Research Fellow at the DFG Center for Advance Studies 2496, University of Tübingen.

Monastic Communities and Canonical Clergy in the Carolingian World (780–840): Categorizing the Church, ed. by Rutger Kramer, Emilie Kurdziel, and Graeme Ward, MMS 8 (Turnhout: Brepols, 2022), pp. 403–423

PUBLISHERS ❧ PUBLISHERS   DOI 10.1484/M.MMS-EB.5.128540

found success. At the council of Quierzy in September 838, Amalarius was condemned for having introduced heretical teachings to the community; by 839 Agobard was restored to his see.[4]

Every aspect of Amalarius's contested tenure at Lyon needs to be reconstructed from the overtly hostile writings of Florus. Taken together, these texts present a dramatic, if wholly one-sided account of reform gone wrong. With a degree of energy which modern scholars continue to characterize as 'zealous', Amalarius appears to have used his new position to push through critical changes to the local liturgy, provoking a backlash in the process.[5] In a letter addressed to a number of prominent west Frankish churchmen in the lead-up to the council of Quierzy in 838, Florus explained that soon after having been appointed, Amalarius convoked a three-day diocesan synod, at which, 'as if a minister of the New Testament', he expounded his ideas about the symbolic meaning of liturgical rituals to the local ecclesiastical hierarchy, wishing 'indelibly to impress all of his assertions upon the fleshy tables of the heart'.[6] To this end, he distributed his own liturgical writings. Amongst these were his *Liber officialis*, a highly influential allegorical commentary on the seasons, texts, and vestments of worship for which today he is primarily known.[7] Also singled out was his antiphoner, a book associated with the celebration of the divine office, which Florus considered to be so full of Amalarius's 'own thoughts that the reader's face is struck with redness and shame on account of his impudent audacity'.[8]

Florus developed his denunciation of Amalarius's antiphoner in another of his tracts, 'On divine psalmody' (*De divina psalmodia*).[9] In this short, sharp polemic, Florus began by railing against 'the stupid and wicked calumniator' who, in his assault on 'our holy church, that is, Lyon', had overhauled liturgical chant, 'as though the solemnities of divine singing were not being performed correctly, adhering neither to paternal custom nor ancient use'. To rectify this

---

4 Boshof, *Erzbischof Agobard*, pp. 290–94, 301–05 and Pezé, 'Florus'.
5 E.g. Zechiel-Eckes, *Florus*, p. 41 ('Amalarius' Reformeifer'); Keefe, *Water and the Word*, I, p. 134 ('a zealous reformer'); Boshof, *Erzbischof Agobard*, p. 301 ('übereifriger Stellvertreter').
6 Florus, *Epistola ad rectores ecclesiae (AM V)*, ed. by Zechiel-Eckes, p. 50: 'immo tanta intentione et studio per totum triduum proponendo, exponendo, exigendo omnibus inculcauit et tradidit, quasi noui testamenti minister tabulis cordis carnalibus cuncta, quae asserebat, indelebiliter uellet imprimere [cf. II Corinthians 3. 3 and 6]'; cf. Florus, *Relatio synodalis (AM VII)*, ed. by Zechiel-Eckes, p. 84.
7 Amalarius, *Liber officialis*, ed. by Hanssens, pp. 13–543; English trans. by Knibbs.
8 Florus, *Epistola ad rectores ecclesiae (AM V)*, ed. by Zechiel-Eckes, p. 50: 'Protulit quoque antiphonarium uelut a se digestum atque correctum, cui talia ex suo sensu inseruit, ut pro eius impudenti audacia frons legentis pudore ac rubore feriatur'. A third book, the so-called *Embolis*, can only be tentatively reconstructed through Florus's writings: see edition by Hanssens, pp. 367–90.
9 Florus, *De divina psalmodia (AM III)*, ed. by Zechiel-Eckes, pp. 35–38 and Zechiel-Eckes, *Florus*, pp. 42–47. Although the text is anonymous, Zechiel-Eckes stated that Florus's 'authorship can be regarded as certain' (p. 60). Cf. Boshof, *Erzbischof Agobard*, pp. 279–81 and Collins, *The Carolingian Debate*, pp. 58–60.

unwarranted disruption, Florus stated that 'it was [deemed] necessary to collect and arrange more diligently and more fully in the little book, which usually they call the antiphoner, the whole sequence of sacred offices performed by the customary ministry of singers all throughout the year in ecclesiastical assemblies'.[10] The legitimacy of this revised antiphoner, furthermore, was assured by a preface written by its creator, identified only as a 'pious and orthodox father', whose 'most tested faith and teaching in the service of God' stood in direct contrast to Amalarius's 'stupidity' and 'wickedness'.[11] There can be little doubt that the unnamed 'father' who wrote the preface to the antiphoner was Agobard.[12] Remarkably, this text survives as Agobard's 'On the antiphoner' (*De antiphonario*), which set out the rationale behind the revised liturgical *libellus* (which itself has not survived).[13] Florus expected his audience already to be familiar with it, implying it was in circulation before *De divina psalmodia* was distributed. 'All the peaceable and prudent sons of the church [of Lyon], in whose hands the text of [Agobard's] booklet arrived', he expressed, would be able to appreciate that their church followed 'the path of the right faith', observed 'paternal custom' and agreed with 'the ancient practice of the church of God'.[14] The wrongs that Amalarius was said to have inflicted on the *ecclesia lugdunensis* through his revisions to the liturgy could be rectified by accepting those previously undertaken by Agobard.

The sharp distinction that Florus drew between the validity of Amalarius's and Agobard's respective alterations to the antiphoner frames my contribution. In what follows, I take the local reaction to Amalarius's leadership as a starting point to explore the role played by liturgy in exercising (as well as contesting)

---

10 Florus, *De divina psalmodia (AM III)*, ed. by Zechiel-Eckes, p. 35: 'Quia nuper stultus et improbus, ipsaque stultitia et improbitate sua omnibus notus calumniator erupit, qui sanctam ecclesiam nostram, id est, Lugdunensem, non solum verbo, sed etiam scriptis lacerare non cessat, quasi non recte, nec more paterno sive usu, divinae decantationis solemnia peragentem, necesse fuit omnem sacrorum officiorum seriem, quae solito cantorum ministerio per totum anni circulum in ecclesiasticis conventibus exhibetur, sicut in eadem ecclesia favente dei gratia custoditur, diligentius et plenius in libello, quem usitato uocabulo antiphonarium nuncupant colligere atque digerere [...]'.
11 Florus, *De divina psalmodia (AM III)*, ed. by Zechiel-Eckes, p. 35: '[...] praemissa scilicet praefatione pii et orthodoxi patris, cuius probatissima fides atque doctrina in munere domini dei nostri omnibus examinata ac declarata caelebriter innotuit [...]'.
12 Zechiel-Eckes, *Florus*, p. 44; Boshof, *Erzbischof Agobard*, p. 280.
13 Agobard of Lyon, *De antiphonario*, ed. by Van Acker. Cf. Boshof, *Erzbischof Agobard*, pp. 274–75, who thought the treatise may have been an epilogue, not a prologue. On the Lyon antiphoner, see most recently Rankin, 'Agobard's Corrections'.
14 Florus, *De divina psalmodia (AM III)*, ed. by Zechiel-Eckes, p. 35: '[...] ut omnes pacifici et prudentes ecclesiae filii, in quorum manus eiusdem libelli textus uenerit, uerissime et euidenter agnoscant praefatam Christi ecclesiam eodem Christo domino gubernante ac protegente nec a recto fidei tramitte deuiasse et paternum morem, quem statuta ecclesiastica declarant, fideliter custodire ac per hoc ab antiquo ecclesiae dei usu nullatenus discrepare nec contempnere alicuius diuersum morem, si constat esse probabilem, sed, iuxta apostolum, ea, quae utiliora et potiora sunt, sequi'.

ecclesiastical authority in the Carolingian Empire. The divine office, it should be noted, was not the primary focus of Florus's attacks, and the charges of heterodoxy that in the end did the most damage were tied to Amalarius's allegorical interpretations of the eucharist.[15] Yet by focusing on the antiphoner as an object of *correctio*, it is possible to view the opposition to Amalarius through a longer lens, which takes into account the wider context of Lyon alongside the modern historiography of Carolingian reform. Concerning Lyon, it is usually assumed that Agobard's (now lost) antiphoner, together with both his *De antiphonario* and Florus's *De divina psalmodia*, were produced between 835 and 838 as part of their anti-Amalarian campaign.[16] There are grounds for thinking that Agobard initially reorganized the Lyon antiphoner before 835. Rather than understanding the text as a direct response to Amalarius, it can be read rather as Agobard's modifications to the initiatives of his archiepiscopal predecessor, Leidrad (c. 799–816). Crucially, Leidrad had made the divine office a key component of his drive to improve the state of the church of Lyon in the first decade of the ninth century;[17] however, unlike Amalarius, whose actions are known only through his opponent's broadsides, Leidrad boasted of his own achievements. As is so often the case, the legitimacy of change depends on the perspective of the sources. In addition to touching upon the representation of reform, this case study also illuminates the place of the divine office in the modern study of Carolingian monastic and liturgical history, not least regarding the central focus of this volume: the Aachen reform councils of 816/17 and the separation of monks and canons. Exploring the implementation of liturgical change in Lyon encourages key aspects of this narrative to be queried. Before doing so, however, it will be helpful not only to sketch this historiographical background but also to introduce the antiphoner, the liturgical book at the heart of this chapter.

Categorizing the Church? Antiphoners and Aachen 816

Antiphoners are liturgical books that contain texts that were sung in the performance of ecclesiastical ritual. The Latin word *antiphonarium* can refer

---

15 On the contrasting theological positions of the protagonists, see Kolping, 'Amalar von Metz'; Pohlen, *Die südeuropäisch-spanisch-gotische Gruppe*, pp. 96–141; Boshof, *Erzbischof Agobard*, pp. 288–90; Zechiel-Eckes, *Florus*, pp. 61–70; Chazelle, 'Amalarius' *Liber Officialis*'; Collins, *Carolingian Debate*, pp. 41–65; on Amalarius's method, see also Bobrycki, 'A Hypothetical Slave'.

16 L. Van Acker favoured a date of 835–38 for *De antiphonario*: see his edition, p. xlvi, as did Boshof, *Erzbischof Agobard*, pp. 278–79 and Zechiel-Eckes, *Florus*, p. 73; Rankin, 'Agobard's Corrections', p. 270 ('at some time after 835'). Hanssens, 'Amalarii vita', p. 80 thought either before 835 or after Agobard's return in 839; Collins, *The Carolingian Debate*, p. 55 suggested Agobard made his revisions before 835 ('Agobard's exasperation is palpable as he relates how under his care the church of Lyon had removed all extrabiblical material from the cathedral's chant, only to see such *humana figmenta* reinstated by Amalarius').

17 Cf. De Jong, 'The State of the Church'.

to the book containing chants for the mass or the divine office.[18] It is unknown precisely when or by whom these various chants were composed, arranged, and compiled together into books, although by the Carolingian period the creation of both the mass and office antiphoners was often attributed to Pope Gregory the Great (590–604).[19] These books, which allege to preserve the ancient Roman liturgy, are extant only in copies produced and edited in Carolingian Francia from the later eighth century onwards, as part of the intertwined concerns of 'correcting' authoritative books and adopting and adapting Roman texts for Frankish use.[20] The complicated and often obscure processes by which these books and the repertories they transmit came into being do not concern me here.[21] Rather, I wish only to touch upon the office antiphoner, and only insofar as it relates to the controversy at Lyon and to the theme of this volume.

At first glance, office antiphoners appear highly germane to the topic of categorizing the church. These books contain antiphons and responsories, short chants connected to psalm singing and night office readings respectively. These chants comprise the central part of the divine office (*officium divinum*), the sequence of 'sung corporate prayer' that structured the lives of members of religious communities.[22] As Charles Dereine stated, the 'essential task' of both monks and canons was 'the chant of the office'.[23] For monks and canons, the basic structure of the office was largely the same, encompassing the chanting of psalms, antiphons, readings, and responsories at defined 'hours' of each day, beginning with matins in the middle of the night, followed by lauds, prime, terce, sext, none, vespers, and finally compline. There were nevertheless distinctions between the monastic and non-monastic regimes of prayer. During the night office on Sundays and feast days, the monastic service consisted of twelve readings and responsories, divided in blocks of four across three nocturns, while the non-monastic office — usually labelled either the secular or Roman office — contained only nine, divided into three rounds of three. The other key distinction lay in how all 150 psalms of the psalter

---

18 Mass antiphoners: Hesbert, ed., *Antiphonale Missarum*; office antiphoners: Hesbert, ed., *Corpus antiphonalium officii*, I–VI.
19 For this reason they are sometimes called Gregorian antiphoners, and the singing associated with them is Gregorian chant; cf. Stäblein, '*Gregorius Praesul*'. Agobard drew attention to the Gregorian authority of the antiphoner, though primarily to critique dubious chants, which he argued should not be associated with that *inlustrissimus doctor*: *De antiphonario*, ed. by Van Acker, 15, pp. 347–48. Amalarius uniquely noted that some antiphoners came with a preface attributed to Pope Hadrian I (772–95): *Prologus antiphonarii*, ed. by Hanssens, p. 361 and *De ordine antiphonarii*, ed. by Hanssens, Prologue, p. 14.
20 For overviews of Romanization, see Hen, 'The Romanization of the Frankish Liturgy' and Steck, '*Secundum usum romanum*'. See also Arthur Westwell in the present volume. Concerning chant Carolingian *correctio*, see Rankin, *Writing Sounds*, pp. 337–61.
21 Rankin, 'The Making'; Huglo, 'L'antiphonaire'.
22 Quote from Harper, *The Forms and Orders of Western Liturgy*, p. 74.
23 Dereine, 'Chanoines', p. 365.

were divided up amongst the various hours of each day of the week.[24] These differences are reflected in the modern bipartite taxonomy of antiphoners. In the critical edition by René-Jean Hesbert, the various exemplars were divided into two main groups: those reflecting the *cursus monasticus* and those reflecting the *cursus romanus*.[25]

Josef Semmler, in his pioneering article of 1960, 'Reichsidee und kirchliche Gesetzgebung bei Ludwig dem Frommen', argued that as a result of the Aachen council of 816, the divine office became a vital way by which monks were to be distinguished from canons.[26] Throughout the reigns of Pippin III and Charlemagne, it was argued, all ecclesiastics, whether monastic or clerical, had been urged to emulate what was understood to be the practice of the Roman church and thus sing the Roman office.[27] In the early ninth century, the court shifted from advocating unity in liturgical practice to stressing differentiation between monastic and clerical *ordines*. After 816, monks and canons were expected not only to swear different 'professions' upon undertaking religious life, but also 'in the liturgy, the innermost domain of each ecclesiastical community, they were to adhere to different forms of the office'. Liturgical concerns thus underpinned the 816 *Reformsynode*.[28] It has even been suggested that the legislation that stemmed from this imperial gathering and its follow-up in 817 bore directly upon the production of antiphoners. In his *History of Liturgical Books*, Eric Palazzo noted that the Aachen councils 'imposed a choice between the Benedictine Rule (twelve responsories at the night office) and the canonical office (Roman or secular, with nine responsories), necessitating for the latter progressive adaptations in the course of the ninth century'.[29]

Palazzo here had in mind the remarkable and unprecedented interest in editing and correcting office antiphoners that took place in the Carolingian Empire between *c.* 819 and *c.* 838. We have already encountered two of the three surviving examples, those of Amalarius and Agobard. Helisachar's antiphoner is the third. In each case, the liturgical books themselves are no longer extant; only accompanying letters, prefaces, and expositions have

---

24 Billett, *The Divine Office*, pp. 13–23. The following discussion is deeply indebted to Billett's work.
25 Hesbert ed., *Corpus antiphonalium officii*, vol. 1 was dedicated to the *cursus romanus* and vol. 2 to the *cursus monasticus*.
26 Semmler, 'Reichsidee', esp. pp. 46–53.
27 Cf. Hen, 'The Romanization of the Frankish Liturgy'.
28 Semmler, 'Reichsidee', pp. 46–48; see also 63–65, at 65: 'Denn die Frage des officium spielte auf der Reichssynode von 816 die zentrale Rolle; erst sie leitete die strenge Scheidung der ordines der canonici und der monachi auch im liturgischen Bereich ein'. Semmler's assessment is repeated, for example, by Marchal, 'Was war das weltliche Kanonikerinstitut', pp. 784–85: 'Sinnfällig kam diese Scheidung [between monks and canons] gerade in dem wichtigen Bereich der Liturgie zum Ausdruck, wo die Mönche auf den cursus s. Benedicti festgelegt wurden, die Kanoniker auf den ordo Romanus'; Picker, *Pastor doctus*, pp. 70–74, esp. 72; Billett, *The Divine Office*, p. 66.
29 Palazzo, *A History of Liturgical Books*, pp. 139–40.

been preserved.[30] Despite differences in how each of the men described or justified their editions, all three can be taken as divergent responses to a shared dissatisfaction with the antiphoners available to them. Agobard's was the most radical of the three. He excised antiphons and responsories of unknown or questionable authorship, leaving behind only 'the purest words of scripture'.[31] As Florus expressed it in his *De divina psalmodia*, if 'nothing but divine words are generally sung during the day at mass, then the same law (*lex*) ought to be observed at night during the sacred vigils'.[32] The texts of the night office were the specific concern at Lyon, as they were for Helisachar, who served as Louis the Pious's imperial chancellor until 7 August 819 before becoming abbot of both St Riquier and St Aubin, Angers. His revisions were carried out in collaboration with Archbishop Nibridius of Narbonne, with whom he was accustomed to celebrate the night office at the Aachen palace chapel while attending court. With respect to the chants of the night office, he came to the conclusion that although the antiphoner 'was properly edited by its author at Rome', it had become 'considerably corrupted' in the process of transmission.[33] Amalarius knew and explicitly drew upon Helisachar's work for his own project, which he undertook not long after returning to Francia after travelling to Rome as an imperial envoy in 831. He sought to compare and contrast Frankish antiphoners that he associated with the Metz with a number of books which, Pope Gregory IV (died 844) himself informed him, had been taken from St Peter's by Abbot Wala to Corbie.[34]

On the one hand, these survivals have much to tell us about the history of liturgical books and the shape of the Roman office in the Carolingian period. In the conspicuous absence of early manuscripts containing antiphoners, the commentaries of Amalarius in particular have contributed greatly to the modern study of the divine office in the eighth and ninth centuries. They supply 'the first systematic description of the Roman office', and have been used to help illustrate the sort of liturgical *ordo* Chrodegang of Metz envisaged for his canonical clergy when in the 750s he instructed them to sing Roman chant; Amalarius even has been used to shed light on the liturgy

---

30 Huglo, 'Les remaniements'; Rankin, *Writing Sounds*, pp. 347–53; Gillis, *Heresy and Dissent*, pp. 217–26 surveys a further example of the correction of the antiphoner.
31 Agobard, *De antiphonario*, ed. by Van Acker, pp. 337–51. For discussion, see Huglo, 'Les remaniements', pp. 102–13 and Rankin, 'Agobard's Corrections'.
32 Florus, *De divina psalmodia (AM III)*, ed. by Zechiel-Eckes, p. 36: 'Certe, si quid sanum cogitare uellet, sufficeret ei ad omnem emendationem et silentium, quod sicut in diebus ad missas non nisi diuina generaliter eloquia decantantur, ita et in noctibus ad sacras deo uigilias exhibendas eadem procul dubio lex debeat obseruari'.
33 Helisachar, *Epistula*, ed. by Dümmler, pp. 307–09. Translation from Levy, 'Abbot Helisachar's Antiphoner', p. 180.
34 See Amalarius, *Prologus antiphonarii*, ed. by Hanssens, pp. 361–63 and Amalarius, *De ordine antiphonarii*, ed. by Hanssens, pp. 13–109.

of papal Rome itself.[35] On the other hand, I am not sure that they can be connected directly back to the Aachen reform councils of 816/17 and the division of monastic and canonical forms of the office allegedly advocated at them. Jesse Billett, for instance, already has demonstrated that the process of making liturgical books conform to the Benedictine cursus was slow and most likely not widely realized until the eleventh century. Before 816 and still long after, monks and canons most likely used the same or very similar office books: as far as the daily celebration of worship was concerned, the two *ordines* appear to have remained entangled throughout much of the ninth century and beyond.[36]

Billett's critique can be taken further. There is a monastic bias built into the master narrative of liturgical development centred on the Aachen reform councils. The need to adopt either Benedictine or canonical observance mainly has been understood as a demand placed upon communities of monks deemed insufficiently Benedictine. This is in part a reflection of the sources. Even if its prescriptions were not realized, the monastic guidelines that stemmed from Aachen 816 urged all monks, many of whom presumably were not already doing so, to sing the office as contained within the *Regula Benedicti*.[37] No exact parallel prescription for the Roman office, however, can be found in the *Institutio canonicorum* or *Institutio sanctimonialium*.[38] To be sure, the performance of the *officium divinum* was considered a vital, defining aspect of the life of canons and canonesses. For example, the expressed intention of the *IC*, especially the rule found at the end of it, was to instil within canonical clergy — or rather, the prelates supervising them — a moral

---

35 Billett, *The Divine Office*, p. 30; Robertson, *The Service-Books*, p. 34: 'The liturgical prescriptions of this Rule [of Chrodegang] were similar to those of the Roman cursus, as described by the ninth-century liturgical commentator Amalarius of Metz'; Leahy, 'Archivio di San Pietro'.
36 Billett, *The Divine Office*, pp. 66–77. See also p. 62: 'The Roman form was used by both monks and secular clerics. There certainly seems to have been no question of different liturgical books for monks and secular clergy. As has already been mentioned, Wala, abbot of Corbie, obtained a copy of the Roman Office antiphoner, presumably for use in his monastery'.
37 *Synodi primae Aquisgranensis*, ed. by Semmler, 3, p. 458: 'Ut officium iuxta quod in regula sancti Benedicti continetur celebrent'; *Chronicon Laurissense breve*, ed. by Schnorr von Carosfeld, 5.3, pp. 38–39: 'Anno III. Hludovichi factum est concilium magnum in Aquisgrani in mense Augusto et praeceptum est, ut monachi omnes cursum sancti Benedicti cantarent ordine regulari [...]'.
38 Billett, *The Divine Office*, p. 65: the *Institutio canonicorum* 'enjoined on canons the recitation of their own Office', while adding that it 'is clear that the Office referred to [...] followed the Roman arrangement, although it is never explicitly named as "Roman"'. Cf. Ling, 'Cloister and Beyond', who has described the Office of the *IC* as 'Isidorean', since its liturgical chapters are drawn largely from Isidore's *De ecclesiasticis officiis*. The office of prime, which was common to monastic and secular practice, was absent, and was added only later in the ninth century in the so-called *Regula longior*. See also Cinzia Grifoni in the present volume.

obligation to worship regularly and correctly.[39] Yet in contrast to Chapters 8–18 of the *Regula Benedicti*, to which Aachen 816 monastic decrees referred, the *IC* did not recommend a specific liturgical cursus to be followed; it gave no indication of what precisely should be chanted or in what order.

It may be that the lack of this sort of liturgical detail is only surprising if it is assumed that it was part of the compilers' remit to supply it. If, for example, such details were present in the (Roman) liturgical books that communities already possessed, there would have been no need to spell them out. Even if this were the case, it still seems that there is some tension here. While adhering to the Benedictine cursus was, or at least gradually would become, a sign of monastic identity, there was no explicit requirement for non-monastic clergy to consciously adopt the *officium romanum*, since most religious communities, canonical or otherwise, already would have been following it in some form or another. Canonical clergy were not categorized by their own distinct cursus, but rather by their rule, property rights, and dress.

The liturgical vagueness of the *Institutio canonicorum*, moreover, may also have been purposeful, to account for the whole range of communities that were expected to become canonical. If, as Rudolf Schieffer stated, the *Institutio* 'aimed at nothing less than subjecting all non-monastic clergy within the empire to a single norm of liturgy and lifestyle', then it stands to reason that considerable room was left to local authorities to decide upon the specifics of worship.[40] Although admittedly obliquely, the various revisions of the antiphoner serve to illustrate this point. The proper, regulated performance of the *officium divinum* was a prerequisite for the canonical way of life, but beyond this basic expectation, the particular books and the choice of chants could be decided by bishops.[41] Rather than understand the various changes to the antiphoner as a direct consequence of Aachen 816, it is more helpful to imagine more dynamic relationships between imperial pronouncements (e.g. the *Institutio canonicorum*) and local initiatives (e.g. revisions to liturgical books): sometimes there could be direct connections, but often local events followed their own logic. Reform can be both top-down and bottom-up, or even a complex symbiosis of both. To illustrate this point, it will be helpful to turn our attention back to Lyon.

---

39 *Institutio canonicorum*, ed. by Werminghoff, 126–37, pp. 406–14. See also, *Institutio canonicorum*, ed. by Werminghoff, 145, pp. 419–20. Picker, *Pastor doctus*, pp. 128–29.
40 Schieffer, *Die Entstehung von Domkapiteln*, p. 232. That the *Institutio canonicorum* was to apply to all non-monastic communities, see also Semmler, 'Die Kanoniker und ihre Regel', pp. 101–02, Gaillard, *D'une réforme à l'autre*, p. 127; for fuller treatment see Kurdziel in the present volume.
41 The production of texts on baptism provides a comparable example of this: Keefe, *Water and the Word*, I, esp. pp. 143–55.

Managing the Liturgy: Lyon between Leidrad and Amalarius

Agobard was one of the four metropolitans whose reception of the official texts of the *Institutio canonicorum* and *Institutio sanctimonialium* is documented.[42] After the conclusion of the 816 Aachen assembly, imperial *missi* were dispatched by the court to communicate the council's outcome to the empire's archdioceses. Copies are recorded as having been sent to Arn of Salzburg and Sicharius of Bordeaux, who were not in attendance, and to Magnus of Sens and Agobard, who were present.[43] The letter to Agobard began by reminding him that he had recently been at the *sacer conventus* at Aachen and, amongst other things, urged him to ensure that 'wherever there are congregations of clerics and canonesses (*sanctimonialium*) anywhere within your province, that they live according to the text of this Rule (*forma institutionis*) as far as circumstances allow'.[44] Yet in the prologue to the *Institutio*, written in the voice of Louis the Pious, it was also acknowledged that 'there were already many who, aided by Christ, did observe the canonical way of life, with their subordinates, in all piety and devotion'.[45] A remarkable letter sent by Archbishop Leidrad of Lyon to Charlemagne (*c.* 809–12) and the lists of names of the religious preserved in the confraternity book from the abbey of Reichenau, the compilation of which began *c.* 824, reveal that at Lyon the canonical way of life had already been instituted by 816 and remained in operation thereafter.[46]

Before Louis's 'most ardent zeal for divine worship' had driven him to seek to 'emend the holy church of God' in 816, Leidrad worked hard to improve ecclesiastical life in Lyon.[47] Sometime between 809 and 812, the ageing *rector* wrote to Charlemagne to inform the emperor on how much progress he had made since being appointed to his post around a decade earlier.[48] He had been dispatched to Lyon with the instruction that he should emend what had been

---

42 Only a fragment survives: *Hludowici imperatoris epistola ad Agobardum missa*, ed. by Conrat, pp. 771–72 and ed. by Levison, pp. 508–09. The text corresponds to the version addressed to Magnus of Sens: *Hludowici imperatoris epistolae ad archiepiscopos missae*, ed. by Werminghoff, pp. 458–64 (second column); the Agobard fragment cuts off at p. 460, line 15. For general analysis, see Kramer, *Rethinking Authority*, pp. 111–21.
43 A copy of the *Institutio canonicorum* is preserved in a Lyon manuscript (Lyon, BM, MS 619), which may even derive from the official copy brought with Egelricus, the imperial missus sent to Lyon.
44 This comes from the letter addressed to Magnus of Sens, *Hludowici imperatoris epistolae ad archiepiscopos missae*, ed. by Werminghoff, p. 462; trans. by Bertram, p. 173.
45 *Institutio canonicorum*, ed. by Werminghoff, Prologue, p. 313; trans. by Bertram, p. 133.
46 Leidrad, *Letter*, ed. by Coville, pp. 283–87; *Das Verbrüderungsbuch*, ed. by Autenrieth, Geuenich, and Schmid, pp. 94–96; the key study of the Lyon material is Oexle, *Forschungen*, pp. 52–63 and 134–62.
47 *Institutio canonicorum*, ed. by Werminghoff, Prologue, p. 312; trans. adapted from Bertram, p. 132.
48 Overview in Reynaud, 'Lyon', pp. 19–33.

previously neglected and guard against future negligence.[49] The *ecclesia* Leidrad encountered upon his appointment in 798 was, he recalls, 'destitute, internally and externally, both in its liturgy and its buildings and other ecclesiastical ministries'.[50] Regarding the material disrepair of the church buildings in Lyon, Leidrad's letter makes reference to five canonical churches as well as two male monasteries and one female monastery. In the three monastic communities, he instituted the 'observance of regular life' which had fallen into abeyance.[51] For the non-monastic clergy, Leidrad 'constructed an enclosure (*claustrum*) [...] in which all now learn to abide under one roof'.[52] According to the *Institutio*, the *claustrum* was a prerequisite for the existence of a canonical community.[53] The *claustrum* built under Leidrad presumably catered for the large community of canons at St Stephen's, which was attached to the cathedral church of St John the Baptist, the city's *ecclesia maxima*.[54] The Reichenau *Liber vitae* named sixty-seven canons at the *domus sancti Stephani protomartyris*, headed by *Agobardus archiepiscopus*.[55] The enclosure may also have served the canons of the other churches mentioned by Leidrad, some of whose names are also recorded in the Reichenau confraternity book. These included the canons of St Just (list of fifteen names under Bishop Agericus), of St Paul (twenty-five canons under *Chorepiscopus* Audinus), of St Georges (eighteen canons under Abbot Motuinus) and St Nizier (nineteen canons under Abbot Ualtarius).[56] Besides these canonical communities, the sources mention the monastery of Île-Barbe (ninety-eight monks listed under Abbot Bartholomeus), the monastery of St Ragnebert (fifty-five monks under Abbot Stephanus) and the female community at St Peter's (forty-one nuns under Abbess Deidona).[57]

---

49 Leidrad, *Letter*, ed. by Coville, p. 283.
50 Leidrad, *Letter*, ed. by Coville, p. 283: 'Erat enim tunc dicta ecclesia multis in rebus in destituta interius exteriusque tam in officiis quam in edificiis vel in caeteris ecclesiasticis ministeriis'.
51 Leidrad, *Letter*, ed. by Coville, p. 287: 'in quibus monasteriis, unum puellarum et duo quoque monachorum, nemo antea erat qui regularem vitam immitari nosset aut vellet, propter quod plurimum laborem et studium impendi ut ad hanc regularis vite observanciam pervenire potuissent, quo nunc pervenisse, Deo auxiliante, videntur'. On Leidrad as a monastic reformer, see Ardo, *Vita Benedicti*, ed. by Waitz, 24, p. 209; Semmler, 'Zu den bayrisch-westfränkischen Beziehungen', pp. 408–10; Oexle, *Forschungen*, pp. 149–52.
52 Leidrad, *Letter*, ed. by Coville, p. 285: 'Claustrum quoque clericorum construxi, in quo nunc omnes sub uno conclavi manere noscuntur'.
53 See for example: *Institutio canonicorum*, ed. by Werminghoff, 117, 144, 145, pp. 398, 418, 420; *Hludowici imperatoris epistolae ad archiepiscopos*, ed. by Werminghoff, p. 460.
54 Leidrad, *Letter*, ed. by Coville, p. 285: '[...] ita ut ejusdem civitatis maximam ecclesiam que est in honorem sancti Johannis Baptiste a novo operuerim et macerias ex parte erexerim'. Oexle, *Forschungen*, p. 146 n. 227: 'Leidrad bestimmte die *maxima ecclesia*, S. Jean, vermutlich zur Kathedralkirche; die Kirche S. Étienne wurde den Kanonikern der Kathedrale zugewiesen. Somit ist für Lyon die Bedeutung der "Doppelkathedrale" geklärt'.
55 *Das Verbrüderungsbuch*, ed. by Autenrieth, Geuenich, and Schmid, p. 94.
56 *Das Verbrüderungsbuch*, ed. by Autenrieth, Geuenich, and Schmid, pp. 94 and 96.
57 *Das Verbrüderungsbuch*, ed. by Autenrieth, Geuenich, and Schmid, pp. 95–96.

The *ecclesia lugdunensis* was a composite community, made up of a number of different social units, comprising both monastic and canonical churches and male and female houses, each under their own authority figure (bishop, chorbishop, abbot, or abbess). The church of Lyon appears almost as a microcosm of the Carolingian *ecclesia*: a multitude of institutions which were distinct from each other yet nevertheless part of a larger whole and subject to an overarching authority, in this case the archbishop. Significantly, Leidrad's overall reorganization of his diverse community took place well before the 816/17 councils, and for this reason Lyon has been seen as a pilot scheme of Carolingian reform.[58] Whether or not this was the case, what the *ecclesia lugdunenesis* certainly offers is a glimpse at the scope individual leaders were granted to make changes within their dioceses. (The size and antiquity of Lyon, to be sure, means it may not be an entirely representative example.) While monastic and canonical reform, and male and female monasticism, are often studied separately today, bishops were ultimately responsible for all the communities under their care. Leidrad did not need to categorize his own church, in the sense that divisions between monks and canons had become blurry and thus had to be reasserted. Rather, he represented his 'reform' as the revitalization of crumbling *ecclesia*. His primary concern was to ensure that the various components of his *ecclesia* were in order and doing what they were expected to do: worship God.

In his seminal study of western Frankish religious communities, Otto Gerhard Oexle argued that 'the regulation of the liturgy and the divine office' was central to Leidrad's creation of a cohesive *ecclesia lugdunensis* and that Chrodegang's reforms at Metz, undertaken in the 750s, were Leidrad's main source of inspiration.[59] Chrodegang and Leidrad, for example, looked out for their cathedral clergy (i.e. canons) as well as monastic houses within their dioceses. The liturgical emphases of Leidrad's letter to Charlemagne, moreover, pointed in this direction. Leidrad wrote that his church now boasted *clerici officiales* ('clerics to perform the liturgy') and expressed gratitude that the emperor had sent to Lyon a cleric from Metz,

> through whom — with God's help and your generous approval — the order of psalmody has been restored in the church of Lyon to such an extent that, so far as our abilities permit, whatever the ordo demands for the complete discharging of the divine office is now performed, in part, according to the rite of the holy palace [i.e. Aachen].[60]

---

58 See Isaïa, 'L'Hagiographie', pp. 83–85. I thank Emilie Kurdziel for this reference. There is unfortunately no indication whether Leidrad's canonical communities followed a rule like the *Institutio canonicorum*.
59 Oexle, *Forschungen*, pp. 146–47 and 154–56.
60 Leidrad, *Letter*, ed. by Coville, p. 284: 'Et ideo officio pietatis vestre placuit, ut ad peticionem meam michi concederetis unum de Metensi ecclesia clericum, per quem, Deo juvante et mercede vestra annuente, ita in Lugdunensi ecclesia instauratus est ordo psallendi, ut juxta

Emulating what had already been institutionalized in Metz, and by implication, the Aachen palace chapel, Leidrad arranged for his church to sing the divine office. Additionally, he established *scholae cantorum* ('schools for singers') and *scholae lectorum* ('schools for readers'), which trained youths in liturgical chant, liturgical reading, and scriptural exegesis. His church was now staffed, and would continue to be staffed, by well-trained *clerici officiales*.[61] Leidrad also established a scriptorium and 'procured priestly vestments and vessels'.[62] His clergy were to be appropriately drilled, equipped, and garbed for worship.[63] These were all things, it should be noted, that the *Institutio* also expected of canonical communities.

With Leidrad's liturgical provisions in mind, we can begin to draw comparisons to and parallels with the mid-830s, when Amalarius's own attempts to shape how the local clergy worshipped God were met with intense hostility. Scholars such as Germain Morin and Jean Michel Hanssens posited a very direct relation between Leidrad and Amalarius. They both thought it quite probable that Amalarius was the very cleric from Metz whom Charlemagne arranged to be dispatched to help Leidrad instruct his *clerici officiales* in liturgical chant. Memories of Amalarius's first imperial secondment thus contributed to the backlash engendered by his second stint at Lyon.[64] Neat as it would be, there is no evidence to support this speculation, and even the basic supposition on which it rests — namely, that Amalarius was from Metz — has been called into question.[65] In fact, the only piece of contemporary evidence that hints towards a Metz connection is to be found in relation to Amalarius's antiphoner, which (as briefly noted above) he created by amalgamating the Roman volumes he was able to scrutinize at Corbie with the Frankish version he previously had known. He referred to this Frankish version as the 'antiphoner of Metz' (*antiphonarius metensis*).[66] Amalarius's designation, however, testifies not to the course of his own ecclesiastical career but to Metz's status as the pre-eminent centre for Roman chant in

---

vires nostras secundum ritum sacri palatii omni ex parte agi videatur quicquid ad divinum persolvendum officium ordo exposcit'. English translation from Billett, *The Divine Office*, pp. 55–56.

61 Leidrad, *Letter*, ed. by Coville, pp. 284–85.
62 Leidrad, *Letter*, ed. by Coville, p. 285.
63 It is unclear whether Leidrad's schools served only the canons at St Stephan's, or all of the see's religious communities.
64 Morin, 'Amalaire', pp. 338–40; Hanssens, 'Amalarii vita', p. 63.
65 Steck, *Der Liturgiker Amalarius*, pp. 119–92.
66 Amalarius, *Prologus antiphonarii*, ed. by Hanssens, p. 362. Comparisons between Metz and Roman antiphoners are found throughout his *De ordine antiphonarii*, ed. by Hanssens, *Opera*, II, pp. 13–109. See for example 29. 1, p. 64: 'Olim quando solus antiphonarius metensis erat mihi notus [...]' (Formerly, when only the antiphoner of Metz was known to me). Cf. *De ordine antiphonarii*, ed. by Hanssens, 8. 12, p. 39; 9. 6, p. 41; 10. 4, p. 41; 23. 1, p. 63; 28. 6, p. 64; 43. 1, pp. 78–79.

the Carolingian world.⁶⁷ More importantly for my purposes, the antiphoner helps tie together some of threads relating to the divine office at Lyon in the first four decades of the ninth century.

The unnamed Metz cleric of Leidrad's letter presumably brought with him a Roman antiphoner and if not, one would have been produced in Lyon's newly established scriptorium, to be used and consulted by the pupils and teachers in the *schola cantorum*. Although there is no direct evidence for this, it can (tentatively) be gleaned from Agobard's *De antiphonario*. Agobard distributed his treatise 'to his most beloved brothers in Christ and especially the singers of the church of Lyon' in order to justify his decision to purge the antiphoner of non-scriptural chants.⁶⁸ Egon Boshof thought that this was undertaken by Agobard 'in order to thwart Amalarius's attempt to reform the liturgy'.⁶⁹ In other words, the *De antiphonario* and the textual corrections it was written to explain were placed squarely in the context of 835–38. Boshof, however, was also of the opinion that Agobard did not remove 'questionable texts' from Amalarius's own antiphoner, but rather from a 'Gallican version […] which was in use in Lyon'.⁷⁰

One 'questionable text' that Agobard took issue with was the responsory '*De illa occulta habitatione sua*', which was sung in the night office on Christmas Eve. Agobard attributed this chant to a '*vane praesumptor*', which Klaus Zechiel-Eckes took as an unmistakeable reference to Amalarius.⁷¹ Yet this text was certainly not composed by Amalarius, but was part of the repertory of chants which office antiphoners transmitted to the Carolingian world and beyond.⁷² A further hint that *De antiphonario* was not written as a reaction to Amalarius can be gleaned from another night office responsory which Agobard attacked, '*Octava decima die mensis*'.⁷³ Amalarius, who drew attention to this same responsory in his *De ordine antiphonarii*, noted that the wording of the text as Agobard presented it reflected how it 'used to be sung amongst the Gauls'; Amalarius discovered that, in the roman [antiphoner],

---

67   Claussen, *The Reform of the Frankish Church*, pp. 275–76; Page, *The Christian West and its Singers*, pp. 339–53.
68   Agobard, *De antiphonario*, ed. by Van Acker, 1, p. 337: 'Dilectissimis in Christo fratribus et praecipue cantoribus Ecclesiae Ludgunensis'. On the impact of Agobard's work, see Rankin, 'Agobard's Corrections'.
69   Boshof, *Erzbischof Agobard*, p. 278.
70   Boshof, *Erzbischof Agobard*, p. 277. See also Huglo, 'Les remaniements', p. 93 and his *Les livres de chant*, pp. 21 and 88. Steck, *Der Liturgiker Amalarius*, p. 161 n. 761. Palazzo, *A History of Liturgical Books*, p. 141.
71   Agobard, *De antiphonario*, ed. by Van Acker, 6, p. 340. Zechiel-Eckes, *Florus*, p. 73 n. 11 ('[…] nur Amalarius gemeint sein kann'); Rankin, 'Agobard's Corrections', p. 271.
72   This responsory appears in all the exemplars and secular and monastic antiphoners edited by Hesbert: see *Corpus antiphonalium officii*, III, p. 100. For chants that Amalarius might have composed, see Hanssens, *Opera*, III, p. 167.
73   Agobard, *De antiphonario*, ed. by Van Acker, 9, p. 343.

it was written 'Vicesima quarta die decimi mensis'.[74] The antiphoner that Agobard corrected in Lyon thus seems to resemble what Amalarius called the 'antiphoner of Metz'.[75]

There is good reason to suppose, therefore, that Agobard produced his revised antiphoner already before 835. This scenario has important implications, not least because it reframes Agobard's project: it was not a direct response to Amalarius's administration, but instead it reflected his own efforts to continue to build upon the foundations which Leidrad had laid. Liturgical reform in Lyon was thus not a one-off event but was an ongoing process,[76] and there is enough evidence to allow us to plot a series of moments within it. Agobard, exasperated by the presence of problematic texts within the antiphoner, took it upon himself to cleanse of non-scriptural chants what he considered to be the 'third book of the liturgy' (after the sacramentary and lectionary).[77] Agobard's work involved making textual changes, but also moral adjustments on the part of his cantors. Only God's words were appropriate for divine praise, and God 'took no pleasure from the artistic pursuit of singing, but from the obedience of [his] commands and the purity of heart'.[78] What is more, Agobard knew that for these moral precepts to take root, they had to be learnt young.[79] Parallels again can be drawn with the *Institutio canonicorum*, in which learning to sing the office was part of growing up in a canonical community.[80]

The liturgical *scholae* (for singers and readers) set up by Leidrad, together with the antiphoner then in use, were the preconditions for the changes Agobard sought to institute while he was archbishop; Agobard himself can be seen as a product of Leidrad's schools. These institutions, furthermore, help us understand Amalarius's actions when he took charge. At Lyon, Amalarius would have found himself amongst well educated clerics who could read, copy, and grasp his allegorical exegesis of the liturgy. There would also have been well-trained singers, who could learn, and more importantly, instruct younger members of the community how to recite the chants of the divine office, as Amalarius rearranged them in his revised antiphoner.

---

74 Amalarius, *De ordine antiphonarii*, ed. by Hanssens, 11. 4, p. 42: 'Notandum quod iste responsorius canebatur in Galliis: *Octava decima die decimi mensis*; pro quo inveni scriptum in romano: *Vicesima quarta die decimi mensis*'. Amalarius claimed that Pope Gregory IV himself confirmed this ('Necnon et de ipso interrogavi apostolicum Gregorium; qui respondit: Non cantamus: "Octava decima die mensis", sed "Vicesima quarta die"').
75 A similar sort of book prompted Helisachar's corrections too: see above, Note 33.
76 Kramer, *Rethinking Authority*; Vanderputten, *Monastic Reform as Process*.
77 Agobard, *De antiphonario*, ed. by Van Acker, 3 and 19, pp. 339 and 351.
78 Agobard, *De antiphonario*, ed. by Van Acker, 17, p. 350: '[…] nec cantilenae artificioso studio, sed obseruantia mandatorum et cordis munditia delectatur'.
79 Agobard, *De antiphonario*, ed. by Van Acker, 19, p. 351.
80 *Institutio canonicorum*, ed. by Werminghoff, 135 and 137, pp. 413 and 414.

Conclusions

If Agobard's revisions to the antiphoner pre-dated his fall from grace and Amalarius's appointment in 835, Florus's *De divina psalmodia* much more obviously appears to have been written *contra Amalarium*. As part of his sustained efforts to disrupt and denigrate Amalarius's caretaker administration, Florus sharply differentiated Agobard's and Amalarius's liturgical initiatives. The former's were righteous and orthodox, the latter's invalid and heterodox. Between 835 and 838, Florus lamented that Lyon had 'a bishop without power and teacher without truth'.[81] When placed in broader context, however, it becomes possible to identify commonalities over and above contrasts between Agobard and Amalarius. As with Leidrad before them, both were engaged in the same core task expected of ecclesiastical leaders: to ensure the regular and correct celebration of the liturgy within communities under their care. The various interconnected snapshots of liturgical change discussed above capture the scope given to bishops (and even those installed to replace them) to ensure that those whom they oversaw were performing the divine office correctly, as they themselves interpreted it. One of the most conspicuous differences between Leidrad, Agobard, and Amalarius, nevertheless, lies not in their respective interpretations of correct worship but in how their various activities were represented and thus the form by which we now must study them. Leidrad sang his own praises in his letter to Charlemagne and Agobard's set out the ideals of divine praise which his revised antiphoner served to inculcate. By contrast, Amalarius's supposed 'reforming zeal' can be accessed only through the writings of his opponents, whose intentions were expressly antagonistic.

Opposition to Amalarius crystallized around the liturgy. Yet it also stemmed from the fact that, as an imperial transplant, his authority evidently was not recognized at Lyon, at least not by certain groups. The episode thus hints towards wider tensions within the Carolingian world as to how the wishes of the imperial court, expressed through conciliar decrees such as those issued at the Aachen 816 council or through appointments such as Amalarius's, were received within the localities of the empire. Resistance to Amalarius was also resistance to Louis the Pious, and Florus appears to have been aware of this. Responding to the authorities who gathered together at Thionville in 835 to depose Agobard, Florus made it clear that in expressing his dissent he was not rebelling against 'divine ordination or a pious imperial provision'. Rather, he claimed to have been motivated by: '[my] hatred of error and love of truth, and the suffering from the wounds [inflicted upon] my mother church, from whose teats I have been nourished since childhood, and in which I have unworthily exercised the place of administration and the office

---

81 Florus, *Sermo synodalis (AM VI)*, ed. by Zechiel-Eckes, p. 69: '[…] ut habeat episcopum sine potestate, magistrum sine veritate'.

of teaching and preaching'.[82] Florus here exemplifies the voice of entrenched local interests: he was born and educated under the auspices of Leidrad and Agobard; he was a product of Lyon's *scholae*. It is therefore not surprising that he did not warm to Amalarius, whom he perceived as interfering with local practice.[83] By characterizing Amalarius's leadership in such resoundingly negative terms, however, he offers insights into the ideals, practicalities, and challenges involved in effecting liturgical change in the Carolingian Church.

Works Cited

Manuscript

Lyon, Bibliothèque Municipale, MS 619 <https://florus.bm-lyon.fr/visualisation.php?cote=MS0619&vue=1> [accessed 8 September 2021]

Primary Sources

Agobard of Lyon, *De antiphonario*, ed. by Lieven Van Acker, Corpus Christianorum Continuatio Medievalis, 52 (Turnhout: Brepols, 1981), pp. 337–51

Amalarius of Metz, *Embolis meorum opusculorum*, ed. by Jean Michel Hanssens, in *Amalarii episocopi opera liturgica omnia*, vol. 1, Studi e Testi, 138 (Vatican City: Bibliotheca Apostolica Vaticana, 1948), pp. 367–90

——, *Prologus antiphonarii*, ed. by Jean Michel Hanssens, in *Amalarii episocopi opera liturgica omnia*, vol. 1, Studi e Testi, 138 (Vatican City: Bibliotheca Apostolica Vaticana, 1948), pp. 360–63

——, *De ordine antiphonarii*, ed. by Jean Michel Hanssens, in *Amalarii episocopi opera liturgica omnia*, vol. 3, Studi e Testi, 140 (Vatican City: Bibliotheca Apostolica Vaticana, 1950), pp. 13–109

——, *Liber officialis*, ed. by Jean Michel Hanssens, in *Amalarii episocopi opera liturgica omnia*, vol. 2, Studi e Testi, 139 (Vatican City: Bibliotheca Apostolica Vaticana, 1950), pp. 13–543; trans. by Eric Knibbs, *Amalar of Metz: On the Liturgy*, 2 vols (Cambridge, MA: Harvard University Press, 2014)

Ardo, *Vita Benedicti abbatis Anianensis et Indensis*, ed. by Georg Waitz, in *Monumenta Germaniae Historica: Scriptores*, xv.1 (Hannover: Hahn, 1887), pp. 198–220

Astronomer, *Vita Hludowici imperatoris*, ed. by Ernst Tremp, *Monumenta Germaniae Historica: Scriptores Rerum Germanicarum in usum scholarum separatim editi*, LXIV (Hannover: Hahn, 1995)

---

82 Florus, *Epistola ad synodum (AM I)*, ed. by Zechiel-Eckes, pp. 4–5. Context: Zechiel-Eckes, *Florus*, pp. 29–34.
83 For a comparable example, see Patzold, 'Konflikte'; see also Cinzia Grifoni and Ingrid Rembold in the present volume.

Chronicon Laurissense breve, ed. by Hans Schnorr von Carolsfeld, *Neues Archiv*, 36 (1911), 15–39

Florus of Lyon, *Opera polemica*, ed. by Klaus Zechiel-Eckes and Erwin Frauenknecht, Corpus Christianorum Continuatio Medievalis, 260 (Brepols: Turnhout, 2014)

Helisachar, *Epistula*, ed. by Ernst Dümmler, in *Monumenta Germaniae Historica: Epistolae*, v, *Epistolae Karolini aevi*, III (Berlin: Weidmann, 1899), pp. 307–09

Hesbert, René-Jean, ed., *Antiphonale Missarum sextuplex* (Brussels: Vromant, 1935)

——, *Corpus antiphonalium officii*, 6 vols (Rome: Herder, 1963–1979)

Hludowici imperatoris epistola ad Agobardum missa, ed. by Max Conrat, *Neues Archiv*, 37 (1912), 771–72; ed. by Wilhelm Levison, 'Handschriften des Museum Meeranno-Westreenianum im Haag', *Neues Archiv*, 38 (1913), 505–24, at 508–09

Hludowici imperatoris epistolae ad archiepiscopos missae, ed. by Albert Werminghoff, in *Monumenta Germaniae Historica: Concilia*, II. 1, *Concilia aevi Karolini*, I (Hannover: Hahn, 1906), pp. 458–64

Institutio Canonicorum, ed. by Albert Werminghoff, in *Monumenta Germaniae Historica: Concilia*, II. 1, *Concilia aevi Karolini*, I (Hannover: Hahn, 1906), pp. 308–421; ed. and trans. by Jerome Bertram, in *The Chrodegang Rules: The Rules for the Common Life of the Secular Clergy from the Eighth and Ninth Centuries; Critical Texts with Translations and Commentary* (Aldershot: Ashgate, 2005), pp. 96–174

Leidrad, *Letter*, ed. by Alfred Coville, *Recherches sur l'histoire de Lyon du Ve siècle au IXe siècle (450–800)* (Paris, 1928), pp. 283–87

Synodi primae Aquisgranensis decreta authentica (a. 816), ed. by Josef Semmler, in *Corpus Consuetudinum Monasticarum*, vol. 1: *Initia Consuetudinis Benedictinae: Consuetudines saeculi octavi et noni* (Siegburg: Schmitt, 1963), pp. 451–68

Das Verbrüderungsbuch der Abtei Reichenau, ed. by Johanne Autenrieth, Dieter Geuenich, and Karl Schmid, *Monumenta Germaniae Historica: Libri memoriales et necrologia*, nova series, I (Hannover: Hahn, 1979)

Secondary Works

Billett, Jesse D., *The Divine Office in Anglo-Saxon England, 597–c. 1000* (London: Boydell, 2014)

Bobrycki, Shane, 'A Hypothetical Slave in Constantinople Amalarius's *Liber Officialis* and the Mediterranean Slave Trade', *The Haskins Society Journal*, 26 (2014), 46–68

Booker, Courtney M., *Past Convictions: The Penance of Louis the Pious and the Decline of the Carolingians* (Philadelphia: University of Pennsylvania Press, 2009)

Boshof, Egon, *Erzbischof Agobard von Lyon: Leben und Werk*, Kölner historische Abhandlungen, 17 (Cologne: Böhlau, 1969)

Bougard, François, Alexis Charansonnet, and Marie-Céline Isaïa, ed., *Lyon dans l'Europe carolingienne: Autour d'Agobard (816–840)* (Brepols: Turnhout, 2019)

Cabaniss, Allen, *Amalarius of Metz* (Amsterdam: North-Holland Pub. Co, 1954)

Chazelle, Celia, 'Amalarius' *Liber Officialis*: Spirit and Vision in Carolingian Liturgical Thought', in *Seeing the Invisible in Late Antiquity and the Early Middle Ages*, ed. by Giselle de Nie, Karl Frederick Morrison, and Marco Mostert (Turnhout: Brepols, 2005), pp. 327–57

Claussen, M. A., *The Reform of the Frankish Church: Chrodegang of Metz and the Regula canonicorum in the Eighth Century* (Cambridge: Cambridge University Press, 2004)

Collins, Samuel W., *The Carolingian Debate over Sacred Space* (New York: Palgrave Macmillan, 2012)

Dereine, Charles, 'Chanoines', in *Dictionnaire d'histoire et de géographie ecclésiastiques*, vol. 12 (Paris: Letouzey et Ané, 1953), cols 353–405

Gaillard, Michèle, *D'une réforme à l'autre (816–934): les communautés religieuses en Lorraine à l'époque carolingienne* (Paris: Publications de la Sorbonne, 2006)

Gillis, Matthew Bryan, *Heresy and Dissent in the Carolingian Empire: The Case of Gottschalk of Orbais* (Oxford: Oxford University Press, 2017)

Hanssens, Jean Michel, 'Amalarii vita', in *Amalarii episocopi opera liturgica omnia*, vol. 1, Studi e Testi, 138 (Vatican City: Bibliotheca Apostolica Vaticana, 1948), pp. 39–82

Harper, John, *The Forms and Orders of Western Liturgy from the Tenth to the Eighteenth Century: A Historical Introduction and Guide for Students and Musicians* (Oxford: Clarendon Press, 1991)

Hen, Yitzhak, 'The Romanization of the Frankish Liturgy: Ideal, Reality, and the Rhetoric of Reform', in *Rome Across Space and Time: Cultural Transmissions and the Exchange of Ideas, c. 500–1400*, ed. by Claudia Bolgia, Rosamond McKitterick, and John Osborne (Cambridge: Cambridge University Press, 2011), pp. 111–24

Huglo, Michel, *Les livres de chant liturgiques*, Typologie des sources du Moyen Âge occidental, 52 (Turnhout: Brepols, 1988)

———, 'Les remaniements de l'antiphonaire grégorien au IXe siècle: Hélisachar, Agobard, Amalaire', in *Culto cristiano, politica imperiale carolingia* (Todi: Presso l'Accademia Tudertina, 1979), pp. 87–120; reprinted in Michel Huglo, *Les sources du plain-chant et de la musique médiévale*, Variorum Collected Studies Series (Aldershot: Ashgate, 2004), X

———, 'L'antiphonaire: archétype ou répertoire originel?', in *Colloques internationaux du CNRS: Grégoire le Grand (Chantilly, 15–19 septembre 1982)*, ed. by Jacques Fontaine (Paris: Éditions du CNRS, 1986), pp. 661–69; reprinted in Michel Huglo, *Les sources du plain-chant et de la musique médiévale*, Variorum Collected Studies Series (Aldershot: Ashgate, 2004), IX

Isaïa, Marie-Céline, 'L'Hagiographie contre la réforme dans l'Église de Lyon ai IX siècle', *Médiévales*, 62 (2012), 83–104

Jones, Christopher A., *A Lost Work by Amalarius of Metz: Interpolation in Salisbury, Cathedral Library MS 154* (Woodbridge: Boydell and Brewer, 2001)

Jong, Mayke de, *The Penitential State: Authority and Atonement in the Age of Louis the Pious, 814–40* (Cambridge: Cambridge University Press, 2009)

———, 'The State of the Church: Ecclesia and Early Medieval State Formation', in *Der frühmittelalterliche Staat: europäische Perspektiven*, ed. by Walter Pohl and Veronika Wieser (Vienna: Österreichische Akademie der Wissenschaften, 2009), pp. 241–54

Keefe, Susan A., *Water and the Word: Baptism and the Education of the Clergy in the Carolingian Empire*, vol. 1: *A Study of Texts and Manuscripts* (Notre Dame: University of Notre Dame Press, 2002)

Knibbs, Eric, 'Introduction', in *Amalar of Metz: On the Liturgy*, 2 vols (Cambridge, MA: Harvard University Press, 2014), vol. 1, pp. vii–xxxvi

Kolping, Adolf, 'Amalar von Metz und Florus von Lyon: Zeugen eines Wandels im liturgischen Mysterienverständnis in der Karolingerzeit', *Zeitschrift für katholische Theologie*, 73 (1951), 424–64

Kramer, Rutger, *Rethinking Authority in the Carolingian Empire: Ideals and Expectations during the Reign of Louis the Pious (813–828)* (Amsterdam: Amsterdam University Press, 2019)

Leahy, Eugene J., 'Archivio di San Pietro, cod. B.79, and Amalarius: Notes on the Development of the Medieval Office', *Manuscripta*, 28 (1984), 79–91

Levy, Kenneth, 'Abbot Helisachar's Antiphoner', *Journal of the American Musicological Society*, 48 (1995), 171–86

Marchal, Guy P., 'Was war das weltliche Kanonikerinstitut im Mittelalter? Dom- und Kollegiatstifte: eine Einführung und eine neue Perspektive', *Revue d'histoire ecclésiastique*, 93 (1999), 761–807 and 95 (2000), 7–53

Morin, Germain, 'Amalaire: esquisse biographique', *Revue Bénédictine*, 9 (1892), 337–51

Oexle, Otto Gerhard, *Forschungen zu monastischen und geistlichen Gemeinschaften in westfränkischen Bereich: Bestandteil des Quellenwerkes Societas et Fraternitas*, Münstersche Mittelalter-Schriften, 31 (Munich: Wilhelm Fink, 1978)

Page, Christopher, *The Christian West and its Singers: The First Thousand Years* (New Haven: Yale University Press, 2010)

Palazzo, Eric, *A History of Liturgical Books: from the Beginning to the Thirteenth Century* (Collegeville: The Liturgical Press, 1998)

Patzold, Steffen, 'Konflikte im Kloster Fulda zur Zeit der Karolinger', *Fuldaer Geschichtsblätter*, 76 (2000), 69–162

Pezé, Warren, 'Florus, Agobard et le concile de Quierzy de 838', in *Lyon dans l'Europe carolingienne: Autour d'Agobard (816–840)*, ed. by François Bougard, Alexis Charansonnet, and Marie-Céline Isaïa (Brepols: Turnhout, 2019), pp. 175–90

Picker, Hanns-Christoph, *Pastor doctus: Klerikerbild und karolingische Reformen bei Hrabanus Maurus* (Mainz: von Zabern, 2001)

Pohlen, Anna Elisabeth Maria, *Die südeuropäisch-spanisch-gotische Gruppe in den geistigen Auseinandersetzungen der Karolingerzeit* (Bonn: Rheinische Friderich-Wilhelms-Universität, 1974)

Rankin, Susan, 'The Making of Carolingian Mass Chant Books', in *Quomodo cantabimus canticum? Studies in Honor of Edward H. Roesner*, ed. by David Butler Cannata, Gabriela Ilnitchi Currie, Rena Charnin Mueller, and John Louis Nádas (Middleton: American Institute of Musicology, 2008), pp. 37–63

——, *Writing Sounds in Carolingian Europe: the Invention of Musical Notation* (Cambridge: Cambridge University Press, 2018)

——, 'Agobard's Corrections to the Antiphoner', in *Lyon dans l'Europe carolingienne: Autour d'Agobard (816–840)*, ed. by François Bougard, Alexis Charansonnet, and Marie-Céline Isaïa (Brepols: Turnhout, 2019), pp. 269–83

Reynaud, Jean-François, 'Lyon à l'époque d'Agobard (816–40)', in *Lyon dans l'Europe carolingienne: Autour d'Agobard (816–840)*, ed. by François Bougard, Alexis Charansonnet, and Marie-Céline Isaïa (Turnhout: Brepols, 2019), pp. 7–33

Robertson, Anne Walters, *The Service-Books of the Royal Abbey of Saint-Denis: Images of Ritual and Music in the Middle Ages* (Oxford: Clarendon Press, 1991)

Rubellin, Michel, 'Introduction', in *Agobard de Lyon: Œuvres*, vol. 1, ed. by Michel Rubellin, Sources Chrétiennes, 583 (Paris: Les Éditions du Cerf, 2016), pp. 15–69

Semmler, Josef, 'Reichsidee und kirchliche Gesetzgebung bei Ludwig dem Frommen', *Zeitschrift für Kirchengeschichte*, 71 (1960), 37–65

——, 'Zu den bayrisch- westfränkischen Beziehungen in karolingischer Zeit', *Zeitschrift für Bayerische Landesgeschichte*, 29 (1966), 344–424

——, *Die Entstehung von Domkapiteln in Deutschland*, Bonner historische Forschungen, 43 (Bonn: Röhrscheid, 1976)

——, 'Die Kanoniker und ihre Regel im 9. Jahrhundert', in *Studien zum weltlichen Kollegiatstift in Deutschland*, ed. by Irene Crusius, Veröffentlichungen des Max-Planck-Instituts für Geschichte, 114 (Göttingen: Vandenhoeck & Ruprecht, 1995) pp. 62–109

Stäblein, Bruno, '*Gregorius Praesul*, der Prolog zum römischen Antiphonale', in *Musik und Verlag: Karl Vötterle zum 65. Geburtstag*, ed. by Richard Baum and Wolfgang Rehm (Kassel: Bärenreiter, 1968), pp. 537–61

Steck, Wolfgang, *Der Liturgiker Amalarius: eine quellenkritische Untersuchung zu Leben und Werk eines Theologen der Karolingerzeit* (St Ottilien: EOS, 2000)

——, '*Secundum usum romanum*: Liturgischer Anspruch und Wirklichkeit zur Karolingerzeit', in *Mittelalterliches Denken: Gestalten, Ideen und Debatten im Kontext*, ed. by Christian H. Schäfer and Martin Thurner (Darmstadt: Wissenschaftliche Buchgesellschaft, 2007), pp. 15–30

Vanderputten, Steven, *Monastic Reform as Process: Realities and Representations in Medieval Flanders* (Ithaca: Cornell University Press, 2016)

Zechiel-Eckes, Klaus, 'Florus von Lyon, Amalarius von Metz und der Traktat über die Bischofswahl: Mit einer kritischen Edition des sog. *Liber de electionibus episcoporum*', *Revue Bénédictine*, 106 (1996), 109–33

——, *Florus von Lyon als Kirchenpolitiker und Publizist*, Quellen und Forschungen zum Recht im Mittelalter, 8 (Stuttgart: Jan Thorbecke, 1999)

ARTHUR WESTWELL

Ordering the Church in the *Ordines Romani*

Introduction

If the Carolingian Empire was, as it has been called, a 'civilization of the liturgy', how much more so was each and every individual monastery and canonical community across that Empire.[1] These communities were intensely invested in liturgy and copied, along with the manuscripts to assist with the performance of it, the puzzling group of texts which editorial practice has grouped under the title *ordines romani*.[2] The title was inherited from when scholars believed the texts accurately represented the practice of the Roman Church (as many claim to do), but the witness from the end of the eighth century to the ninth is entirely Frankish. In modern scholarship, they were treated within an overarching narrative of Carolingian liturgical 'reform', envisaged as the imposition of Roman texts (chiefly the Gregorian Sacramentary, but sometimes the *ordines romani*) upon a largely passive Frankish audience by the imperial court and a restricted intellectual circle, but Michel Andrieu's edition of fifty such texts strains under contradictory manuscript evidence.[3] Rather than passive reception, the manuscripts of the *ordines romani* actually reveal how willing and able the Franks were to edit and reconceive liturgical texts, even those under the august name of the Roman Church, to suit their own needs. Rather than a single, overarching 'Reform' with specific goals set by the elites and imposed on everyone else, the manuscript evidence reveals that those who were most affected, liturgical practitioners themselves, made texts address their own needs and those of

---

[1] Riché, *La vie quotidienne*, pp. 272–89.
[2] Edited by Andrieu, *Les Ordines Romani*, I–V.
[3] Klauser, 'Die liturgischen Austauschbeziehungen', on the *ordines romani*, p. 176; Andrieu, *Les Ordines*, II, pp. xviii–xxi, xlviii; For revisions to this view, McKitterick, 'Unity and Diversity'; Hen, *Royal Patronage*.

Arthur Westwell is a Wissenschaftlicher Mitarbeiter at Universität Regensburg funded by the Deutsche Forschungsgemeinschaft.

Monastic Communities and Canonical Clergy in the Carolingian World (780–840): Categorizing the Church, ed. by Rutger Kramer, Emilie Kurdziel, and Graeme Ward, MMS 8 (Turnhout: Brepols, 2022), pp. 425–445

their congregations and communities. A number of such texts, written in monastic and clerical communities, can therefore shed light on the liturgical creativity and priorities of such communities.

Ordo 15: The *Capitulare Ecclesiastici Ordinis*

A particular collection of such texts survives in St Gall, Stiftsbibliothek, Cod. Sang. 349.[4] The *ordo romanus* section now follows another liturgical document (pp. 1–39), a *Collectarium* or set of 78 Collects. The *ordines* were attached at a later date, pp. 40–124 and, like the *Collectarium*, were a product of the late eighth century and, probably, the *scriptorium* of St Gall. This part is written in Alemannic minuscule, without any attempt at the elaboration which made liturgical texts usable, such as rubrication or a textual hierarchy. After the text of the *Gloria*, the section opens with a significant text, the 412 letter of Pope Innocent to Bishop Decentius of Gubbio (pp. 39–49), an early pope attempting to recommend Rome's liturgical practices as exemplary.[5] This would associate what followed with the pope's recommendations, and papal authority more generally. The manuscript continues (with the significant titles claiming Roman provenance and Andrieu's numbering):

pp. 49–50 Ordo 14, for readings through the church year.[6]
pp. 50–54 A brief anonymous list of books of the Old and New Testament.
pp. 54–67 Ordo 16, entitled:

IN NOMINE SANCTE DOMINI NOSTRI IESU CHRISTI INCIPIT INSTRUCCIO ECCLESIASTICI ORDINIS, qualiter in coenubiis fideliter domino seruientes tam iuxta auctoritatem catholice atque apostolice romane ecclesie quam iuxta dispositione et regulam sancti Benedicti missarum solemniis uel nataliciis sanctorum seu et officiis diuinis annis circoli die noctuque, auxiliante domino, debeant celebrare, sicut in sancta ac romano ecclesia a sapientibus ac uenerabilis patribus nobis traditum.[7]

---

4 St Gall, Stibi, Cod. Sang. 349, for digitized version see Manuscripts; Andrieu, *Les Ordines*, I (repr. 1965), pp. 330–33; Lowe ed., *Codices Latini Antiquiores*, VII, p. 29; the irregular orthography of the manuscript is maintained throughout.
5 Connel, *Church and Worship*.
6 Ordo 14 appears in other manuscripts, generally copied onto spare folios of texts for liturgical reading: St Gall, Stibi, Cod. Sang. 11, pp. 419–20 (Andrieu, *Les Ordines*, I, p. 326), Metz, BM, MS 134, fol. 32[v] (p. 166, destroyed in 1944), BnF, MS lat. 3836, fols 103[v]–104[r] (pp. 272–72) and BAV, Palat. Lat. 277 (Andrieu, *Les Ordines*, III (repr. 1961), p. 26). According to Jeffery, 'The Early Liturgy', the text is an accurate account of the readings in the monasteries serving Saint Peter's Basilica in Rome at an early stage. It is edited at Andrieu, *Les Ordines*, III, pp. 39–41.
7 'In the name of the Lord Jesus Christ, here begins the Instruction of the Order of the Church, how in monasteries, faithfully serving the Lord, according to both the tradition of the catholic and apostolic Roman Church, and also according to the directive and rule of Benedict, the ceremony of festivals and saints' days ought to celebrated, and also the divine

pp. 67–100 Ordo 15, entitled:

IN NOMINE DOMINI IESU CHRISTI INCIPIT CAPITULARE ECCLESIASTICI ORDINIS qualiter a sancta atque apostolice romana ecclesia celebratur, sicuit ibidem a sapientibus et venerabilibus patribus nobis traditum fuit.[8]

pp. 100–04 Ordo 18, entitled:

Item de cursu diurno vel nocturno qualiter oras canonica nuntiatur in sanctae sedis romane ecclesie sive in monastyriis constitutis.[9]

pp. 104–18 Ordo 19, entitled:

ITEM INCIPIT de convivio sive prandio atque cenis monachorum qualiter in monystiria romane ecclesie constitutis est consuetudo.[10]

Andrieu discussed this set of liturgical texts as the *Capitulare* Collection or the Collection of Saint Gall, though two of the *ordines* have a significant textual life beyond this manuscript, and the designation implies more solidity in their transmission than is evident.[11]

Silvo-Tarouca first argued that this manuscript transmits the texts describing Roman liturgical practices which Bede tells us were written down in Anglo-Saxon England by John the *archicantor* and Roman abbot, and preserved in Wearmouth-Jarrow and other monasteries.[12] Thus, Silvo-Tarouca saw these texts as accurate records of Roman liturgical practices of the seventh century, from an unimpeachable source. Unfortunately, nothing in the texts supports identification with John's words.[13] By making bold claims to their own

---

office of the day and night, with the help of the Lord, as in the holy and Roman church from the holy and wise fathers was handed down to us'; edited at Andrieu, *Les Ordines*, III, pp. 147–54.

8 'In the name of the Lord Jesus Christ, here begins the Capitulary of the Order of the Church, how it is celebrated by the Holy and Apostolic Roman Church, as in the same place it was handed down to us by wise and venerable fathers'; edited at Andrieu, *Les Ordines*, III, pp. 95–125.

9 'Then concerning the day and night cursus and how it is established that the canonical hours are announced in the holy Roman church and in monasteries'; edited at Andrieu, *Les Ordines*, III, pp. 205–08.

10 'Here begins those matters concerning the gathering and lunch and dinner of monks, how the custom is established in the monasteries of the Roman church'; Andrieu, *Les Ordines*, III, pp. 217–27.

11 Vogel, *Medieval Liturgy*, pp. 152–54.

12 Silvo-Tarouco, 'Giovanni Archicantor': John is discussed in Bede, *Ecclesiastical History*, ed. by Colgrave and Mynors, IV. 16, pp. 388–41; Baumstark earlier objected to this identification, Baumstark, 'Joannes Archicantor'.

13 Meeder, *The Irish Scholarly Presence at St Gall*, pp. 62–63, while misled by classic studies on Anglo-Saxon history that assumed Silvo-Tarouca's identification, identified a possible exemplar for St Gall, Stibi, Cod. Sang. 349 in the catalogue of the monastery among the books '*scottice scripti*'. The text did not come from England, as Meeder assumed, but perhaps

Roman-ness, the texts encourage identification with an authoritative Roman liturgical tradition, but these claims must be taken with great caution since Carolingian authors did not mean what we now assume when we read a text to be 'Roman'. Andrieu's edition addressed at length and definitively disproved the identification with John's texts, by showing that it was impossible (due to the liturgical peculiarities within, as well as dependence on Frankish texts) that the texts stemmed from a Roman who intended to record accurately Roman liturgical practices. Fragments might represent the practices of the papal see, but these are presented from a Frankish point of view for Frankish purposes and, as a whole, these texts were created by Franks.[14] A supposed Roman provenance was nevertheless revived by Hallinger, who suggested that the texts represented the practice of Roman monasteries from the eighth century without the involvement of John *archicantor*, argued separately by Van Dijk.[15] This was the basis for Semmler's new edition of Ordo 16, 17, 18, 19 and parts of 15 (given subtitles not found in the manuscripts).[16] But neither sufficiently confronted the evidence marshalled by Andrieu. Hallinger, for example, proved that a source Andrieu identified, a monastic rule known as the *Regula Magistri*, was present in Italy as well as Gaul but this hardly suffices to demonstrate Rome as the place of origin.[17] He never addressed Andrieu's proof that certain rituals the *ordines* offered, such as baptism taking place at Epiphany (Ordo 15, nos 70–78), were entirely foreign to Rome, and, in fact, were actively forbidden there.[18] Van Dijk, in turn, asserted that an 'Eastern' influence on the seventh-century papacy could have forced Epiphany baptism on Rome, yet this has left no trace in any Roman Sacramentary and is extremely unlikely.[19] Furthermore, this particular baptism narrative itself was related to the Sacramentary of Gellone, a Frankish text, which also

---

    one copyist of it wrote in Anglo-Saxon script at St Gall.

14 A list of Popes and three (otherwise unknown) abbots who organized the church year is given at the end of Ordo 19 but the information is generic, with only Gregory the Great in detail, as we might expect from a Frankish author. This is part of a broad salvo in favour of following the ritual traditions of Rome, against opponents who apparently appealed to the authority of saints Ambrose, Hilary, Martin, and Germanus (hardly Anglo-Saxon!). The argument here (which may or may not be by the same person who wrote the *ordines*) seems vociferous but must be contextualized by how the *ordines* preceding it creatively reconcile Roman models, and is in fact more equivocal than it appears; See Andrieu, *Les Ordines*, III, pp. 223–24.

15 Hallinger, 'Die römischen Ordines'; van Dijk, 'Urban and Papal Rites'.

16 'Ordines aevi regulae mixtae', ed. by Semmler.

17 *Regula Magistri*, ed. by de Vogüé. It was copied in or near St Gall around this time, in manuscripts St Gall, Stibi, cods. 193 and 194.

18 Jeffery, 'Eastern and Western Elements', pp. 128–30, particularly no. 85: 'other non-Roman liturgical traits that are not particularly monastic, such as the practice of baptizing at Epiphany, go unmentioned or are not really dealt with'; Andrieu, *Les Ordines*, III, pp. 110–12, and analysed at pp. 79–81; Duchesne, *Origines du culte chrétien*, p. 511 details the censure of Epiphany baptism by Popes Siricus, Leo, and Gelasius.

19 Van Dijk, 'Urban and Papal Rites', p. 455.

allows for baptism at Epiphany.[20] Hallinger's error arose partly from his own assumptions about what a Carolingian liturgical 'reform' really looked like, assumptions the manuscript evidence cannot sustain.[21] Like Andrieu, Hallinger envisaged 'Reform' as a straightforward process based on authoritative texts circulated exclusively and passed seamlessly in monasteries from Rome to Francia but the picture given by these *ordines* in their manuscripts is in fact far more ambiguous.

Given this, what do these *ordines* have to offer us for the liturgical priority of monastic (and perhaps canonical) communities in Francia? I intend to discuss the 'family' of significant witnesses (in order of descent): Ordo 15, 16, and 17. Also in the St Gall manuscript, but nowhere else, Ordo 18 (on the *cursus*) and 19 (on monastic meals) are less immediately fruitful. Apart from Ordo 14 (see footnote 6 above), Ordo 15 is the only one of St Gall, Cod. 349's *ordines* which can be found beyond this single manuscript witness. In Andrieu's apparatus, there are three branches of the manuscript tradition. St Gall, Cod. Sang. 349 stands alone, as also does the manuscript Wolfenbüttel, Herzog August Bibliothek, MS Cod. Guelf. 91 Weiss., which offers two short extracts. The third branch is represented by a further four manuscripts. The most complete is Montpellier, Bibliothèque de la faculté de medicine, MS cod. 412, which offers, in Andrieu's numbering, Ordo 15 nos 1–85. The manuscript is of the first or second quarter of the ninth century, and from the *scriptorium* at Tours, in the Abbey of Saint-Martin.[22] Given the dating, Saint-Martin at Tours was likely a community of secular canons when this manuscript was produced, in a key urban centre.[23] The creator of the Montpellier manuscript copied Ordo 15 at the beginning of a set of other *ordines romani* which Andrieu termed 'Collection A'.[24] Interestingly, the *ordines romani* in the manuscripts are all preceded by a copy of Augustine's *Enchiridion*, (fols 1ʳ–86ʳ), and it seems this was originally how the manuscript was conceived. It is curious to find liturgical texts after a work of patristic theology, and this situation makes it less likely that the texts of the *ordines* were here intended as a straightforward script for liturgical performance. This makes it more urgent to probe the other ways these texts could be read, which did not form a part of Andrieu's analysis. Ordo 15 follows (fols 87ʳ–96ʳ) after Augustine, distinguished by a handsome capital letter in a style that seems characteristic of Tours manuscripts. Another capital letter opens the so-called 'Collection

---

20 BnF, MS lat. 12048 (Cambrai, 780–800); *Liber Sacramentorum Gellonensis*, ed. by Dumas, pp. 312–39; Andrieu, *Les Ordines*, III, pp. 81–90.
21 Hallinger, 'Die römischen Ordines', p. 467.
22 Bischoff, *Katalog*, II, p. 209.
23 Oexle, *Forschungen*, pp. 120–33; Noizet, *La fabrique de la ville*, pp. 31–44.
24 Andrieu, *Les Ordines*, I, pp. 467–70; It comprises Ordo 1, 11, 13A, 27, and 42. Andrieu calls Collection A 'The Roman Collection', arguing that the copyists aimed to represent practices of the church of Rome as accurately as possible, yet almost all manuscripts carry non-Roman material.

A' (fols 96ᵛ–133ᵛ) including the texts like Ordo 1 and Ordo 11 upon which Ordo 15 is dependent, and to which it covers liturgical ground that is very similar. This may be why the copy of Ordo 15 is only partial, notably lacking the narrative of baptism at Holy Saturday, which Ordo 11 covered in greater depth. A recension of Ordo 15 very similar to the Montpellier example is found in three manuscripts, each copied one from the other, and all witnesses to the set of canonical texts called the Collection of Saint-Maur and an abridged copy of the *Liber Pontificalis*.[25] The manuscripts are: The Hague, Meermanno Westreeanium, MS cod. 10 B 4 (of the late eighth century, once at Clermont, perhaps from Rheims) fols 47ʳ–50ʳ, which was copied for Vatican Library, MS Reg. lat. 1127 (of the ninth century and copied in the vicinity of Tours, later in Angoulême), fols 52ʳ–56ᵛ and finally Paris, BnF, MS lat. 2400 (from the eleventh century and Angoulême), fols 173ʳ–174ʳ.[26] Ordo 15 was also found in a now lost manuscript of the collection, once in Laon.[27] It is likely that Ordo 15 was added to blank folios in the Hague manuscript, probably during a restoration of fols 31–53 that Lowe identified as a little later than the writing of the original manuscript 'doubtless in a French centre' (it does not appear in the Table of Contents and is not found in another manuscript of the same collection, Paris, BnF, MS lat. 1451).[28] The following manuscripts simply copied it as if it were integral. The manuscript in the Hague also later acquired the only copy of the canons of a council held in Tours under Archbishop Herardus in 853, intensely concerned with liturgical matters.[29] This clearly links some initial transmission of Ordo 15 with Tours. The three manuscripts offer only Ordo 15, nos 1–75, and they end in the middle of Ordo 15, no. 75, without completing the sentence.[30] They all agree with the Montpellier manuscript substantially and maintain the title of Ordo 15 with its reference to the practice of the apostolic church of Rome.

These texts were evidently passing between some of the most significant communities of the empire. Leaving aside the Wolfenbüttel example (whose manuscript represents something like what is later termed a 'pontifical' and was more likely constructed due to the personal initiative of a bishop), we have a recension copied at a monastery at St Gall and one copied around the canonical community at Tours, or at least present there soon afterwards. Can we perceive any sense of the differing priorities of the two communities here, one monastic, the other canonical? Andrieu gives the best summary of the

---

25   On the Collection of Saint-Maur, Kéry, *Canonical Collections*, pp. 45–46.
26   For The Hague MS, Andrieu, *Les Ordines*, I, pp. 140–42, also Levison, 'Handschriften', 513–18; Lowe ed., *Codices Latini Antiquiores*, x, p. 39; for the Vatican MS, BAV, Reg. lat. 1127, Andrieu, *Les Ordines*, I, pp. 322–23, for digitized version see Manuscripts section in the Works Cited below; Paris MS at Andrieu, *Les Ordines*, I, p. 271.
27   Contreni, 'Two Descriptions', p. 47.
28   Andrieu, *Les Ordines*, I, p. 142; As in Reynolds, 'Pseudonymous Liturgica'.
29   Herardus of Tours, *Capitula* ed. by Pokorny and Stratmann.
30   Andrieu, *Les Ordines*, II, p. 112.

contents of Ordo 15.[31] Generally, the text gives an account of the ceremonies in the liturgical year, beginning (as the Sacramentary did) at Advent, then offering brief or more extensive liturgical directives for the feasts of the Conception of Mary, Christmas, Epiphany, Candlemas, Septuagesima, and Lent. Baptism on Holy Saturday and some further rules on chant during the year are given only in the St Gall manuscript. Perhaps rather than a single writer writing the whole text at once, as Andrieu presents it (indeed he viewed the whole 'Collection' in Cod. Sang. 346 as the product of a single author), it is more likely that we have here a disparate collection of liturgical recommendations and rules, including distinct *ordines* for the ceremonies of the Mass and baptism, strung together loosely by a compiler along the structure of the liturgical year. Furthermore, Andrieu believed that the text as it was presented in the St Gall manuscript was the complete original, while the others represent various reductions of it, but the structure of the text presents a different possibility, that the St Gall scribe (or someone from whom he copied) was the one who added various additional rules and customs to the end of the original text. For example, at Ordo 15, no. 152, the text returns to Lent and Easter, which had actually already been treated, to give a few additional rules about the chant of the *Gloria* and other chants.[32] This would also explain why the three manuscripts around Tours offer less complete versions. The text was therefore a less fixed and more interactive transmission than Andrieu had conceived it. The manuscripts of the 'Tours' family do transmit some variants which show words missed or misinterpreted by the St Gall copyist.[33] These were Andrieu's concern as an editor. But we can read the more substantial differences, as well as the interventions made in the source texts, according to the priorities of the communities it circulated in.

For example, one might look at the two narratives of the mass in the text, each one a self-contained *ordo* within the broader narrative. One, Ordo 15 nos 12–65, is found in all of the five manuscripts, the second Ordo 15, nos 133–51 is found only in St Gall, Cod. Sang. 349. The first mass narrative is placed at Christmas. It comes directly after the note that the second mass of this day was celebrated in Rome at Sant'Anastasia and then the third at Saint Peter's Basilica (Ordo 15, no. 11), as the Sacramentary would tell you, but it is explicitly titled as the 'way and custom on this day but also on every Sunday, and Easter, as well as the feast days of saints'.[34] It is fundamentally based on the description of the Roman, papal mass *Ordo Romanus* 1, and thus presents an episcopal Mass, celebrated by a *pontifex* or (at times) the Pope

---

31 Andrieu, *Les Ordines*, III, pp. 59–63.
32 The Wolfenbüttel manuscript, HAB, MS Cod. Guelf. 91 Weiss., also adds a note to the end of the ordo on chant practices on fol. 88. See Ordo 15, no. 84, nota, Andrieu, *Les Ordines*, III, p. 116.
33 Andrieu, *Les Ordines*, III, pp. 46–47, 54–56.
34 Andrieu, *Les Ordines*, III, p. 9 'Modus autem vel consuetudo tam ipsius diei quam omnium dominicorum dierum vel paschalium, seu natalicia sanctorum talis est'.

(*domnus apostolicus*) with numerous assistants. Van Dijk argued that this mass *ordo* was in fact an early form of that source text, Ordo 1 because 'it does not know the complex hierarchy of papal personnel […] the assistants of the *domnus apostolicus* are all clerics: bishops, priests, an archdeacon, deacons and subdeacons etc.'.[35] However these modifications are actually signs of a very early Frankish adaptation of Ordo 1, not an indication that Ordo 15 in any way precedes that text. Additionally the language of the text, too, is changed, from the Latin idiom of Rome, which often used Greek words, in which Ordo 1 was written, to an idiom more characteristic of Frankish liturgical texts. Thus, in places where the text borrows from Ordo 1, *candelabra* for *cereostata*, *turabilus* for *thymiamaterium*, *gradus* for ambo, *sacerdos* instead of *presbyter* and, tellingly for the audience of the text, *clerici* is substituted for *scola cantorum*.[36] The *clerici* or the community surrounding the bishop who take part in this mass include *cantores* (Ordo 15, no. 61) who sing an antiphon pertaining to that day in a custom unknown to Ordo 1. The text also adds some other liturgical customs which can only represent proper practice with which the creators were familiar and felt the text ought to include.[37] Of course, given the relative length of the two texts, the mass text is otherwise much simplified from Ordo 1. These modifications would show the active reception of a source text, Ordo 1, and its adaptation to a Frankish cathedral.

The second mass *ordo* is only to be found in the variant of the text present at St Gall, in Ordo 15, nos 133–51. This has a somewhat unusual title:

> Ordo 15, no. 133: In die vero dominica, uel in aliis precipuis solemnitatibus sanctorum, quando publice missas caelebrant ad sanctam Mariam maiore siue ad presepe uel in monastiria monachorum.[38]

The mention of Santa Maria Maggiore is strange, since the text appears in fact to describe a mass only in a monastery. This reference to the Roman Church is only explicable within Ordo 15's complex, overall relationship to Rome's ecclesiastical topography. This second mass text is no longer based on Ordo 1 at all, and has no points of contact with the preceding mass narrative, but

---

35 Van Dijk, 'Urban and Papal Rites', p. 458.
36 For example Ordo 15, no. 15 '[…] Facit orationem usquedum clerici antiphonam ad introitum cum psalmo et Gloria et repetito verso dixerint' compared to Ordo 1, no. 44 'Et mox incipit prior scolae antiphonam ad introitum' and no. 50 'Et respiciens ad priorem scolae annuit ei ut dicat Gloriam […]'.
37 E.g. the washing of hands at Mass: Ordo 15, no. 27 'Inde dat accolitus aquam manibus adstantes uero duo subdiaconi tenentes linteum ante genua pontifices […]'; saying of the Secret specified to be almost silent: no. 33 'Nouissime duas oblations suas proprias accipiens, eleuatis oculis et manibus cum ipsis ad caelum orat Deum secrete'; no. 35 'Tunc pontifex inclinato uultu in terra, dicit orationem super oblationis, ita ut nullus preter Deum et ipsum audiat, nisi tantum Per omnia secula seculorum'.
38 Andrieu, *Les Ordines*, III, p. 122: 'On Sunday, or on the other high feasts of the saints, when public masses are celebrated at Santa Maria Maggiore or at the crib (ad presepe — an old name of Santa Maria) and in the monasteries of monks'.

is entirely unique. No bishop celebrates the mass, there is only a *sacerdos* and only deacons and acolytes to assist him. Though the main chorus of the mass is given as *clerus*, the setting still seems to be a monastery. Apart from the title, the text gives a clear indication of how the offertory would work within an explicitly monastic hierarchy:

> Ordo 15, no. 145: Et tunc, si in monasterio fuerit, offert abba oblatione, siue secundus seu presbiter uel arciclauius in loco suo pro ipso abate et pre [Andrieu suggests post] ipsis deuoti uel boni christiani.[39]

The *arciclavius* is a somewhat rare term for the treasurer or sacristan, a position of significant importance in a community of secular canons, often entrusted with care of the unfolding of liturgical ceremonies.[40] The term arciclavius is prominent in records of Saint-Martin of Tours at least from 878 onwards, suggesting that this mass text had some roots in that community.[41] The same *arciclavius* is also mentioned in Ordo 18, also only in the St Gall manuscript, where his care of the keys of the church and of liturgical processes are described.[42] The procession to the altar, while the chant *Laudate domini* (nos 135–37) is sung, where the clerics carry 'towers' which held the Eucharistic bread, ('turres tres aut duas uel una') are otherwise attested in such sources as Pseudo-Germanus of Paris and Gregory of Tours, and have no analogue in Rome (though, again implying a potential link to Tours).[43] Suitable for Tours, it presents an audience whose identity as clerics or monks is here not necessarily fixed, yet who resided in what they described as a *monasterium*.[44]

One might briefly consider the text's close attention to Roman churches, focused on the phenomenon of the Roman stational liturgy.[45] As above,

---

39 Andrieu, *Les Ordines*, III, p. 123: 'And then, if this should be in monastery, the abbot offers the offering, and the *secundus* and the priest, or the *archiclavius* in his place for the abbot, and afterwards those of the devoted and good Christians'.
40 Barrow, *The Clergy in the Medieval World*, p. 304.
41 Noizet, *La fabrique de la ville*, pp. 72–73; Boussard 'Le trésorier de Saint-Martin de Tours'.
42 Andrieu, *Les Ordines*, III, p. 206 'Si est consuetudo apud ipsos ut ille archeclavius, qui clavis ecclesiae sive minesterium sacrum sub cura sua habit, ipse costodit'.
43 Andrieu, *Les Ordines*, III, p. 74; Pseudo-Germanus was copied in a manuscript now in Autun, BM, MS S 184, but, according to Bischoff, *Katalog*, I, p. 39, written 'Umkreis von Tours'; Despite his pseudonym and use by liturgists as a testament to the wholly unhelpful construction of a pre-Carolingian 'Gallican rite', Pseudo-Germanus likely wrote in Carolingian times and recorded traditions still living in his time, as these *ordines* show: c.f. McKitterick, *The Frankish Church*, p. 216.
44 Also in *ordines* of Holy Week: Ordo 27, no. 13, for the rite of New Fire, the Roman church's hierarchy struck fire from the church lintel for each day of the Triduum, with increasing stature (*mansionarius*, archdeacon, junior bishop), but an alternative was added for the hierarchy of a monastery (*custos*, provost, abbot), once the text was circulating in Francia, Andrieu, *Les Ordines*, III, pp. 350–51; Ordo 29 (pp. 429–45), written at Lorsch not Corbie, represents an entire reworking of a Roman holy Week *ordo* for a monastery.
45 Baldovin, *The Urban Character*, pp. 109–66.

the text specified two of Christmas's masses at Roman locations, one at Sant'Anastasia and the other at Saint Peter's Basilica, at Ordo 15, no. 11, with processions of 'multa turba populi' (the first mass is noted but not given its place in Santa Maria Maggiore). The text also gives the Roman churches for the three Ember Days of December:

> Ordo 15, no. 3: In ipsa vero ebdomata, quarta et sexta feria seu et sabbatum, stationis puplicas faciunt: prima ad sanctam Mariam ad presepem, secunda ad apostolos Iacobi et Iohannis; tertia cum duocecim leccionibus ad sanctum Petrum.[46]

The text (in all recensions) falsely claims Santi Apostoli was dedicated to the apostles James and John, rather than James and Philip. It also assumes the Frankish and not the Roman localization of this Ember Day (Ordo 15, no. 5) by giving a contingency for if Saturday clashed with Christmas Eve. This would never happen according to the Roman calendar where the Ember Days were immovable, but could occur in the Frankish custom of having them simply in the fourth week of December.[47] At Candlemas (Ordo 15, no. 79), the text mentions the procession from San Adriano al foro to Santa Maria Maggiore. Amidst a text which had clearly been processed for liturgical performance by communities both monastic and cathedral, these notes of Roman detail imply that participation in such rituals had a view towards recreating movements across Rome's ecclesiastical topography, the liturgical expression of a desired bond with Rome, as argued by Häußling.[48]

The four manuscripts around Tours provide some interesting variants. In the brief *ordo* for baptism taking place at Epiphany there are some significant alterations from the text as it was found in Cod. Sang. 349: the clothing of the clerics in white (as in the Sacramentary of Gellone, and Pseudo-Germanus) the invocation of the Holy Trinity at no. 74, and the addition of confirmation soon afterwards by a bishop at no. 77, would all imply the 'correction' of this rite towards a more accurate and comprehensive narrative of baptism.[49] Twice

---

46 Andrieu, *Les Ordines*, III, p. 96 'But on that week, Wednesday and Friday and Saturday, they do public stations: the first is at Santa Maria Maggiore, the second at the church of the Apostles James and John, the third with twelve readings is at Saint Peter's'.

47 Willis, 'Ember Days'; The complex differences between Frankish and Roman practice are laid out by Andrieu, *Les Ordines*, IV, pp. 214–32; see Amalarius of Metz's letter to Hilduin of Saint-Denis: Amalarius of Metz, *Epistula ad Hilduinum*, ed. by Hanssens, I, p. 342.

48 Häußling, *Mönchskonvent*, pp. 67–72, 181–212; Claussen, *The Reform of the Frankish Church*, pp. 276–89 in Metz.

49 Andrieu, *Les Ordines*, III, p. 112: 'Deinde discalciati presbiteri aut diaconi <induentes se aliis vestibus mundis vel candedis>, ingrediuntur ad fontes et acceptis infantibus de parentibus baptizantur eos, ter mergentes in aqua, in nomine patris et filii et spiritus sancti, tantum <sanctam trinitatem> semel invocantes. [...] <Baptizati autem infantes mox deportantur ante episcopum et datur eis gratia spiritus septiformis cum chrisma in fronte et invocatione sanctae trinitatis, id est confirmatio baptismi, vel christianitas>'; compare Ordo 11, nos 99–102; Also *Liber Sacramentorum Gellonensis*, ed. by Dumas, 2319, 2321, 2325, pp. 335–37:

this tradition adds an additional 'explanation' for a liturgical prescription. The first concerns the kiss of peace given during the Christmas mass narrative (an intervention without precedent in the source, Ordo 1 or any other *ordo romanus*):

> Ordo 15, no. 14: Et ut ante altare pervenit, antequam ascendat, inclinat vultum ad oracionem. Et erigens se dat pacem uni episcopo et omnibus diaconibus suis, <hoc autem ita faciens, ut omne ordine sacerdotum vel clero suo pacem et concordiam demonstratem puro corde accedant ad immolandum sacrificum Deo>.[50]

The second such intervention concerns Lenten fasting.

> Ordo 15, no. 81: Et non solum septuagissima, sed et LXma, Lma, XL, XXXma, XXma, XVma et VIIIma semper pro ipso ordine celebrantur, <ut quantum plus cognoverint adproprinquare sanctum diem paschae redemptionis nostrae, tantum amplius ab omni iniquinamento carnis vel inmunditia se abstineant, ut digni sint communicare corpus et sanguinem domini>.[51]

More than liturgical instructions, these suggest the meaning of the rituals in question and the correct means to approach them.[52] They blur the boundaries between *ordines* as purely liturgical texts ruling the performance of rituals (which they rarely were in a simplistic way), liturgical *expositiones* that explain the meaning of liturgical ritual, and 'rules' which regulated the life and defined the mindset of communities. Such directives make implicit theological points too, for example about the stature of the Eucharist and the moral status appropriate for its reception.

One of the text's peculiarities, the attention to the stational liturgy, is somewhat expanded by the Tours examples. The related manuscripts around

---

'Deinde presbiteri aut diaconi, etiam si necesse fuerit et acoliti discalciati, induentes se aliis uestibus mundis uel candedissimis ingrediuntur in fontes intro aquam [...] baptizantur eos sub trinam mersionem tantum sanctam trinitatem semel inuocantes [...] et dat orationem pontifex super eos, cum crisma faciens crucem in frontibus eorum cum innuocatione sanctae trinitatis et tradedit eis septeformem spiritus sancti gratiam'.

50 Andrieu, *Les Ordines*, III, p. 98 'And as he comes before the altar, before he ascends, he inclines his head in prayer. And, rising, he gives peace to each of the bishops and to all his deacons, but he does this so that, having shown peace and concord to every order of priests and to his clerics, they (or he in Montpellier) should rise with a pure heart to offer sacrifice to God'.
51 Andrieu, *Les Ordines*, III, pp. 114–15 'And not only Septuagesima but also Sexagesma, Quinquagesima, Quadragesima, the thirtieth day before Easter, the twentieth day, the fifteenth and the eighth each one in its order should be celebrated, so that they should recognise so much more the approach of the holy day of our redemption, Easter, and they should abstain so much more from any iniquity of the flesh or uncleanness, so that they should be worthy to communicate the body and blood of our Lord'.
52 See also Ordo 15, no. 80, describing how Septuagesima is celebrated so that the people should be aware 'cum tremore et reverentia'.

Tours give a unique witness to an announcement by the archdeacon of the stational church for the feast day of a saint.[53] Of all of them, only the Montpellier manuscript adds an indication that 'public litanies' or processions would take place on the day before Epiphany.[54] At Ordo 15, no. 79, the Montpellier manuscript gives a much expanded account of the processions of the Roman clergy and people from San Adriano al foro to Santa Maria Maggiore that seems to be based on knowledge, or even observation, of Roman practice.[55] These texts show that the details of Roman church names and processional practices were one feature of interest in the copying and editing of *ordines romani*, an interest perhaps even more intense for a community found in an urban centre around a cathedral, as at Tours, though monks certainly appropriated the stational liturgy in innovative ways.[56] Otherwise, the minor interventions of the Tours tradition around Ordo 15 tend to simply add or specify specific points, in the same tradition as the text's original treatment of its sources like Ordo 1, which suggest the text was further refined in the community of Tours to reflect uses they knew.[57]

Ordo 16: The *Instruccio ecclesiastici ordinis*

Evidence that monks still engaged usefully with Ordo 15, is that Ordo 16 comes before it in the single manuscript witness, Cod. Sang. 349. This was probably not the case in the original, since Ordo 16 refers to Ordo 15 twice, as if it were a previous text in the manuscript.[58] Ordo 16 did not, therefore, circulate independently like Ordo 15 did, but was envisaged from the first as being bound to Ordo 15. Thus Semmler's edition, for example, does not

---

53 Ordo 15, no. 56 'Tunc arcidiaconus […] pronuntiat venturam stationem <dicendo: Illa feria veniente, natalis est illius sancti, sive martyrum, sive confessorum, statio in basilica illius, in illo et illo loco. Respondent omnes Deo gratias>'.
54 Andrieu, *Les Ordines*, III, p. 110, Ordo 15, no. 69 'Pridie theophanie, ieiunium publicum <faciunt et hora nona missas celebrantur' (Montpellier 412: 'et laetaniam publicam ad missam faciant')>.
55 Andrieu, *Les Ordines*, III, pp. 113–14 'Postea quidem die secondo mense februario Ypapanti, quod est III nonas ipsius mensis colleguntur omnes tam clerus romanae ecclesiae quam et omnes monachi monasteriorium cum omni populo suburbano seu et copiosa multitudo peregrinorum de quacumque provintia congregati, venientes ad ecclesiam beati Adriani mane prima et accipiunt de manu pontificis unusquis cereo uno […] etc.' The Wolfenbüttel manuscript is further elaborated.
56 Häußling, *Mönchskonvent*, pp. 315–23.
57 Interesting are the orientation of the pontiff to the East at Ordo 15, no. 17, addition of the *Dominus uobiscum* dialogue at Ordo 15, no. 23, and so on.
58 Andrieu, *Les Ordines*, III, p. 150: Ordo 16, no. 25: 'In uigilia natalis domini, tam psalmi nouem cum antephonis uel humilias, cum respunsuriis suis seu et uersibus et matutinis laudibus [sic.] expletis uel missarum solemniis, **ordine quo in priore Capitolare memorauimus** cum magno decore celebrantur' (referring to the Christmas mass) and at no. 27: 'De octabas domini uel de ephifania, **superiore ordine inuenitur** qualiter celebrare debeamus'.

Figure 16.1. The script of Cod. 349; St Gall, Stiftsbibliothek, Cod. Sang. 349, p. 55. Late eighth century. Reproduced with permission of the Sankt Gallen Stiftsbibliothek.

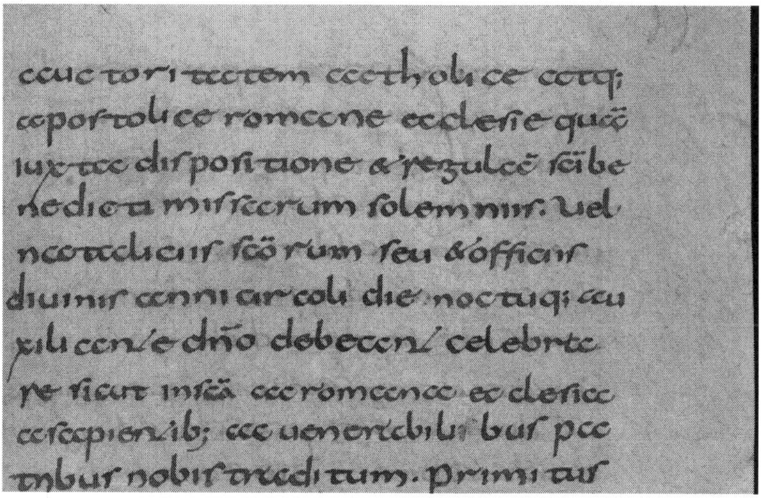
auctoritatem catholice atq;
apostolice romane ecclesie quae
iuxta dispositione & regulae sci be
nedicti missarum solemniis uel
nataliciis scorum seu & officiis
diuinis anni circoli die noctuq; au
xiliante dno debeant celebra
re sicut in sca ac romana ecclesia
a sapientib; ac uenerabilibus pa
tribus nobis traditum. Primitus

replicate how readers encountered it. In its title, the text appealed both to the authority of the Roman Church and the disposition of the monastic Rule established by Benedict of Nursia. But it conforms rather more closely to the Roman *cursus* than the Benedictine, as Billett noted.[59] Notably the author was well aware that the two traditions could contradict each other:

> Ordo 16, no. 15 Responsurius uero tercius, secundum regulam sancti Benedicti, cum Gloria est canendus nouissimi. Sed romana ecclesia omnia responsuria cum Gloria semper cantatur.[60]

Giving both alternatives here implies great openness within the negotiated framework of authoritative liturgical sources, which helps to contextualize the general appeal to Rome within this text and Ordo 15, its source. Allowance for variance would suggest that the title given to these texts was not to be understood, as Andrieu saw it, as a thunder-blast to conformity. In other cases, Ordo 16 goes outside both the Benedictine and Roman traditions, giving, for example, the reading of *passiones* of martyrs and saints during the Night Office at their feasts (Ordo 16 no. 10). Jeffery recapitulated an Irish influence on the text, noting that Ordo 16 agrees with the Bangor Antiphonary by giving Prime

59 Billett, *The Divine Office*, p. 49.

60 Andrieu, *Les Ordines*, III, pp. 148–49 'But the third responsory is to be sung only with the Gloria, according to the Rule of Saint Benedict. But the Roman church always sings every responsory with Gloria'.

at the first or second hour of the day, and, at one particular point, having the *Te Deum* sung after the abbot reads the Gospel on Sunday (Ordo 16 no. 16), whereas the *Regula Benedicti* has the *Te Deum* before.[61] Jeffery (like Andrieu) suggested that the Collection of *ordines* represented by the St Gall manuscript was therefore written in an area of Luxueil's influence.[62] Yet as Fox noted, what little we know of Irish liturgy in this period coheres remarkably with indigenous Frankish traditions, making a firm distinction extremely difficult.[63] In fact, it is likely there was little distinctly 'Irish' to distinguish Luxueil from prevailing trends in Frankish monasticism, so these peculiarities do not really help to locate the Ordo.

Ordo 16 is most clearly distinguished from Ordo 15 by the narrative of Holy Week to Pentecost, Ordo 16, nos 28–50. It ignores the feature of this time of year upon which Ordo 15 dwelt, the baptisms on Holy Saturday. That would be a part of the Holy Week ceremonial with which a cathedral community would be amply familiar, but would be less appropriate for a monastery, since the texts assume the cooperation of the bishop and the presence of the laity. Missing, too, from this account of Holy Week are the blessing of oils on Maundy Thursday and the adoration of the cross on Good Friday, central to both days in their episcopal ceremonies. Paschal candles, perhaps a mistake by the scribe instead of a singular candle, are blessed by a deacon at Ordo 15, no. 40. No bishop is present for these ceremonies, only *sacerdotes*. Furthermore, the Abbot is given a role during the Holy Saturday celebrations at Ordo 16, no. 41, where he stands with the deacons, and no. 44 where he can say the *Gloria*, a striking privilege which was normally afforded to priests only on this day (otherwise an exclusive right for bishops). The Roman church names were removed. Rather than a time for ordination as they were in Ordo 15, the Ember Days were given primarily as fasts, at Ordo 16, no. 22, where ordinations are only mentioned in passing and the fast from Wednesday to Saturday is highlighted, and, particularly, Ordo 16, no. 51, where ordinations are not discussed at all. A striking intervention on the fast from Good Friday to the Easter Vigil at Ordo 16, no. 37, that they should consume only bread and water mixed with vinegar, again blurs the boundaries beyond the strictly liturgical.[64] So too does the instruction that everyone ought to throw themselves to the ground 'with tears and contrition of heart' during the Good Friday prayers.[65] These additions address directly the concerns of

---

61 Andrieu, *Les Ordines*, III, p. 139.
62 Jeffery, 'The Roman Liturgical Year', p. 168.
63 Fox, *Power and Religion*, p. 234.
64 Andrieu, *Les Ordines*, III, p. 152 'His autem expletis, ingrediantur ad vesperum, et ipsa nocte abstenentes se ab omni dilicia corporali, id est, preter tantum pane et aquam cum aceto mixtam, non sumantes; cui autem dominus virtutem dederit, pertranseunt sine cybo usque in vigilia pasche. Hoc autem apud religious et venerabilis viros observantur'.
65 Andrieu, *Les Ordines*, III, p. 151: 'prosternantes se omnes in terra cum lacrimis vel contritione cordis, et iterum admonentur a diacono dicente'.

monastic life surrounding liturgical observance, but also going beyond into the conduct of life. Some of them would not be alien from a monastic Rule.[66]

Ordo 17: The *Breviarium ecclesiastici ordinis*

Found in two manuscripts, Ordo 17 is a reimagining of the traditions of Ordo 15 and 16. The title of this text is identical to Ordo 16 (see above) apart from the substitution of the word *Breviarum* for *Instructio*, and it thus also refers to the traditions of the Roman Church and the Benedictine Rule. The two manuscripts are Vatican Library MS Palat. lat. 574 (once also joined to fols 100–06 of Vatican MS Palat. lat. 493), fols 152^r–165^r produced at Lorsch at the end of the eighth century, and Gotha, Landesbibliothek, MS Membr. I. 85, fols 107^v–112^v, which was once at Murbach, but originally a product of the monastery of Wissembourg, produced at the turn of the ninth century.[67] Gotha, MS Membr.I.85 appears to be a copy of the older manuscript, with the Latin having been lightly edited.[68] Both manuscripts contain the same canonical collection, including extracts from the *Dionysiana* with the decrees of councils and letters of Popes.[69] Ordo 17 appears at the very end. In the Vatican manuscript, the original, the *ordo* was copied onto blank folios seemingly at a later occasion and with several pages separating it from the canonical collection.[70] But the text in Palat. lat. 493 is more deliberately laid out than, say, Cod. Sang. 349's *ordines*, with use of half-uncial and rubrication throughout to divide the work in sections, and it was copied with great care (see fig. 16.2).

---

66 Examples of rules prescribing emotional responses to liturgical actions include: The Benedictine Rule, *The Rule of Saint Benedict*, ed. by Venarde, p. 92, XX On Reverence in Prayer: 'in puritate cordis et conpunctione lacrimarum nos exaudiri sciamus', p. 164, XLVIIII on Lent 'orationi cum fletibus lectioni et conpunctioni cordis atque abstinentiae operam damus'; p. 170, LII on the oratory 'habentur reuerentia Deo [...] non in clamosa voce sed in lacrimis et intentione cordis'; Also in the *Regula Magistri*, ed. de Vogüé, II, p. 204, XLIIII Psalms at Nocturnes 'cognoscitur per bonum liberum arbitrium spiritum prorsus amare quam carnem', particularly pp. 212–17 XLVII on the discipline of psalmody 'debet esse reuerentiae grauitas [...] Ergo si sapienter et cum timore iubet psalli, oportet psallentem inmobili corpore, inclinato capite stare et laudes Domino moderate canere [...] ne alibi sensus eius demigret, ne cum in alia cogitatione sensus noster migrauerit [...] cor pariter cum lingua conueniat cum timore Domino cottidianum debitum redibere', p. 220, XLVIII on reverence in prayer 'Ergo oportet orare cum timore suppliciter'.
67 On BAV, MS Palat. lat. 574, Andrieu, *Les Ordines*, I, pp. 321–22, for digitized version see Manuscripts; Bischoff, *Katalog*, III, p. 414; On Gotha, Andrieu, *Les Ordines*, I, pp. 138–39; Bischoff, *Katalog*, I, p. 297.
68 Andrieu, *Les Ordines*, III, p. 158.
69 Kéry, *Canonical Collections*, pp. 49–50.
70 The quire containing the *Breviarum* was removed from the manuscript, travelled to Saint Blaise in the Black Forest, then to Sankt Paul in Carinthia, but has now been re-attached to its original place in the Vatican manuscript.

Figure 16.2. Script and use of rubrication in Pal.lat.574; Città del Vaticano, Biblioteca Apostolica Vaticana, Pal. lat. 574, fol. 155ʳ. End of the eighth century. © 2021 Biblioteca Apostolica Vaticana. Reproduced by permission of Biblioteca Apostolica Vaticana, with all rights reserved.

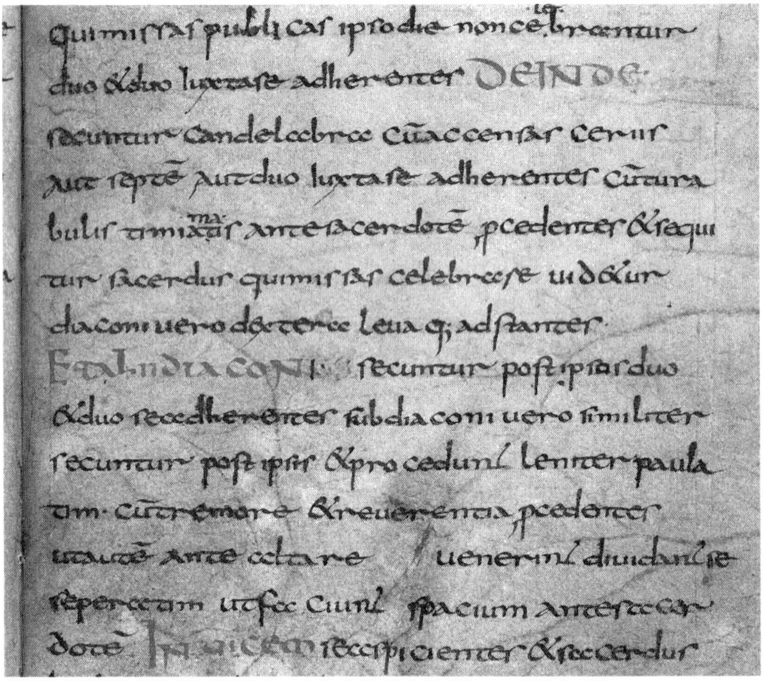

Ordo 17 suggests that monks in these places remained interested in the details of liturgical performance given in Ordo 15, even those which were suppressed in Ordo 16 (which nevertheless is still transmitted with, and refers to, 15). Both texts were here combined. Ordo 17, nos 1–68 is a reprise of the liturgical cycle from Advent to Candlemas, substantially based on Ordo 15. There are some additions, such as the insertion of the feast of Saint Eugenia at no. 7, dealing with the clash of this feast with Christmas. Ordo 17, no. 9 similarly suggests that the creator of the text addressed matters of liturgical confusion or difficulty; here the timing of the Ember Days is explored at length in an attempt to mediate between Roman and Frankish practice.[71] Gregory the Great himself is directly quoted on the celebration of three masses at Christmas

---

71 Andrieu, *Les Ordines*, III, p. 176 'In ipsa autem ordinatione sacerdotum preter quattuor tempora anni nullatenus ordinatur: id est primum ver, quod est ebdomata prima mensis primi marcii, ita tamen si ebdomata infra quadragesima contigerit; deinde sequitur aliut tempus estas, quod venit mensis quarti iunii, quod sequitur ebdomata prima post pentecosten; sequitur tercium tempus auctumni quod est mensis septimi septembrii, quod

at Ordo 17, no. 16.[72] The reprise of Ordo 15 includes the Mass *ordo* for the Christmas Mass, now further removed from its source Ordo 1. The creator of Ordo 17 adapted the text further for the monastic audience, since now here too the *pontifex* and archdeacon were removed and the celebrant is a simple priest. A procession from the sacristy is given in detail (Ordo 17, nos 18–22). At Ordo 17, no. 25, it is made clear that the clergy pray 'for themselves and for the sins of the people' when they prostrate themselves before the altar before mass.[73] The monastic setting is made explicit when, at the moment of offering, in monasteries 'where women do not enter', the priests instead go back to the sacristy and process with the offerings from there up to the altar.[74] Rather than the stations being announced by an archdeacon, as in the 'Tours' variant of Ordo 15, Ordo 17 has the deacon giving the saints' days in the coming week from the martyrology.[75] The second section of Ordo 17 (nos 69–83) gives the readings from Christmas to Pentecost, without substantial changes from Ordo 16. The third section largely again copies from Ordo 16, at Ordo 17, nos 84–120, including that text's narrative of Holy Week which was itself already suited for a monastery. The most significant intervention here fills in a significant gap by replacing Ordo 16's brief reference of a blessing of 'candles' on Holy Saturday, with a much more expanded text with a proper blessing of a single Paschal Candle, at Ordo 17, nos 102–05, which includes a reference to *fratribus*, the monks themselves. Therefore Ordo 17 shows a similar impulse to the original creation of Ordo 16, with monks being clearly keen to rework these pre-existing documents in such a way as to address questions and clarifications, some peculiar to monks, some of general liturgical interest.

Conclusion

These manuscripts defy strict categorization, sharing concerns and freely dialoguing with monastic rules without being bound to them, unsurprising given the texts' employment (openly) of the Rule of Benedict, and (unspoken)

---

agitur tertia ebdomata ipsius mensis; inde sequitur quartum tempus anni hyems, quod est mensis decimi decembrii, sicut supra diximus, hoc est ebdomata prima ante natale domini, ordine quod diximus, quarte et sexta feria seu et sabbatum celeberetur'.

72 Andrieu, *Les Ordines*, III, p. 177: 'celebrant missas sacre nauitatis domini unam postquam gallus cantaverit, aliam mane prima, tertiam in die, sicut mos est in honore sanctae trinitatis sicut sanctus Gregorius in umiliis suis loquitur dicens Quia missarum solempnia ter hodie celebraturi sumus ita et nos oportet ut similiter sanctae natiuitatis domini diem in trinitatis numero missarum solempnia celebramus'.

73 Andrieu, *Les Ordines*, III, p. 179: 'fundens orationem pro se vel pro peccata populi'.

74 Andrieu, *Les Ordines*, III, pp. 180–81: 'Item in monastirio ubi non ingrediuntur femine, postquam primitus sacerdus laveret manus, ingrediuntur sacerdotes cum leuitas in sacrario et accipient oblationes. Et procedant de sacrario'.

75 Andrieu, *Les Ordines*, III, p. 183: 'pronuntians natalicia sanctorum in ipsa ebdomanta venientia [...] secundum martirologium'.

of the *Regula Magistri*. This suggests that boundaries were porous between what have been framed as liturgical texts *strictu sensu* and monastic rules which often touched on liturgical matters. The presentation of Ordo 15, and 17, in canonical manuscripts implies a further openness of such texts to cross genre boundaries and be read in different ways.[76] These manuscripts suggest that, rather than being followed strictly as a prescriptive script for ritual, they might have been simply consulted for specific matters of liturgical confusion or difficulty, as one might consult the canonical collections that often accompany them. For example, the addition about the feast of Saint Eugenia to Ordo 17 n. 7 has less to say about the possible place the text was made (for which Hallinger attempted to use it) and rather more about its function, here addressing a problem the writer, or his community, had encountered: how to resolve the clash of the saint's feast with Christmas. One might even frame these texts as simply the organized repositories for a set of answers to liturgical questions useful to certain communities, in which case it is difficult to see in them anything as systematic or deliberate as the liturgical 'reform' envisaged by Andrieu.[77] Certainly the wider tradition of these *ordines romani* would suggest that questions arising in performance were put to them, and they allowed for adaptation, while being shared from one place to another. Their appeal to Rome (or indeed to the Rule of Benedict) can be seen as answering a certain need or expectation on the part of such readers as well, rather than being the simple seal of authority credulously read, as it was envisaged by Andrieu or Hallinger. Among those questions was certainly how monks received and dealt with these texts, as the successive creations of Ordo 16 and 17 would show. But, whether they surrounded a cathedral or inhabited a monastery, such communities shared these texts in common and exchanged them, and certainly had some interests in common. Among the most interesting found here among several recensions was a continual awareness of the power of liturgy to bring about and recommend certain aspects and habits of mind and emotion deemed suitable to monks and canons alike, be they intercession, purity of heart or repentance.

---

[76] Parkes, *The Making of Liturgy* demonstrates that liturgical manuscripts (of a later date) were doing so many more things than simply being scripts for performance.

[77] Hen, *Royal Patronage*, p. 62 argues briefly that *ordines romani* cannot be seen as deliberately imposed.

Works Cited

Manuscripts

Autun, Bibliothèque Municipale, MS S 184
Gotha, Landesbibliothek, MS Membr. I. 85 <https://dhb.thulb.uni-jena.de/rsc/viewer/ufb_derivate_00015136/Memb-I-00085_00001.tif> [accessed 8 September 2021]
Metz, Bibliothèque Municipale, MS 134
Montpellier, Bibliothèque de la faculté de medicine, MS cod. 412
Paris, Bibliothèque nationale de France, MS fonds latin 3836
———, MS fonds latin 12048
St Gall, Stiftsbibliothek, Cod. Sang. 11
———, Cod. Sang. 193
———, Cod. Sang. 194
———, MS 349 <http://www.e-codices.unifr.ch/en/csg/0349/5> [accessed 8 September 2021]
Città della Vaticano, Biblioteca Apostolica Vaticana, MS Palat. lat. 277
———, MS Palat. lat. 493
———, MS Reg. lat. 1127 <https://digi.vatlib.it/view/MSS_Reg.lat.1127> [accessed 8 September 2021]
———, MS Palat. lat. 574 <https://digi.vatlib.it/view/bav_pal_lat_574> [accessed 8 September 2021]
The Hague, Meermanno Westreeanium, MS cod. 10 B 4
Wolfenbüttel, Herzog August Bibliothek, MS Cod. Guelf. 91 Weiss

Primary Sources

Amalarius of Metz, *Epistula ad Hilduinum*, ed. by Jean-Paul Hanssens, *Amalarii Episcopi Opera Liturgica Omnia*, vol. 1 (Vatican City: Biblioteca Apostolica Vaticana, 1948), pp. 341–58
Andrieu, Michel, ed., *Les Ordines Romani du Haut Moyen Age*, 5 vols (Louvain: Spiciligium Lovaniense, 1931–1961)
Bede, *Ecclesiastical History of the English People*, ed. and trans. by Bertram Colgrave and Roger A. B. Mynors (Oxford: Clarendon Press, 1969)
Herardus of Tours, *Capitula*, ed. by Rudolf Pokorny and Martina Stratmann, *Monumenta Germaniae Historica Capitula Episcoporum* 2 (Hannover: Hahn, 1995), pp. 115–57
Liber Sacramentorum Gellonensis, ed. by Antoine Dumas, Corpus Christianorum Series Latina, 159 (Turnhout: Brepols, 1981)
Lowe, Elias Avery, ed., *Codices Latini Antiquiores: A Palaeographical Guide to Latin Manuscripts Prior to the 9th Century*, vol. 7: *Switzerland*, ed. by Elias Avery Lowe (Oxford: Clarendon Press, 1956); vol. 10: *Austria, Belgium, Czechoslovakia, Denmark, Egypt and Holland* (Oxford: Clarendon Press, 1963)

'Ordines aevi regulae mixtae (post seac. VIII. med.)', ed. by Josef Semmler, in *Corpus Consuetudinum Monasticarum*, vol. 1: *Initia Consuetudinis Benedictinae: Consuetudines saeculi octavi e noni* (Wiesbaden: Harrassowitz, 1962), pp. 3–76

Regula Magistri, ed. by Adalbert de Vogüé, *La Règle du Maître*, Sources Chrétiennes, 105–06, 2 vols (Paris: Les Editions du Cerf, 1964–1965)

The Rule of Saint Benedict, ed. by Bruce L. Venarde, Dumbarton Oaks Medieval Library, 6 (Cambridge, MA: Harvard University Press, 2011)

Secondary Works

Baldovin, John F., *The Urban Character of Christian Worship* (Rome: Oriental Institute Press, 1987)

Barrow, Julia, *The Clergy in the Medieval World: Secular Clerics, their Families and Careers in North-Western Europe, c. 800–c. 1200* (Cambridge: Cambridge University Press, 2015)

Baumstark, Anton, 'Joannes Archicantor und der römische Ordo des Sangall. 349', *Jahrbuch für Liturgiewissenschaft*, 5 (1925), 153–58

Billett, Jesse, *The Divine Office in Anglo Saxon England 597–c. 1000* (London: Henry Bradshaw Society, 2014)

Bischoff, Bernhard, *Katalog der festländischen Handschriften des neunten Jahrhunderts mit Ausnahme der wisigotischen*, vol. 2: *Laon-Paderborn*, ed. by Birgit Ebersperger (Wiesbaden: Harrassowitz, 2004)

Boussard, Jacques, 'Le trésorier de Saint-Martin de Tours', *Revue d'histoire de l'Église de France*, 144 (1961), 67–88

Claussen, M. A., *The Reform of the Frankish Church: Chrodegang of Metz and the Regula Canonicorum in the Eighth Century* (Cambridge: Cambridge University Press, 2004)

Connel, Martin, *Church and Worship in Fifth Century Rome: The Letter of Innocent I to Decentius of Gubbio* (Cambridge: Grove Press, 2002)

Contreni, John, 'Two Descriptions of the Lost Laon Copy of the Collection of Saint-Maur', *Bulletin of Medieval Canon Law*, 10 (1980), 45–51; repr. in John Contreni, *Carolingian Learning, Masters and Manuscripts* (Hampshire: Variorum, 1992), xv

Dijk, Stephen J. P. van, 'Urban and Papal Rites', *Sacris Erudiri*, 12 (1965), 450–65

Duchesne, Louis, *Origines du culte chrétien: étude sur la liturgie latine avant Charlemagne*, 5th edn (Paris: de Bocard, 1920)

Fox, Yaniv, *Power and Religion in Merovingian Gaul: Columbanian Monasticism and the Frankish Elites* (Cambridge: Cambridge University Press, 2014)

Hallinger, Kassius, 'Die römischen Ordines von Lorsch, Murbach und St Gallen', in *Universitas: Dienst an Wahrheit und Leben; Festschrift für Bischof Dr Albert Stohr*, vol. 1, ed. by Ludwig Lenhart (Mainz: Matthias-Gruenwald, 1960), pp. 466–77

Häußling, Angelus Albert, *Mönchskonvent und Eucharistiefeier: Eine Studie über die Messe in der abendländischen Klosterliturgie des frühen Mittelalters und zur Geschichte der Meßhäufigkeit*, Liturgiewissenschaftliche Quellen und Forschungen, 58 (Münster: Aschendorff, 1973)

Hen, Yitzhak, *The Royal Patronage of Liturgy in Frankish Gaul to the Death of Charles the Bald (877)* (London: Henry Bradshaw Society, 2001)

Jeffery, Peter, 'Eastern and Western Elements in the Irish Monastic Prayers of the Hours', in *The Divine Office in the Latin Middle Ages*, ed. by Margot Fassler and Rebecca A. Baltzer (Oxford: Oxford University Press, 2000), pp. 128–30

——, 'The Early Liturgy at St Peter's', in *Old Saint Peter's Rome*, ed. by Rosamond McKitterick, John Osborne, Carol M. Richardson, and Joanna Storey (Cambridge: Cambridge University Press, 2013), pp. 167–76

Kéry, Lotte, *Canonical Collections in the Early Middle Ages (ca.400–1140)* (Washington D.C.: The Catholic University of America Press, 1999)

Klauser, Theodor, 'Die liturgischen Austauschbeziehungen zwischen der römischen und der fränkisch-deutschen Kirche vom achten bis zum elften Jahrhundert', *Historisches Jahrbuch*, 53 (1933), 169–89

Levison, Wilhelm, 'Handschriften des Museum Meermanno-Westreenianum im Haag', *Neues Archiv der Gesellschaft für ältere deutsche Geschichtskunde*, 38 (1913), 503–24

McKitterick, Rosamond, *The Frankish Church and the Carolingian Reforms 789–895* (London: Royal Historical Society, 1977)

——, 'Unity and Diversity in the Carolingian Church', in *Unity and Diversity in the Church*, ed. by Robert N. Swanson, Studies in Church History, 32 (Oxford: Blackwell, 1996), pp. 59–82

Meeder, Sven, *The Irish Scholarly Presence at St Gall: Networks of Knowledge in the Early Middle Ages* (Oxford: Bloomsbury, 2018)

Noizet, Hélène, *La fabrique de la ville: Espace et sociétés à Tours (9e–13e siècle)* (Paris: Publications de la Sorbonne, 2007)

Oexle, Otto Gerhard, *Forschungen zu monastischen und geistlichen Gemeinschaften in westfränkischen Bereich: Bestandteil des Quellenwerkes Societas et Fraternitas*, Münstersche Mittelalter-Schriften, 31 (Munich: Wilhelm Fink, 1978)

Parkes, Henry, *The Making of Liturgy in the Ottonian Church: Books, Music, and Ritual in Mainz, 950–1050* (Cambridge: Cambridge University Press, 2015)

Reynolds, Roger, 'Pseudonymous Liturgica in Early Medieval Canon Law Collections', in Roger E. Reynolds, *Law and Liturgy in the Latin Church, 5th–12th Centuries* (Aldershot: Routledge, 1994), pp. 67–76

Riché, Pierre, *La vie quotidienne dans l'empire carolingien* (Paris: Librairie Hachette, 1973)

Silvo-Tarouco, Carlo, 'Giovanni Archicantor di S. Pietro a Roma e l'ordo Romanus da lui composto (anno 680)', *Atti della Pontificia Accademia di Archeologia*, 3rd ser., Memorie, vol. 1, part 1 (Rome: Tipografia poliglotta vaticana, 1923), pp. 159–219

Vogel, Cyrille, *Medieval Liturgy: An Introduction to the Sources*, trans. by William Storey and Niels Krogh Rasmussen (Washington D.C.: Pastoral Press, 1986)

Willis, Geoffrey Grimshaw, 'Ember Days', in *Essays in Early Roman Liturgy* (London: SPCK, 1964), pp. 49–97

Index

Aachen   131, 179, 245, 268, 394, 409, 414, 415
   Councils of (816–19)   15, 17, 26, 37, 61, 64, 66, 101, 136, 147, 180–84, 189, 190, 197, 200, 206, 218, 222, 226–28, 233, 234, 258, 268, 269, 270, 275, 276, 277, 287, 295, 301, 302, 303, 305, 307, 311, 312, 316, 317, 323, 325, 326, 328, 335, 340, 355, 358, 369–71, 408, 410–12, 418
Adalard of Corbie   159
Admonitio generalis   15, 105, 106, 109, 141, 142, 145, 155, 158, 241, 245–47, 250, 256, 274, 371, 372
Aetherius of Lisieux, bishop   56
Agde, Council of (506)   50, 54
Agobard of Lyon   403–06, 408, 412, 413, 416–18
   De antiphonario   405, 406, 416
Alcuin of Tours   25, 99, 100, 108, 116, 119, 120, 141, 143, 154, 155, 194, 241–43, 245–48, 250, 252–56, 258–60, 286, 291, 292, 294, 304
Amalarius of Metz   26, 106, 242, 251–54, 256, 259, 260, 387, 403–10, 412, 415–19
   De ordine antiphonarii   252, 416
   Liber officialis   402
   Missae expositionis geminus codex   106, 251, 252, 253, 254
Ambrose of Milan   390–91
Andage, abbey   104
Andrieu, Michel   425–31, 433, 437, 442
Angers   341, 409

Angilbert of Saint-Riquier, abbot   40
Angilramn of Metz   244, 245, 248, 250, 253, 254–60
Annales laureshamenses   144, 158, 254, 257
Ardo, hagiographer   34, 84, 119
   Vita Benedicti Anianensis   34, 84
Arles   53, 70, 220, 227
Arles, Council of (813)   105, 114, 154
Arn of Salzburg, bishop   100, 147, 155, 242, 254, 412
Arnulf of Noirmoutier, abbot   305–07
Ars laureshamensis   291
Aschheim, Council of (755–60)   111
Athanasius   223, 228, 229
Audinus, chorbishop   413
Augustine of Hippo   167, 200–03, 205
   De doctrina Christiana   289, 290, 291, 292
   Enchiridion   429
   Regula Augustini/Praeceptum Augustini   340
   Sermo de pastoribus   192, 218

Bartholomeus of Île-Barbe, abbot   413
Basilica Portiana, church in Milan   391
Bathild, queen   247
Baudin of Tours, bishop   52
Baumstark, Anton   26, 381, 382, 384–86, 395, 396

Bavaria, Council of (805)   147, 149
Bede   286, 288, 427
   De temporum ratione   288
Benedict of Aniane   16, 33, 34,
   38–40, 59, 60, 64–66, 71, 84, 90,
   119, 159, 259, 270, 301, 302, 305–09,
   316, 361, 363, 366, 367, 388
   Codex regularum   71, 336, 341–42,
      361, 362, 371
   Concordia regularum   34, 71, 84,
      103, 109, 197
   *Excerptus diuersarum modus
      penitentiarum*   84
Benedict of Nursia   40, 77, 78, 186,
   323, 329, 339, 340, 355, 359, 366–69,
   393, 394, 437
   See also   *Regula Benedicti*
Bertila, abbess of Chelles   69
Bertram, Jerome   183, 207
Billett, Jesse   410, 437
Bisanti, Armando   269
Bodarwé, Katrinette   66
Boniface   46, 103, 140, 141, 243, 271
Bonnerue, Pierre   34
Boshof, Egon   135, 416
Bourges   139
Braga, Council of (561)   386
Brun Candidus/Candidus of
   Fulda   38
Bugyis, Katie Ann-Marie   60, 67
Bullough, Donald   241

Caesaria, sister of Caesarius of
   Arles   71, 227
Caesarius of Arles   70, 71, 223, 224,
   227, 228, 230, 389
   Epistola ad monachos   71
   Regula ad monachos   71
   Regula ad virgins   224, 227
   Vereor   71, 223, 227, 228
Candidus-Wizo, pupil of
   Alcuin   253
Capitula in Auuam directa   64, 77
Capitula Notitiarum   64
Capitula originis incertae   105, 106

*Capitula tractanda cum comitibus,
   episcopis et abbatibus*   251
Capitulare ecclesiasticum   34, 268,
   295
Capitulare missorum generale   112,
   114, 116
Capitulare monasticum   18, 34
Capitularia Regum Francorum   34,
   138
Capitulary of Lestinnes   108
Carloman, son of Pippin III   142
Carloman, son of Charles
   Martel   39
Carloman, son of Charles the
   Bald   309
Cassiodorus   272, 291, 392
   *Historia Ecclesiastica
      Tripartita*   392
   Institutiones   291
Cathwulf   141
Cato   194
Chalcedon, Council of (451)   110
Chalon-sur-Saône, Council of
   (813)   110
Charlemagne   15, 39, 40, 99, 103,
   112, 114, 116, 118, 141–43, 148, 149,
   151, 155, 157–60, 162, 180, 194, 242,
   243, 247, 251, 252, 154, 255–57, 259,
   269, 276, 285, 294, 304, 317, 323,
   329, 371, 381, 382, 389, 408, 412,
   414, 415, 418
Charles Martel   16, 103
Charles the Bald   309
Chelles, abbey   69
Childeric II   308
Chrodegang of Metz, bishop   17,
   34, 61, 66, 69, 86, 102, 133, 140, 141,
   167, 169, 183, 186, 241, 244, 245,
   248, 250, 253, 256, 259, 382, 383,
   387, 409, 414
Chronicle of Fredegar   313
Claussen, Martin Allen   248
Clermont   51, 430
   Council of (535)   50, 54
Clofesho, Council of (747)   243

Clothar II 308
Clovis II 307, 308, 314, 315
Cochelin, Isabelle 61, 89
Codex Theodosianus 54
Collectio Capitularis 59, 60, 64, 65, 90
Collectio Dionysio-Hadriana 158
Columbanus 62, 63, 70, 78, 80, 82
    Regula coenobialis 78, 80, 82
    Regula Columbani 340, 343, 383
    Sermo V 340, 343
Concilium Germanicum 103, 109
Constance 328, 332, 336
Constantine the Great 18, 390, 392
Constantinople 218, 391, 403
Corbie, abbey 390
Corpus Consuetudinum Monasticarum 34, 59, 66, 91, 325
Crusius, Irene 231
Cyprian of Carthage, bishop 223, 226, 227, 229, 285
    De habitu virginum 223, 226, 227

Damasus I, pope 390
De cursu diurno uel nocturno 64
De Jong, Mayke 231, 241, 302, 310
Decentius of Gubbio, bishop 426
Deidona, abbess 413
Demetrias, correspondent of Jerome 225, 226
Dereine, Charles 102, 407
Devisse, Jean 221
Dionysiana 439
Donatus Ortigraphus 291
Dunn, Marilyn 60

Ecgberht of York, archbishop 243
Echternach, abbey 254
Edict of Thessalonica (382) 393
Eigil, abbot of Fulda 36
Einhard of Saint-Wandrille, abbot 35, 38, 117
Elftrude of Flanders 40
Epistola de litteris colendis 256, 292

Ermoldus Nigellus, *Carmen in honorem Hludovici* 34
Eusebius of Vercelli 167
Eustochium, correspondent of Jerome 167
Evagrius of Antioch 228
Evagrius Ponticus 224
Ezekiel, book of the Bible 188, 189, 190, 191, 192, 218, 219

Faremoutiers, abbey 62, 70
Fastrada, queen 257
Faustinus, deacon of Augustine 201
Felten, Franz 223
Ferrières, abbey 243
Florus of Lyon, deacon 403–06, 409, 418, 419
    De divina psalmodia 402–06, 409, 418
Folcuin, chronicler and monk 37, 118
Foucault, Michel 83
Fox, Yaniv 438
Frankfurt, Council of (794) 40, 257, 360
Fridugisus, archchancellor 37, 38, 118
Fulda, abbey 25, 36, 37, 39, 84, 243, 267, 271, 272, 273, 274, 275, 276, 277, 282, 296, 343
Furia, correspondent of Jerome 225, 226

Ganshof, François Louis 183
Gherbald of Liège, bishop 166
Gozbert of Saint-Gall, abbot 328
Gregory IV, pope 409
Gregory of Tours, bishop 52, 53, 56, 139, 247, 433
Gregory the Great, pope 160, 167, 184, 187, 219, 224, 272, 292, 407, 440
    Homeliae in Ezecheliem 187

Regula Pastoralis 160, 219, 279, 288, 292
Grimald, monk at Reichenau 323–25, 329, 332, 334–36
Guillot, Olivier 19

Hadrian I, pope 257
Haistulf of Mainz, archbishop 271, 275, 276
Hallinger, Kassius 34, 324, 428, 429, 442
Hanssens, Jean Michel 415
Harting-Correa, Alice 363, 389
Haudo of Montier-en-Der, abbot 307
Häußling, Angelus Albert 434
Heliodorus of Altino, bishop 193, 194, 198, 222
Helisachar 259, 408, 409
Herardus of Tours, archbishop 430
Hesbert, René-Jean 408
Hilary of Arles, bishop 220, 221
Hildebald of Cologne, archchaplain 259
Hildemar of Corbie 84, 85, 86, 88, 326, 367–71, 388
    Expositio Regulae Sancti Benedicti 84–85, 86, 88, 184, 367–71
Hilduin of Saint-Denis 38, 259, 302, 305, 306, 307, 310, 311, 312, 313, 317
    Gesta Dagoberti 302, 312, 313, 316
Hincmar of Reims 306, 310, 317
Howe, John 20, 180
Hrabanus Maurus 25, 267–96
    De ecclesiastica disciplina 294
    De institutione clericorum 25, 267–96
    De laudibus sanctae crucis 271
    De sacris ordinibus 294

Île-Barbe, abbey 413
Inda, abbey 38

Innocent I, pope 426
Institutio canonicorum 15, 18, 22, 23, 25, 34, 60, 67, 102, 116, 131, 132, 133, 134, 135, 136, 138, 148, 153, 161, 162, 163, 164, 165, 166, 167, 168, 169, 170, 179–207, 217–34, 241, 242, 258–60, 268–70, 274, 275, 277, 279–96, 371, 373, 394, 410–13, 415, 417
Institutio sanctimonialium 15, 18, 22, 25, 34, 66, 67, 71, 131, 156, 179, 180, 217, 223, 410, 412
Inventio sancti Dionysii 313
Isidore of Seville 152, 153, 184, 185, 193, 220, 272, 274, 277, 280, 282, 284–88, 290, 291
    De ecclesiasticis officiis 152, 185, 280–82, 284–86, 288
    De regulis clericorum 152, 153
    Etymologiarum sive Originum libri XX 280, 283, 284, 287, 288, 290, 291

Jacobsen, Werner 41
Januaris, presbyter 200, 201, 203
Jeffery, Peter 437, 438
Jerome 152, 182, 184, 185, 189, 193, 194, 195, 196, 197, 198, 199, 200, 202, 205, 222, 223, 225, 226, 227, 231, 232, 275, 281, 282, 285, 291, 293, 331
    De virginitate servanda 225
    Letter to Nepotian 189, 193, 194, 197, 198, 222, 225, 281
Jerusalem 190, 232
John Cassian 85, 183, 197, 219, 220, 287
    Institutes Coenobiorum 183
John Chrysostom 391
John, archicantor 427, 428
Jonas of Bobbio, abbot 62, 63, 72, 84
    Vita Columbani 62, 84
Jonas of Orléans, *Vita Secunda Sancti Huberti* 104
Jovinian 198, 199

Julianus Pomerius 184, 219, 220
  De vita contemplativa 219–22
Justina, empress 391
Juvencus, poet 291

Kafka, Franz 13, 14, 27

Laeta, correspondent of
  Jerome 225, 231
Landeric of Paris, bishop 307, 308
Langres, Council of (830) 308
Laodicea, Council of (366) 49,
  230, 368, 369, 269
Legatine Capitulary (786) 108,
  141, 155, 245
Leidrad of Lyon, archbishop 168,
  406, 412–19
Leo I, pope 110
Liber Historiae Francorum 313
Liber Pontificalis 392, 430
Lobbes, abbey 37
Lorsch, abbey 87, 439
Louis the German 39
Louis the Pious 15, 17, 19, 24, 26,
  33, 34, 36, 37, 38, 131, 133, 148, 161,
  179, 180, 205, 217, 259, 268, 270,
  276, 277, 302, 304, 305, 306, 310,
  313, 334, 355, 361, 403, 409, 412, 418
Lowe, Elias Avery 430
Luxeuil, abbey 438
Lyon 26, 168, 403, 402, 405, 406,
  407, 409, 411, 412, 413, 414, 415,
  416, 417, 418

Macarius, deacon 253
Mâcon, Council of (585) 53
Magnus of Sens, archbishop 412
Mainz
  Council of (813) 112, 151, 152,
    154, 160, 167, 194
  Council of (847) 153
Marius Victorinus 291
Marmoutier, abbey 291
Masser, Achim 337
Matthew, Gospel of 14, 271, 369

Mattingly, Matthew 61, 72, 78
McCune, James C. 389
McKinnon, James 390, 395
Memoriale qualiter 22, 24, 59–90.
Metz 17, 34, 141, 167, 245, 249, 253,
  254, 409, 414–16, 415, 416
Misonne, Daniel 37
Montecassino, abbey 86, 158, 323,
  329, 336
Montier-en-Der, abbey 307, 308,
  309
Mordek, Hubert 182, 183
Morgand, Claudio 60, 62, 63, 64,
  65, 66, 67, 69, 78, 79, 90
Morin, Germain 254, 415
Motuinus, abbot 413
Münsterschwarzach, abbey 341
Murbach, abbey 243, 439
Muschiol, Gisela 231

Nelson, Janet 251, 317
Nepotian, correspondent of
  Jerome 189, 193, 194, 197, 198,
  222, 225, 281
Nibridius of Narbonne,
  archbishop 409
Nicaea, Council of (325) 19

Oceanus, correspondent of
  Jerome 409
Oexle, Otto Gerhard 38, 39, 414
Ordines Romani 26, 425, 429, 436,
  442
ordo canonicorum, concept of 134,
  136, 138, 139, 148, 149, 157, 158, 162
Ordo Casinensis I 64, 77, 86
Ordo diurnus Anianensis 65, 77
Orléans
  Council of (511) 52
  Council of (538) 51, 54
  Council of (541) 53
Otgar of Mainz, archbishop 271
Othmar of Saint-Gall, *Ordo
  confessionis* 87

Palazzo, Eric   408
Paris, Council of (829)   302, 310
Patroclus, saint   52
Patzold, Steffen   276, 310
Paul the Deacon, *Liber de Episcopis Mettensibus*   245, 255–56
Paula, daughter of Laeta   231, 232
Paulinus of Nola   193, 198, 199, 220
Pelagius   228
Peter of Nonantola, abbot   218
Phelan, Owen   269, 293
Philo of Alexandria   390
Picker, Hanns-Christoph   371, 270, 287, 293, 396
Pippin II of Aquitaine, king   309, 310
Pippin III   102, 118, 133, 142, 243, 304, 279, 382, 408
Poitiers   21, 70
Pölsch, Arnold   49, 52
Prosper of Aquitaine   219
Pseudo-Germanus of Paris   433, 434
Pythagoras   194

Quierzy, Council of (838)   402
Quintilian   291

Radegund, saint and Frankish queen   70
Ratgar of Fulda, abbot   36
Reginbald of Mainz, chorbishop   294
Reginbert, librarian of Reichenau   334
Regula Benedicti   15, 17, 22, 23, 34, 35–40, 60–64, 67, 69, 70, 71, 73, 77–82, 84, 85, 87 89, 90, 119, 132, 135, 143, 147, 148, 152, 155, 158, 159, 160, 161, 163, 164, 165, 186, 217, 218, 244, 274, 286, 287, 295, 296, 302–08, 311, 312, 316, 317, 323–29, 331–36, 345, 447, 339, 340, 342–46, 355–95, 408, 410, 411, 437–39
Regula Basilii   341
Regula cuiusdam ad uirgines   60, 62, 63, 64, 69, 70–73, 75, 78, 79, 80, 81, 82, 84, 89, 90
  See also Jonas of Bobbio
Regula Donati   70, 78
Regula Magistri   60, 62, 387, 428, 442
Regula Monachorum   227
Regula Pauli et Stephani   340, 343
Regula quattuor partum   341
Regula S. Chrodegangi interpolata   61, 66
Regula Chrodegangi   69, 102, 116, 140, 183, 186, 241, 244, 248, 250, 253, 254, 256, 258, 259, 387
Regularis Concordia (966)   62, 87–90
Reichenau, abbey   38, 304, 323, 324, 329, 331–36, 341, 363
  Liber Vitae of 412, 413
Reims   430
  Council of (813)   110, 154, 160
Reuter, Timothy   103
Richbod of Trier, archbishop   253, 254
Riesbach-Friesing-Salzburg, Council of (799/800)   147
Rissel, Maria   269
Rudge, Lindsay   224
  Passio S. Dionysii Rustici et Eleutherii   313
Rusticus, correspondent of Jerome   193, 198, 222

Saint Bavo, patron of Ghent   35
Saint Dionysius   309
Saint Felix of Nola   198
Saint Martin   40, 316
Saint Mary   40, 431
Saint Maurice   315, 316
Saint Omer/Saint Audomarus   118
Saint Ursmer of Lobbes   37
Saint-Amand, abbey   36, 40
Saint-Aubin, abbey in Angers   409
Saint-Baafs, abbey in Ghent   117

Saint-Bertin (or Sithiu), abbey 36, 37, 40, 118
Saint-Denis
  abbey 25, 37, 118, 141, 251, 258, 259, 301–17
  Council of (829/30) 38, 301–03, 305, 307, 308, 309, 310, 311, 314
  Council of (832) 301, 302, 305, 310–12
Saint-Gall/St Gall/Sankt Gallen, abbey 87, 323–25, 327–29, 331, 334–45, 426, 427, 429, 430, 329, 432, 433, 437, 438
Saint-Georges, canonical community 413
Saint-Hilaire, abbey 118, 119, 306
Saint-Jean, abbey 227, 317
Saint-Just, canonical community 413
Saint-Martin of Tours, abbey 40, 99, 100, 116, 117, 119, 120, 143, 247, 251, 253, 304, 306, 314–16, 429, 433
Saint-Maurice d'Augane, abbey 251, 306, 314, 315, 316
Saint-Nizier, canonical community 413
Saint-Omer, abbey 37, 40, 118
Saint-Paul, canonical community 413
St Peter, abbey in Ghent 35, 117
Saint-Pierre de Bèze, abbey 308
Saint-Ragnebert, abbey 413
Saint-Riquier, abbey 37, 40, 41, 409
Saint-Silvester, abbey 218
St Stephen/Saint-Étienne, Lyon, cathedral church 413
St Stephen/Saint-Étienne, Metz, cathedral church 250
Saint-Vaast, abbey 36
Saint-Wandrille, abbey 35, 38
Salmon, Pierre 382
Sant'Anastasia, basilica in Rome 431, 434

Santa Maria Maggiore, basilica in Rome 432, 434, 436
Schäfer, Heinrich 49
Schieffer, Rudolf 50, 51, 134, 139, 411
Schilp, Thomas 230
Schmid, Karl 38
Schmitz, Gerhard 182, 217, 224, 225, 228
Sedulius, poet 291
Semmler, Josef 18, 24, 33, 34, 36, 38, 41, 101, 102, 118, 133, 134, 276, 324, 410, 428, 436
Sicharius of Bordeaux, archbishop 412
Siegwart, Josef 49, 54, 56
Smaragdus of St. Mihiel 60, 71, 84, 85, 361, 362, 363
  Expositio in regulam S. Benedicti 60, 71, 84, 184, 326, 361, 362
Steinová, Evina 331, 332
Sturm of Fulda, abbot 36
Supplex Libellus 84, 275, 276, 295

Taft, Robert 384, 386
Taio of Saragossa, bishop 187, 219, 220, 222, 224
  Sententiae 219, 220, 224
Tatto, monk at Reichenau 323–25, 329, 332, 334–36
Tellenbach, Gerd 38
Theodomar of Montecassino, abbot 86
Theodosius I, emperor 390, 392
Theodulf of Orléans 247, 372, 373
Therasia, wife of Paulinus of Nola 199
Theudebert I 50
Theuderic III 308
Thionville
  palace 254
  synod of (835) 403, 418
Thiotmar, chorbishop 294
Toledo, Council of (633) 168, 386

Tours   119, 225, 246, 255, 341, 431,
    430, 431, 433, 434, 436
  Council of (567)   54, 55, 56
  Council of (813)   105, 106, 114,
    154, 160, 168, 246
  Council of (853)   430

Ualtarius, abbot   413
Usualdo of St Salvatore di Rieti,
    abbot   245

Van Dijk, Stephen J.P.   428, 432
van Rhijn, Carine   247
Venantius Fortunatus   291
Ver, Council of (755)   38, 103, 110,
    111, 147, 244
Vercelli   167
Vita Amandi   313
Vita Bavonis   35
Vita Caesarii   53
Vita Eigilis   36
Vita Bertilae   69

Wala of Corbie, abbot   409
Walahfrid Strabo   358, 363, 364,
    365, 366, 367, 369, 372, 373, 384–87,
    389–96
  *Libellus de Exordiis et incrementis
    quarundam in observationibus
    ecclesiaticis rerum*   363, 384,
    389
Waldo of Reichenau, abbot,
    Translatio sanguinis Domini   304
Wearmouth-Jarrow, abbey   427
Widukind   257
Wigbod, abbot   141
Wollasch, Joachim   38, 335

Zacharias, pope   103, 243, 244
Zechiel-Eckes, Klaus   416
Zimpel, Detlev   268, 269, 279, 296

Medieval Monastic Studies

All volumes in this series are evaluated by an Editorial Board, strictly on academic grounds, based on reports prepared by referees who have been commissioned by virtue of their specialism in the appropriate field. The Board ensures that the screening is done independently and without conflicts of interest. The definitive texts supplied by authors are also subject to review by the Board before being approved for publication. Further, the volumes are copyedited to conform to the publisher's stylebook and to the best international academic standards in the field.

Titles in Series

Women in the Medieval Monastic World, ed. by Janet Burton and Karen Stöber (2015)

Kathryn E. Salzer, *Vaucelles Abbey: Social, Political, and Ecclesiastical Relationships in the Borderland Region of the Cambresis, 1131–1300* (2017)

Michael Carter, *The Art and Architecture of the Cistercians in Northern England, c. 1300–1540* (2019)

Monastic Europe: Medieval Communities, Landscapes, and Settlement, ed. by Edel Bhreathnach, Małgorzata Krasnodębska-D'Aughton, and Keith Smith (2019)

Michael Spence, *The Late Medieval Cistercian Monastery of Fountains Abbey, Yorkshire: Monastic Administration, Economy, and Archival Memory* (2020)

The Medieval Dominicans: Books, Buildings, Music, and Liturgy, ed. by Eleanor J. Giraud and Christian T. Leitmeir (2021)

In Preparation

Joan Barclay Lloyd, *Dominicans and Franciscans in Medieval Rome: History, Architecture, and Art*